UNCTAD/DITE/2(Vol. VI)

United Nations Conference on Trade and Development
Division on Investment, Technology and Enterprise Development

International Investment Instruments: A Compendium

Volume VI

United Nations
New York and Geneva, 2001

Note

UNCTAD serves as the focal point within the United Nations Secretariat for all matters related to foreign direct investment and transnational corporations. In the past, the Programme on Transnational Corporations was carried out by the United Nations Centre on Transnational Corporations (1975-1992) and the Transnational Corporations and Management Division of the United Nations Department of Economic and Social Development (1992-1993). In 1993, the Programme was transferred to the United Nations Conference on Trade and Development. UNCTAD seeks to further the understanding of the nature of transnational corporations and their contribution to development and to create an enabling environment for international investment and enterprise development. UNCTAD's work is carried on through intergovernmental deliberations, technical assistance activities, seminars, workshops and conferences.

The term "country", as used in the boxes added by the UNCTAD secretariat at the beginning of the instruments reproduced in this volume, also refers, as appropriate, to territories or areas; the designations employed and the presentation of the material do not imply the expression of any opinion whatsoever on the part of the Secretariat of the United Nations concerning the legal status of any country, territory, city or area or of its authorities, or concerning the delimitation of its frontiers or boundaries. Moreover, the country or geographical terminology used in the boxes may occasionally depart from standard United Nations practice when this is made necessary by the nomenclature used at the time of negotiation, signature, ratification or accession of a given international instrument.

To preserve the integrity of the texts of the instruments reproduced in this volume, references to the sources of the istruments that are not contained in their original text are identified as "note added by the editor".

The texts of the instruments included in this volume are reproduced as they were written in one of their original languages or as an official translation thereof. When an obvious linguistic mistake has been found, the word "sic" has been added in brackets.

The materials contained in this volume have been reprinted with special permission of the relevant institutions. For those materials under copyright protection, all rights are reserved by the copyright holders.

It should be further noted that this collection of instruments has been prepared for documentation purposes only, and its contents do not engage the responsibility of UNCTAD.

UNCTAD/DITE/2 Vol. VI

UNITED NATIONS PUBLICATION
Sales No. E.01.II.D.34
ISBN 92-1-112546-4

PREFACE

International Investment Instruments: A Compendium contains a collection of international instruments relating to foreign direct investment (FDI) and transnational corporations (TNCs). The collection is presented in six volumes. The first three volumes were published in 1996. Four years later, *Volumes IV* and *V* were published; *Volume VI* brings the collection up to date. This volume also includes a number of instruments adopted in earlier years but not included in the previous volumes.

The collection has been prepared to make the texts of international investment instruments conveniently available to interested policy makers, scholars and business executives. The need for such a collection has increased in recent years as bilateral, regional, interregional and multilateral instruments dealing with various aspects of FDI have proliferated, and as new investment instruments are being negotiated at all levels.

While by necessity selective, the present collection seeks to provide a faithful record of the evolution and present status of intergovernmental cooperation concerning FDI and TNCs. Although the emphasis of the collection is on relatively recent documents (the majority of the instruments reproduced date from after 1990), it was deemed useful to include important older instruments as well, with a view to providing some indications of the historical development of international concerns about FDI in the decades since the end of the Second World War.

The core of this collection consists of legally binding international instruments, mainly multilateral conventions and regional agreements that have entered into force. In addition, a number of "soft law" documents, such as guidelines, declarations and resolutions adopted by intergovernmental bodies, have been included since these instruments also play a role in the elaboration of an international framework for FDI. In an effort to enhance the understanding of the efforts behind the elaboration of this framework, certain draft instruments that never entered into force, or texts of instruments on which the negotiations were not concluded, are also included; and several prototypes of bilateral investment treaties are reproduced. Included also are a number of influential documents prepared by business, consumer and labour organizations, as well as by other non-governmental organizations. It is clear from the foregoing that no implications concerning the legal status or the legal effect of an instrument can be drawn from its inclusion in this collection.

In view of the great diversity of the instruments in this *Compendium* — in terms of subject matter, approach, legal form and extent of participation of States — the simplest possible method of presentation was deemed the most appropriate. Thus, the relevant instruments are distributed among the *six volumes of the Compendium* as follows:

- *Volume I* is devoted to multilateral instruments, that is to say multilateral conventions as well as resolutions and other documents issued by multilateral organizations.

- *Volume II* covers interregional and regional instruments, including agreements, resolutions and other texts from regional organizations with an inclusive geographical context.

- *Volume III* is divided into three annexes covering three types of instruments that differ in their context or their origin from those included in the first two volumes:

  - Annex A reproduces investment-related provisions in free trade and regional integration agreements. The specific function and, therefore, the effect of such provisions are largely determined by the economic integration process which they are intended to promote and in the context of which they operate.

  - Annex B (the only section that departs from the chronological pattern) offers the texts of prototype bilateral treaties for the promotion and protection of foreign investments (BITs) of several developed and developing countries, as well as a list of these treaties concluded up to July 1995. The bilateral character of these treaties differentiates them from the bulk of the instruments included in this *Compendium*. Over 900 such treaties had been adopted by July 1995.

  - Annex C supplies the texts of documents prepared by non-governmental organizations; these give an indication of the broader environment in which the instruments collected here are prepared.

- *Volume IV*, divided into two parts, covers additional multilateral (Part One) and regional instruments (Part Two) not covered in *Volumes I* and *II*, including, but not limited to, those adopted between 1996 and the end of 1999.

- *Volume V* is divided into four parts, as follows:

  - Part One reproduces investment-related provisions in a number of additional free trade and economic integration agreements not covered in *Volume III*.

  - Part Two includes for the first time investment-related provisions in association agreements as well as bilateral and interregional cooperation agreements. These are divided into three annexes. Annex A is devoted to agreements signed between the countries members of the European Free Trade Association (EFTA) and third countries. Annex B covers investment-related provisions in agreements signed between the countries members of the European Community (EC) and third countries as well as other regional groups. Annex C includes types of bilateral agreements related to investment that differ from those covered in other parts.

  - Part Three contains the texts of a number of additional prototype BITs of several developed and developing countries, as well as a list of these treaties concluded between July 1995 and the end of 1998, when the total number of BITs concluded since 1959 reached over 1,730.

  - Part Four reproduces additional texts of recent documents prepared by non-governmental organizations.

- *Volume VI* is divided into the following six parts:

    - Part One contains an additional multilateral instrument.

    - Part Two covers additional interregional and regional instruments, including agreements, resolutions and other texts from regional organizations with an inclusive geographical context.

    - Part Three reproduces investment-related provisions in a number of additional free trade and economic integration agreements not covered in previous volumes.

    - Part Four includes investment-related provisions in association agreements as well as bilateral and interregional cooperation agreements not covered in previous volumes.

    - Part Five contains the texts of a number of additional prototype BITs of several developed and developing countries not covered in previous volumes.

    - Part Six includes for the first time prototype double taxation treaties (DTTs).

Within each of these subdivisions, instruments are reproduced in chronological order, except for the sections dedicated to BIT prototypes.

The multilateral and regional instruments covered differ widely in scope and coverage. Some are designed to provide an overall, general framework for FDI and cover many, although rarely all, aspects of investment operations. Most instruments deal with particular aspects and issues concerning FDI. A significant number address core FDI issues, such as the promotion and protection of investment, investment liberalization, dispute settlement and insurance and guarantees. Others cover specific issues, of direct but not exclusive relevance to FDI and TNCs, such as transfer of technology, intellectual property, avoidance of double taxation, competition and the protection of consumers and the environment. A relatively small number of instruments in this last category have been reproduced, since each of these specific issues often constitutes an entire system of legal regulation of its own, whose proper coverage would require an extended exposition of many kinds of instruments and arrangements.[a]

The *Compendium* is meant to be a collection of instruments, not an anthology of relevant provisions. Indeed, to understand a particular instrument, it is normally necessary to take its entire text into consideration. An effort has been made, therefore, to reproduce complete instruments, even though, in a number of cases, reasons of space and relevance have dictated the inclusion of excerpts.

The UNCTAD secretariat has deliberately refrained from adding its own commentary to the texts reproduced in the *Compendium*. The only exception to this rule is the boxes added to

---

[a] For a collection of instruments (or excerpts therefrom) dealing with transfer of technology, see UNCTAD, *Compendium of International Arrangements on Transfer of Technology: Selected Instruments* (Geneva: United Nations), United Nations publication, Sales No. E.01.II.D.28.

each instrument. They provide some basic facts, such as date of adoption, date of entry into force, status as of 1995 and 1999 respectively, and, where appropriate, signatory countries. Also, in the case of agreements signed between the EFTA countries or the EC countries with third countries or regional groups — where only a few samples of the types of agreements with investment-related provisions are included — a list of similar agreements signed by these two groups of countries has been included to give an indication of the range of countries involved in these types of agreements. Moreover, to facilitate the identification of each instrument in the table of contents, additional information has been added, in brackets, next to each title, on the year of its signature and the name of the relevant institution involved.

Karl P. Sauvant
Director
Division on Investment, Technology
and Enterprise Development
UNCTAD

Geneva, September 2001

ACKNOWLEDGEMENTS

Volume VI of the *Compendium* was prepared by Abraham Negash, under the guidance of Victoria Aranda and the overall direction of Anh-Nga Tran-Nguyen and Karl P. Sauvant. Comments on the table of contents were given by Arghyrios A. Fatouros, Mark Koulen, Peter Muchlinski, Maryse Robert, Patrick Robinson and Joerg Weber. Secretarial assistance was provided by Florence Hudry. The cooperation of the relevant organizations from which the relevant instruments originate is acknowledged with gratitude.

CONTENTS

VOLUME I
MULTILATERAL INSTRUMENTS

VOLUME II
REGIONAL INSTRUMENTS

REGIONAL INSTRUMENTS

VOLUME III

REGIONAL INTEGRATION, BILATERAL AND NON-GOVERNMENTAL INSTRUMENTS

ANNEX C. NON-GOVERNMENTAL INSTRUMENTS

VOLUME IV

MULTILATERAL AND REGIONAL INSTRUMENTS

PART ONE

MULTILATERAL INSTRUMENTS

PART TWO

REGIONAL INSTRUMENTS

VOLUME V

REGIONAL INTEGRATION, BILATERAL AND NON-GOVERNMENTAL INSTRUMENTS

PART ONE

INVESTMENT-RELATED PROVISIONS IN FREE TRADE AND ECONOMIC INTEGRATION AGREEMENTS

PART TWO

INVESTMENT-RELATED PROVISIONS IN ASSOCIATION AGREEMENTS, BILATERAL AND INTERREGIONAL COOPERATION AGREEMENTS

ANNEX A. INVESTMENT-RELATED PROVISIONS IN FREE TRADE AGREEMENTS SIGNED BETWEEN THE COUNTRIES MEMBERS OF THE EUROPEAN FREE TRADE ASSOCIATION AND THIRD COUNTRIES AND LIST OF AGREEMENTS SIGNED (END-1999)

ANNEX B. INVESTMENT-RELATED PROVISIONS IN ASSOCIATION, PARTNERSHIP AND COOPERATION AGREEMENTS SIGNED BETWEEN THE COUNTRIES MEMBERS OF THE EUROPEAN COMMUNITY AND THIRD COUNTRIES AND LIST OF AGREEMENTS SIGNED (END-1999)

ANNEX C.   OTHER BILATERAL INVESTMENT-RELATED AGREEMENTS

PART THREE

PROTOTYPE BILATERAL INVESTMENT TREATIES AND LIST OF BILATERAL INVESTMENT TREATIES (MID-1995 — END-1998)

PART FOUR

NON-GOVERNMENTAL INSTRUMENTS

VOLUME VI

PART ONE

MULTILATERAL INSTRUMENTS

PART TWO

INTERREGIONAL AND REGIONAL INSTRUMENTS

PART THREE

INVESTMENT-RELATED PROVISIONS IN FREE TRADE AND ECONOMIC INTEGRATION AGREEMENTS

PART FOUR

INVESTMENT-RELATED PROVISIONS IN ASSOCIATION AGREEMENTS, BILATERAL AND INTERREGIONAL COOPERATION AGREEMENTS

PART FIVE

PROTOTYPE BILATERAL INVESTMENT TREATIES

PART SIX

PROTOTYPE BILATERAL DOUBLE TAXATION TREATIES

PART ONE

MULTILATERAL INSTRUMENTS

REVISED UNITED NATIONS MODEL DOUBLE TAXATION CONVENTION BETWEEN DEVELOPED AND DEVELOPING COUNTRIES*

The United Nations Model Double Taxation Convention between Developed and Developing Countries of 2000 was intended to revise and update the 1979 Model (reproduced in vol. I of this *Compendium*). The process of revision and updating was initiated in 1995 and concluded in 1999 at the Ninth Meeting of the Group of Experts on Tax Treaties. The Group is composed of 25 members — 10 from developed countries and 15 from developing countries and economies in transition. The Ninth Meeting was attended by representatives from Argentina, Brazil, Burkina Faso, China, Côte d'Ivoire, Egypt, Finland, Germany, Ghana, India, Indonesia, Israel, Jamaica, Mexico, Morocco, Netherlands, Spain, Switzerland, the United Kingdom, the United States and the Palestinian Authority. The commentaries to the Model Convention, which were prepared by the Group, have not been reproduced in this volume.

SUMMARY OF THE CONVENTION

Title and Preamble

CHAPTER I
Scope of the Convention

CHAPTER II
Definitions

CHAPTER III
Taxation of income

---

* *Source*: United Nations (2000). *Articles of the United Nations Model Double Taxation Convention between Developed and Developing Countries*; United Nations document ST/ESA/PAD/SER.E/21, Sales No. E.01.XVI.2 (New York: United Nations). The commentaries on the Articles of the United Nations Model Double Taxation can be found in the same source. [Note added by the editor.]

CHAPTER IV
Taxation of capital

CHAPTER V
Methods for elimination of double taxation

CHAPTER VI
Special provisions

CHAPTER VII
Final provisions

TITLE OF THE CONVENTION

Convention between (State A) and (State B) with respect to taxes on income and on capital[*10]

PREAMBLE OF THE CONVENTION[11]

Chapter I

SCOPE OF THE CONVENTION

Article 1
PERSONS COVERED

This Convention shall apply to persons who are residents of one or both of the Contracting States.

Article 2
TAXES COVERED

1.   This Convention shall apply to taxes on income and on capital imposed on behalf of a Contracting State or of its political subdivisions or local authorities, irrespective of the manner in which they are levied.

2.   There shall be regarded as taxes on income and on capital all taxes imposed on total income, on total capital, or on elements of income or of capital, including taxes on gains from the alienation of movable or immovable property, taxes on the total amounts of wages or salaries paid by enterprises, as well as taxes on capital appreciation.

3.   The existing taxes to which the Convention shall apply are in particular:

(a)   (in State A): ....

(b)   (in State B): ....

4.   The Convention shall apply also to any identical or substantially similar taxes which are imposed after the date of signature of the Convention in addition to, or in place of, the existing taxes. The competent authorities of the Contracting States shall notify each other of significant changes made to their tax law.

---

[*] Footnotes 1-9 are found in the introduction of the United Nations document ST/ESA/PAD/SER.E/21. The introduction has not been reproduced here. [Note added by the editor.]

[10] States wishing to do so may follow the widespread practice of including in the title a reference to either the avoidance of double taxation or to both the avoidance of double taxation and the prevention of fiscal evasion.

[11] The Preamble of the Convention shall be drafted in accordance with the constitutional procedures of the Contracting States.

Chapter II
DEFINITIONS

Article 3
GENERAL DEFINITIONS

1.   For the purposes of this Convention, unless the context otherwise requires:

    (a)   The term "person" includes an individual, a company and any other body of persons;

    (b)   The term "company" means any body corporate or any entity that is treated as a body corporate for tax purposes;

    (c)   The terms "enterprise of a Contracting State" and "enterprise of the other Contracting State" mean respectively an enterprise carried on by a resident of a Contracting State and an enterprise carried on by a resident of the other Contracting State;

    (d)   The term "international traffic" means any transport by a ship or aircraft operated by an enterprise that has its place of effective management in a Contracting State, except when the ship or aircraft is operated solely between places in the other Contracting State;

    (e)   The term "competent authority" means:

        (i)   (In State A): ....

        (ii)   (In State B): ....

    (f)   The term "national" means:

        (i)   Any individual possessing the nationality of a Contracting State

        (ii)   Any legal person, partnership or association deriving its status as such from the laws in force in a Contracting State.

2.   As regards the application of the Convention at any time by a Contracting State, any term not defined therein shall, unless the context otherwise requires, have the meaning that it has at that time under the law of that State for the purposes of the taxes to which the Convention applies, any meaning under the applicable tax laws of that State prevailing over a meaning given to the term under other laws of that State.

Article 4
RESIDENT

1.   For the purposes of this Convention, the term "resident of a Contracting State" means any person who, under the laws of that State, is liable to tax therein by reason of his domicile, residence, place of incorporation, place of management or any other criterion of a similar nature, and also includes that State and any political subdivision or local authority thereof. This term,

however, does not include any person who is liable to tax in that State in respect only of income from sources in that State or capital situated therein.

2.   Where by reason of the provisions of paragraph 1 an individual is a resident of both Contracting States, then his status shall be determined as follows:

(a)   He shall be deemed to be a resident only of the State in which he has a permanent home available to him; if he has a permanent home available to him in both States, he shall be deemed to be a resident only of the State with which his personal and economic relations are closer (centre of vital interests);

(b)   If the State in which he has his centre of vital interests cannot be determined, or if he has not a permanent home available to him in either State, he shall be deemed to be a resident only of the State in which he has an habitual abode;

(c)   If he has an habitual abode in both States or in neither of them, he shall be deemed to be a resident only of the State of which he is a national;

(d)   If he is a national of both States or of neither of them, the competent authorities of the Contracting States shall settle the question by mutual agreement.

3.   Where by reason of the provisions of paragraph 1 a person other than an individual is a resident of both Contracting States, then it shall be deemed to be a resident only of the State in which its place of effective management is situated.

Article 5
PERMANENT ESTABLISHMENT

1.   For the purposes of this Convention, the term "permanent establishment" means a fixed place of business through which the business of an enterprise is wholly or partly carried on.

2.   The term "permanent establishment" includes especially:

(a)   A place of management;

(b)   A branch;

(c)   An office;

(d)   A factory;

(e)   A workshop;

(f)   A mine, an oil or gas well, a quarry or any other place of extraction of natural resources.

3.   The term "permanent establishment" also encompasses:

     (a)   A building site, a construction, assembly or installation project or supervisory activities in connection therewith, but only if such site, project or activities last more than six months;

     (b)   The furnishing of services, including consultancy services, by an enterprise through employees or other personnel engaged by the enterprise for such purpose, but only if activities of that nature continue (for the same or a connected project) within a Contracting State for a period or periods aggregating more than six months within any twelve-month period.

4.   Notwithstanding the preceding provisions of this article, the term "permanent establishment" shall be deemed not to include:

     (a)   The use of facilities solely for the purpose of storage or display of goods or merchandise belonging to the enterprise;

     (b)   The maintenance of a stock of goods or merchandise belonging to the enterprise solely for the purpose of storage or display;

     (c)   The maintenance of a stock of goods or merchandise belonging to the enterprise solely for the purpose of processing by another enterprise;

     (d)   The maintenance of a fixed place of business solely for the purpose of purchasing goods or merchandise or of collecting information, for the enterprise;

     (e)   The maintenance of a fixed place of business solely for the purpose of carrying on, for the enterprise, any other activity of a preparatory or auxiliary character.

     (f)   The maintenance of a fixed place of business solely for any combination of activities mentioned in subparagraphs (a) to (e), provided that the overall activity of the fixed place of business resulting from this combination is of a preparatory or auxiliary character.

5.   Notwithstanding the provisions of paragraphs 1 and 2, where a person -- other than an agent of an independent status to whom paragraph 7 applies -- is acting in a Contracting State on behalf of an enterprise of the other Contracting State, that enterprise shall be deemed to have a permanent establishment in the first-mentioned Contracting State in respect of any activities which that person undertakes for the enterprise, if such a person:

     (a)   Has and habitually exercises in that State an authority to conclude contracts in the name of the enterprise, unless the activities of such person are limited to those mentioned in paragraph 4 which, if exercised through a fixed place of business, would not make this fixed place of business a permanent establishment under the provisions of that paragraph; or

     (b)   Has no such authority, but habitually maintains in the first-mentioned State a stock of goods or merchandise from which he regularly delivers goods or merchandise on behalf of the enterprise.

6.   Notwithstanding the preceding provisions of this article, an insurance enterprise of a Contracting State shall, except in regard to re-insurance, be deemed to have a permanent establishment in the other Contracting State if it collects premiums in the territory of that other State or insures risks situated therein through a person other than an agent of an independent status to whom paragraph 7 applies.

7.   An enterprise of a Contracting State shall not be deemed to have a permanent establishment in the other Contracting State merely because it carries on business in that other State through a broker, general commission agent or any other agent of an independent status, provided that such persons are acting in the ordinary course of their business. However, when the activities of such an agent are devoted wholly or almost wholly on behalf of that enterprise, and conditions are made or imposed between that enterprise and the agent in their commercial and financial relations which differ from those which would have been made between independent enterprises, he will not be considered an agent of an independent status within the meaning of this paragraph.

8.   The fact that a company which is a resident of a Contracting State controls or is controlled by a company which is a resident of the other Contracting State, or which carries on business in that other State (whether through a permanent establishment or otherwise), shall not of itself constitute either company a permanent establishment of the other.

Chapter III
TAXATION OF INCOME

Article 6
INCOME FROM IMMOVABLE PROPERTY

1.   Income derived by a resident of a Contracting State from immovable property (including income from agriculture or forestry) situated in the other Contracting State may be taxed in that other State.

2.   The term "immovable property" shall have the meaning which it has under the law of the Contracting State in which the property in question is situated. The term shall in any case include property accessory to immovable property, livestock and equipment used in agriculture and forestry, rights to which the provisions of general law respecting landed property apply, usufruct of immovable property and rights to variable or fixed payments as consideration for the working of, or the right to work, mineral deposits, sources and other natural resources; ships, boats and aircraft shall not be regarded as immovable property.

3.   The provisions of paragraph 1 shall also apply to income derived from the direct use, letting or use in any other form of immovable property.

4.   The provisions of paragraphs 1 and 3 shall also apply to the income from immovable property of an enterprise and to income from immovable property used for the performance of independent personal services.

Article 7
BUSINESS PROFITS

1.   The profits of an enterprise of a Contracting State shall be taxable only in that State unless the enterprise carries on business in the other Contracting State through a permanent establishment situated therein. If the enterprise carries on business as aforesaid, the profits of the enterprise may be taxed in the other State but only so much of them as is attributable to (a) that permanent establishment; (b) sales in that other State of goods or merchandise of the same or similar kind as those sold through that permanent establishment; or (c) other business activities carried on in that other State of the same or similar kind as those effected through that permanent establishment.

2.   Subject to the provisions of paragraph 3, where an enterprise of a Contracting State carries on business in the other Contracting State through a permanent establishment situated therein, there shall in each Contracting State be attributed to that permanent establishment the profits which it might be expected to make if it were a distinct and separate enterprise engaged in the same or similar activities under the same or similar conditions and dealing wholly independently with the enterprise of which it is a permanent establishment.

3.   In the determination of the profits of a permanent establishment, there shall be allowed as deductions expenses which are incurred for the purposes of the business of the permanent establishment including executive and general administrative expenses so incurred, whether in the State in which the permanent establishment is situated or elsewhere. However, no such deduction shall be allowed in respect of amounts, if any, paid (otherwise than towards reimbursement of actual expenses) by the permanent establishment to the head office of the enterprise or any of its other offices, by way of royalties, fees or other similar payments in return for the use of patents or other rights, or by way of commission, for specific services performed or for management, or, except in the case of a banking enterprise, by way of interest on moneys lent to the permanent establishment. Likewise, no account shall be taken, in the determination of the profits of a permanent establishment, for amounts charged (otherwise than towards reimbursement of actual expenses), by the permanent establishment to the head office of the enterprise or any of its other offices, by way of royalties, fees or other similar payments in return for the use of patents or other rights, or by way of commission for specific services performed or for management, or, except in the case of a banking enterprise, by way of interest on moneys lent to the head office of the enterprise or any of its other offices.

4.   In so far as it has been customary in a Contracting State to determine the profits to be attributed to a permanent establishment on the basis of an apportionment of the total profits of the enterprise to its various parts, nothing in paragraph 2 shall preclude that Contracting State from determining the profits to be taxed by such an apportionment as may be customary; the method of apportionment adopted shall, however, be such that the result shall be in accordance with the principles contained in this article.

5.   For the purposes of the preceding paragraphs, the profits to be attributed to the permanent establishment shall be determined by the same method year by year unless there is good and sufficient reason to the contrary.

6.   Where profits include items of income which are dealt with separately in other articles of this Convention, then the provisions of those articles shall not be affected by the provisions of this article.

(NOTE: The question of whether profits should be attributed to a permanent establishment by reason of the mere purchase by that permanent establishment of goods and merchandise for the enterprise was not resolved. It should therefore be settled in bilateral negotiations).

Article 8
SHIPPING, INLAND WATERWAYS TRANSPORT AND AIR TRANSPORT

Article 8 (alternative A)

1.   Profits from the operation of ships or aircraft in international traffic shall be taxable only in the Contracting State in which the place of effective management of the enterprise is situated.

2.   Profits from the operation of boats engaged in inland waterways transport shall be taxable only in the Contracting State in which the place of effective management of the enterprise is situated.

3.   If the place of effective management of a shipping enterprise or of an inland waterways transport enterprise is aboard a ship or a boat, then it shall be deemed to be situated in the Contracting State in which the home harbour of the ship or boat is situated, or, if there is no such home harbour, in the Contracting State of which the operator of the ship or boat is a resident.

4.   The provisions of paragraph 1 shall also apply to profits from the participation in a pool, a joint business or an international operating agency.

Article 8 (alternative B)

1.   Profits from the operation of aircraft in international traffic shall be taxable only in the Contracting State in which the place of effective management of the enterprise is situated.

2.   Profits from the operation of ships in international traffic shall be taxable only in the Contracting State in which the place of effective management of the enterprise is situated unless the shipping activities arising from such operation in the other Contracting State are more than casual. If such activities are more than casual, such profits may be taxed in that other State. The profits to be taxed in that other State shall be determined on the basis of an appropriate allocation of the over-all net profits derived by the enterprise from its shipping operations. The tax computed in accordance with such allocation shall then be reduced by ... per cent. (The percentage is to be established through bilateral negotiations).

3.   Profits from the operation of boats engaged in inland waterways transport shall be taxable only in the Contracting State in which the place of effective management of the enterprise is situated.

4.   If the place of effective management of a shipping enterprise or of an inland waterways transport enterprise is aboard a ship or boat, then it shall be deemed to be situated in the Contracting State in which the home harbour of the ship or boat is situated, or if there is no such home harbour, in the Contracting State of which the operator of the ship or boat is a resident.

5.   The provisions of paragraphs 1 and 2 shall also apply to profits from the participation in a pool, a joint business or an international operating agency.

Article 9
ASSOCIATED ENTERPRISES

1.   Where:

(a)   an enterprise of a Contracting State participates directly or indirectly in the management, control or capital of an enterprise of the other Contracting State, or

(b)   the same persons participate directly or indirectly in the management, control or capital of an enterprise of a Contracting State and an enterprise of the other Contracting State, and in either case conditions are made or imposed between the two enterprises in their commercial or financial relations which differ from those which would be made between independent enterprises, then any profits which would, but for those conditions, have accrued to one of the enterprises, but, by reason of those conditions, have not so accrued, may be included in the profits of that enterprise and taxed accordingly.

2.   Where a Contracting State includes in the profits of an enterprise of that State -- and taxes accordingly -- profits on which an enterprise of the other Contracting State has been charged to tax in that other State and the profits so included are profits which would have accrued to the enterprise of the first-mentioned State if the conditions made between the two enterprises had been those which would have been made between independent enterprises, then that other State shall make an appropriate adjustment to the amount of the tax charged therein on those profits. In determining such adjustment, due regard shall be had to the other provisions of the Convention and the competent authorities of the Contracting States shall, if necessary, consult each other.

3.   The provisions of paragraph 2 shall not apply where judicial, administrative or other legal proceedings have resulted in a final ruling that by actions giving rise to an adjustment of profits under paragraph 1, one of the enterprises concerned is liable to penalty with respect to fraud, gross negligence or wilful default.

Article 10
DIVIDENDS

1.   Dividends paid by a company which is a resident of a Contracting State to a resident of the other Contracting State may be taxed in that other State.

2.   However, such dividends may also be taxed in the Contracting State of which the company paying the dividends is a resident and according to the laws of that State, but if the beneficial owner of the dividends is a resident of the other Contracting State, the tax so charged shall not exceed:

(a)   ... per cent (the percentage is to be established through bilateral negotiations) of the gross amount of the dividends if the beneficial owner is a company (other than a partnership) which holds directly at least 10 per cent of the capital of the company paying the dividends;

(b)   ... per cent (the percentage is to be established through bilateral negotiations) of the gross amount of the dividends in all other cases.

The competent authorities of the Contracting States shall by mutual agreement settle the mode of application of these limitations.

This paragraph shall not affect the taxation of the company in respect of the profits out of which the dividends are paid.

3.   The term "dividends" as used in this article means income from shares, "jouissance" shares or "jouissance" rights, mining shares, founders' shares or other rights, not being debt-claims, participating in profits, as well as income from other corporate rights which is subjected to the same taxation treatment as income from shares by the laws of the State of which the company making the distribution is a resident.

4.   The provisions of paragraphs 1 and 2 shall not apply if the beneficial owner of the dividends, being a resident of a Contracting State, carries on business in the other Contracting State of which the company paying the dividends is a resident, through a permanent establishment situated therein, or performs in that other State independent personal services from a fixed base situated therein, and the holding in respect of which the dividends are paid is effectively connected with such permanent establishment or fixed base. In such case the provisions of article 7 or article 14, as the case may be, shall apply.

5.   Where a company which is a resident of a Contracting State derives profits or income from the other Contracting State, that other State may not impose any tax on the dividends paid by the company, except in so far as such dividends are paid to a resident of that other State or in so far as the holding in respect of which the dividends are paid is effectively connected with a permanent establishment or a fixed base situated in that other State, nor subject the company's undistributed profits to a tax on the company's undistributed profits, even if the dividends paid or the undistributed profits consist wholly or partly of profits or income arising in such other State.

Article 11
INTEREST

1.   Interest arising in a Contracting State and paid to a resident of the other Contracting State may be taxed in that other State.

2.   However, such interest may also be taxed in the Contracting State in which it arises and according to the laws of that State, but if the beneficial owner of the interest is a resident of the other Contracting State, the tax so charged shall not exceed ... per cent (the percentage is to be established through bilateral negotiations) of the gross amount of the interest. The competent authorities of the Contracting States shall by mutual agreement settle the mode of application of this limitation.

3.   The term "interest" as used in this article means income from debt-claims of every kind, whether or not secured by mortgage and whether or not carrying a right to participate in the debtor's profits, and in particular, income from government securities and income from bonds or debentures, including premiums and prizes attaching to such securities, bonds or debentures. Penalty charges for late payment shall not be regarded as interest for the purpose of this article.

4.   The provisions of paragraphs 1 and 2 shall not apply if the beneficial owner of the interest, being a resident of a Contracting State, carries on business in the other Contracting State

in which the interest arises, through a permanent establishment situated therein, or performs in that other State independent personal services from a fixed base situated therein, and the debt-claim in respect of which the interest is paid is effectively connected with (a) such permanent establishment or fixed base, or with (b) business activities referred to in (c) of paragraph 1 of article 7. In such cases the provisions of article 7 or article 14, as the case may be, shall apply.

5.   Interest shall be deemed to arise in a Contracting State when the payer is a resident of that State. Where, however, the person paying the interest, whether he is a resident of a Contracting State or not, has in a Contracting State a permanent establishment or a fixed base in connection with which the indebtedness on which the interest is paid was incurred, and such interest is borne by such permanent establishment or fixed base, then such interest shall be deemed to arise in the State in which the permanent establishment or fixed base is situated.

6.   Where, by reason of a special relationship between the payer and the beneficial owner or between both of them and some other person, the amount of the interest, having regard to the debt-claim for which it is paid, exceeds the amount which would have been agreed upon by the payer and the beneficial owner in the absence of such relationship, the provisions of this article shall apply only to the last-mentioned amount. In such case, the excess part of the payments shall remain taxable according to the laws of each Contracting State, due regard being had to the other provisions of this Convention.

Article 12
ROYALTIES

1.   Royalties arising in a Contracting State and paid to a resident of the other Contracting State may be taxed in that other State.

2.   However, such royalties may also be taxed in the Contracting State in which they arise and according to the laws of that State, but if the beneficial owner of the royalties is a resident of the other Contracting State, the tax so charged shall not exceed ... per cent (the percentage is to be established through bilateral negotiations) of the gross amount of the royalties. The competent authorities of the Contracting States shall by mutual agreement settle the mode of application of this limitation.

3.   The term "royalties" as used in this article means payments of any kind received as a consideration for the use of, or the right to use, any copyright of literary, artistic or scientific work including cinematograph films, or films or tapes used for radio or television broadcasting, any patent, trade mark, design or model, plan, secret formula or process, or for the use of, or the right to use, industrial, commercial or scientific equipment or for information concerning industrial, commercial or scientific experience.

4.   The provisions of paragraphs 1 and 2 shall not apply if the beneficial owner of the royalties, being a resident of a Contracting State, carries on business in the other Contracting State in which the royalties arise, through a permanent establishment situated therein, or performs in that other State independent personal services from a fixed base situated therein, and the right or property in respect of which the royalties are paid is effectively connected with (a) such permanent establishment or fixed base, or with (b) business activities referred to in (c) of paragraph 1 of article 7. In such cases the provisions of article 7 or article 14, as the case may be, shall apply.

5.   Royalties shall be deemed to arise in a Contracting State when the payer is a resident of that State. Where, however, the person paying the royalties, whether he is a resident of a Contracting State or not, has in a Contracting State a permanent establishment or a fixed base in connection with which the liability to pay the royalties was incurred, and such royalties are borne by such permanent establishment or fixed base, then such royalties shall be deemed to arise in the State in which the permanent establishment or fixed base is situated.

6.   Where by reason of a special relationship between the payer and the beneficial owner or between both of them and some other person, the amount of the royalties, having regard to the use, right or information for which they are paid, exceeds the amount which would have been agreed upon by the payer and the beneficial owner in the absence of such relationship, the provisions of this article shall apply only to the last-mentioned amount. In such case, the excess part of the payments shall remain taxable according to the laws of each Contracting State, due regard being had to the other provisions of this Convention.

Article 13
CAPITAL GAINS

1.   Gains derived by a resident of a Contracting State from the alienation of immovable property referred to in article 6 and situated in the other Contracting State may be taxed in that other State.

2.   Gains from the alienation of movable property forming part of the business property of a permanent establishment which an enterprise of a Contracting State has in the other Contracting State or of movable property pertaining to a fixed base available to a resident of a Contracting State in the other Contracting State for the purpose of performing independent personal services, including such gains from the alienation of such a permanent establishment (alone or with the whole enterprise) or of such fixed base, may be taxed in that other State.

3.   Gains from the alienation of ships or aircraft operated in international traffic, boats engaged in inland waterways transport or movable property pertaining to the operation of such ships, aircraft or boats, shall be taxable only in the Contracting State in which the place of effective management of the enterprise is situated.

4.   Gains from the alienation of shares of the capital stock of a company, or of an interest in a partnership, trust or estate, the property of which consists directly or indirectly principally of immovable property situated in a Contracting State may be taxed in that State. In particular:

   (1)   Nothing contained in this paragraph 4 shall apply to a company, partnership, trust or estate, other than a company, partnership, trust or estate engaged in the business of management of immovable properties, the property of which consists directly or indirectly principally of immovable property used by such company, partnership, trust or estate in its business activities.

   (2)   For the purposes of this paragraph, "principally" in relation to ownership of immovable property means the value of such immovable property exceeding 50 percent of the aggregate value of all assets owned by the company, partnership, trust or estate.

5.   Gains from the alienation of shares other than those mentioned in paragraph 4 representing a participation of ... per cent (the percentage is to be established through bilateral negotiations) in a company which is a resident of a Contracting State may be taxed in that State.

6.   Gains from the alienation of any property other than that referred to in paragraphs 1, 2, 3, 4 and 5 shall be taxable only in the Contracting State of which the alienator is a resident.

Article 14
INDEPENDENT PERSONAL SERVICES

1.   Income derived by a resident of a Contracting State in respect of professional services or other activities of an independent character shall be taxable only in that State except in the following circumstances, when such income may also be taxed in the other Contracting State:

   (a)   If he has a fixed base regularly available to him in the other Contracting State for the purpose of performing his activities; in that case, only so much of the income as is attributable to that fixed base may be taxed in that other Contracting State; or

   (b)   If his stay in the other Contracting State is for a period or periods amounting to or exceeding in the aggregate 183 days in any twelve-month period commencing or ending in the fiscal year concerned; in that case, only so much of the income as is derived from his activities performed in that other State may be taxed in that other State.

2.   The term "professional services" includes especially independent scientific, literary, artistic, educational or teaching activities as well as the independent activities of physicians, lawyers, engineers, architects, dentists and accountants.

Article 15
DEPENDENT PERSONAL SERVICES

1.   Subject to the provisions of articles 16, 18 and 19, salaries, wages and other similar remuneration derived by a resident of a Contracting State in respect of an employment shall be taxable only in that State unless the employment is exercised in the other Contracting State. If the employment is so exercised, such remuneration as is derived therefrom may be taxed in that other State.

2.   Notwithstanding the provisions of paragraph 1, remuneration derived by a resident of a Contracting State in respect of an employment exercised in the other Contracting State shall be taxable only in the first-mentioned State if:

   (a)   The recipient is present in the other State for a period or periods not exceeding in the aggregate 183 days in any twelve-month period commencing or ending in the fiscal year concerned; and

   (b)   The remuneration is paid by, or on behalf of, an employer who is not a resident of the other State; and

   (c)   The remuneration is not borne by a permanent establishment or a fixed base which the employer has in the other State.

3.   Notwithstanding the preceding provisions of this article, remuneration derived in respect of an employment exercised aboard a ship or aircraft operated in international traffic, or aboard a boat engaged in inland waterways transport, may be taxed in the Contracting State in which the place of effective management of the enterprise is situated.

Article 16
DIRECTORS' FEES AND REMUNERATION OF TOP-LEVEL MANAGERIAL OFFICIALS

1.   Directors' fees and other similar payments derived by a resident of a Contracting State in his capacity as a member of the Board of Directors of a company which is a resident of the other Contracting State may be taxed in that other State.

2.   Salaries, wages and other similar remuneration derived by a resident of a Contracting State in his capacity as an official in a top-level managerial position of a company which is a resident of the other Contracting State may be taxed in that other State.

Article 17
ARTISTES AND SPORTSPERSONS

1.   Notwithstanding the provisions of articles 14 and 15, income derived by a resident of a Contracting State as an entertainer, such as a theatre, motion picture, radio or television artiste, or a musician, or as a sportsperson, from his personal activities as such exercised in the other Contracting State, may be taxed in that other State.

2.   Where income in respect of personal activities exercised by an entertainer or a sportsperson in his capacity as such accrues not to the entertainer or sportsperson himself but to another person, that income may, notwithstanding the provisions of articles 7, 14 and 15, be taxed in the Contracting State in which the activities of the entertainer or sportsperson are exercised.

Article 18
PENSIONS AND SOCIAL SECURITY PAYMENTS

Article 18 (alternative A)

1.   Subject to the provisions of paragraph 2 of article 19, pensions and other similar remuneration paid to a resident of a Contracting State in consideration of past employment shall be taxable only in that State.

2.   Notwithstanding the provisions of paragraph 1, pensions paid and other payments made under a public scheme which is part of the social security system of a Contracting State or a political subdivision or a local authority thereof shall be taxable only in that State.

Article 18 (alternative B)

1.   Subject to the provisions of paragraph 2 of article 19, pensions and other similar remuneration paid to a resident of a Contracting State in consideration of past employment may be taxed in that State.

2.   However, such pensions and other similar remuneration may also be taxed in the other Contracting State if the payment is made by a resident of that other State or a permanent establishment situated therein.

3.   Notwithstanding the provisions of paragraphs 1 and 2, pensions paid and other payments made under a public scheme which is part of the social security system of a Contracting State or a political subdivision or a local authority thereof shall be taxable only in that State.

Article 19
GOVERNMENT SERVICE

1.   (a)   Salaries, wages and other similar remuneration, other than a pension, paid by a Contracting State or a political subdivision or a local authority thereof to an individual in respect of services rendered to that State or subdivision or authority shall be taxable only in that State.

        (b)   However, such salaries, wages and other similar remuneration shall be taxable only in the other Contracting State if the services are rendered in that other State and the individual is a resident of that State who:

                (i)   Is a national of that State; or

                (ii)   Did not become a resident of that State solely for the purpose of rendering the services.

2.   (a)   Any pension paid by, or out of funds created by, a Contracting State or a political subdivision or a local authority thereof to an individual in respect of services rendered to that State or subdivision or authority shall be taxable only in that State.

        (b)   However, such pension shall be taxable only in the other Contracting State if the individual is a resident of, and a national of, that other State.

3.   The provisions of articles 15, 16, 17 and 18 shall apply to salaries, wages and other similar remuneration, and to pensions, in respect of services rendered in connection with a business carried on by a Contracting State or a political subdivision or a local authority thereof.

Article 20
STUDENTS

Payments which a student or business trainee or apprentice who is or was immediately before visiting a Contracting State a resident of the other Contracting State and who is present in the first-mentioned State solely for the purpose of his education or training receives for the purpose of his maintenance, education or training shall not be taxed in that State, provided that such payments arise from sources outside that State.

Article 21
OTHER INCOME

1.   Items of income of a resident of a Contracting State, wherever arising, not dealt with in the foregoing articles of this Convention shall be taxable only in that State.

2.   The provisions of paragraph 1 shall not apply to income, other than income from immovable property as defined in paragraph 2 of article 6, if the recipient of such income, being a resident of a Contracting State, carries on business in the other Contracting State through a permanent establishment situated therein, or performs in that other State independent personal services from a fixed base situated therein, and the right or property in respect of which the income is paid is effectively connected with such permanent establishment or fixed base. In such case the provisions of article 7 or article 14, as the case may be, shall apply.

3.   Notwithstanding the provisions of paragraphs 1 and 2, items of income of a resident of a Contracting State not dealt with in the foregoing articles of this Convention and arising in the other Contracting State may also be taxed in that other State.

Chapter IV
TAXATION OF CAPITAL

Article 22
CAPITAL

1.   Capital represented by immovable property referred to in article 6, owned by a resident of a Contracting State and situated in the other Contracting State, may be taxed in that other State.

2.   Capital represented by movable property forming part of the business property of a permanent establishment which an enterprise of a Contracting State has in the other Contracting State or by movable property pertaining to a fixed base available to a resident of a Contracting State in the other Contracting State for the purpose of performing independent personal services, may be taxed in that other State.

3.   Capital represented by ships and aircraft operated in international traffic and by boats engaged in inland waterways transport, and by movable property pertaining to the operation of such ships, aircraft and boats, shall be taxable only in the Contracting State in which the place of effective management of the enterprise is situated

[4.   All other elements of capital of a resident of a Contracting State shall be taxable only in that State].

(The Group decided to leave to bilateral negotiations the question of the taxation of the capital represented by immovable property and movable property and of all other elements of capital of a resident of a Contracting State. Should the negotiating parties decide to include in the Convention an article on the taxation of capital, they will have to determine whether to use the wording of paragraph 4 as shown or wording that leaves taxation to the State in which the capital is located).

Chapter V
METHODS FOR THE ELIMINATION OF DOUBLE TAXATION

Article 23 A
EXEMPTION METHOD

1.   Where a resident of a Contracting State derives income or owns capital which, in accordance with the provisions of this Convention, may be taxed in the other Contracting State, the first-mentioned State shall, subject to the provisions of paragraphs 2 and 3, exempt such income or capital from tax.

2.   Where a resident of a Contracting State derives items of income which, in accordance with the provisions of articles 10, 11 and 12, may be taxed in the other Contracting State, the first-mentioned State shall allow as a deduction from the tax on the income of that resident an amount equal to the tax paid in that other State. Such deduction shall not, however, exceed that part of the tax, as computed before the deduction is given, which is attributable to such items of income derived from that other State.

3.   Where in accordance with any provision of this Convention income derived or capital owned by a resident of a Contracting State is exempt from tax in that State, such State may nevertheless, in calculating the amount of tax on the remaining income or capital of such resident, take into account the exempted income or capital.

Article 23 B
CREDIT METHOD

1.   Where a resident of a Contracting State derives income or owns capital which, in accordance with the provisions of this Convention, may be taxed in the other Contracting State, the first-mentioned State shall allow as a deduction from the tax on the income of that resident an amount equal to the income tax paid in that other State; and as a deduction from the tax on the capital of that resident, an amount equal to the capital tax paid in that other State. Such deduction in either case shall not, however, exceed that part of the income tax or capital tax, as computed before the deduction is given, which is attributable, as the case may be, to the income or the capital which may be taxed in that other State.

2.   Where, in accordance with any provision of this Convention, income derived or capital owned by a resident of a Contracting State is exempt from tax in that State, such State may nevertheless, in calculating the amount of tax on the remaining income or capital of such resident, take into account the exempted income or capital.

Chapter VI
SPECIAL PROVISIONS

Article 24
NON-DISCRIMINATION

1.   Nationals of a Contracting State shall not be subjected in the other Contracting State to any taxation or any requirement connected therewith which is other or more burdensome than the taxation and connected requirements to which nationals of that other State in the same

circumstances, in particular with respect to residence, are or may be subjected. This provision shall, notwithstanding the provisions of article 1, also apply to persons who are not residents of one or both of the Contracting States.

2.   Stateless persons who are residents of a Contracting State shall not be subjected in either Contracting State to any taxation or any requirement connected therewith which is other or more burdensome than the taxation and connected requirements to which nationals of the State concerned in the same circumstances, in particular with respect to residence, are or may be subjected.

3.   The taxation on a permanent establishment which an enterprise of a Contracting State has in the other Contracting State shall not be less favourably levied in that other State than the taxation levied on enterprises of that other State carrying on the same activities. This provision shall not be construed as obliging a Contracting State to grant to residents of the other Contracting State any personal allowances, reliefs and reductions for taxation purposes on account of civil status or family responsibilities which it grants to its own residents.

4.   Except where the provisions of paragraph 1 of article 9, paragraph 6 of article 11, or paragraph 6 of article 12 apply, interest, royalties and other disbursements paid by an enterprise of a Contracting State to a resident of the other Contracting State shall, for the purpose of determining the taxable profits of such enterprise, be deductible under the same conditions as if they had been paid to a resident of the first-mentioned State. Similarly, any debts of an enterprise of a Contracting State to a resident of the other Contracting State shall, for the purpose of determining the taxable capital of such enterprise, be deductible under the same conditions as if they had been contracted to a resident of the first-mentioned State.

5.   Enterprises of a Contracting State, the capital of which is wholly or partly owned or controlled, directly or indirectly, by one or more residents of the other Contracting State, shall not be subjected in the first-mentioned State to any taxation or any requirement connected therewith which is other or more burdensome than the taxation and connected requirements to which other similar enterprises of the first-mentioned State are or may be subjected.

6.   The provisions of this article shall, notwithstanding the provisions of article 2, apply to taxes of every kind and description.

Article 25
MUTUAL AGREEMENT PROCEDURE

1.   Where a person considers that the actions of one or both of the Contracting States result or will result for him in taxation not in accordance with the provisions of this Convention, he may, irrespective of the remedies provided by the domestic law of those States, present his case to the competent authority of the Contracting State of which he is a resident or, if his case comes under paragraph 1 of article 24, to that of the Contracting State of which he is a national. The case must be presented within three years from the first notification of the action resulting in taxation not in accordance with the provisions of the Convention.

2.   The competent authority shall endeavour, if the objection appears to it to be justified and if it is not itself able to arrive at a satisfactory solution, to resolve the case by mutual agreement with the competent authority of the other Contracting State, with a view to the avoidance of

taxation which is not in accordance with this Convention. Any agreement reached shall be implemented notwithstanding any time limits in the domestic law of the Contracting States.

3.   The competent authorities of the Contracting States shall endeavour to resolve by mutual agreement any difficulties or doubts arising as to the interpretation or application of the Convention. They may also consult together for the elimination of double taxation in cases not provided for in the Convention.

4.   The competent authorities of the Contracting States may communicate with each other directly, including through a joint commission consisting of themselves or their representatives, for the purpose of reaching an agreement in the sense of the preceding paragraphs. The competent authorities, through consultations, shall develop appropriate bilateral procedures, conditions, methods and techniques for the implementation of the mutual agreement procedure provided for in this article. In addition, a competent authority may devise appropriate unilateral procedures, conditions, methods and techniques to facilitate the above-mentioned bilateral actions and the implementation of the mutual agreement procedure.

Article 26
EXCHANGE OF INFORMATION

1.   The competent authorities of the Contracting States shall exchange such information as is necessary for carrying out the provisions of this Convention or of the domestic laws of the Contracting States concerning taxes covered by the Convention, in so far as the taxation thereunder is not contrary to the Convention, in particular for the prevention of fraud or evasion of such taxes. The exchange of information is not restricted by article 1. Any information received by a Contracting State shall be treated as secret in the same manner as information obtained under the domestic laws of that State. However, if the information is originally regarded as secret in the transmitting State it shall be disclosed only to persons or authorities (including courts and administrative bodies) concerned with the assessment or collection of, the enforcement or prosecution in respect of, or the determination of appeals in relation to, the taxes which are the subject of the Convention. Such persons or authorities shall use the information only for such purposes but may disclose the information in public court proceedings or in judicial decisions. The competent authorities shall, through consultation, develop appropriate conditions, methods and techniques concerning the matters in respect of which such exchanges of information shall be made, including, where appropriate, exchanges of information regarding tax avoidance.

2.   In no case shall the provisions of paragraph 1 be construed so as to impose on a Contracting State the obligation:

(a)   To carry out administrative measures at variance with the laws and administrative practice of that or of the other Contracting State;

(b)   To supply information which is not obtainable under the laws or in the normal course of the administration of that or of the other Contracting State;

(c)   To supply information which would disclose any trade, business, industrial, commercial or professional secret or trade process, or information, the disclosure of which would be contrary to public policy (ordre public).

Article 27
MEMBERS OF DIPLOMATIC MISSIONS AND CONSULAR POSTS

Nothing in this Convention shall affect the fiscal privileges of members of diplomatic missions or consular posts under the general rules of international law or under the provisions of special agreements.

Chapter VII
FINAL PROVISIONS

Article 28
ENTRY INTO FORCE

1.   This Convention shall be ratified and the instruments of ratification shall be exchanged at .... as soon as possible.

2.   . The Convention shall enter into force upon the exchange of instruments of ratification and its provisions shall have effect:

   (a)   (In State A): ....

   (b)   (In State B): ....

Article 29
TERMINATION

This Convention shall remain in force until terminated by a Contracting State. Either Contracting State may terminate the Convention, through diplomatic channels, by giving notice of termination at least six months before the end of any calendar year after the year ____. In such event, the Convention shall cease to have effect:

   (a)   (In State A): ....

   (b)   (In State B): ....

TERMINAL CLAUSE

   NOTE: The provisions relating to the entry into force and termination and the terminal clause concerning the signing of the Convention shall be drafted in accordance with the constitutional procedure of both Contracting States.

*   *   *

PART TWO

INTERREGIONAL AND REGIONAL INSTRUMENTS

PART TWO

INTERNATIONAL AND REGIONAL INSTRUMENTS

REVISED OECD DECLARATION ON INTERNATIONAL INVESTMENT AND MULTINATIONAL ENTERPRISES, COMMENTARY ON THE OECD GUIDELINES FOR MULTINATIONAL ENTERPRISES, AND COMMENTARY ON THE IMPLEMENTATION PROCEDURES OF THE OECD GUIDELINES FOR MULTINATIONAL ENTERPRISES [*]

(ORGANISATION FOR ECONOMIC CO-OPERATION AND DEVELOPMENT)

The OECD Declaration on International Investment and Multinational Enterprises was adopted by the Governments of OECD member countries on 21 June 1976. It was reviewed in 1979, 1982, 1984, 1991 and 2000. The previous version is reproduced in volume II of this *Compendium*. The Declaration has two Annexes, one containing the OECD Guidelines for Multinational Enterprises and the other dealing with general considerations and practical approaches concerning conflicting requirements imposed on TNCs. The implementation of the Declaration is dealt with in the four procedural Decisions by the OECD Council. Commentaries have been prepared by the Committee on International Investment and Multinational Enterprises that provide further explanations of the Guidelines texts and of the Council Decision on Implementation of the Guidelines. The Commentaries are not part of the Declaration on International Investment and Multinational Enterprises or of the Council Decision on the OECD Guidelines for Multinational Enterprises. As of 27 June 2000, the countries adhering to the Declaration were the 30 OECD members as well as Argentina, Brazil and Chile.

FOREWORD

The OECD has long been a focal point for co-operation among Member countries in the area of international direct investment and multinational enterprises. This co-operation is based on the 1976 Declaration on International Investment and Multinational Enterprises and its associated Decisions of the OECD Council which have been strengthened in various ways over the past twenty-four years. These instruments reflect a consensus based on a shared philosophy and a common approach among twenty-nine OECD and four non-OECD Member countries (Argentina, Brazil, Chile and the Slovak Republic[1]) and contain four inter-related elements:

- **The Guidelines for Multinational Enterprises** provide voluntary principles and standards for responsible business conduct addressed to multinational enterprises themselves;

---

[*] *Source*: Organisation for Economic Co-operation and Development (2000). "The OECD Declaration and Decisions on International Investment and Multinational Enterprises", November 2000, DAFFE/IME(2000)20. [Note added by the editor.]

[1] On 28 September 2000, Slovakia signed an Agreement setting out the terms under which it will become the thirtieth member of the OEC D. The Agreement will now be submitted to the Slovak Parliament for ratification, a process that is expected to take approximately two months.

- **The National Treatment Instrument** sets out member countries' commitment to accord to foreign-controlled enterprises operating in their territories treatment no less favourable than that accorded to domestic enterprises in like situations;

- An instrument on **International Investment Incentives and Disincentives** provides for efforts among member countries to improve co-operation on measures affecting international direct investment; and

- An instrument on **Conflicting Requirements** calls on Member countries to avoid or minimise conflicting requirements imposed on multinational enterprises by governments of different countries.

The OECD Declaration and Decisions have periodically been reviewed[2] (1979, 1982, 1984, 1991). The most recent review concerned the Guidelines for Multinational Enterprises and was completed in June 2000. In comparison with the earlier reviews the changes to the text of the Guidelines are far-reaching and reinforce the core elements – economic, social and environmental – of the sustainable development agenda[3]. They have been developed in constructive dialogue with the business community, labour representatives and non-governmental organisations. The revisions to the implementation procedures maintain the focus on the National Contact Points (NCPs), as the key government institution responsible for furthering effective implementation of the Guidelines; however, they provided more guidance to National Contact Points in fulfilling their role and has also clarified the CIME's role.

In welcoming the updated Guidelines for Multinational Enterprises, OECD Ministers[4] noted that "the Guidelines provide a robust set of recommendations for responsible corporate behaviour worldwide consistent with existing legislation. They are part of the OECD Declaration on International Investment and Multinational Enterprises which provides a balanced framework to improve the international investment climate and encourage the positive contributions multinational enterprises can make to economic, social and environmental goals".

Ministers also noted that "OECD will continue its analytical work in the field of investment policy, including work on maximising the benefits of investment liberalisation, its social and environmental dimensions and on harmful forms of policy-based competition to attract investment. OECD will encourage non-members to adhere to the Declaration on International Investment and Multinational Enterprises".

---

[2] See the Review reports: *International Investment and Multinational Enterprises: Review of the 1976 Declaration and Decisions* (OECD Paris, 1979); *Mid-Term Report on the 1976 Declaration and Decisions* (OECD Paris, 1982); 1984 *Review of the 1976 Declaration and Decisions* (OECD Paris, 1984); The *OECD Declaration and Decisions on International Investment and Multinational Enterprises, 1991 Review* (OECD Paris, 1992).

[3] With the addition of recommendations relating to the elimination of child and forced labour, all internationally recognised core labour standards are now covered by the Guidelines. The environment section now encourages enterprises to raise their environmental performance, through such measures as improved internal environmental management, stronger disclosure of environmental information, and better contingency planning for environmental impacts. A recommendation on human rights has been introduced. New chapters on combating corruption and on consumer protection have also been added. The chapter on disclosure and transparency has been updated to reflect the *OECD Principles on Corporate Governance* and to recognise and encourage progress in enhancing firms' social and environmental accountability.

[4] Extract from the final news release at the OECD Ministerial, June 2000 [http://www.oecd.org/media/release/nw00-70a.htm (paragraph 26)].

The effectiveness of the Declaration and its constituent elements depends on the follow-up which adhering countries will give to it, both nationally and within the procedures set up at the level of OECD.

The ongoing support and involvement of the business community represented by the Business and Industry Advisory committee (BIAC), labour, represented by the Trade Union Advisory Committee (TUAC) and other non-governmental organisations will also be crucial.

I.   DECLARATION ON INTERNATIONAL INVESTMENT AND

MULTINATIONAL ENTERPRISES

27 June 2000

ADHERING GOVERNMENTS[5]

CONSIDERING:

- That international investment is of major importance to the world economy, and has considerably contributed to the development of their countries;

- That multinational enterprises play an important role in this investment process;

- That international co-operation can improve the foreign investment climate, encourage the positive contribution which multinational enterprises can make to economic, social and environmental progress, and minimise and resolve difficulties which may arise from their operations;

- That the benefits of international co-operation are enhanced by addressing issues relating to international investment and multinational enterprises through a balanced framework of inter-related instruments;

DECLARE:

Guidelines for Multinational Enterprises

I.   That they jointly recommend to multinational enterprises operating in or from their territories the observance of the Guidelines, set forth in Annex 1 hereto[6], having regard to the considerations and understandings that are set out in the Preface and are an integral part of them;"

---

5. As at 27 June 2000 adhering governments are those of all OECD Members, as well as Argentina, Brazil, Chile and the Slovak Republic. The European Community has been invited to associate itself with the section on National Treatment on matters falling within its competence.

6 . The text of the Guidelines for Multinational Enterprises is reproduced in Annex 1 of this booklet.

National Treatment

II.1.   That adhering governments should, consistent with their needs to maintain public order, to protect their essential security interests and to fulfil commitments relating to international peace and security, accord to enterprises operating in their territories and owned or controlled directly or indirectly by nationals of another adhering government (hereinafter referred to as "Foreign-Controlled Enterprises") treatment under their laws, regulations and administrative practices, consistent with international law and no less favourable than that accorded in like situations to domestic enterprises (hereinafter referred to as "National Treatment");

2.   That adhering governments will consider applying "National Treatment" in respect of countries other than adhering governments;

3.   That adhering governments will endeavour to ensure that their territorial subdivisions apply "National Treatment";

4.   That this Declaration does not deal with the right of adhering governments to regulate the entry of foreign investment or the conditions of establishment of foreign enterprises;

Conflicting Requirements

III.   That they will co-operate with a view to avoiding or minimising the imposition of conflicting requirements on multinational enterprises and that they will take into account the general considerations and practical approaches as set forth in Annex 2 hereto[7].

International Investment Incentives and Disincentives

IV.1.   That they recognise the need to strengthen their co-operation in the field of international direct investment;

2.   That they thus recognise the need to give due weight to the interests of adhering governments affected by specific laws, regulations and administrative practices in this field (hereinafter called "measures") providing official incentives and disincentives to international direct investment;

3.   That adhering governments will endeavour to make such measures as transparent as possible, so that their importance and purpose can be ascertained and that information on them can be readily available;

Consultation Procedures

V.   That they are prepared to consult one another on the above matters in conformity with the relevant Decisions of the Council;

Review

VI.   That they will review the above matters periodically with a view to improving the effectiveness of international economic co-operation among adhering governments on issues relating to international investment and multinational enterprises.

---

7 . The text of General considerations and Practical Approaches concerning Conflicting Requirements Imposed on Multinational Enterprises is reproduced in Annex 2 of this booklet.

Annex 1

THE OECD GUIDELINES FOR MULTINATIONAL ENTERPRISES

Preface

1.   The *OECD Guidelines for Multinational Enterprises* (the *Guidelines*) are recommendations addressed by governments to multinational enterprises. They provide voluntary principles and standards for responsible business conduct consistent with applicable laws. The *Guidelines* aim to ensure that the operations of these enterprises are in harmony with government policies, to strengthen the basis of mutual confidence between enterprises and the societies in which they operate, to help improve the foreign investment climate and to enhance the contribution to sustainable development made by multinational enterprises. The *Guidelines* are part of the *OECD Declaration on International Investment and Multinational Enterprises* the other elements of which relate to national treatment, conflicting requirements on enterprises, and international investment incentives and disincentives.

2.   International business has experienced far-reaching structural change and the *Guidelines* themselves have evolved to reflect these changes. With the rise of service and knowledge-intensive industries, service and technology enterprises have entered the international marketplace. Large enterprises still account for a major share of international investment, and there is a trend toward large-scale international mergers. At the same time, foreign investment by small- and medium-sized enterprises has also increased and these enterprises now play a significant role on the international scene. Multinational enterprises, like their domestic counterparts, have evolved to encompass a broader range of business arrangements and organisational forms. Strategic alliances and closer relations with suppliers and contractors tend to blur the boundaries of the enterprise.

3.   The rapid evolution in the structure of multinational enterprises is also reflected in their operations in the developing world, where foreign direct investment has grown rapidly. In developing countries, multinational enterprises have diversified beyond primary production and extractive industries into manufacturing, assembly, domestic market development and services.

4.   The activities of multinational enterprises, through international trade and investment, have strengthened and deepened the ties that join OECD economies to each other and to the rest of the world. These activities bring substantial benefits to home and host countries. These benefits accrue when multinational enterprises supply the products and services that consumers want to buy at competitive prices and when they provide fair returns to suppliers of capital. Their trade and investment activities contribute to the efficient use of capital, technology and human and natural resources. They facilitate the transfer of technology among the regions of the world and the development of technologies that reflect local conditions. Through both formal training and on-the-job learning enterprises also promote the development of human capital in host countries.

5.   The nature, scope and speed of economic changes have presented new strategic challenges for enterprises and their stakeholders. Multinational enterprises have the opportunity to implement best practice policies for sustainable development that seek to ensure coherence between social, economic and environmental objectives. The ability of multinational enterprises to promote sustainable development is greatly enhanced when trade and investment are conducted in a context of open, competitive and appropriately regulated markets.

6.   Many multinational enterprises have demonstrated that respect for high standards of business conduct can enhance growth. Today's competitive forces are intense and multinational enterprises face a variety of legal, social and regulatory settings. In this context, some enterprises may be tempted to neglect appropriate standards and principles of conduct in an attempt to gain undue competitive advantage. Such practices by the few may call into question the reputation of the many and may give rise to public concerns.

7.   Many enterprises have responded to these public concerns by developing internal programmes, guidance and management systems that underpin their commitment to good corporate citizenship, good practices and good business and employee conduct. Some of them have called upon consulting, auditing and certification services, contributing to the accumulation of expertise in these areas. These efforts have also promoted social dialogue on what constitutes good business conduct. The *Guidelines* clarify the shared expectations for business conduct of the governments adhering to them and provide a point of reference for enterprises. Thus, the *Guidelines* both complement and reinforce private efforts to define and implement responsible business conduct.

8.   Governments are co-operating with each other and with other actors to strengthen the international legal and policy framework in which business is conducted. The post-war period has seen the development of this framework, starting with the adoption in 1948 of the Universal Declaration of Human Rights. Recent instruments include the ILO Declaration on Fundamental Principles and Rights at Work, the Rio Declaration on Environment and Development and Agenda 21 and the Copenhagen Declaration for Social Development.

9.   The OECD has also been contributing to the international policy framework. Recent developments include the adoption of the Convention on Combating Bribery of Foreign Public Officials in International Business Transactions and of the OECD Principles of Corporate Governance, the OECD Guidelines for Consumer Protection in the Context of Electronic Commerce, and ongoing work on the OECD Guidelines on Transfer Pricing for Multinational Enterprises and Tax Administrations.

10.   The common aim of the governments adhering to the *Guidelines* is to encourage the positive contributions that multinational enterprises can make to economic, environmental and social progress and to minimise the difficulties to which their various operations may give rise. In working towards this goal, governments find themselves in partnership with the many businesses, trade unions and other non-governmental organisations that are working in their own ways toward the same end. Governments can help by providing effective domestic policy frameworks that include stable macroeconomic policy, non-discriminatory treatment of firms, appropriate regulation and prudential supervision, an impartial system of courts and law enforcement and efficient and honest public administration. Governments can also help by maintaining and promoting appropriate standards and policies in support of sustainable development and by engaging in ongoing reforms to ensure that public sector activity is efficient and effective. Governments adhering to the *Guidelines* are committed to continual improvement of both domestic and international policies with a view to improving the welfare and living standards of all people.

I. Concepts and Principles

1.   The *Guidelines* are recommendations jointly addressed by governments to multinational enterprises. They provide principles and standards of good practice consistent with applicable

laws. Observance of the *Guidelines* by enterprises is voluntary and not legally enforceable.

2.   Since the operations of multinational enterprises extend throughout the world, international co-operation in this field should extend to all countries. Governments adhering to the *Guidelines* encourage the enterprises operating on their territories to observe the *Guidelines* wherever they operate, while taking into account the particular circumstances of each host country.

3.   A precise definition of multinational enterprises is not required for the purposes of the *Guidelines*. These usually comprise companies or other entities established in more than one country and so linked that they may co-ordinate their operations in various ways. While one or more of these entities may be able to exercise a significant influence over the activities of others, their degree of autonomy within the enterprise may vary widely from one multinational enterprise to another. Ownership may be private, state or mixed. The *Guidelines* are addressed to all the entities within the multinational enterprise (parent companies and/or local entities). According to the actual distribution of responsibilities among them, the different entities are expected to co-operate and to assist one another to facilitate observance of the *Guidelines*.

4.   The *Guidelines* are not aimed at introducing differences of treatment between multinational and domestic enterprises; they reflect good practice for all. Accordingly, multinational and domestic enterprises are subject to the same expectations in respect of their conduct wherever the *Guidelines* are relevant to both.

5.   Governments wish to encourage the widest possible observance of the *Guidelines*. While it is acknowledged that small- and medium-sized enterprises may not have the same capacities as larger enterprises, governments adhering to the *Guidelines* nevertheless encourage them to observe the *Guidelines* recommendations to the fullest extent possible.

6.   Governments adhering to the *Guidelines* should not use them for protectionist purposes nor use them in a way that calls into question the comparative advantage of any country where multinational enterprises invest.

7.   Governments have the right to prescribe the conditions under which multinational enterprises operate within their jurisdictions, subject to international law. The entities of a multinational enterprise located in various countries are subject to the laws applicable in these countries. When multinational enterprises are subject to conflicting requirements by adhering countries, the governments concerned will co-operate in good faith with a view to resolving problems that may arise.

8.   Governments adhering to the *Guidelines* set them forth with the understanding that they will fulfil their responsibilities to treat enterprises equitably and in accordance with international law and with their contractual obligations.

9.   The use of appropriate international dispute settlement mechanisms, including arbitration, is encouraged as a means of facilitating the resolution of legal problems arising between enterprises and host country governments.

10.   Governments adhering to the *Guidelines* will promote them and encourage their use. They will establish National Contact Points that promote the *Guidelines* and act as a forum for

discussion of all matters relating to the *Guidelines*. The adhering Governments will also participate in appropriate review and consultation procedures to address issues concerning interpretation of the *Guidelines* in a changing world.

II. General Policies

Enterprises should take fully into account established policies in the countries in which they operate, and consider the views of other stakeholders. In this regard, enterprises should:

1. Contribute to economic, social and environmental progress with a view to achieving sustainable development.

2. Respect the human rights of those affected by their activities consistent with the host government's international obligations and commitments.

3. Encourage local capacity building through close co-operation with the local community, including business interests, as well as developing the enterprise's activities in domestic and foreign markets, consistent with the need for sound commercial practice.

4. Encourage human capital formation, in particular by creating employment opportunities and facilitating training opportunities for employees.

5. Refrain from seeking or accepting exemptions not contemplated in the statutory or regulatory framework related to environmental, health, safety, labour, taxation, financial incentives, or other issues.

6. Support and uphold good corporate governance principles and develop and apply good corporate governance practices.

7. Develop and apply effective self-regulatory practices and management systems that foster a relationship of confidence and mutual trust between enterprises and the societies in which they operate.

8. Promote employee awareness of, and compliance with, company policies through appropriate dissemination of these policies, including through training programmes.

9. Refrain from discriminatory or disciplinary action against employees who make *bona fide* reports to management or, as appropriate, to the competent public authorities, on practices that contravene the law, the *Guidelines* or the enterprise's policies.

10. Encourage, where practicable, business partners, including suppliers and sub-contractors, to apply principles of corporate conduct compatible with the *Guidelines*.

11. Abstain from any improper involvement in local political activities.

III. Disclosure

1. Enterprises should ensure that timely, regular, reliable and relevant information is disclosed regarding their activities, structure, financial situation and performance. This information should be disclosed for the enterprise as a whole and, where appropriate, along

business lines or geographic areas. Disclosure policies of enterprises should be tailored to the nature, size and location of the enterprise, with due regard taken of costs, business confidentiality and other competitive concerns.

2.   Enterprises should apply high quality standards for disclosure, accounting, and audit. Enterprises are also encouraged to apply high quality standards for non-financial information including environmental and social reporting where they exist. The standards or policies under which both financial and non-financial information are compiled and published should be reported.

3.   Enterprises should disclose basic information showing their name, location, and structure, the name, address and telephone number of the parent enterprise and its main affiliates, its percentage ownership, direct and indirect in these affiliates, including shareholdings between them.

4.   Enterprises should also disclose material information on:

     1.   The financial and operating results of the company;

     2.   Company objectives;

     3.   Major share ownership and voting rights;

     4.   Members of the board and key executives, and their remuneration;

     5.   Material foreseeable risk factors;

     6.   Material issues regarding employees and other stakeholders;

     7.   Governance structures and policies.

5.   Enterprises are encouraged to communicate additional information that could include:

     a)   Value statements or statements of business conduct intended for public disclosure including information on the social, ethical and environmental policies of the enterprise and other codes of conduct to which the company subscribes. In addition, the date of adoption, the countries and entities to which such statements apply and its performance in relation to these statements may be communicated;

     b)   Information on systems for managing risks and complying with laws, and on statements or codes of business conduct;

     c)   Information on relationships with employees and other stakeholders.

IV. Employment and Industrial Relations

Enterprises should, within the framework of applicable law, regulations and prevailing labour relations and employment practices:

1.   a)   Respect the right of their employees to be represented by trade unions and other bona fide representatives of employees, and engage in constructive negotiations, either individually or through employers' associations, with such representatives with a view to reaching agreements on employment conditions;

      b)   Contribute to the effective abolition of child labour;

      c)   Contribute to the elimination of all forms of forced or compulsory labour;

      d)   Not discriminate against their employees with respect to employment or occupation on such grounds as race, colour, sex, religion, political opinion, national extraction or social origin, unless selectivity concerning employee characteristics furthers established governmental policies which specifically promote greater equality of employment opportunity or relates to the inherent requirements of a job.

2.   a)   Provide facilities to employee representatives as may be necessary to assist in the development of effective collective agreements;

      b)   Provide information to employee representatives which is needed for meaningful negotiations on conditions of employment;

      c)   Promote consultation and co-operation between employers and employees and their representatives on matters of mutual concern.

3.   Provide information to employees and their representatives which enables them to obtain a true and fair view of the performance of the entity or, where appropriate, the enterprise as a whole.

4.   a)   Observe standards of employment and industrial relations not less favourable than those observed by comparable employers in the host country;

      b)   Take adequate steps to ensure occupational health and safety in their operations.

5.   In their operations, to the greatest extent practicable, employ local personnel and provide training with a view to improving skill levels, in co-operation with employee representatives and, where appropriate, relevant governmental authorities.

6.   In considering changes in their operations which would have major effects upon the livelihood of their employees, in particular in the case of the closure of an entity involving collective lay-offs or dismissals, provide reasonable notice of such changes to representatives of their employees, and, where appropriate, to the relevant governmental authorities, and co-operate with the employee representatives and appropriate governmental authorities so as to mitigate to the maximum extent practicable adverse effects. In light of the specific circumstances of each case, it would be appropriate if management were able to give such notice prior to the final decision being taken. Other means may also be employed to provide meaningful co-operation to mitigate the effects of such decisions.

7.   In the context of bona fide negotiations with representatives of employees on conditions of employment, or while employees are exercising a right to organise, not threaten to transfer the

whole or part of an operating unit from the country concerned nor transfer employees from the enterprises' component entities in other countries in order to influence unfairly those negotiations or to hinder the exercise of a right to organise.

8.   Enable authorised representatives of their employees to negotiate on collective bargaining or labour-management relations issues and allow the parties to consult on matters of mutual concern with representatives of management who are authorised to take decisions on these matters.

V. Environment

Enterprises should, within the framework of laws, regulations and administrative practices in the countries in which they operate, and in consideration of relevant international agreements, principles, objectives, and standards, take due account of the need to protect the environment, public health and safety, and generally to conduct their activities in a manner contributing to the wider goal of sustainable development. In particular, enterprises should:

1.   Establish and maintain a system of environmental management appropriate to the enterprise, including:

   a)   Collection and evaluation of adequate and timely information regarding the environmental, health, and safety impacts of their activities;

   b)   Establishment of measurable objectives and, where appropriate, targets for improved environmental performance, including periodically reviewing the continuing relevance of these objectives; and

   c)   Regular monitoring and verification of progress toward environmental, health, and safety objectives or targets.

2.   Taking into account concerns about cost, business confidentiality, and the protection of intellectual property rights:

   a)   Provide the public and employees with adequate and timely information on the potential environment, health and safety impacts of the activities of the enterprise, which could include reporting on progress in improving environmental performance; and

   b)   Engage in adequate and timely communication and consultation with the communities directly affected by the environmental, health and safety policies of the enterprise and by their implementation.

3.   Assess, and address in decision-making, the foreseeable environmental, health, and safety-related impacts associated with the processes, goods and services of the enterprise over their full life cycle. Where these proposed activities may have significant environmental, health, or safety impacts, and where they are subject to a decision of a competent authority, prepare an appropriate environmental impact assessment.

4.   Consistent with the scientific and technical understanding of the risks, where there are threats of serious damage to the environment, taking also into account human health and safety,

not use the lack of full scientific certainty as a reason for postponing cost-effective measures to prevent or minimise such damage.

5.   Maintain contingency plans for preventing, mitigating, and controlling serious environmental and health damage from their operations, including accidents and emergencies; and mechanisms for immediate reporting to the competent authorities.

6.   Continually seek to improve corporate environmental performance, by encouraging, where appropriate, such activities as:

    a)   Adoption of technologies and operating procedures in all parts of the enterprise that reflect standards concerning environmental performance in the best performing part of the enterprise;

    b)   Development and provision of products or services that have no undue environmental impacts; are safe in their intended use; are efficient in their consumption of energy and natural resources; can be reused, recycled, or disposed of safely;

    c)   Promoting higher levels of awareness among customers of the environmental implications of using the products and services of the enterprise; and

    d)   Research on ways of improving the environmental performance of the enterprise over the longer term.

7.   Provide adequate education and training to employees in environmental health and safety matters, including the handling of hazardous materials and the prevention of environmental accidents, as well as more general environmental management areas, such as environmental impact assessment procedures, public relations, and environmental technologies.

8.   Contribute to the development of environmentally meaningful and economically efficient public policy, for example, by means of partnerships or initiatives that will enhance environmental awareness and protection.

VI. Combating Bribery

Enterprises should not, directly or indirectly, offer, promise, give, or demand a bribe or other undue advantage to obtain or retain business or other improper advantage. Nor should enterprises be solicited or expected to render a bribe or other undue advantage. In particular, enterprises should:

1.   Not offer, nor give in to demands, to pay public officials or the employees of business partners any portion of a contract payment. They should not use subcontracts, purchase orders or consulting agreements as means of channelling payments to public officials, to employees of business partners or to their relatives or business associates.

2.   Ensure that remuneration of agents is appropriate and for legitimate services only. Where relevant, a list of agents employed in connection with transactions with public bodies and state-owned enterprises should be kept and made available to competent authorities.

3.   Enhance the transparency of their activities in the fight against bribery and extortion. Measures could include making public commitments against bribery and extortion and disclosing the management systems the company has adopted in order to honour these commitments. The enterprise should also foster openness and dialogue with the public so as to promote its awareness of and co-operation with the fight against bribery and extortion.

4.   Promote employee awareness of and compliance with company policies against bribery and extortion through appropriate dissemination of these policies and through training programmes and disciplinary procedures.

5.   Adopt management control systems that discourage bribery and corrupt practices, and adopt financial and tax accounting and auditing practices that prevent the establishment of "off the books" or secret accounts or the creation of documents which do not properly and fairly record the transactions to which they relate.

6.   Not make illegal contributions to candidates for public office or to political parties or to other political organisations. Contributions should fully comply with public disclosure requirements and should be reported to senior management.

VII. Consumer Interests

When dealing with consumers, enterprises should act in accordance with fair business, marketing and advertising practices and should take all reasonable steps to ensure the safety and quality of the goods or services they provide. In particular, they should:

1.   Ensure that the goods or services they provide meet all agreed or legally required standards for consumer health and safety, including health warnings and product safety and information labels.

2.   As appropriate to the goods or services, provide accurate and clear information regarding their content, safe use, maintenance, storage, and disposal sufficient to enable consumers to make informed decisions.

3.   Provide transparent and effective procedures that address consumer complaints and contribute to fair and timely resolution of consumer disputes without undue cost or burden.

4.   Not make representations or omissions, nor engage in any other practices, that are deceptive, misleading, fraudulent, or unfair.

5.   Respect consumer privacy and provide protection for personal data.

6.   Co-operate fully and in a transparent manner with public authorities in the prevention or removal of serious threats to public health and safety deriving from the consumption or use of their products.

VIII. Science and Technology

Enterprises should:

1. Endeavour to ensure that their activities are compatible with the science and technology (S&T) policies and plans of the countries in which they operate and as appropriate contribute to the development of local and national innovative capacity.

2. Adopt, where practicable in the course of their business activities, practices that permit the transfer and rapid diffusion of technologies and know-how, with due regard to the protection of intellectual property rights.

3. When appropriate, perform science and technology development work in host countries to address local market needs, as well as employ host country personnel in an S&T capacity and encourage their training, taking into account commercial needs.

4. When granting licenses for the use of intellectual property rights or when otherwise transferring technology, do so on reasonable terms and conditions and in a manner that contributes to the long term development prospects of the host country.

5. Where relevant to commercial objectives, develop ties with local universities, public research institutions, and participate in co-operative research projects with local industry or industry associations.

IX. Competition

Enterprises should, within the framework of applicable laws and regulations, conduct their activities in a competitive manner. In particular, enterprises should:

1. Refrain from entering into or carrying out anti-competitive agreements among competitors:

    a) To fix prices;

    b) To make rigged bids (collusive tenders);

    c) To establish output restrictions or quotas; or

    d) To share or divide markets by allocating customers, suppliers, territories or lines of commerce.

2. Conduct all of their activities in a manner consistent with all applicable competition laws, taking into account the applicability of the competition laws of jurisdictions whose economies would be likely to be harmed by anti-competitive activity on their part.

3. Co-operate with the competition authorities of such jurisdictions by, among other things and subject to applicable law and appropriate safeguards, providing as prompt and complete responses as practicable to requests for information.

4. Promote employee awareness of the importance of compliance with all applicable competition laws and policies.

IX. Taxation

It is important that enterprises contribute to the public finances of host countries by making timely payment of their tax liabilities. In particular, enterprises should comply with the tax laws and regulations in all countries in which they operate and should exert every effort to act in accordance with both the letter and spirit of those laws and regulations. This would include such measures as providing to the relevant authorities the information necessary for the correct determination of taxes to be assessed in connection with their operations and conforming transfer pricing practices to the arm's length principle.

Annex 2

GENERAL CONSIDERATIONS AND PRACTICAL APPROACHES CONCERNING CONFLICTING REQUIREMENTS IMPOSED ON MULTINATIONAL ENTERPRISES [8]

GENERAL CONSIDERATIONS

1.   In contemplating new legislation, action under existing legislation or other exercise of jurisdiction which may conflict with the legal requirements or established policies of another Member country and lead to conflicting requirements being imposed on multinational enterprises, the Member countries concerned should:

a)   Have regard to relevant principles of international law;

b)   Endeavour to avoid or minimise such conflicts and the problems to which they give rise by following an approach of moderation and restraint, respecting and accommodating the interests of other Member countries[9];

c)   Take fully into account the sovereignty and legitimate economic, law enforcement and other interests of other Member countries;

d)   Bear in mind the importance of permitting the observance of contractual obligations and the possible adverse impact of measures having a retroactive effect.

2.   Member countries should endeavour to promote co-operation as an alternative to unilateral action to avoid or minimise conflicting requirements and problems arising therefrom. Member countries should on request consult one another and endeavour to arrive at mutually acceptable solutions to such problems.

---

8   The General Considerations and Practical Approaches were endorsed by the Ministers in May 1984. They were annexed to the 1976 Declaration as a result of the 1991 Review exercise.

9   Applying the principle of comity, as it is understood in some Member countries, includes following an approach of this nature in exercising one's jurisdiction. This text is an integral part of the negotiated instruments.

PRACTICAL APPROACHES

3.   Member countries recognised that in the majority of circumstances, effective co-operation may best be pursued on a bilateral basis. On the other hand, there may be cases where the multilateral approach could be more effective.

4.   Member countries should therefore be prepared to:

a)   Develop mutually beneficial, practical and appropriately safeguarded bilateral arrangements, formal or informal, for notification to and consultation with other Member countries;

b)   Give prompt and sympathetic consideration to requests for notification and bilateral consultation on an ad hoc basis made by any Member country which considers that its interests may be affected by a measure of the type referred to under paragraph 1 above, taken by another Member country with which it does not have such bilateral arrangements;

c)   Inform the other concerned Member countries as soon as practicable of new legislation or regulations proposed by their Governments for adoption which have significant potential for conflict with the legal requirements or established policies of other Member countries and for giving rise to conflicting requirements being imposed on multinational enterprises;

d)   Give prompt and sympathetic consideration to requests by other Member countries for consultation in the Committee on International Investment and Multinational Enterprises or through other mutually acceptable arrangements. Such consultations would be facilitated by notification at the earliest stage practicable;

e)   Give prompt and full consideration to proposals which may be made by other Member countries in any such consultations that would lessen or eliminate conflicts.

These procedures do not apply to those aspects of restrictive business practices or other matters which are the subject of existing OECD arrangements.

II.   DECISIONS OF THE OECD COUNCIL

1. The OECD Guidelines for Multinational Enterprises

DECISION OF THE COUNCIL

June 2000

THE COUNCIL,

Having regard to the Convention on the Organisation for Economic Co-operation and Development of 14th December 1960;

Having regard to the OECD Declaration on International Investment and Multinational Enterprises (the "Declaration"), in which the Governments of adhering countries ("adhering countries") jointly recommend to multinational enterprises operating in or from their territories the observance of Guidelines for Multinational Enterprises (the "Guidelines");

Recognising that, since operations of multinational enterprises extend throughout the world, international co-operation on issues relating to the Declaration should extend to all countries;

Having regard to the Terms of Reference of the Committee on International Investment and Multinational Enterprises, in particular with respect to its responsibilities for the Declaration [C(84)171(Final), renewed in C/M(95)21];

Considering the Report on the First Review of the 1976 Declaration [C(79)102(Final)], the Report on the Second Review of the Declaration [C/MIN(84)5(Final)], the Report on the 1991 Review of the Declaration [DAFFE/IME(91)23], and the Report on the 2000 Review of the Guidelines [C(2000)96];

Having regard to the Second Revised Decision of the Council of June 1984 [C(84)90], amended June 1991 [C/MIN(91)7/ANN1];

Considering it desirable to enhance   procedures by which consultations may take place on matters covered by these Guidelines and to promote the effectiveness of the Guidelines;

On the proposal of the Committee on International Investment and Multinational Enterprises:

DECIDES:

To repeal the Second Revised Decision of the Council of June 1984 [C(84)90], amended June 1991 [C/MIN(91)7/ANN1], and replace it with the following:

I. National Contact Points

1.   Adhering countries shall set up National Contact Points for undertaking promotional activities, handling inquiries and for discussions with the parties concerned on all matters

covered by the Guidelines so that they can contribute to the solution of problems which may arise in this connection, taking due account of the attached procedural guidance. The business community, employee organisations, and other interested parties shall be informed of the availability of such facilities.

2.   National Contact Points in different countries shall co-operate if such need arises, on any matter related to the Guidelines relevant to their activities. As a general procedure, discussions at the national level should be initiated before contacts with other National Contact Points are undertaken.

3.   National Contact Points shall meet annually to share experiences and report to the Committee on International Investment and Multinational Enterprises.

II. The Committee on International Investment and Multinational Enterprises

1.   The Committee on International Investment and Multinational Enterprises ("CIME" or "the Committee") shall periodically or at the request of an adhering country hold exchanges of views on matters covered by the Guidelines and the experience gained in their application.

2.   The Committee shall periodically invite the Business and Industry Advisory Committee to the OECD (BIAC), and the Trade Union Advisory Committee to the OECD (TUAC) (the "advisory bodies"), as well as other non-governmental organisations to express their views on matters covered by the Guidelines. In addition, exchanges of views with the advisory bodies on these matters may be held at their request.

3.   The Committee may decide to hold exchanges of views on matters covered by the Guidelines with representatives of non-adhering countries.

4.   The Committee shall be responsible for clarification of the Guidelines. Clarification will be provided as required. If it so wishes, an individual enterprise will be given the opportunity to express its views either orally or in writing on issues concerning the Guidelines involving its interests. The Committee shall not reach conclusions on the conduct of individual enterprises.

5.   The Committee shall hold exchanges of views on the activities of National Contact Points with a view to enhancing the effectiveness of the Guidelines.

6.   In fulfilling its responsibilities for the effective functioning of the Guidelines, the Committee shall take due account of the attached procedural guidance.

7.   The Committee shall periodically report to the Council on matters covered by the Guidelines. In its reports, the Committee shall take account of reports by National Contact Points, the views expressed by the advisory bodies, and the views of other non-governmental organisations and non-adhering countries as appropriate.

III. Review of the Decision

This Decision shall be periodically reviewed. The Committee shall make proposals for this purpose.

Procedural Guidance

I. National Contact Points

The role of National Contact Points (NCP) is to further the effectiveness of the Guidelines. NCPs will operate in accordance with core criteria of visibility, accessibility, transparency and accountability to further the objective of functional equivalence.

A. Institutional Arrangements

Consistent with the objective of functional equivalence, adhering countries have flexibility in organising their NCPs, seeking the active support of social partners, including the business community, employee organisations, and other interested parties, which includes non-governmental organisations.

Accordingly, the National Contact Point:

1. May be a senior government official or a government office headed by a senior official. Alternatively, the National Contact Point may be organised as a co-operative body, including representatives of other government agencies. Representatives of the business community, employee organisations and other interested parties may also be included.

2. Will develop and maintain relations with representatives of the business community, employee organisations and other interested parties that are able to contribute to the effective functioning of the Guidelines.

B. Information and Promotion

National Contact Points will:

1. Make the Guidelines known and available by appropriate means, including through on-line information, and in national languages. Prospective investors (inward and outward) should be informed about the Guidelines, as appropriate.

2. Raise awareness of the Guidelines, including through co-operation, as appropriate, with the business community, employee organisations, other non-governmental organisations, and the interested public.

3. Respond to enquiries about the Guidelines from:

    (a)   Other National Contact Points;

    (b)   The business community, employee organisations, other non-governmental organisations and the public; and

      (c)   Governments of non-adhering countries.

C   Implementation in Specific Instances

The NCP will contribute to the resolution of issues that arise relating to implementation of the Guidelines in specific instances. The NCP will offer a forum for discussion and assist the business community, employee organisations and other parties concerned to deal with the issues raised in an efficient and timely manner and in accordance with applicable law. In providing this assistance, the NCP will:

1.   Make an initial assessment of whether the issues raised merit further examination and respond to the party or parties raising them.

2.   Where the issues raised merit further examination, offer good offices to help the parties involved to resolve the issues. For this purpose, the NCP will consult with these parties and where relevant:

      (a)   Seek advice from relevant authorities, and/or representatives of the business community, employee organisations, other non-governmental organisations, and relevant experts;

      (b)   Consult the National Contact Point in the other country or countries concerned;

      (c)   Seek the guidance of the CIME if it has doubt about the interpretation of the Guidelines in particular circumstances;

      (d)   Offer, and with the agreement of the parties involved, facilitate access to consensual and non-adversarial means, such as conciliation or mediation, to assist in dealing with the issues.

3.   If the parties involved do not reach agreement on the issues raised, issue a statement, and make recommendations as appropriate, on the implementation of the Guidelines.

4.   (a)   In order to facilitate resolution of the issues raised, take appropriate steps to protect sensitive business and other information. While the procedures under paragraph 2 are underway, confidentiality of the proceedings will be maintained. At the conclusion of the procedures, if the parties involved have not agreed on a resolution of the issues raised, they are free to communicate about and discuss these issues. However, information and views provided during the proceedings by another party involved will remain confidential, unless that other party agrees to their disclosure.

      (b)   After consultation with the parties involved, make publicly available the results of these procedures unless preserving confidentiality would be in the best interests of effective implementation of the Guidelines.

5.   If issues arise in non-adhering countries, take steps to develop an understanding of the issues involved, and follow these procedures where relevant and practicable.

D.   Reporting

1.   Each National Contact Point will report annually to the Committee.

2.   Reports should contain information on the nature and results of the activities of the National Contact Point, including implementation activities in specific instances.

II. Committee on International Investment and Multinational Enterprises

1.   The Committee will discharge its responsibilities in an efficient and timely manner.

2.   The Committee will consider requests from NCPs for assistance in carrying out their activities, including in the event of doubt about the interpretation of the Guidelines in particular circumstances.

3.   The Committee will:

(a)   Consider the reports of NCPs.

(b)   Consider a substantiated submission by an adhering country or an advisory body on whether an NCP is fulfilling its responsibilities with regard to its handling of specific instances.

(c)   Consider issuing a clarification where an adhering country or an advisory body makes a substantiated submission on whether an NCP has correctly interpreted the Guidelines in specific instances.

(d)   Make recommendations, as necessary, to improve the functioning of NCPs and the effective implementation of the Guidelines.

4.   The Committee may seek and consider advice from experts on any matters covered by the Guidelines. For this purpose, the Committee will decide on suitable procedures.

ANNEX

COMMENTARIES

COMMENTARY ON THE OECD GUIDELINES FOR MULTINATIONAL ENTERPRISES

(27 June 2000)

Commentary on General Policies

1   The General Policies chapter of the *Guidelines* is the first to contain specific recommendations to enterprises. As such it is important for setting the tone and establishing common fundamental principles for the specific recommendations in subsequent chapters.

2.   Obeying domestic law is the first obligation of business. The *Guidelines* are not a substitute for nor should they be considered to override local law and regulation. They represent supplementary principles and standards of behaviour of a non-legal character, particularly concerning the international operations of these enterprises. While the *Guidelines* extend beyond the law in many cases, they should not and are not intended to place an enterprise in a situation where it faces conflicting requirements.

3.   Enterprises are encouraged to co-operate with governments in the development and implementation of policies and laws. Considering the views of other stakeholders in society, which includes the local community as well as business interests, can enrich this process. It is also recognised that governments should be transparent in their dealings with enterprises, and consult with business on these same issues. Enterprises should be viewed as partners with government in the development and use of both voluntary and regulatory approaches (of which the *Guidelines* are one element) to policies affecting them.

4.   There should not be any contradiction between the activity of multinational enterprises (MNEs) and sustainable development, and the *Guidelines* are meant to foster complementarities in this regard. Indeed, links among economic, social and environmental progress are a key means for furthering the goal of sustainable development.[1] On a related issue, while promoting and upholding human rights is primarily the responsibility of governments, where corporate conduct and human rights intersect enterprises do play a role, and thus MNEs are encouraged to respect human rights, not only in their dealings with employees, but also with respect to others affected by their activities, in a manner that is consistent with host governments' international obligations and commitments. The Universal Declaration of Human Rights and other human rights obligations of the government concerned are of particular relevance in this regard.

5.   The *Guidelines* also acknowledge and encourage the contribution that MNEs can make to local capacity building as a result of their activities in local communities. Similarly, the recommendation on human capital formation is an explicit and forward-looking recognition of the contribution to individual human development that MNEs can offer their employees, and encompasses not only hiring practices, but training and other employee development as well. Human capital formation also incorporates the notion of non-discrimination in hiring practices as well as promotion practices, life-long learning and other on-the-job training.

6.   Governments recommend that, in general, enterprises avoid efforts to secure exemptions not contemplated in the statutory or regulatory framework related to environmental, health, safety, labour, taxation and financial incentives among other issues, without infringing on an enterprise's right to seek changes in the statutory or regulatory framework. The words "or accepting" also draw attention to the role of the sate in offering these exemptions. While this sort of provision has been traditionally directed at governments, it is also of direct relevance to MNES. Importantly, however, there are instances where specific exemptions from laws or other policies can be consistent with these laws for legitimate public policy reasons. The environment and competition policy chapters are examples.

7.   The paragraph devoted to the role of MNEs in corporate governance gives further impetus to the recently adopted OECD Principles of Corporate Governance. Although primary

---

[1]   One of the most broadly accepted definitions of sustainable development is in the 1987 World Commission on Environment and Development (the Brundtland Commission): "Development that meets the needs of the present without compromising the ability of future generations to meet their own needs".

responsibility for improving the legal and institutional regulatory framework lies with governments, enterprises also have an interest in good governance.

8.   An increasing network of non-governmental self-regulatory instruments and actions address aspects of corporate behaviour and the relationships between business and society. Enterprises recognise that their activities often have social and environmental implications. The institution of self-regulatory practices and management systems by enterprises sensitive to reaching these goals -- thereby contributing to sustainable development -- is an illustration of this. In turn, developing such practices can further constructive relationships between enterprises and the societies in which they operate.

9.   Following from effective self-regulatory practices, as a matter of course, enterprises are expected to promote employee awareness of company policies. Safeguards to protect *bona fide* "whistle-blowing" activities are also recommended, including protection of employees who, in the absence of timely remedial action or in the face of reasonable risk of negative employment action, report practices that contravene the law to the competent public authorities. While of particular relevance to anti-bribery and environmental initiatives, such protection is also relevant to other recommendations in the *Guidelines*.

10.   Encouraging, where practicable, compatible principles of corporate responsibility among business partners serves to combine a re-affirmation of the standards and principles embodied in the *Guidelines* with an acknowledgement of their importance to suppliers, contractors, subcontractors, licensees and other entities with which MNEs enjoy a working relationship. It is recognised that there are practical limitations to the ability of enterprises to influence the conduct of their business partners. The extent of these limitations depends on sectoral, enterprise and product characteristics such as the number of suppliers or other business partners, the structure and complexity of the supply chain and the market position of the enterprise vis-à-vis its suppliers or other business partners. The influence enterprises may have on their suppliers or business partners is normally restricted to the category of products or services they are sourcing, rather than to the full range of activities of suppliers or business partners. Thus, the scope for influencing business partners and the supply chain is greater in some instances than in others. Established or direct business relationships are the major object of this recommendation rather than all individual or ad hoc contracts or transactions that are based solely on open market operations or client relationships. In cases where direct influence of business partners is not possible, the objective could be met by means of dissemination of general policy statements of the enterprise or membership in business federations that encourage business partners to apply principles of corporate conduct compatible with the *Guidelines*.

11.   Finally, it is important to note that self-regulation and other initiatives in a similar vein, including the *Guidelines*, should not unlawfully restrict competition, nor should they be considered a substitute for effective law and regulation by governments. It is understood that MNEs should avoid potential trade or investment distorting effects of codes and self-regulatory practices when they are being developed.

Commentary on Disclosure

12.   The purpose of this chapter is to encourage improved understanding of the operations of multinational enterprises. Clear and complete information on enterprises is important to a variety of users ranging from shareholders and the financial community to other constituencies such as employees, local communities, special interest groups, governments and society at large. To

improve public understanding of enterprises and their interaction with society and the environment, enterprises should be transparent in their operations and responsive to the public's increasingly sophisticated demands for information. The information highlighted in this chapter may be a supplement to disclosure required under the national laws of the countries in which the enterprise operates.

13. This chapter addresses disclosure in two areas. The first set of disclosure recommendations is identical to disclosure items outlined in the *OECD Principles of Corporate Governance*. The *Principles* call for timely and accurate disclosure on all material matters regarding the corporation, including the financial situation, performance, ownership, and governance of the company. Companies are also expected to disclose sufficient information on the remuneration of board members and key executives (either individually or in the aggregate) for investors to properly assess the costs and benefits of remuneration plans and the contribution of incentive schemes, such as stock option schemes, to performance. The *Principles* contain annotations that provide further guidance on the required disclosures and the recommendations in the *Guidelines* should be construed in relation to these annotations. They focus on publicly traded companies. To the extent that they are deemed applicable, they should also be a useful tool to improve corporate governance in non-traded enterprises; for example, privately held and state owned enterprises.

14. The *Guidelines* also encourage a second set of disclosure or communication practices in areas where reporting standards are still emerging such as, for example, social, environmental, and risk reporting. Many enterprises provide information on a broader set of topics than financial performance and consider disclosure of such information a method by which they can demonstrate a commitment to socially acceptable practices. In some cases, this second type of disclosure -- or communication with the public and with other parties directly affected by the firms' activities -- may pertain to entities that extend beyond those covered in the enterprises' financial accounts. For example, it may also cover information on the activities of subcontractors and suppliers or of joint venture partners.

15. Many enterprises have adopted measures designed to help them comply with the law and standards of business conduct, and to enhance the transparency of their operations. A growing number of firms have issued voluntary codes of corporate conduct, which are expressions of commitments to ethical values in such areas as environment, labour standards or consumer protection. Specialised management systems are being developed with the aim of helping them respect these commitments - these involve information systems, operating procedures and training requirements. Enterprises are co-operating with NGOs and intergovernmental organisations in developing reporting standards that enhance enterprises' ability to communicate how their activities influence sustainable development outcomes (*e.g.* the Global Reporting Initiative).

16. The *OECD Principles of Corporate Governance* support the development of high quality internationally recognised standards of accounting, financial and non-financial disclosure, and audit, which can serve to improve the comparability of information among countries. Financial audits conducted by independent auditors provide external and objective assurance on the way in which financial statements have been prepared and presented. The transparency and effectiveness of non-financial disclosure may be enhanced by independent verification. Techniques for independent verification of non-financial disclosure are emerging.

17.   Enterprises are encouraged to provide easy and economical access to published information and to consider making use of information technologies to meet this goal. Information that is made available to users in home markets should also be available to all interested users. Enterprises may take special steps to make information available to communities that do not have access to printed media (*e.g.* poorer communities that are directly affected by the enterprise's activities).

18.   Disclosure requirements are not expected to place unreasonable administrative or cost burdens on enterprises. Nor are enterprises expected to disclose information that may endanger their competitive position unless disclosure is necessary to fully inform the investment decision and to avoid misleading the investor.

Commentary on Employment and Industrial Relations.

19.   This chapter opens with a chapeau that includes a reference to "applicable" law and regulations, which is meant to acknowledge the fact that multinational enterprises, while operating within the jurisdiction of particular countries, may be subject to *national, sub-national*, as well as *supra-national* levels of regulation of employment and industrial relations matters. The terms "prevailing labour relations" and "employment practices" are sufficiently broad to permit a variety of interpretations in light of different national circumstances - for example, different bargaining options provided for employees under national laws and regulations.

20.   The International Labour Organisation (ILO) is the competent body to set and deal with international labour standards, and to promote fundamental rights at work as recognised in its 1998 Declaration on Fundamental Principles and Rights at Work of the International Labour Organisation (ILO). The *Guidelines*, as a non-binding instrument, have a role to play in promoting observance of these standards and principles among multinational enterprises. The provisions of the *Guidelines* chapter echo relevant provisions of the 1998 Declaration, as well as the ILO's 1977 Tripartite Declaration of Principles concerning Multinational Enterprises and Social Policy. The Tripartite Declaration sets out principles in the fields of employment, training, working conditions, and industrial relations, while the OECD Guidelines cover all major aspects of corporate behaviour. The OECD Guidelines and the ILO Tripartite Declaration refer to the behaviour expected from enterprises and are intended to parallel and not conflict with each other. The ILO Tripartite Declaration can therefore be of use in understanding the *Guidelines* to the extent that it is of a greater degree of elaboration. However, the responsibilities for the follow-up procedures under the Tripartite Declaration and the *Guidelines* are institutionally separate.

21.   The first paragraph of this chapter is designed to echo all four fundamental principles and rights at work which are contained in the ILO's 1998 Declaration, namely the freedom of association and right to collective bargaining, the effective abolition of child labour, the elimination of all forms of forced or compulsory labour, and non-discrimination in employment and occupation. These principles and rights have been developed in the form of specific rights and obligations in ILO Conventions recognised as fundamental.

22.   The chapter recommends that multinational enterprises contribute to the effective abolition of child labour in the sense of the ILO 1998 Declaration and ILO Convention 182 concerning the worst forms of child labour. Long-standing ILO instruments on child labour are Convention 138 and Recommendation 146 (both adopted in 1973) concerning minimum ages for employment. Through their labour management practices, their creation of high quality, well paid jobs and their contribution to economic growth, multinational enterprises can play a positive

role in helping to address the root causes of poverty in general and of child labour in particular. It is important to acknowledge and encourage the role of multinational enterprises in contributing to the search for a lasting solution to the problem of child labour. In this regard, raising the standards of education of children living in host countries is especially noteworthy.

23.   The chapter also recommends that enterprises contribute to the elimination of all forms of compulsory labour, another principle derived from the 1998 ILO Declaration. The reference to this core labour right is based on the ILO Conventions 29 of 1930 and 105 of 1957. C 29 requests that governments "suppress the use of forced or compulsory labour in all its forms within the shortest possible period", while C. 105 requests of them to "suppress and not to make use of any form of forced or compulsory labour" for certain enumerated purposes (*e.g.* as a means of political coercion or labour discipline), and "to take effective measures to secure [its] immediate and complete abolition". At the same time, it is understood that the ILO is the competent body to deal with the difficult issue of prison labour, in particular when it comes to the hiring-out of prisoners to (or their placing at the disposal of) private individuals, companies or associations.

24.   The principle of non-discrimination with respect to employment and occupation is considered to apply to such terms and conditions as hiring, discharge, pay, promotion, training and retirement. The list of non-permissible grounds for discrimination which is taken from ILO Convention 111 of 1958 considers that any distinction, exclusion or preference on these grounds is in violation of the Convention. At the same time, the text makes clear that the terms do not constitute an exhaustive list. Consistent with the provisions in paragraph 1 d), enterprises are expected to promote equal opportunities for women and men with special emphasis on equal criteria for selection, remuneration, and promotion, and equal application of those criteria, and prevent discrimination or dismissals on the grounds of marriage, pregnancy or parenthood.

25.   The reference to consultative forms of employee participation in paragraph two of the *Guidelines* is taken from ILO Recommendation 94 of 1952 concerning Consultation and Co-operation between Employers and Workers at the Level of the Undertaking. It also conforms to a provision contained in the 1977 ILO Tripartite Declaration of Principles concerning Multinational Enterprises and Social Policy. Such consultative arrangements should not substitute for employees' right to bargain over terms and conditions of employment. A recommendation on consultative arrangements with respect to employment arrangements is also part of paragraph eight.

26.   In paragraph three of this chapter, information provided by companies to their employees is expected to provide a "true and fair view" of performance. It relates to the following: the structure of the enterprise, its economic and financial situation and prospects, employment trends, and expected substantial changes in operations, taking into account legitimate requirements of business confidentiality. Considerations of business confidentiality may mean that information on certain points may not be provided, or may not be provided without safeguards.

27.   In paragraph four, employment and industrial relations standards are understood to include compensation and working-time arrangements. The reference to occupational health and safety implies that MNEs are expected to follow prevailing regulatory standards and industry norms to minimise the risk of accidents and injury to health arising out of, linked with, or occurring in, the course of employment. This encourages enterprises to work to raise the level of performance with respect to occupational health and safety in all parts of their operation even

where this may not be formally required by existing regulations in countries in which they operate. It also encourages enterprises to respect employees' ability to remove themselves from a work situation when there is reasonable justification to believe that it presents an imminent and serious risk to health or safety. Reflecting their importance and complementarities among related recommendations, health and safety concerns are echoed elsewhere in the *Guidelines*, most notably in chapters on Consumer Interests and the Environment.

28.   The recommendation in paragraph five of the chapter encourages MNEs to recruit an adequate workforce share locally, including managerial personnel, and to provide training to them. Language in this paragraph on training and skill levels complements the text in paragraph four of the General Policies chapter on encouraging human capital formation. The reference to local personnel complements the text encouraging local capacity building in paragraph three of the General Policies chapter.

29.   Paragraph six recommends that enterprises provide reasonable notice to the representatives of employees and relevant government authorities, of changes in their operations which would have major effects upon the livelihood of their employees, in particular the closure of an entity involving collective layoffs or dismissals. As stated therein, the purpose of this provision is to afford an opportunity for co-operation to mitigate the effects of such changes. This is an important principle that is widely reflected in the industrial relations laws and practices of adhering countries, although the approaches taken to ensuring an opportunity for meaningful co-operation are not identical in all adhering countries. The paragraph also notes that it would be appropriate if, in light of specific circumstances, management were able to give such notice prior to the final decision. Indeed, notice prior to the final decision is a feature of industrial relations laws and practices in a number of adhering countries. However, it is not the only means to ensure an opportunity for meaningful co-operation to mitigate the effects of such decisions, and the laws and practices of other adhering countries provide for other means such as defined periods during which consultations must be undertaken before decisions may be implemented.

Commentary on the Environment

30.   The text of the Environment Chapter broadly reflects the *principles* and objectives contained in the Rio Declaration on Environment and Development, in Agenda 21 (within the Rio Declaration). It also takes into account the (Aarhus) Convention on Access to Information, Public Participation in Decision-making, and Access to Justice in Environmental Matters and reflects *standards* contained in such instruments as the ISO Standard on Environmental Management Systems.

31.   Sound environmental management is an important part of sustainable development, and is increasingly being seen as both a business responsibility and a business *opportunity*. Multinational enterprises have a role to play in both respects. Managers of these enterprises should therefore give appropriate attention to environmental issues within their business strategies. Improving environmental performance requires a commitment to a systematic approach and to continual improvement of the system. An environmental management system provides the internal framework necessary to control an enterprise's environmental impacts and to integrate environmental considerations into business operations. Having such a system in place should help to assure stockholders, employees and the community that the enterprise is actively working to protect the environment from the impacts of its activities.

32.   In addition to improving environmental performance, instituting an environmental management system can provide economic benefits to companies through reduced operating and insurance costs, improved energy and resource conservation, reduced compliance and liability charges, improved access to capital, improved customer satisfaction, and improved community and public relations.

33.   In the context of these *Guidelines*, "sound environmental management" should be interpreted in its broadest sense, embodying activities aimed at controlling both direct and indirect environmental impacts of enterprise activities over the long-term, and involving both pollution control and resource management elements.

34.   In most enterprises, an internal control system is needed to manage the enterprise's activities. The environmental part of this system may include such elements as targets for improved performance and regular monitoring of progress towards these targets.

35.   Information about the activities of enterprises and associated environmental impacts is an important vehicle for building confidence with the public. This vehicle is most effective when information is provided in a transparent manner and when it encourages active consultation with stakeholders such as employees, customers, suppliers, contractors, local communities and with the public-at-large so as to promote a climate of long-term trust and understanding on environmental issues of mutual interest.

36.   Normal business activity can involve the ex ante assessment of the potential environmental impacts associated with the enterprise's activities. Enterprises often carry out appropriate environmental impact assessments, even if they are not required by law. Environmental assessments made by the enterprise may contain a broad and forward-looking view of the potential impacts of an enterprise's activities, addressing relevant impacts and examining alternatives and mitigation measures to avoid or redress adverse impacts. The *Guidelines* also recognise that multinational enterprises have certain responsibilities in other parts of the product life cycle.

37.   Several instruments already adopted by countries adhering to the *Guidelines*, including Principle 15 of the Rio Declaration on Environment and Development, enunciate a "precautionary approach". None of these instruments is explicitly addressed to enterprises, although enterprise contributions are implicit in all of them.

38.   The basic premise of the *Guidelines* is that enterprises should act as soon as possible, and in a proactive way, to avoid, for instance, serious or irreversible environmental damages resulting from their activities. However the fact that the *Guidelines* are addressed to enterprises means that no existing instrument is completely adequate for expressing this recommendation. The *Guidelines* therefore draw upon, but do not completely mirror, any existing instrument.

39.   The *Guidelines* are not intended to reinterpret any existing instruments or to create new commitments or precedents on the part of governments -- they are intended only to recommend how the precautionary approach should be implemented at the level of enterprises. Given the early stage of this process, it is recognised that some flexibility is needed in its application, based on the specific context in which it is carried out. It is also recognised that governments determine the basic framework in this field, and have the responsibility to periodically consult with stakeholders on the most appropriate ways forward.

40.   The *Guidelines* also encourage enterprises to work to raise the level of environmental performance in all parts of their operations, even where this may not be formally required by existing practice in the countries in which they operate.

41.   For example, multinational enterprises often have access to technologies or operating procedures which could, if applied, help raise environmental performance overall. Multinational enterprises are frequently regarded as leaders in their respective fields, so the potential for a "demonstration effect" on other enterprises should not be overlooked. Ensuring that the environment of the countries in which multinational enterprises operate also benefits from available technologies is an important way of building support for international investment activities more generally.

42.   Enterprises have an important role to play in the training and education of their employees with regard to environmental matters. They are encouraged to discharge this responsibility in as broad a manner as possible, especially in areas directly related to human health and safety.

Commentary on Combating Bribery

43.   Bribery and corruption are not only damaging to democratic institutions and the governance of corporations, but they also impede efforts to reduce poverty. In particular, the diversion of funds through corrupt practices undermines attempts by citizens to achieve higher levels of economic, social and environmental welfare. Enterprises have an important role to play in combating these practices.

44.   Progress in improving the policy framework and in heightening enterprises' awareness of bribery as a management issue has been significant. The OECD *Convention of Combating Bribery of Foreign Public Officials* (*the Convention*) has been signed by 34 countries and entered into force on 15 February 1999. The *Convention*, along with the 1997 revised *Recommendation on Combating Bribery in International Business Transactions* and the 1996 *Recommendation on the Tax Deductibility of Bribes to Foreign Public Officials*, are the core instruments through which members of the anti bribery group co-operate to stop the flow of bribes for the purpose of obtaining or retaining international business. The three instruments target the offering side of the bribery transaction. They aim to eliminate the "supply" of bribes to foreign public officials, with each country taking responsibility for the activities of its companies and what happens on its own territory.[2] A monitoring programme has been established to assure effective and consistent implementation and enforcement of the Convention.

45.   To address the demand side of bribery, good governance practices are important elements to prevent companies from being asked to pay bribes. In addition, governments should assist companies confronted with solicitation of bribes.

---

[2]   For the purpose of the Convention, a "bribe" is defined as an "... offer, promise, or giv(ing) of any undue pecuniary or other advantage, whether directly or through intermediaries, to a foreign public official, for that official or for a third party, in order that the official act or refraim from acting in relation to the performance of official duties, in order to obtain or retain business or other improper advantage in the conduct of international business". The Commentaries to the Convention (paragraph 9) clarify that "(s)mall 'facilitation' payments do not constitute payments made 'to obtain or retain business or other improper advantage' within the meaning of paragraph 1 and, accordingly, are also not an offence. Such payments, which, in some countries, are made to induce public officials to perform their functions, such as issuing licences or permits, are generally illegal in the foreign country concerned. Other countries can and should address this corrosive phenomenon by such means as support for programmes of good governance. ...."

46.   Another important development has been the International Chamber of Commerce's recent update of its *Report on Extortion and Bribery in Business Transactions*. The *Report* contains recommendations to governments and international organisations on combating extortion and bribery as well as a code of conduct for enterprises that focuses on these issues.

47.   Transparency in both the public and private domains is a key concept in the fight against bribery and extortion. The business community, non-governmental organisations and governments and inter-governmental organisations have all co-operated to strengthen public support for anti-corruption measures and to enhance transparency and public awareness of the problems of corruption and bribery. The adoption of appropriate corporate governance practices is a complementary element in fostering a culture of ethics within the enterprise.

Commentary on Consumer Interests

48.   A brief reference to "consumer interests" was first introduced into the *Guidelines* in 1984, to reflect increasingly international aspects of consumer policies and the impact that the expansion of international trade, product packaging, marketing and sales and product safety can have on those policies. Since that time, the development of electronic commerce and the increased globalisation of the marketplace have substantially increased the reach of MNEs and consumer access to their goods and services. In recognition of the increasing importance of consumer issues, a substantial percentage of enterprises in their management systems and codes of conduct include references to consumer interests and protections.

49.   In light of these changes, and with an eye to helping enhance consumer safety and health, a chapter on *consumer interests* has been added to the *Guidelines* as a result of the current Review. Language in this chapter draws on the work of the OECD Committee on Consumer Policy, as well as that embodied in various individual and international corporate codes (such as those of the ICC), the UN Guidelines on Consumer Policy, and the OECD Guidelines for Consumer Protection in the Context of Electronic Commerce.

50.   A variety of consumer protection laws exist that govern business practices. The emerging framework is intended to both protect consumer interests and foster economic growth and places a growing emphasis on the use of self-regulatory mechanisms. As noted, many existing national and international corporate codes of conduct include a reference to some aspect of consumer protection and amplify the commitment of industry to help protect health and safety and build consumer confidence in the marketplace. Ensuring that these sorts of practices provide consumers with effective and transparent protection is essential to help build trust that encourages consumer participation and market growth.

51.   The emphasis on alternative dispute resolution in paragraph 3 of the chapter is an attempt to focus on what may in many cases be a more practicable solution to complaints than legal action which can be expensive, difficult and time consuming for everyone involved. It is particularly important that complaints relating to the consumption or use of a particular product that results in serious risks or damages to public health should be resolved in a fair and timely manner without undue cost or burden to the consumer.

52.   Regarding paragraph 5, enterprises could look to the OECD Guidelines Governing the Protection of Privacy and Transborder Flows of Personal Data as a helpful basis for protecting personal data.

Commentary on Science and Technology

53.   In a knowledge-based and globalised economy where national borders matter less, even for small or domestically oriented enterprises, the ability to access and utilise technology and know-how is essential for improving firm performance. Such access is also important for the realisation of the economy-wide effects of technological progress, including productivity growth and job creation, within the context of sustainable development. Multinational enterprises are the main conduit of technology transfer across borders. They contribute to the national innovative capacity of their host countries by generating, diffusing, and even enabling the use of new technologies by domestic enterprises and institutions. The R&D activities of MNEs, when well connected to the national innovation system, can help enhance the economic and social progress in their host counties. In turn, the development of a dynamic innovation system in the host country expands commercial opportunities for MNEs.

54.   The chapter thus aims to promote, within the limits of economic feasibility, competitiveness concerns and other considerations, the diffusion by multinational enterprises of the fruits of research and development activities among the countries where they operate, contributing thereby to the innovative capacities of host countries. In this regard, fostering technology diffusion can include the commercialisation of products which imbed new technologies, licensing of process innovations, hiring and training of S&T personnel and development of R&D co-operative ventures. When selling or licensing technologies, not only should the terms and conditions negotiated be reasonable, but also MNEs may want to consider the long-term developmental, environmental and other impacts of technologies for the home and host country. In their activities, multinational enterprises can establish and improve the innovative capacity of their international subsidiaries and subcontractors. In addition, MNEs can call attention to the importance of local scientific and technological infrastructure, both physical and institutional. In this regard, MNEs can usefully contribute to the formulation by host country governments of policy frameworks conducive to the development of dynamic innovation systems.

Commentary on Competition

55.   These *Guidelines* are intended to emphasise the importance of competition laws and policies to the efficient operation of both domestic and international markets, to reaffirm the importance of compliance with those laws and policies by domestic and multinational enterprises, and to ensure that all enterprises are aware of developments concerning the number, scope, and severity of competition laws and in the extent of co-operation among competition authorities. The term "competition" law is used to refer to laws, including both "antitrust" and "antimonopoly" laws, that prohibit collective or unilateral action to (a) abuse market power or dominance, (b) acquire market power or dominance by means other than efficient performance, or (c) engage in anti-competitive agreements.

56.   In general, competition laws and policies prohibit (a) hard core cartels; (b) other agreements that are deemed to be anti-competitive; (c) conduct that exploits or extends market dominance or market power; and (d) anti-competitive mergers and acquisitions. Under the 1998 Recommendation of the OECD Council Concerning Effective Action Against Hard Core Cartels, C(98)35/Final, the anti-competitive agreements referred to in sub (a) constitute hard core cartels, but the Recommendation incorporates differences in Member countries' laws, including differences in the laws' exemptions or provisions allowing for an exception or authorisation for activity that might otherwise be prohibited. These *Guidelines* should not be interpreted as

suggesting that enterprises should not avail themselves of such exemptions or provisions. The categories sub (b) and (c) are more general because the effects of other kinds of agreements and of unilateral conduct are more ambiguous, and there is less consensus on what should be considered anti-competitive.

57.   The goal of competition policy is to contribute to overall social welfare and economic growth by creating and maintaining market conditions in which the nature, quality, and price of goods and services are determined by market forces except to the extent a jurisdiction considers necessary to achieve other goals. In addition to benefiting consumers and a jurisdiction's economy as a whole, such a competitive environment rewards enterprises that respond efficiently to consumer demand, and enterprises should provide information and advice when governments are considering laws and policies that might reduce their efficiency or otherwise affect the competitiveness of markets.

58.   Enterprises should be aware that competition laws are being enacted in a rapidly increasing number of jurisdictions, and that it is increasingly common for those laws to prohibit anti-competitive activities that occur abroad if they have a harmful impact on domestic consumers. Moreover, the growth of cross-border trade and investment makes it more likely that anti-competitive conduct taking place in one jurisdiction will have harmful effects in other jurisdictions. As a result, anti-competitive unilateral or concerted conduct that is or may be legal where it occurs is increasingly likely to be illegal in another jurisdiction. Enterprises should therefore take into account both the law of the country in which they are operating and the laws of all countries in which the effects of their conduct are likely to be felt.

59.   Finally, enterprises should understand that competition authorities are engaging in more and deeper co-operation in investigating and challenging anti-competitive activity. See *generally*: Recommendation of the Council Concerning Co-operation between Member Countries on Anticompetitive Practices Affecting International Trade, C(95)130/Final; *Making International Markets More Efficient Through "Positive Comity" in Competition Law Enforcement*, Report of the OECD Committee on Competition Law and Policy, DAFFE/CLP(99)19. When the competition authorities of various jurisdictions are reviewing the same conduct, enterprises' facilitation of co-operation among the authorities promotes consistent and sound decision-making while also permitting cost savings for governments and enterprises.

Commentary on Taxation

60.   Corporate citizenship in the area of taxation implies that enterprises should comply with the taxation laws and regulations in all countries in which they operate, co-operate with authorities and make certain kinds of information available to them. However, this commitment to provide information is not without limitation. In particular, the *Guidelines* make a link between the information that should be provided and its relevance to the enforcement of applicable tax laws. This recognises the need to balance the burden on business in complying with applicable tax laws and the need for tax authorities to have the complete, timely and accurate information to enable them to enforce their tax laws.

61.   A member of an MNE group in one country may have extensive economic relationships with members of the same MNE group in other countries. Such relationships may affect the tax liability of each of the parties. Accordingly, tax authorities may need information from outside their jurisdiction in order to be able to evaluate those relationships and determine the tax liability of the member of the MNE group in their jurisdiction. Again, the information to be provided is

limited to that which is relevant to the proposed evaluation of those economic relationships for the purpose of determining the correct tax liability of the member of the MNE group. MNEs should co-operate in providing that information.

62.   Transfer pricing is another important issue for corporate citizenship and taxation. The dramatic increase in global trade and cross-border direct investment (and the important role played in such trade and investment by MNEs) has meant that transfer pricing tends now to be a significant determinant of the tax liabilities of members of an MNE group. It is recognised that determining whether transfer pricing respects the arm's length standard (or principle) is often difficult both for MNEs and for tax administrations.

63.   The Committee on Fiscal Affairs (CFA) of the OECD undertakes ongoing work to develop recommendations for ensuring transfer pricing reflects the arm's length principle. Its work resulted in the publication in 1995 of the OECD Transfer Pricing Guidelines for Multinational Enterprises and Tax Administrations (OECD Transfer Pricing Guidelines) which was the subject of the Recommendation of the OECD Council on the Determination of Transfer Pricing between Associated Enterprises (members of an MNE group would normally fall within the definition of Associated Enterprises).

64.   The OECD Transfer Pricing Guidelines focus on the application of the arm's length principle to evaluate the transfer pricing of associated enterprises. The Transfer Pricing Guidelines aim to help tax administrations (of both OECD Member countries and non-member countries) and MNEs by indicating mutually satisfactory solutions to transfer pricing cases, thereby minimising conflict among tax administrations and between tax administrations and MNEs and avoiding costly litigation. MNEs are encouraged to follow the guidance in the OECD Transfer Pricing Guidelines, as amended and supplemented, in order to ensure that their transfer prices reflect the arm's length principle.

COMMENTARY ON THE IMPLEMENTATION PROCEDURES OF THE OECD GUIDELINES FOR MULTINATIONAL ENTERPRISES

1.   The Council Decision represents the commitment of adhering countries to further the implementation of the recommendations contained in the text of the *Guidelines*. Procedural guidance for both NCPs and the CIME is attached to the Council Decision.

2.   The Council Decision sets out key adhering country responsibilities for the *Guidelines* with respect to NCPS, summarised as follows:

- Setting up NCPs (which will take due account of the procedural guidance attached to the Decision), and informing interested parties of the availability of *Guidelines*-related facilities.
- NCPs in different countries to co-operate with each other as necessary.
- NCPs to meet annually and report to the CIME.

3.   The Council Decision also establishes CIME's responsibilities for the *Guidelines*, including:

- Organising exchanges of views on matters relating to the *Guidelines*

- Issuing clarifications as necessary
- Holding exchanges of views on the activities of NCPs
- Reporting to the OECD Council on the *Guidelines*

4. CIME is the OECD body responsible for overseeing the functioning of the *Guidelines*. This responsibility applies not only to the *Guidelines*, but to all elements of the Declaration (National Treatment Instrument, and the instruments on International Investment incentives and Disincentives, and Conflicting Requirements). In the Declaration, CIME seeks to ensure that each element is respected and understood, and that they all complement and operate in harmony with each other.

5. Reflecting the increasing relevance of the *Guidelines* to countries outside the OECD, the Decision provides for consultations with non-adhering countries on matters covered by the *Guidelines*. This provision allows CIME to arrange periodic meetings with groups of countries interested in *Guidelines* issues, or to arrange contacts with individual countries if the need arises These meetings and contacts could deal with experiences in the overall functioning of the *Guidelines* or with specific issues. Further guidance concerning CIME and NCP interaction with non-adhering countries is provided in the Procedural Guidance attached to the Decision.

I. Procedural Guidance for NCPs

6. National Contact Points have an important role in enhancing the profile and effectiveness of the *Guidelines*. While it is enterprises that are responsible for observing the *Guidelines* in their day-to-day behaviour, governments can contribute to improving the effectiveness of the implementation procedures. To this end, they have agreed that better guidance for the conduct and activities of NCPs is warranted, including through annul meetings and CIME oversight.

7. Many of the functions in the Procedural Guidance of the Decision are not new, but reflect experience and recommendations developed over the years (*e.g.* the 1984 Review Report C/MIN (84)5 (Final)). By making them explicit the expected functioning of the implementation mechanisms of the *Guidelines* is made more transparent. All functions are now outlined in four parts of the Procedural Guidance pertaining to NCPS: institutional arrangements, information and promotion, implementation in specific instances, and reporting.

8. These four parts are preceded by an introductory paragraph that sets out the basic purpose of NCPS, together with core criteria to promote the concept of "functional equivalence". Since governments are accorded flexibility in the way they organise NCPS, NCPs should function in a visible, accessible, transparent, and accountable manner. These criteria will guide NCPs in carrying out their activities and will also assist the CIME in discussing the conduct of NCPS.

Core Criteria for Functional Equivalence in the Activities of NCPs

Visibility. In conformity with the Decision, adhering governments agree to nominate National Contact Points, and also to inform the business community, employee organisations and other interested parties, including NGOs, about the availability of facilities associated with NCPs in the implementation of the *Guidelines*. Governments are expected to publish information about their contact points and to take an active role in promoting the *Guidelines*, which could include hosting seminars and meetings on the instrument. These events could be arranged in co-operation with business labour, NGOs, and other interested parties, though not necessarily with all groups on each occasion.

Accessibility. Easy access to NCPs is important to their effective functioning. This includes facilitating access by business labour, NGOs, and other members of the public. Electronic communications can also assist in this regard. NCPs would respond to all legitimate requests for information, and also undertake to deal with specific issues raised by parties concerned in an efficient and timely manner.

Transparency. Transparency is an important criterion with respect to its contribution to the accountability of the NCP and in gaining the confidence of the general public. Thus most of the activities of the NCP will be transparent. Nonetheless when the NCP offers its "good offices" in implementing the *Guidelines* in specific instances, it will be in the interests of their effectiveness to take appropriate steps to establish confidentiality of the proceedings. Outcomes will be transparent unless preserving confidentiality is in the best interests of effective implementation of the *Guidelines*.

Accountability. A more active role with respect to enhancing the profile of the *Guidelines* -- and their potential to aid in the management of difficult issues between enterprises and the societies in which they operate -- will also put the activities of NCPs in the public eye. Nationally, parliaments could have a role to play. Annual reports and annual meetings of NCPs will provide an opportunity to share experiences and encourage "best practices" with respect to NCPs. CIME will also hold exchanges of views, where experiences would be exchanged and the effectiveness of the activities of NCPs could be assessed.

Institutional Arrangements

9.   The composition of NCPs should be such that they provide an effective basis for dealing with the broad range of issues covered by the *Guidelines*. Different forms of organisation (*e.g.* representatives from one Ministry, an interagency group, or one that contained representatives from non-governmental bodies) are possible. It may be helpful for the NCP to be headed by a senior official. NCP leadership should be such that it retains the confidence of social partners and fosters the public profile of the *Guidelines*. NCPs, whatever their composition, are expected to develop and maintain relations with representatives of the business community, employee organisations, and other interested parties.

Information and Promotion

10.   The NCP functions associated with information and promotion are fundamentally important to enhancing the profile of the *Guidelines*. These functions also help to put an accent on "pro-active" responsibilities of NCPs.

11.   NCPs are required to make the *Guidelines* better known and available by appropriate means, including in national languages. On-line information may be a cost-effective means of doing this, although it should be noted that universal access to this means of information delivery can not be assured. English and French language versions will be available from the OECD, and website links to the OECD *Guidelines* website are encouraged. As appropriate, NCPs will also provide prospective investors, both inward and outward, with information about the *Guidelines*. A separate provision also stipulates that in their efforts to raise awareness of the *Guidelines*, NCPs will co-operate with a wide variety of organisations and individuals, including, as appropriate, the business community, employee organisations, other non-governmental organisations, and the interested public.

12.   Another basic activity expected of NCPs is responding to legitimate enquiries. Three groups have been singled out for attention in this regard: (i) other National Contact Points (reflecting a provision in the Decision); (ii) the business community, employee organisations, other non-governmental organisations and the public; and (iii) governments of non-adhering countries.

Implementation in Specific Instances

13.   When issues arise relating to implementation of the *Guidelines* in specific instances, the NCP is expected to help resolve them. Generally, issues will be dealt with by the NCP in whose country the issue has arisen. Among adhering countries, such issues will first be raised and discussed on the national level and, where appropriate, pursued at the bilateral level. This section of the Procedural Guidance provides guidance to NCPs on how to handle such situations. The NCP may also take other steps to further the effective implementation of the *Guidelines*.

14.   In making an initial assessment of whether the issue raised merits further examination, the NCP will need to determine whether the issue is *bona fide* and relevant to the implementation of the *Guidelines*. In this context, the NCP will take into account:

- the identity of the party concerned and its interest in the matter;
- whether the issue is material and substantiated;
- the relevance of applicable law and procedures;
- how similar issues have been, or are being, treated in other domestic or international proceedings;
- whether the consideration of the specific issue would contribute to the purposes and effectiveness of the *Guidelines*.

15.   Following its initial assessment, the NCP is expected to respond to the party or parties having raised the issue. If the NCP decides that the issue does not merit further consideration, it will give reasons for its decision.

16.   Where the issues raised merit further consideration, the NCP would discuss the issue further with parties involved and offer "good offices" in an effort to contribute informally to the resolution of issues. Where relevant, NCPs will follow the procedures set out in paragraph 2a) through 2d). This could include seeking the advice of relevant authorities, as well as representatives of the business community, labour organisations, other non-governmental organisations, and experts Consultations with NCPs in other countries, or seeking guidance on issues related to the interpretation of the *Guidelines* may also help to resolve the issue.

17.   As part of making available good offices, and where relevant to the issues at hand, NCPs will offer, or facilitate access to, consensual and non-adversarial procedures, such as conciliation or mediation, to assist in dealing with the issues at hand, such as conciliation or mediation. In common with accepted practices on conciliation and mediation procedures, these procedures would be used only upon agreement of the parties concerned.

18.   If the parties involved fail to reach agreement on the issues raised, the NCP will issue a statement, and make recommendations as appropriate, on the implementation of the *Guidelines*. This procedure makes it clear that an NCP will issue a statement, even when it feels that a specific recommendation is not called for.

19.   Transparency is recognised as a general principle for the conduct of NCPs in their dealings with the public (see para. 8 in "Core Criteria" section, above). However, paragraph C-4 recognises that there are specific circumstances where confidentiality is important. The NCP will take appropriate steps to protect sensitive business information. Equally, other information, such as the identity of individuals involved in the procedures, should be kept confidential in the interests of the effective implementation of the *Guidelines*. It is understood that proceedings include the facts and arguments brought forward by the parties. Nonetheless, it remains important to strike a balance between transparency and confidentiality in order to build confidence in the *Guidelines* procedures and to promote their effective implementation. Thus, while para. C-4 broadly outlines that the proceedings associated with implementation will normally be confidential, the results will normally be transparent.

20.   As noted in para. 2 of the "Concepts and Principles" chapter, enterprises are encouraged to observe the *Guidelines* wherever they operate, taking into account the particular circumstances of each host country.

- In the event *Guidelines*-related issues arise in a non-adhering country, NCPs will take steps to develop an understanding of the issues involved. While it may not always be practicable to obtain access to all pertinent information, or to bring all the parties involved together, the NCP may still be in a position to pursue enquiries and engage in other fact finding activities. Examples of such steps could include contacting the management of the firm in the home country, and, as appropriate, government officials in the non-adhering country.

- Conflicts with host country laws, regulations, rules and policies may make effective implementation of the *Guidelines* in specific instances more difficult than in adhering counties. As noted in the commentary to the General Policies chapter, while the *Guidelines* extend beyond the law in many cases, they should not and are not intended to place an enterprise in a situation where it faces conflicting requirements.

- The parties involved will have to be advised of the limitations inherent in implementing the *Guidelines* in non-adhering countries.

- Issues relating to the *Guidelines* in non-adhering countries could also be discussed at NCP annual meetings with a view to building expertise in handling issues arising in non-adhering countries.

Reporting

21.   Reporting would be an important responsibility of NCPs that would also help to build up a knowledge base and core competencies in furthering the effectiveness of the *Guidelines*. In reporting on implementation activities in specific instances, NCPs will comply with transparency and confidentiality considerations as set out in para. C 4.

II. Procedural Guidance for the CIME

22.   The Procedural Guidance to the Council Decision provides additional guidance to the Committee in carrying out its responsibilities, including:

- Discharging its responsibilities in an efficient and timely manner
- Considering requests from NCPs for assistance
- Holding exchanges of views on the activities of NCPs
- Providing for the possibility of seeking advice from experts

23.   The non-binding nature of the *Guidelines* precludes the Committee from acting as a judicial or quasi-judicial body. Nor should the findings and statements made by the NCP (other than interpretations of the *Guidelines*) be questioned by a referral to CIME. The provision that CIME shall not reach conclusions on the conduct of individual enterprises has been maintained in the Decision itself.

24.   CIME will consider requests from NCPs for assistance, including in the event of doubt about the interpretation of the *Guidelines* in particular circumstances. This paragraph reflects paragraph C-2c) of the Procedural Guidance to the Council Decision pertaining to NCPs, where NCPs are invited to seek the guidance of the CIME if they have doubt about the interpretation of the *Guidelines* in these circumstances.

25.   When discussing NCP activities, it is not intended that CIME conduct annual reviews of each individual NCP, although the CIME will make recommendations, as necessary, to improve their functioning, including with respect to the effective implementation of the *Guidelines*.

26.   A substantiated submission by an adhering country or an advisory body that an NCP was not fulfilling its procedural responsibilities in the implementation of the *Guidelines* under the Decision, or acting consistently with regard to the procedures followed in its handling of specific instances, will also be considered by the CIME. This complements provisions in the section of the annex pertaining to NCPs reporting on their activities.

27.   Clarifications of the meaning of the *Guidelines* at the multilateral level would remain a key responsibility of the CIME to ensure that the meaning of the *Guidelines* is consistent with CIME interpretations will also be considered. This may not be needed often, but would provide a vehicle to ensure consistent interpretations of the *Guidelines*.

28.   Finally, the Committee may wish to call on experts to address and report on issues (e.g. child labour, human rights), or individual issues, or to improve the effectiveness of procedures. For this purpose, CIME could call on OECD in-house expertise, international organisations, the advisory bodies, NGOs, academics, and others. It is understood that this will not become a panel to settle individual issues.

*   *   *

SHORT-TERM MEASURES TO ENHANCE ASEAN INVESTMENT CLIMATE[*]

(ASSOCIATION OF SOUTH EAST ASIAN NATIONS)

The Short-Term Measures to Enhance ASEAN Investment Climate were adopted by the members of the Association of South East Asian Nations to stimulate investment in the region. In particular, they apply to companies that submitted relevant applications to the ASEAN Investment Agencies from 1 January 1999 to 31 December 2000, approved thereafter, with regard to investment projects in the manufacturing sector.

Section 1

Privileges Granted to New Investments/Projects or Expansion of Existing Investment Operations

1.   Fiscal Incentives

Companies will be given:

      i.   minimum of 3 years corporate income tax exemption or a minimum 30% corporate income tax allowance. This tax exemption is not granted on an incremental basis over and above existing incentive provisions.

      ii.   duty exemption on imported capital goods required by the promoted investment projects.

2.   Domestic Market Access

Companies will be given free market access to the domestic market of the host country.

3.   Foreign Equity Ownership

Companies will be allowed 100% foreign equity ownership.

4.   Right of Use of Industrial Land

Companies will be given the right of use or lease of factory or industrial land for a minimum period of 30 years.

---

[*]   *Source*: Association of South East Asian Nations (2000). "Short-Term Measures to Enhance ASEAN Investment Climate"; available on the Internet (http:// www.asean.org.id). [Note added by the editor.]

5.   Customs Clearance

Approved investment projects will be given speedy customs clearance through the ASEAN CEPT Green Lane or equivalent procedures adopted by the ASEAN Member Countries for all raw materials and capital goods required by the investment projects.

6.   Employment of Foreign Personnel

The privileges cover more relaxed policy on the following:

   i.   Approval of foreign professional, managerial and technical personnel posts required by the investor;

   ii.   At least one-year renewable multiple entry visas and exit permits for all foreign professional, managerial and technical personnel and their family members, where applicable; and

   iii.   Restrictions and levies on the employment of foreign professional, managerial and technical personnel, if any.

Section 2

Privileges Granted to Investors Injecting Equity Into Existing Companies

All privileges available under Section 1, except for corporate tax incentives and land use privileges, also apply to investors under Section 2. However, with regard to tax incentives, the remaining period of the tax privileges enjoyed by the company being taken over, or into which capital is injected, will continue to be available to the new equity owners.

Section 3

Highlights of Specific Measures Extended by ASEAN Member Countries

Brunei Darussalam

Brunei Darussalam will allow 100% foreign equity ownership in high-technology manufacturing and export-oriented industries.

Indonesia

Indonesia offers wholesale and retail trade up to 100% foreign equity ownership to qualified investors, in addition to 100% foreign equity in all areas of the manufacturing sector. Indonesia has also reduced the processing time for approval in principle, for investments less than US$100 million, to 10 working days. In the banking sector, listed banks are open for 100% foreign equity ownership.

Lao PDR

Lao PDR allows duty exemption on imported capital goods required by the promoted investment projects.

Malaysia

Malaysia offers 100% foreign equity ownership in the manufacturing sector with no export conditions imposed on all new investments, expansions and diversifications (except for seven specific activities and products).

With limited exceptions, foreigners can also own land in Malaysia.

Myanmar

Myanmar will extend minimum of three years corporate tax exemption to all investment projects in all sectors. In addition, Myanmar will also extend duty free import of raw materials to all industrial investments for the first three years of operation.

Philippines

Philippines will open retail trade and distribution business to foreign equity. In addition, the Philippines has opened private construction in the domestic market to foreign companies.

Singapore

Singapore has substantially reduced business costs as part of a cost reduction package that amounts to S$10 billion in savings in addition to extending 30% corporate investment tax allowance on a liberal basis to industrial projects and to selected service industries in respect of productive equipment. These activities include manufacturing, engineering or technical services and computer-related services.

Thailand

Thailand allows 100% foreign equity ownership for manufacturing projects regardless of location. Furthermore, agricultural projects which export 80% of sales will receive import duty exemption on machinery, regardless of location.

Vietnam

Vietnam extends duty exemption on imported capital goods for all projects. In respect of inport of raw materials for production for specially encouraged investments and for projects located in mountainous or remote regions for the first 5 years of operation. Issuance of investment licenses for several types of projects has been reduced to 15 days from the receipt of proper simplified documents. In addition, investment licensing for projects under US$ 5 million has been decentralised to all provinces and cities.

Section 4

Conditions

To qualify for the privileges stipulated in the above sections of this Memorandum, investors must satisfy the following specific conditions:

    i.   Meet the minimum investment level specified by the host country, if any;

ii.   The industry must be in the published priority list for tax incentives to enjoy this particular privilege;

iii.   The industry must not be in any negative list, if any; and

iv.   The investor must show proof that foreign funds have been brought in for the entire amount of the investment, if required by the host country.

Some details on specific privileges are contained in the table below.

MEASURES	COMMENTS
1. Fiscal Incentives	Details of incentives, priority list and other terms and conditions can be obtained from the individual Member Countries' websites or the individual Member Countries' contact points listed in Section 6.
2. Duty exemption on the import of capital goods	Malaysia - duty-free for export zones and exemption for export-oriented projects. For others, applicable, if not locally manufactured. Philippines - only in export-zones, free ports and selected sectors covered by special laws. Thailand - duty free for export-oriented and special projects located in all zones and projects located in zone 3, if not manufactured locally.
3. Free market access to domestic market	Indonesia - covers all industries except those in the negative list and those in the bonded zones. Lao PDR - export condition may be imposed on selected products. Myanmar – only a certain amount will be allowed for domestic market. Malaysia, Philippines, Singapore, Thailand and Vietnam - covers all industries except those listed in the negative list.
4. 100% foreign equity ownership	Brunei Darussalam - only for high-technology manufacturing and export-oriented projects. Indonesia - after 15 years, companies must have at least some local equity ownership Indonesia, Malaysia Philippines, Singapore Thailand And Vietnam - covers all industries except those listed in the negative list.
5. Removal of Restrictions and Levies on the Employment of Foreign Nationals, if any	Indonesia - any individuals must pay an exit tax but this is deductible against income tax. Malaysia - Foreign professionals, managerial and technical personnel paying income tax are exempted from paying levy.

The priority list of industries, the negative list of the respective Member Countries and other details relating to the privileges are available in the ASEAN website as well as the individual Member Countries' investment agencies websites or through the individual Member Countries contact points listed in Section 6.

The Investment Agencies are required to complete processing of the relevant applications within 60 working days from receipt of fully completed applications.

In addition to the specific conditions, an investor must submit an application to the Investment Agency of the host country before 31 December 2000. Investors or companies will receive official confirmation of privileges relating to incentives, market access and equity ownership in writing on approval of their applications.

Section 5

Duration of Privileges

Privileges will, unless otherwise specified in this Memorandum, or at the time of issue of approval, continue for the life of the investment project or such other period as may be specified by individual Member Countries at their websites. This will apply even if there are subsequent changes in the investment or other laws of the host country. If any approved project, under this Memorandum, is not implemented according to the project implementation schedule agreed to between the investor and the host government, during the promotion period, the above privileges may be withdrawn.

Section 6

Contact Points for Further Information and Enquiries

Brunei Darussalam

Brunei Industrial Development Authority (BINA)
Ministry of Industry and Primary Resources
Jalan Menteri Besar 2065
Bandar Seri Begawan
Brunei Darussalam
Tel : (673) 2 383 811
Fax : (673) 2 382 838
Web Site: http://www.brunet.bn/aseansummit/summit.htm
E-mail: BinaL1@brunet.bn

Indonesia

Deputy Chairman for Promotion
Investment Coordinating Board (BKPM)
No. 44, Jalan Gatot Subroto, Jakarta
Indonesia
Tel: (62) 21 525 2008/525 5041
Fax (62) 21 525 4945

Web Site: http://www.bkpm.go.id
E-mail: sysadm@bkpm.go.id

Lao PDR

Committee for Investment and Foreign Economic Cooperation
Luang Prabang Road-Vientiane
Lao People's Democratic Republic
Tel: (856) 21 216 563
Fax: (856) 21 216 563

Malaysia

Investment Promotion Division
Malaysian Industrial Development Authority
Wisma Damansara, Ground 9 & 11 Floor
Jalan Semantan, Damansara Heights
P.O. Box 101618
50720 Kuala Lumpur
Malaysia
Tel: (603) 255 3633
Fax: (603) 255 7970/255 0697/253 8507
Web Site: http://www.mida.gov.my
E-mail: promotion@mida.gov.my

Myanmar

The Office of Myanmar Investment Commission
653-691 Merchant Street
Pabedan Township
Yangon
Union of Myanmar
Tel: (951) 241 918
Fax: (951) 282 101

Philippines

Technical Services Group
Board of Investments
Department of Trade and Industry
Industry and Investments Building
385 Senator Gil J. Puyat Avenue
Makati, Metro Manila
Philippines
Tel: (632) 897 7895
Fax: (632) 895 3978
Web Site: http://www.dti.gov.ph/boi
E-Mail: boitsg@mnl.sequel.net

Singapore

International Policy Group
Economic Development Board
250 North Bridge Road#24-00
Raffles City Tower
Singapore 179101
Tel: (65) 336 2288
Fax: (65) 339 5203
Web Site: http://www.sedb.com
E-Mail: international@edb.gov.sg

Thailand

Investment Service Centre
Office of the Board of Investment
555 Vipavadee Rangsit Road
Jatuchak, Bangkok 10900
Thailand
Tel: (662) 537 8111
Fax: (662) 537 8188
Web Site: http://www.boi.go.th
E-Mail: head@boi.go.th

Vietnam

Ministry of Planning and Investment (MPI)
Investment Legislation and Promotion Department
56 Quoc Tu Giam
Hanoi, Vietnam
Tel: (844) 823 5606/8258142
Fax (844) 845 9271/8232890/8234453
E-Mail: mp-ii@hn.vnn.vn

*   *   *

DRAFT FINAL ACT OF THE INTERNATIONAL CONFERENCE, DRAFT SUPPLEMENTARY TREATY TO THE ENERGY CHARTER TREATY, DRAFT DECISION OF THE ENERGY CHARTER CONFERENCE, DRAFT DECLARATION ON ENVIRONMENTAL AND SOCIAL STANDARDS, AND GUIDELINES TO INVESTORS *

> Article 10(4) of the Energy Charter Treaty (reproduced in vol. II of this *Compendium*) required signatories to commence negotiations on a supplementary treaty not later than 1 January 1995, with a view to concluding it by 1 January 1998. The aim of the Supplementary Treaty is to provide a non-discriminatory basis for making investments in the energy sector while grandfathering existing discriminatory measures and catering for specific reservations in respect of privatizations. As of the time of the printing of this volume, broad agreement had been reached on the draft texts, with a few outstanding issues remaining to be solved. Discussions continue in the Energy Charter Investment Group on those issues. The draft texts consist of the following parts: the draft Final Act, the draft text of the Supplementary Treaty, the draft Decisions and the draft Declaration on Environmental and Social Standards, and Guidelines to Investors.

DRAFT **

FINAL ACT OF THE INTERNATIONAL CONFERENCE AND DRAFT DECISION OF THE ENERGY CHARTER CONFERENCE

I.   Acting in accordance with Article 10(4) of the Energy Charter Treaty, negotiations for a supplementary treaty began in December 1994 by the setting up of a Working Group to prepare the text. The Provisional Energy Charter Conference met a number of times and concluded the negotiations on the Supplementary Treaty to the Energy Charter Treaty (hereinafter referred to as the "Supplementary Treaty") in December 1997. A Conference to adopt the Supplementary Treaty was held at Brussels in three sessions on 23-24 April, on 24-25 June 1998 and on [...].

Representatives of the Republic of Albania, the Republic of Armenia, Australia, the Republic of Austria, the Azerbaijani Republic, the Kingdom of Belgium, the Republic of Belarus, Bosnia and Herzegovina, the Republic of Bulgaria, the Republic of Croatia, the Republic of Cyprus, the Czech Republic, the Kingdom of Denmark, the Republic of Estonia, the European Communities, the Republic of Finland, the French Republic, the Republic of Georgia, the Federal Republic of Germany, the Hellenic Republic, the Republic of Hungary, the Republic of Iceland, Ireland, the Italian Republic, Japan, the Republic of Kazakhstan, the Republic of Kyrgyzstan, the Republic of Latvia, the Principality of Liechtenstein, the Republic of Lithuania, the Grand Duchy of

---

*   *Source*: Energy Charter Conference (1998). "Draft Final Act of the International Conference, Draft Supplementary Treaty to the Energy Charter Treaty and Decision of the Energy Charter Conference, Draft Declaration on Environmental and Social Standards and Guidelines to Investors"; (Brussels: Energy Charter Secretariat); available on the Internet (http://www.encharter.org). [Note added by the editor.]

**   This text reflects a work in progress, and has been produced for documentary purposes without involving the responsibility on the Energy Charter Conference or its Secretariat. Permission to reproduce the text should be obtained from the Enregy Charter Secretariat.

Luxembourg, the Republic of Malta, the Republic of Moldova, the Kingdom of the Netherlands, the Kingdom of Norway, the Republic of Poland, the Portuguese Republic, Romania, the Russian Federation, the Slovak Republic, the Republic of Slovenia, the Kingdom of Spain, the Kingdom of Sweden, the Swiss Confederation, the Republic of Tajikistan, the former Yugoslav Republic of Macedonia, the Republic of Turkey, Turkmenistan, Ukraine, the United Kingdom of Great Britain and Northern Ireland and the Republic of Uzbekistan (hereinafter referred to as "the representatives") participated in the Conference, as did invited observers from certain countries and international organisations.

II.   The Energy Charter Conference, which was definitively established on the entry into force on 16 April 1998 of the Energy Charter Treaty, also met in Brussels in April and June 1998 and on [...] to consider adoption of the Supplementary Treaty.

DRAFT

SUPPLEMENTARY TREATY TO THE ENERGY CHARTER TREATY

III.   The text of the Supplementary Treaty which is set out in Annex 1 and Decisions with respect thereto which are set out in Annex 2 were adopted and it was agreed that the Supplementary Treaty would be open for signature at [...] from [...] to [...].

UNDERSTANDINGS

IV.   The following Understandings were adopted with respect to the Supplementary Treaty:

1.   With respect to Article 10(2)

    a.   With respect to the foundation and establishment of banks and their licensing it is understood that Article 10(2) places on Contracting Parties no obligations relating to economic activities other than Economic Activities in the Energy Sector.

    b.   The obligation in Article 10(2) on a Contracting Party to accord treatment no less favourable than that which it accords to its own Investors or their Investments does not apply to the disposal by a Contracting Party of an asset described in Article 1(6)(a) of the Energy Charter Treaty which has a value of less than 75.000 Special Drawing Rights. However, a Contracting Party can not artificially partition an asset in order to evade the obligations of Article 10(2).

    c.   Public ownership and/or participation in the energy sector, including in monopolized and demonopolized sectors, is not as such regarded as contravening Article 10(2).

        For the avoidance of doubt, and consistent with the Supplementary Treaty, a Contracting Party, when demonopolizing an activity, may establish transparent, objective, non-discriminatory conditions and requirements on the basis of which new entrants may take up the previously monopolized activity.

2.   With respect to Article 10(3)

Restrictions in the constituent instruments of companies on the shareholdings or powers of Investors of other Contracting Parties and their Investments are regarded as contravening Article 10(2) if imposed or requested by a Contracting Party.

However, existing restrictions in such constituent instruments on the subsequent acquisition of privatised shares by Investors of other Contracting Parties are not affected by Article 10(2).

3.   With respect to Article 10(3)(a)

It is understood that the individual exceptions in Annex EX do not affect the scope or interpretation of the Energy Charter Treaty.

4.   With respect to Article 10(3)(b)

  a   Restrictions on the percentage or type of shares which can be owned by a single holder or association of such holders are not a contravention of Article 10(2) unless such restrictions discriminate against Investors of other Contracting Parties and their Investments.

  b.   Reservation of a minority of shares in a privatised enterprise to particular categories of Investors, employees, customers or small shareholders, or preferential terms given to such categories, are not regarded as contravening Article 10(2) provided there is no legal discrimination against members of such categories that are nationals or legal entities of other Contracting Parties.

  c.   The enquiry points designated under Article 20(3) of the Energy Charter Treaty shall be ready, if the designating Contracting Party so wishes, to make information available either free or for a reasonable charge about plans and intentions regarding privatisation and reduction of exclusive and special privileges. They should be ready to supply to Investors all the non-confidential information needed to tackle specific problems concerning Investments.

  d.   Contracting Parties acknowledge that special share arrangements are compatible with Article 10(2), unless they explicitly or intentionally favour Investors or Investments of a Contracting Party or discriminate against Investors or Investments of another Contracting Party on the grounds of their nationality or permanent residency.

5.   With respect to Article 10(2) to (5)

For the avoidance of doubt, the Decisions and Understandings which form part of the Final Act of the European Energy Charter Conference done in Lisbon on 17 December 1994 apply to the Supplementary Treaty.

DECLARATIONS

V.   The following Declarations were made with respect to the Supplementary Treaty:

1.   The Charter Conference will proceed to a review of the Investor-State dispute settlement provisions. In so doing it shall take account of relevant international legal developments in the field of investor protection.

The review shall commence once such developments are manifest, but no later than 2005.

2.   The representatives have taken note of the position of a significant number of delegations that they attach importance to high standards of environmental protection and conservation and in the field of labour, and that they reaffirm their commitment to sustainable development, taking into account the principles on environmental standards already set out in Article 19 of the Energy Charter Treaty and the Energy Charter Protocol on Energy Efficiency and Related Environmental Aspects, together with measures incorporating social and labour considerations. The representatives also took note that there was broad support for including a strong commitment in future on those issues. [See separate Declaration]

3.   Contracting Parties undertake that in the light of the results of the efforts underway in other international fora to establish and further develop multilateral rules governing investment, they will commence consideration, not later than 2005 or the entry into force of this Treaty, whichever is the later, of appropriate amendments to this Treaty with a view to the adoption of any such amendments by the Charter Conference.

VI.   The representatives also noted the following Declarations that were made with respect to the Supplementary Treaty:

DOCUMENTATION

VII.   The records of negotiations of the Supplementary Treaty will be deposited with the Secretariat.

Done at [...] on [...].

DRAFT

SUPPLEMENTARY TREATY TO THE ENERGY CHARTER TREATY

PREAMBLE

The Contracting Parties to this Treaty,

Having regard to the Energy Charter Treaty done at Lisbon on 17 December 1994;

Acting in accordance with Article 10(4) of the Energy Charter Treaty which calls for negotiation of a supplementary treaty that will, subject to the conditions laid down therein, oblige each party thereto to accord to Investors of other parties, as regards the Making of Investments in its Area, the Treatment described in Article 10(3) of the Energy Charter Treaty;

Recalling Understanding No. 10 adopted at the signature of the Final Act of the European Energy Charter Conference in Lisbon on 17 December 1994, which specifies that those conditions will include, inter alia, provisions relating to the sale or other divestment of state assets (privatisation) and to the dismantling of monopolies (demonopolization);

Considering the important contribution that foreign investment can make to the development of energy sectors of the Contracting Parties;

Desiring to liberalise further the existing regimes relating to the Making of Investments in the energy sector;

Wishing to establish stable, equitable, favourable and transparent market conditions to achieve this purpose;

Confirming the importance of effective dispute settlement procedures,

HAVE AGREED as follows:

PART I:

INVESTMENT PROMOTION AND PROTECTION

ARTICLE 1
DEFINITION

In this Treaty "Contracting Party" means a state or Regional Economic Integration Organisation which has consented to be bound by this Treaty and for which this Treaty is in force.

ARTICLE 2
TREATMENT OF THE MAKING OF INVESTMENTS

1.   As among the Contracting Parties, Article 10(2) to (5) of the Energy Charter Treaty shall read as follows:

2.   Each Contracting Party shall accord to Investors of other Contracting Parties and their Investments in its Area, as regards the Making of Investments in its Area, treatment no less favourable than that which it accords to its own Investors or their Investments, or to Investors of any other Contracting Party or any third state or their Investments, whichever is the most favourable.

3.   a.   Paragraph (2) shall not apply to :

      i.   any non-conforming measure that is maintained by a Contracting Party as set out n Annex EX;

      ii.   the continuation or prompt renewal of such non-conforming measure; or

      iii.   an amendment to such non-conforming measure to the extent that the amendment does not decrease the conformity of the measure, as it existed immediately before the amendment, with paragraph (2).

   b.   The obligation in paragraph (2) to accord treatment no less favourable than that which a Contracting Party accords to its own Investors or their Investments shall not apply to measures concerning privatisation as provided for in Annex PR.

4.   In the event of any inconsistency between paragraphs (2) and (3) of Article 10 and paragraph (7) of Article 10 the provision or provisions more favourable to the Investor or Investment shall prevail.

5.   Each Contracting Party shall, as regards the Making of Investments in its Area, endeavour to:

   a.   limit to the minimum the application of measures referred to in paragraph (3);

   b.   progressively remove existing restrictions affecting Investors of other Contracting Parties or their Investments;

   c.   i.   progressively reduce the scope of application inscribed against its name in Annex PR; and

          ii.   remove its name from the list of Annex PR.

              The Charter Conference shall review Annex PR annually with a view to encouraging Contracting Parties listed therein to remove their names from that Annex.

              In this light the Charter Conference shall, not later than 1 January 2004, conduct a comprehensive assessment of Annex PR taking into account the results of the annual reviews and any notifications by Contracting Parties of reliance on exceptions provided for in Annex PR.

2.   As a consequence of paragraph 1. of this Article, the reference in paragraph (10) of Article 10 to paragraph (3) shall read paragraph (2).

PART II:

FINAL PROVISIONS

ANNEX EX

NON-CONFORMING MEASURES MAINTAINED BY A CONTRACTING PARTY AND ANY COMMITMENTS WITH REGARD TO THEM

(in accordance with Article 10(3)(a)(i))

[See the "Blue Book" for measures notified in accordance Article 10(9) of the Energy Charter Treaty]

ANNEX PR
EXCEPTIONS RELATING TO PRIVATISATION MEASURES

(In accordance with Article 10(3)(b))

1.   Contracting Party listed below may, subject to the scope of application inscribed against its name, reserve a right for its own Investors to acquire all or some of the shares of a state enterprise or assets owned by the state or a state enterprise which it is privatising, or may sell or dispose of such shares or assets to its own Investors on preferential terms.

Country   **Scope of Application**

2.   Any Contracting Party may reduce the scope of application inscribed against its name or remove its name from the list by notifying the Secretariat. The Secretariat shall forthwith inform other Contracting Parties and update Annex PR accordingly.

DRAFT

DECISIONS WITH RESPECT TO THE ENERGY CHARTER TREATY AND THE SUPPLEMENTARY TREATY

The following Decisions were adopted with respect to the Energy Charter Treaty and the Supplementary Treaty:

1.   With respect to Article 10(8)

Given that there do not appear to be any programmes maintained by signatories to the Energy Charter Treaty that come within the terms of Article 10(8) of that Treaty, the modalities of application of Article 10(7) of the Energy Charter Treaty to any such programmes shall be reserved for further consideration by the Charter Conference at an appropriate time.

2.   With respect to the application of the institutional arrangements of the Energy Charter Treaty to the Supplementary Treaty

The Energy Charter Conference and the Secretariat established under the Energy Charter Treaty (referred to in the Supplementary Treaty and Decisions and Understandings respectively as the Charter Conference and the Secretariat) shall perform relevant duties and functions with respect to the Supplementary Treaty.

3.   With respect to Article 10(3)(a)

Given that historically those few Contracting Parties with reciprocity exceptions have seldom relied on them and that the Supplementary Treaty represents substantial progress in meeting the conditions of such exceptions, the Contracting Parties concerned shall, where they have invoked or acted under such exceptions, notify the Secretariat, which shall inform the Charter Conference.

4.   With respect to Article 10(9)

Having regard to the value gained from the first review of the reports submitted to the Secretariat under Article 10(9) of the Energy Charter Treaty:

  a.   The Contracting Parties shall continue to include material illustrating the overall opportunities for investors of other Contracting Parties to Make Investments in their Areas. Such material shall cover in particular the existence and nature of relevant state entities, monopoly situations and exclusive and special privileges.

  b.   The Charter Conference should further define, as and when appropriate, the details of information to be included in such explanatory material.

Each Contracting Party listed in Annex PR to the Supplementary Treaty shall on an annual basis notify the Secretariat of any reliance on an exception provided for in Annex PR that relates to the obligation in Article 10(2) on a Contracting Party to accord treatment no less favourable than that it accords to its own Investors or their Investments. The Charter Conference may review the information provided.

5.   With respect to Article 10(3)(b)

A Contracting Party which is not listed in Annex PR may, regarding an exception inscribed in Annex PR by a Contracting Party which is listed in Annex PR but not Annex T, invoke an equivalent exception to its obligation in Article 10(2) in relation to the Investors of that other Contracting Party or their Investments in its own privatisation operations.

DRAFT

DECLARATION ON ENVIRONMENTAL AND SOCIAL STANDARDS, AND GUIDELINES TO INVESTORS

SOCIAL AND ENVIRONMENTAL STANDARDS

A.   The Contracting Parties declare that, as regards measures taken in the context of investment promotion, they shall endeavour to ensure:

i.   that such measures are consistent with internationally recognised fundamental health, safety and labour standards, and relevant international environmental obligations; and

ii.   that no measure taken by a Contracting Party shall derogate from its domestic health, safety, labour or environmental laws and regulations, so as to induce an Investor to make an Investments within its Area.

B.   The Charter Conference may, at the request of one or more Contracting Parties, review compliance with the terms set out in paragraph A(ii) above.

GUIDELINES TO INVESTORS

C.   The Contracting parties further declare that they jointly recommend to multinational enterprises engaged in Economic Activity in the Energy Sector the observance of the Guidelines for Multinational Enterprises annexed to this Declaration. The Charter Conference shall consider any subsequent revisions of the Guidelines with a view of recommending them.

*   *   *

PROTOCOL AMENDING THE TREATY ESTABLISHING THE CARIBBEAN COMMUNITY (PROTOCOL VIII: COMPETITION POLICY, CONSUMER PROTECTION, DUMPING AND SUBSIDIES)*
[excerpts]

(CARIBBEAN COMMUNITY)

> The Protocol Amending the Treaty Establishing the Caribbean Community (Protocol VIII: Competition Policy, Consumer Protection, Dumping and Subsidies) was opened for signature in March 2000.

PREAMBLE

The States parties to the Treaty Establishing the Caribbean Community (hereinafter referred to as **"the Member States"**):

Noting that competition policy has become more important with the deepening of the integration arrangements and the liberalisation of the markets of the Region;

Aware that the benefits expected from the establishment of the CARICOM Single Market and Economy (CSME) may be frustrated by anti-competitive business conduct whose object or effect is to prevent, restrict, or distort competition.

Determined to promote and maintain competition through the establishment and enforcement of applicable laws and rules.

Determined further to promote consumer interest and welfare;

Conscious that the provision of subsidies by Member States and the practice of dumping could have an adverse impact on the promotion and development of competition in the CSME;

Convinced that the application and convergence of national competition policies and the cooperation of competition authorities in the Community would promote the objectives of the CSME,

Have Agreed as follows:

---

* *Source*: The Caribbean Community (2000). "Protocol Amending the Treaty Establishing the Caribbean Community (Protocol VIII: Competition Policy, Consumer Protection, Dumping and Subsidies)"; available on the Internet (http://www.caricom.org/protocolviii.htm). [Note added by the editor.]

PART I
PRELIMINARY

Article I
Use of Terms

1.   In this Protocol, unless the context otherwise requires:

"anti-competitive business conduct" has the meaning assigned to it in Article 30(i);

"business" means any activity carried on for gain or reward or in the course of which goods or services are produced, manufactured or supplied;

"Commission" means the Competition Commission established by Article 30(c);

"Community" includes the CARICOM Single Market and Economy to be established by the Protocols amending or replacing the Caribbean Common Market Annex to the Treaty;

"Community Council of Ministers" (hereinafter referred to as "the Community Council") means the Organ of the Community so named in Article 8 (1) of the Treaty;

"competent authority" means the authority legally authorised to perform a function;

"Conference" means the Conference of Heads of Government of the Community;

"Council for Trade and Economic Development (COTED)" means the Organ of the Community so named in Article 6(2)(a) of the Treaty, and for the purposes of this Protocol shall be deemed to include the interim Committee established pursuant to Rule 34 of the Rules of Procedure of the COTED;

"Court" means the Court established by Article III of the Agreement Establishing the Caribbean Court of Justice;

"enterprise" means any person or type of organisation involved in the production of or the trade in goods, or the provision of services (other than a non-profit organisation);

"goods" means all kinds of property other than real property, money, securities or choses in action;

"Regional Judicial and Legal Services Commission" means the Commission established by Article V of the Agreement Establishing the Caribbean Court of Justice;

"rules of competition" includes the rules set out in Articles 30(i), 30(h) and 30(k) of this Protocol and any other rules made pursuant to Article 30(b) 1(a)(i);

"Secretary-General" means the Secretary-General of the Community;

"services" means services provided against remuneration other than wages in an approved sector and "the provision of services" means the supply of services:

(a)   from the territory of one Member State into the territory of another Member State;

(b)   in the territory of one Member State to a service consumer of another Member State;

(c)   by a service supplier of one Member State through commercial presence in the territory of another Member State; and

(d)   by a service supplier of one Member State through the presence of natural persons of a Member State in the territory of another Member State;

"subsidies" includes the subsidies set out in Schedule V of Protocol IV - Trade Policy and shall apply only in relation to goods;

"trade" includes any business, industry, profession or occupation relating to the supply or acquisition of goods or services;

"Treaty" means the Treaty Establishing the Caribbean Community signed at Chaguaramas on the 4th day of July 1973 and includes any amendments thereto which take effect either provisionally or definitively (hereinafter referred to as "the Treaty").

2.   Where in this Protocol there is a requirement for notification to be given, such notification shall be in writing.

Article II
Amendment

Replace Articles 19 and 30 of the Caribbean Common Market Annex to the Treaty with the following:

Article 30
Scope of Parts I, II and III

The rules of competition shall not apply to -

(a)   combinations or activities of employees for their own reasonable protection as employees;

(b)   arrangements for collective bargaining on behalf of employers or employees for the purpose of fixing terms and conditions of employment;

(c)   business conduct within the meaning of Article 30(i) duly notified to the COTED in accordance with Article 30(b);

(d)   negative clearance rulings within the meaning of Article 30(l) or exemptions within the meaning of Articles 30(m) and 30(o);

(e)   activities of professional associations designed to develop or enforce professional standards of competence reasonably necessary for the protection of the public and approved by the Commission.

Article 30(a)
Objectives of Community Competition Policy

1.   The goal of the Community Competition Policy shall be to ensure that the benefits expected from the establishment of the CARICOM Single Market and Economy (CSME) are not frustrated by anti-competitive business conduct.

2.   In fulfillment of the goal set out in paragraph 1 of this Article, the Community shall pursue the following objectives:

   (a)   promote and maintain competition and enhance economic efficiency in production, trade and commerce;

   (b)   subject to the Treaty, prohibit anti-competitive business conduct which prevents, restricts or distorts competition or which constitutes the abuse of a dominant position in the market;

   (c)   promote consumer welfare and protect consumer interest;.

Article 30(b)
Implementation of Community Competition Policy

1.   In order to achieve the objectives of the Community Competition Policy,

   (a)   the Community shall:

      (i)   subject to the Treaty, establish appropriate norms and institutional arrangements to prohibit and penalise anti-competitive business conduct;

      (ii)   establish and maintain information systems to enable enterprises and consumers to be kept informed about the operation of markets within the CSME;

   (b)   Member States shall:

      (i)   take the necessary legislative measures to ensure consistency and compliance with the rules of competition and provide penalties for anti-competitive business conduct;

      (ii)   provide for the dissemination of relevant information to facilitate consumer choice;

      (iii)   establish and maintain institutional arrangements and administrative procedures to enforce competition laws;

      (iv)   take effective measures to ensure access by nationals of other Member States to competent enforcement authorities including the courts on an equitable, transparent and non-discriminatory basis.

2.   A Member State shall establish and maintain a national competition authority for the purpose of facilitating the implementation of the rules of competition.

3.   A Member State shall require its national competition authority to:

   (a)   co-operate with the Commission in achieving compliance with the rules of competition;

   (b)   investigate any allegations of anti-competitive business conduct being allegations referred to the authority by the Commission or another Member State.

   (c)   cooperate with other national competition authorities in the detection and prevention of anti-competitive business conduct, and the exchange of information relating to such conduct.

4.   Nothing in this Article shall be construed as requiring a Member State to disclose confidential information, the disclosure of which would be prejudicial to the public interest or to the legitimate commercial interests of enterprises, public or private. Confidential or proprietary information disclosed in the course of an investigation shall be treated on the same basis as that on which it was provided.

5.   Within 24 months of the entry into force of this Protocol, Member States shall notify the COTED of existing legislation, agreements and administrative practices inconsistent with the provisions of this Protocol. Within 36 months of entry into force of this Protocol, the COTED shall establish a programme providing for the termination of such legislation, agreements and administrative practices.

PART II
COMPETITION COMMISSION

Article 30 (c)
Establishment of the Competition Commission

For the purposes of implementation of the Community Competition Policy, there is hereby established a Competition Commission (hereinafter called "the Commission") having the composition, functions and powers hereinafter set forth.

Article 30(d)
Composition of the Commission

1.   The Commission shall comprise seven members appointed by the Regional Judicial and Legal Services Commission to serve on the Commission. The Regional Judicial and Legal Services Commission shall appoint a Chairman from among the members so appointed. Notwithstanding the foregoing, the Chairman and Members of the Commission shall be appointed by Conference on the recommendation of the COTED as long as the Parties to the Agreement Establishing the Caribbean Court of Justice are less than seven.

2.   The Commission shall comprise persons, collectively having expertise or experience in commerce, finance, economics, law, competition policy and practice, international trade and such other areas of expertise or experience as may be necessary.

3.   A Commissioner shall be appointed for a term of five years and such appointment may be renewed for a further period of not more than five years as determined by the Regional Judicial and Legal Services Commission.

4.   A Commissioner may be removed from office only for inability to perform the functions of his office or for misbehaviour.

5.   A Commissioner shall be removed only on the vote of the Judicial and Legal Services Commission that represents not less than three-quarters of all the Members of the Commission.

6.   A Commissioner may at any time resign the office of Commissioner by writing under his hand addressed to the Chairman of the Judicial and Legal Services Commission.

7.   A Commissioner shall not enter upon the duties of the office unless he has taken and subscribed before the Chairman of the Judicial and Legal Services Commission, the Oath of Office set out in Annex V to this Protocol.

Article 30(e)
Functions of the Commission

1.   The Commission shall:

   (a)   apply the rules of competition in respect of anti-competitive cross-border business conduct;

   (b)   promote competition in the Community and co-ordinate the implementation of the Community Competition Policy; and

   (c)   perform any other function conferred on it by any competent body of the Community.

2.   In discharging the functions set out in paragraph 1, the Commission shall:

   (a)   monitor anti-competitive practices of enterprises operating in the CSME, and investigate and arbitrate cross-border disputes;

   (b)   keep the Community Competition Policy under review and advise and make recommendations to the COTED to enhance its effectiveness;

   (c)   promote the establishment of institutions and the development and implementation of harmonised competition laws and practices by Member States to achieve uniformity in the administration of applicable rules;

   (d)   review the progress made by Member States in the implementation of the legal and institutional framework for enforcement;

(e)   co-operate with competent authorities in Member States;

(f)   provide support to Member States in promoting and protecting consumer welfare;

(g)   facilitate the exchange of relevant information and expertise; and

(h)   develop and disseminate information about competition policy, and consumer protection policy.

3.   The Commission may, by directions in writing and subject to such conditions as it thinks fit, delegate any of its functions to one or more of its members.

Article 30(f)
Powers of the Commission

1.   Subject to Articles 30(g) and 30(h), the Commission may, in respect of cross-border transactions or transactions with cross-border effects, monitor, investigate, detect, make determinations or take action to inhibit and penalise enterprises whose business conduct prejudices trade or prevents, restricts or distorts competition within the CSME.

2.   The Commission may, in accordance with applicable national laws, in the conduct of its investigations:

(a)   secure the attendance of any person before it to give evidence;

(b)   require the discovery or production of any document or part thereof; and

(c)   take such other action as may be necessary in furtherance of the investigation.

3.   The Commission may, on the basis of its investigations, make determinations regarding the compatibility of business conduct with the rules of competition and other related provisions of the Treaty.

4.   The Commission shall, to the extent required to remedy or penalise anti-competitive business conduct referred to in Article 30(i):

(a)   order the termination or nullification as the case may require, of agreements, conduct, activities or decisions prohibited by Article 30(i);

(b)   direct the enterprise to cease and desist from anti-competitive business conduct and to take such steps as are necessary to overcome the effects of abuse of its dominant position in the market, or any other business conduct inconsistent with the principles of fair competition set out in this Protocol;

(c)   order payment of compensation to persons affected; and

(d)   impose fines for breaches of the rules of competition.

5.   The Commission may enter into such arrangements for the provision of services as may be necessary for the efficient performance of its functions.

6.   Member States shall enact legislation to ensure that determinations of the Commission are enforceable in their jurisdictions.

7.   The Commission may establish its own rules of procedure.

Article 30(g)
Determination of Anti-Competitive Business Conduct:
Procedure of Commission on Request

1.   A Member State may request an investigation referred to in paragraph 1 of Article 30(f) where it has reason to believe that business conduct by an enterprise located in another Member State prejudices trade and prevents, restricts or distorts competition in the territory of the requesting Member
State.

2.   Where the COTED has reason to believe that business conduct by an enterprise in the CSME prejudices trade and prevents, restricts or distorts competition within the CSME and has or is likely to have cross-border effects, the COTED may request an investigation referred to in paragraph 1 of
Article 30(f).

3.   Requests under paragraphs 1 and 2 shall be in writing and shall disclose sufficient information for the Commission to make a preliminary assessment whether it should proceed with the investigation.

4.   Upon receipt of a request mentioned in paragraph 3, the Commission shall consult with the interested parties and shall determine on the basis of such consultations whether:

  (a)   the investigation is within the jurisdiction of the Commission; and

  (b)   the investigation is justified in all the circumstances of the case.

5.   The consultations shall be concluded within 30 days of the date of receipt of the request for investigation, unless the parties agree to continue the consultations for a longer period.

6.   Where the Commission decides to conduct the investigation, the Commission shall:

  (a)   notify the interested parties and the COTED;

  (b)   complete the investigation within 120 days from the date of receipt of the request for the investigation; and

  (c)   where the circumstances so warrant, extend the time period for completion of the investigation and notify the interested Parties.

7.   Where the Commission decides to conduct an enquiry following an investigation, the Commission shall afford any party complained of the opportunity to defend its interest.

8.   At the conclusion of an enquiry, the Commission shall notify the interested parties of its determination.

9.   Where the Commission determines that a party has engaged in anti-competitive business conduct, it shall also require the party to take the action necessary to remove the effects of the anti-competitive business conduct.

10.   Where a specific course of action is required under paragraph 9, the enterprise concerned shall take the appropriate course of action within 30 days of the date of notification. If the concerned enterprise cannot comply, it shall notify the Commission and request an extension.

11.   If the enterprise cannot comply within the time period specified and fails to inform the Commission, the Commission may apply to the Court for an order.

12.   A party which is aggrieved by a determination of the Commission under paragraph 4 of Article 30(f) in any matter may apply to the Court for a review of that determination.

Article 30(h)
<u>Determination of Anti-Competitive Business Conduct;</u>
<u>Procedure of Commission Proprio Motu</u>

1.   Where the Commission has reason to believe that business conduct by an enterprise in the CSME prejudices trade and prevents, restricts, or distorts competition within the CSME and has cross-border effects, the Commission shall request the competent national authority to undertake a preliminary examination of the business conduct of the enterprise.

2.   Where a request is made under paragraph 1, the national authority shall examine the matter and report its findings to the Commission within such time as may be determined by the Commission.

3.   Where the Commission is not satisfied with the outcome of its request, the Commission may initiate its own preliminary examination into the business conduct of the enterprise referred to in paragraph 1.

4.   Where the findings of the preliminary examination under paragraphs 2 and 3 require investigation, the Commission and the Member State concerned shall hold consultations to determine and agree on who should have jurisdiction to investigate.

5.   If there is a difference of opinion between the Commission and the Member State regarding the nature and effects of the business conduct or the jurisdiction of the investigating authority, the Commission shall:

    (a)   cease any further examination of the matter; and

    (b)   refer the matter to the COTED for its decision.

6.   Nothing in this Article shall prejudice the right of the Member State to initiate proceedings before the Court at any time.

7.   Where there is a finding that the Commission has jurisdiction to investigate the matter, the Commission shall follow the procedures set out in paragraphs 5, 6, 7 and 8 of Article 30(g).

PART III
RULES OF COMPETITION

Article 30(i)
Prohibition of Anti-Competitive Business Conduct

1.   A Member State shall, within its jurisdiction, prohibit as being anti-competitive business conduct, the following:

     (a)   agreements between enterprises, decisions by associations of enterprises, and concerted practices by enterprises which have as their object or effect the prevention, restriction or distortion of competition within the Community;

     (b)   actions by which an enterprise abuses its dominant position within the Community; or

     (c)   any other like conduct by enterprises whose object or effect is to frustrate the benefits expected from the establishment of the CSME.

2.   Anti-competitive business conduct within the meaning of paragraph 1 includes the following:

     (a)   the direct or indirect fixing of purchase or selling prices,

     (b)   the limitation or control of production, markets, investment or technical development;

     (c)   the artificial dividing up of markets or restriction of supply sources;

     (d)   the application of unequal conditions to parties undertaking equivalent engagements in commercial transactions thereby placing them at a competitive disadvantage;

     (e)   making the conclusion of a contract subject to the acceptance by the other party to the contract of additional obligations which, by their nature or according to commercial practice, have no connection with the subject matter of the contract;

     (f)   unauthorised denial of access to networks or essential infrastructure;

     (g)   predatory pricing;

     (h)   price discrimination;

     (i)   loyalty discounts or concessions;

     (j)   exclusionary vertical restrictions; and

     (k)   bid-rigging.

3.   Subject to Article 30, a Member State shall ensure that all agreements and decisions within the meaning of paragraph 1 of this Article shall be null and void within its jurisdiction.

4.   An enterprise shall not be treated as engaging in anti-competitive business conduct if it establishes that the activity complained of:

(a)   contributes to:

(i)   the improvement of production or distribution of goods and services; or

(ii)   the promotion of technical or economic progress;

while allowing consumers a fair share of the resulting benefit;

(b)   imposes on the enterprises affected only such restrictions as are indispensable to the attainment of the objectives mentioned in sub-paragraph (a); or

(c)   does not afford the enterprise engaged in the activity the possibility of eliminating competition in respect of a substantial part of the market for goods or services concerned.

Article 30(j)
Determination of Dominant Position

For the purposes of this Protocol:

(a)   an enterprise holds a dominant position in a market if by itself or together with an interconnected company, it occupies such a position of economic strength as will enable it to operate in the market without effective constraints from its competitors or potential competitors;

(b)   any two companies shall be treated as interconnected companies if one of them is a subsidiary of the other or both of them are subsidiaries of the same parent company.

Article 30(k)
Abuse of a Dominant Position

1.   Subject to paragraph 2 of this Article, an enterprise abuses its dominant position in a market if it prevents, restricts or distorts competition in the market and, in particular but without prejudice to the generality of the foregoing, it:

(a)   restricts the entry of any enterprise into a market;

(b)   prevents or deters any enterprise from engaging in competition in a market;

(c)   eliminates or removes any enterprise from a market;

(d)   directly or indirectly imposes unfair purchase or selling prices or other restrictive practices;

(e)   limits the production of goods or services for a market to the prejudice of consumers;

(f)   as a party to an agreement, makes the conclusion of such agreement subject to acceptance by another party of supplementary obligations which, by their nature or according to commercial usage, have no connection with the subject of the agreement;

(g)   engages in any business conduct that results in the exploitation of its customers or suppliers, so as to frustrate the benefits expected from the establishment of the CSME.

2.   In determining whether an enterprise has abused its dominant position, consideration shall be given to:

(a)   the relevant market defined in terms of the product and the geographic context;

(b)   the concentration level before and after the relevant activity of the enterprise measured in terms of annual sales volume, the value of assets and the value of the transaction;

(c)   the level of competition among the participants in terms of number of competitors, production capacity and product demand;

(d)   the barriers to entry of competitors; and

(e)   the history of competition and rivalry between participants in the sector of activity.

3.   An enterprise shall not be treated as abusing its dominant position if it is established that:

(a)   its behaviour was directed exclusively to increasing efficiency in the production, provision or distribution of goods or services or to promoting technical or economic progress and that consumers were allowed a fair share of the resulting benefit;

(b)   the enterprise reasonably enforces or seeks to enforce a right under or existing by virtue of a copyright, patent, registered trade mark or design; or

(c)   the effect or likely effect of its behaviour on the market is the result of superior competitive performance of the enterprise concerned.

Article 30(l)
Negative Clearance Rulings

1.   In any case where a Member State is uncertain whether business conduct is prohibited by paragraph 1 of Article 30(i), such a Member State may apply to the Commission for a ruling on the matter. If the Commission determines that such conduct is not prohibited by paragraph 1 of Article 30(i), it shall issue a negative clearance ruling to this effect.

2.   A negative clearance ruling shall be conclusive of the matters stated therein in any judicial proceedings in the Community.

Article 30(m)
De Minimis Rule

The Commission may exempt from the provisions of this Part any business conduct referred to it if it considers that the impact of such conduct on competition and trade in the CSME is minimal.

Article 30(n)
Powers of the COTED Respecting Community
Competition Policy and Rules

Subject to the Treaty, the COTED shall develop and establish appropriate policies and rules of competition within the Community including special rules for particular sectors.

Article 30(o)
Exemptions

1.   Where the COTED determines, pursuant to Article 30(n), that special rules shall apply to specific sectors of the Community, it may suspend or exclude the application of Article 30(i) to such sectors pending adoption of the relevant rules.

2.   The COTED may, on its own initiative or pursuant to an application by a Member State in that behalf, exclude or suspend the application of Article 30(i) to any sector or any enterprise or group of enterprises in the public interest.

PART IV
DUMPING AND SUBSIDIES

Article 30(p)
Determination of a Subsidy

For the purposes of this Part, a subsidy shall be deemed to exist if there is a financial contribution by a Government or any public body within the territory of a Member State (hereinafter referred to as "government") where:

(a)   government practice involves direct transfer of funds (e.g., grants, loans and equity infusion) or potential direct transfer of funds or liabilities (e.g., loan guarantees);

(b)   government revenue that is otherwise due is foregone or not collected (e.g., fiscal incentives, such as tax credits);

(c)   a government purchases goods or provides goods or services other than general infrastructure; or

(d)   a government makes payments to a funding mechanism, or directs or entrusts to a private body the conduct of activities mentioned in sub-paragraphs (a), (b) and (c) which are normally conducted by governments; or

(e)   there is any form of income or price support, and a benefit is thereby conferred.

Article 30(p)(bis)
<u>Types of Subsidies</u>

1.   Member States may take action against products from another Member State which benefit from a subsidy within the meaning of Article 30(p) being -

(a)   a prohibited subsidy;

(b)   a subsidy which:

     (i)   causes injury to a domestic industry; or

     (ii)   results in nullification or impairment of benefits accruing directly or indirectly to any Member State; or

     (iii)   seriously prejudices the interests of any Member State; or

(c)   a subsidy which causes serious adverse effects to a domestic industry of any Member State such as to cause damage which would be difficult to repair:

Provided that the subsidy is specific to an enterprise or industry or group of enterprises or industries within the jurisdiction of the granting Member State.

2.   For the purpose of this Protocol a determination of whether a subsidy as defined in Article 30(p) is specific shall be governed by the following principles:

(a)   in order to determine whether a subsidy referred to in paragraph 1 of this Article is specific to an enterprise or industry or group of enterprises or industries (referred to in this Protocol as "certain enterprises") within the jurisdiction of the granting authority, the following principles shall apply:

     (i)   where the granting authority, or the legislation pursuant to which the granting authority operates, explicitly limits access to a subsidy to certain enterprises, such a subsidy shall be specific;

     (ii)   where the granting authority, or the legislation pursuant to which the granting authority operates, establishes objective criteria or conditions governing the eligibility for, and the amount of, a subsidy, specificity shall not exist, provided that the eligibility is automatic and that such criteria and conditions are strictly adhered to. The criteria or conditions must be clearly spelled out in law, regulation, or other official document, so as to be capable of verification;

     (iii)   if, notwithstanding any appearance of non-specificity resulting from the application of the principles laid down in sub-sub-paragraphs (i) and (ii), there are reasons to believe that the subsidy may in fact be specific, other factors may be considered. Such factors are: use of a subsidy programme by a limited number of certain enterprises, predominant use of certain enterprises, the granting of disproportionately large amounts of subsidy to certain enterprises, and the manner in which discretion has been exercised by the granting authority in the decision to grant a subsidy. In applying this sub-paragraph, account shall be taken of the extent of diversification of economic activities within the jurisdiction of the granting authority, as well as of the length of time during which the subsidy programme has been in operation;

(b)   a subsidy which is limited to certain enterprises located within a designated geographical region within the jurisdiction of the granting authority shall be specific. It is understood that the setting or change of generally applicable tax rates by all levels of government entitled to do so shall not be deemed to be a specific subsidy for the purposes of this Protocol;

(c)   any subsidy falling under the provisions of Article 30(p)(quater) shall be deemed to be specific;

(d)   any determination of specificity under the provisions of this Article shall be clearly substantiated on the basis of positive evidence.

Article 30(p)(ter)
Entitlement to Take Action Against Subsidised Products

1.   A Member State may take action against subsidised products where:

(a)   the products have benefited from a prohibited subsidy;

(b)   the subsidy is specific and has caused any of the effects referred to in Article 30(t); and

(c)   the subsidy is specific and does not conform to the provisions of Article 30(z).

2.   Notwithstanding the provisions of paragraph 1, a Member State shall not take definitive action against products which are believed to be benefiting from subsidies referred to in Article 30(p)(bis)) if the Member State aggrieved thereby has not:

(a)   promulgated legislation to permit the introduction of counter measures or countervailing duties against subsidised imports;

(b)   consulted with the Member State which is alleged to have introduced or to be maintaining subsidies identified in Article 30(p)(bis);

(c)   notified the COTED of the alleged subsidisation based on preliminary investigations and failure of consultations; and

(d)   received authorisation from the COTED to introduce countervailing duties or countermeasures as a result of a definitive determination of the existence of prohibited subsidies which cause nullification, impairment, serious prejudice or adverse effects caused by subsidisation.

3.   Consultations for the purposes of this Part shall follow the procedures set out in Annex II to this Protocol.

Article 30(p)(quater)
Prohibited Subsidies

1.   Subject to the Treaty, a Member State shall neither grant nor maintain subsidies referred to in paragraph 2.

2.   The following subsidies within the meaning of Article 30(p)(bis) shall be prohibited:

(a)   subsidies contingent, in law or in fact, whether solely or as one of several other conditions, upon export performance, including those listed in Schedule 5 of Protocol IV - Trade Policy; and

(b)   subsidies contingent, whether solely or as one of several other conditions, upon the use of domestic over imported goods.

3.   Nothing in this Article shall be construed as applying to agricultural commodities produced in the Community.

Article 30(p)(quinquies)
Preliminary Investigation of Prohibited Subsidies

1.   An application for an investigation may be made in writing by or on behalf of a domestic industry to its competent authority where the industry has reason to believe that a prohibited subsidy referred to in Article 30(p)(quater) has been granted or maintained by another Member State. The authority shall examine the application and determine, on the basis of the facts available, whether to initiate an investigation.

2.   An investigation initiated pursuant to paragraph 1 of this Article shall be deemed to be a preliminary investigation. The authority shall give public notice of the preliminary investigation to inform the concerned Member State, other Member States and the interested parties all of whom shall be afforded adequate time to submit information required and to make comments.

3.   The authority shall make a preliminary determination whether a prohibited subsidy has been granted or maintained and, where the determination is affirmative, invite the concerned Member States and interested parties to defend their interests.

4.   Wherever the term "domestic industry" is used in this Protocol, it shall mean domestic industry as defined in Annex 1. A request for investigation by the domestic industry under this Article or under Article 30(u) or 30(aa) be accompanied by information set out in the Illustrative List at Annex 111(a).

Article 30(p)(sex)
Request for Consultations Relating to Prohibited Subsidies

1.   Whenever a Member State has reason to believe, pursuant to Article 30(p)(quater) that a prohibited subsidy has been granted or is maintained by a Member State, the aggrieved or any other Member State may request consultations with the Member State believed to be granting or

maintaining the subsidy. The aggrieved Member State shall notify the COTED of the request for consultations. A request for consultations shall include a statement of the available evidence with regard to the existence and nature of the alleged prohibited subsidy.

2.   Upon receipt of a request for consultations under paragraph 1, the Member State believed to be granting or maintaining the subsidy shall reply within 10 days and shall furnish the relevant information requested and shall promptly enter into consultations which shall be concluded within 30 days of the date of request for such consultations unless the parties agree to extend the consultations to a mutually agreed date. The purpose of the consultations shall be to clarify the facts relating to the existence and type of the alleged subsidy and to arrive at a mutually agreed solution.

Article 30(q)
Reference to COTED to Investigate Prohibited Subsidies

1.   If no mutually agreed solution is reached at the completion of 30 days from the date of the request for the consultations referred to in Article 30(p)(sex), or at such time as the parties agree, or if the Member State believed to be granting or maintaining the subsidy refuses to co-operate, the Member State requesting consultations or any other Member State interested in such consultations may refer the matter to the COTED which shall carry out an investigation to establish whether the subsidy in question is a prohibited subsidy.

2.   The referral of the matter to the COTED for an investigation shall not prevent the aggrieved Member State from taking, on a provisional basis, which shall not be sooner than 60 days from the date of initiation of investigations under paragraph 1 of Article 30(p)(quinquies),. countermeasures to forestall injury or to prevent further injury to its domestic industry.

Article 30(r)
Investigation by COTED of Prohibited Subsidies

1.   Whenever the COTED decides to carry out an investigation pursuant to Article 30(q), such an investigation by the COTED shall proceed as expeditiously as possible. The COTED may appoint competent experts to advise whether the subsidy falls to be classified as a prohibited subsidy, in which case the COTED shall set a time limit for the examination of the evidence by the competent experts. The COTED shall make its determination and issue its report which shall, unless extenuating circumstances arise, not exceed 90 days from the date of receipt of request for the investigation.

2.   The results of an investigation carried out pursuant to Article 30(q) shall be made available to all Member States for information and to afford the concerned Member States an opportunity to arrive at a mutually agreed solution within 30 days from the date of issue of the report failing which the COTED shall adopt the recommendations of the report.

3.   If the COTED is satisfied, based on the results of the investigation, that the subsidy in question is a prohibited subsidy and that the concerned Member States cannot reach a mutually agreed solution, it shall subject to Article 30(s), require the offending Member State to withdraw the subsidy within a specified time-frame. Where the offending Member State fails to comply, the COTED shall authorise the aggrieved Member State to take counter-measures on the products which benefit from such a subsidy.

Article 30(s)
Withdrawal of Prohibited Subsidies

1.   Notwithstanding the investigation confirming the existence of a prohibited subsidy in paragraph 3 of Article 30(r), the COTED shall not impose a requirement for Member States to withdraw such a subsidy sooner than specified in this paragraph as follows:

(a)   with respect to subsidies contingent upon export performance:

(i)   Member States with per capita GNP of less than one thousand United States dollars shall be allowed to maintain such subsidies; and

(ii)   other Member States shall be allowed to maintain such subsidies until 1 January 2003;

(b)   with respect to subsidies contingent upon the use of domestic over imported inputs, Member States with per capita GNP of less than one thousand United States dollars shall be allowed to maintain such subsidies until 2003.

2.   Whenever the results of an investigation by the COTED prove that the alleged subsidy is not a prohibited subsidy, any provisional countervailing measures which might have been imposed shall be promptly withdrawn and any bond or deposit which might have been effected, released or refunded, as the case may be. If the provisional measures referred to in this paragraph have materially retarded the exports of the Member State which was wrongfully alleged to have introduced or maintained prohibited subsidies, the COTED shall, upon application from such a Member State, assess the effects of the provisionally applied measures and determine the nature and extent of compensation which is warranted and recommend compensation in accordance with its assessment.

3.   From the date of entry into force of this Protocol until the expiration of the dates mentioned in paragraph 1, no provisional measures shall be imposed where it has been determined by preliminary investigations that prohibited subsidies are maintained.

Article 30(t)
Subsidies Causing Injury, Nullification, Impairment or Serious Prejudice

A Member State may take action against subsidised imports from any other Member State where it can be established, based on an investigation, that the effect of the subsidy has been:

(a)   injury to its domestic industry;

(b)   nullification or impairment of benefits which it expects under this Treaty; or

(c)   serious prejudice to its interests.

2.   Serious prejudice shall be deemed to exist in the case of:

(a)   the total ad valorem subsidisation of a product exceeding 5 per cent;

(b)   subsidies to cover operating losses sustained by an industry;

(c)   subsidies to cover operating losses sustained by an enterprise, other than one-time measures which are non-recurrent and cannot be repeated for that enterprise and which are given merely to provide time for the development of long-term solutions and to avoid acute social problems; or

(d)   forgiveness of government-held debt and government grants to cover debt repayment.

3.   Notwithstanding the provisions of this Article, serious prejudice shall not be found if the Member State granting the subsidy in question demonstrates that the effect of the subsidy has not been:

(a)   to displace or impede the imports of like products from the Member State exporting to the Member State which has introduced or maintains the subsidy;

(b)   to displace or impede the exports of a like product from the affected exporting Member State into the market of a third Member State;

(c)   a significant price undercutting by the subsidised product as compared with the price of a like product of another Member State in the same market or a significant price suppression or price depression;

(d)   lost sales of another Member State in the same market; or

(e)   an increase in its market share within the CSME..

4.   The provisions of this Article shall not apply to Part V.

Article 30(u)
Preliminary Investigation of Subsidies Causing Injury, Nullification, Impairment or Serious Prejudice

1.   An application for an investigation may be made in writing by or on behalf of a domestic industry to the national authority where the industry has reason to believe that a subsidy referred to in Article 30(t) has been granted or is maintained by another Member State and has caused injury, or resulted in nullification, impairment or serious prejudice to its interests.

2.   An application under paragraph 1 shall include sufficient information about the existence of a subsidy and, if possible, its amount, injury and a causal link between the subsidised products and the alleged injury.

3.   An application to initiate an investigation shall be considered to have been made by or on behalf of a domestic industry if it is supported by those domestic producers whose collective output constitutes more than 50 per cent of the total production of the like product by that proportion of the domestic industry expressing support for or opposition to the application. The investigation shall not be initiated where the domestic producers expressly supporting the application account for less than 25 per cent of the total production of the like product produced by the domestic industry.

4.   Upon receipt of a request for such an investigation, the authority shall examine the application and determine, on the basis of the facts available, whether to initiate an investigation. If the authority decides to initiate an investigation, it shall issue a public notice to that effect, invite the concerned Member State, other interested Member States and interested parties to submit required information and comments.

5.   An investigation initiated pursuant to paragraph 2 shall be deemed to be a preliminary investigation. The authority shall inform the concerned Member State and all interested parties of the results of the investigation.

Article 30(v)
Request for Consultations Relating to Subsidies Causing Injury, Nullification, Impairment or Serious Prejudice

1.   Whenever a Member State has reason to believe that a subsidy within the meaning of Article 30(p) has been granted or is maintained by another Member State, and that imports from such a Member State have resulted in any of the effects mentioned in paragraph 1(b) of Article 30(p)(bis), the first-mentioned Member State may approach the Member States believed to be granting a subsidy with a request for consultations.

2.   A request for consultations shall include a statement of available evidence with regard to

(a)   the existence and nature of the subsidy; and

(b)   the injury caused to the domestic industry; or

(c)   the impairment or nullification of benefits of exporting to other Member States in the Community; or

(d)   serious prejudice to its interests.

3.   Upon receipt of a request for consultations under paragraph 1, the Member State believed to be granting or maintaining the subsidy shall reply within 10 days, furnish relevant information, and enter into consultations within 30 days of the date of the request. The purpose of the consultations shall be to clarify the facts relating to the existence, type and effect of the alleged subsidy and to arrive at a mutually agreed solution.

Article 30(w)
Reference to COTED to Investigate Subsidies Causing Injury, Nullification, Impairment or Serious Prejudice

1.   If no mutually agreed solution is reached at the completion of 60 days from the date of request for consultations, or on a date mutually agreed, the Member State requesting consultations may refer the matter to the COTED which shall initiate an investigation, make a determination to resolve the dispute and issue a report within 120 days of the date of the request for an investigation by the aggrieved Member State.

2.   A decision by the COTED to initiate an investigation shall not prevent the aggrieved Member State from taking, on a provisional basis, countermeasures which shall not be sooner

than 60 days from the date of initiation of a preliminary investigation by the national authority to forestall or prevent further adverse effects.

Article 30(x)
Investigation by COTED of Subsidies Causing Injury, Nullification, Impairment or Serious Prejudice

1.   In order to arrive at a determination of the existence, degree and effect of subsidisation, and remedial action which may be taken pursuant to the referral of a complaint of alleged subsidisation mentioned in Article 30(w), the COTED shall -

(a)   carry out an investigation into the circumstances relating to the alleged grant or maintenance of the subsidy by the offending Member State; the investigation is to be completed within 120 days of the date of receipt of a complaint regarding alleged subsidisation by an offending Member State; and

(b)   upon receipt of the report arising from the investigation, promptly make available the report to the concerned Member States to facilitate consultation and to permit the Member states concerned to arrive at a mutually acceptable solution.

Article 30(y)
Consequences of Failure to Remove Subsidies Causing Injury, Nullification, Impairment or Serious Prejudice

1.   If no mutually acceptable solution is reached within 30 days of the date of issue of the report by the COTED, and the COTED is satisfied:

(a)   of the existence of a subsidy within the meaning of Article 30(t); and

(b)   that the subsidy has caused injury to the enterprise in the complaining Member State; or

(c)   that the subsidy has impaired or nullified benefits expected of the complaining Member State with respect to its exports to the Community; or

(d)   that the effect of the subsidy was to seriously prejudice the interests of the Member State,

then in such a case, the COTED shall request the Member State which has granted or maintained the subsidy to take appropriate steps to remedy the effects of the subsidy within six months of the date of the issue of the report by the COTED.

2.   If, at the end of the period of six months allowed by COTED to the Member State granting or maintaining the subsidy to remedy the effects of the subsidy, the Member State fails to comply and in the absence of agreement on compensation the COTED shall authorise the aggrieved Member State to impose countervailing duties at a rate equivalent to the amount of subsidisation for such time and under such conditions as the COTED may prescribe.

Article 30(z)
Types of Subsidies Causing Serious Adverse Effects

1.   Member States shall not ordinarily impose or introduce countervailing duties or take countermeasures on products which benefit from:

(a)   subsidies which are not specific within the meaning of Article 30(p)(bis); or

(b)   subsidies which are specific within the meaning of Article 30(p)(bis) but which satisfy all of the conditions set out in this sub-paragraph hereunder:

    (i)   subsidies which are not specific, in terms of the granting authority or the enabling legislation it applies -

        (a)   not explicitly limiting access to such subsidies by certain enterprises;

        (b)   establishing objective criteria or conditions governing the eligibility for and the amount of, a subsidy where eligibility is automatic and such criteria and conditions are strictly adhered to; or

        (c)   not limiting a subsidy programme or its predominant or disproportionate use to certain enterprises;

    (ii)   subsidies granted for research activities conducted by enterprises or by higher education or research establishments on a contract basis with firms if: the assistance covers not more than 75 per cent of the costs of industrial research or 50 per cent of the costs of pre-competitive development activity; and provided that such assistance is limited exclusively to:

        (a)   costs of personnel (researchers, technicians and other supporting staff employed exclusively in the research activity);

        (b)   costs of instruments, equipment, land and buildings used exclusively and permanently (except when disposed of on a commercial basis) for the research activity;

    (iii)   subsidies granted to assist disadvantaged regions within the territory of a Member State given pursuant to a general framework of regional development and non-specific within eligible regions provided that:

        (a)   each disadvantaged region must be a clearly designated contiguous geographical area with a definable economic and administrative identify;

        (b)   the region is considered as disadvantaged on the basis of neutral and objective criteria, indicating that the region's difficulties arise out of more than temporary circumstances; such criteria must be clearly spelled out in law, regulation, or other official document, so as to be capable of verification;

(c) the criteria shall include a measurement of economic development which shall be based on at least one of the following factors:

(i) one of either income per capita or household income per capita, or GDP per capita, which must not be above 85 per cent of the average for the territory concerned;

(ii) unemployment rate, which must be at least 110 per cent of the average for the territory concerned;

(iv) subsidies granted to assist entities in the adaptation of existing facilities to new environmental requirements imposed by law and/or regulations which result in greater constraints and financial burden on enterprises provided that the subsidies -

(a) are a one-time non-recurring measure; and

(b) are limited to 20 per cent of the cost of adaptation; and

(c) do not cover the cost of replacing and operating the assisted investment, which must be fully borne by firms; and

(d) are directly linked to and proportionate to a firm's planned reduction of nuisances and pollution, and does not cover any manufacturing cost savings which may be achieved; and

(e) are available to all firms which can adopt the new equipment and/or production processes.

(v) subsidies granted to assist enterprises to undertake training or retraining of employees, whether or not the enterprise is new, and the upgrading of existing facilities to facilitate transition to competitive status within the Community, provided that such subsidies are not specific.

2. Member States shall notify the COTED of any subsidy mentioned in paragraph 1. Any Member State may request further information regarding a notified subsidy programme and the COTED shall review annually all notified subsidies referred to in paragraph 1.

Article 30(aa)
Preliminary Investigation of Subsidies Causing Serious Adverse Effects

1. A domestic industry may submit to the competent authority an application for an investigation to verify that serious adverse effects have been caused by imports which benefit from subsidies referred to in Article 30(z).

2.   Upon receipt of an application for an investigation to verify adverse effects, the authority shall examine the application, and, on the basis of the available facts, determine whether to initiate an investigation.

3.   The investigation referred to in paragraph 2 shall be deemed a preliminary investigation. The authority shall give public notice of its decision to initiate a preliminary investigation and the concerned Member State, other interested Member States, and the interested parties shall all be invited to provide relevant information and make comments.

4.   The results of the preliminary investigation shall be made available to the concerned Member State, other interested Member States and the interested parties to enable them to defend their interests.

Article 30(bb)
Request for Consultations Relating to Subsidies Causing Serious Adverse Effects

1.   Whenever a Member State has reason to believe that imports from another Member State benefited from subsidies within the meaning of Article 30(z) and such imports have resulted in serious adverse effects to a domestic industry so as to cause damage which would be difficult to repair, the Member State aggrieved may request consultations with the Member State granting or maintaining the subsidy.

2.   The Member State alleged to be granting the subsidy which caused adverse effects shall reply within 10 days of the date of the request for consultations and shall enter into the consultations requested by the aggrieved Member State. If there is no mutual agreement within 60 days of the date of the request for such consultations or on a later date which was mutually agreed or if the Member State refuses to cooperate, the aggrieved Member State may refer the matter to the COTED and request the COTED to carry out an investigation.

Article 30(cc)
Investigation by COTED of Subsidies Causing Serious Adverse Effects

1.   The referral of the matter to the COTED for an investigation shall not prevent the aggrieved Member State from imposing on a provisional basis, which shall not be sooner than 60 days from the date of initiation of the preliminary investigation referred to in Article 30(aa), countermeasures to forestall or prevent further adverse effects.

2.   If the COTED is satisfied that the investigation requested is justified, the COTED shall carry out the investigation, make a determination and issue a report within 120 days from the date when the request was referred.

3.   Where the results of the investigation carried out by the COTED demonstrated that the subsidised imports caused serious adverse effects to the domestic industry of the aggrieved Member State requesting the investigation, the COTED shall recommend that the offending Member State modify the programme of subsidies in such a way as to remove the adverse effects complained of.

Article 30(dd)
Consequences of Failure to Eliminate or
Establish Adverse Effects of Subsidies

1.   If the offending Member State fails to implement the recommendations of the COTED within 6 months of the date of issue of the report referred to in paragraph 2 of Article 30(cc), the COTED shall authorise the aggrieved Member State to impose appropriate countervailing duties commensurate with the nature and degree of serious adverse effects determined to exist.

2.   Whenever the results of an investigation by COTED prove that serious adverse effects have not been caused by subsidised imports referred to in paragraph 1 of Article 30(z), the Member State alleging that its domestic industry has suffered serious adverse effects shall promptly refund any duties which might have been provisionally imposed and where such provisional duties had materially retarded the exports of the Member State complained against, the COTED shall, upon application from such State, assess the effects of the provisionally applied duties and determine the nature and extent of compensation which is warranted and require compensation in accordance with its assessment.

Article 30(ee)
Imposition of Provisional Measures and Countervailing Duties

1.   Notwithstanding anything to the contrary in this Protocol, a Member State aggrieved by the application or maintenance of prohibited subsidies or by subsidies which cause injury, or result in nullification, impairment, or serious prejudice, or cause serious adverse effects, as the case may be, shall introduce provisional measures only on the basis of the following rules:

   (a)   Provisional measures may be applied only if -

      (i)   a preliminary investigation has been initiated in accordance with the provisions of this Protocol, a public notice has been given to that effect and interested parties have been given adequate opportunities to submit information and make comments;

      (ii)   an affirmative preliminary determination has been made of the existence of a prohibited subsidy, or a subsidy causing injury, nullification, impairment, serious prejudice, or a subsidy causing serious adverse effects, as the case may be;

      (iii)   consultations were requested and/or undertaken, the COTED was notified and requested to investigate and the authorities concerned judge such measures necessary to prevent injury being caused during the investigation;

   (b)   Provisional measures may take the form of provisional countervailing duties guaranteed by cash deposits or bond equal to the amount of the provisionally calculated amount of subsidisation;

   (c)   Provisional measures shall not be applied sooner than 60 days from the date of initiation of the preliminary investigation;

    (d)   The application of provisional measures shall be limited to as short a period as possible, not exceeding 120 days.

2.   Where investigations by the COTED continue beyond the period allowed for the maintenance of provisional measures under sub-paragraph 1(d), the Member State imposing the measures may continue with such measures until a definitive determination is made by the COTED.

3.   The Member States which are parties to an investigation to verify the existence and the effect of alleged subsidisation, may seek or accept, as the case may be, undertakings from the Member State alleged to have granted or to be maintaining a subsidy. Undertakings may take the form of:

    (a)   withdrawal, or limiting the amount of, the subsidy to such an extent that injury, nullification, impairment, serious prejudice or serious adverse effects, as the case may be, are eliminated; or

    (b)   a guarantee from the exporter benefiting from the subsidy to raise his price to such an extent that the injurious effect is eliminated.

4.   If a Member State accepts a voluntary guarantee pursuant to sub-paragraph 3(b), then the accepting Member State shall notify the COTED and promptly suspend proceedings, and any provisional measures which may have been imposed shall be withdrawn with immediate effect.

5.   In the event that investigations to determine subsidisation have been concluded and the evidence proves injury, nullification, impairment or serious prejudice, or serious adverse effects, as the case may be, a Member State may impose countervailing duties retroactively to account for the entire period during which provisional measures have been in force. Such retroactively applied duties shall take into account the definitively assessed countervailing duties and the amount guaranteed by cash deposit or bond and:

    (a)   where the definitive countervailing duties are higher than the provisional duties, the difference shall not be collected;

    (b)   where the definitive countervailing duties are lower than the provisional duties, the excess of the deposit shall be refunded or the bond released promptly.

6.   No Member State shall impose countervailing duties other than provisional countervailing duties without prior authorisation from the COTED and the determination and imposition of definitive countervailing duties shall be governed by the relevant provisions of the World Trade Organisation (WTO) Agreement on Subsidies and Countervailing Measures.

7.   The COTED shall keep under review all counter-measures imposed by Member States and shall ensure that Member States observe the conditions and timetable for review and withdrawal of counter-measures that it may have authorised.

8.   Member States undertake to co-operate in establishing harmonised legislation and procedures in accordance with the provisions of this Protocol.

Article 30(ff)
Action Against Dumping

A Member State may take action against dumped imports if such imports cause injury or pose a serious threat of injury to a domestic industry.

Article 30(gg)
Determination of Dumping

1.   For the purposes of this Protocol, a product is to be considered to be dumped, that is to say, introduced into the commerce of another country at less than its normal value if the export price of the product exported from one Member state to another Member State is less than the comparable price, in the ordinary course of trade, for the like product when destined for consumption in the exporting Member State.

2.   When there are no sales of the like product in the ordinary course of trade in the domestic market of the exporting country or when, because of the particular market situation or the low volume of the sales in the domestic market of the exporting country, such sales do not permit a proper comparison, the margin of dumping shall be determined by comparison with a comparable price of the like product when exported to an appropriate third country, provided that this price is representative, or with the cost of production in the country of origin plus a reasonable amount for administrative, selling and general costs and for profits.

3.   In cases where there is no export price or where it appears to the authorities concerned that the export price is unreliable because of association or a compensatory arrangement between the exporter and importer or a third party, the export price may be constructed on the basis of the price at which the imported products are first resold to an independent buyer, or if the products are not resold to an independent buyer, or not resold in the condition as imported, on such reasonable basis as the authorities may determine.

4.   A fair comparison shall be made between the export price and the normal value. This comparison shall be made at the same level of trade, normally at the ex-factory level, and in respect of sales made at as nearly as possible the same time. Due allowance shall be made in each case, on its merits, for differences which affect price comparability, including differences in conditions and terms of sale, taxation, levels of trade, quantities, physical characteristics, and any other differences which are also demonstrated to affect price comparability. In the cases referred to in paragraph 3, allowances for costs, including duties and taxes incurred between importation and resale, and for profits accruing, should also be made. If in these cases price comparability has been affected, the authorities shallestablish the normal value at a level of trade equivalent to the level of trade of the constructed export price, or shall make due allowance as warranted under this paragraph. The authorities shall indicate to the parties in question what information is necessary to ensure a fair comparison and shall not impose an unreasonable burden of proof on those parties.

5.   In the case where products are not imported directly from the country of origin but are exported to the importing Member from an intermediate country, the price at which the products are sold from the country of export to the importing Member shall normally be compared with the comparable price in the country of export. However, comparison may be made with the price in the country of origin, if, for example, the products are merely transshipped through the

country of export, or such products are not produced in the country of export, or there is no comparable price for them in the country of export.

6.   For the purpose of this Protocol "like product" shall be interpreted to mean a product which is identical, i.e., alike in all respects to the product under consideration, or in the absence of such a product, another product, which, although not alike in all respects, has characteristics closely resembling those of the product under consideration.

Article 30(hh)
Determination of Injury

1.   For the purpose of Article 30(ff), injury shall, unless otherwise specified, be taken to mean material injury to a domestic industry, threat of material injury to a domestic industry or material retardation of the establishment of such an industry.

2.   A determination of injury within the meaning of paragraph 1 shall be based on positive evidence and involve an objective examination of:

(a)   the volume of the dumped imports and the effect of such imports on prices in the domestic market for like products; and

(b)   the consequent impact of the dumped imports on domestic producers of such products.

3.   In making a determination regarding the existence of a threat of material injury, the competent authorities shall consider, inter alia:

(a)   significant rate of increase of dumped imports into the domestic market indicating the likelihood of substantially increased importation;

(b)   sufficient freely disposable, or an imminent, substantial increase in, capacity of the exporter indicating the likelihood of substantially increased dumped exports to the importing Member's market taking into account the availability of other export markets to absorb any additional exports;

(c)   whether imports are entering at prices that will have a significant depressing or suppressing effect on domestic prices, and would likely increase demand for further imports; and

(d)   inventories of the product being investigated.

Article 30(ii)
Definition of Domestic Industry

1.   For the purposes of this Protocol, the term "domestic industry" shall mean "domestic industry" as defined in Annex I.

Article 30(jj)
Initiation of Preliminary Investigations

1.   If a domestic industry in a Member State has reason to believe that it is being injured or faces the threat of injury as a result of dumped imports, an application may be submitted in writing by the industry or on its behalf by an association representing the industry or by employees employed by the producers of the like product to the competent authority to initiate an investigation in order to verify the existence of dumped imports and injury caused or the existence of a serious threat of injury as the case may be.

2.   The application shall be considered to have been made by or on behalf of the domestic industry if it is supported by those domestic producers whose collective output constitutes more than 50 per cent of the total production of the like product produced by that portion of the domestic industry expressing either support for or opposition to the request. However, no investigation shall be initiated when domestic producers expressly supporting the request account for less than 25 per cent of total production of the like product produced by the domestic industry.

3.   The authority shall examine the application and determine if an investigation is justified and if it is satisfied, it shall issue a public notice to that effect and request the concerned Member State, other interested Member States and the interested parties, all of whom may be requested to and shall be afforded an opportunity to provide required information and comments.

4.   A decision by the authority to initiate an investigation shall be considered a decision to initiate a preliminary investigation, the results of which shall be made available by a public notice.

5.   Where a preliminary investigation provides sufficient evidence that dumped imports have entered into the commerce of the Member State and such imports seriously threaten or have injured a domestic industry, it may submit to the competent authority of the exporting Member State a request for consultations which shall be notified to the COTED.

6.   The purpose of the request for consultations shall be to establish whether imports have been dumped and injury has been caused or there is a serious threat of injury and if the injury or the serious threat thereof is directly the result of dumped imports.

7.   Interested parties who have been requested to provide information shall be allowed 30 days from the date of submission of the application by or on behalf of a domestic industry under paragraph 2 to reply unless the authorities concerned agree to a later date.

8.   For the purpose of this Protocol, "interested parties" shall include:

(a)   an exporter or foreign producer or the importer of a product subject to investigation, or a trade or business association, a majority of the members of which are producers, exporters or importers of such product;

(b)   the government of the exporting Member State; and

(c)   a producer of the like product in the importing Member State or a trade and business association, a majority of the members of which produce the like product in the territory of the importing Member State.

9.   A request for investigations to be undertaken by the competent authority of a Member State or by the COTED shall include but shall not necessarily be limited to the information indicated in the Illustrative List attached to this Protocol as Annex III(b). If, however, an aggrieved Member State is satisfied that the offending party had not made satisfactory efforts to afford consultations, to provide requested information or otherwise unreasonably impede an investigation which has been initiated, the competent authority of the Member State aggrieved may impose on a provisional basis anti-dumping measures and may refer the request for investigation to the COTED. A public notice of the imposition of provisional anti-dumping measures shall be issued by the Member State which has imposed such measures.

Article 30(kk)
Provisional Measures

1.   Provisional measures may be applied only if -

(a)   an investigation has been initiated in accordance with the provisions of paragraph 4 of Article 30(jj), a public notice has been given to that effect and interested parties have been given adequate opportunities to submit information and make comments;

(b)   a preliminary affirmative determination has been made of dumping and consequent injury to a domestic industry; and

(c)   the authorities concerned judge such measures necessary to prevent injury being caused during the investigation.

2.   Provisional measures may take the form of a provisional duty or preferably, a security - by cash deposit or bond - equal to the amount of the anti-dumping duty provisionally estimated, being not greater than the provisionally estimated margin of dumping. Withholding of appraisement is an appropriate provisional measure, provided that the normal duty and the estimated amount of the anti-dumping duty be indicated and as long as the withholding of appraisement is subject to the same conditions as other provisional measures.

3.   Provisional measures shall not be applied sooner than 60 days from the date of initiation of the investigation by a competent authority.

4.   The application of provisional measures shall be limited to as short a period as possible, not exceeding 120 days or, on decision of the authorities concerned, upon request by exporters representing a significant percentage of the trade involved, to a period not exceeding 180 days. When authorities, in the course of an investigation, examine whether a duty lower than the margin of dumping would be sufficient to remove injury, these periods may be 180 and 270 days, respectively.

Article 30(ll)
Conduct of Investigations leading to Definitive Determination of Injury

1.   Whenever the COTED receives a request for investigation, referred to it under paragraph 9 of Article 30(jj), the COTED shall determine whether the information accompanying the request justifies the continuation of investigations and if it is satisfied, cause an investigation to be completed within 12 months but not longer than 18 months after the date of receipt of the request. If the COTED is not satisfied that there is sufficient justification to initiate an investigation, it shall inform the applicant in writing of its refusal to investigate.

2.   Investigations either initiated by a competent authority of a Member State or undertaken by the COTED shall be terminated promptly whenever:

(a)   the margin of dumping is determined to be less than two per cent; and

(b)   the volume of dumped imports from a particular country is less than three per cent of imports of the like product in the importing Member State, unless countries which individually account for less than three per cent of the imports of the like product into the importing Member State collectively account for more than seven per cent of the imports of the like product in the importing Member State,

and a public notice of the termination of investigations under this paragraph shall be made by the Member State terminating investigations or by the COTED, as the case may be.

3.   Member States recognise that an investigation into the circumstances of alleged dumping based on a request by another Member State on behalf of a domestic industry will require the full co-operation of the competent authority and the parties alleged to be responsible for dumped imports, in the Member State from which such imports originated; all of whom shall provide relevant information in the time specified in this Article.

4.   In the conduct of an investigation to determine the existence and effect of dumped imports, competent authorities of Member States and the parties concerned shall observe the rights of the parties providing information with regard to confidentiality of any information provided and shall not disclose any such information without the prior written approval of the parties providing the information.

5.   Where an industry within the Single Market and Economy has suffered injury or faces the threat of serious injury based on evidence of dumped imports by third States, the competent authority for requesting investigation on behalf of the affected industry shall be the COTED.

6.   Nothing in this Article shall be construed so as to prevent an injured party or a Member State from initiating and proceeding with an investigation into alleged dumping having regard to the rights of such parties under international agreements to which they are signatories.

Article 30(mm)
Co-operation by Competent Authorities and Interested Parties

1.   Where an applicant for an investigation who receives information pursuant to dumping investigations requires verification of the information, the competent authority and the parties

alleged to be responsible for dumped imports shall co-operate in allowing the applicant to carry out verifications in the offending Member State.

2.   The results of any investigations carried out by a competent authority of a Member State aggrieved or by the COTED shall be disclosed promptly to the competent authority and the parties alleged to be responsible for dumped imports in the offending Member State. A public notice of the conclusions of the investigations shall be issued by the Member State or by the COTED, as the case may be.

3.   The purpose of the disclosure referred to in paragraph 2 shall be to present the facts of the case and to allow the parties alleged to be responsible for the dumped imports to defend their interests.

Article 30(nn)
Imposition of Anti-Dumping Measures

1.   The COTED shall, after consideration of the available evidence and having been satisfied of the existence of dumped imports, injury caused by dumped imports or the threat of serious injury from dumped imports, authorise the Member State aggrieved to take anti-dumping action:

(a)   if the parties alleged to be responsible for dumped imports refuse to cooperate within the time specified so as to frustrate or otherwise impede an investigation;

(b)   if there is a serious threat of injury or if injury has resulted.

2.   In authorising the imposition of anti-dumping measures, the COTED shall set the date, duration and conditions for the imposition of the measures as the case may require.

3.   Anti-dumping action taken pursuant to this Article, shall be based on the calculated margin of dumping and may be applied as follows:

(a)   if the evidence arising from definitive investigations of dumping proves the existence of dumping and that injury was caused by dumping, a Member State may impose anti-dumping duties sufficient to eliminate the margin of dumping. The COTED may authorise all affected Member States to impose similar anti-dumping duties for such time and under such conditions as the COTED may prescribe;

(b)   in the imposition of anti-dumping duties, Member States imposing the measure shall not discriminate among the sources of all dumped imports based on country of origin or nationality of the exporters;

(c)   an exporter whose exports are the subject of anti-dumping duties may request at any time the Member State imposing the duties to review the application of the duties against the relevant exports;

(d)   if an applicant for review of anti-dumping duties applied to exports mentioned in sub-paragraph (c) is not satisfied that the competent authorities in the importing Member States have given adequate consideration to the request for review within 30 days of the receipt of the request, the applicant may refer the request to the

COTED which shall recommend to the Member State maintaining the anti-dumping duty to take the appropriate action if it is satisfied that the application for review is justified;

(e) in the event that investigations have been concluded and the evidence proves that injury has been caused, a Member State may impose anti-dumping duties retroactively to account for the entire period during which provisional anti-dumping duties have been in force preceding the date of imposition of definitive anti-dumping duties. If, however, the definitive anti-dumping duties are higher than the provisional duties paid or payable or the amount estimated for the purpose of security, the difference shall not be collected. If the definitive duties are lower than the provisional duties payable, or the amount estimated for the purpose of security, the difference shall be reimbursed or the duties recalculated as the case may require.

(f) if however the investigations reveal that injury was not caused by dumped imports as alleged, but the provisional measures have materially retarded exports of the Member State complained against, the COTED shall, upon application by such State, assess the effects of the provisionally applied duties and determine the nature and extent of compensation which is warranted and require the Member State applying provisional measures to withdraw the measure and pay compensation in accordance with its assessment;

(g) a Member State may accept a voluntary price guarantee from an exporter who is believed to be exporting dumped products, to raise the price of the export sufficiently to forestall a serious threat of injury or to eliminate injury caused by dumped imports;

(h) if a Member State has initiated investigations based on evidence of dumped imports and the Member State had imposed provisional measures, the Member State may, upon the receipt of a voluntary guarantee from the exporter referred to in sub-paragraph (g), promptly suspend the investigation and withdraw any provisional measures it may have imposed as appropriate.

4. The COTED shall keep under review all anti-dumping measures imposed by Member States and shall ensure that Member States observe the conditions and the timetable for review and withdrawal of anti-dumping measures that it may have authorised.

5. Member States undertake to co-operate in the establishment of harmonised anti-dumping legislation and procedures in accordance with the provisions of this Protocol.

PART V
SUBSIDIES TO AGRICULTURE

Article 30(oo)
Definition

1. For the purposes of this Protocol an agricultural subsidy is defined as any form of domestic support, financial or otherwise, including revenue foregone, provided by government

or any public agency in favour of the producers of a specific agricultural product or to the agricultural sector as a whole. This includes:

(a)   assistance provided by government or any public agency to foster agricultural and rural development or to assist low income or resource poor producers;

(b)   financial concessions granted by government or a public agency to offset the cost of agricultural inputs or to encourage investments in agriculture;

(c)   any other financial concession which has the effect of providing price or income support to producers of agricultural products which is administered either through direct payments to the producers or processors of an agricultural product or indirectly through government or other publicly funded programmes;

(d)   payments in kind to agricultural producers.

2.   **"Agricultural products"** refers to the products listed in Chapters 1-24 of the Harmonised System (HS) of Product Classification, not including fish and fish products, forestry and forest products, and including the products listed in <u>Annex IV</u>.

Article 30(pp)
<u>Rights</u>

Having regard to the general use of subsidies in Member States to encourage agricultural and rural development, to promote investments in agriculture generally and to assist low-income or resource-poor producers, Member States may grant subsidies to meet those objectives, consistent with their obligations under international agreements and subject to the provisions of this Protocol.

Article 30(qq)
<u>Obligations</u>

1.   Notwithstanding the right to grant subsidies indicated in Article 30(pp), a Member State shall not use such subsidies in a manner to distort the production of and intraregional trade in the product or products benefiting from such subsidies.

2.   Accordingly, subsidies provided by a Member State to agriculture shall not involve transfers from consumers, or direct payments to producers or processors which would have the effect of providing price support to producers.

3.   Subsidies provided by a Member State to agriculture shall be made through publicly funded programmes which benefit the agricultural sector generally, in areas such as research, training, extension and advisory services, pest and disease control, inspection services, marketing and promotion services and infrastructural services.

4.   Where a Member State makes direct payments of a subsidy to agricultural producers or processors through such schemes as crop insurance, disaster relief, income safety-net programmes, regional assistance programmes and structural adjustment assistance programmes , that Member State shall ensure that these payments, whether financial or otherwise, have no or

minimal production and trade distortion effect and do not constitute price support to producers of the product or products benefiting from the use of such schemes.

Article 30(rr)
Regulation

1.   Any subsidy provided by a Member State in favour of the production of an agricultural product entering regional trade, except for the provision of general services programmes or direct payments satisfying the conditions stated in Article 30(qq), shall not exceed 10 per cent of the total value of that Member State's annual production of such tradeable agricultural product in any one year.

2.   Any subsidy provided by a Member State in favour of agricultural producers or processors in general, except for the provision of general services programmes or direct payments satisfying the conditions stated in Article 30(qq), shall not exceed 10 per cent of the total value of that Member State's annual total agricultural
output, in any one year.

3.   Where a Member State provides a subsidy, except for the provision of general services programmes or direct payments satisfying the conditions stated in Article 30(qq), in excess of the levels prescribed in paragraphs 1 and 2, such a subsidy shall be considered as a subsidy causing injury, nullification, impairment or
serious prejudice.

Article 30(ss)
Discipline

1.   Each Member State shall ensure that any subsidy in favour of agricultural producers conforms with the provisions of Article 30(qq) and Article 30(rr).

2.   Any subsidy in favour of agricultural producers that cannot be shown to satisfy the provisions in Article 30(qq) and Article 30(rr), shall be subject to the provisions of Article30(u) to Article 30(y) inclusive.

3.   A subsidies programme undertaken in conformity with the provisions of this Part shall be subject to action based on Article 30(u) to 30(y) inclusive where a determination of injury or threat thereof is made in accordance with the provisions of this Part.

4.   In the determination of a threat of injury, the investigating authorities shall consider, inter alia, such factors as:

(i)   nature of the subsidy or subsidies in question and the trade effects likely to arise therefrom;

(ii)   a significant rate of increase of subsidized imports into the domestic market indicating the likelihood of substantially increased importations;

(iii)   sufficient freely disposable or an imminent, substantial increase in capacity of the exporter indicating the likelihood of substantially increased subsidized exports to the importing country's market, taking into account the availability of other export markets to absorb any additional exports;

(iv)   whether imports are entering at prices that will have a significant depressing or suppressing effect on domestic prices, and would likely increase demand for further imports;

(v)   inventories of the product being investigated.

Article 30(tt)
Due Restraint

Where it has been determined that a subsidy causes injury or threatens to cause such injury, in accordance with the provisions of this Protocol, the aggrieved Member State shall exercise due restraint in initiating any action in retaliation.

Article 30(uu)
Notification

1.   Member States shall notify the COTED of any subsidy programme pursuant to Article 30(oo) prior to implementation.

2.   In addition to the notification to be submitted under this Article, any new subsidy or modification of an existing measure shall be notified promptly. This notification shall contain details of the new or modified subsidy and its conformity with the agreed criteria as set out in Article 30(qq) and Article 30(rr).

3.   Any Member State may bring to the attention of the COTED any measure which it considers ought to have been notified by another Member State.

Article 30(uu)(bis)
Review

1.   The COTED shall undertake a review of the implementation of the provisions on subsidies to agriculture on the basis of notifications of the subsidies programmes submitted by Member States, as well as on the basis of any other documentation which the COTED may request to be prepared to facilitate its review.

2.   Any Member State may bring to the attention of the COTED any measure which it considers ought to have been notified by another Member State.

PART VI
CONSUMER PROTECTION

Article 30(vv)
Promotion of Consumer Interests in the Community

1.   Member States shall promote the interests of consumers in the Community by appropriate measures that:

(a)   provide for the production and supply of goods and the provision of services to ensure the protection of life, health and safety of consumers;

(b)   ensure that goods supplied and services provided in the CARICOM Single Market and Economy (CSME) satisfy regulations, standards, codes and licensing requirements established or approved by competent bodies in the Community;

(c)   provide, where the regulations, standards, codes and licensing requirements referred to in paragraph (b) do not exist, for their establishment and implementation;

(d)   encourage high levels of ethical conduct for those engaged in the production and distribution of goods and services to consumers;

(e)   encourage fair and effective competition in order to provide consumers with greater choice among goods and services at lowest cost;

(f)   promote the provision of adequate information to consumers to enable the making of informed choices;

(g)   ensure the availability of adequate information and education programmes for consumers and suppliers;

(h)   protect consumers by prohibiting discrimination against producers and suppliers of goods produced in the Community and against service providers who are nationals of other Member States of the Community;

(i)   encourage the development of independent consumer organisations;

(j)   provide adequate and effective redress for consumers.

2.   For the purpose of this Part,

"consumer" means any person:

(a)   to whom goods are supplied or intended to be supplied in the course of business; or

(b)   for whom services are supplied or intended to be supplied in the course of business, carried on by a supplier or potential supplier and who does not receive the goods or services in the course of a business carried on by him.

Article 30(ww)
Protection of Consumer Interests in the Community

Member States shall enact harmonised legislation to provide, inter alia:

(a)   for the fundamental terms of a contract and the implied obligations of parties to a contract for the supply of goods or services;

(b)   for the prohibition of the inclusion of unconscionable terms in contracts for the sale and supply of goods or services to consumers;

(c)   for the prohibition of unfair trading practices particularly such practices relating to misleading or deceptive or fraudulent conduct;

(d)   for the prohibition of production and supply of harmful and defective goods and for the adoption of measures to prevent the supply or sale of such goods including measures requiring the removal of defective goods from the market;

(e)   that the provision of services is in compliance with the applicable regulations, standards, codes and licensing requirements;

(f)   that goods supplied to consumers are labeled in accordance with standards and specifications prescribed by the competent authorities;

(g)   that hazardous or other goods whose distribution and consumption are regulated by law are sold or supplied in accordance with applicable regulations;

(h)   that goods or materials the production or use of which is likely to result in potentially harmful environmental effects, are labeled and supplied in accordance with applicable standards and regulations;

(i)   that producers and suppliers are liable for defects in goods and for violation of product standards and consumer safety standards which occasion loss or damage to consumers;

(j)   that violations of consumer safety standards by producers / suppliers are appropriately sanctioned and relevant civil or criminal defences to such violations are available to defendants.

Article 30(xx)
Action by the Commission to Provide Support in the
Promotion and Protection of Consumer Welfare

1.   The Commission shall, for the purpose of providing support to Member States in the enhancement of consumer education and consumer welfare:

(a)   promote in the Community the elaboration, publication and adoption of fair contract terms between suppliers and consumers of goods and services produced or traded in the CARICOM Single Market and Economy;

(b)   take such measures as it considers necessary to ensure that Member States discourage and eliminate unfair trading practices, including misleading or deceptive conduct, false advertising, bait advertising, referral selling and pyramid selling;

(c)   promote in Member States product safety standards as part of a programme of consumer education in order to assist the consumer to make informed choices concerning the purchase of consumer goods;

(d) keep under review the carrying on of commercial activities in Member States which relate to goods supplied to consumers in such States or produced with a view to their being so supplied, or which relate to services supplied for consumers with a view to identifying practices which may adversely affect the interest of consumers;

(e) educate and guide consumers generally in the practical resolution of their problems and in the best use of their income and credit, using such techniques and means of communications as are available;

(f) confer, on request, with consumer organisations of Member States and offer such advice and information as may be appropriate for the resolution of their consumer problems;

(g) establish the necessary co-ordination with government agencies and departments for the effective education and guidance of consumers having regard to the programmes, activities and resources of each agency or department;

(h) conduct research and collect and collate information in respect of matters affecting the interests of consumers;

(i) compile, evaluate and publicise enactments for the protection of consumers in such States and recommend to the COTED the enactment of legislation considered necessary or desirable for the protection of consumers;

(j) promote, after consultation with the competent standardising agency and other public and private agencies or organisations, the establishment of quality standards for consumer products;

(k) promote and monitor, after consultation with relevant agencies and departments of Government, the enforcement of legislation affecting the interests of consumers, including, but not limited to, legislation relating to weights and measures, food and drugs adulteration, the control of standards and price controls;

(l) make recommendations to the COTED for the enactment of legislation by the Member States for the effective enforcement of the rights of consumers.

2. The Commission shall:

(a) draw to the attention of the COTED business conduct by enterprises which impact adversely on consumer welfare;

(b) collaborate with competent Organs of the Community to promote consumer education and consumer welfare.

ARTICLE III
Signature

This Protocol shall be open for signature by any Member State.

ARTICLE IV
Ratification

This Protocol shall be subject to ratification by signatory States in accordance with their respective constitutional procedures. Instruments of ratification shall be deposited with the Secretariat which shall transmit certified copies to the Government of each Member State.

ARTICLE V
Entry into Force

This Protocol shall enter into force one month after the date on which the last instrument of ratification is deposited with the Secretariat.

ARTICLE VI
Provisional Application

1.   A Member State may, upon the signing of this Protocol or at any later date before it enters into force, declare its intention to apply it provisionally.

2.   Upon such declaration, the provisions of this Protocol shall be applied provisionally pending its entry into force in accordance with Article V.

IN WITNESS WHEREOF the undersigned duly authorised in that behalf by their respective Governments have executed this Protocol

DONE at --on the --------------------------- day

of------------------------------2000.

ANNEX I

DEFINITION OF DOMESTIC INDUSTRY

1.   For the purposes of this Protocol, the term "domestic industry" shall, except as provided in paragraph 4, be interpreted as referring to the domestic producers as a whole of the like products or to those of them whose collective output of the products constitutes a major proportion of the total domestic production of those products, except that when producers are related to the exporters or importers or are themselves importers of the allegedly subsidised or dumped product or a like product from other countries, the term "domestic industry" may be interpreted as referring to the rest of the producers.

2.   In exceptional circumstances, the territory of a Member State may, for the production in question, be divided into two or more competitive markets and the producers within each market may be regarded as a separate industry if (a) the producers within such market sell all or almost all of their production of the product in question in that market, and (b) the demand in that market is not to any substantial degree supplied by producers of the product in question located elsewhere in the territory. In such circumstances, injury may be found to exist even where a major portion of the total domestic industry is not injured, provided there is a concentration of subsidised for dumped imports into such an isolated market and provided further that the

subsidised imports are causing injury to the producers of all or almost all of the production within such market.

3.   When the domestic industry has been interpreted as referring to the producers in a certain area, i.e., a market as defined in paragraph 2, countervailing duties shall be levied only on the products in question consigned for final consumption to that area. When the constitutional law of the importing Member State does not permit the levying of countervailing or anti-dumping on such a basis, the importing Member State may levy the relevant duties without limitation only of (a) the exporters shall have been given an opportunity to cease exporting at subsidised or dumped prices to the area concerned or otherwise give assurances pursuant to Article 30(cc) or 30(oo) and adequate assurances in this regard have not been promptly given, and (b) such duties cannot be levied only on products of specific producers which supply the area in question.

4.   Whenever an investigation is being undertaken by the Community on behalf of the domestic industry which has alleged injury from extra-regional imports, the domestic industry in the CSME shall be taken to be the industry referred to in paragraphs 1 and 2 consistent with the provisions of paragraph 8(a) of Article XXIV of GATT 1994.

ANNEX II

CONSULTATIONS

1.   As soon as possible after an application for an investigation is accepted and in any event before the initiation of any investigation, a Member State whose products may be subject to such investigation, shall be invited for consultations with the aim of clarifying the situation and arriving at a mutually agreed solution.

2.   Furthermore, throughout the period of investigation, a Member State whose products are the subject of the investigation shall be afforded a reasonable opportunity to continue consultations, with a view to clarifying the factual situation and to arriving at a mutually agreed solution.

3.   Without prejudice to the obligation to afford reasonable opportunity for consultations, these provisions regarding consultations are not intended to prevent the authorities of a Member State from proceeding expeditiously with regard to initiating the investigation, reaching preliminary or final determinations, whether affirmative or negative, or from applying provisional or final measures, in accordance with the provisions of this Agreement.

4.   The Member State which intends to initiate any investigation or is conducting such an investigation shall permit, upon request, the Member State whose products are subject to such investigation access to non-confidential evidence, including any non-confidential summary of confidential data being used for initiating or conducting the investigation.

ANNEX III(a)

ILLUSTRATIVE LIST OF INFORMATION
REQUIRED BY ARTICLE 30 (JJ)

(i)   The identity of the applicant and a description of the volume and value of the domestic production of the like product by the applicant. Where a written application is made on behalf of the domestic industry, the application shall identify the industry on behalf of which the application is made by a list of all known domestic producers of the like product (or associations of domestic producers of the like product) and, to the extent possible, a description of the volume and value of domestic production of the like product accounted for by such producers;

(ii)   a complete description of the <u>allegedly subsidised</u> product, the names of the country or countries of origin or export in question, the identity of each known exporter or foreign producer and a list of known persons importing the product in question;

(iii)   evidence with regard to the existence, amount and nature of the subsidy in question;

(iv)   evidence that alleged injury to a domestic industry is caused by subsidised imports through the effects of the subsidies; this evidence includes information on the evolution of the volume of the allegedly subsidised imports, the effect of these imports on prices of the like product in the domestic market and the consequent impact of the imports on domestic industry, as demonstrated by relevant factors and indices having a bearing on the state of the domestic industry.

ANNEX III (b)

ILLUSTRATIVE LIST OF INFORMATION
REQUIRED BY ARTICLE 30 (JJ)

(i)   The identity of the applicant and a description of the volume and value of the domestic production of the like product by the applicant. Where a written application is made on behalf of the domestic industry, the application shall identify the industry on behalf of which the application is made by a list of all known domestic producers of the like product (or associations of domestic producers of the like product) and, to the extent possible, a description of the volume and value of domestic production of the like product accounted for by such producers;

(ii)   A complete description of the allegedly dumped product, the names of the country or countries of origin or export in question, the identity of each known exporter or foreign producer and a list of known persons importing the product in question;

(iii)   Information on prices at which the product in question is sold when destined for consumption in the domestic markets of the country or countries of origin or export (or, where appropriate, information on the prices at which the product is sold from the country or countries of origin or export to a third country or countries, or on the constructed value of the product) and information on export prices or, where appropriate, on the prices at which the product is first resold to an independent buyer in the territory of the importing Member State;

(iv)   Information on the evolution of the volume of the allegedly dumped imports, the effect of these imports on prices of the like product in the domestic market and the consequent impact of the imports on the domestic industry, as demonstrated by relevant factors and indices having a bearing on the state of the domestic industry, such as those referred to in Article 30(ii).

ANNEX IV

PRODUCT COVERAGE[1]

2.   This Protocol shall cover the following products:

(i)   HS Chapters 1-24 less fish and fish products, forestry and forest products plus*;

ii)	HS Code 2905.43	(mannitol)
	HS Code 2905.44	(sorbitol)
	HS Heading 3301	(essential oils)
	HS Heading 35.01 to 35.05	(albuminoidal substances, modified starches, glues)
	HS Code 3809.10	(Fishing agents)
	HS Code 3823.60	(Sorbitol n.e.p)
	HS Headings 41.01 to 41.03	(Hides and skins)
	HS Headings 43.01	(raw furskins)
	HS Headings 50.01 to 50.03	(Raw silk and silk waste)
	HS Headings 52.01 to 52.03	(Wool and animal hair)
	HS Headings 52.01 to 52.03	(Raw cotton, waste and cotton carded or combed)
	HS Heading 53.01	(Raw flax)
	HS Heading 53.02	(Raw hemp)

* The product descriptions in round brackets are not necessarily exhaustive.

ANNEX V

OATH OF OFFICE

I ....do hereby swear (or solemnly affirm) that I will faithfully exercise the office of Commissioner of the Competition Commission without fear or favour, affection or ill-will.

(so help me God (to be omitted in affirmation)).

*   *   *

---

[1]   The product coverage is the same as that of the WTO Agreement on Agriculture.

CIVIL LAW CONVENTION ON CORRUPTION[*]

(COUNCIL OF EUROPE)

The Civil Law Convention on Corruption was adopted by the Committee of Ministers on 9 September 1999, at its 678th meeting, and opened for signature by the member States, the non-member States that participated in its elaboration and the European Community, on 4 November 1999.

Preamble

The member States of the Council of Europe, the other States and the European Community, signatories hereto,

Considering that the aim of the Council of Europe is to achieve a greater unity between its members;

Conscious of the importance of strengthening international co-operation in the fight against corruption;

Emphasising that corruption represents a major threat to the rule of law, democracy and human rights, fairness and social justice, hinders economic development and endangers the proper and fair functioning of market economies;

Recognising the adverse financial consequences of corruption to individuals, companies and States, as well as international institutions;

Convinced of the importance for civil law to contribute to the fight against corruption, in particular by enabling persons who have suffered damage to receive fair compensation;

Recalling the conclusions and resolutions of the 19th (Malta, 1994), 21st (Czech Republic, 1997) and 22nd (Moldova, 1999) Conferences of the European Ministers of Justice;

Taking into account the Programme of Action against Corruption adopted by the Committee of Ministers in November 1996;

Taking also into account the feasibility study on the drawing up of a convention on civil remedies for compensation for damage resulting from acts of corruption, approved by the Committee of Ministers in February 1997;

Having regard to Resolution (97) 24 on the 20 Guiding Principles for the Fight against Corruption, adopted by the Committee of Ministers in November 1997, at its 101st Session, to Resolution (98) 7 authorising the adoption of the Partial and Enlarged Agreement establishing

---

[*] *Source*: Council of Europe (1999). "Civil Law Convention on Corruption (ETS No. 174)"; available on the Internet: (http://conventions.coe.int/treaty/en/Treaties/Html/174.htm). [Note added by the editor.]

the "Group of States against Corruption (GRECO)", adopted by the Committee of Ministers in May 1998, at its 102nd Session, and to Resolution (99) 5 establishing the GRECO, adopted on 1st May 1999;

Recalling the Final Declaration and the Action Plan adopted by the Heads of State and Government of the member States of the Council of Europe at their 2nd summit in Strasbourg, in October 1997,

Have agreed as follows:

CHAPTER I – MEASURES TO BE TAKEN AT NATIONAL LEVEL

Article 1 – Purpose

Each Party shall provide in its internal law for effective remedies for persons who have suffered damage as a result of acts of corruption, to enable them to defend their rights and interests, including the possibility of obtaining compensation for damage.

Article 2 – Definition of corruption

For the purpose of this Convention, "corruption" means requesting, offering, giving or accepting, directly or indirectly, a bribe or any other undue advantage or prospect thereof, which distorts the proper performance of any duty or behaviour required of the recipient of the bribe, the undue advantage or the prospect thereof.

Article 3 – Compensation for damage

1.   Each Party shall provide in its internal law for persons who have suffered damage as a result of corruption to have the right to initiate an action in order to obtain full compensation for such damage.

2.   Such compensation may cover material damage, loss of profits and non-pecuniary loss.

Article 4 – Liability

1.   Each Party shall provide in its internal law for the following conditions to be fulfilled in order for the damage to be compensated:

    i   the defendant has committed or authorised the act of corruption, or failed to take reasonable steps to prevent the act of corruption;

    ii   the plaintiff has suffered damage; and

    iii   there is a causal link between the act of corruption and the damage.

2.   Each Party shall provide in its internal law that, if several defendants are liable for damage for the same corrupt activity, they shall be jointly and severally liable.

Article 5 – State responsibility

Each Party shall provide in its internal law for appropriate procedures for persons who have suffered damage as a result of an act of corruption by its public officials in the exercise of their functions to claim for compensation from the State or, in the case of a non-state Party, from that Party's appropriate authorities.

Article 6 – Contributory negligence

Each Party shall provide in its internal law for the compensation to be reduced or disallowed having regard to all the circumstances, if the plaintiff has by his or her own fault contributed to the damage or to its aggravation.

Article 7 – Limitation periods

1.   Each Party shall provide in its internal law for proceedings for the recovery of damages to be subject to a limitation period of not less than three years from the day the person who has suffered damage became aware or should reasonably have been aware, that damage has occurred or that an act of corruption has taken place, and of the identity of the responsible person. However, such proceedings shall not be commenced after the end of a limitation period of not less than ten years from the date of the act of corruption.

2.   The laws of the Parties regulating suspension or interruption of limitation periods shall, if appropriate, apply to the periods prescribed in paragraph 1.

Article 8 – Validity of contracts

1   Each Party shall provide in its internal law for any contract or clause of a contract providing for corruption to be null and void.

2   Each Party shall provide in its internal law for the possibility for all parties to a contract whose consent has been undermined by an act of corruption to be able to apply to the court for the contract to be declared void, notwithstanding their right to claim for damages.

Article 9 – Protection of employees

Each Party shall provide in its internal law for appropriate protection against any unjustified sanction for employees who have reasonable grounds to suspect corruption and who report in good faith their suspicion to responsible persons or authorities.

Article 10 – Accounts and audits

1   Each Party shall, in its internal law, take any necessary measures for the annual accounts of companies to be drawn up clearly and give a true and fair view of the company's financial position.

2   With a view to preventing acts of corruption, each Party shall provide in its internal law for auditors to confirm that the annual accounts present a true and fair view of the company's financial position.

Article 11 – Acquisition of evidence

Each Party shall provide in its internal law for effective procedures for the acquisition of evidence in civil proceedings arising from an act of corruption.

Article 12 – Interim measures

Each Party shall provide in its internal law for such court orders as are necessary to preserve the rights and interests of the parties during civil proceedings arising from an act of corruption.

CHAPTER II – INTERNATIONAL CO-OPERATION AND MONITORING OF IMPLEMENTATION

Article 13 – International co-operation

The Parties shall co-operate effectively in matters relating to civil proceedings in cases of corruption, especially concerning the service of documents, obtaining evidence abroad, jurisdiction, recognition and enforcement of foreign judgements and litigation costs, in accordance with the provisions of relevant international instruments on international co-operation in civil and commercial matters to which they are Party, as well as with their internal law.

Article 14 – Monitoring

The Group of States against Corruption (GRECO) shall monitor the implementation of this Convention by the Parties.

CHAPTER III – FINAL CLAUSES

Article 15 – Signature and entry into force

1   This Convention shall be open for signature by the member States of the Council of Europe, by non-member States that have participated in its elaboration and by the European Community.

2   This Convention is subject to ratification, acceptance or approval. Instruments of ratification, acceptance or approval shall be deposited with the Secretary General of the Council of Europe.

3   This Convention shall enter into force on the first day of the month following the expiration of a period of three months after the date on which fourteen signatories have expressed their consent to be bound by the Convention in accordance with the provisions of paragraph 1. Any such signatory, which is not a member of the Group of States against Corruption (GRECO) at the time of ratification, acceptance or approval, shall automatically become a member on the date the Convention enters into force.

4   In respect of any signatory which subsequently expresses its consent to be bound by it, the Convention shall enter into force on the first day of the month following the expiration of a period of three months after the date of the expression of their consent to be bound by the Convention in accordance with the provisions of paragraph 1. Any signatory, which is not a member of the Group of States against Corruption (GRECO) at the time of ratification, acceptance or approval, shall automatically become a member on the date the Convention enters into force in its respect.

5   Any particular modalities for the participation of the European Community in the Group of States against Corruption (GRECO) shall be determined as far as necessary by a common agreement with the European Community.

Article 16 – Accession to the Convention

1   After the entry into force of this Convention, the Committee of Ministers of the Council of Europe, after consulting the Parties to the Convention, may invite any State not a member of the Council and not having participated in its elaboration to accede to this Convention, by a decision taken by the majority provided for in Article 20.d. of the Statute of the Council of Europe and by the unanimous vote of the representatives of the Parties entitled to sit on the Committee.

2   In respect of any State acceding to it, the Convention shall enter into force on the first day of the month following the expiration of a period of three months after the date of deposit of the instrument of accession with the Secretary General of the Council of Europe. Any State acceding to this Convention shall automatically become a member of the GRECO, if it is not already a member at the time of accession, on the date the Convention enters into force in its respect.

Article 17 – Reservations

No reservation may be made in respect of any provision of this Convention.

Article 18 – Territorial application

1   Any State or the European Community may, at the time of signature or when depositing its instrument of ratification, acceptance, approval or accession, specify the territory or territories to which this Convention shall apply.

2   Any Party may, at any later date, by a declaration addressed to the Secretary General of the Council of Europe, extend the application of this Convention to any other territory specified in the declaration. In respect of such territory the Convention shall enter into force on the first day of the month following the expiration of a period of three months after the date of receipt of such declaration by the Secretary General.

3   Any declaration made under the two preceding paragraphs may, in respect of any territory specified in such declaration, be withdrawn by a notification addressed to the Secretary General. The withdrawal shall become effective on the first day of the month following the expiration of a period of three months after the date of receipt of such notification by the Secretary General.

Article 19 – Relationship to other instruments and agreements

1   This Convention does not affect the rights and undertakings derived from international multilateral instruments concerning special matters.

2   The Parties to the Convention may conclude bilateral or multilateral agreements with one another on the matters dealt with in this Convention, for purposes of supplementing or strengthening its provisions or facilitating the application of the principles embodied in it or, without prejudice to the objectives and principles of this Convention, submit themselves to rules on this matter within the framework of a special system which is binding at the moment of the opening for signature of this Convention.

3   If two or more Parties have already concluded an agreement or treaty in respect of a subject which is dealt with in this Convention or otherwise have established their relations in respect of that subject, they shall be entitled to apply that agreement or treaty or to regulate these relations accordingly, in lieu of the present Convention.

Article 20 – Amendments

1   Amendments to this Convention may be proposed by any Party, and shall be communicated by the Secretary General of the Council of Europe to the member States of the Council of Europe, to the non member States which have participated in the elaboration of this Convention, to the European Community, as well as to any State which has acceded to or has been invited to accede to this Convention in accordance with the provisions of Article16.

2   Any amendment proposed by a Party shall be communicated to the European Committee on Legal Co-operation (CDCJ) which shall submit to the Committee of Ministers its opinion on that proposed amendment.

3   The Committee of Ministers shall consider the proposed amendment and the opinion submitted by the European Committee on Legal Co-operation (CDCJ) and, following consultation of the Parties to the Convention which are not members of the Council of Europe, may adopt the amendment.

4   The text of any amendment adopted by the Committee of Ministers in accordance with paragraph 3 of this article shall be forwarded to the Parties for acceptance.

5   Any amendment adopted in accordance with paragraph 3 of this article shall come into force on the thirtieth day after all Parties have informed the Secretary General of their acceptance thereof.

Article 21 – Settlement of disputes

1   The European Committee on Legal Co-operation (CDCJ) of the Council of Europe shall be kept informed regarding the interpretation and application of this Convention.

2   In case of a dispute between Parties as to the interpretation or application of this Convention, they shall seek a settlement of the dispute through negotiation or any other peaceful means of their choice, including submission of the dispute to the European Committee on Legal

Co-operation (CDCJ), to an arbitral tribunal whose decisions shall be binding upon the Parties, or to the International Court of Justice, as agreed upon by the Parties concerned.

Article 22 – Denunciation

1   Any Party may, at any time, denounce this Convention by means of a notification addressed to the Secretary General of the Council of Europe.

2   Such denunciation shall become effective on the first day of the month following the expiration of a period of three months after the date of receipt of the notification by the Secretary General.

Article 23 – Notification

The Secretary General of the Council of Europe shall notify the member States of the Council and any other signatories and Parties to this Convention of:

    a   any signature;

    b   the deposit of any instrument of ratification, acceptance, approval or accession;

    c   any date of entry into force of this Convention, in accordance with Articles 15 and 16;

    d   any other act, notification or communication relating to this Convention.

In witness whereof the undersigned, being duly authorised thereto, have signed this Convention.

Done at Strasbourg, the 4th day of November 1999, in English and in French, both texts being equally authentic, in a single copy which shall be deposited in the archives of the Council of Europe. The Secretary General of the Council of Europe shall transmit certified copies to each member State of the Council of Europe, to the non-member States which have participated in the elaboration of this Convention, to the European Community, as well as to any State invited to accede to it.

*   *   *

RESOLUTION (97) 24 ON THE TWENTY GUIDING PRINCIPLES FOR THE FIGHT AGAINST CORRUPTION[*]
(COUNCIL OF EUROPE)

Resolution (97) 24 on the Twenty Guiding Principles for the Fight Against Corruption was adopted by the Committee of Ministers of the Council of Europe on 6 November 1997 at its 101st Session.

The Committee of Ministers,

Considering the Declaration adopted at the Second Summit of Heads of State and Government, which took place in Strasbourg on 10 and 11 October 1997 and in pursuance of the Action Plan, in particular section III, paragraph 2 "Fighting corruption and organised crime";

Aware that corruption represents a serious threat to the basic principles and values of the Council of Europe, undermines the confidence of citizens in democracy, erodes the rule of law, constitutes a denial of human rights and hinders social and economic development;

Convinced that the fight against corruption needs to be multi-disciplinary and, in this respect having regard to Programme of Action against Corruption as well as to the resolutions adopted by the European Ministers of Justice at their 19th and 21st Conferences held in Valletta and Prague respectively;

Having received the draft 20 guiding principles for the fight against corruption, elaborated by the Multidisciplinary Group on Corruption (GMC);

Firmly resolved to fight corruption by joining the efforts of our countries,

AGREES TO ADOPT **THE 20 GUIDING PRINCIPLES** FOR THE FIGHT AGAINST CORRUPTION, SET OUT BELOW:

1. to take effective measures for the prevention of corruption and, in this connection, to raise public awareness and promoting ethical behaviour;

2. to ensure co-ordinated criminalisation of national and international corruption;

3. to ensure that those in charge of the prevention, investigation, prosecution and adjudication of corruption offences enjoy the independence and autonomy appropriate to their functions, are free from improper influence and have effective means for gathering evidence, protecting the persons who help the authorities in combating corruption and preserving the confidentiality of investigations;

---

[*] *Source*: Council of Europe (1997). "Resolution (97) 24 on the twenty guiding principles for the fight against corruption"; adopted by the Committee of Ministers on 6 November 1997 at its 101st session; available on the Internet (http://www.greco.coe.int/docs/ResCM(1997)24E.htm). [Note added by the editor.]

4. to provide appropriate measures for the seizure and deprivation of the proceeds of corruption offences;

5. to provide appropriate measures to prevent legal persons being used to shield corruption offences;

6. to limit immunity from investigation, prosecution or adjudication of corruption offences to the degree necessary in a democratic society;

7. to promote the specialisation of persons or bodies in charge of fighting corruption and to provide them with appropriate means and training to perform their tasks;

8. to ensure that the fiscal legislation and the authorities in charge of implementing it contribute to combating corruption in an effective and co-ordinated manner, in particular by denying tax deductibility, under the law or in practice, for bribes or other expenses linked to corruption offences;

9. to ensure that the organisation, functioning and decision-making processes of public administrations take into account the need to combat corruption, in particular by ensuring as much transparency as is consistent with the need to achieve effectiveness;

10. to ensure that the rules relating to the rights and duties of public officials take into account the requirements of the fight against corruption and provide for appropriate and effective disciplinary measures; promote further specification of the behaviour expected from public officials by appropriate means, such as codes of conduct;

11. to ensure that appropriate auditing procedures apply to the activities of public administration and the public sector;

12. to endorse the role that audit procedures can play in preventing and detecting corruption outside public administrations;

13. to ensure that the system of public liability or accountability takes account of the consequences of corrupt behaviour of public officials;

14. to adopt appropriately transparent procedures for public procurement that promote fair competition and deter corruptors;

15. to encourage the adoption, by elected representatives, of codes of conduct and promote rules for the financing of political parties and election campaigns which deter corruption;

16. to ensure that the media have freedom to receive and impart information on corruption matters, subject only to limitations or restrictions which are necessary in a democratic society;

17. to ensure that civil law takes into account the need to fight corruption and in particular provides for effective remedies for those whose rights and interests are affected by corruption;

18. to encourage research on corruption;

19. to ensure that in every aspect of the fight against corruption, the possible connections with organised crime and money laundering are taken into account;

20. to develop to the widest extent possible international co-operation in all areas of the fight against corruption.

AND, IN ORDER TO PROMOTE A DYNAMIC PROCESS FOR EFFECTIVELY PREVENTING AND COMBATING CORRUPTION, THE COMMITTEE OF MINISTERS

1. invites national authorities to apply these Principles in their domestic legislation and practice;

2. instructs the Multidisciplinary Group on Corruption (GMC) rapidly to complete the elaboration of international legal instruments pursuant to the Programme of Action against Corruption;

3. instructs the Multidisciplinary Group on Corruption (GMC) to submit without delay a draft text proposing the establishment of an appropriate and efficient mechanism, under the auspices of the Council of Europe, for monitoring observance of these Principles and the implementation of the international legal instruments to be adopted.

*   *   *

PART THREE

INVESTMENT-RELATED PROVISIONS IN FREE TRADE AND ECONOMIC INTEGRATION AGREEMENTS

AGREEMENT ON THE ESTABLISHMENT OF A FREE TRADE AREA BETWEEN THE GOVERNMENT OF ISRAEL AND THE GOVERNMENT OF THE UNITED STATES OF AMERICA*
[excerpts]

The Agreement on the Establishment of a Free Trade Area between the Government of Israel and the Government of the United States of America was signed on 22 April 1985. It entered into force on 1 September 1985.

ARTICLE 13
TRADE-RELATED PERFORMANCE REQUIREMENTS

Neither Party shall impose, as a condition of establishment, expansion or maintenance of investments by nationals or companies of the other Party, requirements to export any amount of production resulting from such investments or to purchase locally-produced goods and services. Moreover, neither Party shall impose requirements on investors to purchase locally-produced goods and services as a condition for receiving any type of governmental incentives.

ARTICLE 14
INTELLECTUAL PROPERTY

The Parties reaffirm their obligations under bilateral and multilateral agreements relating to intellectual property rights, including industrial property rights, in effect between the Parties. Accordingly, nationals and companies of each Party shall continue to be accorded national and most favored nation treatment with respect to obtaining, maintaining and enforcing patents of invention, with respect to obtaining and enforcing copyrights, and with respect to rights in trademarks, service marks, tradenames, trade labels, and industrial property of all kinds.

ARTICLE 16
TRADE IN SERVICES

The Parties recognize the importance of trade in services and the need to maintain an open system of services exports which would minimize restrictions on the flow of services between the two nations. To this end, the Parties agree to develop means for cooperation on trade in services pursuant to the provisions of a Declaration to be made by the Parties.

---

* *Source*: The Government of the United States and the Government of Israel (1985). "Agreement on the Establishment of a Free Trade Area between the Government of Israel and the Government of the United States of America", *KITVEI-AMANA Treaty Series 972, vol. 28*; available also on the Internet (http://www. amcham. co.il/ agree. html). [Note added by the editor.]

In Witness Whereof, the respective representatives, having been duly authorized, have signed this Agreement.

Done in duplicate, in the Hebrew and English languages, both equally authentic, at Washington, D.C., this twenty second day of April 1985, which corresponds to this first day of Iyar, 5745.

*   *   *

ACUERDO DE COMPLEMENTACIÓN ECONÓMICA MERCOSUR-CHILE [*]
[excerpts]

> The Economic Complementation Agreement between MERCOSUR member States, namely Argentina, Brazil, Paraguay and Uruguay, and Chile, was signed at Potrero de los Funes on 25 June 1996. It entered into force on 1 October 1996.

Los Gobiernos de la República Argentina, de la República Federativa del Brasil, de la República del Paraguay y de la República Oriental del Uruguay, Estados Partes del Mercado Común del Sur (MERCOSUR), y el Gobierno de la República de Chile serán denominados Partes Signatarias. Las Partes Contratantes del presente Acuerdo son el MERCOSUR y la República de Chile.

CONSIDERANDO:

La necesidad de fortalecer el proceso de integración de América Latina, a fin de alcanzar los objetivos previstos en el Tratado de Montevideo 1980, mediante la concertación de acuerdos abiertos a la participación de los demás países miembros de la Asociación Latinoamericana de Integración (ALADI), que permitan la conformación de un espacio económico ampliado;

Que la conformación de áreas de libre comercio en América Latina constituye un elemento relevante para aproximar los esquemas de integración existentes, además de ser una etapa fundamental para el proceso de integración y el establecimiento de un área de libre comercio hemisférica;

Que la integración económica regional constituye uno de los instrumentos esenciales para que los países de América Latina avancen en su desarrollo económico y social, asegurando una mejor calidad de vida para sus pueblos;

Que la vigencia de las instituciones democráticas constituye un elemento esencial para el desarrollo del proceso de integración regional;

Que los Estados Partes del MERCOSUR, a través de la suscripción del Tratado de Asunción de 1991, han dado un paso significativo hacia la consecución de los objetivos de integración latinoamericana;

Que el Acuerdo de Marrakesh, por el que se crea la Organización Mundial del Comercio (OMC), constituye un marco de derechos y obligaciones al que se ajustarán las políticas comerciales y los compromisos del presente Acuerdo;

Que el proceso de integración entre MERCOSUR y Chile tiene como objetivo la libre circulación de bienes y servicios, facilitar la plena utilización de los factores productivos en el espacio económico ampliado, impulsar las inversiones recíprocas y promover el desarrollo y la utilización de la infraestructura física;

---

[*] *Source*: MERCOSUR and the Government of Chile (1996). "Acuerdo De Complementación Económica Mercosur-Chile"; available on the Internet (http://www.sice.OAS.org/trade/msch/ACUERDO.asp). [Note added by the editor.]

El interés compartido de las Partes Contratantes en el desarrollo de relaciones comerciales y de cooperación económica con los países del área del Pacífico y la conveniencia de aunar esfuerzos y acciones en los foros de cooperación existentes en dichas áreas;

Que el establecimiento de reglas claras, previsibles y durables es fundamental para que los operadores económicos puedan utilizar plenamente los mecanismos de integración regional;

Que el presente Acuerdo constituye un importante factor para la expansión del intercambio comercial entre el MERCOSUR y Chile, y establece las bases para una amplia complementación e integración económica recíproca;

CONVIENEN:

En celebrar el presente Acuerdo de Complementación Económica, al amparo del Tratado de Montevideo 1980, de la Resolución N° 2 del Consejo de Ministros de la ALADI y de las normas que se establecen a continuación.

TÍTULO I: OBJETIVOS

Artículo 1: El presente Acuerdo tiene por objetivos:

Establecer el marco jurídico e institucional de cooperación e integración económica y física que contribuya a la creación de un espacio económico ampliado que tienda a facilitar la libre circulación de bienes y servicios y la plena utilización de los factores productivos;

Formar un área de libre comercio entre las Partes Contratantes en un plazo máximo de 10 años, mediante la expansión y diversificación del intercambio comercial y la eliminación de las restricciones arancelarias y no arancelarias que afectan el comercio recíproco;

Promover el desarrollo y la utilización de la infraestructura física, con especial énfasis en el establecimiento de interconexiones bioceánicas;

Promover e impulsar las inversiones recíprocas entre los agentes económicos de las Partes Signatarias;

Promover la complementación y cooperación económica, energética, científica y tecnológica.

TÍTULO VI: DEFENSA DE LA COMPETENCIA Y DEL CONSUMIDOR

Artículo 18: Las Partes Contratantes promoverán acciones para acordar, a la brevedad, un esquema normativo basado en disposiciones y prácticas internacionalmente aceptadas, que constituya el marco adecuado para disciplinar eventuales prácticas anti competitivas.

Artículo 19: Las Partes Contratantes desarrollarán acciones conjuntas tendientes al establecimiento de normas y compromisos específicos, para que los productos provenientes de ellas gocen de un tratamiento no menos favorable que el que se concede a los productos nacionales similares, en aspectos relacionados con la defensa de los consumidores.

Artículo 20: Los organismos competentes en estas materias en las Partes Signatarias implementarán un esquema de cooperación que permita alcanzar a corto plazo un primer nivel de entendimiento sobre estas cuestiones y un esquema metodológico para la consideración de situaciones concretas que pudieran presentarse.

TÍTULO VIII: SOLUCIÓN DE CONTROVERSIAS

Artículo 22: Las controversias que surjan sobre la interpretación, la aplicación o el incumplimiento del presente Acuerdo y de los Protocolos celebrados en el marco del mismo, serán dirimidas de conformidad con el Régimen de Solución de Controversias contenido en el Anexo 14.

La Comisión Administradora deberá iniciar, a partir de la fecha de su constitución, las negociaciones necesarias para definir y acordar un procedimiento arbitral, que entrará en vigor al iniciarse el cuarto año de vigencia del Acuerdo.

Si vencido el plazo señalado en el párrafo anterior no hubieran concluido las negociaciones pertinentes o no hubiese acuerdo sobre dicho procedimiento, las Partes adoptarán el procedimiento arbitral previsto en el Capítulo IV del Protocolo de Brasilia.

TÍTULO XI: APLICACIÓN Y UTILIZACIÓN DE INCENTIVOS A LAS EXPORTACIONES

Artículo 30: Las Partes Signatarias se atendrán, en la aplicación y utilización de los incentivos a las exportaciones, a los compromisos asumidos en el ámbito de la OMC.

La Comisión Administradora efectuará, transcurridos no más de 12 meses de vigencia del Acuerdo, un relevamiento y examen de los incentivos a las exportaciones vigentes en cada una de las Partes Signatarias.

Artículo 31: Los productos que incorporen en su fabricación insumos importados temporariamente, o bajo régimen de draw-back, no se beneficiarán del Programa de Liberación establecido en el presente Acuerdo, una vez cumplimentado el quinto año de su entrada en vigencia.

TÍTULO XIII: SERVICIOS

Artículo 34: Las Partes Signatarias promoverán la liberación, expansión y diversificación progresiva del comercio de servicios en sus territorios, en un plazo a ser definido, y de acuerdo con los compromisos asumidos en el Acuerdo General sobre Comercio de Servicios (GATS).

Artículo 35: A los fines del presente Título, se define el "comercio de servicios" como la prestación de un servicio:

a)   Del territorio de una de las Partes Signatarias al territorio de la otra Parte;

b)   En el territorio de una Parte Signataria a un consumidor de servicios de la otra Parte Signataria;

c)   Por un proveedor de servicios de una Parte Signataria mediante presencia comercial en el territorio de la otra Parte Signataria;

d)   Por un proveedor de servicios de una Parte Signataria mediante la presencia de personas físicas de una Parte Signataria en el territorio de la otra Parte Signataria.

Artículo 36:   Para la consecución de los objetivos enunciados en el Artículo 34 precedente, las Partes Contratantes acuerdan iniciar los trabajos tendientes a avanzar en la definición de los aspectos del Programa de Liberación para los sectores de servicios objeto de comercio.

TÍTULO XV: INVERSIONES

Artículo 41:   Los acuerdos bilaterales sobre promoción y protección recíproca de las inversiones, suscritos entre Chile y los Estados Partes del MERCOSUR, mantendrán su plena vigencia.

TÍTULO XVI: DOBLE TRIBUTACIÓN

Artículo 42:   A fin de estimular las inversiones recíprocas, las Partes Signatarias procurarán celebrar acuerdos para evitar la doble tributación. Nada de lo dispuesto en el presente Acuerdo afectará los derechos y obligaciones de cualquiera de las Partes que se deriven de cualquier convenio tributario suscrito o que se suscriba a futuro.

TÍTULO XVII: PROPIEDAD INTELECTUAL

Artículo 43:   Las Partes Signatarias se regirán por el Acuerdo sobre los Aspectos de los Derechos de Propiedad Intelectual Relacionados con el Comercio, incluido en el Anexo 1 C) del Acuerdo por el que se establece la OMC.

TÍTULO XXII: ADHESIÓN

Artículo 54:   En cumplimiento de lo establecido en el Tratado de Montevideo 1980, el presente Acuerdo está abierto a la adhesión, mediante negociación previa, de los demás países miembros de ALADI.

La adhesión será formalizada una vez negociados sus términos entre las Partes Contratantes y el país adherente, mediante la celebración de un Protocolo Adicional al presente Acuerdo que entrará en vigor 30 días después de ser depositado en la Secretaría General de la ALADI.

TÍTULO XXIII: VIGENCIA

Artículo 55: El presente Acuerdo entrará en vigencia el 1º de octubre de 1996 y tendrá duración indefinida.

*   *   *

AGREEMENT ESTABLISHING THE FREE TRADE AREA BETWEEN THE CARIBBEAN COMMUNITY AND THE DOMINICAN REPUBLIC*
[excerpts]

The Agreement Establishing the Free Trade Area between the Caribbean Community and the Dominican Republic was signed at Santo Domingo in the Dominican Republic on 22 August 1998. It entered into force on 1 January 1999.

ANNEX III: AGREEMENT ON RECIPROCAL PROMOTION AND PROTECTION OF INVESTMENTS

The Caribbean Community (CARICOM) and the Dominican Republic, "the Parties":

Interested in promoting greater economic cooperation amongst themselves, above all in the field of investments made by natural and juridical persons of one Party in the territory of the other Party;

Recognising the need to stimulate and protect investments in a manner that will promote economic growth and development of both Parties;

Recognising that the strengthening of economic ties can contribute to the well-being of workers in both Parties and promote respect for workers' rights;

Agreeing that these objectives can be achieved without relaxing health, safety and environmental measures of general application;

Acknowledging the importance of respect for the sovereignty and laws of the Party within whose territory the investment takes place.

Resolved to conclude this Agreement on Reciprocal Promotion and Protection of Investments.

Have decided the following:

ARTICLE I - DEFINITIONS

For the purposes of this Agreement:

(i)   Investments: means every kind of asset and in particular, though not exclusively, includes:

---

* *Source*: The Caribbean Community and the Government of the Dominican Republic (1998). "Agreement Establishing the Free Trade Area between the Caribbean Community and the Dominican Republic"; available on the Internet (http://www.sice.oas.org/Trade/Ccdr/Ccdr_an3.asp#annexiii) [Note added by the editor.]

(a)   movable and immovable property and any other property rights such as mortgages, liens or pledges;

(b)   shares, stocks and debentures of companies or int-erests in the property of such companies;

(c)   a claim to money or a claim to any performance having financial value;

(d)   intellectual and industrial property rights, including rights with respect to copyrights, patents, trademarks, trade names, industrial designs, trade secrets, technical processes and know-how and goodwill;

(e)   business concessions conferred by law or under contract, including concessions to search for, cultivate, extract, or exploit natural resources.

(ii)

(a)   An investor: means -

(i)   any natural person possessing the citizenship of a Party in accordance with its laws: and

(ii)   any corporation, company, association, partnership, or other organization, legally constituted under the laws of a Party, whether or not organized for pecuniary gain, or privately, or governmentally owned or controlled.

(b)   Returns: means the amount yielded by an investment and, in particular, though not exclusively, includes profits, interests, capital gains, dividends, royalties or fees.

ARTICLE II - ADMISSION AND PROMOTION

1.   Each Party shall in its territory promote, as far as possible, the investment made in its territory by investors of the other Party, and shall admit these investments in accordance with its laws. To that end, they shall, within six months of the entry into force of the Agreement, consult with each other through their designated agencies, with a view to identifying the most effective ways of achieving that purpose.

2.   Each Party, shall, subject to its laws, grant the necessary authorisations for these investments, allow licensing agreements for manufacturing and for technical, commercial, financial and administrative assistance, and grant the necessary permits for the activities of the professional staff and consultants hired by the investors of the other Party.

ARTICLE III - GENERAL PRINCIPLES GOVERNING TREATMENT

1.   Each Party shall admit and treat investments in a manner not less favourable than the treatment granted in similar situations to investments of its investors except for investments in areas to be identified in the Appendix to this Annex.

2.   Each Party shall admit and treat investments in a manner not less favourable than the treatment granted in similar situations to areas related to Most-Favoured-Nation treatment except for investments in the areas identified in the Appendix to this Annex.

3.   The obligation to grant treatment no less favourable than is granted to third States does not apply to:

(i)   any treatment or advantage resulting from any existing or future customs union or free trade area or common market or monetary union or similar agreement to which a Party is a party: or

(ii)   any international agreement or arrangement relating wholly or mainly to taxation.

ARTICLE IV - FAIR AND EQUITABLE TREATMENT

Each Party shall ensure, at all times, fair and equitable treatment for investments and returns, which shall thus enjoy full protection and security, and shall not receive a treatment less favourable than established under international law.

ARTICLE V - COMPLIANCE WITH OBLIGATIONS

Each Party shall comply with its commitments regarding investment and shall, in no way, impair, through the adoption of arbitrary and discriminatory measures, the management, development, maintenance, utilisation, usufruct, acquisition, expansion or transfer of said investments.

ARTICLE VI - ENTRY AND STAY OF FOREIGNERS

Subject to the laws governing the entry and stay of foreigners and any arrangements which the Parties may negotiate, investors of each Party shall be allowed to enter and remain in the territory of the other Party for the purposes of establishing, developing or administering investments, or to advise on the establishment, development and administration of investments in which they have committed or are about to commit a substantial amount of capital or resources.

ARTICLE VII - PERFORMANCE REQUIREMENTS

No Party shall impose any performance requirements which are contrary to the World Trade Organisation Agreement on Trade Related Investment Measures as a condition for establishing, expanding or maintaining investments.

ARTICLE VIII

Each Party shall provide appropriate means and procedures for asserting claims and enforcing rights regarding investments and investment agreements.

ARTICLE IX - TRANSPARENCY

Each Party shall publish all laws, judgments, administrative practices and procedures regarding investments, or which may affect the same.

ARTICLE X - COMPENSATION FOR LOSSES

Investors of one Party whose investments in the territory of the other Party suffer losses owing to war or other armed conflict, revolution, a state of national emergency, revolt, insurrection or riot in the territory of the latter Party shall be accorded by the latter Party treatment, as regards restitution, indemnification, compensation or other settlement, no less favourable than that which the latter Party accords to investors of any third State.

ARTICLE XI - CONDITIONS FOR EXPROPRIATION

Investments shall not be expropriated or nationalised either directly or indirectly through the application of measures equivalent to expropriation, except for reasons of public interest, in non-discriminatory fashion, and after payment of prompt, adequate and effective compensation, in a freely convertible currency and in accordance with due process of law and with the general principles of treatment established in Articles III and IV.

ARTICLE XII - FREE CONVERTIBILITY AND FREE TRANSFER

Each Party in whose territory an investment has been made shall grant in respect of such investment the right to the unrestricted transfer of -

(i)   returns;

(ii)   the proceeds from the total or partial liquidation of an investment; provided however, that in periods of serious balance of payments difficulties such transfers may be phased over a period of three years;

(iii)   amounts for the repayment of loans incurred for the investment;

(iv)   the net earnings of nationals of one Party who are employed and allowed to work in connection with an investment in the territory of the other Party;

(v)   payments deriving from indemnifications arising from expropriations and compensation for losses provided for in Articles X and XI of this Agreement.

2.   Such transfers shall be in freely convertible currency and at the exchange rate applicable at the time of remittance.

3.   Notwithstanding the above paragraph, a Party may prevent a transfer through the equitable, non-discriminatory and good faith application of its laws relating to:

(i)   bankruptcy, insolvency or the protection of the rights of creditors;
(ii)   issuing, trading or dealing in securities;
(iii)   criminal or penal offences;
(iv)   reports of transfers of currency or other monetary instruments; or
(v)   ensuring the

*   *   *

TRATADO DE LIBRE COMERCIO ENTRE LOS GOBIERNOS DE CENTROAMERICA Y EL GOBIERNO DE LA REPÚBLICA DE CHILE *
[excerpts]

The Agreement on the Establishment of a Free Trade Area between the Governments of the Countries of Central American and the Government of Chile was signed on 18 October 1999.

CUARTA PARTE

INVERSIÓN, SERVICIOS Y ASUNTOS RELACIONADOS

CAPÍTULO 10
INVERSIÓN

Artículo 10.01 Ámbito de aplicación

1. Se incorporan a este Tratado y serán parte integrante del mismo los acuerdos que se señalan en el Anexo 10.01.

2. En caso de incompatibilidad entre este Capítulo y cualquier otro Capítulo de este Tratado, prevalecerá el primero en la medida de la incompatibilidad, salvo respecto a los Capítulos 1 (Disposiciones iniciales), 18 (Administración del Tratado), 19 (Solución de controversias) y 21 (Disposiciones finales).

Artículo 10.02 Programa de trabajo futuro

1. Dentro del plazo de dos (2) años a partir de la entrada en vigor de este Tratado, todas las Partes analizarán la posibilidad de desarrollar y ampliar la cobertura de las normas y disciplinas establecidas en los acuerdos señalados en el Anexo 10.01. El desarrollo y ampliación de estos acuerdos serán parte integrante de este Tratado.

2. No obstante lo establecido en el párrafo 1, Chile y un país centroamericano podrán acordar el desarrollo y la ampliación de la cobertura de las normas y disciplinas establecidas en los acuerdos señalados en el Anexo 10.01. El desarrollo y ampliación de estos acuerdos serán parte integrante de este Tratado.

---

* *Source*: The Government of Costa Rica, the Government of El Salvador, the Government of Guatemala, the Government of Honduras, the Government of Nicaragua and the Government of Chile (1999). "Tratado de Libre Comercio entre los Gobiernos de Centroamérica y el Gobierno de la República de Chile"; available on the Internet (http://www.sice.oas.org/trade/chicam/chicam11.asp#Xt). [Note added by the editor.]

ANEXO 10.01

ÁMBITO DE APLICACIÓN

Se incorporan a este Tratado los siguientes acuerdos:

a) Acuerdo entre la República de Chile y la República de Costa Rica para la Promoción y Protección Recíproca de las Inversiones, suscrito el 11 de julio de 1996;

b) Acuerdo entre la República de Chile y la República de El Salvador para la Promoción y Protección Recíproca de las Inversiones, suscrito entre El Salvador y Chile el 8 de noviembre de 1996;

c) Acuerdo entre la República de Chile y la República de Guatemala para la Promoción y Protección Recíproca de las Inversiones, suscrito el 8 de noviembre de 1996;

d) Acuerdo entre la República de Chile y la República de Honduras para la Promoción y Protección Recíproca de las Inversiones, suscrito el 11 de noviembre de 1996; y

e) Acuerdo entre la República de Chile y la República de Nicaragua para la Promoción y Protección Recíproca de las Inversiones, suscrito el 8 de noviembre de 1996.

CAPÍTULO 11

COMERCIO TRANSFRONTERIZO DE SERVICIOS

Artículo 11.01 Definiciones

Para efectos de este Capítulo, se entenderá por:

Prestador de servicios de una Parte: una persona de otra Parte que preste o pretenda prestar transfronterizamente un servicio;

Restricción cuantitativa: una medida no discriminatoria que impone limitaciones sobre:

a) el número de prestadores de servicios, sea a través de una cuota, monopolio o una prueba de necesidad económica o por cualquier otro medio cuantitativo;

b) las operaciones de cualquier prestador de servicios, sea a través de una cuota o de una prueba de necesidad económica, o por cualquier otro medio cuantitativo;

Servicios aéreos especializados: los servicios transfronterizos de cartografía aérea, topografía aérea, fotografía aérea, control de incendios forestales, extinción de incendios, publicidad aérea, remolque de planeadores, servicios transfronterizos de paracaidismo, servicios transfronterizos aéreos para la construcción, transporte aéreo de madera en trozas o troncos, vuelos panorámicos, vuelos de entrenamiento, inspección y vigilancia aéreas yrociamiento aéreo;

Servicios o funciones gubernamentales: todo servicio transfronterizo prestado por una institución pública, que no se preste en condiciones comerciales ni en competencia con uno o varios prestadores de servicios;

Servicios profesionales: los servicios transfronterizos que para su prestación requieren educación superior técnica o universitaria o adiestramiento o experiencia equivalentes y cuyo ejercicio es autorizado, restringido o regulado por una Parte, pero no incluye los servicios prestados por personas que practican un oficio o a los tripulantes de barcos mercantes o aeronaves; y

Servicio transfronterizo: la prestación de un servicio:

a)   desde territorio de una Parte a territorio de otra Parte;

b)   en territorio de una Parte a un consumidor de otra Parte; y

c)   por un prestador de servicios mediante la presencia de personas físicas de una Parte en territorio de otra Parte;

pero no incluye la prestación de un servicio en territorio de una Parte mediante una inversión, en ese territorio.

Artículo 11.02 Ámbito de aplicación

1.   Este Capítulo se aplicará a las medidas que una Parte adopte o mantenga sobre servicios transfronterizos, que realicen los prestadores de servicios de otra Parte, incluidas las relativas a:

a)   la producción, la distribución, la comercialización, la venta y la prestación de un servicio transfronterizo;

b)   la compra, el uso o el pago de un servicio transfronterizo;

c)   el acceso a y el uso de sistemas de distribución y transporte relacionados con la prestación de un servicio transfronterizo;

d)   la presencia en su territorio de un prestador de servicios transfronterizos de otra Parte; y

e)   el otorgamiento de una fianza u otra forma de garantía financiera, como condición para la prestación de un servicio transfronterizo.

2.   Para efectos de este Capítulo, se entenderá que medidas que adopte o mantenga una Parte incluye a las medidas adoptadas o mantenidas por instituciones u organismos no gubernamentales en ejercicio de facultades reglamentarias, administrativas u otras de carácter gubernamental en ellos delegadas por esa Parte.

3.   Este Capítulo no se aplicará a:

a)   los subsidios o donaciones otorgados por una Parte o una empresa del Estado, incluidos los préstamos, garantías y seguros apoyados por una Parte;

b)   los servicios aéreos, incluidos los de transporte aéreo nacional e internacional, regulares y no regulares, así como las actividades auxiliares de apoyo a los servicios aéreos, salvo:

   i)   los servicios de reparación y mantenimiento de aeronaves durante el período en que se retira una aeronave de servicio;

   ii)   los servicios aéreos especializados; y

   iii)   los sistemas computarizados de reservación;

c)   los servicios o funciones gubernamentales, tales como la ejecución de las leyes, servicios de readaptación social, pensión o seguro de desempleo o servicios de seguridad social, bienestar social, educación pública, capacitación pública, salud y atención infantil o protección de la niñez;

d)   los servicios financieros transfronterizos; y

e)   las compras gubernamentales hechas por una Parte o empresa del Estado.

4.   No obstante lo dispuesto en el párrafo 3(c), si un prestador de servicios de una Parte, debidamente autorizado, presta servicios o lleva a cabo funciones gubernamentales, tales como servicios de readaptación social, pensión o seguro de desempleo o servicios de seguridad social, bienestar social, educación pública, capacitación pública, salud y atención infantil o protección de la niñez en territorio de otra Parte, la prestación de esos servicios estará protegida por las disposiciones de este Capítulo.

5.   Ninguna disposición de este Capítulo se interpretará en el sentido de imponer a una Parte obligación alguna respecto a un nacional de otra Parte que pretenda ingresar a su mercado de trabajo o que tenga empleo permanente en su territorio, ni de conferir algún derecho a ese nacional, respecto a ese ingreso o empleo.

Artículo 11.03 Trato nacional

1.   Cada Parte otorgará a los servicios transfronterizos y a los prestadores de servicios de otra Parte, un trato no menos favorable que el que conceda a sus propios servicios similares o prestadores de servicios similares.

2.   Cada Parte podrá cumplir lo prescrito en el párrafo 1 otorgando a los servicios transfronterizos y a los prestadores de servicios de otra Parte un trato formalmente idéntico o formalmente diferente al que dispense a sus propios servicios transfronterizos similares y prestadores de servicios similares.

3. Se considerará que un trato formalmente idéntico o formalmente diferente es menos favorable si modifica las condiciones de competencia a favor de los servicios transfronterizos o prestadores de servicios de una Parte en comparación con los servicios transfronterizos similares o los prestadores de servicios similares de otra Parte.

Artículo 11.04 Trato de nación más favorecida

Cada Parte otorgará inmediata e incondicionalmente a los servicios transfronterizos y a los prestadores de servicios de otra Parte un trato no menos favorable que el que conceda a los servicios similares y a los prestadores de servicios similares de cualquier otro país.

Artículo 11.05 Nivel de trato

Cada Parte otorgará a los servicios transfronterizos y a los prestadores de servicios de otra Parte el mejor de los tratos requeridos por los artículos 11.03 y 11.04.

Artículo 11.06 Presencia local

Ninguna Parte exigirá a un prestador de servicios de otra Parte que establezca o mantenga una oficina de representación u otro tipo de empresa, o que resida en su territorio, como condición para la prestación de un servicio transfronterizo.

Artículo 11.07 Otorgamiento de permisos, autorizaciones, licencias o certificaciones

Con el objeto de garantizar que toda medida que una Parte adopte o mantenga en relación con los requisitos y procedimientos para el otorgamiento de permisos, autorizaciones, licencias o certificaciones a los nacionales de otra Parte no constituya una barrera innecesaria a los servicios transfronterizos, cada Parte procurará garantizar que dichas medidas:

    a) se sustenten en criterios objetivos y transparentes, tales como la capacidad y la aptitud para prestar un servicio transfronterizo;

    b) no sean más gravosas de lo necesario para asegurar la calidad de un servicio transfronterizo; y

    c) no constituyan una restricción encubierta a la prestación de un servicio transfronterizo.

Artículo 11.08 Reservas

    1. Los artículos 11.03, 11.04 y 11.06 no se aplicarán a:

        a) cualquier medida disconforme existente que sea mantenida por una Parte en todos sus niveles de gobierno, tal como se indica en su Lista del Anexo I;

b) la continuación o la pronta renovación de cualquier medida disconforme a que se refiere el literal a); ni

c) la reforma de cualquier medida disconforme a que se refiere el literal a), siempre que dicha reforma no disminuya el grado de conformidad de la medida, tal como estaba en vigor inmediatamente antes de la reforma, con los artículos 11.03, 11.04 y 11.06.

2. Los artículos 11.03, 11.04 y 11.06 no se aplicarán a cualquier medida que una Parte adopte o mantenga respecto a los sectores, subsectores o actividades, tal como se indica en su Lista del Anexo II.

3. Para efectos de este artículo y del artículo 11.09, existente significa al 18 de agosto de 1998, salvo en el caso entre Chile y Honduras en el que será al 30 de junio de 1999.

Artículo 11.09 Restricciones cuantitativas no discriminatorias

1. Cada Parte elaborará una lista de medidas existentes que constituyan restricciones cuantitativas no discriminatorias, las que se consignan en el Anexo III.

2. Cada Parte notificará a otra Parte cualquier medida que constituya una restricción cuantitativa no discriminatoria, que sea adoptada después de la entrada en vigor de este Tratado, e indicará la restricción en la lista a que se refiere el párrafo 1.

3. Periódicamente, al menos una vez cada dos (2) años, las Partes procurarán negociar para liberalizar o eliminar:

a) restricciones cuantitativas existentes que mantenga una Parte, según la lista a que se refiere el párrafo 1;

b) restricciones cuantitativas que haya adoptado una Parte después de la entrada en vigor de este Tratado.

Artículo 11.10 Denegación de beneficios

Previa notificación y realización de consultas, conforme a los artículos 17.04 (Suministro de información) y 19.06 (Consultas), una Parte podrá denegar los beneficios derivados de este Capítulo a un prestador de servicios de otra Parte, cuando determine que el servicio está siendo prestado por una empresa que no realiza actividades comerciales sustanciales en territorio de esa otra Parte y que, de conformidad con la legislación vigente de esa otra Parte, es propiedad o está bajo control de personas de un país no Parte.

Artículo 11.11 Liberalización futura

A través de negociaciones futuras a ser convocadas por la Comisión, las Partes profundizarán la liberalización alcanzada en los diferentes sectores de servicios, con miras a lograr la eliminación de las restricciones remanentes listadas de conformidad con el artículo 11.08(1) y (2).

Artículo 11.12 Procedimientos

Las Partes establecerán procedimientos para:

a)   que una Parte notifique a otra Parte e incluya en sus listas pertinentes:

i)   las reformas a medidas a las cuales se hace referencia en el artículo 11.08(1) y (2); y

ii)   las restricciones cuantitativas, de conformidad con el artículo 11.09;

b)   indicar sus compromisos para liberalizar restricciones cuantitativas, requisitos para el otorgamiento de licencias, y otras medidas no discriminatorias; y

c)   las consultas sobre reservas, restricciones cuantitativas o compromisos, tendientes a lograr una mayor liberalización.

Artículo 11.13 Servicios profesionales

En el Anexo 11.13 sobre servicios profesionales se establecen las reglas que observarán las Partes para armonizar las medidas que normarán los servicios profesionales mediante el otorgamiento de autorizaciones para el ejercicio profesional.

Articulo 11.14 Comité de Inversión y Servicios Transfronterizos

1.   Las Partes establecen el Comité de Inversión y Servicios Transfronterizos, cuya composición se señala en el Anexo 11.14.

2.   El Comité conocerá los asuntos relativos a este Capítulo y al Capítulo 10 (Inversión).

ANEXO 11.13

SERVICIOS PROFESIONALES

Reconocimiento de títulos

1.   Cuando una Parte reconozca de manera unilateral o por acuerdo con otro país, los títulos obtenidos en territorio de otra Parte o país no Parte:

a) nada de lo dispuesto en el artículo 11.04, se interpretará en el sentido de exigir a esa Parte que reconozca los títulos obtenidos en territorio de otra Parte; y

b) la Parte proporcionará a otra Parte, la oportunidad para demostrar que los títulos obtenidos en territorio de esa otra Parte también podrán reconocerse, o para negociar o celebrar un arreglo o acuerdo que tenga efectos equivalentes.

Bases para el reconocimiento de títulos y autorización para el ejercicio profesional

2. Las Partes acuerdan que los procesos de mutuo reconocimiento de títulos y el otorgamiento de autorizaciones para el ejercicio profesional, se harán sobre la base de mejorar la calidad de los servicios profesionales a través del establecimiento de normas y criterios para esos procesos, protegiendo al mismo tiempo a los consumidores y salvaguardando el interés público.

3. Las Partes alentarán a los organismos pertinentes, entre otros, a autoridades gubernamentales competentes y a las asociaciones y colegios profesionales, cuando corresponda, para:

a) elaborar tales criterios y normas; y

b) formular y presentar recomendaciones sobre el mutuo reconocimiento de títulos profesionales y el otorgamiento de licencias para el ejercicio profesional.

4. La elaboración de normas y criterios a que se refiere el párrafo 3, podrá considerar la legislación de cada Parte y a título indicativo los elementos siguientes: educación, exámenes, experiencia, conducta y ética, desarrollo profesional y renovación de la certificación, ámbito de acción, conocimiento local, supervisión y protección al consumidor.

5. Las Partes proporcionarán la información detallada y necesaria para el reconocimiento de títulos y el otorgamiento de licencias para el ejercicio profesional, incluyendo la correspondiente a cursos académicos, guías y materiales de estudio, pago de derechos, fechas de exámenes, horarios, ubicaciones, afiliación a sociedades o colegios profesionales. Esta información incluirá la legislación, las directrices administrativas y las medidas de aplicación general de carácter central y las elaboradas por instituciones gubernamentales y no gubernamentales.

ANEXO 11.14

COMITÉ DE INVERSIÓN Y SERVICIOS TRANSFRONTERIZOS

El Comité de Inversión y Servicios Transfronterizos establecido en el artículo 11.14 estará integrado:

a) para el caso de Chile, por la Dirección General de Relaciones Económicas Internacionales del Ministerio de Relaciones Exteriores, o su sucesora;

b) para el caso de Costa Rica, por el Ministerio de Comercio Exterior, o su sucesor;

c)   para el caso de El Salvador, por el Ministerio de Economía, o su sucesor;

d)   para el caso de Guatemala, por el Ministerio de Economía, o su sucesor;

e)   para el caso de Honduras, por la Secretaría de Industria y Comercio, o su sucesora;

f)   para el caso de Nicaragua, por el Ministerio de Fomento, Industria y Comercio, o su sucesor.

*   *   *

TREATY FOR THE ESTABLISHMENT OF THE EAST AFRICAN COMMUNITY[*]
[excerpts]

> The Treaty for the Establishment of the East African Community was signed between Kenya, Uganda and the United Republic of Tanzania on 30 November 1999. It entered into force on 7 June 2000.

12. CO-OPERATION IN INVESTMENT AND INDUSTRIAL DEVELOPMENT

Article 79
Industrial Development

In order to promote the achievement of the objectives of the Community as set out in Article 5 of this Treaty, the Partner States shall take such steps in the field of industrial development that will:

a.   promote self-sustaining and balanced industrial growth;

b.   improve the competitiveness of the industrial sector so as to enhance the expansion of trade in industrial goods within the Community and the export of industrial goods from the Partner States in order to achieve the structural transformation of the economy that would foster the overall socio-economic development in the Partner States; and

c.   encourage the development of indigenous entrepreneurs.

Article 80
Strategy and Priority Areas

1.   For purposes of Article 79 of this Treaty, the Partner States shall take measures to:

a.   develop an East African Industrial Development Strategy:

b.   promote linkages among industries within the Community through diversification. specialisation and complementarity, in order to enhance the spread effects of industrial growth and to facilitate the transfer of technology;

c.   facilitate the development of:

i.   small and medium scale industries including subcontracting and other relations between larger and smaller firms;

---

* *Source*: East African Community (1999). "Treaty for the Establishment of the East African Community"; available on the Internet (http://www.newafrica.com/eac/treaty/index.htm). [Note added by the editor.]

    ii.   basic capital and intermediate goods industries for the purposes of obtaining the advantages of economies of scale; and

    iii.   food and agro industries;

d.   rationalise investments and the full use of established industries so as to promote efficiency in production;

e.   promote industrial research and development and the transfer, acquisition, adaptation and development of modern technology, training, management and consultancy services through the establishment of joint industrial institutions and other infrastructural facilities:

f.   harmonise and rationalise investment incentives including those relating to taxation of industries particularly those that use local materials and labour with a view to promoting the Community as a single investment area;

g.   disseminate and exchange industrial and technological information;

h.   avoid double taxation; and

i.   maintain the standardisation quality assurance, metrology and testing currently applicable and such other standards as may be adopted by the Council after the signing of this Treaty for goods and services produced and traded among the Partner States pending the conclusion of a protocol under paragraph 4 of Article 81 of this Treaty

2.   The Partners States shall take such other measures for the purposes of Article 79 of this Treaty as the Council may determine.

17. FREE MOVEMENT OF PERSONS, LABOUR, SERVICES, RIGHT OF ESTABLISHMENT AND RESIDENCE

Article 104
Scope of Co-operation

1.   The Partner States agree to adopt measures to achieve the free movement of persons, labour and services and to ensure the enjoyment of the right of establishment and residence of their citizens within the Community.

2.   For purposes of paragraph 1 of this Article the Partner States agree to conclude a Protocol on the Free Movement of Persons, Labour, Services and Right of Establishment and Residence at a time to be determined by the Council.

3.   The Partner States shall as may be determined by the Council:

a.   ease border crossing by citizens of the Partner States;

b.   maintain common standard travel documents for their citizens;

c.   effect reciprocal opening of border posts and keep the posts opened and manned for twenty four hours;

d.   maintain common employment policies;

e.   harmonise their labour policies, programmes and legislation including those on occupational health and safety:

f.   establish a region centre for productivity and employment promotion and exchange information on the availability of employment

g.   make their training facilities available to persons from other Partner States: and

h.   enhance the activities of the employers and workers organisations with a view to strengthening them.

4.   The Partner States undertake to co-operate in the enhancement of the social partnership between the governments, employers and employees so as to increase the productivity of labour through efficient production.

*   *   *

TRATADO DE LIBRE COMERCIO ENTRE LOS ESTADOS UNIDOS MEXICANOS Y LAS REPUBLICAS DE EL SALVADOR, GUATEMALA Y HONDURAS*
[excerpts]

The Free Trade Agreement between Mexico and El Salvador, Guatemala and Honduras (commonly known as the "Northern Trangle") was signed on 29 June 2000. It entered into force on 15 March 2001 between Mexico and Guatemala, and Mexico and El Salvador, and on 1 June 2001 between Mexico and Honduras.

Capítulo XIV

INVERSIÓN

Sección A

Inversión

ARTÍCULO 14-01
Definiciones.

Para efectos de este capítulo, se entenderá por:

CIADI: el Centro Internacional de Arreglo de Diferencias Relativas a Inversiones;

Convención Interamericana: la Convención Interamericana sobre Arbitraje Comercial Internacional, celebrada en Panamá el 30 de enero de 1975;

Convenio del CIADI: el Convenio sobre Arreglo de Diferencias Relativas a Inversiones entre Estados y Nacionales de otros Estados, celebrado en Washington, D.C., el 18 de marzo de 1965;

Convención de Nueva York: la Convención de las Naciones Unidas sobre el Reconocimiento y Ejecución de Sentencias Arbitrales Extranjeras, celebrada en Nueva York el 10 de junio de 1958;

demanda: la reclamación sometida por un inversionista contendiente contra una Parte, cuyo fundamento sea una presunta violación a las disposiciones contenidas en este capítulo;

empresa: una "empresa", tal como se define en el artículo 2-01, y la sucursal de una empresa;

---

* *Source*: The Government of Mexico, the Government of El Salvador, the Government of Guatemala and the Government of Honduras (2000). "Tratado de Libre Comercio entre los Estados Unidos Mexicanos y las Republicas de El Salvador, Guatemala y Honduras "; available on the Internet (http://www. sice.oas .org /Trade/ mextnorte/indice.asp). [Note added by the editor.]

empresa de una Parte: una empresa constituida u organizada de conformidad con la legislación de una Parte y una sucursal de una empresa ubicada en el territorio de una Parte que desempeñe actividades comerciales en el mismo;

inversión:

a)   una empresa;

b)   acciones de una empresa;

c)   instrumentos de deuda de una empresa:

      i)   cuando la empresa es una filial del inversionista; o

      ii)   cuando la fecha de vencimiento original del instrumento de deuda sea por lo menos de tres años, pero no incluye un instrumento de deuda de una empresa del Estado, independientemente de la fecha original del vencimiento;

d)   un préstamo a una empresa;

      i)   cuando la empresa es una filial del inversionista; o

      ii)   cuando la fecha de vencimiento original del préstamo sea por lo menos de tres años, pero no incluye un préstamo a una empresa del Estado, independientemente de la fecha original del vencimiento;

e)   na participación en una empresa, que le permita al propietario participar en los ingresos o en las utilidades de la empresa;

f)   una participación en una empresa que otorgue derecho al propietario para participar del haber social de esa empresa en una liquidación, siempre que éste no derive de una obligación o un préstamo excluidos conforme a los literales c) o d);

g)   bienes raíces u otra propiedad, tangibles o intangibles, adquiridos o utilizados con el propósito de obtener un beneficio económico o para otros fines empresariales; y

h)   la participación que resulte del capital u otros recursos destinados para el desarrollo de una actividad económica en el territorio de otra Parte, entre ellos, conforme a:

      i)   contratos que involucran la presencia de la propiedad de un inversionista en el territorio de otra Parte, incluidos, las concesiones, los contratos de construcción y de llave en mano; o

      ii)   contratos donde la remuneración depende sustancialmente de la producción, ingresos o ganancias de una empresa;

pero inversión no significa:

i)   un instrumento de deuda del Estado;

j)   reclamaciones pecuniarias derivadas exclusivamente de:

  i)   contratos comerciales para la venta de bienes o servicios por un nacional o empresa en territorio de una Parte a una empresa en el territorio de otra Parte; o

  ii)   el otorgamiento de crédito en relación con una transacción comercial, como el financiamiento al comercio, salvo un préstamo cubierto por las disposiciones del literal d); ni

k)   cualquier otra reclamación pecuniaria que no conlleve los tipos de interés dispuestos en los literales a) al i);

inversión de un inversionista de una Parte: la inversión propiedad o bajo control directo o indirecto de un inversionista de una Parte en el territorio de otra Parte;

inversionista de una Parte: una Parte o una empresa de la misma, un nacional o una empresa de esa Parte, que lleve a cabo los actos materiales tendientes a realizar una inversión o, en su caso, realice o haya realizado una inversión en el territorio de otra Parte;

inversionista de un país no Parte: un inversionista que no es inversionista de una Parte que pretende realizar, realiza o ha realizado una inversión;

inversionista contendiente: un inversionista que somete una demanda en los términos de la sección B;

Parte contendiente: la Parte contra la cual se somete una demanda en los términos de la sección B;

parte contendiente: el inversionista contendiente o la Parte contendiente;

partes contendientes: el inversionista contendiente y la Parte contendiente;

Reglas de Arbitraje de la CNUDMI: las Reglas de Arbitraje de la Comisión de Naciones Unidas sobre Derecho Mercantil Internacional (CNUDMI), aprobadas por la Asamblea General de las Naciones Unidas el 15 de diciembre de 1976;

Secretario General: el Secretario General del CIADI;

transferencias: las remisiones y pagos internacionales;

tribunal: un tribunal arbitral establecido conforme al artículo 14-22; y

tribunal de acumulación: un tribunal arbitral establecido conforme al artículo 14-29.

Artículo 14-02
Ámbito de aplicación y extensión de las obligaciones.

1. Este capítulo se aplica a las medidas que adopte o mantenga una Parte relativas a:

    a) los inversionistas de otra Parte, en todo lo relativo a su inversión;

    b) las inversiones de inversionistas de otra Parte realizadas en el territorio de la Parte; y

    c) en lo que respecta al artículo 14-07, todas las inversiones en el territorio de la Parte.

2. Este capítulo no se aplica a:

    a) las actividades económicas reservadas a cada Parte, tal y como se señalan en el Anexo III;

    b) las medidas que adopte o mantenga una Parte en materia de servicios financieros;

    c) las medidas que adopte una Parte para restringir la participación de las inversiones de inversionistas de otra Parte en su territorio, por razones de seguridad nacional u orden público; y

    d) las controversias o reclamaciones surgidas con anterioridad a la entrada en vigor de este tratado, o relacionadas con hechos acaecidos con anterioridad a su vigencia, incluso si sus efectos permanecen aún después de ésta.

3. Este capítulo se aplica en todo el territorio de las Partes y en cualquier nivel u orden de gobierno, a pesar de las medidas incompatibles que pudieran existir en sus respectivas legislaciones.

4. Ninguna disposición de este capítulo se interpretará en el sentido de impedir a una Parte prestar servicios o llevar a cabo funciones relacionadas con la ejecución de las leyes, servicios de readaptación social, pensión o seguro de desempleo o servicios de seguridad social, bienestar social, educación pública, salud y protección de la niñez.

Artículo 14-03
Nivel mínimo de trato.

Cada Parte otorgará a los inversionistas de otra Parte y a sus inversiones, un trato acorde con el derecho internacional, incluido el trato justo y equitativo, así como protección y seguridad jurídica dentro de su territorio.

Artículo 14-04
Trato nacional.

Cada Parte otorgará al inversionista de una Parte y a la inversión de un inversionista de una Parte, un trato no menos favorable que el que otorgue, en circunstancias similares, a sus propios inversionistas y a las inversiones de dichos inversionistas en lo referente al establecimiento, adquisición, expansión, administración, conducción, operación, venta u otra disposición de las inversiones.

Artículo 14-05
Trato de nación más favorecida.

1.   Cada Parte otorgará al inversionista de una Parte y a la inversión de un inversionista de una Parte, un trato no menos favorable que el que otorgue, en circunstancias similares, al inversionista y a la inversión de un inversionista de una Parte o de un país no Parte, en lo referente al stablecimiento, adquisición, expansión, administración, conducción, operación, venta u otra disposición de las inversiones.

2.   Si una Parte hubiere otorgado un trato especial al inversionista de un país no Parte o a la inversión de un inversionista de un país no Parte, en virtud de convenios que establezcan disposiciones para evitar la doble tributación, zonas de libre comercio, uniones aduaneras, mercados comunes, uniones económicas o monetarias e instituciones similares, dicha Parte no estará obligada a otorgar el tratamiento que se trate al inversionista de una Parte o a la inversión de un inversionista de una Parte.

Artículo 14-06
Trato en caso de pérdidas.

Cada Parte otorgará al inversionista de una Parte, respecto de las inversiones que sufran pérdidas en su territorio debidas a conflictos armados o contiendas civiles, caso fortuito o fuerza mayor, un trato no discriminatorio respecto de cualquier medida que adopte o mantenga en vinculación con esas pérdidas.

Artículo 14-07
Requisitos de desempeño.

1.   Ninguna Parte podrá imponer u obligar al cumplimiento de los siguientes requisitos o compromisos, en relación con el establecimiento, adquisición, expansión, administración, conducción u operación de una inversión de un inversionista de una Parte o de un país no Parte en su territorio para:

   a)   exportar un determinado tipo, nivel o porcentaje de bienes o servicios;

   b)   alcanzar un determinado grado o porcentaje de contenido nacional;

   c)   adquirir, utilizar u otorgar preferencia a bienes producidos o a servicios prestados en su territorio, o adquirir bienes de productores o servicios de prestadores de servicios en su territorio;

   d)   relacionar en cualquier forma el volumen o valor de las importaciones con el volumen o valor de las exportaciones, o con el monto de las entradas de divisas asociadas con dicha inversión;

e) restringir las ventas en su territorio de los bienes o servicios que tal inversión produzca o preste, relacionando de cualquier manera dichas ventas al volumen o valor de sus exportaciones o a ganancias que generen en divisas;

f) transferir a una persona en su territorio, tecnología, proceso productivo u otro conocimiento reservado, salvo cuando el requisito se imponga por un tribunal judicial o administrativo o autoridad competente, para reparar una supuesta violación a las leyes en materia de competencia o para actuar de una manera que no sea incompatible con otras disposiciones de este tratado; o

g) actuar como el proveedor exclusivo de los bienes que produzca o servicios que preste para un mercado específico, regional o mundial.

Este párrafo no se aplica a ningún otro requisito distinto a los señalados en el mismo.

2. La medida que exija que una inversión emplee una tecnología para cumplir con requisitos de salud, ambiente o seguridad de aplicación general, no se considerará incompatible con el párrafo 1 literal f). Para brindar mayor certeza, los artículos 14-04 y 14-05 se aplican a la citada medida.

3. Ninguna Parte podrá condicionar la recepción de una ventaja o que se continúe recibiendo la misma, en relación con una inversión en su territorio por parte de un inversionista de una Parte o de un país no Parte, al cumplimiento de cualquiera de los siguientes requisitos:

a) adquirir, utilizar u otorgar preferencia a bienes producidos en su territorio o a comprar bienes de productores en su territorio;

b) alcanzar un determinado grado o porcentaje de contenido nacional;

c) relacionar en cualquier forma el volumen o valor de las importaciones con el volumen o valor de las exportaciones, o con el monto de las entradas de divisas asociadas con dicha inversión; o

d) restringir las ventas en su territorio de los bienes o servicios que tal inversión produzca o preste, relacionando de cualquier manera dichas ventas al volumen o valor de sus exportaciones o a ganancias que generen en divisas.

Este párrafo no se aplica a ningún otro requisito distinto a los señalados en el mismo.

4. Nada de lo dispuesto en el párrafo 3 se interpretará como impedimento para que una Parte imponga en relación con una inversión de un inversionista de una Parte o de un inversionista de un país no Parte en su territorio, requisitos legalmente establecidos relativos a localización geográfica de unidades productivas, de generación de empleo o capacitación de mano de obra, o de realización de actividades en materia de investigación y desarrollo.

5. En caso que, a juicio de una Parte, la imposición por otra Parte de cualquier otro requisito no previsto en el párrafo 1 afecte negativamente el flujo comercial, o constituya una barrera significativa a la inversión, el asunto será considerado por el Comité de Comercio

Transfronterizo de Servicios e Inversión, al que se hace referencia en el artículo 10-10 de este tratado.

6.   Si el Comité considera que, el requisito en cuestión afecta negativamente el flujo comercial, recomendará a la Comisión la suspensión de la práctica respectiva.

7.   Este artículo no se aplica a cualquier compromiso, obligación o requisito entre partes privadas.

Artículo 14-08
Alta dirección empresarial y consejos de administración.

1.   Ninguna Parte podrá exigir que una empresa de esa Parte, designe a individuos de alguna nacionalidad en particular para ocupar puestos de alta dirección, sin perjuicio de lo establecido en su legislación.

2.   Una Parte podrá exigir que la mayoría de los miembros de los órganos de administración o de cualquier comité de tales órganos de una empresa de esa Parte que sea una inversión de un inversionista de la otra Parte, sea de una nacionalidad en particular, o sea residente en territorio de la Parte, siempre que el requisito no menoscabe significativamente la capacidad del inversionista para ejercer el control de su inversión.

Artículo 14-09
Reservas y excepciones.

1.   Los artículos 14-04, 14-05, 14-07 y 14-08 no se aplican a:

    a)   cualquier medida incompatible existente que mantenga una Parte, sea cual fuere el nivel u orden de gobierno, como se estipula en su lista del Anexo I o del Anexo III;

    b)   la continuación o pronta renovación de cualquier medida incompatible a que se refiere el literal a); ni

    c)   la reforma a cualquier medida incompatible a que se refiere el literal a), siempre que dicha reforma no disminuya el grado de compatibilidad de la medida, tal y como estaba en vigor antes de la reforma, con los artículos 14-04, 14-05, 14-07 y 14-08.

2.   El trato otorgado por una Parte de conformidad con el artículo 14-05 no se aplica a los tratados o sectores estipulados en su lista del Anexo IV.

3.   Los artículos 14-04, 14-05 y 14-08 no se aplican a:

    a)   las compras realizadas por una Parte o por una empresa del Estado; ni

    b)   subsidios o aportaciones, incluyendo los préstamos, garantías y seguros gubernamentales otorgados por una Parte o por una empresa del Estado, salvo por lo dispuesto en el artículo 14-06.

4.   Las disposiciones contenidas en:

a)   los literales a), b) y c) del párrafo 1 y los literales a) y b) del párrafo 3, del artículo 14-07, no se aplicarán en lo relativo a los requisitos para calificación de los bienes y servicios con respecto a programas de promoción a las exportaciones y de ayuda externa;

b)   los literales b), c), f) y g) del párrafo 1 y los literales a) y b) del párrafo 3 del artículo14-07, no se aplican a las compras realizadas por una Parte o por una empresa del Estado; y

c)   los literales a) y b) del párrafo 3, del artículo 14-07, no se aplican a los requisitos impuestos por una Parte importadora relacionados con el contenido necesario de bienes para calificar respecto de aranceles o cuotas preferenciales.

Artículo 14-10
Transferencias.

1.   Cada Parte permitirá que en su territorio todas las transferencias relacionadas con la inversión de un inversionista de otra Parte, se hagan libremente y sin demora. Dichas transferencias incluyen:

a)   ganancias, dividendos, intereses, ganancias de capital, pagos por regalías, gastos de administración, asistencia técnica y otros cargos, ganancias en especie y otros montos derivados de la inversión;

b)   productos derivados de la venta o liquidación, total o parcial, de la inversión;

c)   pagos realizados conforme a un contrato del que sea parte un inversionista o su inversión, incluidos pagos efectuados conforme a un convenio de préstamo;

d)   pagos derivados de indemnizaciones por concepto de expropiación; y

e)   pagos que provengan de la aplicación de las disposiciones relativas al mecanismo de solución de controversias contenido en la sección B.

2.   Para efectos de este capítulo, una transferencia se considera realizada sin demora cuando se ha efectuado dentro del plazo normalmente necesario para el cumplimiento de las formalidades de transferencia.

3.   Ninguna Parte podrá exigir a sus inversionistas que efectúen transferencias de sus ingresos, ganancias, o utilidades u otros montos derivados de, o atribuibles a, inversiones llevadas a cabo en el territorio de otra Parte, ni los sancionará en caso que no realicen la transferencia.

4.   Cada Parte permitirá que las transferencias se realicen en divisas de libre convertibilidad al tipo de cambio vigente de mercado en la fecha de la transferencia.

5.   No obstante lo dispuesto en los párrafos 1 y 4, cada Parte podrá impedir la realización de transferencias, mediante la aplicación equitativa, no discriminatoria y de buena fe de medidas:

a)   para proteger los derechos de los acreedores;

b)   relativas a asegurar el cumplimiento de las leyes y reglamentos:

  i)   para la emisión, transmisión y negociación de valores, futuros y derivados; o

  ii)   relativos a reportes o registros de transferencias; o

c)   relacionadas con infracciones penales o resoluciones en procedimientos administrativos o judiciales.

6.   No obstante lo dispuesto en este artículo, cada Parte podrá establecer controles temporales a las operaciones cambiarias, siempre y cuando la balanza de pagos de la Parte de que se trate, presente un serio desequilibrio e instrumente un programa de acuerdo con los criterios internacionalmente aceptados.

Artículo 14-11
Expropiación e indemnización.

1.   Ninguna Parte podrá nacionalizar ni expropiar, directa o indirectamente, una inversión de un inversionista de una Parte en su territorio, ni adoptar medida alguna equivalente a la expropiación o nacionalización de esa inversión, salvo que sea:

a)   por causa de utilidad pública de conformidad con lo dispuesto en el anexo;

b)   sobre bases no discriminatorias;

c)   con apego al principio de legalidad; y

d)   mediante indemnización de conformidad con los párrafos 2 al 4.

2.   La indemnización será equivalente al valor justo de mercado que tenga la inversión expropiada inmediatamente antes que la medida expropiatoria se haya llevado a cabo (fecha de expropiación), y no reflejará ningún cambio en el valor, debido a que la intención de expropiar se haya conocido con antelación a la fecha de expropiación. Los criterios de valuación incluirán el valor fiscal declarado de bienes tangibles, así como otros criterios que resulten apropiados para determinar el valor justo de mercado.

3.   El pago de la indemnización se hará sin demora y será completamente liquidable.

4.   La cantidad pagada no será inferior a la cantidad equivalente que por indemnización se hubiera pagado en una divisa de libre convertibilidad en el mercado financiero internacional, en la fecha de expropiación, y esta divisa se hubiese convertido a la cotización de mercado vigente en la fecha de valuación, más los intereses que hubiese generado a una tasa bancaria o comercial hasta la fecha del día del pago.

Artículo 14-12
Formalidades especiales y requisitos de información.

1.   Nada de lo dispuesto en el artículo 14-04 se interpretará en el sentido de impedir a una Parte adoptar o mantener una medida que prescriba formalidades especiales conexas al establecimiento de inversiones por inversionistas de otra Parte, tales como que las inversiones se constituyan conforme a la legislación de la Parte, siempre que dichas formalidades no menoscaben sustancialmente la protección otorgada por una Parte conforme a este capítulo.

2.   No obstante lo dispuesto en los artículos 14-04 y 14-05, cada Parte podrá exigir, en su territorio, a un inversionista de otra Parte, que proporcione información rutinaria, referente a su inversión, exclusivamente con fines de información o estadística. La Parte protegerá la información que sea confidencial, de cualquier divulgación que pudiera afectar negativamente la situación competitiva de la inversión o del inversionista.

Artículo 14-13
Relación con otros capítulos.

En caso de incompatibilidad entre una disposición de este capítulo y una disposición de otro, prevalecerá la de este último en la medida de la incompatibilidad.

Artículo 14-14
Denegación de beneficios.

1.   Una Parte, previa notificación y consulta con otra Parte, podrá denegar los beneficios de este capítulo a un inversionista de esa Parte que sea una empresa de la misma y a las inversiones de tal inversionista, si inversionistas de un país no Parte son propietarios mayoritarios o controlan la empresa y ésta no tiene actividades empresariales sustanciales en el territorio de la Parte conforme a cuya ley está constituida u organizada.

2.   Una Parte podrá denegar los beneficios de este capítulo a un inversionista de otra Parte que sea una empresa de esa Parte y a las inversiones de dicho inversionista, si dicha empresa es propiedad de o está controlada por inversionistas de un país no Parte y:

   a)   la Parte que deniegue los beneficios no mantiene relaciones diplomáticas con el país no Parte; o

   b)   la Parte que deniegue los beneficios adopta o mantiene medidas en relación con el país no Parte, que prohiben transacciones con esa empresa o que serían violadas o eludidas si los beneficios de este capítulo se otorgan a esa empresa o a sus inversiones.

Artículo 14-15
Aplicación extraterritorial de la legislación de una Parte.

1.   Las Partes, en relación con las inversiones de sus inversionistas, constituidas y organizadas conforme a la legislación de otra Parte, no podrán ejercer jurisdicción ni adoptar medida alguna que tenga por efecto la aplicación extraterritorial de su legislación o la obstaculización del comercio entre las Partes, o entre una Parte y un país no Parte.

2.   Si alguna de las Partes incumpliere lo dispuesto por el párrafo 1, la Parte en donde la inversión se hubiere constituido podrá, a su discreción, adoptar las medidas y ejercitar las acciones que considere necesarias, a fin de dejar sin efecto la legislación o la medida que se trate y los obstáculos al comercio consecuencia de las mismas.

Artículo 14-16
Medidas relativas al ambiente.

1.   Nada de lo dispuesto en este capítulo se interpretará como impedimento para que una Parte adopte, mantenga o ponga en ejecución cualquier medida, compatible con este capítulo, que considere apropiada para asegurar que las inversiones en su territorio observen la legislación en materia ambiental.

2.   Las Partes reconocen que es inadecuado fomentar la inversión por medio de un relajamiento de las medidas internas aplicables a la salud, seguridad o relativas al ambiente. En consecuencia, ninguna Parte deberá eliminar o comprometerse a eximir de la aplicación de esas medidas a la inversión de un inversionista, como medio para inducir el establecimiento, la adquisición, la expansión o conservación de la inversión en su territorio. Si una Parte estima que otra Parte ha fomentado una inversión de tal manera, podrá solicitar consultas con esa otra Parte.

Artículo 14-17
Promoción de inversiones e intercambio de información.

1.   Con la intención de incrementar significativamente la participación recíproca de las inversiones, las Partes podrán promover y apoyar la elaboración de documentos de promoción de oportunidades de inversión y el diseño de mecanismos para su difusión. Así mismo, las Partes podrán crear, mantener y perfeccionar mecanismos financieros que hagan viable las inversiones de una Parte en el territorio de otra Parte.

2.   Las Partes darán a conocer información disponible sobre oportunidades de:

a)   inversión en su territorio, que puedan ser desarrolladas por inversionistas de otra Parte;

b)   alianzas estratégicas entre inversionistas de las Partes, mediante la investigación y conjugación de intereses y oportunidades de asociación; y

c)   inversión en sectores económicos específicos que interesen a las Partes y a sus inversionistas, de acuerdo a la solicitud expresa que haga cualquier Parte.

3.   Las Partes se mantendrán informadas y actualizadas respecto de:

a)   la legislación que, directa o indirectamente, afecte a la inversión extranjera incluyendo, entre otros, regímenes cambiarios y de carácter fiscal;

b)   el comportamiento de la inversión extranjera en sus respectivos territorios; y

c)   las oportunidades de inversión a que se refiere el párrafo 2, incluyendo la difusión de los instrumentos financieros disponibles que coadyuven al incremento de la inversión en el territorio de las Partes.

Sección B

Solución de Controversias entre una Parte y un Inversionista de otra Parte

Artículo 14-18
Objetivo.

Sin perjuicio de lo dispuesto en el capítulo XIX, esta sección establece un mecanismo para la solución de controversias en materia de inversión que se susciten, a partir de la entrada en vigor del presente tratado, y que asegura, tanto el trato igual entre inversionistas de las Partes de acuerdo con el principio de reciprocidad internacional, como el debido ejercicio de la garantía de audiencia y defensa dentro de un proceso legal ante un tribunal arbitral.

Artículo 14-19
Demanda del inversionista de una Parte, por cuenta propia o en representación de una empresa.

1.   e conformidad con esta sección, el inversionista de una Parte podrá, por cuenta propia o en representación de una empresa de otra Parte que sea de su propiedad o que esté bajo su control directo o indirecto, someter a arbitraje una demanda cuyo fundamento sea el que otra Parte o una empresa controlada directa o indirectamente por esa Parte, ha violado una obligación establecida en este capítulo, siempre y cuando el inversionista o su inversión hayan sufrido pérdidas o daños en virtud de la violación o como consecuencia de ella.

2.   El inversionista no podrá presentar una demanda conforme a esta sección, si han transcurrido más de tres años a partir de la fecha en la cual tuvo conocimiento o debió haber tenido conocimiento de la presunta violación cometida a su inversión, así como de las pérdidas o daños sufridos.

3.   Cuando un inversionista presente una demanda en representación de una empresa que sea de su propiedad o que esté bajo su control directo o indirecto, y de manera paralela un inversionista que no tenga el control de una empresa presente una demanda por cuenta propia como consecuencia de los mismos actos que dieron lugar a la presentación de una demanda de acuerdo con este artículo, y dos o más demandas se sometan a arbitraje en los términos del artículo 14-22, el tribunal de acumulación establecido de conformidad con el artículo 14-29, examinará conjuntamente dichas demandas, salvo que ese tribunal determine que los intereses de una parte contendiente se verían perjudicados.

4.   Una inversión no podrá someter una demanda a arbitraje conforme a esta sección.

Artículo 14-20
Solución de controversias mediante consultas y negociaciones.

Las partes contendientes primero intentarán dirimir la controversia por vía de consulta o negociación.

Artículo 14-21
Notificación de la intención de someter la demanda a arbitraje.

El inversionista contendiente notificará por escrito a la Parte contendiente su intención de someter una demanda a arbitraje, cuando menos 90 días antes que se presente formalmente la demanda. La notificación señalará lo siguiente:

a) el nombre y domicilio del inversionista contendiente y, cuando la demanda se haya presentado en representación de una empresa, la denominación o razón social y el domicilio de la misma;

b) los hechos en que se funde la demanda;

c) las disposiciones de este capítulo presuntamente incumplidas y cualquier otra disposición aplicable; y

d) la reparación que se solicite y el monto aproximado de los daños reclamados.

Artículo 14-22
Sometimiento de la demanda al arbitraje.

1. Salvo lo dispuesto en el párrafo 3 y siempre que hayan transcurrido seis meses desde que tuvieron lugar los actos que motivan la demanda, un inversionista contendiente podrá someter la demanda arbitraje de acuerdo con:

a) el Convenio del CIADI, siempre que tanto la Parte contendiente como la Parte del inversionista sean Estados parte del mismo;

b) Las Reglas del Mecanismo Complementario del CIADI, cuando la Parte contendiente o la Parte del inversionista, pero no ambas, sea parte del Convenio del CIADI; o

c) las Reglas de Arbitraje de la CNUDMI.

2. Las reglas de arbitraje elegidas, regirán el arbitraje, salvo en la medida de lo modificado por esta sección.

3. Cuando una empresa de una Parte que sea propiedad de un inversionista de otra Parte o que esté bajo su control directo o indirecto, en procedimientos ante un tribunal judicial o administrativo que resulte competente según la legislación de cada Parte, alegue que la primera Parte ha violado presuntamente una obligación a las que se refiere la sección A, el o los inversionistas no podrán alegar la presunta violación en un procedimiento arbitral conforme a esta sección.

Artículo 14-23
Condiciones previas al sometimiento de una demanda al procedimiento arbitral.

1. Un inversionista contendiente por cuenta propia podrá someter una demanda al procedimiento arbitral de conformidad con esta sección, sólo si:

a)   consiente someterse al arbitraje en los términos de los procedimientos establecidos en esta sección; y

b)   el inversionista y, cuando la reclamación se refiera a pérdida o daño en una participación en una empresa de la otra Parte que sea propiedad del inversionista o que esté bajo su control directo o indirecto, la empresa renuncian a su derecho a iniciar cualquier procedimiento ante un tribunal nacional competente conforme al derecho de la Parte contendiente u otros procedimientos de solución de controversias respecto a la medida de la Parte contendiente presuntamente violatoria de las disposiciones a las que se refiere el artículo 14-19, salvo los procedimientos en que se solicite la aplicación de medidas precautorias de carácter suspensivo, declarativo o extraordinario, que no impliquen el pago de daños ante el tribunal nacional competente, conforme a la legislación de la Parte contendiente, tales como el agotamiento de los recursos administrativos ante las propias autoridades ejecutoras de la medida presuntamente violatoria, previstos en la legislación de la Parte contendiente.

2.   Un inversionista contendiente, en representación de una empresa, podrá someter una reclamación al procedimiento arbitral de conformidad con esta sección, sólo si tanto el inversionista como la empresa:

a)   consienten en someterse al arbitraje en los términos de los procedimientos establecidos en esta sección; y

b)   renuncian a su derecho de iniciar cualquier procedimiento con respecto a la medida de la Parte contendiente que presuntamente sea una de las violaciones a las que se refiere el artículo 14-19 ante cualquier tribunal nacional competente conforme a la legislación o derecho de una Parte u otros procedimientos de solución de controversias, salvo los procedimientos en que se solicite la aplicación de medidas precautorias de carácter suspensivo, declarativo o extraordinario, que no impliquen el pago de daños ante el tribunal nacional competente, conforme a la legislación o derecho de la Parte contendiente, tales como el agotamiento de los recursos administrativos ante las propias autoridades ejecutoras de la medida presuntamente violatoria, previstos en la legislación de la Parte contendiente.

3.   El consentimiento y la renuncia requeridos por este artículo se manifestarán por escrito, se entregarán a la Parte contendiente y se incluirán en el sometimiento de la reclamación a arbitraje.

4.   Sólo en el caso que la Parte contendiente haya privado al inversionista contendiente del control de una empresa:

a)   no se requerirá la renuncia de la empresa conforme a los literales b) de los párrafos 1 ó 2; y

b)   no será aplicable el párrafo 3 del artículo 14-22.

Artículo 14-24
Consentimiento al arbitraje.

1.   Cada Parte consiente en someter demandas a arbitraje con apego a los procedimientos y requisitos señalados en esta sección.

2.   El sometimiento de una demanda a arbitraje por parte de un inversionista contendiente cumplirá con los requisitos señalados en:

a)   el Capítulo II del Convenio del CIADI (Jurisdicción del Centro) y las Reglas del Mecanismo Complementario que exigen el consentimiento por escrito de las Partes;

b)   el Artículo II de la Convención de Nueva York, que exige un acuerdo por escrito; o

c)   el Artículo I de la Convención Interamericana, que requiere un acuerdo.

Artículo 14-25
Número de árbitros y método de nombramiento.

Con excepción de lo dispuesto por el artículo 14-29, y sin perjuicio que las partes contendientes acuerden algo distinto, el tribunal estará integrado por tres árbitros. Cada una de las partes contendientes nombrará a un árbitro. El tercer árbitro, quien será el presidente del tribunal, será designado por las partes contendientes de común acuerdo.

Artículo 14-26

Integración del tribunal en caso que una parte contendiente no designe árbitro o no se logre un acuerdo en la designación del presidente del tribunal.

En caso que una parte contendiente no designe árbitro o no se logre un acuerdo en la designación del presidente del tribunal:

a)   el Secretario General nombrará a los árbitros en los procedimientos de arbitraje, de conformidad con esta sección;

b)   cuando un tribunal, que no sea el establecido de conformidad con el artículo 14-29, no se integre en un plazo de 90 días a partir de la fecha en que la demanda se someta a arbitraje, el Secretario General, a petición de cualquiera de las partes contendientes, nombrará, a su discreción, al árbitro o árbitros no designados todavía, pero no al presidente del tribunal, quién será designado conforme a lo dispuesto en el literal c);

c)   el Secretario General designará al presidente del tribunal de entre los árbitros de la lista a que se refiere el artículo 14-27, asegurándose que el presidente del tribunal no sea nacional de la Parte contendiente o nacional de la Parte del inversionista contendiente. En caso que no se encuentre en la lista un árbitro disponible para presidir el tribunal, el Secretario General designará, del panel de árbitros del

CIADI, al presidente del tribunal, siempre que sea de nacionalidad distinta a la de la Parte contendiente o a la de la Parte del inversionista contendiente.

Artículo 14-27
Lista de árbitros.

A la fecha de entrada en vigor de este tratado, las Partes establecerán y mantendrán una lista de 40 árbitros, como posibles presidentes del tribunal, o para nombrar los árbitros de un tribunal de acumulación, según el párrafo 4 del artículo 14-29, que reúnan las mismas cualidades a que se refiere el Convenio del CIADI, las Reglas del Mecanismo Complementario del CIADI o las Reglas de Arbitraje de la CNUDMI y que cuenten con experiencia en derecho internacional y en asuntos en materia de inversiones. Los miembros de la lista serán designados por consenso sin importar su nacionalidad.

Artículo 14-28
Consentimiento para la designación de árbitros.

Para efectos del Artículo 39 del Convenio del CIADI y del Artículo 7 de la Parte C de las Reglas del Mecanismo Complementario del CIADI, y sin perjuicio de objetar a un árbitro con fundamento en el literal c) del artículo 14-26, o sobre base distinta a la de nacionalidad:

a) la Parte contendiente acepta la designación de cada uno de los miembros de un tribunal establecido de conformidad con el Convenio del CIADI o con las Reglas del Mecanismo Complementario del CIADI; y

b) un inversionista contendiente, sea por cuenta propia o en representación de una empresa, podrá someter una demanda a arbitraje o continuar el procedimiento conforme al Convenio del CIADI, o a las Reglas del Mecanismo Complementario del CIADI, únicamente a condición de que el inversionista contendiente y, en su caso, la empresa que representa, manifiesten su consentimiento por escrito sobre la designación de cada uno de los miembros del tribunal.

Artículo 14-29
Acumulación de procedimientos.

1. Un tribunal de acumulación establecido conforme a este artículo se instalará con apego a las Reglas de Arbitraje de la CNUDMI y procederá de conformidad con lo establecido en dichas reglas, salvo lo que disponga esta sección.

2. Cuando un tribunal de acumulación determine que las demandas sometidas a arbitraje de acuerdo con el artículo 14-22, plantean cuestiones de hecho y derecho en común, el tribunal de acumulación, en interés de su resolución justa y eficiente, y habiendo escuchado a las partes contendientes, podrá asumir jurisdicción, dar trámite y resolver:

a) todas o parte de las demandas, de manera conjunta; o

b) una o más de las demandas en el entendido que ello contribuirá a la resolución de las otras.

3.   Una parte contendiente que pretenda obtener una orden de acumulación en los términos del párrafo 2, solicitará al Secretario General que instale un tribunal de acumulación y especificará en su solicitud:

    a)   el nombre de la Parte contendiente o de los inversionistas contendientes contra los cuales se pretenda obtener la orden de acumulación;

    b)   la naturaleza de la orden de acumulación solicitada; y

    c)   el fundamento en que se apoya la solicitud.

4.   En un plazo de 60 días contado a partir de la fecha de la recepción de la solicitud, el Secretario General instalará un tribunal de acumulación integrado por tres árbitros. El Secretario General nombrará de la lista de árbitros a que se refiere el artículo 14-27, al presidente del tribunal de acumulación, quien no será nacional de la Parte contendiente ni nacional de la Parte del inversionista contendiente. En caso que no se encuentre en la lista un árbitro disponible para presidir el tribunal de acumulación, el Secretario General designará, del panel de árbitros del CIADI, al presidente de dicho tribunal, quien no será nacional de la Parte contendiente ni nacional de la Parte del inversionista contendiente. El Secretario General designará a los otros dos integrantes del tribunal de acumulación de la lista de árbitros que se refiere el artículo 14-27 y, cuando no estén disponibles en dicha lista, los seleccionará del panel de árbitros del CIADI. De no haber disponibilidad de árbitros en ese panel, el Secretario General hará discrecionalmente los nombramientos faltantes. Uno de los miembros será nacional de la Parte contendiente y el otro miembro del tribunal de acumulación será nacional de una Parte de los inversionistas contendientes.

5.   Cuando se haya establecido un tribunal de acumulación conforme a este artículo, el inversionista contendiente que haya sometido una demanda a arbitraje conforme al artículo 14-19, y no haya sido mencionado en la solicitud de acumulación hecha de acuerdo con el párrafo 3, podrá solicitar por escrito al tribunal de acumulación que se le incluya en una orden de acumulación formulada de acuerdo con el párrafo 2, y especificará en dicha solicitud:

    a)   el nombre y domicilio del inversionista contendiente y, en su caso, la denominación o razón social y el domicilio de la empresa;

    b)   la naturaleza de la orden de acumulación solicitada; y

    c)   los fundamentos en que se apoya la solicitud.

6.   El tribunal de acumulación proporcionará, a costa del inversionista interesado, copia de la petición de acumulación a los inversionistas contendientes que quedarían sujetos a la resolución de acumulación.

7.   Un tribunal no tendrá jurisdicción para resolver una demanda, o parte de ella, respecto de la cual haya asumido jurisdicción un tribunal de acumulación. 8. A solicitud de una parte contendiente, un tribunal de acumulación podrá, en espera de su decisión conforme al párrafo 2, disponer que los procedimientos de un tribunal se suspendan, hasta en tanto se resuelva sobre la procedencia de la acumulación. Lo ordenado por el tribunal de acumulación deberá ser acatado por el tribunal.

Artículo 14-30
Notificaciones.

1.   Dentro del plazo de 15 días contado a partir de la fecha de su recepción, la Parte contendiente hará llegar al Secretariado una copia de:

a)   una solicitud de arbitraje hecha de conformidad con el párrafo 1 del Artículo 36 del Convenio del CIADI;

b)   una notificación de arbitraje en los términos del Artículo 2 de la Parte C de las Reglas del Mecanismo Complementario del CIADI; o

c)   una notificación de arbitraje en los términos previstos por las Reglas de Arbitraje de la CNUDMI.

2.   La Parte contendiente entregará al Secretariado copia de la solicitud formulada en lostérminos del párrafo 3 del artículo 14-29:

a)   en un plazo de 15 días contado a partir de la recepción de la solicitud, en el caso de una petición hecha por el inversionista contendiente; o

b)   en un plazo de 15 días contado a partir de la fecha de la solicitud, en el caso de una petición hecha por la Parte contendiente.

3.   La Parte contendiente entregará al Secretariado copia de una solicitud formulada en los términos del párrafo 5 del artículo 14-29 en un plazo de 15 días contado a partir de la fecha de recepción de la solicitud.

4.   El Secretariado conservará un registro público de los documentos a los que se refieren los párrafos 1, 2 y 3.

5.   La Parte contendiente entregará a las otras Partes:

a)   notificación escrita de una demanda que se haya sometido a arbitraje a más tardar 30 días después de la fecha de sometimiento de la demanda a arbitraje; y

b)   copias de todos los escritos presentados en el procedimiento arbitral.

Artículo 14-31
Participación de una Parte.

Previa notificación escrita a las partes contendientes, una Parte podrá presentar escritos a un tribunal establecido conforme a esta sección, sobre cuestiones de interpretación de este tratado, que se estén discutiendo ante dicho tribunal.

Artículo 14-32
Documentación.

1.   Una Parte tendrá, a su costa, derecho a recibir de una parte contendiente una copia de:

a)   las pruebas ofrecidas a un tribunal establecido conforme a esta sección, y

b)   los argumentos escritos presentados por las partes contendientes.

2.   Una Parte que reciba información conforme a lo dispuesto en el párrafo 1, dará tratamiento a dicha información como si fuera una Parte contendiente.

Artículo 14-33
Sede del procedimiento arbitral.

Salvo que las partes contendientes acuerden otra cosa, un tribunal establecido conforme a esta sección, llevará a cabo el procedimiento arbitral en el territorio de una Parte que sea miembro de la Convención de Nueva York, el cual será elegido de conformidad con:

a)   las Reglas del Mecanismo Complementario del CIADI, si el arbitraje se rige por esas reglas o por el Convenio del CIADI; o

b)   las Reglas de Arbitraje de la CNUDMI, si el arbitraje se rige por esas reglas.

Artículo 14-34
Derecho aplicable.

1.   Un tribunal establecido conforme a esta sección, decidirá las controversias que se sometan a su consideración de conformidad con este tratado y con las disposiciones aplicables del derecho internacional.

2.   La interpretación que formule la Comisión sobre una disposición de este tratado, será obligatoria para un tribunal establecido conforme a esta sección.

Artículo 14-35
Interpretación de los anexos.

1.   Cuando una Parte alegue como defensa que una medida presuntamente violatoria cae en el ámbito de una reserva o excepción consignada en cualquiera de los anexos, a petición de la Parte contendiente, un tribunal establecido conforme a esta sección, solicitará a la Comisión una interpretación sobre ese asunto. La Comisión, en un plazo de 60 días contado a partir de la entrega de la solicitud, presentará por escrito a dicho tribunal su interpretación.

2.   La interpretación de la Comisión sometida conforme al párrafo 1 será obligatoria para un tribunal establecido conforme a esta sección. Si la Comisión no somete una interpretación dentro de un plazo de 60 días, dicho tribunal decidirá sobre el asunto.

Artículo 14-36
Dictámenes de expertos.

Sin perjuicio de la designación de otro tipo de expertos cuando lo autoricen las reglas de arbitraje aplicables, el tribunal establecido conforme a esta sección, a petición de una parte contendiente, o por iniciativa propia a menos que las partes contendientes no lo acepten, podrá designar uno o másexpertos para dictaminar por escrito cualquier cuestión que haya planteado una parte contendiente en un procedimiento, de acuerdo a los términos y condiciones que acuerden las partes contendientes.

Artículo 14-37
Medidas provisionales o precautorias.

Un tribunal establecido conforme a esta sección, podrá solicitar a los tribunales nacionales, o dictar a las partes contendientes, medidas provisionales o precautorias para preservar los derechos de la parte contendiente o para asegurar que la jurisdicción del tribunal establecido conforme a esta sección, surta plenos efectos. Ese tribunal no podrá ordenar el acatamiento o la suspensión de la medida presuntamente violatoria a que se refiere el artículo 14-19.

Artículo 14-38
Laudo definitivo.

1.   Cuando un tribunal establecido conforme a esta sección, dicte un laudo definitivo desfavorable a una Parte, dicho tribunal sólo podrá ordenar:

  a)   el pago de daños pecuniarios y los intereses correspondientes; o

  b)   la restitución de la propiedad, en cuyo caso el laudo dispondrá que la Parte contendiente pueda pagar daños pecuniarios, más los intereses que procedan, en lugar de la restitución.

2.   Un tribunal establecido conforme a esta sección, podrá también ordenar el pago de costas de acuerdo con las reglas de arbitraje aplicables.

3.   Cuando la demanda la haga un inversionista en representación de una empresa con base en el artículo 14-19:

  a)   el laudo que prevea la restitución de la propiedad dispondrá que se otorgue a la empresa; y

  b)   . el laudo que conceda daños pecuniarios e intereses correspondientes dispondrá que la suma de dinero se pague a la empresa.

4.   Un tribunal establecido conforme a esta sección, no podrá ordenar que una Parte pague daños de carácter punitivo.

5.   El laudo se dictará sin perjuicio de los derechos que cualquier persona con interés jurídico tenga sobre la reparación de los daños que haya sufrido, de conformidad con la legislación aplicable.

Artículo 14-39
Definitividad y ejecución del laudo.

1.   El laudo dictado por un tribunal establecido conforme a esta sección, será obligatorio sólo para las partes contendientes y únicamente respecto del caso concreto.

2.   De conformidad con lo dispuesto en el párrafo 3 y al procedimiento de revisión aplicable a un laudo provisional, una parte contendiente acatará y cumplirá con el laudo sin demora.

3.   Una parte contendiente podrá solicitar la ejecución de un laudo definitivo siempre que:

   a)   en el caso de un laudo definitivo dictado conforme al Convenio del CIADI:

      i)   hayan transcurrido 120 días desde la fecha en que se dictó el laudo sin que alguna parte contendiente haya solicitado la aclaración, revisión o anulación del mismo; o

      ii)   hayan concluido los procedimientos de aclaración, revisión y anulación; o

   b)   en el caso de un laudo definitivo conforme a las Reglas del Mecanismo Complementario del CIADI o a las Reglas de arbitraje de la CNUDMI:

      i)   hayan transcurrido 90 días desde la fecha en que se dictó el laudo sin que alguna parte contendiente haya iniciado un procedimiento de interpretación, rectificación, laudo adicional o anulación; o

      ii)   hayan concluido los procedimientos de interpretación, rectificación o laudo adicional, o haya sido resuelta por un tribunal judicial de la Parte contendiente una solicitud de anulación y esta resolución no sea susceptible de ser impugnada.

4.   Cada Parte dispondrá la debida ejecución de un laudo en su territorio.

5.   Cuando una Parte contendiente incumpla o no acate un laudo definitivo, la Comisión, a la recepción de una solicitud de una Parte cuyo inversionista fue parte en el procedimiento de arbitraje, integrará un tribunal arbitral conforme al capítulo XIX. La Parte solicitante podrá invocar dichos procedimientos para obtener:

   a)   una determinación en el sentido que el incumplimiento o desacato de los términos del laudo definitivo es contrario a las obligaciones de este tratado; y

   b)   una recomendación en el sentido que la Parte cumpla y acate el laudo definitivo.

6.   El inversionista contendiente podrá recurrir a la ejecución de un laudo arbitral conforme al Convenio del CIADI, la Convención de Nueva York o la Convención Interamericana, independientemente que se hayan iniciado o no los procedimientos contemplados en el párrafo 5.

7.   Para efectos del Artículo I de la Convención de Nueva York y del Artículo I de la Convención Interamericana, se considerará que la demanda que se somete a arbitraje conforme a esta sección, surge de una relación u operación comercial.

Artículo 14-40
Disposiciones generales.

Momento en que la demanda se considera sometida a arbitraje

1.   Una demanda se considera sometida a arbitraje en los términos de esta sección cuando:

a) la solicitud para un arbitraje conforme al párrafo 1 del Artículo 36 del Convenio del CIADI ha sido recibida por el Secretario General;

b) la notificación de arbitraje, de conformidad con el Artículo 2 de la Parte C de las Reglas del Mecanismo Complementario del CIADI, ha sido recibida por el Secretario General; o

c) la notificación de arbitraje contemplada en las Reglas de Arbitraje de la CNUDMI, se ha recibido por la Parte contendiente.

Entrega de documentos

2. La entrega de la notificación y otros documentos a una Parte se hará en el lugar designado por ella, de conformidad con el anexo 14-40 (2).

Pagos conforme a contratos de seguro o garantía

3. En un procedimiento arbitral solicitado de conformidad con lo dispuesto en esta sección, una Parte no aducirá como defensa, contrademanda, derecho de compensación, u otros, que el inversionista contendiente recibió o recibirá, de acuerdo con un contrato de seguro o garantía, indemnización u otra compensación por todos o parte de los presuntos daños cuya restitución solicite.

Publicación de laudos

4. La publicación de laudos se realizará de conformidad con lo establecido en las reglas de procedimiento.

Artículo 14-41
Exclusiones.

Las disposiciones de solución de controversias de esta sección, y las del capítulo XIX no se aplicarán a las resoluciones que adopte una Parte en virtud del párrafo 2, literal c) del artículo 14-02, ni a los supuestos contenidos en el anexo 14-41.

Artículo 14-42
Subrogación.

En caso que una Parte o la entidad por ella designada haya otorgado cualquier garantía financiera sobre riesgos no comerciales en relación con una inversión efectuada por sus inversionistas en el territorio de otra Parte y desde el momento en que la primera Parte o su entidad designada haya realizado pago alguno con cargo a la garantía concedida, dicha Parte o la entidad designada será beneficiaria directa de todo tipo de pagos a los que pudiese ser acreedor el inversionista. En caso de controversia, únicamente el inversionista podrá iniciar o participar en los procedimientos ante un tribunal establecido conforme a esta sección.

Artículo 14-41
Exclusiones.

Las disposiciones de solución de controversias de esta sección, y las del capítulo XIX no se aplicarán a las resoluciones que adopte una Parte en virtud del párrafo 2, literal c) del artículo 14-02, ni a los supuestos contenidos en el anexo 14-41.

Artículo 14-42
Subrogación.

En caso que una Parte o la entidad por ella designada haya otorgado cualquier garantía financiera sobre riesgos no comerciales en relación con una inversión efectuada por sus inversionistas en el territorio de otra Parte y desde el momento en que la primera Parte o su entidad designada haya realizado pago alguno con cargo a la garantía concedida, dicha Parte o la entidad designada será beneficiaria directa de todo tipo de pagos a los que pudiese ser acreedor el inversionista. En caso de controversia, únicamente el inversionista podrá iniciar o participar en los procedimientos ante un tribunal establecido conforme a esta sección.

Anexo 14-11
Utilidad Pública.

Para efectos del literal a) del párrafo 1 del artículo 14-11 se entienden comprendidos en el término de utilidad pública:

a)   para el caso de El Salvador: utilidad pública o interés social;

b)   para el caso de Guatemala: utilidad colectiva, beneficio social o interés público;

c)   para el caso de Honduras: necesidad o interés público; y

d)   para el caso de México: utilidad pública.

Anexo 14-40(2)
Entrega de Notificaciones y otros Documentos.

1.   Para efectos del artículo 14-40 (2), el lugar para la entrega de notificaciones y otros documentos será:

a)   para el caso de El Salvador:

Dirección de Política Comercial, Ministerio de Economía Alameda Juan Pablo II, Calle Guadalupe, Edificio C-2, Planta 3, Centro de Gobierno San Salvador, El Salvador

b)   para el caso de Guatemala:

Ministerio de Economía 8ª. Avenida 10-43 zona 1 Guatemala, Guatemala

c)   ara el caso de Honduras:

Dirección General de Integración Económica y Política Comercial, Secretaría de Estado en los Despachos de Industria y Comercio Avenida Jeréz, Edificio Larach, Piso 10 Tegucigalpa, M.D.C., Honduras

d) para el caso de México:
Dirección General de Inversión Extranjera, Secretaría de Comercio y Fomento Industrial Insurgentes Sur 1940, Piso 8, Colonia Florida, C.P. 01030 México, D.F.

2. Las Partes comunicarán cualquier cambio del lugar designado para la entrega de notificaciones y otros documentos.

Anexo 14-41
Exclusiones

No estarán sujetas a los mecanismos de solución de controversias dispuestos en la sección B o el capítulo XIX:

a) para el caso de Honduras: las resoluciones que adopte la Secretaría de Estado en los Despachos de Industria y Comercio en aplicación de los artículos 11 y 18 de la Ley de Inversión Extranjera referente a la salud, la seguridad nacional y la preservación del ambiente.

b) para el caso de México, las resoluciones que adopte la Comisión Nacional de Inversiones Extranjeras que prohiban o restrinjan la adquisición de una inversión en el territorio de los Estados Unidos Mexicanos que sea propiedad o esté controlada por sus nacionales, o por parte de uno o más inversionistas de otra Parte, así como las resoluciones relativas a las disposiciones del Anexo I, página I-M-F-4.

ANNEXOS

RESERVAS DE SERVICIOS E INVERSIÓN

Anexo I

1. Para los efectos de este Anexo se entenderá por:

carga internacional para las reservas de México, los bienes que tienen su origen o destino fuera del territorio de una Parte;

cláusula de exclusión de extranjeros para las reservas de México, la disposición expresa en los estatutos internos de una empresa, que establece que no se permitirá a extranjeros, de manera directa o indirecta, ser socios o poseer acciones de la sociedad;

CMAP los dígitos de la Clasificación Mexicana de Actividades y Productos, tal como están establecidos en la Clasificación Mexicana de Actividades y Productos, 1988 del Instituto Nacional de Estadística, Geografía e Informática;

concesión para las reservas de México, una autorización otorgada por el Estado a una persona para explotar recursos naturales o prestar un servicio, para lo cual, los mexicanos y las empresas mexicanas serán preferidos sobre los extranjeros;

CPC los dígitos de la Clasificación Central de Productos (CPC), tal como han sido establecidos por la Oficina de Estadísticas de las Naciones Unidas, Documentos Estadísticos, Series M, No. 77, Provisional Central Product Classification, 1991; y

empresa mexicana para las Reservas de México, una empresa constituida conforme a las leyes mexicanas.

2.   La Lista de una Parte indica, de conformidad con los artículos 10-06 (1) y 14-09 (1), las reservas tomadas por una Parte con relación a medidas vigentes que sean disconformes con las obligaciones impuestas por:

   a)   los Artículos 10-04 ó 14-04 "Trato nacional";

   b)   los Artículos 10-03 ó 14-05 "Trato de nación más favorecida";

   c)   el Artículo 10-05 "Presencia local";

   d)   el Artículo 14-07 "Requisitos de desempeño"; o

   e)   el Artículo 14-08 "Alta dirección empresarial y consejos de administración", y que, en ciertos casos, indican compromisos de liberalización inmediata o futura.

3.   Cada reserva establece los siguientes elementos:

   a)   Sector se refiere al sector en general en el que se ha tomado la reserva;

   b)   Subsector se refiere al sector específico en el que se ha tomado la reserva;

   c)   Clasificación Industrial se refiere, cuando sea pertinente, a la actividad que abarca la reserva, de acuerdo con los códigos nacionales de clasificación industrial.

La Clasificación Central de Productos (CPC) tiene un carácter meramente ilustrativo;

   d)   Tipo de Reserva especifica la obligación mencionada en el párrafo 2 sobre la cual se toma una reserva;

   e)   Nivel de Gobierno indica el nivel de gobierno que mantiene la medida sobre la cual se toma la reserva;

   f)   Medidas identifica las leyes, reglamentos u otras medidas, tal como se califica, donde ello se indica, con el elemento Descripción, respecto de las cuales se ha tomado la reserva. Una medida mencionada en el elemento Medidas:

      i)   significa la medida, modificada, continuada o renovada, a partir de la fecha de entrada en vigor de este tratado, e

      ii)   incluye cualquier medida subordinada, adoptada o mantenida bajo la facultad de dicha medida y consecuente con ella;

g)   Descripción establece los compromisos de liberalización, cuando éstos se hayan tomado, a partir de la fecha de entrada en vigor de este tratado, y los aspectos disconformes restantes de las medidas vigentes sobre los que la reserva es tomada; y

h)   Calendario de Reducción indica los compromisos de liberalización, cuando éstos se hayan tomado, después de la fecha de entrada en vigor de este tratado.

4.   En la interpretación de una reserva, todos los elementos de la reserva serán considerados. Una reserva será interpretada a la luz de las disposiciones pertinentes del capítulo contra el que la reserva es tomada. En la medida que:

a)   el elemento Calendario de Reducción establezca una reducción gradual de los aspectos disconformes de las medidas, este elemento prevalecerá sobre todos los otros elementos;

b)   el elemento Medidas esté calificado por un compromiso de liberalización en el elemento Descripción, el elemento Medidas, tal como se califica, prevalecerá sobre todos los otros elementos; y

c)   el elemento Medidas no esté así calificado, el elemento Medidas prevalecerá sobre todos los demás elementos, a menos que alguna discrepancia entre el elemento Medidas y los otros elementos, considerados en su totalidad, sea tan sustancial y significativa, que no sería razonable concluir que el elemento Medidas deba prevalecer; en este caso, los otros elementos prevalecerán en la medida de esa discrepancia.

5.   Cuando una Parte mantenga una medida que exija al prestador de un servicio ser nacional, residente permanente o residente en su territorio como condición para la prestación de un servicio en su territorio, al tomarse una reserva sobre una medida con relación a los Artículos 10-03, 10-04 ó 10-05, o los Artículos 11-05, 11-06 u 11-07, operará como una reserva con relación a los artículos 14-04, 14-05 ó 14-07 en lo que respecta a tal medida.

6.   No obstante lo dispuesto en el artículo 14-09 1 (a), (b) y (c), exclusivamente los artículos 14-04, 14-07 ó 14-08, no se aplicarán a las actividades listadas por El Salvador en la Sección "B" de su lista de reservas contenida en este Anexo, durante los plazos establecidos en las reservas respectivas.

Transcurridos los plazos de referencia, las medidas vigentes que mantenga El Salvador en las actividades listadas, que sean incompatibles con los artículos 14-04, 14-07 ó 14-08 deberán serconsolidadas en la Sección "A" de su lista de reservas contenida en este Anexo, y deberán de ser notificadas por El Salvador en la primera reunión del Comité de Comecio Transfronterizo de Servicios e Inversión, que se celebre con posterioridad al vencimiento del plazo establecido en la reserva que corresponda.

El Salvador no podrá exigir, de conformidad con cualquier medida adoptada después de la entrada en vigor de este tratado y comprendida en la sección "B" de la lista de El Salvador, a un inversionista de México que venda o disponga de alguna otra manera de una inversión existente al momento en que la medida cobre vigencia.

6 bis. Cada reserva de la Sección "B" de la lista de reservas de El Salvador contenida en este Anexo establece los siguientes elementos:

a)　　Sector se refiere al sector en general en el que se ha tomado la reserva;

b)　　Subsector se refiere al sector específico en el que se ha tomado la reserva;

c)　　Clasificación Industrial se refiere, cuando sea pertinente a la actividad que abarca la reserva, de acuerdo con los códigos nacionales de clasificación industrial. Para los propósitos de la Sección "B" de la Lista de El Salvador, se entenderá por CPC, los dígitos de la Clasificación Central de Productos, tal como han sido establecidos por la Oficina de Estadísticas de las Naciones Unidas, documentos estadísticos, Series M, No. 77, Provisional Central Product Classification, 1991.

d)　　Tipo de Reserva especifica la obligación mencionada en el párrafo 6 sobre la cual se toma una reserva;

e)　　Nivel de Gobierno indica el nivel de gobierno que mantiene la medida sobre la cual se toma la reserva;

f)　　Medidas Vigentes identifica, con propósitos de transparencia las medidas vigentes que se aplican al sector, subsector o actividades cubiertas por la reserva, y que podrán ser modificadas en el plazo señalado en cada una de las reservas;

g)　　Descripción describe la cobertura del sector, subsector o actividades cubiertas por la reserva; y

h)　　Plazo establece el período, a partir de la entrada en vigor de este tratado, en el que no aplicarán los artículos reservados a las actividades listadas;

En la interpretación de las reservas contenidas en la Sección "B" de la lista de reservas de El Salvador contenida en este Anexo, todos los elementos serán considerados. El elemento Plazo en primer lugar y, el elemento Descripción en segundo lugar, prevalecerán sobre los demás elementos.

Anexo II

1.　　Para los efectos de este Anexo se entenderá por:

CMAP los dígitos de la Clasificación Mexicana de Actividades y Productos (CMAP), establecidos en la Clasificación Mexicana de Actividades y Productos, 1988, del Instituto Nacional de Estadística, Geografía e Informática; y CPC los dígitos de la Clasificación Central de Productos (CPC), tal como han sido establecidos por la Oficina de Estadísticas de las Naciones Unidas, Documentos Estadísticos, Series M, No. 77, Provisional Central Product Classification, 1991.

2.   La Lista de cada Parte indica las reservas tomadas por esa Parte, de conformidad con el artículo 10-06 (3) con respecto a sectores, subsectores o actividades específicas para los cuales podrá mantener o adoptar medidas nuevas o más restrictivas que sean disconformes con las obligaciones impuestas por:

    a)   el Artículo 10-03 "Trato de nación más favorecida";

    b)   el Artículo 10-04 "Trato nacional"; o

    c)   el Artículo 10-05 "Presencia local".

3.   Cada reserva contiene los siguientes elementos:

    a)   Sector se refiere al sector en general en el que se ha tomado la reserva;

    b)   Subsector se refiere al sector específico en el que se ha tomado la reserva;

    c)   Clasificación Industrial se refiere, cuando sea pertinente, a la actividad que abarca la reserva, de acuerdo con los códigos de clasificación industrial;

    d)   Tipo de Reserva especifica la obligación de entre aquellas mencionadas en el párrafo 2 sobre la cual se ha tomado la reserva;

    e)   Descripción describe la cobertura del sector, subsector o actividades cubiertas por la reserva; y

    f)   Medidas Vigentes identifica, con propósitos de transparencia, las medidas vigentes que se aplican al sector, subsector o actividades cubiertas por la reserva.

4.   En la interpretación de una reserva todos sus elementos serán considerados. El elemento Descripción prevalecerá sobre los demás elementos.

Anexo III

1.   Las actividades establecidas en la Sección A están reservadas a las Partes y la inversión de capital privado está prohibida bajo la legislación de las Partes. Si una Parte permite la participación de inversiones privadas en tales actividades a través de contratos de servicios, concesiones, préstamos o cualquier otro tipo de actos contractuales, no podrá interpretarse que a través de dicha participación se afecta la reserva de la Parte en esas actividades.

2.   Si la legislación de las Partes se reforma para permitir la inversión de capital privado en las actividades señaladas en la Sección A, las Partes podrán imponer restricciones a la participación de la inversión extranjera no obstante lo indicado por el Artículo 14-04 (Trato nacional) debiendo indicarlas en el Anexo I (Medidas disconformes existentes y compromisos de liberalización). Las Partes también podrán imponer excepciones al artículo 14-04 con respecto a la participación de la inversión extranjera en el caso de la venta de activos o de la participación en el capital de una empresa involucrada en las actividades señaladas en la Sección A, debiendo indicarlas en el Anexo I.

3.	Las medidas referidas están incluidas para efectos de transparencia e incluyen cualquier medida subordinada, adoptada o mantenida bajo la autoridad de y consistente con tales medidas.

ANEXO I
LISTA DE GUATEMALA

Sector:	Todos los sectores
Subsector:	
Clasificación Industrial:	
Tipo de Reserva:	Trato nacional (Artículo 14-04)
Nivel de Gobierno:	Nacional
Medidas:	Decreto No. 118-96 que reforma los Decretos No. 38-71 y 48-72, Artículos 1 y 2
Descripción:	Inversión Solamente podrán ser beneficiarios de tierras nacionales, en el Departamento del Petén, por medio de adjudicación en propiedad, arrendamiento o usufructo, los guatemaltecos de origen, que no sean propietarios de bienes inmuebles rústicos en cualquier parte del territorio nacional mayores de 45 hectáreas y/o de empresas de carácter industrial, minero o comercial que les permitan los medios necesarios para su propia subsistencia y la de sus familias. También pueden ser beneficiarias de adjudicación de tierras en el Departamento del Petén, las personas jurídicas cuyo capital social pertenezca en un 100% a personas que reúnan los requisitos enumerados en el párrafo anterior.
Calendario de Reducción:	Ninguno

Sector:	Todos los sectores
Subsector:	
Clasificación Industrial:	
Tipo de Reserva:	Trato nacional (Artículo 14-04)
Nivel de Gobierno:	Nacional
Medidas:	Ley de Titulación Supletoria, Decreto 49-79, Artículo 2
Descripción:	Inversión Sólo los guatemaltecos naturales pueden obtener titulación supletoria de bienes inmuebles; si se tratare de personas jurídicas, éstas deberán estar integradas mayoritaria o totalmente por guatemaltecos, circunstancia que deberá probarse fehacientemente al formular la solicitud respectiva.
Calendario de Reducción:	Ninguno

Sector:	Todos los sectores
Subsector:	
Clasificación Industrial:	
Tipo de Reserva:	Trato nacional (Artículo 14-04)
Nivel de Gobierno:	Nacional
Medidas:	Constitución Política de la República de Guatemala, Artículo 122
Descripción:	Inversión Los extranjeros necesitan autorización del Ejecutivo, para adquirir en propiedad, inmuebles situados en zonas urbanas y los bienes sobre los que existen derechos inscritos en el Registro General de la Propiedad.

<table>
<tr><td colspan="2">con anterioridad al 1° de marzo de 1956, ubicados en:

a) Una faja terrestre de tres kilómetros a lo largo de los océanos;

b) 200 metros alrededor de las orillas de los lagos;

c) 100 metros a cada lado de las riberas de los ríos navegables; y

d) 50 metros alrededor de las fuentes y manantiales donde nazcan aguas que surtan a las poblaciones.</td></tr>
<tr><td>**Calendario de Reducción:**</td><td>Ninguno</td></tr>
</table>

Sector:	Todos los sectores
Subsector:	
Clasificación Industrial:	
Tipo de Reserva:	Trato nacional (Artículo 14-04)
Nivel de Gobierno:	Nacional
Medidas:	Constitución Política de la República de Guatemala, Artículo 123 Ley Reguladora de las Areas de Reservas Territoriales del Estado de Guatemala, Decreto 126-97, Artículo 5
Descripción:	Inversión Sólo los guatemaltecos de origen, o las sociedades cuyos socios tengan la misma calidad, podrán ser propietarios o poseedores de inmuebles situados en la faja de 15 kilómetros de ancho a lo largo de las fronteras, medidos desde la línea divisoria. Se exceptúan los bienes urbanos y los derechos inscritos con anterioridad al 1° de marzo de 1956. El Estado podrá dar en arrendamiento inmuebles ubicados dentro de las áreas de reserva territorial del Estado a personas naturales o jurídicas; para el caso de las últimas que se encuentren legalmente constituidas en Guatemala.
Calendario de reducción:	Ninguno

Sector:	Todos los sectores
Subsector:	
Clasificación Industrial:	
Tipo de Reserva:	Trato nacional (Artículo 14-04)
Nivel de Gobierno:	Nacional
Medidas:	Código de Comercio, Decreto 2-70 y sus reformas, contenidas en el Decreto 62-95, Artículo 215
Descripción:	Inversión Para que una sociedad legalmente constituida con arreglo a las leyes extranjeras (sociedad extranjera), pueda establecerse en el país o tener en él sucursales o agencias, deberá constituir un capital asignado para sus operaciones en la República y una fianza a favor de terceros por una cantidad razonable, no menor al equivalente en quetzales de 50 mil dólares de los Estados Unidos de América, que fijará el Registro Mercantil, que deberá permanecer vigente durante todo el tiempo que dicha sociedad opere en el país.
Calendario de Reducción:	Ninguno

Sector:	Forestal
Subsector:	
Clasificación Industrial:	CPC. 31 Extracción de madera CPC. 88140 Servicios relacionados con la agricultura y la extracción de

	madera
Tipo de Reserva:	Trato nacional (Artículo 14-04)
Nivel de Gobierno:	Nacional
Medidas:	Constitución Política de la República de Guatemala, Artículo 126
Descripción:	Inversión La explotación de todos los recursos forestales y su renovación, corresponderá exclusivamente a personas guatemaltecas, individuales o jurídicas.
Calendario de Reducción:	Ninguno

Sector:	Servicios a las empresas
Subsector:	Servicios profesionales
Clasificación Industrial:	CPC. 861 Servicios jurídicos (aplica únicamente a Notarios)
Tipo de Reserva:	Trato nacional (Artículo 10-04) Presencia local (Artículo 10-05)
Nivel de Gobierno:	Nacional
Medidas:	Código de Notariado, Decreto 314, Art. 2
Descripción:	Servicios transfronterizos Para ejercer el Notariado se requiere ser guatemalteco natural, domiciliado en la República y haber obtenido el título facultativo en la República o la incorporación con arreglo a la ley.
Calendario de Reducción:	Ninguno

Sector:	Servicios a las empresas
Subsector:	Servicios profesionales
Clasificación Industrial:	
Tipo de Reserva:	Trato nacional (Artículo 10-04 y 14-04) Presencia local (Artículo 10-05)
Nivel de Gobierno:	Nacional
Medidas:	Código de Comercio Decreto 2-70, Artículo 213
Descripción:	Servicios transfronterizos e Inversión Queda prohibido el funcionamiento de sociedades extranjeras que se dediquen a la prestación de servicios profesionales, para cuyo ejercicio se requiere grado, título o diploma universitarios legalmente reconocidos. Se entiende como sociedad extranjera la constituida en el extranjero.
Calendario de Reducción:	Ninguno

Sector:	Servicios a las empresas
Subsector:	Servicios profesionales (únicamente agentes aduaneros)
Clasificación Industrial:	
Tipo de Reserva:	Trato de nación más favorecida (Artículo 10-03) Trato nacional (Artículo 10-04) Presencia local (Artículo 10-05)
Nivel de Gobierno:	Nacional
Medidas:	Decreto Ley 169, Protocolo al Tratado General de Integración Económica Centroamericana que contiene el Código Aduanero Uniforme Centroamericano (CAUCA), publicado el 10 de abril de 1964 (Países miembros: Guatemala, El Salvador, Honduras, Nicaragua y Costa Rica)
Descripción:	Servicios transfronterizos La persona natural que tenga interés en que se le autorice como agente aduanero deberá tener la nacionalidad de alguno de los Estados signatarios del CAUCA y tener su domicilio en el país donde realice su actividad.

	Las personas jurídicas que tengan interés en que se les autorice como agencia aduanal deberán tener su domicilio en el país donde realice su actividad.
Calendario de Reducción:	Ninguno

Sector:	
Subsector:	Servicios profesionales
Clasificación Industrial:	
Tipo de Reserva:	Trato de nación más favorecida (Artículo10-03)
Nivel de Gobierno:	Nacional
Medidas:	Constitución Política de la República de Guatemala, Artículo 87 Estatutos de la Universidad de San Carlos de Guatemala, Artículos 135 y 136
Descripción:	Servicios transfronterizos Los títulos otorgados por universidades centroamericanas tendrán plena validez en Guatemala al lograrse la unificación básica de los planes de estudio. Solamente podrán ejercer en Guatemala profesiones liberales, los titulados o incorporados en la Universidad de San Carlos de Guatemala y quienes se encuentren amparados por los tratados internacionales aceptados por Guatemala, siempre que haya reciprocidad.
Calendario de Reducción:	Ninguno

Sector:	Servicios a las empresas
Subsector:	Servicios profesionales
Clasificación Industrial:	
Tipo de Reserva:	Trato de nación más favorecida (Artículo 10-03) Presencia local (Artículo 10-05)
Nivel de Gobierno:	Nacional
Medidas:	Convenio sobre el Ejercicio de Profesiones Universitarias y Reconocimiento de Estudios Universitarios, vigente desde el 7 de julio de 1962. (países miembros: Guatemala, El Salvador, Honduras y Costa Rica) Artículos: 1, 3, 4, 6, 9 y 10
Descripción:	Servicios transfronterizos El centroamericano por nacimiento que haya obtenido en alguno de los Estados parte del Convenio sobre el Ejercicio de Profesiones Universitarias y Reconocimiento de Estudios Universitarios, un título profesional o diploma académico equivalente, que lo habilite en forma legal para ejercer una profesión universitaria, será admitido al ejercicio de esas actividades en los otros países miembros del Convenio, siempre que cumpla con los mismos requisitos y formalidades que, para dicho ejercicio, exigen a sus nacionales graduados universitarios, las leyes del Estado en donde desea ejercer la profesión de que se trate. La anterior disposición será aplicable mientras el interesado conserve la nacionalidad de uno de los países de Centroamérica. Las disposiciones anteriores son aplicables al centroamericano por nacimiento que hubiere obtenido su título universitario fuera de Centroamérica, siempre que haya sido incorporado a una Universidad Centroamericana legalmente autorizada para ello. Se reconoce la validez en cada uno de los Estados parte del presente Convenio de los estudios académicos aprobados en las universidades de cualquiera de los otros Estados. A los centroamericanos emigrados o perseguidos por razones políticas que deseen ejercer sus profesiones o continuar sus estudios universitarios

	en cualquiera de los Estados parte del presente Convenio, se les extenderán licencias provisionales, en tanto sea dable a los interesados obtener la documentación del caso. Para otorgarlas, las entidades correspondientes de cada país seguirán información sumaria, a fin de comprobar los extremos necesarios. Para gozar de los beneficios de este Convenio, los centroamericanos por naturalización deberán haber residido en forma continua por más de cinco años en territorio centroamericano, después de obtener la naturalización. Para los efectos de este Instrumento, se entiende que la expresión "centroamericanos por nacimiento" comprende a todas las personas que gozan de la calidad jurídica de nacionales por nacimiento en cualquiera de los Estados signatarios. Así mismo, se entiende que la expresión "centroamericanos por naturalización" se refiere a quienes no siendo originarios de alguno de los Estados que suscriben este Convenio, se hayan naturalizado en cualquiera de ellos.
Calendario de Reducción:	Ninguno

Sector:	Servicios de construcción y servicios de ingeniería
Subsector:	Todos los subsectores
Clasificación Industrial:	CPC. 511 Trabajos previos a la construcción en obras de construcción CPC. 512 Trabajos de construcción para la edificación CPC. 513 Trabajos de construcción para la ingeniería civil CPC. 514 Armado e instalación de construcciones prefabricadas CPC. 515 Trabajos de construcción especializados CPC. 516 Trabajos de instalación
Tipo de Reserva:	Trato de nación más favorecida (Artículo 10-03)
Nivel de Gobierno:	Nacional
Medidas:	Tratado General de Integración Económica Centroamericana, Artículo XVI, vigente desde el 4 de junio de 1961. (Países miembros: Guatemala, El Salvador, Honduras, Nicaragua y Costa Rica)
Descripción:	Servicios transfronterizos Los Estados contratantes del Tratado General de Integración Económica Centroamericana otorgarán el mismo tratamiento que a las empresas nacionales, a las empresas de los nacionales de los otros Estados signatarios que se dediquen a la construcción de carreteras, puentes, presas, sistemas de riego, electrificación, vivienda y otras obras que tiendan al desarrollo de la infraestructura económica centroamericana.
Calendario de Reducción:	Ninguno

Sector:	Servicios de esparcimiento, culturales y deportivos
Subsector:	Servicios de espectáculos (incluidos los de cine, teatro, danza, música, recital, conferencias, circo, eventos deportivos, corridas de toros, peleas de gallos, bandas y orquestas)
Clasificación Industrial:	CPC. 96191 Servicios artísticos de productores de teatro, grupos de cantantes, bandas y orquestas CPC. 96192 Servicios proporcionados por autores, compositores y otros, a título individual CPC. 96194 Servicios de circos, parques de atracciones
Tipo de Reserva:	Trato nacional (Artículo 10-04)
Nivel de Gobierno:	Nacional
Medidas:	Ley de Espectáculos Públicos, Decreto 574, Artículos 36, 37 y 49 Acuerdo Ministerial No. 592-99 del Ministerio de Cultura y Deportes
Descripción:	Servicios transfronterizos e Inversión Para la contratación de conjuntos, compañías o artistas extranjeros.

	previamente se deberá obtener autorización de la Dirección de Espectáculos.
	Para la presentación de artistas o grupos artísticos internacionales en Guatemala, se deberá acompañar entre otros requisitos, una carta anuencia de cualquiera de los Sindicatos de artistas legalmente reconocidos en el País.
	En las funciones mixtas, formadas por una o varias películas y número de variedades, se dará preferencia, si las circunstancias de elenco, programa y contrato lo permitan, a elementos nacionales.
Calendario de Reducción:	Ninguno

Sector:	Servicios de turismo y servicios relacionados con los viajes
Subsector:	Servicios de guías de turismo
Clasificación Industrial:	CPC. 7472 Servicios de guías de turismo
Tipo de Reserva:	Trato nacional (Artículo 10-04)
	Presencia local (Artículo 10-05)
Nivel de Gobierno:	Nacional
Medidas:	Funcionamiento de Guías de Turismo, Acuerdo No. 219-87, Artículo 6, del Instituto Guatemalteco de Turismo -INGUAT-
Descripción:	Servicios transfronterizos
	La persona que preste servicios como guía de turismo deberá ser guatemalteco o residente.
Calendario de Reducción:	Ninguno

Sector:	Transporte
Subsector:	Transporte aéreo
Clasificación Industrial:	CPC. 731 Transporte de Pasajeros por Vía Aérea (limitado a pilotos de aeronaves)
Tipo de Reserva:	Trato de nación más favorecida (Artículo 10-03)
Nivel de Gobierno:	Nacional
Medidas:	Ley de Aviación Civil, Decreto 100-97 del Congreso, Artículo 29
Descripción:	Servicios transfronterizos
	Las licencias de piloto extendidas en el extranjero serán aceptadas de acuerdo con las normas y tratados internacionales de aeronavegación ratificados por Guatemala, siempre y cuando exista reciprocidad en el trato con el país donde se haya expedido.
Calendario de Reducción:	Ninguno

Sector:	Transporte
Subsector:	Transporte de carga por carretera
	Transporte de personas por carretera
Clasificación Industrial:	CPC. 7121 Otros tipos de transporte regular de pasajeros
	CPC. 7122 Otros tipos de transporte no regular de pasajeros
	CPC. 7123 Transporte de carga
Tipo de Reserva:	Trato de nación más favorecida (Artículo 10-03)
	Trato nacional (Artículo 10-04 y 14-04)
Nivel de Gobierno:	Nacional
Medidas:	Ley de Transportes, Decreto 253, Artículo 4
	Ley de Inversión Extranjera, Decreto 9-98, Artículo 19
	Protocolo al Tratado General de Integración Económica Centroamericana, vigente desde el 16 de agosto de 1995, Artículos 15 y 28

	Reglamento del Servicio de Transporte de Equipos de Carga, Acuerdo Gubernativo 135-94, Artículos 3, 9 y 10 Capítulo VIII del Reglamento de Transportes Extraurbanos aprobado por el Acuerdo Gubernativo del 24 de octubre de 1967, Artículo 77 Reglamento del Servicio de Transporte Extraurbano de Pasajeros por Carretera, Acuerdo Gubernativo 42-94, Artículos 5 y 9 Reglamento para el control de pesos y dimensiones de vehículos automotores y sus combinaciones, Acuerdo Gubernativo 1084-92, Artículo 8 Acuerdo Gubernativo del 10 de marzo de 1965, Artículos 2 y 3
Descripción:	Servicios transfronterizos e Inversión El servicio público de transporte de pasajeros o carga podrá ser prestado por personas individuales, tanto nacionales como extranjeras. Adicionalmente, dicho servicio público podrá ser prestado también por personas jurídicas, siempre y cuando su capital social esté aportado, como mínimo, en un 51% por accionistas guatemaltecos. Ningún vehículo automotor, con placas o matrículas extranjeras, podrá transportar carga comercial entre puntos dentro del territorio nacional. Se exceptúan de la anterior prohibición los vehículos remolques o semiremolques matriculados en cualquiera de los Estados centroamericanos que ingresen temporalmente al país. Los servicios intercentroamericanos de transporte de personas, podrán ser operados por empresas individuales o jurídicas, cuyo capital esté integrado en un 51%, como mínimo, con aportaciones de centroamericanos naturales.
Calendario de Reducción:	Servicios transfronterizos Ninguno Inversión Accionistas extranjeros podrán aportar o invertir en el capital social de personas jurídicas que se dediquen al transporte de pasajeros o carga, de conformidad con las disposiciones siguientes: **1.** A partir del 1º de enero del año 2001, con una aportación máxima del 51% del capital social respectivo; y **2.** A partir del 1º de enero del año 2004, con una aportación del 100% del capital social.

Sector:	Transporte
Subsector:	Transporte terrestre Transporte marítimo Transporte aéreo
Clasificación Industrial:	CPC. 7121 Otros tipos de transporte regular de pasajeros CPC. 7122 Otros tipos de transporte no regular de pasajeros CPC. 7123 Transporte de carga CPC. 7211 Transporte de pasajeros por vía marítima CPC. 7212 Transporte de carga por vía marítima CPC. 731 Transporte de pasajeros por vía aérea CPC. 732 Transporte de carga por vía aérea
Tipo de Reserva:	Trato de nación más favorecida (Artículo10-03)
Nivel de Gobierno:	Nacional
Medidas:	Tratado Multilateral de Libre Comercio e Integración Económica Centroamericana, Artículo XV, vigente desde el 2 de junio de 1959. (Países miembros: Guatemala, El Salvador y Nicaragua)
Descripción:	Servicios transfronterizos Las naves marítimas o aéreas, comerciales o particulares, de cualquiera de los Estados contratantes, serán tratadas en los puertos y aeropuertos abiertos al tráfico internacional de los otros Estados. en iguales términos

	que las naves y aeronaves nacionales correspondientes. Igual tratamiento se extenderá a los pasajeros, tripulantes y carga de los otros Estados contratantes. Los vehículos terrestres matriculados en uno de los Estados firmantes gozarán en el territorio de los otros Estados, durante su permanencia temporal, del mismo tratamiento que los matriculados en el país de visita. Las empresas que en los Países signatarios se dediquen a prestar servicios intercentroamericanos de transporte automotor de pasajeros y mercaderías recibirán trato nacional en los territorios de los otros Estados. Las embarcaciones de cualquiera de los Estados contratantes que presten servicios entre puertos centroamericanos recibirán en los puertos de los otros Estados, el tratamiento nacional de cabotaje.
Calendario de Reducción:	Ninguno

Sector:	Transporte
Subsector:	Servicios de transporte terrestre de carga por carretera
Clasificación Industrial:	CPC. 7123 Transporte de carga
Tipo de Reserva:	Trato de nación más favorecida (Artículo 10-03)
Nivel de Gobierno:	Nacional
Medidas:	Resolución No. 64-98, aprobada por el Consejo de Ministros Responsables de la Integración Económica y Desarrollo Regional (COMRIEDRE), el 19 de enero de 1998
Descripción:	Servicios transfronterizos Se establece un mecanismo de tratamiento recíproco y no discriminatorio para el servicio de transporte de carga entre los seis Estados miembros del Protocolo de Tegucigalpa (Costa Rica, El Salvador, Guatemala, Honduras, Nicaragua y Panamá) que comprende lo siguiente: **a.** Plena libertad de tránsito a través de sus territorios para los medios de transporte de carga terrestre de mercancías destinadas de Panamá hacia cualquier país centroamericano, y de cualquier país centroamericano hacia Panamá. **b.** La libertad de tránsito implica la garantía de libre competencia en la contratación del transporte sin perjuicio del país de origen o destino y el trato nacional al transporte de todos los Estados en el territorio de cualquiera de ellos, con los orígenes y destinos señalados supra.
Calendario de Reducción:	Ninguno

ANEXO II
LISTA DE GUATEMALA

Sector:	Servicios a las empresas
Subsector:	Servicios profesionales
Clasificación Industrial:	
Tipo de Reserva:	Trato de nación más favorecida (Artículo 10-03) Trato nacional (Artículo 10-04) Presencia local (Artículo 10-05)
Nivel de Gobierno:	Nacional
Descripción:	Servicios transfronterizos Guatemala se reserva el derecho de adoptar o mantener cualquier medida

	que restrinja la prestación transfronteriza de servicios profesionales. Guatemala reitera los derechos y obligaciones adquiridos en la Convención sobre el Ejercicio de Profesiones Liberales.
Medidas Vigentes:	Constitución Política de la República de Guatemala, Artículo 90 Ley de Colegiación Profesional Obligatoria, Decreto 62-91 Convención sobre el Ejercicio de Profesiones Liberales, del 28 de enero de 1902; publicada en el Diario Oficial el 23 de enero de 1903

Sector:	Servicios de construcción
Subsector:	
Clasificación Industrial:	
Tipo de Reserva:	Trato de nación más favorecida (Artículo 10-03) Trato nacional (Artículo 10-04) Presencia local (Artículo 10-05)
Nivel de Gobierno:	Nacional
Descripción:	Servicios transfronterizos Guatemala se reserva el derecho de adoptar o mantener cualquier medida que restrinja la prestación transfronteriza de servicios de construcción durante los dos años posteriores a la entrada en vigor del tratado. Transcurrido el plazo indicado en el párrafo anterior, las medidas vigentes a esa fecha, estarán sujetas a las disposiciones establecidas en el Artículo 10-06 (1).
Medidas Vigentes:	

ANEXO III
LISTA DE GUATEMALA

Guatemala se reserva el derecho exclusivo de desempeñar y negarse a autorizar el establecimiento de inversiones en la siguiente actividad:

1. Emisión de la moneda

    a) Descripción de actividades:

Es potestad exclusiva del Estado, emitir y regular la moneda, así como, formular y realizar las políticas que tiendan a crear y mantener condiciones cambiarias y crediticias favorables al desarrollo ordenado de la economía nacional.

    b) Medidas:

    Constitución Política de la República de Guatemala, Artículo 132

ANEXO IV
LISTA DE GUATEMALA

Guatemala exceptúa la aplicación del Artículo 14-05 (Trato de nación más favorecida) al tratamiento otorgado bajo aquellos acuerdos en vigor o firmados después de la fecha de entrada en vigor de este tratado, en materia de:

    a) aviación;

b)   pesca; o

c)   asuntos marítimos, incluyendo salvamento.

Para mayor certeza, el Artículo 14-05 no se aplica a ningún programa presente o futuro de cooperación internacional para promover el desarrollo económico.

LISTA DE HONDURAS

Sector:	Todos los sectores
Subsector:	Todos los subsectores
Clasificación Industrial:	
Tipo de Reserva:	Trato nacional (Artículo 14-04)
Nivel de Gobierno:	Nacional
Medidas:	Medidas: Constitución de la República, Título III, Capítulo II, Artículo 107, Decreto N. 131 Ley para la Adquisición de Bienes Urbanos en las Áreas que delimita el Artículo 107 de la Constitución de la República Decreto N° 90-90, Artículo 1 y 4 Ley para la Declaratoria, Planeamiento y Desarrollo de las Zonas de Turismo, Decreto No 968, Titulo V, Capítulo V, Artículo 16
Descripción:	Inversión Los terrenos del Estado, ejidales, comunales o de propiedad privada situados en la zona limítrofe a los Estados vecinos, o en el litoral de ambos mares, en una extensión de cuarenta kilómetros hacia el interior del país, y los de las islas, cayos, arrecifes, escolladeros, peñones, sirtes y bancos de arena, solo podrán ser adquiridos o poseídos o tenidos a cualquier título por hondureños de nacimiento, por sociedades integradas en su totalidad por socios hondureños y por las instituciones del Estado, bajo pena de nulidad del respectivo acto o contrato. No obstante lo anterior, se permite la adquisición de inmuebles urbanos señalados supra, por personas naturales que no sean hondureñas por nacimiento y por sociedades que no estén integradas en su totalidad por socios hondureños, cuando sean destinados a proyectos turísticos, de desarrollo económico, desarrollo social o de interés público calificados y aprobados por la Secretaría en los Despachos de Turismo. Tratándose de extranjeros rentistas que destinen la tierra exclusivamente para su habitación, podrán obtener el uso, goce o usufructo de ella, conforme a contratos de arrendamiento u otras formas contractuales no traslaticias de dominio por un término de hasta cuarenta (40) años prorrogables. Tales contratos y sus prórrogas deberán ser previamente aprobados por la Secretaría de Turismo. El Poder Ejecutivo a través de la Secretaría de Estado en los Despachos de Gobernación y Justicia, podrá establecer toda clase de restricciones, modalidades o prohibiciones para la adquisición, uso, goce y usufructo de terrenos por parte de personas que no sean hondureñas por nacimiento o por sociedades que no estén integradas en su totalidad por socios hondureños, por razones fundamentales de conveniencia nacional en aquellas áreas urbanas ubicadas en las zonas limítrofes con los países vecinos.
Calendario de Reducción:	Ninguno

Sector:	Todos los Sectores
Subsector :	Todos los subsectores
Clasificación Industrial:	
Tipo de Reserva:	Presencia local (Artículo 10-05)
Nivel de Gobierno:	Nacional
Medidas:	Código del Comercio, Capítulo IX, Artículos N. 308 y 310
Descripción:	Servicios transfronterizos Para que una sociedad constituida con arreglo a las leyes extranjeras pueda dedicarse al ejercicio del comercio en Honduras deberá: **a)** Tener permanentemente en la República cuando menos un representante con amplias facultades para realizar todos los actos y negocios jurídicos que hayan de celebrarse y surtir efecto en el territorio nacional. **b)** Constituir un patrimonio afecto a la actividad mercantil que haya de desarrollar en la República. Se consideran sociedades constituidas con arreglo a las leyes extranjeras las que no tengan su domicilio legal en Honduras.
Calendario de Reducción:	Ninguno

Sector:	Todos los Sectores
Subsector :	Todos los subsectores
Clasificación Industrial:	
Tipo de Reserva:	Trato nacional (Artículo 14-04)
Nivel de Gobierno:	Nacional
Medidas:	Constitución de la República de Honduras, Título VI, Capítulo I, Artículo 337, Decreto No. 131 Reglamento de la Ley de Inversiones, Capítulos I y VI, Artículos 3 y 49 (definiciones), Acuerdo No. 345-92
Descripción:	Inversión La industria y el comercio en pequeña escala, constituyen patrimonio de los hondureños. Los inversionistas extranjeros no podrán dedicarse a la industria y el comercio en pequeña escala, excepto en aquellos casos que hayan adquirido la carta de naturalización como hondureños, debiendo presentar la documentación que acredite la respectiva naturalización, siempre y cuando en su país de origen exista reciprocidad. La inversión excluyendo, terrenos, edificios y vehículos no será mayor al equivalente de ciento cincuenta mil lempiras (Lps 150,000.00).
Calendario de Reducción:	Ninguno

Sector:	Todos los sectores
Subsector:	Todos los subsectores
Clasificación Industrial:	Tipo de Reserva: Trato nacional (Artículo 14-04)
Nivel de Gobierno:	Nacional
Medidas:	Ley de Cooperativas de Honduras, Titulo II, Capítulo I, Artículo 10, Decreto No. 65-87 de fecha 20 de mayo de 1987
Descripción:	Inversión Las cooperativas no hondureñas podrán operar en el país con permiso previo del Organismo rector del cooperativismo, para concederlo se tomará en cuenta: **a)** La conveniencia económica y social de la expansión de la cooperativa

	b) La seguridad de que la regional o filial no perjudican los intereses de otra cooperativa hondureña organizada en la zona o región de que se trate **c)** La reciprocidad en el país de origen.
Calendario de Reducción:	Ninguno

Sector:	Todos los sectores
Subsector:	Todos los subsectores
Clasificación Industrial:	
Tipo de Reserva:	Presencia local (Articulo 10-05)
Nivel de Gobierno:	Nacional
Medidas:	Ley de Promoción y Desarrollo de Obras Públicas y de Infraestructura Nacional, Capítulo I, Artículos 6 y 7, Decreto 283-98 Código de Trabajo, Artículo 544
Descripción:	Servicios transfronterizos Serán admisibles las ofertas de compañías, sociedades y consorcios extranjeros en las licitaciones o subastas públicas y concursos públicos, nacionales o internacionales, siempre que, cuando la modalidad para la prestación del servicio público lo requiera y así se determine en el pliego de condiciones, se obligue, de resultar adjudicatarios, a constituir una sociedad mercantil con domicilio en Honduras con la finalidad de prestación de los servicios bajo los términos y condiciones que dispongan los respectivos pliegos; y en su caso, el contrato o la licencia.
Calendario de Reducción:	Ninguno

Sector:	Todos los sectores
Subsector:	Todos los subsectores
Clasificación Industrial:	
Tipo de Reserva:	Trato de nación más favorecida (Artículo 10-03)
Nivel de Gobierno:	Nacional
Medidas:	Decreto No. 177-94, de fecha 01 de marzo de 1995
Descripción:	Servicios transfronterizos Integración progresiva de los servicios de diversa naturaleza (aplica para Guatemala, El Salvador, Nicaragua, Costa Rica y Panamá)
Calendario de Reducción:	Ninguno

Sector:	Agrícola
Subsector:	
Clasificación Industrial:	CPC Sección 0
Tipo de Reserva:	Trato nacional (Artículo 14-04)
Nivel de Gobierno:	Nacional
Medidas:	Ley para la Modernización y Desarrollo del Sector Agrícola Artículo 79, reformado mediante Decreto Legislativo No. 31-9 Reglamento de Adjudicación de Tierras en la Reforma Agraria, Artículo 2, Acuerdo No 2124-92
Descripción:	Inversión Para ser adjudicatario o adjudicataria de tierras de la reforma agraria, se requiere que los campesinos, hombres o mujeres sean hondureños por nacimiento. Los beneficiarios de la reforma agraria solo podrán ser personas naturales, cooperativas de campesinos, empresas asociativas de

	campesinos.
Calendario de Reducción:	Ninguno

Sector:	Pesca
Subsector:	Fluvial, lacustre y marítima
Clasificación Industrial:	CPC 04 Pescado y otros productos de la pesca
Tipo de Reserva: Trato nacional (Artículos 10-04 y 14-04)	
Nivel de Gobierno:	Nacional
Medidas:	Decreto No 154, Ley de Pesca, Capítulos I, III, IV Acuerdo No 345-92, Reglamento Ley de Inversiones, Capítulo VI, Artículo 50
Descripción :	Servicios transfronterizos e Inversión Con fines de explotación o lucro, solo podrán obtener permisos o licencias de pescar, los hondureños residentes y las personas jurídicas hondureñas en que por lo menos el cincuenta y uno por ciento (51%) del capital pertenezca a hondureños. Solo los hondureños de nacimiento podrán ser patrones o capitanes de barcos de pesca de cualquier especie. Únicamente podrán dedicarse a las actividades de la pesca en las aguas territoriales, las embarcaciones que ostenten el pabellón hondureño.
Calendario de Reducción:	Ninguno

Sector:	Servicios de Comunicaciones
Subsector:	Servicios privados de mensajería
Clasificación Industrial:	CPC 7511 Servicios postales
Tipo de Reserva:	Trato de nación más favorecida (Artículo 10-03) Trato nacional (Artículos 10-04 y 14-04) Presencia local (Artículo 10-05)
Nivel de Gobierno:	Nacional
Medidas:	Artículo No. 3, Ley Orgánica de la Empresa Hondureña de Correos, Decreto No. 120-93 Artículo No. 1, 4 y 7 del Reglamento Regulador de la Prestación de Servicios de Mensajería por parte de Empresas Privadas, aprobado por la Junta Directiva de la Empresa de Correos de Honduras y publicado en el Diario Oficial La Gaceta el 17 de agosto, 1996
Descripción:	Servicios transfronterizos Se entiende por servicio de mensajería privada, la clase de servicio postal registrado, prestado con independencia de las redes oficiales de correo nacional e internacional que exige la aplicación y adopción de características especiales para la admisión, recolección y entrega de envíos de correspondencia y demás objetos postales, transportados vía superficie marítima o aérea, en el ámbito nacional e internacional. Ninguna persona natural o jurídica podrá prestar servicios de mensajería privada sin haber obtenido licencia previamente de HONDUCOR. Tampoco podrán prestar los servicios de admisión, clasificación y entrega de envíos de correspondencia. Se requiere autorización para ejercer el servicio de mensajería privada. La prestación del servicio de mensajería privada nacional e internacional se concederá a personas naturales o jurídicas mediante licencia. Para el otorgamiento de licencia se requiere entre otros requisitos estar declarado como comerciante individual en el caso de personas naturales, o estar constituido como sociedad mercantil, y debidamente autorizada para ejercer el comercio en Honduras. Para cada sucursal a establecer se requiere permiso de operaciones o de Negocios del establecimiento principal y de cada una de las sucursales.

	extendido por las municipalidades correspondientes, en su defecto se aceptará una constancia de trámite. Los servicios de mensajería privada estarán sujeta a la aplicación del principio de reciprocidad equitativa. Inversión La inversión en materia de servicios privados de mensajería se regulará por las siguientes reglas: **a)** Preferentemente la inversión en este rubro estará reservada a los hondureños por nacimiento. **b)** También podrán participar en este rubro las personas jurídicas donde el 60% de los socios o asociados sean hondureños por nacimiento y que su capital otorgado y pagado no sea inferior al 60% del total invertido. **c)** No obstante con carácter excepcional y en casos calificados por la Junta Directiva de HONDUCOR, ésta podrá autorizar la inversión extranjera, en los casos en que, con arreglo a los literales anteriores los hondureños no calificaran. La inversión privada extranjera será autorizada, registrada y supervisada por HONDUCOR; será complementaria y jamas substitutiva de las inversiones de origen nacional.
Calendario de Reducción:	Ninguno

Sector:	Servicios de Comunicaciones
Subsector:	Telecomunicaciones
Clasificación Industrial:	CPC 752. Servicios de Telecomunicaciones (excepto 7524)
Tipo de Reserva:	Trato de nación más favorecida (Artículo 10-03)
Nivel de Gobierno:	Nacional
Medidas:	Decreto No 177-94 publicado en el diario Oficial "la Gaceta" el 1 de marzo de 1995
Descripción:	Servicios transfronterizos Se establecen facilidades para el establecimiento, operación, mantenimiento, expansión y modernización de los sistemas regionales de telecomunicaciones. (Aplicable a Guatemala, El Salvador, Nicaragua y Costa Rica).
Calendario de Reducción:	Ninguno

Sector:	Servicios de Comunicaciones
Subsector:	Telecomunicaciones
Clasificación Industrial:	CPC 752. Servicios de telecomunicaciones
Tipo de Reserva:	Trato nacional (Artículo 10-04)
Nivel de Gobierno:	Nacional
Medidas:	Ley Marco del Sector Telecomunicaciones Capítulo I, Artículo No. 26, Decreto No 185-95 Reglamento General de la Ley Marco del Sector de Telecomunicaciones, Acuerdo No. 89-97 publicado el 2 de agosto de 1997. Artículo 93, Titulo III, Capítulo I, Acuerdo No 89/97
Descripción:	Servicios transfronterizos Los gobiernos extranjeros no podrán participar en forma directa en la prestación de servicios públicos de telecomunicaciones.
Calendario de Reducción:	Ninguno
Sector:	Servicios de Comunicaciones

Subsector:	Telecomunicaciones
Clasificación Industrial:	CPC 752. Servicios de telecomunicaciones (exclusivamente servicios portadores, telex, telefonía y telegrafía).
Tipo de Reserva:	Trato nacional (Artículos 10-04 y 14-04)
Nivel de Gobierno:	Nacional
Medidas:	Decreto No. 244-98 del 19 de septiembre de 1998, publicado en el Diario Oficial la Gaceta el 02 de octubre de 1998, Artículo 1 Decreto No. 89-99 del 30 de junio de 1999, Artículo 4
Descripción:	Servicios transfronterizos e Inversión La Empresa Hondureña de Telecomunicaciones (HONDUTEL) goza de una concesión para que ésta provea en todo el territorio de la República de Honduras, los servicios de telecomunicaciones nacionales e internacionales, tales como: servicios portadores, telex, telefonía y telegrafía, incluyendo los servicios de telegrafía en aquellos lugares donde no haya otro medio de comunicación con el resto del país. HONDUTEL gozará de exclusividad hasta el veinticuatro (24) de diciembre del año dos mil cinco (2005) para operar dichos servicios. La Empresa Hondureña de Telecomunicaciones (HONDUTEL) está autorizada para asociarse con un inversionista estratégico seleccionado, bajo la condición de que este adquiera el cincuenta y uno por ciento (51%) de las acciones representativas del capital de la Compañía Hondureña de Telecomunicaciones, S.A. de C.V. (COHONDETEL, S.A. de C.V.).
Calendario de reducción:	A partir del 25 de diciembre del año dos mil cinco (2005) HONDUTEL no gozará de la exclusividad para operar los servicios de telecomunicaciones nacionales e internacionales, tales como: servicios portadores, telex, telefonía y telegrafía, incluyendo los servicios de telegrafía en aquellos lugares donde no haya otro medio de comunicación con el resto del país.

Sector:	Servicios de Comunicaciones
Subsector:	Telecomunicaciones
Clasificación Industrial:	CPC 752. Servicios de Telecomunicaciones (excepto 7524)
Tipo de Reserva:	Trato nacional (Artículo 14-04)
Nivel de Gobierno:	Nacional
Medidas:	Decreto No 244-98 de fecha 19 de septiembre de 1998, publicado en el Diario Oficial la Gaceta el 02 de octubre de 1998, Artículos 6 y 15 Decreto No. 89-99 del 30 de junio de 1999, Artículos 4 y 9
Descripción:	Inversión Se autoriza a la Empresa Hondureña de Telecomunicaciones (HONDUTEL) a asociarse con un inversionista estratégico bajo la condición de que este adquiera el cincuenta y uno porciento (51%) de las acciones representativas del capital de la Compañía Hondureña de Telecomunicaciones S.A. de C.V. (COHONDETEL, S.A. de C.V.). Mientras dure el proceso de Capitalización de la Compañía Hondureña de Telecomunicaciones SA de CV (COHONDETEL, SA de CV), e inicie sus operaciones, HONDUTEL continuará operando el sistema de telecomunicaciones, incluyendo el plan de expansión previsto hasta esa fecha. La Compañía Hondureña de telecomunicaciones SA de CV (COHONDETEL, SA de CV), queda obligada a expandir la telefonía rural en todas la comunidades de quinientos (500) o más habitantes requiriendo para cada comunidad la instalación de por lo menos dos (2) teléfonos públicos o del sistema comunitario dentro del periodo de exclusividad, conforme a los términos y condiciones que señala el contrato de concesión: asimismo queda obligada a mantener y restablecer

	el sistema de telegrafía en aquellas comunidades que cuentan o contaban con este sistema, mientras se instale el sistema telefónico permanente y que estén distante de centros poblacionales.
Calendario de Reducción:	Ninguno

Sector:	Servicios de Comunicaciones
Subsector:	Telecomunicaciones
Clasificación Industrial:	CPC 752. Servicios de Telecomunicaciones
Tipo de Reserva:	Presencia local (Artículo 10-05)
Nivel de Gobierno:	Nacional
Medidas:	Decreto No 185-95 Ley Marco del Sector Telecomunicaciones, Titulo III, Capítulo I, Artículo 25 Acuerdo No 89/97 Reglamento General de la Ley Marco del Sector Telecomunicaciones, Titulo III, Capítulo I, II, IV, V, Artículos 90, 93, 124 y 148
Descripción:	Servicios Transfronterizos Para la prestación de servicios de telecomunicaciones se requiere concesión (servicios públicos portadores y finales básicos), permiso (servicios complementarios, de radiocomunicación, de difusión y redes privadas, así como los servicios privados) o registro (servicios de valor agregado) otorgado por CONATEL. Sin perjuicio de lo anterior, los servicios que necesiten para su prestación del uso del espectro radioeléctrico requerirán además licencia otorgada por CONATEL. Las empresas extranjeras para solicitar los respectivos títulos habilitantes (concesión, permiso, registro y licencia) deberán señalar domicilio en el país y nombrar un representante legal igualmente domiciliado, quien asumirá todas las responsabilidades que sean de ley.
Calendario de Reducción:	Ninguno

Sector:	Servicios de Comunicaciones
Subsector:	Servicios de radio, televisión y periódicos
Clasificación Industrial:	CPC 7524. Servicios de transmisión de programas CPC 9613. Servicios de radio y televisión CPC 96211. Servicios de suministro de noticias impresas CPC 96220. Servicios de agencias de noticias a emisoras de radio CPC 96231. Servicios de reportajes de noticias para estaciones de televisión CPC 96232. Servicios en directo de agencias de noticias para estaciones de televisión CPC 96290. Otros servicios de agencias de noticias
Tipo de Reserva:	Alta dirección empresarial y consejos de administración (Artículo 14-08)
Nivel de Gobierno:	Nacional
Medidas:	Decreto No 131, Constitución de la República de Honduras, Capítulo II, Artículo 73, párrafo tercero Decreto No. 6, Ley de Emisión del Pensamiento, Capítulo IV, Artículo 30
Descripción:	Inversión La dirección de los periódicos impresos, radiales o televisados y la orientación intelectual, política y administrativa de los mismos, será ejercida exclusivamente por hondureños por nacimiento. Los extranjeros no podrán dirigir publicaciones periodísticas, escritas o habladas.
Calendario de Reducción:	Ninguno

Sector:	Servicios de Construcción y servicios de ingeniería conexos
Subsector:	Todos los subsectores
Clasificación Industrial:	CPC 511. Trabajos previos a la construcción en obras de edificación y construcción CPC 512. Construcción de edificios CPC 513. Trabajos generales de construcción en obras de ingeniería civil CPC 514. Montaje e instalación de construcciones prefabricadas CPC 515. Trabajos de construcción especializados CPC 516. Trabajos de instalación CPC 517. Trabajos de acabado de edificios
Tipo de Reserva:	Trato de nación más favorecida (Artículo 10-03) Trato nacional (Artículos 10-04 y 14-04) Presencia local (10-05)
Nivel de Gobierno:	Nacional
Medidas:	Ley Orgánica del Colegio de Arquitectos de Honduras y su Reglamento Ley Orgánica del Colegio de Ingenieros Agrónomos de Honduras y su Reglamento Ley Orgánica del Colegio de Ingenieros Civiles de Honduras y su Reglamento Ley Orgánica del Colegio de Ingenieros Mecánicos, Electricistas y Químicos de Honduras y su Reglamento
Descripción:	Inversión Ingeniería Civil Se consideran firmas nacionales de consultoría o de construcción aquellas donde al menos el 70% del capital social sea de nacionales hondureños. Servicios transfronterizos Los Estados Contratantes del Tratado General de Integración Económica Centroamericana otorgarán el mismo tratamiento que a las compañías nacionales, a las empresas de otros Estados signatarios que se dediquen a la construcción de carreteras, puentes, presas, sistemas de riego, electrificación, vivienda y otras obras que tiendan al desarrollo de la infraestructura económica centroamericana. Arquitectura Toda empresa extranjera constructora de obras de arquitectura o consultora de arquitectura, esta obligada a registrarse y clasificarse provisionalmente en el Comité Intercolegial de Registro y Clasificación de Empresas Constructoras y Consultoras en Ingeniería y Arquitectura, para cada proyecto específico, como paso previo para inscribirse en el Colegio de Arquitectos de Honduras (CAH), y no podrá participar en licitaciones publicas o privadas o concursos para prestación de servicios profesionales diferentes al objeto de inscripción. En caso de salir favorecida deberá inscribirse en forma definitiva en el Colegio de Arquitectos de Honduras, para la ejecución del proyecto específico. Las empresas extranjeras que se dediquen a la arquitectura serán inscritas en el Colegio de Arquitectos de Honduras únicamente para proyectos específicos y no podrán ejecutar otros proyectos o trabajos para los cuales no estén autorizados. Ingeniería Agronómica Toda empresa extranjera constructora de obras o consultora esta obligada a registrarse y clasificarse provisionalmente en el Comité Intercolegial de Registro y Clasificación de Empresas Constructoras de Ingeniería, para cada proyecto específico como paso previo para poder inscribirse en el Colegio de Ingenieros Agrónomos de Honduras y poder participar en licitaciones publicas o privadas y concursos para prestación de servicios profesionales. En caso de salir favorecida deberá inscribirse en forma definitiva en el Colegio de Ingenieros Agrónomos, previa calificación

respectiva para la ejecución de proyectos específicos.

Las empresas extranjeras que tengan como finalidad dedicarse al ejercicio de actividades propias de la profesión agronómica, de acuerdo a lo señalado en la ley serán inscritas previa clasificación en el Comité Intercolegial de Registro y Clasificación de Empresas Constructoras y Consultoras de Ingeniería, únicamente para proyectos específicos y no podrán ejecutar otros proyectos o trabajos para los cuales no fueron autorizados.

Ingenierías Mecánica, Eléctrica y Química

Las empresas extranjeras que se dediquen a la ingeniería mecánica, eléctrica o química serán inscritas en el Comité Intercolegial de Registro y Clasificación de Empresas de Construcción únicamente para proyectos específicos y no podrán ejecutar otros proyectos o trabajos para los cuales no fueron autorizados.

Toda empresa extranjera constructora o consultora de ingeniería mecánica, eléctrica o química esta obligada a registrarse y clasificarse provisionalmente en el Comité Intercolegial de Registro y Clasificación de Empresas de Construcción para cada proyecto específico como paso previo para poder inscribirse en el Colegio de Ingenieros Mecánicos, Eléctricos y Químicos (CIMEQH) y poder participar en licitaciones públicas o privadas y concursos para prestación de servicios profesionales. En caso de salir favorecida deberá inscribirse en forma definitiva en el CIMEQH.

Ingeniería Civil

Las empresas extranjeras que se dediquen a la ingeniería civil, serán inscritas en el Comité Intercolegial de Registro y Clasificación de Empresas de Construcción únicamente para proyectos específicos y no podrán ejecutar otros proyectos o trabajos para los cuales no estén autorizadas.

Toda empresa extranjera constructora o consultora de ingeniería civil esta obligada a registrarse y clasificarse provisionalmente en el Comité Intercolegial de Registro y Clasificación de Empresas de Construcción para cada proyecto específico como paso previo para poder inscribirse en el Colegio de Ingenieros Civiles de Honduras (CICH) y poder participar en licitaciones publicas o privadas y concursos para prestación de servicios profesionales. En caso de salir favorecida deberá inscribirse en forma definitiva en el Colegio de Ingenieros Civiles para la ejecución del proyecto específico.

Para el registro de compañías constructoras o consultoras extranjeras para la ejecución de un proyecto específico, se exige que la compañía este autorizada a ejercer el comercio en Honduras. Asímismo, se exige que se presente copia del contrato para la ejecución del proyecto específico. Adicionalmente, se requiere autorización del CICH para que el personal técnico extranjero pueda trabajar en Honduras.

Una firma extranjera será considerada asesora cuando una empresa nacional consultora o constructora presente o negocie directamente una oferta de servicios profesionales y proponga al dueño del proyecto la utilización de los servicios de una firma extranjera como Asesora, la cual debe participar en el proyecto en forma limitada, ya sea en las etapas conceptuales del proyecto o en ciertas áreas del mismo con personal especializado.

Cuando una firma nacional contemple la utilización de una firma asesora extranjera, ésta última deberá registrarse provisionalmente, conforme al procedimiento usual, previa a la presentación o negociación de la oferta en la cual la firma extranjera sea incluida y a un pago por registro.

Una firma extranjera será calificada como asesora cuando reúna los siguientes requisitos:

a) que sea propuesta como tal por una firma nacional;

	b) que los servicios y relaciones profesionales de la firma extranjera sean realizados a través de la firma nacional; **c)** que la relación contractual de la firma extranjera sea únicamente con la firma nacional; **d)** que los servicios de la firma extranjera sean prestados en su país de origen o en forma periódica limitada en Honduras; **e)** que el alcance de los servicios de la firma extranjera sean limitados a aspectos conceptuales de un proyecto o en aspectos específicos de áreas limitadas del mismo; **f)** que el personal que provea la firma extranjera en sus servicios sea altamente especializado y no podrá ser destacado en Honduras por periodos continuos mayores de tres meses por especialidad; **g)** que el costo de los servicios que preste la firma extranjera sea de un monto reducido en comparación con el valor total del Contrato y que por consiguiente sea evidente a la Junta Directiva del Colegio de Ingenieros Civiles de Honduras, CICH, que los mismos no cubrirán los costos envueltos en el registro definitivo. Para este aspecto la Junta Directiva del CICH, analizará los conceptos de tasas unitarias, salarios, gastos generales y honorarios de los contratos de la firma extranjera y la nacional; y **h)** las firmas extranjeras proporcionaran al CICH cualquier otro elemento que pueda ser útil a la Junta Directiva para calificarla. Si la Junta Directiva del CICH, en base a los requisitos del artículo anterior estima que la firma extranjera sea calificada como asesora, podrá autorizar a dicha firma para que preste su asesoramiento sin que se requiera el registro definitivo usual. Para que una firma extranjera pueda brindar en forma definitiva sus servicios como asesora, deberá solicitar la respectiva autorización al Colegio para cada proyecto específico. La firma asesora no deberá estar operando en Honduras en forma contractual directamente, u operar como firma asesora en forma continua durante varios años en distintos proyectos simultáneamente. En el caso que una firma extranjera sea utilizada como asesora en diferentes proyectos en el país, la Junta Directiva del CICH evaluará la participación de la misma en todos los proyectos desde un período dado, como un solo proyecto para el mismo período. Si del examen de dichos proyectos resultare que la firma está devengando un monto razonable de honorarios será requerida a registro en forma definitiva para proyecto específico. Si la firma extranjera es autorizada por la Junta Directiva del CICH, para brindar sus servicios como asesora, se le extenderá una constancia como tal para un proyecto específico previo el pago de según el monto del proyecto y por cada profesional extranjero que sea propuesto por la firma extranjera durante el tiempo que estos sean asignados al proyecto específico, más una cuota inicial de cada uno de ellos. Existen tarifas diferenciadas para extranjeros para el registro de empresas en el Colegio de Ingenieros Civiles de Honduras.
Calendario de Reducción:	Ninguno

Sector:	Servicios de Distribución
Subsector:	Representantes, distribuidores y agentes de empresas nacionales y extranjeras
Clasificación Industrial:	CPC 61. Servicios de venta, mantenimiento y reparación de vehículos

	automotores y motocicletas (excluyendo 6120 y 61220) CPC 622. Servicios comerciales al por mayor CPC 63. Servicios comerciales al por menor; servicios de reparación de artículos personales y domésticos (excluyendo 6330.) CPC 96113. Servicios relacionados con la distribución de películas cinematográficas o cintas de vídeo
Tipo de Reserva:	Presencia local (Artículo 10-05) Trato nacional (Artículo 14-04)
Nivel de Gobierno:	Nacional
Medidas:	Ley de Representantes, Distribuidores y Agentes de Empresas Nacionales y Extranjeras, Decreto No 549 Capítulo I, Artículo 4. Reformado por Decreto No 804 Acuerdo No 669-79 Reglamento de la Ley de Representantes, Distribuidores y Agentes de Empresas Nacionales y Extranjeras, Artículo 2
Descripción:	Servicios transfronterizos e Inversión Para ser concesionario se requiere: **a)** ser hondureño o sociedad mercantil hondureña; **b)** estar afiliado a la correspondiente Cámara de Comercio; **c)** licencia extendida por la Secretaría de Industria y Comercio. Para dedicarse a la representación, agencia o distribución, las personas naturales deberán estar constituidas como comerciante individual. Se tendrá por sociedad hondureña aquella en cuyo capital social predomine una inversión netamente hondureña, en una proporción no inferior al cincuenta y uno porciento (51%).
Calendario de educción:	Ninguno

Sector:	Servicios de Distribución
Subsector:	Instalación y funcionamiento de estaciones y depósitos de combustible líquidos, derivados del petróleo Gasolina automotriz Diesel Kerosene LPG
Clasificación Industrial:	CPC 613. Venta al por menor de carburante CPC 62271. Servicios comerciales al por mayor de combustibles sólidos, líquidos y gaseosos y productos conexos CPC 63297. Venta al por menor de gasóleo, gas envasado, carbón y madera
Tipo de Reserva:	Presencia local (Artículo 10-05) Trato nacional (Artículo 14-04)
Nivel de Gobierno :	Nacional
Medidas :	Decreto No 319, Ley de Transporte, Capítulo II, Artículo 11 Decreto No 549 Ley de Representantes, Distribuidores y Agentes de Empresas Nacionales y Extranjeras, Capítulo I y VI, Artículos 4 y 25 Decreto No 804, reforma el Artículo 4 de la Ley de Representantes, Distribuidores y Agentes de Empresas Nacionales y Extranjera Acuerdo 000489, Reglamento para la Instalación y Funcionamiento de Estaciones y Depósitos de Combustible Líquidos Derivados del Petróleo, Capitulo IV, Artículo 19
Descripción :	Servicios transfronterizos e Inversión El establecimiento de estaciones de combustible y depósitos de combustible esta sujeto a autorización de la Dirección General de

	Transporte de la Secretaría de Obras Publicas, Transporte y Vivienda (SOPTRAVI). Los titulares o arrendatarios de las estaciones de servicios autorizadas para la venta al consumidor de productos derivados del petróleo se consideran distribuidores. En tal sentido, son aplicables los limites de capital establecidos en la Ley de Representantes y Distribuidores y Agentes de Empresas Nacionales y Extranjeras, que consideran a una sociedad hondureña aquella en cuyo capital social predomine una inversión netamente hondureña, en una proporción no inferior al cincuenta y uno porciento (51%). Las personas naturales deberán estar constituidas como comerciante individual, se tendrá por sociedad hondureña aquella cuyo capital social no sea inferior al cincuenta y uno por ciento. Para el obtenimiento de los permisos de instalación y de operación deberá presentarse escritura que acredite la condición de sociedad legalmente constituida o de comerciante individual.
Calendario de Reducción:	Ninguno

Sector :	Servicios de Enseñanza
Subsector:	Escuelas privadas Universidades privadas Servicios de educación preescolar (jardines de niños) Servicios privados de educación primaria Servicios privados de educación secundaria Servicios privados de educación superior (Universidades) Programas Especiales
Clasificación Industrial	CPC 921. Servicios de enseñanza primaria CPC 922. Servicios de enseñanza secundaria CPC 923. Servicios enseñanza superior
Tipo de Reserva:	Trato nacional (Artículo 10-04) Presencia local (Artículo 10-05) Alta dirección empresarial y consejos de administración (Artículo 14-08)
Nivel de Gobierno:	Nacional
Medidas:	Constitución de la República, Decreto No 131, Título III, Capítulo VIII, Artículos 151 al 160 Ley Orgánica de Educación, Decreto No 79, Artículo 65 Ley de Educación Superior, Decreto No 142-89, Sección A y B, Capítulo V, Artículos 15 c) y ch); 20 ch) y 32 Ley de Escalafón del Magisterio, Artículo 4 Reglamento de Educación Primaria, Acuerdo No 4118EP, Artículos 140, 150, 151 y 152 Reglamento de Educación Media, Acuerdo No 4118EP, Artículos 502, 503, 504, 505 y 506 Reglamento General de la Ley de Educación Superior, Artículo 64 b) y 70 a) Reglamento de la Ley de Inversiones, Acuerdo No. 345-92 Artículo No. 51
Descripción:	Inversión Los cargos de dirección y supervisión en los establecimientos de enseñanza solo podrán ser desempeñados por maestros hondureños por nacimiento. Servicios transfronterizos La enseñanza de la Constitución, educación cívica, geografía e historia de Honduras, solo podrán ser desempeñados por maestros hondureños por nacimiento. Se reconoce a las personas jurídicas hondureñas, creadas especialmente para ello, la iniciativa de promover la fundación de centros o universidades particulares dentro del respeto a la Constitución y las leyes.

	Se requiere autorización de la Secretaría de Educación Publica de Honduras, para la prestación de servicios de Jardines de Niños, escuelas, institutos y academias privados. Para la obtención de la autorización se requiere, entre otros requisitos, una certificación de que se ha obtenido personería jurídica. La creación y funcionamiento de centros de educación superior públicos o privados, requiere la aprobación del Consejo de Educación Superior previo dictamen del Consejo Técnico Ejecutivo. Los centros de Educación Superior por su naturaleza y constitución podrán ser Públicos o estatales y Privados o particulares, cuando sean constituidos como asociaciones o fundaciones civiles o sociedades mercantiles y cualquier otra forma de asociación, sea nacional o extranjera. Para la presentación de solicitud para la creación, organización y funcionamiento de centros estatales o públicos se deberá acreditar la Constitución y organización legal del solicitante Para el ejercicio de la docencia en cualquiera de los niveles del sistema educativo, a que se refiere la ley, se requiere poseer título docente y ser ciudadano hondureño por nacimiento, natural o naturalizado, excepto en los casos en que no haya personal nacional capacitado para la enseñanza de asignaturas especiales en el nivel medio y magisterial. Los maestros sin título docente tendrán el carácter de interinos. Para inscribirse en el Escalafón del Magisterio se requiere ser hondureño por nacimiento, natural o naturalizado. Para que un extranjero pueda ejercer la docencia en la educación media, debe estar legalmente incorporado.
Calendario de educción:	Ninguno

Sector :	Servicios de Enseñanza
Subsector:	Escuelas privadas Servicios de educación preescolar (jardines de niños) Servicios privados de educación primaria Servicios privados de educación secundaria Programas especiales
Clasificación Industrial	CPC 921. Servicios de enseñanza primaria CPC 922. Servicios de enseñanza secundaria
Tipo de Reserva:	Trato nacional (Artículo 10-04) Presencia local (Artículo 10-05)
Nivel de Gobierno:	Nacional
Medidas:	Ley Orgánica de Educación, Decreto No 79, Artículo 64 Reglamento General de la Educación Media, Artículo 110 Ley del Estatuto del Docente No 136-97, Artículos 7 y 8
Descripción:	Servicios transfronterizos Para el ejercicio de la docencia en cualquiera de los niveles del sistema educativo a que se refiere la Ley Orgánica de Educación, se requiere poseer título docente y ser ciudadano hondureño por nacimiento, natural o naturalizado, excepto en los casos en que no haya personal nacional capacitado para la enseñanza de asignaturas especiales en el nivel medio y magisterial. Los maestros sin título docente tendrán el carácter de interinos. Para ingresar a la carrera docente se requiere ser hondureño por nacimiento. Los docentes centroamericanos y de otra nacionalidad podrán ingresar a la carrera docente, siempre que en su país de origen exista reciprocidad. Para que un extranjero pueda ejercer la docencia en la educación media, debe estar legalmente incorporado.
Calendario de Reducción:	Ninguno

Sector:	Servicios de Esparcimiento
Subsector:	Artistas musicales
Clasificación Industrial:	CPC 96192. Servicios proporcionados por actores, compositores, escultores, artistas del espectáculo y otros artistas a título individual (exclusivamente artistas musicales)
Tipo de Reserva:	Trato nacional (Artículo 10-04) Requisitos de desempeño (Artículo 14-07) Nivel de Gobierno: Nacional
Medidas:	Ley de Protección a los Artistas Musicales, Decreto No 123, Artículos 1, 2, 3, 4, 7 y 8
Descripción:	Servicios transfronterizos e Inversión
	Los artistas musicales extranjeros para trabajar eventualmente en Honduras ya sea en forma individual o en conjunto deberán previo pagarle al sindicato musical más representativo del país un DIEZ POR CIENTO (10%) de sus honorarios como "cuota de paso" y el empresario o arrendatario deberá contratar para el mismo espectáculo artistas musicales del país, por lo menos en igualdad de condiciones de número, calidad y honorarios, conforme a tarifas establecidas o que se establezcan en la localidad de que se trata.
	Cuando no hubiere disponibles artistas musicales en igualdad de condiciones, de numero, clase y honorario según dictamen del sindicato, se pagará únicamente la cuota expresada, pero si el empresario o arrendatario no deseare los servicios de artistas nacionales, se pagará en concepto de cuota de paso UN CUARENTA POR CIENTO (40%) de los honorarios pactados por los artistas musicales extranjeros. Si hubiere artistas musicales del país disponibles en la localidad de que se trate, en el mismo acto el empresario o arrendatario deberá acordar con el sindicato la ocupación de estos bajo las condiciones previstas en el artículo que antecede el sindicato para este fin hará consulta con los conjuntos musicales nacionales y aplicará en cada caso una tabla de sistema rotativo que deberá de establecerse por localidad o bien por zona según lo considere conveniente.
	Si los honorarios de los músicos extranjeros según los contratos respectivos, fueren inferiores a los establecidos en la localidad, para los efectos de pago de la "cuota de paso", los porcentajes determinados en los párrafos anteriores serán calculados conforme a las tarifas locales.
	Antes del ingreso de los artistas musicales extranjeros, el contratante de los mismos o quien los represente deberá obtener del sindicato indicado en el párrafo primero su autorización escrita para actuar en el país. Dicha autorización se dará con vista del contrato respectivo y previo pago de la cantidad de dinero que corresponda deducir de los honorarios conforme a los porcentajes señalados según el caso.
	Quedan excluidos de las obligaciones económicas anteriores los artistas de la música cuando actúen para fines de asistencia social o esencialmente culturales, ya sea por iniciativa propia o por patrocinio de entidades nacionales o extranjeras de carácter público o privado.
	Los artistas musicales extranjeros que ingresen al país para actuar ocasionalmente al amparo de esta ley, no les será aplicable la prohibición de ejercer trabajos lucrativos, señalados en el artículo 4 de la Ley de Migración.
Calendario de Reducción:	Ninguno

Sector::	Servicios de Esparcimiento, Culturales y Deportivos
Subsector:	Campeonatos y competencias de fútbol
Clasificación Industrial:	CPC. 96412 Servicios de organización de espectáculos deportivos
Tipo de Reserva:	Trato de nación más favorecida (Artículo 10-03) Trato nacional (Artículo 10-04)

	Presencia local (Artículo 10-05)
Nivel de Gobierno:	Nacional
Medidas:	Reglamento de Campeonatos y Competencias Liga Nacional de Fútbol No Aficionado de Primera División
Descripción:	Servicios Transfronterizos
	Para la inscripción de jugadores extranjeros se exigirá constancia extendida por el Ministerio de Gobernación y Justicia expresando que el documento de residencia está en trámite. Cada club afiliado podrá inscribir un máximo de cuatro (4) jugadores extranjeros, siendo uno de ellos obligatoriamente de nacionalidad centroamericana.
Calendario de Reducción:	Ninguno

Sector:	Servicios de esparcimiento, culturales y deportivos
Subsector:	Casinos de juegos de envite o azar (abarca juegos de ruleta, damas, baraja, punto y banca, bacará máquinas tragamonedas y otros similares)
Clasificación Industrial:	CPC 96492. Servicios de juegos de azar y apuestas
Tipo de Reserva:	Trato nacional (Artículo 10-04) Presencia local (Artículo 10-05)
Nivel de Gobierno:	Nacional
Medidas:	Decreto No 488, Ley de Casinos de Juegos de Envite o Azar, Artículo 3-Acuerdo No 520 Reglamento Ley de Casinos de Juegos de Envite o Azar
Descripción:	Servicios transfronterizos Solamente los hondureños por nacimiento y las personas jurídicas constituidas de conformidad a las leyes del país, podrán solicitar al poder ejecutivo, licencia para la operación de casinos de juegos de envite o azar.
Calendario de Reducción:	Ninguno

Sector:	Servicios Prestados a las Empresas
Subsector:	Agentes aduanales y agencias aduaneras
Clasificación Industrial:	CPC 87909. Otros servicios a las empresas n.c.p.
Tipo de Reserva:	Trato nacional (Artículos 10-04 y 14-04) Presencia local (Artículo 10-05) Nivel de Gobierno: Nacional
Medidas:	Ley de Aduanas, Decreto No 212-87, Título IX, Capítulo I, Sección Primera y Tercera, Artículos 176, 177, 180 y 182
Descripción:	Servicios transfronterizos e Inversión Las agencias aduaneras para poder operar en las aduanas del país, deberán inscribirse en la Secretaría de Finanzas, que autorizará su operación siempre y cuando se disponga de los servicios profesionales de un agente aduanal con licencia valida y extendida en legal forma. Para obtener licencia de agente aduanal se requiere ser ciudadano hondureño por nacimiento y estar en pleno ejercicio de sus derechos civiles. Es obligación de los agentes aduanales mantener abierta una oficina en el lugar donde radique la aduana o aduanas donde ejerza sus funciones. Los empleados auxiliares que designe el agente aduanal para gestionar en su nombre y representación, trámites antes las administraciones de aduanas, deberán ser ciudadanos hondureños por nacimiento y en el pleno ejercicio de sus derechos civiles.
Calendario de Reducción:	Ninguno

Sector:	Servicios Prestados a las empresas
Subsector:	Almacenes generales de depósito
Clasificación Industrial:	CPC 742. Servicios de almacenamiento
Tipo de Reserva:	Presencia local (Artículo 10-05)
Nivel de Gobierno:	Nacional
Medidas:	Acuerdo No. 1055, Reglamento de los Almacenes Generales de Depósitos, Artículo 3
Descripción:	Servicios transfronterizos Para prestar los servicios de almacenes generales de depósito, deberá de constituirse en Honduras una sociedad anónima de capital fijo y con finalidad única.
Calendario de Reducción:	Ninguno

Sector :	Servicios Prestados a las Empresas
Subsector:	Servicios de investigación y seguridad
Clasificación Industrial:	CPC 873. Servicios de investigación y seguridad
Tipo de Reserva:	Presencia local (Artículo 10-05) Trato nacional (Artículo 14-04) Alta dirección empresarial y consejos de administración (Artículo 14-08)
Nivel de Gobierno:	Nacional
Medidas:	Ley Orgánica de la Policía Nacional, Artículo 91, Decreto No. 156-98
Descripción:	Servicios transfronterizos e Inversión La Secretaría de Estado en el Despacho de Seguridad, previo dictamen de la Dirección respectiva, podrá autorizar la operación de servicios privados de seguridad (servicios de vigilancia preventiva, servicios de investigación privada y servicios de capacitación de sus miembros). Las empresas extranjeras que solicitaren permiso para la prestación de servicios privados de seguridad, deberán asociarse con empresas hondureñas dedicadas a la misma actividad y nombrar un gerente hondureño por nacimiento.
Calendario de Reducción:	Ninguno

Sector:	Transporte
Subsector:	Transporte marítimo: navegación de cabotaje
Clasificación Industrial:	CPC 72. Servicios de transporte por vía acuática
Tipo de Reserva:	Trato de nación más favorecida (Artículo 10-03) Presencia local (Artículo 10-05) Trato nacional (Artículo 14-04)
Nivel de Gobierno:	Nacional
Medidas:	Decreto No 167-94, de fecha 2 de enero de 1995, Ley Orgánica de la Marina Mercante Nacional, Título III, Capítulos I, II y VII, Artículos 40 al 42 y 48 Acuerdo No. 000764, Reglamento de Transporte Marítimo del 13 de diciembre de 1997
Descripción:	Servicios transfronterizos e Inversión Se entiende por navegación de cabotaje, la que no siendo navegación interior, se efectúa entre puertos o puntos situados dentro del territorio nacional. La navegación de cabotaje con finalidad mercantil esta reservada a buques mercantes hondureños. Excepcionalmente cuando no existan buques mercantes hondureños o no se encuentren disponibles y por el tiempo que perdure tal circunstancia, la Dirección General de la Marina Mercante Nacional podrá autorizar que buques mercantes extranjeros, en particular de nacionalidad centroamericana, puedan prestar servicios de

	cabotaje en Honduras. La empresa naviera deberá estar constituida de conformidad con la leyes de país, que de su capital social suscrito y pagado como mínimo, un 51% pertenezca a ciudadanos hondureños y que el domicilio de la empresa esté en el país.
Calendario de Reducción:	Ninguno

Sector:	Transporte
Subsector:	Servicios de transporte aéreo
Clasificación Industrial:	CPC 73. Servicios de transporte por vía aérea
Tipo de Reserva:	Trato nacional (Artículo 14-04) Alta dirección empresarial y consejos de administración (Artículo 14-08)
Nivel de Gobierno:	Nacional
Medidas:	Decreto No 146, Ley de Aeronáutica Civil, Capítulo X, Sección segunda, tercera y cuarta, Artículos 75 al 102 Acuerdo No 001518, Reglamento de Certificados de Explotación y Permisos Provisionales para la Prestación de Servicio Aéreo de Transporte Publico Nacional e Internacional de Pasajeros Carga y Correo
Descripción:	Inversión Solo las personas naturales o jurídicas hondureñas podrán inscribir en el Registro Aeronáutico Administrativo Hondureño aeronaves destinadas a servicio de transporte público o a trabajos aéreos por remuneración. Solo las personas naturales o jurídicas de nacionalidad hondureña tendrán derecho a explotar servicios aéreos de transporte público, ya sean estos servicios regulares o no regulares, internos o internacionales, por medio de aeronave que se ampare con la bandera de Honduras. Las personas jurídicas a las que se refiere el numeral anterior, deberán reunir además los siguientes requisitos: a) el 51% de su capital, por lo menos debe pertenecer a hondureños; y b) el control, efectivo de la empresa y la dirección de la misma, deberán estar igualmente en poder de hondureños. Los servicios aéreos de transporte público entre dos puntos cualesquiera del territorio nacional, quedan reservados a las aeronaves hondureñas.
Calendario de Reducción:	Ninguno

Sector:	Transporte
Subsector:	Servicios de transporte aéreo (limitado a inscripción de aeronaves, servicios aéreos especializados, y personal técnico aeronáutico)
Clasificación Industrial:	CPC 73. Servicios de transporte por vía aérea (limitado a inscripción de aeronaves, servicios aéreos especializados y personal técnico aeronáutico)
Tipo de Reserva:	Trato de nación más favorecida (Artículo 10-03) Trato nacional (Artículo 10-04)
Nivel de Gobierno:	Nacional
Medidas:	Decreto No 146, Ley de Aeronáutica Civil, Capítulo X, Secciones segunda, tercera y cuarta, Artículos 75 al 102 Acuerdo No 001518, Reglamento de Certificados de Explotación y Permisos Provisionales para la Prestación de Servicio Aéreo de Transporte Público Nacional e Internacional de Pasajeros Carga y Correo
Descripción:	Servicios transfronterizos

	Solo las personas naturales o jurídicas hondureñas podrán inscribir en el Registro Aeronáutico Administrativo Hondureño aeronaves destinadas a servicio de transporte público o a trabajos aéreos por remuneración. Para realizar servicios privados por remuneración se requiere autorización de la Secretaría de Obras Publicas Transporte y Vivienda y ser persona natural o jurídica hondureña. Solo personal técnico aeronáutico hondureño, podrá ejercer en Honduras actividades remuneradas de aeronáutica nacional. A falta de este personal se podrá permitir que ejerzan dichas actividades pilotos u otros miembros de personal técnico extranjero, dando preferencia en este caso al personal de cualquier otro país del istmo centroamericano.
Calendario de Reducción:	Ninguno

Sector:	Transporte
Subsector:	Ferrocarril
Clasificación Industrial:	CPC 711. Servicio de transporte por ferrocarril
Tipo de Reserva:	Trato nacional (Artículo 14-04)
Nivel de Gobierno:	Nacional
Medidas:	Decreto No. 48, Ley Constitutiva del Ferrocarril Nacional de Honduras, Capítulos I y VIII, Artículos 1, 32 y 34, Artículo 12 reformado mediante Decreto No. 54.
Descripción:	Inversión El Ferrocarril Nacional de Honduras (Ferrocarril Nacional) es un organismo autónomo del Estado con personería, patrimonio propio y duración indefinida. Si el Ferrocarril Nacional optare por establecer empresas subsidiarias, queda facultado para vigilar y supervisar la marcha de dichas empresas. En casos especiales, el Ferrocarril Nacional podrá vender dichas empresas subsidiarias a empresarios particulares de nacionalidad hondureña quienes se encargarán de continuar prestando los mismos servicios. Para ser gerente del Ferrocarril Nacional, se requiere ser hondureño por nacimiento. El auditor, que será un contador público autorizado, debe ser hondureño por nacimiento.
Calendario de Reducción:	Ninguno

Sector:	Transporte
Subsector:	Servicios de Transporte terrestre por carretera
Clasificación Industrial :	CPC 712. Otros servicios de transporte por vía terrestre
Tipo de Reserva:	Trato de nación más favorecida (Artículo 10-03) Trato nacional (Artículos 10-04, 14-04) Presencia local (Artículo 10-05)
Nivel de Gobierno:	Nacional
Medidas:	Decreto No 319, Ley de Transporte, Artículos 3, 5 y 17 Reglamento de la Ley de Transporte, Artículo 7
Descripción:	Servicios transfronterizos e Inversión Se reserva exclusivamente a las personas naturales o jurídicas hondureñas, de interés público o particular, el derecho de prestar el servicio de transporte interno. El servicio público de transporte internacional podrá prestarse también por empresas extranjeras a base del principio de reciprocidad equitativa. Se requiere certificado o permiso de explotación extendido por el Poder Ejecutivo o por la Dirección General de Transporte respectivamente, para la prestación de servicios de transporte terrestre. El certificado de

	explotación y el permiso se otorgarán a hondureños por nacimiento y a personas jurídicas en cuyo capital social predomine la inversión nacional. En todo caso, el capital netamente hondureño no podrá ser inferior al 51% del capital social. Los servicios y actividades de transporte, estarán sujetos a las siguientes condiciones: **a)** El servicio público de transporte interno, solamente podrán prestarlo los hondureños y las personas jurídicas constituidas en Honduras, conforme a las leyes nacionales y cuyo capital por lo menos en un 51% pertenezca a hondureños. En igualdad de condiciones se preferirá a hondureños por nacimiento. **b)** El servicio internacional de pasajeros y carga será prestado preferentemente por personas naturales o jurídicas hondureñas, quienes podrán hacerlo por sí o en combinación con empresas extranjeras. Tales convenios deberán ser aprobados por la Dirección General de Transporte. Estas previsiones dejan a salvo los convenios y tratados celebrados por Honduras con otros Estados así como el principio de reciprocidad equitativa.
Calendario de Reducción:	Ninguno

Sector:	Transporte
Subsector:	Servicios de transporte terrestre por carretera
Clasificación Industrial:	CPC 712. Otros servicios de transporte por vía terrestre
Tipo de Reserva:	Trato de nación más favorecida (Artículo 10-03)
Nivel de Gobierno:	Nacional
Medidas:	Decreto No. 177-94 del 1 de marzo de 1995
Descripción:	Servicios transfronterizos El gobierno de la República de Honduras tiene la discreción de expedir licencias y autorizaciones sobre la base de reciprocidad.
Calendario de Reducción:	Ninguno

Sector:	Transporte
Subsector:	Servicios de transporte terrestre de carga por carretera
Clasificación Industrial:	CPC 7123. Transporte de carga
Tipo de Reserva:	Trato de nación más favorecida (Artículo 10-03)
Nivel de Gobierno:	Nacional
Medidas:	Resolución No. 64-98 (COMRIEDRE), aprobada por el Consejo de Ministros Responsables de la Integración Económica y Desarrollo Regional el 19 de enero de 1998.
Descripción:	Servicios transfronterizos Se establece un mecanismo de tratamiento recíproco y no discriminatorio para el servicio de transporte de carga entre los seis Estados miembros del Protocolo de Tegucigalpa (Costa Rica, El Salvador, Guatemala, Honduras, Nicaragua y Panamá) que comprende lo siguiente: a) Plena libertad de tránsito a través de sus territorios para los medios de transporte de carga terrestre de mercancías destinadas de Panamá hacia cualquier país centroamericano, y de cualquier país centroamericano hacia Panamá. b) La libertad de tránsito implica la garantía de libre competencia en la contratación del transporte sin perjuicio del país de origen o destino y el trato nacional al transporte de todos los Estados en el territorio de

	cualquiera de ellos, con los orígenes y destinos señalados supra.
Calendario de Reducción:	Ninguno

LISTA DE HONDURAS

Sector:	Servicios de Aeroportuarios
Subsector:	Servicios auxiliares de navegación aérea
Clasificación Industrial:	CPC 74620. Servicio de control de trafico aéreo CPC 74690. Otros servicios auxiliares del transporte aéreo
Tipo de Reserva:	Trato de nación más favorecida (Artículo 10-03) Trato nacional (Artículo 10-04) Presencia local (Artículo 10-05)
Nivel de Gobierno:	Nacional
Descripción:	Servicios Transfronterizos Honduras se reserva el derecho de adoptar o mantener cualquier medida que aplique el suministro de los servicios auxiliares de navegación aérea.
Medidas Vigentes:	Ley de Aeronáutica Civil, Decreto No 146, Capítulo VIII, Artículo 60

Sector:	Servicios de Comunicaciones
Subsector:	Correos
Clasificación Industrial:	CPC 75111. Servicios postales: cartas
Tipo de Reserva:	Trato de nación más favorecida (Artículo 10-03) Trato nacional (Artículo 10-04) Presencia local (Artículo 10-05)
Nivel de Gobierno:	Nacional
Descripción:	Servicios transfronterizos La operación del sistema de correos en el ámbito nacional e internacional, vía superficie, marítima y aérea está a cargo exclusivo de HONDUCOR. El ejercicio de la potestad reguladora corresponde al Estado, a través de HONDUCOR.
Medidas Vigentes:	Reglamento Regulador de la Prestación de Servicios de Mensajería por parte de Empresas Privadas, Artículos 2 y 3

Sector:	Energía Eléctrica
Subsector:	
Clasificación Industrial:	CPC 17100. Energía eléctrica
Tipo de Reserva:	Trato de nación más favorecida (Artículo 10-03) Trato nacional (Artículo 10-04) Presencia local (Artículo 10-05)
Nivel de Gobierno:	Nacional
Descripción:	Servicios transfronterizos Transmisión de energía eléctrica, conducción de la operación del sistema de transmisión y centro de despacho.
Medidas Vigentes:	Ley Marco del Sub Sector Eléctrico, Decreto No 158-94,Capítulo V, Artículo 15

Sector:	Servicios de Esparcimiento, Culturales y Deportivos
Subsector:	Loterías
Clasificación Industrial:	

Tipo de Reserva:	Trato de nación más favorecida (Artículo 10-03) Trato Nacional (Artículo 10-04) Presencia local (Artículo 10-05)
Nivel de Gobierno:	Nacional
Descripción:	Servicios transfronterizos Corresponde al Patronato Nacional de la Infancia (PANI) la administración de la lotería nacional (lotería mayor y lotería menor) y otras loterías no tradicionales que en el futuro pueda crear o autorizar el PANI.
Medidas Vigentes:	Decreto No 438, publicado el 23 de abril de 1977

Sector:	Servicios Prestados a las Empresas
Subsector:	Servicios profesionales
Clasificación Industrial:	
Tipo de Reserva:	Trato de nación más favorecida (Artículo 10-03) Presencia local (Artículo 10-05)
Nivel de Gobierno :	Nacional
Descripción:	Servicios transfronterizos El centroamericano por nacimiento que haya obtenido en alguno de los Estados partes del Convenio, un título profesional o diploma Académico equivalente, que lo habilite en forma legal para ejercer una profesión universitaria, será admitido al ejercicio de esas actividades en los otros países, siempre que cumpla con los requisitos y formalidades que, para dicho ejercicio, exigen a sus nacionales graduados universitarios, las leyes del Estado donde se desea ejercer la profesión de que se trate. La anterior disposición será aplicable mientras el interesado conserve la nacionalidad de uno de los países de Centroamérica. Las disposiciones anteriores son aplicables al centroamericano por nacimiento que hubiere obtenido título universitario fuera de Centroamérica, siempre que se haya incorporado a una universidad centroamericana legalmente autorizada para ello. Se reconoce la validez en cada uno de los Estados partes del Convenio de los estudios académicos aprobados en las universidades de cualquiera de los otros Estados. A los centroamericanos emigrados o perseguidos por razones políticas que deseen ejercer sus profesiones o continuar sus estudios universitarios en cualquiera de los Estados partes del Convenio, se les extenderán licencias provisionales, en tanto sea dable a los interesados obtener la documentación del caso. Para otorgarlas, las entidades correspondientes de cada país seguirán información sumaria, a fin de comprobar los extremos necesarios. Para gozar de los beneficios del Convenio, los centroamericanos por naturalización deberán haber residido en forma continua por mas de cinco años en territorio centroamericano, después de obtener la naturalización. Para los efectos del Convenio, se entiende que la expresión "centroamericano por nacimiento" comprende todas las personas que gozan de la calidad jurídica de nacionales por nacimiento en cualquiera de los Estados signatarios. Asímismo, se entiende que la expresión "centroamericanos por naturalización" se refiere a quienes no siendo originarios de alguno de los Estados que suscriben el Convenio, se hayan naturalizado en cualquiera de ellos.
Medidas Vigentes:	Convenio sobre el Ejercicio de Profesiones Universitarias y Reconocimiento de Estudios Universitarios, vigente desde el 22 de junio de 1962. (Costa Rica, El Salvador, Guatemala, Honduras y Nicaragua)

Sector:	Servicios Prestados a las Empresas
Subsector:	Servicios profesionales
Clasificación Industrial:	CPC
Tipo de Reserva:	Trato de nación más favorecida (Artículo 10-03) Trato nacional (Artículo 10-04) Presencia local (Artículo 10-05)
Nivel de Gobierno :	Nacional
Descripción:	Servicios transfronterizos La autorización para el ejercicio profesional se concede en base a prescripciones de reciprocidad. Solo tendrán validez oficialmente en Honduras a nivel de enseñanza superior y educación profesional los títulos de carácter académico o diplomas reconocidos y otorgados por la Universidad Nacional Autónoma de Honduras (UNAH). El reconocimiento del título o diploma obtenidos en el extranjero, produce la incorporación del profesional a la UNAH. Solo las personas que ostenten título válido, podrán ejercer actividades profesionales. Para la incorporación de extranjeros no centroamericano se requiere acreditar residencia legal en el país. Se establece la colegiación profesional obligatoria para el ejercicio de las profesiones. Para la colegiación se exige entre otros requisitos el Acuerdo de incorporación en la UNAH. De no existir un colegio profesional específico para la profesión de que se trate, los profesionales universitarios deberán afiliarse al Colegio Profesional que tenga mayores afinidades con su profesión. Se requiere residencia legal para optar a la colegiación
Medidas Vigentes:	Constitución de la República de Honduras, Capítulo VIII, Artículo No 177 Ley de Colegiación Profesional Obligatoria, Artículos 1 y 2 Reglamento para el Reconocimiento de Estudios Universitarios e Incorporación de Profesionales, aprobado por el Consejo Universitario de la Universidad Nacional Autónoma de Honduras Decreto No. 177-94, de fecha 1 de marzo de 1995

Sector:	Servicios Prestados a las Empresas
Subsector:	Servicios profesionales: Administradores de empresas y carreras afines
Clasificación Industrial:	CPC 8640. Servicios de estudios de mercado y realización de encuestas de la opinión publica CPC 8650. Servicios de consultores en administración CPC 8660. Servicios relacionados con los consultores en administración
Tipo de Reserva:	Trato de nación más favorecida (Artículo 10-03) Trato nacional (Artículo 10-04)
Nivel de Gobierno :	Nacional
Descripción:	Servicios transfronterizos Para la Colegiación se exige reciprocidad, en el país de origen, hasta donde esta se extienda, a licenciados en administración de empresas y carreras afines graduados en el extranjero. La contratación de personas naturales extranjeras como consultores en Administración de Empresas o disciplinas afines solo podrá realizarse previo dictamen favorable del Colegio de Administradores de Empresas de Honduras. Existen costos de inscripción diferenciados para empresas consultoras extranjeras. La contratación de firmas extranjeras en administración de empresas solo podrá efectuarse por razones de especialidades que no se encuentren en el país, o bien por exigencias contractuales ineludibles y previo dictamen favorable del Colegio de Administradores de Empresas.

	La contratación de firmas extranjeras en administración de empresas solo podrá efectuarse a través de sociedades o consorcios con firmas nacionales debidamente inscritas en el Colegio de Administradores de Empresas. Para su inscripción en el Colegio de Administradores de Empresas de Honduras, las empresas extranjeras que pretendan dedicarse a prestar servicios de consultoría deberán acreditar la contratación de sus servicios profesionales acompañando copia del respectivo contrato.
Medidas Vigentes:	Ley Orgánica del Colegio de Administradores de Empresas de Honduras y su Reglamento

Sector:	Servicios Prestados a las Empresas
Subsector:	Servicios profesionales: arquitectos
Clasificación Industrial:	CPC 8671. Servicios de arquitectura CPC 8674. Servicios de planificación urbana y de arquitectura paisajista
Tipo de Reserva:	Trato de nación más favorecida (Artículo 10-03) Trato nacional (Artículo 10-04) Presencia local (Artículo 10-05)
Nivel de Gobierno :	Nacional
Descripción:	Servicios Transfronterizos Para la colegiación de extranjeros residentes legales en Honduras, graduados en el extranjero, se exige: **a)** constancia de reciprocidad del país de origen; **b)** constancia de que se ha cumplido con el servicio social; y **c)** constancia de buena conducta emitida por autoridad competente o cartas de tres (3) personas de moralidad reconocida. Las empresas extranjeras que se dediquen a la arquitectura serán inscritas únicamente para proyectos específicos y no podrán ejecutar otros proyectos o trabajos para los cuales no estén autorizados. Toda empresa extranjera constructora de obra de arquitectura o consultoras de arquitectura, esta obligada a registrarse y clasificarse provisionalmente en el Comité Intercolegial de Registro y Clasificación de Empresas Constructoras y Consultores en Ingeniería, para cada proyecto específico, como paso previo para poder inscribirse en el Colegio de Arquitectos de Honduras y podrá participar en licitaciones públicas o privadas y concursos para la prestación de servicios profesionales.
Medidas Vigentes:	Ley Orgánica del Colegio de Arquitectos de Honduras y su Reglamento

Sector:	Servicios Prestados a las Empresas
Subsector:	Servicios profesionales: enfermeras
Clasificación Industrial:	CPC 93191. Servicios proporcionados por comadronas, enfermeros, fisioterapeutas y personal paramédico
Tipo de Reserva:	Trato de nación más Favorecida (Artículo 10-03) Trato nacional (Artículo 10-04) Presencia local (Artículo 10-05)
Nivel de Gobierno :	Nacional
Descripción:	Servicios Transfronterizos Las enfermeras graduadas en el extranjero están obligadas a presentar examen de incorporación. Se requiere que todo profesional de enfermería cuya lengua materna no sea el español acredite a satisfacción del Colegio de Profesionales de la Enfermería hablar y escribir en forma suficiente el español para ejercer la

	profesión. Las enfermeras profesionales que ingresen al país en calidad de asesoras o consultoras de programas especiales, deben presentar sus credenciales al colegio. Para la inscripción en el Colegio las enfermeras extranjeras deben presentar además de su título, la partida de nacimiento autenticada o su pasaporte y el permiso de trabajo extendido por la oficina de migración. Se exige reciprocidad en el país de origen.
Medidas Vigentes:	Ley Orgánica del Colegio de Profesionales de la Enfermería

Sector:	Servicios Prestados a las Empresas
Subsector:	Servicios profesionales: economistas
Clasificación Industrial:	CPC 85202. Servicios de investigación y desarrollo en las ciencias económicas
Tipo de Reserva:	Presencia local (Artículo 10-05) Nivel de Gobierno: Nacional
Descripción:	Servicios transfronterizos Las firmas extranjeras de consultoría deberán estar representadas por un miembro del Colegio Hondureño de Economistas.
Medida Vigentes:	Ley Orgánica del Colegio Hondureño de Economistas

Sector:	Servicios Prestados a las Empresas
Subsector:	Servicios profesionales: ingenieros mecánicos, electricistas y químicos
Clasificación Industrial:	CPC 8672. Servicios de asesores y consultores en ingeniería CPC 86723. Servicios de diseño técnico de instalaciones mecánicas y eléctricas para edificios CPC 86726. Servicios de diseño técnico CPC 86729. Otros servicios de ingeniería CPC 86751. Servicios de prospección geológica, geofísica y de otros tipos de prospección científica CPC 8676. Servicios de ensayos y análisis técnicos
Tipo de Reserva:	Trato de nación más favorecida (Artículo 10-03)
Nivel de Gobierno :	Nacional
Descripción:	Servicios transfronterizos Se exige constancia de reciprocidad en el país de origen en el ejercicio profesional para la colegiación en el Colegio de Ingenieros Mecánicos, Eléctricos y Químicos.
Medidas Vigentes:	Ley Orgánica del Colegio de Ingenieros Mecánicos, Electricistas y Químicos de Honduras y su Reglamento

Sector:	Servicios Prestados a las Empresas
Subsector:	Servicios profesionales: Ingenieros civiles
Clasificación Industrial	CPC 8672. Servicios de ingeniería (excepto 86723 y 86725) CPC 8673. Servicios integrados de ingeniería CPC 8675. Servicios conexos de consultores en ciencia y tecnología (exclusivamente 86751, 86752, 86753 y 86754)
Tipo de Reserva:	Trato nacional (Artículo 10-04) Presencia local (Artículo 10-05)
Nivel de Gobierno:	Nacional
Descripción:	Servicios transfronterizos Para la colegiación de extranjeros se les exige la aprobación de un examen profesional ante el Colegio de Ingenieros Civiles de Honduras (CICH). Se exige el registro de título en el colegio para la realización de un trabajo específico, siempre que el colegio los autorice previa

comprobación de la necesidad de sus servicios y el plazo de permanencia en el país.

Si el profesional extranjero fuere autorizado por el CICH para actuar como asesor individual, deberá registrar su título en el Colegio de Ingenieros Civiles de Honduras y pagar una cuota inicial mas una cuota mensual durante el período que dure su asignación.

Las firmas nacionales que presten en su nómina de personal técnico en ofertas y concursos de manera individual a profesionales extranjeros ingenieros no colegiados y que no tengan su residencia en Honduras, deberán solicitar previamente la autorización del CICH, la cual se concederá cuando la necesidad de sus servicios sea debidamente comprobada, sin perjuicio de que en caso de obtener el contrato, dichos profesionales quedan obligados a inscribir sus títulos en el Colegio previa comprobación del plazo de su permanencia en el país y el pago de los derechos correspondientes.

Cuando una firma nacional contemple la utilización de asesores extranjeros individuales en una oferta, deberá previamente a la presentación de la oferta, solicitar la autorización provisional del CICH, debiendo acompañar el Curriculum Vitae de cada profesional, la justificación, alcance y duración de sus servicios.

Asimismo indicará el nombre del proyecto en que dicho personal participará y cualquier otro dato que la Junta Directiva estime conveniente mas un pago por asesor.

En caso de que la firma nacional saliera favorecida con la adjudicación del contrato deberá solicitar la autorización del CICH para que los Asesores Extranjeros puedan prestarle sus servicios profesionales y cumplir además con lo dispuesto en el reglamento en lo que le fuere aplicable y que servirá de base para ser calificados como asesores.

Si una firma nacional contempla la utilización de varios asesores extranjeros individuales, la participación de tales asesores será evaluada como conjunto conforme al reglamento y si resultara que la participación del conjunto es significativa dentro del alcance de los servicios y montos del contrato, entonces el Colegio exigirá de la firma nacional que pague una cuota anual de registro, debiendo efectuar la inscripción de los títulos de cada uno de los asesores de conformidad con lo dispuesto en la Ley Orgánica del CICH y pagar una cuota inicial y cuotas mensuales por cada uno de los asesores mientras duren sus servicios.

El personal profesional extranjero de una firma extranjera que presente una oferta, no será requerido a obtener una autorización provisional, pero si el contrato es adjudicado a la firma, el personal extranjero deberá inscribir su título en el CICH y pagar una cuota inicial y otra cuota mensual durante el tiempo que esté asignado al proyecto.

Los profesionales extranjeros no deben estar incluidos en nominas de personal técnico de ofertas de firmas nacionales o extranjeras, o como asesores, si no que deben haber sido contratados en forma directa para la realización de un trabajo específico por parte de una institución estatal o municipal. El personal profesional extranjero contratado por una institución estatal, municipal deberá inscribir su título y pagar una cuota inicial y una mensualidad durante el tiempo que dure el proyecto específico.

El personal profesional de la ingeniería extranjero de organismos internacionales no están obligados a registrar sus títulos para el desempeño de sus funciones en el país, mientras estén asignados por tales organismos en misiones oficiales, pero el organismo internacional deberá certificar el grado académico de dicho personal.

Cuando un gobierno u organismo extranjero efectúe donaciones o ayudas al país a través de personas o firmas extranjeras en la forma de asistencia técnica éstas y su personal están exentos de registro y del pago de la cuota correspondiente, pero el organismo internacional deberá certificar

	el grado académico de dicho personal. A efectos de lo anterior el gobierno u organismo extranjero o la institución nacional beneficiada deberá cumplir con los requisitos siguientes: **a)** Solicitud de excepción de pago y demás requisitos al CICH firmada por el funcionario responsable; y **b)** copia del Tratado o Convenio entre el país donante u organismo extranjero y el gobierno de Honduras.
Medidas Vigentes:	Ley Orgánica del Colegio de Ingenieros Civiles de Honduras y su Reglamento

Sector:	Servicios Prestados a las Empresas
Subsector:	Servicios profesionales: Ingenieros forestales
Clasificación Industrial:	CPC 86729. Otros servicios de ingeniería
Tipo de Reserva:	Trato nacional (Artículo 10-04) Presencia local (Artículo 10-05)
Nivel de Gobierno:	Nacional
Descripción:	Servicios transfronterizos Los extranjeros para ejercer actividades de consultoría y construcción en actividades propias de la ingeniería forestal deberán estar inscritos en el Colegio de Ingenieros Forestales de Honduras. Temporalmente serán incorporados al Colegio los profesionales graduados en el extranjero que presten sus servicios en Honduras en misiones de buena voluntad. Se requiere acreditar residencia legal para la colegiación de profesionales extranjeros de la ingeniería forestal especializados, y ser contratados, previa comprobación de la necesidad de sus servicios y autorización del Colegio. Cuando se trate de sociedades consultoras extranjeras éstas deberán contratar entre los miembros colegiados una contraparte nacional que sea significativa en relación a la magnitud del proyecto.
Medidas Vigentes:	Ley Orgánica del Colegio de Ingenieros Forestales de Honduras

Sector:	Servicios Prestados a las Empresas
Subsector:	Servicios profesionales: Cirujanos dentistas
Clasificación Industrial:	CPC 93123. Servicios de odontología
Tipo de Reserva:	Trato de nación más favorecida (Artículo 10-03) Trato nacional (Artículo 10-04) Presencia local (Artículo 10-05)
Nivel de Gobierno:	Nacional
Descripción:	Servicios transfronterizos Para ser miembro del Colegio de Cirujanos Dentistas de Honduras se requiere entre otros requisitos para los extranjeros: **a)** Constancia de haber realizado un año de servicio social ad-honorem autorizado y coordinado por el Colegio de Cirujanos Dentistas de Honduras, en el área rural del país, según conste en los archivos respectivos; **b)** constancia de haber residido en el país en forma permanente durante cinco años o más, después de haber obtenido título profesional. Se exime de este requisito a los dentistas extranjeros casados con hondureños, con dos o más años de matrimonio; y **c)** constancia de reciprocidad que especifique que odontólogos hondureños pueden ejercer la profesión en análoga circunstancia en el

	país de origen.
Medidas Vigentes:	Ley Orgánica del Colegio de Cirujanos Dentistas de Honduras y su Reglamento

Sector:	Servicios Prestados a las Empresas
Subsector:	Servicios profesionales: Contadores públicos
Clasificación Industrial	CPC 862. Servicios de contabilidad, auditoría y teneduría de libros CPC 863. Servicios de asesoramiento tributario
Tipo de Reserva:	Trato de nación más favorecida (Artículo 10-03) Trato nacional (Artículo 10-04) Presencia local (Artículo 10-05)
Nivel de Gobierno :	Nacional
Descripción:	Servicios transfronterizos Para ser miembro del Colegio Hondureño de Profesionales Universitarios en Contaduría Publica los extranjeros requieren acreditar: **a)** residencia legal; y **b)** reciprocidad en el país de origen
Medidas Vigentes:	Ley Orgánica del Colegio Hondureño de Profesionales Universitarios de Contaduría Publica

Sector:	Servicios Prestados a las Empresas
Subsector:	Servicios profesionales: Contadores públicos
Clasificación Industrial:	CPC 862. Servicios de contabilidad, auditoría y teneduría de libros CPC 863. Servicios de asesoramiento tributario
Tipo de Reserva:	Trato de nación más favorecida (Artículo 10-03) Presencia local (Artículo 10-05)
Nivel de Gobierno:	Nacional
Descripción:	Servicios transfronterizos Para la incorporación al Colegio de Peritos Mercantiles y Contadores Públicos de Honduras se exige reciprocidad. Las sociedades y firmas individuales de contadores públicos extranjeros que no estén legalmente constituidas en el país, no podrán operar en Honduras en actividades profesionales reguladas por la Ley Orgánica del Colegio de Peritos Mercantiles y Contadores Públicos de Honduras.
Medidas Vigentes:	Ley Orgánica del Colegio de Peritos Mercantiles y Contadores Públicos de Honduras. Decreto No. 74, publicado el 10 de octubre de 1996, con reformas del Decreto No. 117, publicado el 12 de febrero de 1971 Reglamento de la Ley Orgánica del Colegio de Peritos Mercantiles y Contadores Públicos de Honduras. Artículos 8 y 9

Sector:	Servicios Prestados a las Empresas
Subsector:	Servicios profesionales: psicólogos
Clasificación Industrial:	CPC 85201. Servicios de investigación y desarrollo en las letras, la sociología y la psicología
Tipo de Reserva:	Presencia local (Artículo 10-05) Nivel de Gobierno: Nacional
Descripción:	Servicios transfronterizos Para ser miembro del Colegio de Psicólogos de Honduras y obtener autorización para el ejercicio de la profesión, un extranjero requiere acreditar que cuenta con carnet de residencia y carnet de trabajo.
Medidas Vigentes:	Ley Orgánica del Colegio de Psicólogos de Honduras y su Reglamento

Sector:	Servicios Prestados a las Empresas
Subsector:	Servicios profesionales: Médicos veterinarios
Clasificación Industrial:	CPC 932. Servicios veterinarios
Tipo de Reserva:	Trato de nación más favorecida (Artículo 10-03) Trato nacional (Artículo 10-04) Presencia local (Artículo 10-05)
Nivel de Gobierno:	Nacional
Descripción:	Servicios transfronterizos Para que médicos veterinarios extranjeros sean miembros del colegio de médicos veterinarios de Honduras se requiere entre otros requisitos: **a)** Acreditar residencia legal; **b)** antecedentes de buena conducta en el país de origen; **c)** autorización de la Secretaría de Trabajo para poder laborar en el país; **d)** someterse a examen de admisión ante Comisión nombrada por la Junta Directiva del Colegio; y **e)** hablar y escribir correctamente el español. Se exceptúan de la ley los contratos en virtud de disposiciones contenidas en convenios de préstamos internacionales o tratados de asistencia técnica, de los cuales Honduras sea signatario. Existen costos de colegiación diferenciados para Centroamericanos y extranjeros no Centroamericanos. Para ser miembro de la Junta Directiva del Colegio Médico Veterinario de Honduras se requiere ser de nacionalidad hondureña.
Medidas Vigentes:	Ley Orgánica del Colegio de Médicos Veterinarios de Honduras y su Reglamento

Sector:	Servicios Prestados a las Empresas
Subsector:	Servicios Profesionales: Médicos
Clasificación Industrial:	CPC 85105. Servicios de investigación y desarrollo en las ciencias medicas y farmacéuticas CPC 93121. Servicios de medicina general CPC 93122. Servicios de médicos especialistas
Tipo de Reserva:	Trato nacional (Artículo 10-04)
Nivel de Gobierno :	Nacional
Descripción:	Servicios Transfronterizos Para ser miembro de la Junta Directiva del Colegio Médico de Honduras, se requiere ser hondureño por nacimiento. Se dará colegiación provisional a los médicos centroamericanos o extranjeros que quieran establecer su residencia en el país, como un medio para que puedan practicar là medicina durante el servicio médico social, exijiendose para ello presentar Constancia de finalizar sus dos (2) años de servicio médico social ad-honorem avalado por el Ministerio de Salud Pública y el Delegado del Colegio Médico del Departamento donde realizó su servicio médico social. Para la obtención de la colegiación provisional, en caso de ser extranjero, se deberá presentar la documentación que acredite la residencia legal en el país. Los médicos extranjeros que sean llamados en consulta, de conformidad al artículo 76 de la Ley Orgánica del Colegio Médico de Honduras, tendrán la obligación primordial de atender el o los casos para los cuales fueron expresamente llamados; para atender otras consultas será obligatoria la autorización del Colegio Médico de Honduras.
Medidas Vigentes:	Ley Orgánica del Colegio Médico de Honduras Reglamento Interno del Colegio Médico de Honduras Reglamento de

	Colegiación Profesional Artículos 1,2 y 4

Sector:	Servicios Prestados a las Empresas
Subsector:	Servicios profesionales: notarios
Clasificación Industrial:	CPC 85203. Servicios de investigación y desarrollo en el derecho CPC 861. Servicios jurídicos
Tipo de Reserva:	Trato nacional (Artículo 10-04)
Nivel de Gobierno:	Nacional
Descripción:	Servicios transfronterizos Para ejercer el notariado se requiere: **a)** ser abogado; **b)** ser mayor de veintiún años, ciudadano hondureño en ejercicio de sus derechos; y **c)** haber obtenido el correspondiente exequátur de la Corte Suprema de Justicia
Medidas Vigentes:	Ley del Notariado

Sector:	Servicios Prestados a las Empresas
Subsector:	Servicios profesionales: Periodistas
Clasificación Industrial:	CPC 962. Servicios de agencias de noticias
Tipo de Reserva:	Trato de nación más favorecida (Artículo 10-03) Trato nacional (Artículo 10-04) Presencia local (Artículo 10-05)
Nivel de Gobierno :	Nacional
Descripción:	Servicios transfronterizos Para ejercer las funciones de director, subdirector, jefe de redacción y jefe de información se requiere ser hondureño. Para ser miembro del Colegio de Periodistas de Honduras, entre otros requisitos se exige a los extranjeros: **a)** si hubiere adquirido sus conocimientos en el ejercicio práctico de la profesión, deberá presentar constancia de estar colegiado en el país de origen y haber residido por lo menos cinco (5) años consecutivos en Honduras; **b)** demostrar reciprocidad de los tratados y leyes entre Honduras y el país de origen en el ejercicio profesional del periodismo; **c)** tener actualizada su cédula de residencia; **d)** tener carnet de trabajo autorizado por el Ministerio de Trabajo; y **e)** para ser miembro de la Junta Directiva del Colegio de Periodistas de Honduras, se requiere ser hondureño por nacimiento.
Medidas Vigentes:	Ley Orgánica del Colegio de Periodistas de Honduras Reglamento Interno de los Miembros del Colegio de Periodistas de Honduras, Artículo 19

Sector:	Servicios Prestados a las Empresas
Subsector:	Servicios profesionales: Microbiólogos y clínicos
Clasificación Industrial:	
Tipo de Reserva:	Trato nacional (Artículo 10-04) Nivel de Gobierno: Nacional

Descripción:	Servicios transfronterizos Los extranjeros deberán cumplir con los siguientes requisitos: **a)** hacer servicio social de la carrera; y **b)** pagar una cuota de inscripción diferenciada al del nacional
Medidas Vigentes:	Reglamento del Colegio de Microbiólogos y Químicos Clínicos. Artículos 7 y 8

Sector:	Servicios Prestados a las Empresas
Subsector:	Servicios profesionales: Pedagogos
Clasificación Industrial:	
Tipo de Reserva:	Trato de nación más favorecida (Artículo 10-03) Trato nacional (Artículo 10-04)
Nivel de Gobierno:	Nacional
Descripción:	Servicios transfronterizos Los extranjeros solamente podrán dentro de los límites que establezca la ley, desempeñar empleos en la enseñanza de las ciencias y de las artes y prestar al Estado servicios técnicos y de asesoramiento, cuando no haya hondureños que puedan desempeñar dichos empleos y prestar tales servicios La enseñanza de la Constitución de la República, de la historia y geografía nacionales es obligatoria y estará a cargo de profesionales hondureños. Los docentes centroamericanos y de otra nacionalidad podrán ingresar a la carrera docente, siempre que en su país de origen exista reciprocidad.
Medidas Vigentes:	Constitución de la República, Artículos 34 y 168 Estatuto del Colegio de Pedagogos, Artículo 8

Sector:	Servicios Prestados a las Empresas
Subsector:	Servicios profesionales: Químicos y farmacéuticos
Clasificación Industrial:	CPC 85102. Servicios y desarrollo en la química y la biología CPC 85015 Servicios de investigación y desarrollo de las ciencias médicas farmacéuticas
Tipo de Reserva:	Trato de nación más favorecida (Artículo 10-03) Trato nacional (Artículo 10-04) Presencia local (Artículo 10-05)
Nivel de Gobierno :	Nacional
Descripción:	Servicios transfronterizos Honduras se reserva el derecho de adoptar o mantener cualquier medida que aplique a la colegiación profesional obligatoria de los doctores en química y farmacia.
Medidas Vigentes	

Sector:	Servicios Prestados a las Empresas
Subsector:	Servicios profesionales: Ingenieros agrónomos
Clasificación Industrial:	CPC 86729. Otros servicios de ingeniería
Tipo de Reserva:	Trato de nación más favorecida (Artículo 10-03) Trato nacional (Artículo 10-04) Presencia local (Artículo 10-05)
Nivel de Gobierno :	Nacional
Descripción:	Servicios Transfronterizos Honduras se reserva el derecho de adoptar o mantener cualquier medida que aplique a la colegiación profesional obligatoria de los ingenieros agrónomos

Medidas Vigentes	

Sector:	Servicios Relacionados con el Medio Ambiente
Subsector:	Servicios de alcantarillado, Abastecimiento de agua potable, ornato, aseo e higiene municipal Lucha contra la contaminación del medio marino
Clasificación Industrial:	CPC 94. Alcantarillado y eliminación de residuos, servicios de saneamiento y similares (excepto 94050)CPC 18000. Agua natural
Tipo de Reserva:	Trato de nación más favorecida (Artículo 10-03) Trato nacional (Artículo 10-04) Presencia Local (Artículo 10-05)
Nivel de Gobierno:	Nacional
Descripción:	Servicios Transfronterizos Honduras se reserva el derecho de adoptar o mantener cualquier medida que aplique sobre: **a)** Servicios de Alcantarillado, corresponde al Servicio Nacional de Acueductos y Alcantarillados (SANAA) la promoción, el desarrollo de los abastecimientos públicos de agua potable y alcantarillados sanitarios y pluviales en todo el país. Le corresponde a las municipalidades la construcción de acueductos, mantenimiento y administración del agua potable, alcantarillado sanitario y pluvial. **b)** Recolección, tratamiento y disposición de residuos sólidos y orgánicos. Les corresponde a las municipalidades el ornato, aseo e higiene municipal Corresponde a las municipalidades en consulta con la Secretaría de Estado en el Despacho de Salud Pública u otros organismos técnicos, adoptar un sistema de recolección, tratamiento y disposición final de los residuos sólidos y orgánicos, incluyendo las posibilidades de su reutilización o reciclaje. La prestación de servicios públicos municipales podrá realizarse por contrato con las municipalidades correspondientes. **c)** La lucha contra la contaminación del medio marino : El servicio de lucha contra la contaminación del medio marino se prestará por la Dirección General de la Marina Mercante con la colaboración de las demás dependencias del Poder Ejecutivo, en particular de las Secretarías de Estado en el Despacho de Recursos Naturales y Ambiente, de las Fuerza Naval y de la Autoridad Portuaria.
Medidas Vigentes:	Ley de Municipalidades, Decreto No 134-90, Artículo 13, numerales 3, 4 y 15

LISTA DE HONDURAS

Honduras se reserva el derecho exclusivo de desempeñar y de negarse a autorizar el establecimiento de inversiones en las siguientes actividades:

1. **Energía Eléctrica:**

   a) Descripción de actividades:

   Transmisión de energía eléctrica: conducción de la operación del sistema de transmisión y centro de despacho.

   b) Medidas

   Ley Marco del Sub Sector Eléctrico, Decreto No 158-94, Capítulo V, Artículo 15

2. Industria de Armas:

   a) Descripción de actividades:

   Explosivos, armas de fuego y cartuchos; fabricación, importación, distribución y venta de armas, municiones y artículos similares.

Se entenderá por armas, municiones y artículos similares, los siguientes:

- municiones;
- aeroplanos de Guerra,
- fusiles militares,
- pistolas y Revólveres de toda clase, calibre 41 o mayor;
- pistolas reglamentarias del Ejército de Honduras;
- silenciadores para toda clase de armas de fuego;
- armas de fuego;
- accesorios y municiones;
- cartuchos para armas de fuego;
- aparatos y demás accesorios indispensables para la carga de cartucho;
- pólvora, explosivos, fulminantes y mechas;
- mascaras protectoras contra gases asfixiantes;
- escopetas de viento.

   b) Medidas

   Constitución de la República, Título V, Capítulo X, Artículo 292

   Ley de Inversiones, Decreto No 80-92, Capítulo VI, Artículo 16

3. Servicios de Comunicaciones:

   a) Descripción de actividades:

Servicios de correos: La operación del servicio de correos en el ámbito nacional e internacional, vía superficie, marítima y aérea está a cargo exclusivo de HONDUCOR.

El ejercicio de la potestad reguladora corresponde al Estado, a través de HONDUCOR.

b) Medidas :
Reglamento Regulador de la Prestación de Servicios de Mensajería por parte de Empresas Privadas, Artículo 2 y 3

4. Servicios Relacionados con el Medio Ambiente:

a) Descripción de actividades:

i) Servicios de alcantarillado, corresponde al Servicio Nacional de Acueductos y Alcantarillados (SANAA) la promoción, el desarrollo de los abastecimientos públicos de agua potable y alcantarillados sanitarios y pluviales en todo el país.

Le corresponde a las municipalidades la construcción de acueductos, mantenimiento y administración del agua potable, alcantarillado sanitario y pluvial.

ii) recolección, tratamiento y disposición de residuos sólidos y orgánicos les corresponde a las municipalidades el ornato, aseo e higiene municipal.

Corresponde a las municipalidades en consulta con la Secretaría de Estado en el Despacho de Salud Pública u otros organismos técnicos, adoptar un sistema de recolección, tratamiento y disposición final de los residuos sólidos y orgánicos, incluyendo las posibilidades de su reutilización o reciclaje.

La prestación de servicios públicos municipales podrá realizarse por contrato con las unicipalidades correspondientes.

iii) Lucha contra la contaminación del medio marino: el servicio de lucha contra la contaminación del medio marino se prestara por la Dirección General de la Marina Mercante con la colaboración de las demás dependencias del Poder Ejecutivo, en particular de las Secretarías de Estado en el Despacho de Recursos Naturales y Ambiente, de la Fuerza Naval y de la Autoridad Portuaria

b) Medidas:

Ley de Municipalidades, Decreto No. 134-90, Artículos 13, numeral 4) numerales 3) y 15)

Reglamento de la Ley de Inversiones, Acuerdo No. 345-92 Artículo No.50

Ley General del Ambiente, Decreto No. 104-93, Artículo 67

Ley Orgánica de la Marina Mercante Nacional, Decreto 167-94, Artículo No.100

5.   Servicios de Esparcimiento, Culturales y Deportivos:

    a)   Descripción de actividades:

        Loterías: Corresponde al Patronato Nacional de la Infancia (PANI) la administración de la Lotería Nacional (Lotería Mayor y Lotería Menor) y otras loterías no tradicionales que en el futuro pueda crear o autorizar el PANI.

    b)   Medidas

        Decreto No. 438 publicado el 23 de abril de 1977

6.   Explotación de Servicios Aeroportuarios:

    a)   Descripción de actividades:

        Es atribución del Estado el control y suministro de los servicios auxiliares de navegación aérea.

    b)   Medidas:

        Ley de Aeronáutica Civil, Decreto No. 146, Capítulo VIII, Artículo No. 60.

7.   Emisión de Moneda:

    a)   Descripción de actividades:

        La emisión monetaria es potestad exclusiva del Estado, que la ejercerá por medio del Banco Central de Honduras

    b)   Medidas:

        Constitución de la República, Decreto No 131, Capítulo II, Artículo 342

        Ley del Banco Central de Honduras, Artículo 26 reformado mediante Decreto No. 228-96

        Ley Monetaria, Decreto No 51, Artículo 5

ANEXO IV
LISTA DE HONDURAS

Honduras exceptúa la aplicación del Artículo 14-05 (Trato de nación más favorecida), al tratamiento otorgado bajo aquellos acuerdos en vigor o firmados después de la fecha de entrada en vigor de este tratado, en materia de:

a)   aviación;

b)   pesca; o

c)   asuntos marítimos, incluyendo salvamento.

Para mayor certeza, el Artículo 14-05 no se aplica a ningún programa presente o futuro de cooperación internacional para promover el desarrollo económico.

ANEXO I
LISTA DE MEXICO

Sector:	Todos los sectores
Subsector :	
Clasificación Industrial:	
Tipo de Reserva:	Trato nacional (Artículo 14-04)
Nivel de Gobierno:	Federal
Medida:	Constitución Política de los Estados Unidos Mexicanos, Artículo 27 Ley de Inversión Extranjera, Diario Oficial, diciembre 27, 1993, Título II, Capítulos I y II Reglamento de la Ley de Inversión Extranjera y del Registro Nacional de Inversiones Extranjeras, D.O.F., Noviembre 1998, Título Segundo
Descripción:	Inversión Los extranjeros o las empresas extranjeras, no podrán adquirir el dominio directo sobre tierras y aguas en una faja de 100 kilómetros a lo largo de las fronteras y de 50 en las playas (la Zona Restringida). Las empresas mexicanas sin cláusula de exclusión de extranjeros podrán adquirir el dominio de bienes inmuebles destinados a la realización de actividades no residenciales ubicados en la Zona Restringida, debiendo dar aviso de dicha adquisición a la Secretaría de Relaciones Exteriores (SRE), dentro de los sesenta días hábiles siguientes a aquél en el que se realice la adquisición. Las empresas mexicanas sin cláusula de exclusión de extranjeros no podrán adquirir el dominio de bienes inmuebles destinados a fines residenciales ubicados en la Zona Restringida. Las empresas mexicanas sin cláusula de exclusión de extranjeros podrán adquirir conforme al procedimiento que se describe, derechos para la utilización y aprovechamiento sobre bienes inmuebles sobre la Zona Restringida, que sean destinados a fines residenciales. Dicho procedimiento también aplicará a los nacionales o empresas extranjeras para el mismo caso de conformidad con lo siguiente: Se requiere permiso de la SRE para que instituciones de crédito

	adquieran como fiduciarias, derechos sobre bienes inmuebles ubicados en la Zona Restringida,□cuando el objeto del fideicomiso sea permitir la utilización y el aprovechamiento de tales bienes sin constituir derechos reales sobre ellos.
	Se entenderá por utilización y aprovechamiento de los bienes inmuebles ubicados en la Zona Restringida los derechos al uso o goce de los mismos, incluyendo en su caso la obtención de frutos, productos y, en general, cualquier rendimiento que resulte de la operación y explotación lucrativa a través de terceros o de la institución fiduciaria.
	La duración de los fideicomisos a que esta reserva se refiere, será por un período máximo de cincuenta años, mismo que podrá prorrogarse a solicitud del interesado.
	La SRE podrá verificar en cualquier tiempo el cumplimiento de las condiciones, la presentación y veracidad bajo las cuales se otorguen los permisos.
	La SRE resolverá sobre los permisos, considerando el beneficio económico y social que la realización de estas operaciones implique para la Nación.
	Los nacionales extranjeros o las empresas extranjeras que pretendan adquirir bienes inmuebles fuera de la Zona Restringida, deberán presentar previamente ante la SRE, un escrito en el que convengan considerarse nacionales mexicanos para estos efectos y renunciar a invocar la protección de sus gobiernos respecto de dichos bienes.
Calendario de Reducción:	Ninguno

Sector:	Todos los sectores
Subsector :	
Clasificación Industrial:	
Tipo de Reserva:	Trato nacional (Artículo 14-04)
Nivel de Gobierno:	Federal
Medida:	Ley de Inversión Extranjera, Diario Oficial, diciembre 27, 1993, Título VI, Capítulo III
Descripción:	Inversión
	La Comisión Nacional de Inversiones Extranjeras (CNIE) para determinar la conveniencia de autorizar las solicitudes presentadas a su consideración para la adquisición o establecimiento de inversiones en las actividades restringidas, en las que se requiera dicha autorización, de conformidad con el presente Anexo deberá tomar en cuenta los siguientes criterios:
	a) el impacto sobre el empleo y la capacitación de los trabajadores;
	b) la contribución tecnológica;
	c) el cumplimiento de las disposiciones en materia ambiental contenidas en los ordenamientos ecológicos que rigen la materia; o
	d) en general, la aportación para incrementar la competitividad de la planta productiva de México.
	La CNIE al resolver sobre la procedencia de una solicitud, sólo podrá imponer Requisitos de desempeño que no distorsionen el comercio internacional y que no estén prohibidos por el Artículo de Requisitos de desempeño del capítulo de Inversión.
Calendario de Reducción:	Ninguno

Sector:	Todos los sectores
Subsector :	
Clasificación Industrial:	
Tipo de Reserva:	Trato nacional (Artículo 14-04)

Nivel de Gobierno:	Federal
Medida:	Ley de Inversión Extranjera, Diario Oficial, diciembre 27, 1993, Título I, Capítulo III Tal como la califica el elemento Descripción
Descripción:	Inversión Se requiere resolución favorable de la Comisión Nacional de Inversiones Extranjeras (CNIE) para que en las sociedades mexicanas donde la Inversión extranjera pretenda participar, directa o indirectamente, en una proporción mayor al 49 por ciento de su capital social, únicamente cuando el valor total de los activos de las sociedades de que se trate, al momento de someter la solicitud de adquisición, rebase el umbral aplicable.
Calendario de Reducción:	Para los inversionistas e inversiones de El Salvador, Guatemala y Honduras el umbral aplicable para la revisión de la adquisición de una empresa mexicana será de 150 millones de dólares de EE.UU. a partir del 1 de enero del año 2003. A partir del 1 de enero del año 2004, los umbrales serán ajustados anualmente de acuerdo a la tasa de crecimiento nominal del Producto Interno Bruto de México, de conformidad con lo que publique el Instituto Nacional de Estadística Geografía e Informática.

Sector:	Todos los sectores
Subsector :	
Clasificación Industrial:	
Tipo de Reserva:	Trato nacional (Artículo 14-04) Alta dirección empresarial y consejos de administración (Artículo 14-08)
Nivel de Gobierno:	Federal
Medida:	Constitución Política de los Estados Unidos Mexicanos, Artículo 25 Ley General de Sociedades Cooperativas, Diario Oficial, agosto 3, 1994, Título I, Capítulo Único Ley de Inversión Extranjera, Diario Oficial, diciembre 27, 1993, Título I, Capítulo III
Descripción:	Inversión No más del 10 por ciento de los miembros que integren una sociedad cooperativa de producción mexicana podrán ser extranjeros. Los extranjeros no podrán desempeñar puestos de dirección o de administración general en las sociedades cooperativas.
Calendario de Reducción:	Ninguno

Sector:	Todos los sectores
Subsector :	
Clasificación Industrial:	
Tipo de Reserva:	Trato nacional (Artículo 14-04)
Nivel de Gobierno:	Federal
Medida:	Ley Federal para el Fomento de la Microindustria y la Actividad Artesanal, Diario Oficial, julio 22, 1991, Capítulos I, II y III
Descripción:	Inversión Sólo los nacionales mexicanos podrán solicitar cédula para calificar como empresa microindustrial. Una "empresa microindustrial" mexicana no podrá tener como socios a personas de nacionalidad extranjera. La Ley Federal para el Fomento de la Microindustria y la Actividad Artesanal define a la "empresa microindustrial" como, entre otras cosas, aquélla que cuenta hasta con 15 trabajadores, que se dedican a la

	transformación de bienes y cuyas ventas anuales no excedan los montos determinados periódicamente por la Secretaría de Comercio y Fomento Industrial, los cuales se publicarán en el Diario Oficial de la Federación.
Calendario de Reducción:	Ninguno

Sector:	Agricultura, ganadería, silvicultura y actividades madereras
Subsector :	Agricultura, ganadería o silvicultura
Clasificación Industrial:	CMAP 1111 Agricultura CMAP 1112 Ganadería y caza (limitado a ganadería) CMAP 1200 Silvicultura y tala de árboles
Tipo de Reserva:	Trato nacional (Artículo 14-04)
Nivel de Gobierno:	Federal
Medida:	Constitución Política de los Estados Unidos Mexicanos, Artículo 27 Ley Agraria, Diario Oficial, julio 7, 1993, Títulos V y VI Ley de Inversión Extranjera, Diario Oficial, diciembre 27, 1993, Título I, Capítulo III
Descripción:	Inversión Sólo los nacionales mexicanos o las empresas mexicanas podrán ser propietarios de tierra destinada para propósitos agrícolas, ganaderos o forestales. Tales empresas deberán emitir una serie especial de acciones (acciones "T"), que representan el valor de la tierra al momento de su adquisición. Los inversionistas de las otras Partes o sus inversiones sólo podrán adquirir hasta el 49 por ciento de participación en las acciones serie "T".
Calendario de Reducción:	Ninguno

Sector:	Comercio
Subsector :	Comercio de productos no alimenticios en establecimientos especializados
Clasificación Industrial:	CMAP 623087 Comercio al por menor de armas de fuego, cartuchos y Municiones CMAP 612024 Comercio al por mayor no clasificado en otra parte (limitado a armas de fuego, cartuchos y municiones)
Tipo de Reserva:	Trato nacional (Artículo 14-04)
Nivel de Gobierno:	Federal
Medida:	Ley de Inversión Extranjera, Diario Oficial, diciembre 27, 1993, Título I, Capítulo III
Descripción:	Inversión Los inversionistas de las otras Partes o sus inversiones sólo podrán adquirir, hasta un 49 por ciento de la participación en una empresa establecida o por establecerse en el territorio de México que se dedique a la venta de explosivos, armas de fuego, cartuchos, municiones y fuegos artificiales, sin incluir la adquisición de explosivos para actividades industriales y extractivas, ni la elaboración de mezclas explosivas para el consumo de dichas actividades. Para efectos de determinar este límite máximo de participación, no se computará la Inversión extranjera que, de manera indirecta, sea realizada en esta actividad a través de sociedades mexicanas con mayoría de capital mexicano, siempre que estas últimas no se encuentren controladas por la Inversión extranjera.
Calendario de Reducción:	Ninguno

Sector:	Comunicaciones
Subsector :	Servicios de esparcimiento (radiodifusión, sistemas de distribución multipunto MDS/MMDS, música continua, DTH y DBS y televisión de alta definición)
Clasificación Industrial:	CMAP 941104 Servicios privados de producción y transmisión privada de programas de radio (limitadas a producción y transmisión de programas de radio, MDS/MMDS y música continua) CMAP 941105 Servicios privados de producción, transmisión y repetición de programas de televisión, (limitados a la transmisión y repetición de programas de televisión, MDS/MMDS, sistemas directos de distribución (DTH y DBS) y televisión de alta definición)
Tipo de Reserva:	Trato nacional (Artículos 10-04 y 14-04) Presencia local (Artículo 10-05)
Nivel de Gobierno:	Federal
Medida:	Constitución Política de los Estados Unidos Mexicanos, Artículo 32 Ley de Vías Generales de Comunicación, Diario Oficial, febrero 19, 1940, Libro I, Capítulo III Ley Federal de Telecomunicaciones, Diario Oficial, junio 7, 1995, Capítulo III, Sección I Ley Federal de Radio y Televisión, Diario Oficial, enero 19, 1960, Título III, Capítulo I Reglamento de la Ley Federal de Radio y Televisión y de la Ley de la Industria Cinematográfica Relativo al Contenido de las Transmisiones de Radio y Televisión, Diario Oficial, enero 19, 1960, Título III Ley de Inversión Extranjera, Diario Oficial, diciembre 27, 1993, Título I, Capítulo II
Descripción:	Servicios transfronterizos e Inversión Se requiere concesión otorgada por la Secretaría de Comunicaciones y Transportes para prestar servicios de radiodifusión, sistemas de distribución multipunto MDS/MMDS, música continua, DTH y DBS y televisión de alta definición. Sólo los nacionales mexicanos y las empresas mexicanas con cláusula de exclusión de extranjeros podrán prestar servicios o realizar inversiones en las actividades mencionadas en el párrafo anterior. Esta reserva no se aplica a la producción, venta o autorización de derechos de programas de radio o televisión.
Calendario de Reducción:	Ninguno
Sector:	Comunicaciones
Subsector :	Servicios de esparcimiento (radiodifusión, sistemas de distribución multipunto (MDS/MMDS) y televisión por cable)
Clasificación Industrial:	CMAP 941104 Producción y transmisión privada de programas de radio (limitados a producción y transmisión de programas de radio, MDS/MMDS y música continua) CMAP 941105 Servicios privados de producción, transmisión y repetición de programas de televisión (limitado a producción, transmisión y repetición de programas de televisión, MDS/MMDS, sistemas directos de distribución (DTH y DBS), televisión de alta definición y televisión por cable)
Tipo de Reserva:	Trato nacional (Artículo 10-04) Requisitos de desempeño (Artículo 14-07)
Nivel de Gobierno:	Federal
Medidas:	Ley Federal de Radio y Televisión, Diario Oficial, enero 19, 1960 Título IV, Capítulo III Reglamento de la Ley Federal de Radio y Televisión y de la Ley de la Industria Cinematográfica Relativo al Contenido de las Transmisiones de

	Radio y Televisión, Diario Oficial, enero 19, 1960, Título III Reglamento del Servicio de Televisión por Cable, Diario Oficial, enero 18, 1979, Capítulo VI
Descripción:	Servicios transfronterizos e Inversión Para proteger los derechos de autor, el concesionario de una estación comercial de radiodifusión o de un sistema de televisión por cable, requiere previa autorización de la Secretaría de Gobernación para importar de cualquier forma programas de radio o televisión con el fin de retransmitirlos o distribuirlos en el territorio de México. La autorización será concedida siempre que la solicitud lleve adjunta la documentación comprobatoria de el o los derechos de autor para la retransmisión o distribución de tales programas.
Calendario de Reducción:	Ninguno

Sector:	Comunicaciones
Subsector :	Servicios de esparcimiento (limitado a radiodifusión, transmisión y sistemas de distribución multipunto (MDS/MMDS) y televisión por cable)
Clasificación Industrial:	CMAP 941104 Producción y transmisión privada de programas de radio (limitado a producción y repetición de programas de radio, MDS/MMDS y música continua) CMAP 941105 Servicios privados de producción, transmisión y repetición de programas de televisión (limitado a la producción, transmisión y repetición de programas de televisión, MDS/MMDS, sistemas directos de distribución (DTH y DBS), televisión de alta definición, televisión por cable y radiodifusión)
Tipo de Reserva:	Trato nacional (Artículo 10-04) Requisitos de desempeño (Artículo 14-07)
Nivel de Gobierno:	Federal
Medida:	Ley Federal de Radio y Televisión, enero 19, 1960, Título IV, Capítulo III y Capítulo V Reglamento de la Ley Federal de Radio y Televisión y de la Ley de la Industria Cinematográfica Relativo al Contenido de las Transmisiones de Radio y Televisión, enero 19, 1960, Título III Reglamento del Servicio de Televisión por Cable, enero 18, 1979, Capítulo VI
Descripción:	Servicios transfronterizos e Inversión Se requiere el uso del idioma español o subtítulos en español en los anuncios radiodifundidos o de otro modo distribuidos en el territorio de México. La publicidad incluida en los programas transmitidos directamente desde fuera del territorio de México no puede ser distribuida cuando los programas son retransmitidos en el territorio de México. Se requiere el uso del idioma español para la transmisión, distribución por cable o por sistemas de distribución multipunto de programas de radio y televisión, excepto cuando la Secretaría de Gobernación autorice el uso de otro idioma. La mayor parte del tiempo de la programación diaria radiodifundida que utilice actuación personal deberá ser cubierta por nacionales mexicanos. En México los locutores y animadores de radio o televisión que no sean nacionales mexicanos deberán obtener una autorización de la Secretaría de Gobernación para desempeñar dichas actividades.
Calendario de Reducción:	Ninguno

243

Sector:	Comunicaciones
Subsector :	Servicios de esparcimiento (televisión por cable)
Clasificación Industrial:	CMAP 941105 Servicios privados de producción, transmisión y repetición de programas de televisión (limitado a televisión por cable)
Tipo de Reserva:	Trato nacional (Artículos 10-04 y 14-04) Presencia local (Artículo 10-05)
Nivel de Gobierno:	Federal
Medidas:	Constitución Política de los Estados Unidos Mexicanos, Artículo 32 Ley de Vías Generales de Comunicación, Diario Oficial, febrero 19, 1940, Libro I, Capítulo III Ley de Nacionalidad, Diario Oficial, junio 21, 1993, Capítulo I, II y IV Ley Federal de Radio y Televisión, Diario Oficial, enero 19, 1960, Título III, Capítulos I, II y III Ley de Inversión Extranjera, Diario Oficial, diciembre 27, 1993, Título, I, Capítulo III Ley Federal de Telecomunicaciones, Diario Oficial, junio 7, 1995, Capítulo III Reglamento del Servicio de Televisión por Cable, Diario Oficial, enero 18, 1979, Capítulo II
Descripción:	Servicios transfronterizos Se requiere una concesión otorgada por la Secretaría de Comunicaciones y Transportes para construir y operar, o sólo operar, un sistema de televisión por cable. Tal concesión sólo podrá ser otorgada a nacionales mexicanos o empresas mexicanas. Inversión Los inversionistas de El Salvador, Guatemala y Honduras o sus inversiones sólo podrán adquirir, hasta un 49 por ciento de la participación en empresas establecidas o por establecerse en el territorio de México que posean o exploten sistemas de televisión por cable o que suministren servicios de televisión por cable. Para efectos de determinar este límite máximo de participación, no se computará la Inversión extranjera que, de manera indirecta, sea realizada en esta actividad a través de sociedades mexicanas con mayoría de capital mexicano, siempre que estas últimas no se encuentren controladas por la Inversión extranjera.
Calendario de Reducción:	Ninguno

Sector:	Comunicaciones
Subsector :	Servicios y redes públicas de telecomunicaciones (comercializadoras)
Clasificación Industrial:	CMAP 720006 Otros servicios de telecomunicaciones (limitado a comercializadoras)
Tipo de Reserva:	Trato nacional (Artículos 10-04 y 14-04) Trato de nación más favorecida (Artículo 10-03) Presencia local (Artículo 10-05)
Nivel de Gobierno:	Federal
Medidas:	Constitución Política de los Estados Unidos Mexicanos, Artículo 32 Ley de Vías Generales de Comunicación, Diario Oficial, febrero 19, 1940 Ley Federal de Telecomunicaciones, Diario Oficial, junio 7, 1995, Capítulo III, Sección IV, art.30 y sección V y Capítulo IV, Sección III Reglamento del Servicio de Telefonía Pública, Diario Oficial, diciembre 16, 1996, Capítulo IV
Descripción:	Servicios transfronterizos e Inversión Empresas comercializadoras son aquéllas que, sin ser propietarias o poseedoras de medios de transmisión, proporcionan a terceros servicios

	de telecomunicaciones mediante el uso de capacidad arrendada de un concesionario de redes públicas de telecomunicaciones.
	Se requiere permiso otorgado por la Secretaría de Comunicaciones y Transportes (SCT) para prestar servicios de comercialización de telecomunicaciones. Sólo las empresas constituidas conforme a las leyes mexicanas pueden obtener tal permiso.
	Salvo aprobación expresa de la SCT, los concesionarios de redes públicas de telecomunicaciones no podrán participar, directa o indirectamente, en el capital de una empresa comercializadora de telecomunicaciones.
	El establecimiento y operación de las empresas comercializadoras deberá sujetarse invariablemente a las disposiciones reglamentarias respectivas. La SCT no otorgará permisos para el establecimiento de una comercializadora hasta emitir la reglamentación correspondiente.
	El tráfico internacional debe ser enrutada a través de las instala ciones de una empresa con una concesión otorgada por la SCT.
Calendario de Reducción:	Ninguno

Sector:	Comunicaciones
Subsector :	Servicios y redes públicas de telecomunicaciones
Clasificación Industrial:	CMAP 720006 Otros servicios de telecomunicaciones (limitado a telecomunicación marítima, servicios de transmisión de datos con conmutación de paquetes y de circuitos, servicios de facsímil, servicios de circuitos privados arrendados, servicios de radio localización móvil de personas y servicios de localización de vehículos y otros objetos)
Tipo de Reserva:	Trato nacional (Artículos 10-04 y 14-04) Trato de nación más favorecida (Artículo 10-03) Presencia local (Artículo 10-05)
Nivel de Gobierno:	Federal
Medida:	Constitución Política de los Estados Unidos Mexicanos, Artículo 32 Ley de Vías Generales de Comunicación, Diario Oficial, febrero 19, 1940, Libro I, Capítulo III Ley Federal de Telecomunicaciones, Diario Oficial, junio 7, 1995, Capítulo III, Sección I, II y IV. Art. 30 Ley de Inversión Extranjera, Diario Oficial, diciembre 27, 1993, Título I, Capítulo III Reglamento de Comunicación Vía Satélite, Diario Oficial, agosto 1, 1997
Descripción:	Servicios transfronterizos e Inversión Se requiere concesión otorgada por la Secretaría de Comunicaciones y Transportes (SCT) para prestar los servicios de transmisión de datos con conmutación de paquetes y circuitos; servicios de circuitos privados arrendados; servicios de localización de personas; servicios de localización de vehículos y otros objetos; para instalar, operar o explotar redes públicas de telecomunicaciones; para ocupar posiciones orbitales geoestacionarias y órbitas satelitales asignadas al país y explotar sus respectivas bandas de fre cuencias; y para explotar los derechos de emisión y recepción de señales de bandas de frecuencias asociadas a sistemas satelitales extranjeros que cubran y puedan prestar servicios en el territorio nacional. Sólo los nacionales mexicanos o las empresas mexicanas pueden obtener tal concesión. Se requiere registro ante la SCT para prestar servicio público de facsímil. Se requiere concesión para usar, aprovechar o explotar bandas de frecuencias del espectro radioeléctrico en el territorio nacional mexicano. Las concesiones sobre bandas de frecuencia del espectro para usos determinados se otorgarán mediante licitación pública. El tráfico internacional debe ser enrutado a través de las instalaciones de una empresa con una concesión otorgada por la SCT. Los operadores de redes privadas que pretendan explotar comercialmente los servicios. deberán obtener concesión otorgada por la SCT adoptando

	tales redes al carácter de red pública de telecomunicaciones. Telecomunicaciones de México tiene los derechos exclusivos para los enlaces con Intelsat e Inmarsat. Los servicios distintos a los de larga distancia internacional que requieran del uso de satélites hasta el año 2002, deberán utilizar infraestructura satelital mexicana. México se reserva el derecho de mantener cualquier medida con respecto a la Inversión en telecomunicación marítima. Los inversionistas de las otras Partes o sus inversiones podrán participar hasta en un 49 por ciento en empresas concesionarias que presten los servicios de transmisión de datos con conmutación de paquetes y circuitos, servicios de circuitos privados arrendados, servicios de localización de personas, servicios de localización de vehículos y otros objetos. Para efectos de determinar este límite máximo de participación, no se computará la Inversión extranjera que, de manera indirecta, sea realizada en estas actividades a través de sociedades mexicanas con mayoría de capital mexicano, siempre que estas últimas no se encuentren controladas por la Inversión extranjera.
Calendario de Reducción:	Ninguno

Sector:	Comunicaciones
Subsector :	Servicios y redes públicas de telecomunicaciones (telefonía)
Clasificación Industrial:	CMAP 720003 Servicios telefónicos (incluye servicios de telefonía celular en las bandas "A" y "B") CMAP 720004 Servicios de casetas telefónicas CMAP 502003 Instalaciones de telecomunicaciones
Tipo de Reserva:	Trato nacional (Artículos 10-04 y 14-04) Trato de nación más favorecida (Artículo 10-03) Presencia local (Artículo 10-05)
Nivel de Gobierno:	Federal
Medidas:	Constitución Política de los Estados Unidos Mexicanos, Artículo 32 Ley Federal de Telecomunicaciones, Diario Oficial, junio 7, 1995, Capítulo III, Sección I, II y IV. Artículo 30 Ley de Vías Generales de Comunicación, Diario Oficial, febrero 19, 1940, Libro I, Capítulo III Ley de Inversión Extranjera, Diario Oficial, diciembre 27, 1993, Título I, Capítulo III Reglamento del Servicio de Telefonía Pública, Diario Oficial, diciembre 16, 1996, Capítulo IV Reglamento de Comunicación Vía Satélite, Diario Oficial, agosto 1, 1997

Descripción:	Servicios transfronterizos
	Los servicios de telecomunicaciones comprendidos en esta reserva, sean o no prestados al público, entrañan el tiempo real de transmisión de la información suministrada al usuario entre dos o más puntos, sin cambio de punto a punto en la forma o en el contenido de la información del usuario.
	Se requiere concesión otorgada por la Secretaría de Comunicaciones y Transportes (SCT) para prestar los servicios telefónicos; para instalar, operar o explotar redes públicas de telecomunicaciones; para ocupar posiciones orbitales geoestacionarias y órbitas satelitales asignadas al país y explotar sus respectivas bandas de frecuencias; y para explotar los derechos de emisión y recepción de señales de bandas de frecuencias asociadas a sistemas satelitales extranjeros
	que cubran y puedan prestar servicios en el territorio nacional. Sólo los nacionales mexicanos o empresas mexicanas pueden obtener tal concesión.
	Se requiere permiso expedido por la SCT para establecer, operar o explotar una comercializadora de telefonía pública. Sólo los nacionales mexicanos o empresas mexicanas pueden obtener tal permiso.
	Los operadores de redes privadas que pretendan explotar comercialmente los servicios, deberán obtener concesión otorgada por la SCT adoptando tales redes al carácter de red pública de telecomunicaciones.
	Las redes públicas de telecomunicaciones incluyen las instalaciones para prestar servicios de telefonía.
	Se requiere concesión para usar, aprovechar o explotar bandas de frecuencias del espectro radioeléctrico en el territorio nacional mexicano. Las concesiones sobre bandas de frecuencias del espectro para usos determinados se otorgarán mediante licitación pública.
	El tráfico internacional debe ser enrutado a través de las instalaciones de una empresa con una concesión otorgada por la SCT.
	Telecomunicaciones de México tiene los derechos exclusivos para los enlaces con Intelsat e Inmarsat. Los servicios distintos a los de larga distancia internacional que requieran del uso de satélites hasta el año 2002 deberán utilizar infraestructura satelital mexicana.
	Inversión
	Los inversionistas de las otras Partes o sus inversiones podrán participar, hasta en un 49 por ciento en empresas concesionarias que presten los servicios telefónicos, los servicios de casetas telefónicas y de las instalaciones de telecomunicaciones.
	Para efectos de determinar este límite máximo de participación, no se computará la Inversión extranjera que, de manera indirecta, sea realizada en estas actividades a través de sociedades mexicanas con mayoría de capital mexicano, siempre que estas últimas no se encuentren controladas por la Inversión extranjera. Se requiere resolución favorable de la Comisión Nacional de Inversiones Extranjeras para que la Inversión extranjera participe, directa o indirectamente, en la prestación de servicios de telefonía celular en un porcentaje mayor al 49 por ciento.
Calendario de Reducción:	Ninguno

Sector:	Comunicaciones
Subsector :	Transporte y Telecomunicaciones
Clasificación Industrial:	CMAP 7200 Comunicaciones CMAP 7100 Transporte
Tipo de Reserva:	Trato nacional (Artículo 14-04)
Nivel de Gobierno:	Federal
Medidas:	Ley de Vías Generales de Comunicación, Diario Oficial, febrero 19, 1940, Libro I, Capítulos III y V

	Ley de Puertos, Diario Oficial, julio 19, 1993, Capítulo IV Ley de Navegación, Diario Oficial, enero 4, 1994, Título I, Capítulo I Ley Reglamentaria del Servicio Ferroviario, Diario Oficial, mayo 12, 1995, Capítulo II, Sección Tercera Ley de Aviación Civil, Diario Oficial, mayo 12, 1995, Capítulo III, Sección Tercera Ley de Aeropuertos, Diario Oficial, diciembre 22, 1995, Capítulo IV Ley de Caminos, Puentes y Autotransporte Federal, Diario Oficial, diciembre 22, 1993, Título I, Capítulo III Ley Federal de Telecomunicaciones, Diario Oficial, junio 7, 1995, Capítulo I y III, Sección Sexta Reglamento de Telecomunicaciones, Diario Oficial, octubre 29, 1990, Capítulo III
Descripción:	Inversión Los gobiernos extranjeros y las empresas de Estado extranjeras o sus inversiones no podrán invertir directa o indirectamente en empresas mexicanas que proporcionen servicios relacionados con las comunicaciones, el transporte y otras vías generales de comunicación.
Calendario de Reducción:	Ninguno

Sector:	Construcción
Subsector :	
Clasificación Industrial:	CMAP 501322 Construcción para la conducción de petróleo y sus derivados (limitado sólo a contratistas especializados) CMAP 503008 Servicios y trabajos de exploración y perforación de petróleo y gas (limitado a sólo contratistas especializados)
Tipo de Reserva:	Trato nacional (Artículo 14-04)
Nivel de Gobierno:	Federal
Medidas:	Constitución Política de los Estados Unidos Mexicanos, Artículo 27 Ley Reglamentaria del Artículo 27 Constitucional en el Ramo del Petróleo, Diario Oficial, noviembre 29, 1958 Ley de Inversión Extranjera, Diario Oficial, diciembre 27, 1993, Título I, Capítulo III Reglamento de la Ley Reglamentaria del Artículo 27 Constitucional en el Ramo del Petróleo, Diario Oficial, agosto 25, 1959, Capítulo I, V, IX y XII
Descripción:	Inversión Están prohibidos los contratos de riesgo compartido. Se requiere aprobación previa de la Comisión Nacional de Inversiones Extranjeras para que un inversionista de las otras Partes o sus inversiones adquieran, directa o indirectamente, más del 49 por ciento de participación en empresas establecidas o por establecerse en el territorio de México involucradas en contratos diferentes a los de riesgo compartido relacionados con trabajos de exploración y perforación de pozos de petróleo y gas y la construcción de ductos para la transportación de petróleo y sus derivados.
Calendario de Reducción:	Ninguno

Sector:	Construcción
Subsector :	Transporte terrestre y transporte por agua
Clasificación Industrial:	CMAP 501421 Obras marítimas y fluviales CMAP 501422 Construcción de obras viales y para el transporte terrestre
Tipo de Reserva:	Trato nacional (Artículo 10-04) Presencia local (Artículo 10-05)

Nivel de Gobierno:	Federal
Medidas:	Constitución Política de los Estados Unidos Mexicanos, Artículo 32 Ley de Caminos, Puentes y Autotransporte Federal, Diario Oficial, diciembre 22, 1993, Título I, Capítulo III Ley de Puertos, Diario Oficial, julio 19, 1993, Capítulo IV Ley de Navegación, Diario Oficial, enero 4, 1994, Título I, Capítulo II
Descripción:	Servicios transfronterizos Se requiere una concesión otorgada por la Secretaría de Comunicaciones y Transportes para construir y operar, o sólo operar, obras en mares o ríos o caminos para el transporte terrestre. Tal concesión sólo podrá ser otorgada a los nacionales mexicanos y las empresas mexicanas.
Calendario de Reducción:	Ninguno

Sector:	Energía
Subsector :	Productos del petróleo
Clasificación Industrial:	CMAP 626000 Comercio al por menor de gasolina y diesel (incluye aceites, lubricantes y aditivos para su venta en gasolineras)
Tipo de Reserva:	Trato nacional (Artículo 14-04)
Nivel de Gobierno:	Federal
Medidas:	Ley de Inversión Extranjera, Diario Oficial, diciembre 27, 1993, Título I, Capítulo II Reglamento de la Ley Reglamentaria del Artículo 27 Constitucional en el Ramo del Petróleo, Diario Oficial, agosto 25, 1959, Capítulos I, II, III, V, VII, IX y XII
Descripción:	Inversión Sólo los nacionales mexicanos y las empresas mexicanas con cláusula de exclusión de extranjeros podrán adquirir, establecer u operar gasolineras para la venta o distribución al por menor de gasolina, diesel, lubricantes, aditivos o aceites.
Calendario de Reducción:	Ninguno

Sector:	Energía
Subsector :	Productos del petróleo
Clasificación Industrial:	CMAP 623050 Comercio al por menor de gas licuado de petróleo
Tipo de Reserva:	Trato nacional (Artículo 14-04)
Nivel de Gobierno:	Federal
Medidas:	Ley Reglamentaria del Artículo 27 Constitucional en el Ramo del Petróleo, Diario Oficial, noviembre 29, 1958 Ley de Inversión Extranjera, Diario Oficial, diciembre 27, 1993, Título I, Capítulo II Reglamento de la Ley Reglamentaria del Artículo 27 Constitucional en el Ramo del Petróleo, Diario Oficial, agosto 25, 1959, Capítulos I, IX y XII Reglamento de Distribución de Gas Licuado de Petróleo, Diario Oficial, noviembre 25, 1993, Capítulos II, III y V
Descripción:	Inversión Sólo los nacionales mexicanos y las empresas mexicanas con cláusula de exclusión de extranjeros podrán distribuir, transportar, almacenar o vender gas líquido de petróleo, e instalar depósitos fijos.
Calendario de Reducción:	Ninguno

Sector:	Energía
Subsector :	Productos del petróleo (suministro de combustible, lubricantes de aeronaves y equipo ferroviario)
Clasificación Industrial:	
Tipo de Reserva:	Trato nacional (Artículo 14-04)
Nivel de Gobierno:	Federal
Medidas:	Ley de Inversión Extranjera, Diario Oficial, diciembre 27, 1993, Título I, Capítulo III
Descripción:	Inversión Los inversionistas de las otras Partes o sus inversiones podrán participar, hasta en un 49 por ciento en el capital de una empresa mexicana que suministre combustibles y lubricantes para embarcaciones, aeronaves y equipo ferroviario. Para efectos de determinar este límite máximo de participación, no se computará la Inversión extranjera que, de manera indirecta, sea realizada en esta actividad a través de sociedades mexicanas con mayoría de capital mexicano, siempre que estas últimas no se encuentren controladas por la Inversión extranjera.
Calendario de Reducción:	Ninguno

Sector:	Imprentas, editoriales e industrias conexas
Subsector :	Publicación de periódicos
Clasificación Industrial:	CMAP 342001 Edición de Periódicos
Tipo de Reserva:	Trato nacional (Artículo 14-04)
Nivel de Gobierno:	Federal
Medidas:	Ley de Inversión Extranjera, Diario Oficial, diciembre 27, 1993, Título I, Capítulo III Tal como la califica el elemento Descripción
Descripción:	Inversión Los inversionistas de las otras Partes o sus inversiones podrán, directa o indirectamente, detentar el 100 por ciento de la participación en una empresa establecida o por establecerse en el territorio de México que se dedique a la impresión y/o distribución de un periódico que se publique de manera simultánea fuera del territorio de México. Los inversionistas de las otras Partes o sus inversiones sólo podrán adquirir, hasta un 49 por ciento de la participación en empresas establecidas o por establecerse en el territorio de México que impriman y/o publiquen periódicos para circulación exclusiva en territorio nacional. Para efectos de determinar este límite máximo de participación, no se computará la Inversión extranjera que, de manera indirecta, sea realizada en esta actividad a través de socie dades mexicanas con mayoría de capital mexicano, siempre que estas últimas no se encuentren controladas por la Inversión extranjera. Para efectos de esta reserva se considera un periódico aquél que se publica por lo menos cinco días a la semana.
Calendario de Reducción:	Ninguno

ANEXO I
LISTA DE MEXICO

Sector:	Industria manufacturera
Subsector :	Explosivos artificiales, fuegos artificiales, armas de fuego y cartuchos
Clasificación Industrial:	CMAP 352236 Fabricación de explosivos y fuegos artificiales CMAP 382208 Fabricación de armas de fuego y cartuchos
Tipo de Reserva:	Trato nacional (Artículo 14-04)
Nivel de Gobierno:	Federal
Medidas:	Ley de Inversión Extranjera, Diario Oficial, diciembre 27, 1993, Título I, Capítulo III
Descripción:	Inversión Los inversionistas de las otras Partes o sus inversiones sólo podrán adquirir, hasta un 49 por ciento de participación en las empresas establecidas o por establecerse en el territorio de México que fabriquen explosivos, fuegos artificiales, armas de fuego, cartuchos y municiones, sin incluir la adquisición y utilización de explosivos para actividades industriales y extractivas, ni la elaboración de mezclas explosivas para el consumo de dichas actividades. Para efectos de determinar este límite máximo de participación, no se computará la Inversión extranjera que, de manera indirecta, sea realizada en esta actividad a través de sociedades mexicanas con mayoría de capital mexicano, siempre que estas últimas no se encuentren controladas por la Inversión extranjera.
Calendario de Reducción:	Ninguno

Sector:	Manufactura de bienes
Subsector :	
Clasificación Industrial:	
Tipo de Reserva:	Requisitos de desempeño (Artículo 14-07)
Nivel de Gobierno:	Federal
Medidas:	Ley de Comercio Exterior, Diario Oficial, diciembre 27, 1993, Título I, Título II, Capítulos I, II y III, y Título III Ley Aduanera, Diario Oficial, diciembre 30, 1989, Título III, Capítulo IV, Título IV, Capítulos I y III Decreto que Establece Programas de Importación Temporal para Producir Artículos de Exportación (Decreto PITEX), Diario Oficial, mayo 3, 1990
Descripción:	Inversión Las personas autorizadas por la Secretaría de Comercio y Fomento Industrial para operar conforme al Decreto PITEX deben exportar, por lo menos: a) el 30 por ciento de sus ventas totales anuales para permitírseles b) importar temporalmente libre de impuestos de: i) maquinaria, equipo, instrumentos, moldes y herramental duradero destinados al proceso productivo, y equipo usado para el manejo de materiales directamente relacionados con los bienes de exportación, y ii) aparatos, equipos, accesorios y otros relacionados con la producción de bienes de exportación incluyendo aquellos destinados a la investigación, seguridad industrial, control de calidad, comunicación, capacitación de personal, informática, y para fines ambientales; y b) el 10 por ciento de sus ventas totales anuales o quinientos mil dólares

	de EE.UU. anuales para que se les permita la importación temporal libre de impuestos de:
	i) materias primas, partes y componentes que se destinen totalmente a integrar mercancías de exportación;
	ii) envases, empaques, contenedores y cajas de trailers que se destinen totalmente a contener mercancías de exportación; y
	iii) combustibles, lubricantes, materiales auxiliares, herramientas de reparación y equipo, consumidos en la producción de una mercancía de exportación.
Calendario de Reducción:	A partir del 1 de enero del 2001, tales personas no estarán obligadas a cumplir con los requisitos de porcentaje indicados en el elemento Descripción.

Sector:	Manufactura de bienes
Subsector :	
Clasificación Industrial:	
Tipo de Reserva:	Requisitos de desempeño (Artículo 14-07)
Nivel de Gobierno:	Federal
Medidas:	Ley de Comercio Exterior, Diario Oficial, diciembre 27, 1993, Título I, Título II, Capítulos I, II y III, Título III Decreto para el Fomento y Operación de las Empresas Altamente Exportadoras (Decreto ALTEX), Diario Oficial, mayo 3, 1990
Descripción:	Inversión Los "exportadores directos", como se definen en el Decreto ALTEX, autorizados por la Secretaría de Comercio y Fomento Industrial para operar conforme a tal decreto deben exportar por lo menos el 40 por ciento de sus ventas totales anuales o dos millones de dólares de EE.UU. Los "Exportadores indirectos", como se definen en el Decreto ALTEX, autorizados por la Secretaría de Comercio y Fomento Industrial para operar conforme a tal decreto deben exportar por lo menos el 50 por ciento de sus ventas totales anuales.
Calendario de Reducción:	A partir del 1 de enero del 2001, los exportadores directos e indirectos no estarán sujetos a los requisitos de porcentajes indicados en el elemento Descripción.

Sector:	Manufactura de bienes
Subsector :	Industria automotriz
Clasificación Industrial:	CMAP 383103 Fabricación de partes y accesorios para el sistema eléctrico automotriz CMAP 3841 Industria automotriz CMAP 384121 Fabricación y ensamble de carrocerías y remolques para automóviles y camiones CMAP 384122 Fabricación de motores y sus partes para automóviles y camiones CMAP 384123 Fabricación de partes para el sistema de transmisión de automóviles y camiones CMAP 384124 Fabricación de partes para el sistema de suspensión de automóviles y camiones CMAP 384125 Fabricación de partes y accesorios para el sistema de frenos de automóviles y camiones CMAP 384126 Fabricación de otras partes y accesorios para automóviles y camiones
Tipo de Reserva:	Requisitos de desempeño (Artículo 14-07)

Nivel de Gobierno:	Federal
Medidas:	Decreto para el Fomento y Modernización de la Industria Automotriz, Diario Oficial, diciembre 11, 1989 (Decreto Automotriz) Acuerdo que Determina Reglas para la Aplicación del Decreto para el Fomento y Modernización de la Industria Automotriz, Diario Oficial, noviembre 30, 1990
Descripción:	Inversión Tal como se indica en el Decreto Automotriz y en el Acuerdo que Determina Reglas para la Aplicación del Decreto para el Fomento y Modernización de la Industria Automotriz, los requisitos de desempeño que son contrarios al Artículo 14-07 (Requisitos de desempeño).
Calendario de Reducción:	Conforme a los plazos contenidos en el Decreto Automotriz y en el Acuerdo que Determina Reglas para la Aplicación del Decreto para el Fomento y Modernización de la Industria Automotriz.

Sector:	Manufactura de bienes
Subsector :	Industria maquiladora
Clasificación Industrial:	
Tipo de Reserva:	Requisitos de desempeño (Artículo 14-07)
Nivel de Gobierno:	Federal
Medidas:	Ley Aduanera, Diario Oficial, diciembre 30, 1989, Título IV, Capítulos I y III, Título V, Capítulo II, y Título VI Decreto para el Fomento y Operación de la Industria Maquiladora de Exportación, Diario Oficial, diciembre 22, 1989
Descripción:	Inversión Las personas autorizadas por la Secretaría de Comercio y Fomento Industrial para operar bajo el Decreto para el Fomento y Operación de la Industria Maquiladora de Exportación no podrán vender en el mercado doméstico más del 80 por ciento del valor total de sus exportaciones que hayan realizado el año anterior.
Calendario de Reducción:	Las ventas de una maquiladora al mercado doméstico no podrán ser superiores a partir del 1 de enero de 2000, al 85 por ciento del valor total de sus exportaciones anuales del año anterior. A partir del 1 de enero del 2001, las ventas de la industria maquiladora al mercado doméstico no estarán sujetas a ningún requisito de porcentaje.

Sector:	Pesca
Subsector :	
Clasificación Industrial:	CMAP 1300 Pesca
Tipo de Reserva:	Trato nacional (Artículo 10-04) Trato de nación más favorecida (Artículo 10-03) Presencia local (Artículo 10-05)
Nivel de Gobierno:	Federal
Medidas:	Constitución Política de los Estados Unidos Mexicanos, Artículo 32 Ley de Pesca, Diario Oficial, junio 25, 1992, Capítulos I y II Ley de Navegación, Diario Oficial, enero 4, 1994, Título II, Capítulo I Reglamento de la Ley de Pesca, Diario Oficial, julio 21, 1992, Capítulos I, III, IV, V, VI, IX y XV
Descripción:	Servicios transfronterizos Se requiere de una concesión o de permiso expedido por la Secretaría del Medio Ambiente, Recursos Naturales y Pesca (SEMARNAP) para participar en actividades pesqueras en aguas de jurisdicción mexicanas. Sólo los nacionales mexicanos y las empresas mexicanas, que utilizan embarcaciones con bandera mexicana, podrán obtener tales concesiones o permisos. Los permisos podrán ser expedidos excepcionalmente para personas que operan naves abanderadas en un país extranjero que

	proporcionen trato equivalente a las naves de bandera mexicana para desempeñar o realizar actividades pesqueras en la zona económica exclusiva. Sólo los nacionales mexicanos y las empresas mexicanas podrán obtener autorización de la SEMARNAP para pescar en alta mar en naves con bandera mexicana, colocar aparejos, recolectar larvas, postlarvas, crías, huevos, semillas o alevines del medio natural, con fines de producción acuícola o de investigación e introducción de especies vivas dentro de las aguas de jurisdicción mexicanas y para la pesca didáctica que determinen los programas de enseñanza de las instituciones de educación pesquera del país.
Calendario de Reducción:	Ninguno

Sector:	Pesca
Subsector :	
Clasificación Industrial:	CMAP 130011 Pesca en alta mar CMAP 130012 Pesca costera CMAP 130013 Pesca en agua dulce
Tipo de Reserva:	Trato nacional (Artículo 14-04) Trato de nación más favorecida (Artículo 14-05)
Nivel de Gobierno:	Federal
Medidas:	Ley de Pesca, Diario Oficial, junio 25, 1992, Capítulos I, II y IV Ley de Navegación, Diario Oficial, enero 4, 1994, Título III, Capítulo I Ley Federal del Mar, Diario Oficial, enero 8, 1986, Título I y Capítulo I Ley de Aguas Nacionales, Diario Oficial, diciembre 1, 1992, Título I y Título IV, Capítulo I Ley de Inversión Extranjera, Diario Oficial, diciembre 27, 1993, Título I, Capítulo III Reglamento de la Ley de Pesca, Diario Oficial, julio 21, 1992, Capítulos I, II, III, V, VI, IX y XV Acuerdo de Pesca entre los Estados Unidos Mexicanos y la República de Cuba, 21 de julio de 1976.
Descripción:	Inversión Con respecto a las empresas establecidas o por establecerse en el territorio de México, que realicen pesca en agua dulce, costera y en la zona económica exclusiva, sin incluir acuacultura, los inversionistas de la otras Partes o sus inversiones sólo podrán adquirir, hasta un 49 por ciento de la participación en tales empresas. Para efectos de determinar este límite máximo de participación, no se computará la Inversión extranjera que, de manera indirecta, sea realizada en esta actividad a través de sociedades mexicanas con mayoría de capital mexicano, siempre que estas últimas no se encuentren controladas por la Inversión extranjera. En relación con las empresas establecidas o por establecerse en el territorio de México que realicen pesca en tráfico de altura, se requiere aprobación previa de la Comisión Nacional de Inversiones Extranjeras para que los inversionistas de las otras Partes o sus inversiones adquieran, directa o indirectamente, más del 49 por ciento de la participación en tales empresas.
Calendario de Reducción:	Ninguno

Sector:	Servicios a la agricultura
Subsector :	
Clasificación Industrial:	CMAP 971010 Prestación de servicios agrícolas

Tipo de Reserva:	Trato nacional (Artículo 10-04) Presencia local (Artículo 10-05)
Nivel de Gobierno:	Federal
Medidas:	Constitución Política de los Estados Unidos Mexicanos, Artículo 32 Ley Federal de Sanidad Vegetal, Diario Oficial, enero 5, 1994, Capítulo IV Reglamento de la Ley de Sanidad Fitopecuaria de los Estados Unidos Mexicanos, Diario Oficial, enero 18, 1980, Capítulo VII
Descripción:	Servicios transfronterizos Se requiere de una concesión otorgada por la Secretaría de Agricultura, Ganadería y Desarrollo Rural para aplicar pesticidas. Sólo los nacionales mexicanos o las empresas mexicanas podrán obtener tal concesión.
Calendario de Reducción:	Tres años después de la entrada en vigor de este tratado: **a)** el requisito de concesión será reemplazado por el de permiso; y **b)** el requisito de ciudadanía será eliminado.

Sector:	Servicios educativos
Subsector:	Escuelas privadas
Clasificación Industrial:	CMAP 921101 Servicios privados de educación preescolar CMAP 921102 Servicios privados de educación primaria CMAP 921103 Servicios privados de educación secundaria CMAP 921104 Servicios privados de educación media superior CMAP 921105 Servicios privados de educación superior CMAP 921106 Servicios privados de educación que combinan los niveles de enseñanza preescolar, primaria, secundaria, media superior y superior
Tipo de Reserva:	Trato nacional (Artículo 14-04)
Nivel de Gobierno:	Federal
Medidas:	Ley de Inversión Extranjera, Diario Oficial, diciembre 27, 1993, Título I, Capítulo III Ley para la Coordinación de la Educación Superior, Diario Oficial, diciembre 29, 1978, Capítulo II Ley General de Educación, Diario Oficial, julio 13, 1993, Capítulo III
Descripción:	Inversión Se requiere aprobación previa de la Comisión Nacional de Inversiones Extranjeras para que los inversionistas de la otra Parte o sus inversiones adquieran, directa o indirectamente, más del 49 por ciento de la participación en una empresa establecida o por establecerse en el territorio de México que preste servicios privados de educación preescolar, primaria, secundaria, media superior, superior y combinados.
Calendario de Reducción:	Ninguno

Sector:	Servicios profesionales, técnicos y especializados
Subsector :	Médicos
Clasificación Industrial:	CMAP 9231 Servicios médicos, odontológicos y veterinarios prestados por el sector privado (limitado a servicios médicos y odontológicos)
Tipo de Reserva:	Trato nacional (Artículo 10-04)
Nivel de Gobierno:	Federal
Medidas:	Ley Federal del Trabajo, Diario Oficial, abril 1, 1970, Capítulo I
Descripción:	Servicios transfronterizos Sólo nacionales mexicanos con cédula para ejercer como médicos en el territorio de México, podrán ser contratados para prestar servicios médicos al personal de las empresas mexicanas.

Calendario de Reducción:	Ninguno

Sector:	Servicios profesionales, técnicos y especializados
Subsector :	Personal especializado
Clasificación Industrial:	CMAP 951012 Agentes aduanales y servicios de agencias aduanales y de representación (limitado a declaraciones de embarques de importación y exportación)
Tipo de Reserva:	Trato nacional (Artículos 10-04 y 14-04)
Nivel de Gobierno:	Federal
Medidas:	Ley Aduanera, Diario Oficial, diciembre 30, 1989, Título II, Capítulo I y III, y Título VII, Capítulo Único Ley de Inversión Extranjera, Diario Oficial, diciembre 27, 1993, Título I, Capítulo II
Descripción:	Servicios transfronterizos e Inversión Sólo los mexicanos por nacimiento podrán ser agentes aduanales. Unicamente los agentes aduanales que actúen como consignatarios o mandatarios de un determinado importador o exportador, así como los apoderados aduanales, podrán llevar a cabo los trámites relacionados con el despacho de las mercancías de dicho importador o exportador. Los inversionistas de las otras Partes o sus inversiones no podrán participar, directa o indirectamente, en una agencia aduanal.
Calendario de Reducción:	Ninguno

Sector:	Servicios profesionales, técnicos y especializados
Subsector :	Servicios especializados (Corredores Públicos)
Clasificación Industrial:	
Tipo de Reserva:	Trato nacional (Artículos 10-04 y 14-04)
Nivel de Gobierno:	Federal
Medidas:	Ley Federal de Correduría Pública, Diario Oficial, diciembre 29, 1992, Artículo 8 Ley de Inversión Extranjera, Diario Oficial, diciembre 27, 1993, Título I, Capítulo II
Descripción:	Servicios transfronterizos e Inversión Sólo los nacionales mexicanos podrán estar autorizados para ejercer como corredores públicos. Los corredores públicos no podrán asociarse con ninguna persona que no sea corredor público en México para prestar un servicio de corredor público. Un corredor público tiene funciones tales como: **a)** actuar como agente mediador para transmitir e intercambiar propuestas entre dos o más partes y asesorar en la celebración o ajustes de cualquier contrato mercantil; **b)** fungir como perito valuador; **c)** asesorar jurídicamente a los comerciantes en las actividades propias del comercio; **d)** actuar como árbitro a solicitud de las partes en la solución de controversias de naturaleza mercantil; y **e)** actuar como fedatario público para hacer constar los contratos, convenios, actos y hechos de naturaleza mercantil.
Calendario de Reducción:	Ninguno

Sector:	Servicios profesionales, técnicos y especializados
Subsector :	Servicios Profesionales
Clasificación Industrial:	CMAP 951002 Servicios legales (incluye consultores legales extranjeros)
Tipo de Reserva:	Trato nacional (Artículos 10-04 y 14-04)

	Trato de nación más favorecida (Artículos 10-03 y 14-05)
Nivel de Gobierno:	Federal
Medidas:	Ley Reglamentaria del Artículo 5 Constitucional, relativo al ejercicio de las profesiones en el Distrito Federal, Diario Oficial, mayo 26, 1945 Ley de Inversión Extranjera, Diario Oficial, diciembre 27, 1993, Título I, Capítulo II
Descripción:	Inversión Se requiere resolución favorable de la Comisión Nacional de Inversiones Extranjeras para que la Inversión extranjera participe directa e indirectamente, en un porcentaje mayor al 49 por ciento en las empresas establecidas o por establecerse en el territorio de México que presten servicios legales. Servicios transfronterizos Cuando no hubiere tratado en la materia, el ejercicio profesional de los extranjeros estará sujeto a la reciprocidad en el lugar de residencia del solicitante y al cumplimiento de los demás requisitos establecidos por las leyes mexicanas. Salvo lo establecido en esta reserva, sólo los abogados autorizados para ejercer en México podrán participar en un despacho de abogados constituido en el territorio de México. Los abogados con autorización para ejercer en El Salvador, Guatemala y Honduras podrán asociarse con abogados con autorización para ejercer en México. El número de abogados con autorización para ejercer en El Salvador, Guatemala y Honduras que sean socios en una sociedad en México no podrá exceder al número de abogados con autorización para ejercer en México que sean socios de esa sociedad. Los abogados con autorización para ejercer en El Salvador, Guatemala y Honduras podrán ejercer y dar consultas jurídicas sobre derecho mexicano, siempre y cuando cumplan con los requisitos para el ejercicio de la profesión de abogado en México.☐Un despacho de abogados establecido por una sociedad entre abogados con autorización para ejercer en El Salvador, Guatemala y Honduras y abogados con autorización para ejercer en México podrán contratar como empleados a abogados con autorización para ejercer en México.
Calendario de Reducción:	Ninguno

Sector:	Servicios profesionales, técnicos y especializados
Subsector :	Servicios profesionales
Clasificación Industrial:	CMAP 9510 Servicios profesionales, técnicos y especializados (limitado a servicios profesionales)
Tipo de Reserva:	Trato de nación más favorecida (Artículo 10-03) Trato nacional (Artículo 10-04) Presencia local (Artículo 10-05)
Nivel de Gobierno:	Federal
Medidas:	Ley Reglamentaria del Artículo 5 Constitucional, Relativo al Ejercicio de las Profesiones en el Distrito Federal, Diario Oficial, mayo 26, 1945, Capítulo III, Sección Tercera, Capítulos IV y V Ley General de Población, Diario Oficial, enero 7, 1974, Título III, Capítulo III Reglamento de la Ley Reglamentaria del Artículo 5 Constitucional, relativo al ejercicio de las profesiones en el Distrito Federal, Capítulo III, Diario Oficial, octubre 1, 1945
Descripción:	Servicios transfronterizos Con sujeción a lo previsto en los tratados internacionales de que México sea parte los extranjeros podrán ejercer en el Distrito Federal las

	profesiones establecidas en la Ley Reglamentaria del Artículo 5 Constitucional, Relativo al Ejercicio de las Profesiones en el Distrito Federal. Cuando no hubiere tratado en la materia, el ejercicio profesional de los extranjeros estará sujeto a la reciprocidad en el lugar de residencia del solicitante y al cumplimiento de los demás requisitos establecidos por las leyes mexicanas. Los profesionistas extranjeros deberán tener un domicilio en México. Se entenderá por domicilio: el lugar en el que el sujeto pueda oír y recibir notificaciones y documentos.
Calendario de Reducción:	Ninguno

Sector:	Servicios religiosos
Subsector :	
Clasificación Industrial:	CMAP 929001 Servicios de organizaciones religiosas
Tipo de Reserva:	Presencia local (Artículo 10-05) Alta dirección empresarial y consejos de administración (Artículo 14-08)
Nivel de Gobierno:	Federal
Medidas:	Ley de Asociaciones Religiosas y Culto Público, Diario Oficial, julio 15, 1992, Título II, Capítulos I y II
Descripción:	Servicios transfronterizos Para obtener registro constitutivo, las asociaciones religiosas deberán acreditar que han realizado actividades religiosas en la República Mexicana por un mínimo de cinco años y establecido su domicilio en México. Inversión Los representantes de las asociaciones religiosas deben ser nacionales mexicanos.
Calendario de Reducción:	Ninguno

Sector:	Transporte
Subsector :	Transporte aéreo
Clasificación Industrial:	CMAP 384205 Fabricación, ensamble y reparación de aeronaves (limitado a reparación de aeronaves)
Tipo de Reserva:	Presencia local (Artículo 10-05)
Nivel de Gobierno:	Federal
Medidas:	Ley de Aviación Civil, Diario Oficial, mayo 12, 1995, Capítulo III Reglamento de Talleres Aeronáuticos, Diario Oficial, abril 20, 1988, Capítulo I
Descripción:	Servicios transfronterizos Se requiere de permiso otorgado por la Secretaría de Comunicaciones y Transportes para el establecimiento y operación de talleres de aeronáutica y centros de capacitación y adiestramiento.
Calendario de Reducción:	Ninguno

Sector:	Transporte
Subsector :	Transporte aéreo
Clasificación Industrial:	CMAP 973301 Servicios a la navegación aérea CMAP 973302 Servicios de administración de aeropuertos y helipuertos
Tipo de Reserva:	Trato nacional (Artículos 10-04 y 14-04) Presencia local (Artículo 10-05)
Nivel de Gobierno:	Federal
Medidas:	Constitución Política de los Estados Unidos Mexicanos, Artículo 32

	Ley de Vías Generales de Comunicación, Diario Oficial, febrero 19, 1940, Libro I, Capítulos I, II y III Ley de Inversión Extranjera, Diario Oficial, diciembre 27, 1993, Título I, Capítulo III Ley de Nacionalidad, Diario Oficial, junio 21, 1993 Ley de Aviación Civil, Diario Oficial, mayo 12, 1995, Capítulos I y IV Ley de Aeropuertos, Diario Oficial, diciembre 22, 1995, Capítulo III
Descripción:	Servicios transfronterizos e Inversión Se requiere de una concesión otorgada por la Secretaría de Comunicaciones y Transportes para construir y operar, o sólo operar aeropuertos y helipuertos. Sólo las sociedades mercantiles mexicanas podrán obtener tal concesión. Se requiere aprobación previa de la Comisión Nacional de Inversiones Extranjeras (CNIE) para que un inversionista de las otras Partes o sus inversiones adquieran, directa o indirectamente, más del 49 por ciento de la participación de una sociedad establecida o por establecerse en el territorio de México que sea concesionaria o permisionaria de aeródromos de servicio al público. La CNIE deberá considerar al resolver, que se propicie el desarrollo nacional y tecnológico, y se salvaguarde la integridad soberana de la nación.
Calendario de Reducción:	Ninguno

Sector:	Transporte
Subsector :	Transporte aéreo
Clasificación Industrial:	CMAP 713001 Servicios de transporte en aeronaves con matrícula nacional CMAP 713002 Servicios de transporte en aerotaxis
Tipo de Reserva:	Trato nacional (Artículo 14-04) Alta dirección empresarial y consejos de administración (Artículo 14-08)
Nivel de Gobierno:	Federal
Medidas:	Ley de Aviación Civil, Diario Oficial, mayo 12, 1995, Sección Tercera Ley de Inversión Extranjera, Diario Oficial, diciembre 27, 1993, Título I, Capítulo III Tal como la califica el elemento Descripción
Descripción:	Inversión Los inversionistas de las otras Partes o sus inversiones sólo podrán adquirir, hasta un 25 por ciento de acciones con derecho a voto de una empresa establecida o por establecerse en el territorio de México que preste servicios aéreos comerciales en aeronaves con matrícula mexicana. El presidente y por lo menos dos terceras partes del consejo de administración y dos terceras partes de los puestos de alta dirección de tales empresas deben ser nacionales mexicanos. Para efectos de determinar este límite máximo de participación, no se computará la Inversión extranjera que, de manera indirecta, sea realizada en esta actividad a través de sociedades mexicanas con mayoría de capital mexicano, siempre que estas últimas no se encuentren controladas por la Inversión extranjera. Sólo los nacionales mexicanos y las empresas mexicanas en las que el 75 por ciento de acciones con derecho a voto, sean propiedad o estén controladas por nacionales mexicanos y en las que, el presidente y al menos dos terceras partes de los puestos de alta dirección sean nacionales mexicanos, podrán registrar una aeronave en México.
Calendario de Reducción:	Ninguno

Sector:	Transporte
Subsector:	Servicios aéreos especializados
Clasificación Industrial:	
Tipo de Reserva:	Trato nacional (Artículos 10-04 y 14-04) Presencia local (Artículo 10-05) Alta dirección empresarial y consejos de administración (Artículo 14-08)
Nivel de Gobierno:	Federal
Medidas:	Ley de Inversión Extranjera, Diario Oficial, diciembre 27, 1993, Título I, Capítulo III Ley de Aviación Civil, Diario Oficial, mayo 12, 1995, Capítulos I, II, IV y IX Tal como la califican los párrafos 2, 3, 4 y 5 del elemento de Descripción
Descripción:	Servicios transfronterizos **1)** Se requiere de un permiso otorgado por la Secretaría de Comunicaciones y Transportes (SCT) para prestar todos los servicios aéreos especializados en el territorio mexicano. **2)** Una persona de El Salvador, Guatemala y Honduras podrá obtener tal permiso para prestar en el territorio mexicano, sujeto al cumplimiento de las reglas mexicanas de seguridad, los servicios de vuelo de entrenamiento, control de incendios forestales, extinción de incendios, remolque de planeadores, paracaidismo, publicidad aérea, vuelos panorámicos, servicios aéreos para la construcción y el transporte aéreo de troncos. **3)** Tal permiso no se otorgará a personas de El Salvador, Guatemala y Honduras para prestar servicios aéreos especializados de: inspección, vigilancia, cartografía, fotografía, topografía y de rociamiento. Inversión **4)** Los inversionistas de las otras Partes o sus inversiones sólo podrán adquirir, hasta un 25 por ciento de acciones con derecho a voto de las empresas establecidas o por establecerse en el territorio de México que presten servicios aéreos especializados utilizando aeronaves con matrícula mexicana. El presidente y por lo menos dos terceras partes del consejo de administración y dos terceras partes de los puestos de alta dirección de tales empresas deben ser nacionales mexicanos. Sólo los nacionales mexicanos y las empresas mexicanas con 75 por ciento de acciones que sean propiedad o estén bajo control de nacionales mexicanos y que el presidente y al menos dos terceras partes de los puestos de alta dirección sean nacionales mexicanos, podrán matricular aeronaves en México. **5)** Para efectos de determinar este límite máximo de participación, no se computará la Inversión extranjera que, de manera indirecta, sea realizada en esta actividad a través de sociedades mexicanas con mayoría de capital mexicano, siempre que estas últimas no se encuentren controladas por la Inversión extranjera.
Calendario de Reducción:	Inversión Ninguno

Sector:	Transporte
Subsector :	Transporte por agua
Clasificación Industrial:	CMAP 973203 Administración portuaria integral
Tipo de Reserva:	Trato nacional (Artículo 14-04)
Nivel de Gobierno:	Federal
Medidas:	Ley de Puertos, Diario Oficial, julio 19, 1993, Capítulos IV y V Ley de Inversión Extranjera, Diario Oficial, diciembre 27, 1993, Título I, Capítulo III

Descripción:	Inversión
	Los inversionistas de las otras Partes o sus inversiones podrán participar hasta en un 49 por ciento, en el capital de una empresa mexicana que sea autorizado como administrador portuario integral.
	Para efectos de determinar este límite máximo de participación, no se computará la Inversión extranjera que, de manera indirecta, sea realizada en esta actividad a través de sociedades mexicanas con mayoría de capital mexicano, siempre que estas últimas no se encuentren controladas por la Inversión extranjera.
	Existe administración portuaria integral cuando la planeación, programación, desarrollo y demás actos relativos a los bienes y servicios de un puerto, se encomienden en su totalidad a una sociedad mercantil, mediante la concesión para el uso, aprovechamiento y explotación de los bienes y la prestación de los
	servicios respectivos.
Calendario de Reducción:	Ninguno

Sector:	Transporte
Subsector:	Transporte por agua
Clasificación Industrial:	CMAP 384201 Construcción y reparación de embarcaciones
Tipo de Reserva:	Trato nacional (Artículo 10-04)
	Presencia local (Artículo 10-05)
Nivel de Gobierno:	Federal
Medidas:	Constitución Política de los Estados Unidos Mexicanos, Artículo 32
	Ley de Vías Generales de Comunicación, Diario Oficial, febrero 19, 1940, Libro I, Capítulos I, II y III, Libro III, Capítulo XV
	Ley de Navegación, Diario Oficial, enero 4, 1994, Título I, Capítulo II
	Ley de Nacionalidad, Diario Oficial, junio 21, 1993, Capítulo II
	Ley de Puertos, Diario Oficial, julio 19, 1993, Capítulo IV
Descripción:	Servicios transfronterizos
	Se requiere de una concesión otorgada por la Secretaría de Comunicaciones y Transportes para establecer y operar, o sólo operar, un astillero. Sólo los nacionales mexicanos y las empresas mexicanas podrán obtener tal concesión.
Calendario de Reducción:	Ninguno

Sector:	Transporte
Subsector:	Transporte por agua
Clasificación Industrial:	CMAP 973201 Servicios de carga y descarga, vinculados con el transporte por agua (incluye operación y mantenimiento de muelles; carga y descarga costera de embarcaciones; manejo de carga marítima; operación y mantenimiento de embarcaderos; limpieza de embarcaciones; estiba; transferencia de carga entre embarcaciones y camiones, trenes, ductos y muelles; operaciones de terminales portuarias)
Tipo de Reserva:	Trato nacional (Artículos 10-04 y 14-04)
	Presencia local (Artículo 10-05)
Nivel de Gobierno:	Federal
Medidas:	Constitución Política de los Estados Unidos Mexicanos, Artículo 32
	Ley de Navegación, Diario Oficial, enero 4, 1994, Título I, Capítulo II y Título II, Capítulos IV y V
	Ley de Puertos, Diario Oficial, julio 19, 1993, Capítulos II, IV y VI
	Ley de Vías Generales de Comunicación, Diario Oficial, febrero 19, 1940, Libro I, Capítulos I, II y III
	Reglamento para el Uso y Aprovechamiento del Mar Territorial, Vías

	Navegables, Playas, Zona Federal Marítimo Terrestre y Terrenos Ganados al Mar, Diario Oficial, agosto 21, 1991, Capítulo II, Sección II Ley de Inversión Extranjera, Diario Oficial, diciembre 27, 1993, Título I, Capítulo III Tal como la califica el elemento Descripción en Inversión
Descripción:	Servicios transfronterizos Se requiere de una concesión otorgada por la Secretaría de Comunicaciones y Transportes (SCT) para construir y operar, o sólo operar, terminales marítimas, incluyendo muelles, grúas y actividades conexas. Sólo los nacionales mexicanos y las empresas mexicanas podrán obtener tal concesión. Se requiere de un permiso otorgado por la SCT para prestar servicios de almacenaje y estiba. Sólo los nacionales mexicanos y las empresas mexicanas podrán obtener tal permiso. Inversión Se requiere aprobación previa de la Comisión Nacional de Inversiones Extranjeras para que un inversionista de la otra Parte o sus inversiones sea propietario, directa o indirectamente, de más del 49 por ciento de la participación en una empresa establecida o por establecerse en el territorio de México que preste a terceras personas los siguientes servicios: servicios portuarios a las embarcaciones para realizar sus operaciones de navegación interior, tales como el remolque, amarre de cabos y lanchaje.
Calendario de Reducción:	Ninguno

Sector:	Transporte
Subsector:	Transporte por agua
Clasificación Industrial:	CMAP 973203 Servicios portuarios de pilotaje
Tipo de Reserva:	Trato nacional (Artículo 14-04)
Nivel de Gobierno:	Federal
Medidas:	Ley de Navegación, Diario Oficial, enero 4, 1994, Título III, Capítulo III Ley de Inversión Extranjera, Diario Oficial, diciembre 27, 1993, Título I, Capítulo III Ley de Puertos, Diario Oficial, julio 19, 1993, Capítulos IV y VI
Descripción:	Inversión Los inversionistas de las otras Partes o sus inversiones podrán participar, hasta en un 49 por ciento en empresas mexicanas dedicadas a prestar servicios portuarios de pilotaje a las embarcaciones para realizar operaciones de navegación interior. Para efectos de determinar este límite máximo de participación, no se computará la Inversión extranjera que, de manera indirecta, sea realizada en esta actividad a través de sociedades mexicanas con mayoría de capital mexicano, siempre que estas últimas no se encuentren controladas por la Inversión extranjera.
Calendario de Reducción:	Ninguno

Sector:	Transporte
Subsector:	Transporte por agua
Clasificación Industrial:	CMAP 712011 Servicio de transporte marítimo de altura CMAP 712012 Servicio de transporte marítimo de cabotaje CMAP 712013 Servicio de remolque en altamar y costero CMAP 712021 Servicio de transporte fluvial y lacustre CMAP 712022 Servicio de transporte en el interior de puertos
Tipo de Reserva:	Trato nacional (Artículos 10-04 v 14-04)

	Trato de nación más favorecida (Artículos 10-03 y 14-05)
Nivel de Gobierno:	Federal
Medidas:	Ley de Navegación, Diario Oficial, enero 4, 1994, Título III, Capítulo I Ley de Inversión Extranjera, Diario Oficial, diciembre 27, 1993, Título I, Capítulo III Ley Federal de Competencia Económica, Diario Oficial, diciembre 24, 1992, Capítulo IV Decreto para el Fomento y Modernización de la Industria Automotriz, Diario Oficial, diciembre 11, 1989 (Decreto Automotriz) Acuerdo que Determina Reglas para la Aplicación del Decreto para el Fomento y Modernización de la Industria Automotriz, Diario Oficial, noviembre 30, 1990 Tal como la califica el elemento Descripción
Descripción:	Servicios transfronterizos e Inversión La operación o explotación de embarcaciones en navegación de altura, incluyendo transporte y el remolque marítimo internacional, está abierta para los navieros y las embarcaciones de todos los países, cuando haya reciprocidad en los términos de los tratados internacionales. La Secretaría de Comunicaciones y Transportes (SCT), previa opinión de la Comisión Federal de Competencia Económica (CFCE), podrá reservar, total o parcialmente, determinado transporte internacional de carga de altura, para que sólo pueda realizarse por empresas navieras mexicanas, con embarcaciones mexicanas o reputadas como tales, cuando no se respeten los principios de libre competencia y se afecte la economía nacional. La operación y explotación de embarcaciones de navegación interior está reservada a navieros mexicanos con embarcaciones mexicanas. Cuando no existan embarcaciones mexicanas adecuadas y disponibles, o el interés público lo exija, la SCT podrá otorgar a navieros mexicanos, permisos temporales de navegación para operar y explotar con embarcaciones extranjeras, o en caso de no existir navieros mexicanos interesados, podrá otorgar estos permisos a empresas navieras extranjeras. La operación y explotación de embarcaciones en navegación de cabotaje, podrá realizarse por navieros mexicanos o extranjeros, con embarcaciones mexicanas o extranjeras. En el caso de navieras o embarcaciones extranjeras, se requerirá permiso de la SCT, previa verificación de que existan condiciones de reciprocidad y equivalencia con el país en que se encuentre matriculada la embarcación y con el país donde el naviero tenga su domicilio social y su sede real y efectiva de negocios. Los importes de los fletes que se contraten con compañías salvadoreñas, guatemaltecas y hondureñas serán considerados como contratados con compañías mexicanas para los efectos del Artículo 22 del Acuerdo que Determina Reglas para la Aplicación del Decreto para el Fomento y Modernización de la Industria Automotriz y sus posteriores modificaciones. La operación y explotación en navegación interior y de cabotaje de cruceros turísticos, así como de dragas y artefactos navales para la construcción, conservación y operación portuaria, podrá realizarse por navieros mexicanos o extranjeros, con embarcaciones o artefactos navales mexicanos o extranjeros. La SCT, previa opinión de la CFCE, podrá resolver que, total o parcialmente determinados tráficos de cabotaje, sólo puedan realizarse por navieros mexicanos con embarcaciones mexicanas o reputadas como tales, cuando no se respeten los principios de competencia y se afecte la economía nacional. Los inversionistas de las otras Partes o sus inversiones podrán participar, en el capital de una sociedad naviera mexicana establecida o por

	establecerse hasta en un 49 por ciento, la cual se dedique a la explotación comercial de embarcaciones para la navegación interior y de cabotaje, con excepción de cruceros turísticos y la explotación de dragas y artefactos navales para la construcción, conservación y operación portuaria. Para efectos de determinar este límite máximo de participación, no se computará la Inversión extranjera que, de manera indirecta, sea realizada en esta actividad a través de sociedades mexicanas con mayoría de capital mexicano, siempre que estas últimas se encuentren controladas por la Inversión mexicana. Se requiere previa aprobación de la Comisión Nacional de Inversiones Extranjeras para que los inversionistas de las otras Partes o sus inversiones detenten, directa o indirectamente, más del 49 por ciento de la participación en sociedades navieras establecidas o por establecerse en el territorio de México, dedicadas a la explotación de embarcaciones exclusivamente en tráfico de altura.
Calendario de Reducción:	Ninguno

Sector:	Transporte
Subsector:	Ductos diferentes a los que transportan energéticos
Clasificación Industrial:	
Tipo de Reserva:	Trato nacional (Artículo 10-04) Presencia local (Artículo 10-05)
Nivel de Gobierno:	Federal
Medidas:	Constitución Política de los Estados Unidos Mexicanos, Artículo 32 Ley de Vías Generales de Comunicación, Diario Oficial, febrero 19, 1940, Libro I, Capítulos I, II y III Ley de Aguas Nacionales, Diario Oficial, diciembre 1, 1992, Título I, Capítulo II, Título IV, Capítulo II Ley de Nacionalidad, Diario Oficial, junio 21, 1993, Capítulo II
Descripción:	Servicios transfronterizos Se requiere de una concesión, otorgada por la Secretaría de Comunicaciones y Transportes, para construir, y operar ductos que transporten bienes distintos a los energéticos o a los productos petroquímicos básicos. Sólo los nacionales mexicanos y las empresas mexicanas podrán obtener tal concesión.
Calendario de Reducción:	Ninguno

Sector:	Transporte
Subsector:	Personal especializado
Clasificación Industrial:	CMAP 951023 Otros servicios de personal especializado (limitado a capitanes; pilotos; patrones; maquinistas; mecánicos; comandantes de aeródromos; capitanes de puerto; pilotos de puerto; personal que tripule cualquier embarcación o aeronave con bandera o insignia mercante mexicana)
Tipo de Reserva:	Trato nacional (Artículo 10-04)
Nivel de Gobierno:	Federal
Medidas:	Constitución Política de los Estados Unidos Mexicanos, Artículo 32
Descripción:	Servicios transfronterizos Sólo los mexicanos por nacimiento podrán ser: **a)** capitanes, pilotos, patrones, maquinistas, mecánicos y tripulación de embarcaciones o aeronaves con bandera mexicana:

	b) capitanes de puerto, pilotos de puerto y comandantes de aeródromos.
Calendario de Reducción:	Ninguno

Sector:	Transporte
Subsector:	Transporte por ferrocarril
Clasificación Industrial:	CMAP 711101 Transporte por ferrocarril
Tipo de Reserva:	Trato nacional (Artículo 14-04)
Nivel de Gobierno:	Federal
Medidas:	Ley de Inversión Extranjera, Diario Oficial, diciembre 27, 1993, Título I, Capítulo III Ley Reglamentaria del Servicio Ferroviario, Diario Oficial, mayo 12, 1995, Capítulo I y Capítulo II, Sección III
Descripción:	Inversión Se requiere resolución favorable de la Comisión Nacional de Inversiones Extranjeras para que la Inversión extranjera participen directa o indirectamente, en un porcentaje mayor al 49 por ciento, en las actividades económicas y sociedades dedicadas a la construcción, operación y explotación de vías férreas que sean vía general de comunicación y prestación de servicio público de transporte ferroviario.
Calendario de Reducción:	Ninguno

Sector:	Transporte
Subsector:	Transporte terrestre
Clasificación Industrial:	CMAP 973101 Servicio de administración de centrales camioneras de pasajeros y servicios auxiliares (terminales camioneras y estaciones de camiones y autobuses)
Tipo de Reserva:	Trato nacional (Artículos 10-04 y 14-04) Trato de nación más favorecida (Artículo 10-03) Presencia local (Artículo 10-05)
Nivel de Gobierno:	Federal
Medidas:	Ley de Inversión Extranjera, Diario Oficial, diciembre 27, 1993, Artículo Sexto Transitorio Ley de Caminos, Puentes y Autotransporte Federal, Diario Oficial, diciembre 22, 1993, Título I, Capítulo III Reglamento para el Aprovechamiento del Derecho de Vía de las Carreteras Federales y Zonas Aledañas, Diario Oficial, febrero 5, 1992, Capítulos II y IV Reglamento de Autotransporte Federal y Servicios Auxiliares, Diario Oficial, noviembre 22, 1994, Capítulo I
Descripción:	Servicios transfronterizos Se requiere de permiso otorgado por la Secretaría de Comunicaciones y Transportes para establecer u operar una estación o terminal de autobuses o camiones. Sólo los nacionales mexicanos y empresas mexicanas podrán obtener tal permiso. Inversión Los inversionistas de las otras Partes o sus inversiones podrán participar, hasta un 49 por ciento en empresas establecidas o por establecerse en el territorio de México dedicadas al establecimiento u operación de estaciones o terminales de camiones o autobuses. Para efectos de determinar este límite máximo de participación, no se computará la Inversión extranjera que, de manera indirecta, sea realizada en esta actividad a través de sociedades mexicanas con mayoría de capital mexicano, siempre que estas últimas no se encuentren controladas por la Inversión extranjera.

Calendario de Reducción:	Servicios transfronterizos Ninguno Inversión Con respecto a empresas establecidas o por establecerse en el territorio de México dedicadas al establecimiento u operación de terminales de autobús o camioneras y estaciones de camiones y autobuses, los inversionistas de las otras Partes o sus inversiones sólo podrán detentar, directa o indirectamente: **a)** a partir del 1 de enero del 2001, hasta un 51 por ciento en la participación de las empresas; y **b)** a partir del 1 de enero del 2004, hasta un 100 por ciento en la participación de las empresas sin necesidad de obtener la resolución favorable de la Comisión Nacional de Inversiones Extranjeras.

Sector:	Transporte
Subsector:	Transporte terrestre
Clasificación Industrial:	CMAP 973102 Servicio de administración de caminos, puentes y servicios auxiliares
Tipo de Reserva:	Trato nacional (Artículo 10-04) Presencia local (Artículo 10-05)
Nivel de Gobierno:	Federal
Medidas:	Constitución Política de los Estados Unidos Mexicanos, Artículo 32 Ley de Caminos, Puentes y Autotransporte Federal, Diario Oficial, diciembre 22, 1993, Título I, Capítulo III
Descripción:	Servicios transfronterizos Se requiere de una concesión otorgada por la Secretaría de Comunicaciones y Transportes para prestar los servicios de administración de caminos, puentes y servicios auxiliares. Sólo los nacionales mexicanos y las empresas mexicanas podrán obtener tal concesión.
Calendario de Reducción:	Ninguno

Sector:	Transporte
Subsector:	Transporte terrestre
Clasificación Industrial:	CMAP 711201 Servicio de autotransporte de materiales de construcción CMAP 711202 Servicio de autotransporte de mudanzas CMAP 711203 Otros servicios de autotransporte especializado de carga CMAP 711204 Servicio de autotransporte de carga en general CMAP 711311 Servicio de transporte foráneo de pasajeros en autobús CMAP 711318 Servicio de transporte escolar y turístico (limitado a servicios de transporte turístico)
Tipo de Reserva:	Trato nacional (Artículos 10-04 y 14-04) Trato de nación más favorecida (Artículo 10-03) Presencia local (Artículo 10-05)
Nivel de Gobierno:	Federal
Medidas:	Ley de Inversión Extranjera, Diario Oficial, diciembre 27, 1993, Artículo Sexto Transitorio Ley de Caminos, Puentes y Autotransporte Federal, Diario Oficial, diciembre 22, 1993, Título I, Capítulo III, Título V Reglamento de Autotransporte Federal y Servicios Auxiliares, Diario Oficial, noviembre 22, 1994, Capítulo I
Descripción:	Servicios transfronterizos Se requiere de un permiso expedido por la Secretaría de Comunicaciones y Transportes (SCT) para proporcionar los servicios de autobús

<table>
<tr><td></td><td>interurbano, servicios de transportación turística y servicios de transporte de carga, desde o hacia el territorio de México. Sólo los nacionales mexicanos y empresas mexicanas con cláusula de exclusión de extranjeros podrán proporcionar tales servicios.

Sólo los nacionales mexicanos y las empresas mexicanas con cláusula de exclusión de extranjeros, utilizando equipo registrado en México que haya sido construido en México o legalmente importado y con conductores que sean nacionales mexicanos podrán obtener permiso para prestar servicios de camión o autobús para transportar bienes o pasajeros entre dos puntos en el territorio de México.

Se requiere permiso de la SCT para prestar servicios de mensajería y paquetería. Estos permisos se otorgarán a mexicanos o a sociedades constituidas conforme a las leyes mexicanas.

El autotransporte internacional de pasajeros, turismo y carga se ajustará a los términos y condiciones previstos en los tratados internacionales aplicables.

Inversión

Los inversionistas de la otras Partes o sus inversiones no podrán participar, directa o indirectamente, en empresas establecidas o por establecerse en el territorio de México para prestar los servicios de transporte de camión o autobús indicados en el elemento Clasificación Industrial.

Con respecto a empresas establecidas o por establecerse en el territorio de México que presten servicios de transporte interurbano de pasajeros, de transporte turístico o de transporte de carga internacional entre puntos en el territorio de México, los inversionistas de la otra Parte o sus inversiones podrán detentar, hasta un 49 por ciento de la participación en tales empresas.

Para efectos de determinar este límite máximo de participación, no se computará la Inversión extranjera que, de manera indirecta, sea realizada en esta actividad a través de sociedades mexicanas con mayoría de capital mexicano, siempre que estas últimas no se encuentren controladas por la Inversión extranjera.</td></tr>
<tr><td>**Calendario de Reducción:**</td><td>Servicios transfronterizos
Ninguno
Inversión
Con respecto a empresas establecidas o por establecerse en el territorio de México que presten servicios de transporte interurbano de pasajeros, de transporte turístico o de transporte de carga internacional entre puntos en el territorio de México, los inversionistas de las otras Partes o sus inversiones sólo podrán detentar, directa o indirectamente:
a) a partir del 1 de enero del 2001, sólo hasta un 51 por ciento de la participación en tales empresas; y
b) a partir del 1 de enero del 2004, hasta el 100 por ciento de la participación en tales empresas.
Los inversionistas de las otras Partes o sus inversiones, no podrán, directa o indirectamente, participar en empresas que proporcionen servicios de transporte de carga nacional.</td></tr>
</table>

Sector:	Transporte
Subsector:	Transporte terrestre
Clasificación Industrial:	CMAP 711101 Servicio de transporte por ferrocarril (limitado a la tripulación ferroviaria)
Tipo de Reserva:	Trato nacional (Artículo 10-04)
Nivel de Gobierno:	Federal
Medidas:	Ley Federal del Trabajo, Diario Oficial, abril 1, 1970, Título VI, Capítulo V

Descripción:	Servicios transfronterizos Sólo los nacionales mexicanos podrán ser empleados en las tripulaciones de los ferrocarriles en México.
Calendario de Reducción:	Ninguno

Sector:	Transporte
Subsector:	Transporte terrestre
Clasificación Industrial:	CMAP 711312 Servicio de transporte urbano y suburbano de pasajeros en autobús CMAP 711315 Servicio de transporte en automóvil de ruleteo CMAP 711316 Servicio de transporte en automóvil de ruta fija CMAP 711317 Servicio de transporte en automóvil de sitio CMAP 711318 Servicio de transporte escolar y turístico (limitado al servicio de transporte escolar)
Tipo de Reserva:	Trato nacional (Artículos 10-04 y 14-04)
Nivel de Gobierno:	Federal
Medidas:	Ley de Inversión Extranjera, Diario Oficial, diciembre 27, 1993, Título I, Capítulo II Ley de Vías Generales de Comunicación, Diario Oficial, febrero 19, 1940, Libro I, Capítulos I y II Ley de Caminos Puentes y Autotransporte Federal, Diario Oficial, diciembre 22, 1993, Título I, Capítulo III Reglamento de Autotransporte Federal y Servicios Auxiliares, Diario Oficial, noviembre 22, 1994, Capítulo I
Descripción:	Servicios transfronterizos e Inversión Sólo los nacionales mexicanos y las empresas mexicanas con cláusula de exclusión de extranjeros podrán proporcionar el servicio de transporte urbano y suburbano de pasajeros en autobús, los servicios de autobús escolar, taxi, ruleteo y de otros servicios de transporte colectivo.
Calendario de Reducción:	Ninguno

Sector:	Todos los sectores
Subsector:	
Clasificación Industrial:	
Tipo de Reserva:	Trato nacional (Artículo 10-04)
Nivel de Gobierno:	Estatal (Estado de Baja California Sur)
Medida:	Constitución Política del Estado de Baja California Sur, Boletín Oficial, diciembre 9, 1993, Capítulo III
Descripción:	Servicios transfronterizos Los sudcalifornianos serán preferidos para toda clase de concesiones en que sea indispensable la calidad de ciudadano.
Calendario de Reducción:	Ninguno

Sector:	Todos los sectores
Subsector :	
Clasificación Industrial:	
Tipo de Reserva:	Trato nacional (Artículo 14-04) Trato de nación más favorecida (Artículo 14-05) Requisitos de desempeño (Artículo 14-07)
Nivel de Gobierno:	Estatal (Estado de Jalisco)

Medida:	Ley para el Fomento Económico del Estado de Jalisco, Periódico Oficial, diciembre 31, 1994, Capítulo VI, Artículo 11 Tal como se califica en el elemento Descripción
Descripción:	Inversión Para el otorgamiento de incentivos, se deberán utilizar los criterios de rentabilidad social, tomando en consideración el volumen de exportaciones, entre otros. Para efectos de esta reserva se entiende por existente la medida vigente al 1 de enero de 1994.
Calendario de Reducción:	Ninguno

Sector:	Todos los sectores
Subsector :	
Clasificación Industrial:	
Tipo de Reserva:	Trato nacional (Artículo 14-04) Requisitos de desempeño (Artículo 14-07)
Nivel de Gobierno:	Estatal (Estado de Puebla)
Medida:	Ley Orgánica de la Administración Pública del Estado de Puebla, Periódico Oficial, junio 4, 1996, Capítulo V, Artículo 32
Descripción:	Inversión La Secretaría de Desarrollo Económico será la encargada de dirigir, coordinar y controlar la ejecución de los programas de fomento y promoción económica para el desarrollo integral, regional y sectorial de la entidad.
Calendario de Reducción:	Ninguno

Sector:	Todos los sectores
Subsector :	
Clasificación Industrial:	
Tipo de Reserva:	Requisitos de desempeño (Artículo 14-07)
Nivel de Gobierno:	Estatal (Estado de Puebla)
Medida:	Código Fiscal del Estado de Puebla, Periódico Oficial, diciembre 29, 1987, Artículos 13, 14 y 41
Descripción:	Inversión Las autoridades fiscales tienen facultades para autorizar el pago a plazos, ya sea diferido o en parcialidades de las contribuciones omitidas y sus accesorios, bajo los requisitos establecidos en este código. Así mismo, conocerán y resolverán de las solicitudes de condonación o exención total o parcial del pago de contribuciones y sus accesorios. Además, concederá subsidios y estímulos fiscales.
Calendario de Reducción:	Ninguno

Sector:	Todos los sectores
Subsector :	
Clasificación Industrial:	
Tipo de Reserva:	Trato nacional (Artículo 14-04) Requisitos de desempeño (Artículo 14-07)
Nivel de Gobierno:	Estatal (Estado de Tamaulipas)
Medida:	Ley de Fomento y Protección a la Industria, Periódico Oficial, abril 1, 1964, Capítulo I, Artículo 7
Descripción:	Inversión Se condiciona el otorgamiento de franquicias fiscales a las industrias nuevas o necesarias de ensamble que armen mercancías con partes que en

	su totalidad sean fabricadas en el país y las que con sus propios equipos, produzcan no menos del 25 por ciento del costo directo de la totalidad de las partes con las que armen sus productos, pero, que en ningún caso utilicen piezas de origen extranjero que representen más del 40 por ciento de dicho costo.
Calendario de Reducción:	Ninguno

Sector:	Todos los sectores
Subsector :	
Clasificación Industrial:	
Tipo de Reserva:	Trato nacional (Artículos 10-04 y 14-04)
Nivel de Gobierno:	Estatal (Estado de Sinaloa)
Medida:	Constitución Política del Estado de Sinaloa, Periódico Oficial, julio 20, 1922, Capítulo II, Artículo 10, fracción III
Descripción:	Servicios transfronterizos e Inversión Es prerrogativa del ciudadano sinaloense ser preferido en igualdad de circunstancias a los que no sean ciudadanos sinaloenses, en toda clase de concesiones del gobierno del Estado y Municipios.
Calendario de Reducción:	Ninguno

Sector:	Agua
Subsector :	Captación, potabilización y distribución de agua
Clasificación Industrial:	CMAP 420000 Captación, tratamiento, conducción y distribución de agua
Tipo de Reserva:	Trato nacional (Artículos 10-04 y 14-04)
Nivel de Gobierno:	Estatal (Estado de Guerrero)
Medida:	Ley del Sistema Estatal de Agua Potable, Alcantarillado y Saneamiento del Estado de Guerrero, Diario Oficial, abril 26, 1994, Capítulo V, Artículo 39
Descripción:	Servicios transfronterizos e Inversión La autorización para la distribución comercial de agua potable sólo se otorgará a mexicanos o sociedades constituidas en términos de ley cuando el suministro de agua potable a la población así lo requiera.
Calendario de Reducción:	Ninguno

Sector:	Comercio
Subsector :	Comercio de productos alimenticios, bebidas y tabaco al por mayor y al por menor
Clasificación Industrial:	CMAP 614012 Comercio al por mayor de cerveza CMAP 614013 Comercio al por mayor de vinos y licores CMAP 621016 Comercio al por menor de cerveza CMAP 621017 Comercio al por menor de vinos y licores CMAP 931011 Servicio de restaurantes y fondas CMAP 931020 Servicios de cabaretes y centros nocturnos CMAP 931031 Servicio de cantinas y bares CMAP 931032 Servicio de cervecerías CMAP 931033 Servicio de pulquerías
Tipo de Reserva:	Trato nacional (Artículo 14-04)
Nivel de Gobierno:	Estatal (Estado de Quintana Roo)
Medida:	Ley para el Control de Ventas y Consumo de Bebidas Alcohólicas en el Estado de Quintana Roo, Periódico Oficial, enero 15, 1991, Capítulo III,

	Artículo 27 y 30
Descripción:	Inversión La patente para la venta de bebidas alcohólicas se otorga a personas físicas y a sociedades mercantiles constituidas conforme a las leyes del país. En el caso de personas físicas extranjeras, se deberá acompañar el documento que avale su capacidad financiera. El otorgamiento de patentes es un acto discrecional del C. Gobernador del Estado.
Calendario de Reducción:	Ninguno

Sector:	Comercio
Subsector :	Comercio de productos alimenticios, bebidas y tabaco al por mayor y al por menor
Clasificación Industrial:	CMAP 614012 Comercio al por mayor de cerveza CMAP 614013 Comercio al por mayor de vinos y licores CMAP 621016 Comercio al por menor de cerveza CMAP 621017 Comercio al por menor de vinos y licores CMAP 931011 Servicio de restaurantes y fondas CMAP 931020 Servicios de cabaretes y centros nocturnos CMAP 931031 Servicio de cantinas y bares CMAP 931032 Servicio de cervecerías CMAP 931033 Servicio de pulquerías
Tipo de Reserva:	Trato nacional (Artículos 10-04 y 14-04)
Nivel de Gobierno:	Estatal (Estado de Sonora)
Medida:	Ley número 119 que regula la Operación y Funcionamiento de los Establecimientos destinados a la Fabricación, Envasamiento, Distribución, Guarda, Transportación, Venta y Consumo de Bebidas con contenido Alcohólico en el Estado de Sonora, Boletín Oficial, junio 25, 1992, Capítulo VI, Artículo 47
Descripción:	Servicios transfronterizos e Inversión Se requiere licencia para la apertura y funcionamiento de los establecimientos destinados a la fabricación, envasamiento, distribución, guarda, transportación, venta y consumo de bebidas con contenido alcohólico. Esta licencia se otorga a mexicanos.
Calendario de Reducción:	Ninguno

Sector:	Comercio
Subsector :	Comercio de productos alimenticios, bebidas y tabaco al por mayor y al por menor
Clasificación Industrial:	CMAP 614012 Comercio al por mayor de cerveza CMAP 614013 Comercio al por mayor de vinos y licores CMAP 621016 Comercio al por menor de cerveza CMAP 621017 Comercio al por menor de vinos y licores CMAP 931011 Servicio de restaurantes y fondas CMAP 931020 Servicios de cabaretes y centros nocturnos CMAP 931031 Servicio de cantinas y bares CMAP 931032 Servicio de cervecerías CMAP 931033 Servicio de pulquerías
Tipo de Reserva:	Trato nacional (Artículos 10-04 y 14-04)
Nivel de Gobierno:	Estatal (Estado de Tabasco)
Medida:	Ley que Reglamenta la Venta, Distribución y Consumo de Bebidas Alcohólicas y Cervezas en el Estado, Periódico Oficial, diciembre 26, 1981, Capítulo IV, Artículos 26 y 28
Descripción:	Servicios transfronterizos e Inversión

	Se requiere licencia para la apertura y funcionamiento de los establecimientos dedicados a la venta y consumo de bebidas alcohólicas. Esta licencia se otorga a mexicanos.
Calendario de Reducción:	Ninguno

Sector:	Comercio al por menor
Subsector :	
Clasificación Industrial:	CMAP 62 Comercio al por menor
Tipo de Reserva:	Trato nacional (Artículos 10-04 y 14-04)
Nivel de Gobierno:	Estatal (Estado de Veracruz)
Medida:	Reglamento de Mercados para el Estado, Gaceta Oficial, abril 25, 1959, Capítulo III, Artículos 17 y 18
Descripción:	Servicios transfronterizos e Inversión Los comerciantes permanentes y temporales que deseen obtener un local en los mercados del Estado deberán ser mexicanos por nacimiento.
Calendario de Reducción:	Ninguno

Sector:	Comercio
Subsector :	Comercio de productos alimenticios, bebidas y tabaco al por mayor y al por menor
Clasificación Industrial:	CMAP 614012 Comercio al por mayor de cerveza CMAP 614013 Comercio al por mayor de vinos y licores CMAP 621016 Comercio al por menor de cerveza CMAP 621017 Comercio al por menor de vinos y licores CMAP 931011 Servicio de restaurantes y fondas CMAP 931020 Servicios de cabaretes y centros nocturnos CMAP 931031 Servicio de cantinas y bares CMAP 931032 Servicio de cervecerías CMAP 931033 Servicio de pulquerías
Tipo de Reserva:	Trato nacional (Artículos 10-04 y 14-04)
Nivel de Gobierno:	Estatal (Estado de Zacatecas)
Medida:	Ley sobre el Funcionamiento y Operación de Establecimientos destinados al Almacenaje, Distribución, Venta y Consumo de Bebidas Alcohólicas, Periódico Oficial, diciembre 29, 1996, Artículos 8 y 9
Descripción:	Servicios transfronterizos e Inversión Para obtener la licencia para la operación de establecimientos destinados al almacenaje, distribución, venta y consumo de bebidas alcohólicas, se requiere la nacionalidad mexicana de las personas físicas y la constitución legal de las personas morales.
Calendario de Reducción:	Ninguno

Sector:	Servicios profesionales, técnicos y especializados
Subsector :	
Clasificación Industrial:	
Tipo de Reserva:	Trato nacional (Artículo 10-04)
Nivel de Gobierno:	Estatal (Estado de Baja California Sur)
Medida:	Ley de Profesiones del Estado de Baja California Sur, Boletín Oficial, junio 14, 1989, Capítulo V y Tercero Transitorio
Descripción:	Servicios transfronterizos Se requiere ser mexicano por nacimiento o por naturalización para ejercer en el Estado las siguientes profesiones técnico-científicas:

	medicina; las ciencias biológicas; las ciencias de la alimentación y nutrición; la rehabilitación; la fisioterapia; la medicina veterinaria; la actuaría; la física y la química experimentales aplicadas; la arquitectura; el urbanismo; las ciencias de la tierra; la oceanología; la ingeniería en todas sus ramas; y cualquier otra licenciatura que en forma instrumental implique el manejo del medio inorgánico, de habitat y del entorno humano; la abogacía; la economía; la contaduría; el trabajo social; la antropología; la ciencia de la conducta; las ciencias de la educación; la docencia en la educación preescolar, primaria y secundaria; la administración en sus diferentes ramas; así como, cualquier otra licenciatura que tenga incidencia en las ciencias sociales, humanidades o en las económico administrativas.
Calendario de Reducción:	Ninguno

Sector:	Servicios profesionales, técnicos y especializados
Subsector :	
Clasificación Industrial:	
Tipo de Reserva:	Trato nacional (Artículo 10-04)
Nivel de Gobierno:	Estatal (Estado de Colima)
Medida:	Ley de Profesiones en el Estado de Colima, Periódico Oficial, diciembre 26, 1964, Capítulos I y III
Descripción:	Servicios transfronterizos Se requiere ser mexicano por nacimiento o por naturalización para que los siguientes profesionistas ejerzan en el Estado: arquitecto; antropólogo; bacteriólogo; biólogo; cirujano dentista; contador en sus diversas especialidades; enfermera; partera; homeópata; farmacéutico; ingeniero; licenciado en derecho, en economía, en ciencias políticas y sociales y en administración de empresas; médico; veterinario; profesor de educación y otras especialidades; y químico en sus diversas especialidades.
Calendario de Reducción:	Ninguno

Sector:	Servicios profesionales, técnicos y especializados
Subsector :	
Clasificación Industrial:	
Tipo de Reserva:	Trato nacional (Artículo 10-04)
Nivel de Gobierno:	Estatal (Estado de Chihuahua)
Medida:	Código Administrativo del Estado de Chihuahua, Periódico Oficial, agosto 2, 1950, Título Unico, Capítulos I y III, Sección IV
Descripción:	Servicios transfronterizos Ningún extranjero en el Estado podrá ejercer como: actuario; agrónomo; arquitecto; bacteriólogo; biólogo; cirujano dentista; contador público; enfermera; enfermera y partera; ingeniero en sus diversas ramas profesionales; licenciado en administración, en derecho, en economía, en filosofía, en letras; médico en sus diversas ramas profesionales; médico veterinario; metalúrgico; piloto aviador; profesor de educación preescolar, primaria y secundaria; químico en sus diversas ramas profesionales; topógrafo-hidrógrafo; y trabajador social.
Calendario de Reducción:	Ninguno

Sector:	Servicios profesionales, técnicos y especializados
Subsector :	
Clasificación Industrial:	
Tipo de Reserva:	Trato nacional (Artículo 10-04)
Nivel de Gobierno:	Estatal (Estado de Durango)

Medida:	Ley de Profesiones para el Estado de Durango, Periódico Oficial, junio 4, 1987, Capítulo II, Sección IV, Artículo 11 y Capítulo IV, Artículo 17
Descripción:	Servicios transfronterizos Se requiere ser mexicano para que los siguientes profesionistas ejerzan en el Estado: actuario; arquitecto; bacteriólogo; cirujano dentista; contador; corredor; dibujantes técnicos; economistas; enfermera; partera; ingeniero; licenciado en administración de empresas, en derecho, en economía; médico; veterinario; metalúrgico; Notario Público; optometrista; piloto aviador; profesor de educación preescolar, primaria, secundaria y superior; psicólogo; químico; y trabajador social.
Calendario de Reducción:	Ninguno

Sector:	Servicios profesionales, técnicos y especializados
Subsector :	
Clasificación Industrial:	
Tipo de Reserva:	Trato nacional (Artículo 10-04)
Nivel de Gobierno:	Estatal (Estado de México)
Medida:	Ley del Ejercicio Profesional para el Estado de México, Gaceta Oficial, abril 24, 1957, Capítulo I, Sección III, Artículo 15
Descripción:	Servicios transfronterizos Se requiere ser mexicano por nacimiento o por naturalización para que los siguientes profesionistas ejerzan en el Estado: arquitecto; bacteriólogo; biólogo; cirujano; dentista; contador; corredor; enfermera; enfermera y partera; ingeniero en sus diversas ramas profesionales, licenciado en derecho, en economía; médico en sus diversas ramas profesionales; médico veterinario; metalúrgico; piloto aviador; profesor de educación primaria, secundaria y maestro de especialidades; químico en sus diversas ramas profesionales; trabajador social; y las demás ramas que comprendan los planes de estudio de la Universidad Autónoma del Estado, de la Universidad Autónoma de México, del Instituto Politécnico Nacional, del Colegio Militar, de la Escuela Médico Militar y los Centros Universitarios y de estudios profesionales reconocidos por la Dirección de Educación en el Estado en concordancia con la Dirección General de Profesiones.
Calendario de Reducción:	Ninguno

Sector:	Servicios profesionales, técnicos y especializados
Subsector :	
Clasificación Industrial:	
Tipo de Reserva:	Trato nacional (Artículo 10-04)
Nivel de Gobierno:	Estatal (Estado de Nayarit)
Medida:	Ley para el Ejercicio de las Profesiones y Actividades Técnicas en el Estado de Nayarit, Periódico Oficial, enero 31, 1987, Capítulo VI, Artículo 18
Descripción:	Servicios transfronterizos Para ejercer en el Estado de Nayarit cualquiera de las profesiones que requieren título profesional y las actividades técnicas que necesitan diploma para su ejercicio en el Estado, se requiere ser mexicano por nacimiento o naturalización.
Calendario de Reducción:	Ninguno

Sector:	Servicios profesionales, técnicos y especializados

Subsector :	
Clasificación Industrial:	
Tipo de Reserva:	Trato nacional (Artículo 10-04)
Nivel de Gobierno:	Estatal (Estado de Nuevo León)
Medida:	Ley de Profesiones del Estado de Nuevo León, Periódico Oficial, julio 25, 1984, Capítulo II, Artículo 5 y Capítulo V, Artículo 16
Descripción:	Serviciostransfronterizos Se requiere ser mexicano por nacimiento o por naturalización para que los siguientes profesionistas ejerzan en el Estado: arquitecto; biólogo; contador público y auditor; cirujano dentista; ingeniero en agronomía, bioquímica, civil, electricidad, administración de sistemas, control e instrumentación, en control y computación, en electrónica y comunicaciones, industrias alimentarias o en alimentos, planificación y diseño, sistemas computacionales, electrónicos u operacionales, físico industrial, industrial administrador, industrial de sistemas, mecánica, metalurgia, química; licenciado en administración, antropología física o social, banca y finanzas, ciencias computacionales, ciencias de la comunicación o información, ciencias de la comunidad, derecho o ciencias jurídicas, ciencias políticas y administración pública, ciencias químicas, criminología, diseño gráfico o industrial, economía, educación o pedagogía, enfermería, estadística social, filosofía, física, historia, hotelería y turismo, informática administrativa, lengua inglesa, letras, matemáticas, mercadotecnia, nutrición, organización deportiva, sicología, química, relaciones humanas, sistemas de computación administrativa.
Calendario de Reducción:	Ninguno

Sector:	Servicios profesionales, técnicos y especializados
Subsector :	
Clasificación Industrial:	
Tipo de Reserva:	Trato nacional (Artículo 10-04)
Nivel de Gobierno:	Estatal (Estado de Querétaro)
Medida:	Ley de Profesiones, Periódico Oficial, junio 26, 1964, Capítulo I, Artículos 2 y 15
Descripción:	Servicios transfronterizos Ningún extranjero podrá ejercer en el estado las siguientes profesiones: actuario; arquitecto; bacteriólogo; biólogo; cirujano dentista; contador; corredor; enfermera; enfermera y partera; ingeniero en sus diversas ramas profesionales; abogado; licenciado en administración y en economía; médico en sus diversas ramas profesionales; médico veterinario; metalúrgico; piloto aviador; maestros de educación primaria, secundaria y de especialidades; químico en sus diversas ramas profesionales; y trabajador social.
Calendario de Reducción:	Ninguno

Sector:	Servicios profesionales, técnicos y especializados
Subsector :	
Clasificación Industrial:	
Tipo de Reserva:	Trato nacional (Artículo 10-04)
Nivel de Gobierno:	Estatal (Estado de Sonora)
Medida:	Ley Reglamentaria para el ejercicio de las Profesiones en el Estado de Sonora Boletín Oficial, diciembre 3, 1932, Capítulo I, Artículo 1 y Capítulo III, Artículo 12
Descripción:	Servicios transfronterizos Se requiere ser de nacionalidad mexicana para ejercer en el Estado cualquiera de las profesiones siguientes: agrónomo; arquitecto;

	bacteriólogo; biólogo; cirujano dentista; contador; enfermero; partero; ingeniero civil, electricista, industrial, mecánico, de minas, petrolero químico, topógrafo e hidrógrafo y sus diversas ramas de estas profesiones; licenciado en derecho y en economía; médico en sus diversas ramas; farmaceuta; y profesor de educación preescolar, primaria y secundaria.
Calendario de Reducción:	Ninguno

Sector:	Servicios profesionales, técnicos y especializados
Subsector :	
Clasificación Industrial:	
Tipo de Reserva:	Trato nacional (Artículo 10-04)
Nivel de Gobierno:	Estatal (Estado de Veracruz)
Medida:	Ley del Ejercicio Profesional para el Estado, Gaceta Oficial, diciembre 24, 1963, Capítulo I, Artículo 2; Capítulo III, Sección III, Artículo 14 y Capítulo V, Artículo 19
Descripción:	Servicios transfronterizos Se requiere ser mexicano por nacimiento o por naturalización para ejercer en el Estado cualquiera de las siguientes profesiones: arquitecto; biólogo; cirujano dentista; contador; enfermera; enfermera y partera; ingeniero en sus diversas ramas profesionales; licenciado en derecho y en economía; médico cirujano o médico en sus diversas ramas profesionales; médico veterinario; metalúrgico; piloto aviador; antropólogo; arqueólogo; trabajador social; educadora de párvulos, profesores de educación primaria, maestro de segunda enseñanza en sus diversas especialidades y maestro de enseñanza superior, también en sus diversas especialidades; químico en sus diversas ramas profesionales; licenciado en administración de empresas, ciencias físicas, estadística, matemáticas, psicología, biología; técnico en estadigrafía, dentista y de laboratorio.
Calendario de Reducción:	Ninguno

Sector:	Servicios públicos
Subsector :	
Clasificación Industrial:	
Tipo de Reserva:	Trato nacional (Artículos 10-04 y 14-04)
Nivel de Gobierno:	Distrito Federal
Medida:	Ley Orgánica del Departamento del Distrito Federal, Diario Oficial, diciembre 29, 1978, Capítulo III
Descripción:	Servicios transfronterizos e Inversión Se requiere concesión para prestar servicios públicos. La concesión se otorgará a personas físicas o morales de nacionalidad mexicana.
Calendario de Reducción:	Ninguno

Sector:	Servicios públicos
Subsector :	
Clasificación Industrial:	
Tipo de Reserva:	Trato nacional (Artículos 10-04 y 14-04) Presencia local (Artículo 10-05)
Nivel de Gobierno:	Estatal (Estado de Guerrero)
Medida:	Ley que Establece las Bases para el Régimen de Permisos, Licencias y

	Concesiones para la Prestación de Servicios Públicos y la Explotación y Aprovechamiento de Bienes de Dominio del Estado y los Ayuntamientos, Diario Oficial, octubre 10, 1989, Capítulo V, Artículo 34
Descripción:	Servicios transfronterizos e Inversión Se requiere concesiones para la prestación de servicios públicos, así como para la explotación y aprovechamiento de bienes del dominio del Estado. Estas concesiones se otorgarán a mexic anos y, preferentemente, a vecinos del municipio en donde se encuentre el servicio que se pretenda prestar. Las personas morales deberán estar constituidas conforme a la ley.
Calendario de Reducción:	Ninguno

Sector:	Servicios profesionales, técnicos y especializados
Subsector :	Corredores públicos
Clasificación Industrial:	
Tipo de Reserva:	Trato nacional (Artículo 10-04)
Nivel de Gobierno:	Estatal (Estado de Nuevo León)
Medida:	Reglamento de Corredores del Estado de Nuevo León, Periódico Oficial, agosto 2, 1985, Artículo 12
Descripción:	Servicios transfronterizos Para ejercer como corredor público en la entidad se requiere ser ciudadano mexicano.
Calendario de Reducción:	Ninguno

Sector:	Servicios profesionales, técnicos y especializados
Subsector :	Inspector de ganadería
Clasificación Industrial:	
Tipo de Reserva:	Trato nacional (Artículo 10-04)
Nivel de Gobierno:	Estatal (Estado de Michoacán)
Medida:	Ley de Ganadería en el Estado de Michoacán, Periódico Oficial, diciembre 30, 1954, Capítulo IV, Artículo 15
Descripción:	Servicios transfronterizos Para ser inspector de ganadería, se requiere ser ciudadano mexicano.
Calendario de Reducción:	Ninguno

Sector:	Servicios profesionales, técnicos y especializados
Subsector :	Ingenieros y arquitectos
Clasificación Industrial:	
Tipo de Reserva:	Trato nacional (Artículo 10-04)
Nivel de Gobierno:	Estatal (Estado de Nayarit)
Medida:	Reglamento de los Peritos de Obra, Periódico Oficial, diciembre 18, 1985, Artículo séptimo.
Descripción:	Servicios transfronterizos Para tener derecho a inscribirse en el Registro de Peritos Responsables de Obra se requiere ser ciudadano mexicano.
Calendario de Reducción:	Ninguno

Sector:	Servicios profesionales, técnicos y especializados
Subsector :	Ingenieros y arquitectos
Clasificación Industrial:	
Tipo de Reserva:	Trato nacional (Artículo 10-04)
Nivel de Gobierno:	Estatal (Estado de Oaxaca)

Medida:	Reglamento de Construcciones Públicas y Privadas para el Estado de Oaxaca, Periódico Oficial, mayo 18, 1978, Título Segundo, Capítulo VI, Artículo 38
Descripción:	Servicios transfronterizos Para obtener el registro como director responsable de obra, se requiere acreditar la nacionalidad mexicana.
Calendario de Reducción:	Ninguno

Sector:	Servicios profesionales, técnicos y especializados
Subsector :	Ingenieros y arquitectos
Clasificación Industrial:	
Tipo de Reserva:	Trato nacional (Artículo 10-04)
Nivel de Gobierno:	Estatal (Estado de Veracruz)
Medida:	Reglamento de Construcciones para el Estado de Veracruz, Gaceta Oficial, agosto 23, 1979, Título II, Capítulo I, Artículo 41
Descripción:	Servicios transfronterizos Se requiere ser mexicano para obtener el registro como director responsable de obra.
Calendario de Reducción:	Ninguno

Sector:	Servicios profesionales, técnicos y especializados
Subsector :	Ingenieros y arquitectos
Clasificación Industrial:	
Tipo de Reserva:	Trato nacional (Artículo 10-04)
Nivel de Gobierno:	Estatal (Estado de Michoacán)
Medida:	Reglamento de Construcciones, Periódico Oficial, mayo 22, 1990, Título VI, Capítulo XXXVII, Artículo 458
Descripción:	Servicios transfronterizos Para ser director responsable de obra, se necesita ser ciudadano mexicano.
Calendario de Reducción:	Ninguno

Sector:	Servicios profesionales, técnicos y especializados
Subsector :	Inspector ganadero
Clasificación Industrial:	
Tipo de Reserva:	Trato nacional (Artículo 10-04)
Nivel de Gobierno:	Estatal (Estado de Puebla)
Medida:	Ley Ganadera del Estado de Puebla, Periódico Oficial, noviembre 16, 1984, Capítulo IV, Artículo 11
Descripción:	Servicios transfronterizos Para ser inspector de ganadería se requiere ser ciudadano mexicano.
Calendario de Reducción:	Ninguno

Sector:	Servicios profesionales, técnicos y especializados
Subsector :	Inspector ganadero
Clasificación Industrial:	
Tipo de Reserva:	Trato nacional (Artículo 10-04) Presencia local (Artículo 10-05)
Nivel de Gobierno:	Estatal (Estado de Sonora)

Medida:	Ley de Ganadería para el Estado de Sonora, Boletín Oficial, junio 8, 1992, Título I, Capítulo II, Artículo 9
Descripción:	Servicios transfronterizos Para ser inspector ganadero de zona, se requiere ser mexicano y tener residencia en el municipio de la zona de que se trate con antigüedad mínima de 2 años.
Calendario de Reducción:	Ninguno

Sector:	Servicios profesionales, técnicos y especializados
Subsector :	Inspector ganadero
Clasificación Industrial:	
Tipo de Reserva:	Trato nacional (Artículo 10-04) Presencia local (Artículo 10-05)
Nivel de Gobierno:	Estatal (Estado de Tabasco)
Medida:	Ley de Ganadería del Estado, Periódico Oficial, enero 28, 1959, Capítulo VI, Artículo 56
Descripción:	Servicios transfronterizos Para ser inspector ganadero de zona, se requiere ser ciudadano mexicano y vecino de la zona.
Calendario de Reducción:	Ninguno

Sector:	Servicios profesionales, técnicos y especializados
Subsector :	Inspector de ganadería
Clasificación Industrial:	
Tipo de Reserva:	Trato nacional (Artículo 10-04) Presencia local (Artículo 10-05)
Nivel de Gobierno:	Estatal (Estado de Tlaxcala)
Medida:	Ley Ganadera del Estado de Tlaxcala, Periódico Oficial, julio 5, 1978, Título II, Capítulo VI, Artículo 89
Descripción:	Servicios transfronterizos Para ser inspector de ganadería, se requiere ser ciudadano mexicano residente del estado.
Calendario de Reducción:	Ninguno

Sector:	Servicios de esparcimiento, culturales, recreativos y deportivos
Subsector :	Fútbol Soccer
Clasificación Industrial:	CMAP 949102 Servicios privados de promoción y presentación de espectáculos deportivos, taurinos y circos CMAP 949202 Servicios públicos de promoción y presentación de espectáculos deportivos y taurinos
Tipo de Reserva:	Trato nacional (Artículo 10-04)
Nivel de Gobierno:	Distrito Federal
Medida:	Decreto que crea un cuerpo colegiado que se denominará Comisión de Fomento Deportivo del Distrito Federal, Diario Oficial, enero 24, 1945, Artículo Undécimo
Descripción:	Servicios transfronterizos En la celebración de juegos, ligas o campeonatos nacionales de fútbol soccer como espectáculo público de paga, se requiere que por lo menos siete jugadores sean mexicanos por nacimiento.
Calendario de Reducción:	Ninguno

Sector:	Servicios profesionales, técnicos y especializados

Subsector :	Notariado
Clasificación Industrial:	CMAP 951001 Servicios de notarías públicas
Tipo de Reserva:	Trato nacional (Artículos 10-04 y 14-04) Presencia local (Artículo 10-05)
Nivel de Gobierno:	Estatal (Estado de Aguascalientes)
Medida:	Ley del Notariado para el Estado de Aguascalientes, Periódico Oficial, junio 1, 1980, Título II, Capítulo III
Descripción:	Servicios transfronterizos e Inversión Para obtener el fiat de Notario se requiere ser mexicano por nacimiento y estar registrado con una práctica profesional en la entidad de por lo menos tres años previos a la fecha en que presente su solicitud. Un Notario Público sólo puede asociarse con otro Notario Público para prestar servicios notariales.
Calendario de Reducción:	Ninguno

Sector:	Servicios profesionales, técnicos y especializados
Subsector :	Notariado
Clasificación Industrial:	CMAP 951001 Servicios de notarías pública
Tipo de Reserva:	Trato nacional (Artículos 10-04 y 14-04) Presencia local (Artículo 10-05)
Nivel de Gobierno:	Estatal (Estado de Baja California)
Medida:	Ley del Notariado para el Estado de Baja California, Periódico Oficial, septiembre 30, 1965, Título I, Capítulo Tercero
Descripción:	Servicios transfronterizos e Inversión Para obtener patente de aspirante al ejercicio del notariado, se requiere ser mexicano por nacimiento. Además, es requisito una residencia efectiva y no interrumpida en la entidad, ejerciendo la profesión en cualesquier rama del Derecho por un término no menor de tres años antes de la iniciación de su práctica. Se exige la práctica de tres años ininterrumpidos de la profesión y un mínimo de cinco años de residencia en el Estado. Un Notario Público sólo puede asociarse con otro Notario Público para prestar servicios notariales.
Calendario de Reducción:	Ninguno

Sector:	Servicios profesionales, técnicos y especializados
Subsector :	Notariado
Clasificación Industrial:	CMAP 951001 Servicios de notarías públicas
Tipo de Reserva:	Trato nacional (Artículos 10-04 y 14-04) Presencia local (Artículo 10-05)
Nivel de Gobierno:	Estatal (Estado de Baja California Sur)
Medida:	Ley del Notariado del Estado de Baja California Sur, Boletín Oficial, diciembre 31, 1977, Título I, Capítulo II
Descripción:	Servicios transfronterizos e Inversión Para obtener la patente de aspirante de Notario se requiere ser mexicano por nacimiento, ser ciudadano del estado y tener residencia efectiva en el mismo cuando menos tres años anteriores a la fecha de la solicitud. Un Notario Público sólo puede asociarse con otro Notario Público para prestar servicios notariales.
Calendario de Reducción:	Ninguno

Sector:	Servicios profesionales, técnicos y especializados
Subsector :	Notariado
Clasificación Industrial:	CMAP 951001 Servicios de notarías públicas
Tipo de Reserva:	Trato nacional (Artículos 10-04 y 14-04) Presencia local (Artículo 10-05)
Nivel de Gobierno:	Estatal (Estado de Campeche)
Medida:	Ley del Notariado del Estado de Campeche, Periódico Oficial, octubre 9, 1944, Capítulo I
Descripción:	Servicios transfronterizos e Inversión Para obtener el fiat de Notario Público se requiere ser ciudadano mexicano por nacimiento o por naturalización y haber realizado práctica notarial por un año en la entidad. Un Notario Público sólo puede asociarse con otro Notario Público para prestar servicios notariales.
Calendario de Reducción:	Ninguno

Sector:	Servicios profesionales, técnicos y especializados
Subsector :	Notariado
Clasificación Industrial:	CMAP 951001 Servicios de notarías públicas
Tipo de Reserva:	Trato nacional (Artículos 10-04 y 14-04)
Nivel de Gobierno:	Estatal (Estado de Chiapas)
Medida:	Ley del Notariado del Estado de Chiapas, Periódico Oficial, marzo 21, 1993, Título I, Capítulo III
Descripción:	Servicios transfronterizos e Inversión Para ser aspirante al ejercicio del notariado se requiere ser mexicano y comprobar práctica notarial en el estado por un año. Un Notario Público sólo puede asociarse con otro Notario Público para prestar servicios notariales.
Calendario de Reducción:	Ninguno

Sector:	Servicios profesionales, técnicos y especializados
Subsector :	Notariado
Clasificación Industrial:	CMAP 951001 Servicios de Notarías Públicas
Tipo de Reserva:	Trato nacional (Artículos 10-04 y 14-04) Presencia local (Artículo 10-05)
Nivel de Gobierno:	Estatal (Estado de Chihuahua)
Medida:	Ley del Notariado del Estado de Chihuahua, Periódico Oficial, agosto 2, 1950, Capítulo III
Descripción:	Servicios transfronterizos e Inversión Para obtener la patente de aspirante al ejercicio del notariado se requiere ser mexicano y tener residencia en la entidad por más de dos años. Un Notario Público sólo puede asociarse con otro Notario Público para prestar servicios notariales.
Calendario de Reducción:	Ninguno

Sector:	Servicios profesionales, técnicos y especializados
Subsector :	Notariado
Clasificación Industrial:	CMAP 951001 Servicios de notarías públicas
Tipo de Reserva:	Trato nacional (Artículos 10-04 y 14-04) Presencia local (Artículo 10-05)
Nivel de Gobierno:	Estatal (Estado de Coahuila)

Medida:	Ley del Notariado del Estado de Coahuila, Periódico Oficial, febrero 6, 1979, Título II, Capítulo III
Descripción:	Servicios transfronterizos e Inversión Para obtener la patente de aspirante a Notario se requiere ser ciudadano mexicano por nacimiento y realizar práctica notarial por un año. Un Notario Público sólo puede asociarse con otro Notario Público para prestar servicios notariales.
Calendario de Reducción:	Ninguno

Sector:	Servicios profesionales, técnicos y especializados
Subsector :	Notariado
Clasificación Industrial:	CMAP 951001 Servicios de notarías públicas
Tipo de Reserva:	Trato nacional (Artículos 10-04 y 14-04) Presencia local (Artículo 10-05)
Nivel de Gobierno:	Estatal (Estado de Colima)
Medida:	Ley del Notariado del Estado de Colima, Periódico Oficial, enero 4, 1964, Título II, Capítulo III
Descripción:	Servicios transfronterizos e Inversión Para obtener el nombramiento de Notario y ejercer como tal es requisito indispensable ser mexicano por nacimiento, con un mínimo de cinco años de ejercicio profesional y ser vecino del estado. Un Notario Público sólo puede asociarse con otro Notario Público para prestar servicios notariales.
Calendario de Reducción:	Ninguno

Sector:	Servicios profesionales, técnicos y especializados
Subsector :	Notariado
Clasificación Industrial:	CMAP 951001 Servicios de notarías públicas
Tipo de Reserva:	Trato nacional (Artículos 10-04 y 14-04) Presencia local (Artículo 10-05)
Nivel de Gobierno:	Distrito Federal
Medida:	Ley del Notariado para el Distrito Federal, Diario Oficial, enero 8, 1990, Capítulo II, Sección Segunda
Descripción:	Servicios transfronterizos e Inversión Para obtener la patente de aspirante al notariado, el interesado deberá ser mexicano por nacimiento y haber realizado práctica notarial bajo la dirección y responsabilidad de algún Notario de la entidad, por lo menos ocho meses ininterrumpidos e inmediatamente anteriores a la solicitud de examen. Un Notario Público sólo puede asociarse con otro Notario Público para prestar servicios notariales.
Calendario de Reducción:	Ninguno

Sector:	Servicios profesionales, técnicos y especializados
Subsector :	Notariado
Clasificación Industrial:	CMAP 951001 Servicios de notarías públicas
Tipo de Reserva:	Trato nacional (Artículos 10-04 y 14-04) Presencia local (Artículo 10-05)
Nivel de Gobierno:	Estatal (Estado de Durango)
Medida:	Ley del Notariado del Estado de Durango, Periódico Oficial, junio 17, 1974, Título II, Capítulo III, Artículo 70

Descripción:	Servicios transfronterizos e Inversión Para obtener la patente de aspirante a Notario, el interesado deberá ser mexicano por nacimiento y vecino del estado. Un Notario Público sólo puede asociarse con otro Notario Público para prestar servicios notariales.
Calendario de Reducción:	Ninguno

Sector:	Servicios profesionales, técnicos y especializados
Subsector :	Notariado
Clasificación Industrial:	CMAP 951001 Servicios de notarías públicas
Tipo de Reserva:	Trato nacional (Artículos 10-04 y 14-04) Presencia local (Artículo 10-05)
Nivel de Gobierno:	Estatal (Estado de México)
Medida:	Ley Orgánica del Notariado del Estado de México, Gaceta Oficial, octubre 11, 1972, Título Primero, Capítulo Primero, Artículo 10-A.
Descripción:	Servicios transfronterizos e Inversión Para ser aspirante a notariado se requiere ser ciudadano mexicano por nacimiento. Tener residencia efectiva en el estado de cuando menos tres años anteriores a la solicitud y haber realizado prácticas en alguna notaria establecida en el estado por un período mínimo de un año. Un Notario Público sólo puede asociarse con otro Notario Público para prestar servicios notaria les.
Calendario de Reducción:	Ninguno

Sector:	Servicios profesionales, técnicos y especializados
Subsector :	Notariado
Clasificación Industrial:	CMAP 951001 Servicios de notarías públicas
Tipo de Reserva:	Trato nacional (Artículos 10-04 y 14-04) Presencia local (Artículo 10-05)
Nivel de Gobierno:	Estatal (Estado de Guanajuato)
Medida:	Ley del Notariado para el Estado de Guanajuato, Periódico Oficial, enero 8, 1959, Artículo 6
Descripción:	Servicios transfronterizos e Inversión Para obtener el fíat de Notario se requiere ser mexicano por nacimiento y haber realizado una práctica mínima de un año en alguna notaría del estado. Un Notario Público sólo puede asociarse con otro Notario Público para prestar servicios notariales.
Calendario de Reducción:	Ninguno

Sector:	Servicios profesionales, técnicos y especializados
Subsector :	Notariado
Clasificación Industrial:	CMAP 951001 Servicios de notarías públicas
Tipo de Reserva:	Trato nacional (Artículos 10-04 y 14-04) Presencia local (Artículo 10-05)
Nivel de Gobierno:	Estatal (Estado de Guerrero)
Medida:	Ley del Notariado para el Estado de Guerrero, Diario Oficial, agosto 6, 1988, Capítulo III, Artículo 97
Descripción:	Servicios transfronterizos e Inversión Para obtener patente de aspirante al ejercicio del notariado se requiere ser mexicano por nacimiento y haber realizado práctica notarial por un mínimo de cinco años. Un Notario Público sólo puede asociarse con otro Notario Público para

	prestar servicios notariales.
Calendario de Reducción:	Ninguno

Sector:	Servicios profesionales, técnicos y especializados
Subsector :	Notariado
Clasificación Industrial:	CMAP 951001 Servicios de notarías públicas
Tipo de Reserva:	Trato nacional (Artículos 10-04 y 14-04) Presencia local (Artículo 10-05)
Nivel de Gobierno:	Estatal (Estado de Hidalgo)
Medida:	Ley del Notariado para el Estado de Hidalgo, Periódico Oficial, mayo 18, 1992, Título II, Capítulo II, Artículo 17
Descripción:	Servicios transfronterizos e Inversión Para obtener nombramiento de Notario titular se requiere ser mexicano por nacimiento y ser ciudadano hidalguense. Un Notario Público sólo puede asociarse con otro Notario Público para prestar servicios notariales.
Calendario de Reducción:	Ninguno

Sector:	Servicios profesionales, técnicos y especializados
Subsector :	Notariado
Clasificación Industrial:	CMAP 951001 Servicios de notarías públicas
Tipo de Reserva:	Trato nacional (Artículos 10-04 y 14-04) Presencia local (Artículo 10-05)
Nivel de Gobierno:	Estatal (Estado de Jalisco)
Medida:	Ley del Notariado del Estado de Jalisco, Periódico Oficial, octubre 14, 1993, Título I, Capítulo II, Artículo 10
Descripción:	Servicios transfronterizos e Inversión Para obtener la patente de aspirante al ejercicio del notariado se requiere ser mexicano por nacimiento y tener su domicilio civil en la entidad. Un Notario Público sólo puede asociarse con otro Notario Público para prestar servicios notariales.
Calendario de Reducción:	Ninguno

Sector:	Servicios profesionales, técnicos y especializados
Subsector :	Notariado
Clasificación Industrial:	CMAP 951001 Servicios de notarías públicas
Tipo de Reserva:	Trato nacional (Artículos 10-04 y 14-04) Presencia local (Artículo 10-05)
Nivel de Gobierno:	Estatal (Estado de Michoacán)
Medida:	Ley del Notariado del Estado, Periódico Oficial, febrero 15, 1980, Título II, Capítulo II, Artículo 21
Descripción:	Servicios transfronterizos e Inversión Para obtener nombramiento de Notario se requiere ser mexicano por nacimiento y tener residencia ininterrumpida en el estado por más de tres años. Un Notario Público sólo puede asociarse con otro Notario Público para prestar servicios notariales.
Calendario de Reducción:	Ninguno

Sector:	Servicios profesionales, técnicos y especializados
Subsector :	Notariado

Clasificación Industrial:	CMAP 951001 Servicios de notarías públicas
Tipo de Reserva:	Trato nacional (Artículos 10-04 y 14-04) Presencia local (Artículo 10-05)
Nivel de Gobierno:	Estatal (Estado de Morelos)
Medida:	Ley del Notariado del Estado de Morelos, Periódico Oficial, agosto 3, 1983, Capítulo II, Sección II, Artículo 11
Descripción:	Servicios transfronterizos e Inversión Para obtener el registro de aspirante al notariado, el interesado deberá ser morelense y tener una residencia no menor de 10 años en el estado. Un Notario Público sólo puede asociarse con otro Notario Público para prestar servicios notariales.
Calendario de Reducción:	Ninguno

Sector:	Servicios profesionales, técnicos y especializados
Subsector :	Notariado
Clasificación Industrial:	CMAP 951001 Servicios de notarías públicas
Tipo de Reserva:	Trato nacional (Artículos 10-04 y 14-04) Presencia local (Artículo 10-05)
Nivel de Gobierno:	Estatal (Estado de Nayarit)
Medida:	Ley del Notariado del Estado de Nayarit, Periódico Oficial, enero 28, 1987, Título II, Capítulo I, Artículo 7
Descripción:	Servicios transfronterizos e Inversión Para obtener el nombramiento de Notario, se requiere ser mexicano por nacimiento y tener ejercicio profesional en la entidad de por lo menos cinco años. Un Notario Público sólo puede asociarse con otro Notario Público para prestar servicios notariales.
Calendario de Reducción:	Ninguno

Sector:	Servicios profesionales, técnicos y especializados
Subsector :	Notariado
Clasificación Industrial:	CMAP 951001 Servicios de notarías públicas
Tipo de Reserva:	Trato nacional (Artículos 10-04 y 14-04) Presencia local (Artículo 10-05)
Nivel de Gobierno:	Estatal (Estado de Nuevo León)
Medida:	Ley del Notariado del Estado de Nuevo León, Periódico Oficial, diciembre 26, 1983, Título I, Capítulo III, Artículo 18
Descripción:	Servicios transfronterizos e Inversión Para obtener el nombramiento de Notario se requiere ser mexicano por nacimiento y residir en el estado. Un Notario Público sólo puede asociarse con otro Notario Público para prestar servicios notariales.
Calendario de Reducción:	Ninguno

Sector:	Servicios profesionales, técnicos y especializados
Subsector :	Notariado
Clasificación Industrial:	CMAP 951001 Servicios de Notarías Públicas
Tipo de Reserva:	Trato nacional (Artículos 10-04 y 14-04) Presencia local (Artículo 10-05)
Nivel de Gobierno:	Estatal (Estado de Oaxaca)
Medida:	Ley del Notariado para el Estado de Oaxaca, Periódico Oficial, julio 30, 1994, Título II, Capítulo I, Artículo 12

Descripción:	Servicios transfronterizos e Inversión Para obtener la patente de Notario Titular, se requiere ser mexicano por nacimiento y tener una residencia en el estado no menor de cinco años. Un Notario Público sólo puede asociarse con otro Notario Público para prestar servicios notariales.
Calendario de Reducción:	Ninguno

Sector:	Servicios profesionales, técnicos y especializados
Subsector :	Notariado
Clasificación Industrial:	CMAP 951001 Servicios de notarías públicas
Tipo de Reserva:	Trato nacional (Artículos 10-04 y 14-04) Presencia local (Artículo 10-05)
Nivel de Gobierno:	Estatal (Estado de Puebla)
Medida:	Ley del Notariado de Puebla, Periódico Oficial, agosto 6, 1976, Capítulo IV, Artículo 27
Descripción:	Servicios transfronterizos e Inversión Para obtener la patente de Notario, se requiere ser mexicano por nacimiento y ser vecino del estado, con residencia no menor de cinco años ininterrumpidos anteriores a su nombramiento. Un Notario Público sólo puede asociarse con otro Notario Público para prestar servicios notariales.
Calendario de Reducción:	Ninguno

Sector:	Servicios profesionales, técnicos y especializados
Subsector :	Notariado
Clasificación Industrial:	CMAP 951001 Servicios de notarías públicas
Tipo de Reserva:	Trato nacional (Artículos 10-04 y 14-04) Presencia local (Artículo 10-05)
Nivel de Gobierno:	Estatal (Estado de Querétaro)
Medida:	Ley del Notariado del Estado de Querétaro, Periódico Oficial, octubre 28, 1976, Capítulo III, Artículo 11
Descripción:	Servicios transfronterizos e Inversión Para obtener el nombramiento de Notario Titular, se requiere ser mexicano por nacimiento y tener residencia ininterrumpida en el estado por más de tres años anteriores a su nombramiento. Un Notario Público sólo puede asociarse con otro Notario Público para prestar servicios notariales.
Calendario de Reducción:	Ninguno
Sector:	Servicios profesionales, técnicos y especializados
Subsector :	Notariado
Clasificación Industrial:	CMAP 951001 Servicios de notarías públicas
Tipo de Reserva:	Trato nacional (Artículos 10-04 y 14-04) Presencia local (Artículo 10-05)
Nivel de Gobierno:	Estatal (Estado de Quintana Roo)
Medida:	Ley Orgánica del Notariado del Estado de Quintana Roo, Periódico Oficial, noviembre 25, 1976, Capítulo II, Artículo 10
Descripción:	Servicios transfronterizos e Inversión Para ser Notario se requiere ser ciudadano mexicano, de preferencia quintanarroense, con residencia en el estado cuando menos con tres años anteriores a la designación. Un Notario Público sólo puede asociarse con otro Notario Público para prestar servicios notariales.

Calendario de Reducción:	Ninguno

Sector:	Servicios profesionales, técnicos y especializados
Subsector :	Notariado
Clasificación Industrial:	CMAP 951001 Servicios de notarías públicas
Tipo de Reserva:	Trato nacional (Artículos 10-04 y 14-04) Presencia local (Artículo 10-05)
Nivel de Gobierno:	Estatal (Estado de Sinaloa)
Medida:	Ley del Notariado del Estado de Sinaloa, Periódico Oficial, agosto 12, 1969, Capítulo IV, Artículo 109
Descripción:	Servicios transfronterizos e Inversión Para obtener autorización para ejercer como Notario Público, se requiere ser ciudadano mexicano y haber realizado práctica con Notario Titular por dos años ininterrumpidos. Un Notario Público sólo puede asociarse con otro Notario Público para prestar servicios notariales.
Calendario de Reducción:	Ninguno

Sector:	Servicios profesionales, técnicos y especializados
Subsector :	Notariado
Clasificación Industrial:	CMAP 951001 Servicios de notarías públicas
Tipo de Reserva:	Trato nacional (Artículos 10-04 y 14-04) Presencia local (Artículo 10-05)
Nivel de Gobierno:	Estatal (Estado de Sonora)
Medida:	Ley del Notariado del Estado de Sonora, Boletín Oficial, julio 4, 1970, Título II, Capítulo Tercero, Artículo 80
Descripción:	Servicios transfronterizos e Inversión Para obtener el nombramiento y ejercer como Notario, se requiere ser mexicano por nacimiento y vecino del estado. Un Notario Público sólo puede asociarse con otro Notario Público para prestar servicios notariales.
Calendario de Reducción:	Ninguno

Sector:	Servicios profesionales, técnicos y especializados
Subsector :	Notariado
Clasificación Industrial:	CMAP 951001 Servicios de notarías públicas
Tipo de Reserva:	Trato nacional (Artículos 10-04 y 14-04) Presencia local (Artículo 10-05)
Nivel de Gobierno:	Estatal (Estado de Tabasco)
Medida:	Ley del Notariado para el Estado de Tabasco, Periódico Oficial, noviembre 10, 1976, Capítulo II, Artículo 6, fracciones I y IV
Descripción:	Servicios transfronterizos e Inversión Para obtener el fiat o nombramiento de Notario, se requiere ser mexicano por nacimiento y ser vecino del estado, con residencia efectiva no menor de cinco años. Un Notario Público sólo puede asociarse con otro Notario Público para prestar servicios notariales.
Calendario de Reducción:	Ninguno

Sector:	Servicios profesionales, técnicos y especializados
Subsector :	Notariado
Clasificación Industrial:	CMAP 951001 Servicios de notarías públicas
Tipo de Reserva:	Trato nacional (Artículos 10-04 y 14-04) Presencia local (Artículo 10-05)
Nivel de Gobierno:	Estatal (Estado de Tamaulipas)
Medida:	Ley del Notariado para el Estado de Tamaulipas, Periódico Oficial, enero 30, 1993, Artículo 13
Descripción:	Servicios transfronterizos e Inversión El Ejecutivo del Estado expedirá patente de aspirante al cargo de Notario a quien acredite ser mexicano por nacimiento y con residencia en el estado de 3 años por lo menos. Un Notario Público sólo puede asociarse con otro Notario Público para prestar servicios notariales.
Calendario de Reducción:	Ninguno

Sector:	Servicios profesionales, técnicos y especializados
Subsector :	Notariado
Clasificación Industrial:	CMAP 951001 Servicios de notarías públicas
Tipo de Reserva:	Trato nacional (Artículos 10-04 y 14-04) Presencia local (Artículo 10-05)
Nivel de Gobierno:	Estatal (Estado de Tlaxcala)
Medida:	Ley del Notariado para el Estado de Tlaxcala, Periódico Oficial, enero 5, 1983, Título III, Capítulo I, Artículo 29 y 30
Descripción:	Servicios transfronterizos e Inversión Para obtener la constancia de aspirante a Notario Público se requiere ser mexicano por nacimiento y tener su domicilio civil en el Estado de Tlaxcala con una antigüedad de cinco años por lo menos. Un Notario Público sólo puede asociarse con otro Notario Público para prestar servicios notariales.
Calendario de Reducción:	Ninguno

Sector:	Servicios profesionales, técnicos y especializados
Subsector :	Notariado
Clasificación Industrial:	CMAP 951001 Servicios de notarías públicas
Tipo de Reserva:	Trato nacional (Artículos 10-04 y 14-04) Presencia local (Artículo 10-05)
Nivel de Gobierno:	Estatal (Estado de Veracruz)
Medida:	Ley del Notariado, Gaceta Oficial, junio 1, 1965, Título I, Capítulo IV, Artículo 37, fracciones I y VI
Descripción:	Servicios transfronterizos e Inversión Para obtener el nombramiento de Notario se requiere ser mexicano por nacimiento y vecino del estado. Un Notario Público sólo puede asociarse con otro Notario Público para prestar servicios notariales.
Calendario de Reducción:	Ninguno

Sector:	Servicios profesionales, técnicos y especializados
Subsector :	Notariado
Clasificación Industrial:	CMAP 951001 Servicios de notarías públicas
Tipo de Reserva:	Trato nacional (Artículos 10-04 y 14-04)
Nivel de Gobierno:	Estatal (Estado de Yucatán)

Medida:	Ley del Notariado del Estado de Yucatán, Diario Oficial, julio 4, 1977, Capítulo II, Artículos 10 y 12
Descripción:	Servicios transfronterizos e Inversión La patente de aspirante a Notario será extendida por el Ejecutivo del estado a ciudadanos mexicanos. Un Notario Público sólo puede asociarse con otro Notario Público para prestar servicios notariales.
Calendario de Reducción:	Ninguno

Sector:	Servicios profesionales, técnicos y especializados
Subsector :	Notariado
Clasificación Industrial:	CMAP 951001 Servicios de notarías públicas
Tipo de Reserva:	Trato nacional (Artículos 10-04 y 14-04) Presencia local (Artículo 10-05)
Nivel de Gobierno:	Estatal (Estado de Zacatecas)
Medida:	Ley del Notariado del Estado de Zacatecas, Periódico Oficial, enero 14, 1990, Capítulo II, Artículo 69
Descripción:	Servicios transfronterizos e Inversión Para obtener el nombramiento y ejercer como Notario, se requiere ser mexicano por nacimiento y tener por lo menos cinco años de residencia en el estado. Asimismo, acreditar haber practicado durante un año ininterrumpido bajo la dirección y responsabilidad de un Notario de la entidad. Un Notario Público sólo puede asociarse con otro Notario Público para prestar servicios notariales.
Calendario de Reducción:	Ninguno

Sector:	Servicios profesionales, técnicos y especializados
Subsector :	Perito valuador
Clasificación Industrial:	
Tipo de Reserva:	Trato nacional (Artículo 10-04) Presencia local (Artículo 10-05)
Nivel de Gobierno:	Estatal (Estado de Colima)
Medida:	Ley que crea el Registro de Peritos Valuadores del Estado de Colima, Periódico Oficial, noviembre 28, 1992, Capítulo I
Descripción:	Servicios transfronterizos Para inscribirse en el Registro de Peritos Valuadores técnico-comercial del estado, principalmente respecto de bienes inmuebles y de empresas, se requiere la ciudadanía mexicana y tener residencia efectiva en la entidad no menor a tres años anteriores a la fecha de solicitud.
Calendario de Reducción:	Ninguno
Sector:	Servicios profesionales, técnicos y especializados
Subsector :	Perito Valuador
Clasificación Industrial:	
Tipo de Reserva:	Trato nacional (Artículo 10-04) Presencia local (Artículo 10-05)
Nivel de Gobierno:	Estatal (Estado de Durango)
Medida:	Reglamento de Registro de Peritos Valuadores para el Estado de Durango, Periódico Oficial, noviembre 21, 1993, Capítulo I, Artículo 5, fracciones I y V
Descripción:	Servicios transfronterizos

	Para inscribirse en el Registro de Peritos Valuadores del estado, se requiere la ciudadanía mexicana y tener residencia efectiva en la entidad no menor a tres años anteriores a la fecha de solicitud.
Calendario de Reducción:	Ninguno

Sector:	Servicios profesionales, técnicos y especializados
Subsector :	Perito valuador
Clasificación Industrial:	
Tipo de Reserva:	Trato nacional (Artículo 10-04)
Nivel de Gobierno:	Estatal (Estado de Tamaulipas)
Medida:	Reglamento para el Registro de Peritos en el Estado de Tamaulipas, Periódico Oficial, febrero 6, 1993, Artículo 12
Descripción:	Servicios transfronterizos Se requiere ser ciudadano mexicano para obtener el registro de perito valuador inmobiliario.
Calendario de Reducción:	Ninguno

Sector:	Servicios educativos
Subsector :	Servicios privados de educación
Clasificación Industrial:	CMAP 921104 Servicios privados de educación media superior CMAP 921106 Servicios privados de educación que combinan los niveles de enseñanza preescolar, primaria, secundaria, media superior y superior
Tipo de Reserva:	Trato nacional (Artículo 14-04) Alta dirección empresarial y consejos de administración (Artículo 14-08)
Nivel de Gobierno:	Estatal (Estado de Chihuahua)
Medida:	Código Administrativo del Estado, Periódico Oficial, agosto 2, 1950, Título IV, Capítulo II
Descripción:	Servicios transfronterizos e Inversión Para establecer e incorporar escuelas sostenidas por la iniciativa privada se requiere que su director sea mexicano.
Calendario de Reducción:	Ninguno

Sector:	Servicios profesionales, técnicos y especializados
Subsector :	Servicios de seguridad privada
Clasificación Industrial:	CMAP 951019 Servicios de protección y de custodia
Tipo de Reserva:	Trato nacional (Artículos10-04 y 14-04) Alta dirección empresarial y consejos de administración (Artículo 14-08)
Nivel de Gobierno:	Distrito Federal
Medida:	Ley de Seguridad Pública del Distrito Federal, Diario Oficial, julio 19, 1993, Título IX, Capítulo Unico Acuerdo No. A/011/94 del Procurador General de Justicia del Distrito Federal en el que se establecen las reglas generales del título noveno de la Ley de Seguridad Pública del Distrito Federal, Diario Oficial, marzo 31, 1994, Capítulo III
Descripción:	Servicios transfronterizos e Inversión Sólo podrán prestar los servicios privados de seguridad las personas físicas o morales de nacionalidad mexicana. El personal directivo y operativo debe ser de nacionalidad mexicana.
Calendario de Reducción:	Ninguno

Sector:	Servicios profesionales, técnicos y especializados
Subsector :	Servicios privados de seguridad

Clasificación Industrial:	CMAP 951019 Servicios de protección y de custodia
Tipo de Reserva:	Trato nacional (Artículo 10-04)
Nivel de Gobierno:	Estatal (Estado de Jalisco)
Medida:	Reglamento de los Servicios Privados de Seguridad en Jalisco, Periódico Oficial, mayo 21, 1994, Capítulo II, Artículo 9
Descripción:	Servicios transfronterizos Para obtener registro y autorización para prestar servicios privados de seguridad se requiere la nacionalidad mexicana.
Calendario de Reducción:	Ninguno

Sector:	Servicios profesionales, técnicos y especializados
Subsector :	Servicios de asociaciones comerciales, profesionales y laborales
Clasificación Industrial:	CMAP 925001 Servicios de cámaras, asociaciones y agrupaciones de productores y comerciantes (incluye las industriales, comerciales y agropecuarias)
Tipo de Reserva:	Alta dirección empresarial y consejos de administración (Artículo 14-08)
Nivel de Gobierno:	Estatal (Estado de Sinaloa)
Medida:	Ley de Organizaciones Agrícolas del Estado de Sinaloa, Periódico Oficial, marzo 31, 1997, Título Primero, Capítulo VII, Artículo 55 y Título Segundo, Capítulo VI, Artículo 89
Descripción:	Inversión El Presidente, Vicepresidente, Secretario, Tesorero y Vocales de una asociación agrícola en la entidad deberán ser mexicanos. Asimismo, para ser consejero propietario o suplente de la Confederación de Asociaciones Agrícolas del estado de Sinaloa se requiere ser mexicano.
Calendario de Reducción:	Ninguno

Sector:	Servicios de esparcimiento, culturales, recreativos y deportivos
Subsector :	
Clasificación Industrial:	CMAP 949102 Servicios privados de promoción y presentación de espectáculos deportivos, taurinos y circos CMAP 949202 Servicios públicos de promoción y presentación de espectáculos deportivos y taurinos
Tipo de Reserva:	Trato nacional (Artículo 10-04) Requisitos de desempeño (Artículo 14-07)
Nivel de Gobierno:	Distrito Federal
Medida:	Reglamento Taurino para el Distrito Federal, Diario Oficial, noviembre 11, 1987, Capítulos II y IV
Descripción:	Servicios transfronterizos e Inversión Para la celebración de espectáculos taurinos en el Distrito Federal se requiere de autorización expedida por la Delegación correspondiente. Los actuantes extranjeros, en las categorías de corrida de toros, novilladas y festivales taurinos y becerradas, no podrán exceder del 50 por ciento de los diestros y actuantes programados. Todos los carteles deberán estar integrados por el 50 por ciento de actuantes mexicanos como mínimo.
Calendario de Reducción:	Ninguno

Sector:	Servicios de esparcimiento, culturales, recreativos y deportivos
Subsector :	
Clasificación Industrial:	CMAP 949202 Servicios públicos de promoción y presentación de espectáculos deportivos y taurinos
Tipo de Reserva:	Trato nacional (Artículo 10-04) Alta dirección empresarial y consejos de administración (Artículo 14-08)

Nivel de Gobierno:	Distrito Federal
Medida:	Reglamento para el Funcionamiento de Establecimientos Mercantiles y Celebración de Espectáculos Públicos en el Distrito Federal, DiarioOficial, julio 31, 1989, Título Tercero, Capítulo III, Sección Primera
Descripción:	Servicios transfronterizos e Inversión Para el desarrollo técnico de los espectáculos de box, lucha libre, frontón, fútbol, básquetbol, béisbol, automovilismo, motociclismo, ciclismo, atletismo, y similares, el Departamento del Distrito Federal contará para cada tipo de espectáculo deportivo con una Comisión. Para poder integrar cualquiera de las Comisiones de espectáculos deportivos se requiere ser ciudadano mexicano.
Calendario de Reducción:	Ninguno

Sector:	Servicios profesionales, técnicos y especializados
Subsector :	
Clasificación Industrial:	CMAP 951008 Servicios de publicidad y actividades conexas
Tipo de Reserva:	Trato nacional (Artículo 10-04) Requisitos de desempeño (Artículo 14-07)
Nivel de Gobierno:	Estatal (Estado de Sinaloa)
Medida:	Reglamento para el Aprovechamiento del Derecho de Vía de las Carreteras Estatales y Zonas Aledañas, Periódico Oficial, junio 28, 1993, Capítulo II, Artículo 5, Capítulo V, Artículo 31
Descripción:	Servicios transfronterizos e Inversión Se requiere permiso para la instalación de anuncios o construcción de obras con fines de publicidad en los terrenos adyacentes al derecho de vía de las carreteras estatales. Los anuncios y obras publicitarias, además de lo requerido por las disposiciones de la materia, deberán estar redactados en lenguaje claro y accesible en idioma español. Sólo se autorizará el uso de diale ctos de nombres de productos, marcas o establecimientos en lengua extranjera cuando se justifique su uso.
Calendario de Reducción:	Ninguno

Sector:	Servicios profesionales, técnicos y especializados
Subsector :	
Clasificación Industrial:	CMAP 951008 Servicios de publicidad y actividades conexas
Tipo de Reserva:	Trato nacional (Artículo 10-04) Requisitos de desempeño (Artículo 14-07)
Nivel de Gobierno:	Distrito Federal
Medida:	Reglamento de Anuncios para el Distrito Federal, Diario Oficial, septiembre 2, 1988, Capítulo I
Descripción:	Servicios transfronterizos e Inversión En la fijación, instalación, colocación y distribución de anuncios en los sitios y en los lugares a los que tenga acceso el público o que sean visibles en la vía pública, el texto de los anuncios deberá redactarse en idioma español con sujeción a las reglas de la gramática. No se pueden emplear palabras de otro idioma, salvo que se trate de dialectos nacionales o de nombres propios de productos, marcas o nombres comerciales en la lengua extranjera que estén registrados en la Secretaría de Comercio y Fomento Industrial.
Calendario de Reducción:	Ninguno

Sector:	Trabajadores no asalariados
Subsector :	

Clasificación Industrial:	
Tipo de Reserva:	Trato nacional (Artículo 10-04) Alta dirección empresarial y consejos de administración (Artículo 14-08)
Nivel de Gobierno:	Distrito Federal
Medida:	Reglamento de los Trabajadores no Asalariados del Distrito Federal, Diario Oficial, mayo 2, 1975, Capítulo III
Descripción:	Servicios transfronterizos e Inversión Para ser miembro de la directiva de las Uniones de Trabajadores no Asalariados se requiere ser mexicano por nacimiento.
Calendario de Reducción:	Ninguno

Sector:	Transporte
Subsector :	Transporte terrestre
Clasificación Industrial:	CMAP 711201 Servicio de autotransporte de materiales de construcción CMAP 711202 Servicio de autotransporte de mudanzas CMAP 711203 Otros servicios de autotransporte especializado de carga CMAP 711204 Servicio de autotransporte de carga en general CMAP 711311 Servicio de transporte foráneo de pasajeros en autobús CMAP 711312 Servicio de transporte urbano y suburbano de pasajeros en autobús CMAP 711315 Servicio de transporte en automóvil de ruleteo CMAP 711316 Servicio de transporte de automóvil de ruta fija CMAP 711317 Servicio de transporte en automóvil de sitio CMAP 711318 Servicio de transporte escolar CMAP 711319 Servicio de alquiler de automóviles CMAP 973105 Servicio de grúa para vehículos
Tipo de Reserva:	Trato nacional (Artículos 10-04 y 14-04) Presencia local (Artículo 10-05)
Nivel de Gobierno:	Estatal (Estado de Baja California)
Medida:	Ley de Tránsito y Transportes del Estado de Baja California, Periódico Oficial, agosto 10, 1982, Capítulo VII
Descripción:	Servicios transfronterizos e Inversión Se requiere concesión o permiso para la explotación del servicio público de transporte. Sólo los nacionales mexicanos pueden obtener tales concesiones o permisos. Para el otorgamiento de las concesiones se preferirá, en igualdad de circunstancias, a las sociedades cooperativas, uniones, sindicatos obreros, ligas y asociaciones formadas por trabajadores.
Calendario de Reducción:	Ninguno

Sector:	Transporte
Subsector :	Transporte terrestre
Clasificación Industrial:	CMAP 711201 Servicio de autotransporte de materiales de construcción CMAP 711202 Servicio de autotransporte de mudanzas CMAP 711203 Otros servicios de autotransporte especializado de carga CMAP 711204 Servicio de autotransporte de carga en general CMAP 711311 Servicio de transporte foráneo de pasajeros en autobús CMAP 711312 Servicio de transporte urbano y suburbano de pasajeros en autobús CMAP 711315 Servicio de transporte en automóvil de ruleteo CMAP 711317 Servicio de transporte en automóvil de sitio CMAP 711318 Servicio de transporte escolar CMAP 973105 Servicio de grúa para vehículos
Tipo de Reserva:	Trato nacional (Artículos 10-04 y 14-04)

	Presencia local (Artículo 10-05)
Nivel de Gobierno:	Estatal (Estado de Baja California Sur)
Medida:	Ley de Tránsito y Transporte del Estado de Baja California Sur, Boletín Oficial, noviembre 22, 1990, Capítulo Unico
Descripción:	Servicios transfronterizos e Inversión Se requiere concesión para prestar servicios de transporte público. En igualdad de circunstancias, tendrán preferencia para obtener las concesiones de explotación del servicio público de transporte los sudcalifornianos.
Calendario de Reducción:	Ninguno

Sector:	Transporte
Subsector :	Transporte Terrestre
Clasificación Industrial:	CMAP 973101 servicio de administración de centrales camioneras de pasajeros y servicios auxiliares (terminales camioneras y estaciones de camiones y autobuses)
Tipo de Reserva:	Trato nacional (Artículos 10-04 y 14-04) Presencia local (Artículo 10-05)
Nivel de Gobierno:	Estatal (Estado de Campeche)
Medida:	Ley de Vialidad, Comunicaciones y Transportes para el Estado de Campeche, Periódico Oficial, abril 30, 1987, Capítulo III
Descripción:	Servicios transfronterizos e Inversión Se requiere concesión para establecer estaciones terminales para el aprovechamiento de los sistemas de transporte de jurisdicción estatal. Las concesiones se otorgarán a personas morales mexicanas. En igualdad de circunstancias, se preferirá a las sociedades integradas por concesionarios del servicio público de transporte que exploten cuando menos el 51 por ciento de los vehículos que deban servir en esas terminales.
Calendario de Reducción:	Ninguno

Sector:	Transporte
Subsector :	Transporte Terrestre
Clasificación Industrial:	CMAP 711201 Servicio de autotransporte de materiales de construcción CMAP 711202 Servicio de autotransporte de mudanzas CMAP 711203 Otros servicios de autotransporte especializado de carga CMAP 711204 Servicio de autotransporte de carga en general CMAP 711311 Servicio de transporte foráneo de pasajeros en autobús CMAP 711312 Servicio de transporte urbano y suburbano de pasajeros en autobús CMAP 711318 Servicio de transporte escolar CMAP 711319 Servicio de alquile r de automóviles CMAP 973105 Servicio de grúa para vehículos
Tipo de Reserva:	Trato nacional (Artículos 10-04 y 14-04) Presencia local (Artículo 10-05)
Nivel de Gobierno:	Estatal (Estado de Campeche)
Medida:	Ley de Vialidad, Comunicaciones y Transportes para el Estado de Campeche, Periódico Oficial, abril 30, 1987, Título III, Capítulo III
Descripción:	Servicios transfronterizos e Inversión Se requiere concesión para prestar servicios de transporte público. Las personas físicas que deseen obtener una concesión para la prestación del servicio público de transporte deben ser mexicanas por nacimiento. Las personas morales deben estar organizadas conforme a las leyes del país y constituidas exclusivamente por socios mexicanos de nacimiento.

Calendario de Reducción:	Ninguno

Sector:	Transporte
Subsector :	Transporte terrestre
Clasificación Industrial:	CMAP 711201 Servicio de autotransporte de materiales de construcción CMAP 711202 Servicio de autotransporte de mudanzas CMAP 711203 Otros servicios de autotransporte especializado de carga CMAP 711204 Servicio de autotransporte de carga en general CMAP 711311 Servicio de transporte foráneo de pasajeros en autobús CMAP 711312 Servicio de transporte urbano y suburbano de pasajeros en autobús CMAP 711317 Servicio de transporte en automóvil de sitio
Tipo de Reserva:	Trato nacional (Artículos 10-04 y 14-04) Presencia local (Artículo 10-05)
Nivel de Gobierno:	Estatal (Estado de Coahuila)
Medida:	Ley de Tránsito y Transportes del Estado de Coahuila de Zaragoza, Periódico Oficial, enero 19, 1996, Capítulo VI
Descripción:	Servicios transfronterizos e Inversión Se requiere concesión para prestar servicios de transporte público. Las concesiones sólo podrán otorgarse a personas físicas mexicanas o a personas morales constituidas conforme a la ley.
Calendario de Reducción:	Ninguno

Sector:	Transporte
Subsector :	Transporte terrestre
Clasificación Industrial:	CMAP 711201 Servicio de autotransporte de materiales de construcción CMAP 711202 Servicio de autotransporte de mudanzas CMAP 711203 Otros servicios de autotransporte especializado de carga CMAP 711204 Servicio de autotransporte de carga en general CMAP 711311 Servicio de transporte foráneo de pasajeros en autobús CMAP 711312 Servicio de transporte urbano y suburbano de pasajeros en autobús CMAP 711318 Servicio de transporte escolar CMAP 711319 Servicio de alquiler de automóviles
Tipo de Reserva:	Trato nacional (Artículos 10-04 y 14-04) Presencia local (Artículo 10-05)
Nivel de Gobierno:	Estatal (Estado de Colima)
Medida:	Reglamento de Vialidad y Transporte, Periódico Oficial, marzo 13, 1993, Capítulo XVIII
Descripción:	Servicios transfronterizos e Inversión El solicitante de concesión de servicio público de transporte deberá ser mexicano por nacimiento en el caso de persona física; las personas morales deberán estar debidamente constituidas conforme a la ley.
Calendario de Reducción:	Ninguno

Sector:	Transporte
Subsector :	Transporte terrestre
Clasificación Industrial:	CMAP 711201 Servicio de autotransporte de materiales de construcción CMAP 711202 Servicio de autotransporte de mudanzas CMAP 711203 Otros servicios de autotransporte especializado de carga CMAP 711204 Servicio de autotransporte de carga en general CMAP 711311 Servicio de transporte foráneo de pasajeros en autobús

	CMAP 711312 Servicio de transporte urbano y suburbano de pasajeros en autobús CMAP 711315 Servicio de transporte en automóvil de ruleteo CMAP 711316 Servicio de transporte de automóvil de ruta fija CMAP 711317 Servicio de transporte en automóvil de sitio CMAP 711318 Servicio de transporte escolar CMAP 711319 Servicio de alquiler de automóviles CMAP 973105 Servicio de grúa para vehículos
Tipo de Reserva:	Trato nacional (Artículos 10-04 y 14-04) Presencia local (Artículo 10-05)
Nivel de Gobierno:	Estatal (Estado de Chiapas)
Medida:	Reglamento de Tránsito del Estado de Chiapas, Periódico Oficial, mayo 30, 1972 Decreto que establece diversas disposiciones en materia de servicio público de autotransporte de carga en el Estado de Chiapas, marzo 21, 1990
Descripción:	Servicios transfronterizos e Inversión Se requiere permiso para la explotación total o parcial de los servicios públicos estatales de transporte. El permiso se otorga a mexicanos por nacimiento o naturalización y a sociedades mexicanas legalmente constituidas.
Calendario de Reducción:	Ninguno

Sector:	Transporte
Subsector :	Transporte terrestre
Clasificación Industrial:	CMAP 711201 Servicio de autotransporte de materiales de construcción CMAP 711202 Servicio de autotransporte de mudanzas CMAP 711203 Otros servicios de autotransporte especializado de carga CMAP 711204 Servicio de autotransporte de carga en general CMAP 711311 Servicio de transporte foráneo de pasajeros en autobús CMAP 711312 Servicio de transporte urbano y suburbano de pasajeros en autobús CMAP 711315 Servicio de transporte en automóvil de ruleteo CMAP 711316 Servicio de transporte de automóvil de ruta Fija CMAP 711317 Servicio de transporte en automóvil de sitio CMAP 711318 Servicio de transporte escolar CMAP 711319 Servicio de alquiler de automóvil CMAP 973105 Servicio de grúa para vehículo
Tipo de Reserva:	Trato nacional (Artículos 10-04 y 14-04) Presencia local (Artículo 10-05)
Nivel de Gobierno:	Estatal (Estado de Chihuahua)
Medida:	Ley de Comunicaciones y Transportes del Estado de Chihuahua, Periódico Oficial, julio 13, 1987, Capítulo III
Descripción:	Servicios transfronterizos e Inversión Se requiere concesión o permiso para prestar servicios de transporte público. Las concesiones y permisos se otorgarán únicamente a personas físicas mexicanas o a personas morales constituidas conforme a la ley.
Calendario de Reducción:	Ninguno

Sector:	Transporte
Subsector :	Transporte terrestre
Clasificación Industrial:	CMAP 711101 Servicio de transporte en tranvías y trolebuses CMAP 711201 Servicio de autotransporte de materiales de construcción CMAP 711202 Servicio de autotransporte de mudanzas

	CMAP 711203 Otros servicios de autotransporte especializado de carga CMAP 711204 Servicio de autotransporte de carga en general CMAP 711312 Servicio de transporte urbano y suburbano de pasajeros en autobús CMAP 711315 Servicio de transporte en automóvil de ruleteo CMAP 711316 Servicio de transporte de automóvil de ruta fija CMAP 711317 Servicio de transporte en automóvil de sitio CMAP 711318 Servicio de transporte escolar CMAP 711319 Servicio de alquiler de automóviles CMAP 973105 Servicio de grúa para vehículos
Tipo de Reserva:	Trato nacional (Artículos 10-04 y 14-04) Presencia local (Artículo 10-05)
Nivel de Gobierno:	Distrito Federal
Medida:	Ley que fija las Bases Generales a que habrán de sujetarse el Tránsito y los Transportes en el Distrito Federal, Diario Oficial, marzo 23, 1942, Artículo 7, incisos a) y b) Reglamento de Transporte Urbano de Carga para el Distrito Federal, Diario Oficial, febrero 16, 1993, Capítulo Segundo, Artículo 16, fracción I, inciso a) Reglamento para el Servicio Público de Transporte de Pasajeros en el Distrito Federal, Diario Oficial, abril 14, 1942, Artículos 17 y 23
Descripción:	Servicios transfronterizos e Inversión Se requiere concesión o permiso para establecer y operar líneas locales de transporte público. Las concesiones y permisos se otorgarán a personas físicas mexicanas por nacimiento. Tratándose de personas morales, éstas deberán estar organizadas conforme a las leyes del país.
Calendario de Reducción:	Ninguno

Sector:	Transporte
Subsector :	Transporte terrestre
Clasificación Industrial:	CMAP 711201 Servicio de autotransporte de materiales de construcción CMAP 711202 Servicio de autotransporte de mudanzas CMAP 711203 Otros servicios de autotransporte especializado de carga CMAP 711204 Servicio de autotransporte de carga en general CMAP 711311 Servicio de transporte foráneo de pasajeros en autobús CMAP 711312 Servicio de transporte urbano y suburbano de pasajeros en autobús CMAP 711317 Servicio de transporte en automóvil de sitio CMAP 711318 Servicio de transporte escolar
Tipo de Reserva:	Trato nacional (Artículos 10-04 y 14-04) Presencia local (Artículo 10-05)
Nivel de Gobierno:	Estatal (Estado de Durango)
Medida:	Ley de Transporte de Durango, Periódico Oficial, diciembre 10, 1996, Capítulo IV, Artículos 23, 24, 33 y 34 Reglamento General de la Ley de Tránsito y Transporte del Estado de Durango, Periódico Oficial, agosto 11, 1991, Capítulo XX, Artículo 176
Descripción:	Servicios transfronterizos e Inversión Se requiere concesión o permiso para prestar servicios de transporte público. Las concesiones o permisos se otorgan a ciudadanos mexicanos, así como a sindicatos y a otras organizaciones de carácter social constituidas por aquellos, de acuerdo a las leyes mexicanas.
Calendario de Reducción:	Ninguno

Sector:	Transporte
Subsector :	Transporte terrestre
Clasificación Industrial:	CMAP 711201 Servicio de autotransporte de materiales de construcción CMAP 711202 Servicio de autotransporte de mudanzas CMAP 711203 Otros servicios de autotransporte especializado de carga CMAP 711204 Servicio de autotransporte de carga en general CMAP 711311 Servicio de transporte foráneo de pasajeros en autobús CMAP 711312 Servicio de transporte urbano y suburbano de pasajeros en autobús CMAP 711315 Servicio de transporte en automóvil de ruleteo CMAP 711316 Servicio de transporte en automóvil de ruta fija CMAP 711317 Servicio de transporte en automóvil de sitio CMAP 711318 Servicio de transporte escolar CMAP 711319 Servicio de alquiler de automóviles CMAP 711320 Otro tipo de transporte de pasajeros, incluye vehículos de tracción animal CMAP 973105 Servicio de grúa para vehículo
Tipo de Reserva:	Trato nacional (Artículos 10-04 y 14-04) Presencia local (Artículo 10-05)
Nivel de Gobierno:	Estatal (Estado de México)
Medida:	Ley de Tránsito y Transportes del Estado de México, Gaceta Oficial, abril 21, 1971, Capítulo IV, Artículo 25
Descripción:	Servicios transfronterizos e Inversión Se requiere concesiones para explotar el servicio público de transporte en sus diferentes ramas y modalidades. Estas sólo se podrán otorgar a mexicanos por nacimiento o sociedades mercantiles integradas por éstos y que estén legalmente constituidas conforme a las leyes del país.
Calendario de Reducción:	Ninguno

Sector:	Transporte
Subsector :	Transporte terrestre
Clasificación Industrial:	CMAP 711201 Servicio de autotransporte de materiales de construcción CMAP 711202 Servicio de autotransporte de mudanzas CMAP 711203 Otros servicios de autotransporte especializado de carga CMAP 711204 Servicio de autotransporte de carga en general CMAP 711311 Servicio de transporte foráneo de pasajeros en autobús CMAP 711312 Servicio de transporte urbano y suburbano de pasajeros en autobús CMAP 711315 Servicio de transporte en automóvil de ruleteo CMAP 711317 Servicio de transporte en automóvil de sitio CMAP 711318 Servicio de transporte escolar
Tipo de Reserva:	Trato nacional (Artículos 10-04 y 14-04) Presencia local (Artículo 10-05)
Nivel de Gobierno:	Estatal (Estado de Guanajuato)
Medida:	Ley de Tránsito y Transporte del Estado de Guanajuato, Periódico Oficial, agosto 20, 1993, Título III, Capítulo II, Artículo 90
Descripción:	Servicios transfronterizos e Inversión Se requiere concesión para la prestación del servicio público de transporte. Estas se otorgarán única y exclusivamente en favor de personas físicas o morales de nacionalidad mexicana.
Calendario de Reducción:	Ninguno

Sector:	Transporte
Subsector :	Transporte terrestre
Clasificación Industrial:	CMAP 711201 Servicio de autotransporte de materiales de construcción CMAP 711202 Servicio de autotransporte de mudanzas CMAP 711203 Otros servicios de autotransporte especializado de carga CMAP 711204 Servicio de autotransporte de carga en general CMAP 711311 Servicio de transporte foráneo de pasajeros en autobús CMAP 711312 Servicio de transporte urbano y suburbano de pasajeros en autobús CMAP 711318 Servicio de transporte escolar CMAP 711319 Servicio de alquiler de automóviles
Tipo de Reserva:	Trato nacional (Artículos 10-04 y 14-04) Presencia local (Artículo 10-05)
Nivel de Gobierno:	Estatal (Estado de Guerrero)
Medida:	Ley de Transporte y Vialidad del Estado de Guerrero, Diario Oficial, junio 6, 1989, Capítulo VII, Artículo 52
Descripción:	Servicios transfronterizos e Inversión Se requiere concesión o permiso para prestar servicios de transporte público. Las concesiones y permisos sólo se otorgarán a mexicanos o a sociedades constituidas conforme a la ley. En igualdad de condiciones se preferirá a trabajadores guerrerenses del transporte, núcleos agrarios, organizaciones representativas de los trabajadores del transporte, personas morales del sector social, a quienes cuenten con mejor equipo, infraestructura y experiencia para la eficiente prestación de los servicios públicos de transporte y a quien haya resultado afectado por expropiaciones agrarias o por razón de equidad social.
Calendario de Reducción:	Ninguno

Sector:	Transporte
Subsector :	Transporte terrestre
Clasificación Industrial:	CMAP 973101 Servicio de administración de centrales camioneras e pasajeros y servicios auxiliares (terminales camioneras y estaciones de camiones y autobuses)
Tipo de Reserva:	Trato nacional (Artículos 10-04 y 14-04) Presencia local (Artículo 10-05)
Nivel de Gobierno:	Estatal (Estado de Hidalgo)
Medida:	Ley de Vías de Comunicación y Tránsito del Estado de Hidalgo, Periódico Oficial, enero 8, 1970, Título VI, Capítulo V, Artículos 170, 182, fracción II y Artículo 206
Descripción:	Servicios transfronterizos e Inversión Se requiere concesión para construir y explotar estaciones centrales y terminales de paso. Las concesiones se otorgarán a mexicanos por nacimiento o a personas morales constituidas conforme a las leyes del país. Se declaran improcedentes las solicitudes hechas por extranjeros.
Calendario de Reducción:	Ninguno

Sector:	Transporte
Subsector :	Transporte terrestre
Clasificación Industrial:	CMAP 711201 Servicio de autotransporte de materiales de construcción CMAP 711202 Servicio de autotransporte de mudanzas CMAP 711203 Otros servicios de autotransporte especializado de carga CMAP 711204 Servicio de autotransporte de carga en general CMAP 711311 Servicio de transporte foráneo de pasajeros en autobús

	CMAP 711312 Servicio de transporte urbano y suburbano de pasajeros en autobús CMAP 711317 Servicio de transporte en automóvil de sitio
Tipo de Reserva:	Trato nacional (Artículos 10-04 y 14-04) Presencia local (Artículo 10-05)
Nivel de Gobierno:	Estatal (Estado de Hidalgo)
Medida:	Ley de Vías de Comunicación y Tránsito del Estado de Hidalgo, Periódico Oficial, enero 8, 1970, Título VI, Capítulo V, Artículos 170 y 180, fracción II y Artículo 182, fracción II
Descripción:	Servicios transfronterizos e Inversión Se requiere concesión o permiso para la explotación del servicio público de transporte. Para obtener la concesión y permiso, se requiere ser mexicano por nacimiento ser persona moral constituida conforme a las leyes del país. Se declaran improcedentes las solicitudes hechas por extranjeros.
Calendario de Reducción:	Ninguno
Sector:	Transporte
Subsector :	Transporte terrestre
Clasificación Industrial:	CMAP 711201 Servicio de autotransporte de materiales de construcción CMAP 711202 Servicio de autotransporte de mudanzas CMAP 711203 Otros servicios de autotransporte especializado de carga CMAP 711204 Servicio de autotransporte de carga en general CMAP 711311 Servicio de transporte foráneo de pasajeros en autobús CMAP 711312 Servicio de transporte urbano y suburbano de pasajeros en autobús CMAP 711315 Servicio de transporte en automóvil de ruleteo CMAP 711317 Servicio de transporte en automóvil de sitio CMAP 711318 Servicio de transporte escolar CMAP 711319 Servicio de alquiler de automóviles CMAP 711320 Otro tipo de transporte de pasajeros, incluye vehículos de tracción animal CMAP 973105 Servicio de grúa para vehículos
Tipo de Reserva:	Trato nacional (Artículos 10-04 y 14-04) Presencia local (Artículo 10-05)
Nivel de Gobierno:	Estatal (Estado de Jalisco)
Medida:	Ley del Servicio de Tránsito del Estado de Jalisco, Periódico Oficial, agosto 5, 1941, Capítulo VI, Artículos 42 y 44 Reglamento de la Ley del Servicio de Tránsito, Periódico Oficial, agosto 5, 1941, Título V, Capítulo I, Artículo 168
Descripción:	Servicios transfronterizos e Inversión Se requiere permiso para la explotación de servicio de transporte público. Este permiso se otorga a mexicanos por nacimiento. Se declaran improcedentes las solicitudes de permisos cuando sean hechas por extranjeros.
Calendario de Reducción:	Ninguno

Sector:	Transporte
Subsector :	Transporte Terrestre
Clasificación Industrial:	CMAP 711201 Servicio de autotransporte de materiales de construcción CMAP 711202 Servicio de autotransporte de mudanzas CMAP 711203 Otros servicios de autotransporte especializado de carga CMAP 711204 Servicio de autotransporte de carga en general CMAP 711311 Servicio de transporte foráneo de pasajeros en autobús CMAP 711312 Servicio de transporte urbano y suburbano de pasajeros

	en autobús CMAP 711315 Servicio de transporte en automóvil de ruleteo CMAP 711316 Servicio de transporte de automóvil de ruta fija CMAP 711317 Servicio de transporte en automóvil de sitio CMAP 711318 Servicio de transporte escolar CMAP 711319 Servicio de alquiler de automóviles CMAP 711320 Otro tipo de transporte de pasajeros, incluye vehículos de tracción animal CMAP 973105 Servicio de grúa para vehículo
Tipo de Reserva:	Trato nacional (Artículo 10-04 y 14-04) Presencia local (Artículo 10-05)
Nivel de Gobierno:	Estatal (Estado de Michoacán)
Medida:	Ley de Comunicaciones y Transportes del Estado de Michoacán, Periódico Oficial, julio 19, 1982,Título I, Artículo 3
Descripción:	Servicios transfronterizos e Inversiòn Se requiere concesión para prestar servicios de transporte público. Las concesiones sólo se otorgarán a ciudadanos mexicanos o a sociedades mexicanas constituidas conforme a las leyes del país. En igualdad de circunstancias, tendrán preferencia para obtener estas concesiones los michoacanos por nacimiento, los mexicanos con residencia de más de un año en el estado y las sociedades mexicanas registradas en Michoacán.
Calendario de Reducción:	Ninguno

Sector:	Transporte
Subsector :	Transporte terrestre
Clasificación Industrial:	CMAP 711201 Servicio de autotransporte de materiales de construcción CMAP 711202 Servicio de autotransporte de mudanzas CMAP 711203 Otros servicios de autotransporte especializado de carga CMAP 711204 Servicio de autotransporte de carga en general CMAP 711311 Servicio de transporte foráneo de pasajeros en autobús CMAP 711312 Servicio de transporte urbano y suburbano de pasajeros en autobús CMAP 711315 Servicio de transporte en automóvil de ruleteo CMAP 711316 Servicios de transporte en automóvil de ruta fija CMAP 711317 Servicio de transporte en automóvil de sitio
Tipo de Reserva:	Trato nacional (Artículos 10-04 y 14-04) Presencia local (Artículo 10-05)
Nivel de Gobierno:	Estatal (Estado de Morelos)
Medida:	Reglamento de Servicio Público de Transporte del Estado de Morelos, Periódico Oficial, octubre 25, 1989, Artículo 37
Descripción:	Servicios transfronterizos e Inversión Se requiere concesiones para la prestación del servicio público de transporte. Estas concesiones se otorgarán a personas físicas o morales mexicanas, por nacimiento las primeras, y con cláusula de exclusión las segundas.
Calendario de Reducción:	Ninguno

Sector:	Transporte
Subsector :	Transporte terrestre
Clasificación Industrial:	CMAP 711201 Servicio de autotransporte de materiales de construcción CMAP 711202 Servicio de autotransporte de mudanzas CMAP 711203 Otros servicios de autotransporte especializado de carga CMAP 711204 Servicio de autotransporte de carga en general CMAP 711311 Servicio de transporte foráneo de pasajeros en autobús

	CMAP 711312 Servicio de transporte urbano y suburbano de pasajeros en autobús CMAP 711316 Servicio de transporte de automóvil de ruta fija CMAP 711317 Servicio de transporte en automóvil de sitio CMAP 711318 Servicio de transporte escolar CMAP 711319 Servicio de alquiler de automóviles CMAP 973105 Servicio de grúa para vehículos
Tipo de Reserva:	Trato nacional (Artículos 10-04 y 14-04) Presencia local (Artículo 10-05)
Nivel de Gobierno:	Estatal (Estado de Nayarit)
Medida:	Ley de Tránsito y Transportes para el Estado de Nayarit, Periódico Oficial, octubre 24, 1970, Capítulo XVIII, Artículos 113 y 129
Descripción:	Servicios transfronterizos e Inversión Se requiere permisos de ruta para explotar los servicios de transporte público. Estos permisos se otorgarán a los mexicanos por nacimiento y, preferentemente, a los miembros de las sociedades cooperativas y de las uniones de trabajadores establecidas conforme a la ley.
Calendario de Reducción:	Ninguno

Sector:	Transporte
Subsector :	Transporte terrestre
Clasificación Industrial:	CMAP 711201 Servicio de autotransporte de materiales de construcción CMAP 711202 Servicio de autotransporte de mudanzas CMAP 711203 Otros servicios de autotransporte especializado de carga CMAP 711204 Servicio de autotransporte de carga en general CMAP 711311 Servicio de transporte foráneo de pasajeros en autobús CMAP 711312 Servicio de transporte urbano y suburbano de pasajeros en autobús CMAP 711315 Servicio de transporte en automóvil de ruleteo CMAP 711317 Servicio de transporte en automóvil de sitio CMAP 711318 Servicio de transporte escolar CMAP 711319 Servicio de alquiler de automóviles CMAP 973105 Servicio de grúa para vehículos
Tipo de Reserva:	Trato nacional (Artículos 10-04 y 14-04) Presencia local (Artículo 10-05)
Nivel de Gobierno:	Estatal (Estado de Nuevo León)
Medida:	Ley de Comunicaciones y Transportes para el Estado de Nuevo León, Periódico Oficial, diciembre 14, 1984, Capítulo III, Artículos 27 y 29
Descripción:	Servicios transfronterizos e Inversión Se requiere concesiones para la prestación del servicio público de transporte. Las concesiones y permisos sólo se otorgarán a ciudadanos mexicanos o a sociedades mexicanas constituidas conforme a las leyes del país.
Calendario de Reducción:	Ninguno

Sector:	Transporte
Subsector :	Transporte terrestre
Clasificación Industrial:	CMAP 711201 Servicio de autotransporte de materiales de construcción CMAP 711202 Servicio de autotransporte de mudanzas CMAP 711203 Otros servicios de autotransporte especializado de carga CMAP 711204 Servicio de autotransporte de carga en general CMAP 711311 Servicio de transporte foráneo de pasajeros en autobús CMAP 711312 Servicio de transporte urbano y suburbano de pasajeros

	en autobús CMAP 711315 Servicio de transporte en automóvil de ruleteo CMAP 711317 Servicio de transporte en automóvil de sitio CMAP 711319 Servicio de alquiler de automóviles
Tipo de Reserva:	Trato nacional (Artículos 10-04 y 14-04) Presencia local (Artículo 10-05)
Nivel de Gobierno:	Estatal (Estado de Oaxaca)
Medida:	Ley de Tránsito Reformada, Periódico Oficial, diciembre 25, 1976, Capítulo IV, Artículo 21
Descripción:	Servicios transfronterizos e Inversión Se requiere concesiones o permisos para la prestación del servicio público de transporte. Las concesiones o permisos se otorgarán únicamente a mexicanos y a sociedades mercantiles constituidas conforme a las leyes del país.
Calendario de Reducción:	Ninguno

Sector:	Transporte
Subsector :	Transporte terrestre
Clasificación Industrial:	CMAP 711201 Servicio de autotransporte de materiales de construcción CMAP 711202 Servicio de autotransporte de mudanzas CMAP 711203 Otros servicios de autotransporte especializado de carga CMAP 711204 Servicio de autotransporte de carga en general CMAP 711311 Servicio de transporte foráneo de pasajeros en autobús CMAP 711312 Servicio de transporte urbano y suburbano de pasajeros en autobús CMAP 711315 Servicio de transporte en automóvil de ruleteo CMAP 711316 Servicio de transporte de automóvil de ruta fija CMAP 711317 Servicio de transporte en automóvil de sitio CMAP 711318 Servicio de transporte escolar CMAP 711319 Servicio de alquiler de automóviles
Tipo de Reserva:	Trato nacional (Artículos 10-04 y 14-04) Presencia local (Artículo 10-05)
Nivel de Gobierno:	Estatal (Estado de Puebla)
Medida:	Reglamento de Tránsito del Estado de Puebla, Periódico Oficial, octubre 19, 1984, Título 6, Capítulo I, Artículo 161
Descripción:	Servicios transfronterizos e Inversión Se requiere concesiones para la prestación del servicio público de transporte. No se otorgarán concesiones cuando el solicitante sea extranjero o la sociedad, en su caso, sea anónima.
Calendario de Reducción:	Ninguno

Sector:	Transporte
Subsector :	Transporte Terrestre
Clasificación Industrial:	CMAP 711201 Servicio de autotransporte de materiales de construcción CMAP 711202 Servicio de autotransporte de mudanzas CMAP 711203 Otros servicios de autotransporte especializado de carga CMAP 711204 Servicio de autotransporte de carga en general CMAP 711311 Servicio de transporte foráneo de pasajeros en autobús CMAP 711312 Servicio de transporte urbano y suburbano de pasajeros en autobús CMAP 711315 Servicio de transporte en automóvil de ruleteo CMAP 711316 Servicio de transporte de automóvil de ruta fija CMAP 711317 Servicio de transporte en automóvil de sitio

	CMAP 711318 Servicio de transporte escolar
Tipo de Reserva:	Trato nacional (Artículos 10-04 y 14-04) Presencia local (Artículo 10-05)
Nivel de Gobierno:	Estatal (Estado de Querétaro)
Medida:	Ley de Seguridad Pública y Tránsito del Estado de Querétaro. Periódico Oficial, diciembre 17, 1987, Artículo 102, fracciones I y II
Descripción:	Servicios transfronterizos e Inversión Se requiere concesiones para prestar el servicio público de transporte. Las concesiones podrán otorgarse a personas físicas mexicanas por nacimiento o a personas morales integradas por mexicanos.
Calendario de Reducción:	Ninguno

Sector:	Transporte
Subsector :	Transporte terrestre
Clasificación Industrial:	CMAP 711201 Servicio de autotransporte de materiales de construcción CMAP 711202 Servicio de autotransporte de mudanzas CMAP 711203 Otros servicios de autotransporte especializado de carga CMAP 711204 Servicio de autotransporte de carga en general CMAP 711311 Servicio de transporte foráneo de pasajeros en autobús CMAP 711312 Servicio de transporte urbano y suburbano de pasajeros en autobús CMAP 711315 Servicio de transporte en automóvil de ruleteo CMAP 711316 Servicio de transporte de automóvil de ruta fija CMAP 711317 Servicio de transporte en automóvil de sitio CMAP 711318 Servicio de transporte escolar CMAP 711319 Servicio de alquiler de automóviles
Tipo de Reserva:	Trato nacional (Artículos 10-04 y 14-04) Presencia local (Artículo 10-05)
Nivel de Gobierno:	Estatal (Estado de Quintana Roo)
Medida:	Constitución Política de los Estados Unidos Mexicanos, Artículo 32 Ley de Tránsito, Transporte y Explotación de Vías y Carreteras del Estado de Quintana Roo, Periódico Oficial, diciembre 16, 1996, Título V, Capítulo I, Artículos 32 y 34
Descripción:	Servicios transfronterizos e Inversión Se requiere concesión o permiso para la prestación del servicio público de autotransporte. El otorgamiento de estas concesiones o permisos se expedirán discrecionalmente por el Gobernador del Estado a las personas físicas o morales que lo soliciten.
Calendario de Reducción:	Ninguno

Sector:	Transporte
Subsector :	Transporte terrestre
Clasificación Industrial:	CMAP 711201 Servicio de autotransporte de materiales de construcción CMAP 711202 Servicio de autotransporte de mudanzas CMAP 711203 Otros servicios de autotransporte especializado de carga CMAP 711204 Servicio de autotransporte de carga en general CMAP 711311 Servicio de transporte foráneo de pasajeros en autobús CMAP 711312 Servicio de transporte urbano y suburbano de pasajeros en autobús CMAP 711315 Servicio de transporte en automóvil de ruleteo CMAP 711316 Servicio de transporte de automóvil de ruta fija CMAP 711317 Servicio de transporte en automóvil de sitio CMAP 711318 Servicio de transporte escolar CMAP 711319 Servicio de alquiler de automóviles

Tipo de Reserva:	Trato nacional (Artículos 10-04 y 14-04) Presencia local (Artículo 10-05)
Nivel de Gobierno:	Estatal (Estado de San Luis Potosí)
Medida:	Ley de Transporte Público del Estado de San Luis Potosí, Periódico Oficial, agosto 30, 1996, Artículos 9, 13 y 20
Descripción:	Servicios transfronterizos e Inversión Se requiere concesión o permiso para prestar el servicio público de transporte. Las concesiones o permisos únicamente se otorgarán a personas de nacionalidad mexicana, físicas o morales, según el servicio de que se trate, creadas o constituidas conforme a las leyes del país.
Calendario de Reducción:	Ninguno

Sector:	Transporte
Subsector :	Transporte terrestre
Clasificación Industrial:	CMAP 711201 Servicio de autotransporte de materiales de construcción CMAP 711202 Servicio de autotransporte de mudanzas CMAP 711203 Otros servicios de autotransporte especializado de carga CMAP 711204 Servicio de autotransporte de carga en general CMAP 711311 Servicio de transporte foráneo de pasajeros en autobús CMAP 711312 Servicio de transporte urbano y suburbano de pasajeros en autobús CMAP 711315 Servicio de transporte en automóvil de ruleteo CMAP 711316 Servicio de transporte de automóvil de ruta fija CMAP 711317 Servicio de transporte en automóvil de sitio CMAP 711319 Servicio de alquiler de automóviles
Tipo de Reserva:	Trato nacional (Artículos 10-04 y 14-04) Presencia local (Artículo 10-05)
Nivel de Gobierno:	Estatal (Estado de Sinaloa)
Medida:	Reglamento General de la Ley de Tránsito y Transportes, Periódico Oficial, agosto 21, 1970, Título VI, Capítulo II, Artículo 70
Descripción:	Servicios transfronterizos e Inversión Se requiere concesión o permiso para prestar servicio público de transporte. Para obtener la concesión y permiso, se requiere la nacionalidad mexicana.
Calendario de Reducción:	Ninguno

Sector:	Transporte
Subsector :	Transporte terrestre
Clasificación Industrial:	CMAP 973101 Servicio de administración de centrales camioneras de pasajeros y servicios auxiliares (terminales camioneras y estaciones de camiones y autobuses)
Tipo de Reserva:	Trato nacional (Artículos 10-04 y 14-04) Presencia local (Artículo 10-05)
Nivel de Gobierno:	Estatal (Estado de Sonora)
Medida:	Ley Número 120 de Transportes para el Estado de Sonora, Boletín Oficial, julio 20, 1992, Capítulo IV, Artículo 22, 23 y 54
Descripción:	Servicios transfronterizos e Inversión Se requiere concesión para el establecimiento de centrales y terminales de pasaje y de carga para explotar los servicios públicos de transporte. Las concesiones se otorgan a ciudadanos mexicanos por nacimiento. Las sociedades deberán estar conformadas por socios mexicanos por nacimiento.

Calendario de Reducción:	Ninguno

Sector:	Transporte
Subsector :	Transporte terrestre
Clasificación Industrial:	CMAP 711201 Servicio de autotransporte de materiales de construcción CMAP 711202 Servicio de autotransporte de mudanzas CMAP 711203 Otros servicios de autotransporte especializado de carga CMAP 711204 Servicio de autotransporte de carga en general CMAP 711311 Servicio de transporte foráneo de pasajeros en autobús CMAP 711312 Servicio de transporte urbano y suburbano de pasajeros en autobús CMAP 711318 Servicio de transporte escolar CMAP 711319 Servicio de alquiler de automóviles
Tipo de Reserva:	Trato nacional (Artículos 10-04 y 14-04) Presencia local (Artículo 10-05)
Nivel de Gobierno:	Estatal (Estado de Sonora)
Medida:	Ley número 120 de Transporte para el Estado de Sonora, Boletín Oficial, julio 20, 1992, Título II, Capítulo III, Artículos 22 y 23
Descripción:	Servicios transfronterizos e Inversión Se requiere concesión para prestar el servicio público de transporte. La concesión se otorga a mexicanos por nacimiento. Las sociedades deberán estar conformadas por socios mexicanos por nacimiento.
Calendario de Reducción:	Ninguno

Sector:	Transporte
Subsector :	Transporte terrestre
Clasificación Industrial:	CMAP 711201 Servicio de autotransporte de materiales de construcción CMAP 711202 Servicio de autotransporte de mudanzas CMAP 711203 Otros servicios de autotransporte especializado de carga CMAP 711204 Servicio de autotransporte de carga en general CMAP 711311 Servicio de transporte foráneo de pasajeros en autobús CMAP 711312 Servicio de transporte urbano y suburbano de pasajeros en autobús CMAP 711315 Servicio de transporte en automóvil de ruleteo CMAP 711316 Servicio de transporte de automóvil de ruta fija CMAP 711317 Servicio de transporte en automóvil de sitio CMAP 711318 Servicio de transporte escolar CMAP 711319 Servicio de alquiler de automóviles CMAP 973105 Servicio de grúa para vehículos
Tipo de Reserva:	Trato nacional (Artículos 10-04 y 14-04) Presencia local (Artículo 10-05)
Nivel de Gobierno:	Estatal (Estado de Tabasco)
Medida:	Ley de Vías de Comunicación y Transporte del Estado, Periódico Oficial, agosto 1, 1984, Título II, Capítulo II, Artículos 26 y 28
Descripción:	Servicios transfronterizos e Inversión Se requiere concesión para la explotación del servicio público de transporte. La concesión se otorga a mexicanos por nacimiento, en el caso de las personas físicas, y tratándose de personas morales, los socios deberán ser mexicanos por nacimiento.
Calendario de Reducción:	Ninguno

Sector:	Transporte
Subsector :	Transporte terrestre

Clasificación Industrial:	CMAP 973101 Servicio de administración de centrales camioneras de pasajeros y servicios auxiliares (terminales camioneras y estaciones de camiones y autobuses)
Tipo de Reserva:	Trato nacional (Artículos 10-04 y 14-04) Presencia local (Artículo 10-05)
Nivel de Gobierno:	Estatal (Estado de Tabasco)
Medida:	Ley de Vías de Comunicación y Transporte del Estado, Periódico Oficial, agosto 1, 1984, Título II, Capítulo III, Artículo 49
Descripción:	Servicios transfronterizos e Inversión Se requiere concesión para la construcción y explotación de estaciones terminales en el aprovechamiento de los sistemas de transporte de jurisdicción estatal. Estas concesiones se otorgarán a personas morales mexicanas. En igualdad de circunstancias, se preferirá a las sociedades integradas por concesionarios del servicio público de transporte que exploten cuando menos el 51 por ciento de los vehículos que deban servir en esas terminales.
Calendario de educción:	Ninguno

Sector:	Transporte
Subsector :	Transporte terrestre
Clasificación Industrial:	CMAP 711201 Servicio de autotransporte de materiales de construcción CMAP 711202 Servicio de autotransporte de mudanzas CMAP 711203 Otros servicios de autotransporte especializado de carga CMAP 711204 Servicio de autotransporte de carga en general CMAP 711311 Servicio de transporte foráneo de pasajeros en autobús CMAP 711312 Servicio de transporte urbano y suburbano de pasajeros en autobús CMAP 711315 Servicio de transporte en automóvil de ruleteo CMAP 711316 Servicio de transporte en automóvil de ruta fija CMAP 711317 Servicio de transporte en automóvil de sitio CMAP 711318 Servicio de transporte escolar CMAP 711319 Servicio de alquiler de automóviles
Tipo de Reserva:	Trato nacional (Artículos 10-04 y 14-04) Presencia local (Artículo 10-05)
Nivel de Gobierno:	Estatal (Estado de Tamaulipas)
Medida:	Ley de Tránsito y Transporte, Periódico Oficial, noviembre 30, 1987, Capítulo VI, Artículos 28 y 33
Descripción:	Servicios transfronterizos e Inversión Se requiere concesiones o permisos para el servicio público de transporte. Las concesiones o permisos se otorgarán en favor de personas físicas o morales mexicanas.
Calendario de Reducción:	Ninguno

Sector:	Transporte
Subsector :	Transporte terrestre
Clasificación Industrial:	CMAP 711201 Servicio de autotransporte de materiales de construcción CMAP 711202 Servicio de autotransporte de mudanzas CMAP 711203 Otros servicios de autotransporte especializado de carga CMAP 711204 Servicio de autotransporte de carga en general CMAP 711311 Servicio de transporte foráneo de pasajeros en autobús CMAP 711312 Servicio de transporte urbano y suburbano de pasajeros en autobús CMAP 711315 Servicio de transporte en automóvil de ruleteo CMAP 711316 Servicio de transporte de automóvil de ruta fija CMAP 711317 Servicio de transporte en automóvil de sitio

	CMAP 711319 Servicio de alquiler de automóviles
Tipo de Reserva:	Trato nacional (Artículos 10-04 y 14-04) Presencia local (Artículo 10-05)
Nivel de Gobierno:	Estatal (Estado de Tlaxcala)
Medida:	Ley de Comunicaciones y Transportes en el Estado de Tlaxcala, Periódico Oficial, junio 22, 1983, Capítulo I, Artículo 2 y Capítulo III, Artículo 14
Descripción:	Servicios transfronterizos e Inversión Se requiere concesión para prestar el servicio público de transporte. En igualdad de circunstancias, tendrán preferencia para obtener las concesiones los tlaxcaltecas por nacimiento, los mexicanos con residencia de más de un año en el estado y las sociedades mexicanas registradas en Tlaxcala.
Calendario de Reducción:	Ninguno

Sector:	Transporte
Subsector :	Transporte terrestre
Clasificación Industrial:	CMAP 711201 Servicio de autotransporte de materiales de construcción CMAP 711202 Servicio de autotransporte de mudanzas CMAP 711203 Otros servicios de autotransporte especializado de carga CMAP 711204 Servicio de autotransporte de carga en general CMAP 711311 Servicio de transporte foráneo de pasajeros en autobús CMAP 711312 Servicio de transporte urbano y suburbano de pasajeros en autobús CMAP 711315 Servicio de transporte en automóvil de ruleteo CMAP 711316 Servicio de transporte en automóvil de ruta fija CMAP 711317 Servicio de transporte en automóvil de sitio CMAP 711318 Servicio de transporte escolar
Tipo de Reserva:	Trato nacional (Artículos 10-04 y 14-04) Presencia local (Artículo 10-05)
Nivel de Gobierno:	Estatal (Estado de Veracruz)
Medida:	Ley número 100 de Tránsito y Transporte para el Estado de Veracruz, Gaceta Oficial, enero 19, 1988, Capítulo VI, Artículos 20 y 25 Reglamento de la Ley de Tránsito y Transporte para el Estado de Veracruz, Gaceta Oficial, noviembre 24, 1988, Capítulo III, Artículo 161, fracción I
Descripción:	Servicios transfronterizos e Inversión Se requiere concesión para prestar el servicio público de transporte. Las concesiones se otorgan a ciudadanos mexicanos y a las sociedades mercantiles constituidas por éstos.
Calendario de Reducción:	Ninguno

Sector:	Transporte
Subsector :	Transporte terrestre
Clasificación Industrial:	CMAP 711201 Servicio de autotransporte de materiales de construcción CMAP 711202 Servicio de autotransporte de mudanzas CMAP 711203 Otros servicios de autotransporte especializado de carga CMAP 711204 Servicio de autotransporte de carga en general CMAP 711311 Servicio de transporte foráneo de pasajeros en autobús CMAP 711312 Servicio de transporte urbano y suburbano de pasajeros en autobús CMAP 711315 Servicio de transporte en automóvil de ruleteo CMAP 711316 Servicio de transporte de automóvil de ruta fija CMAP 711317 Servicio de transporte en automóvil de sitio

	CMAP 711318 Servicio de transporte escolar CMAP 711319 Servicio de alquiler de automóviles CMAP 711320 Otro tipo de transporte de pasajeros, incluye vehículos de tracción animal CMAP 973105 Servicio de grúa para vehículo
Tipo de Reserva:	Trato nacional (Artículos 10-04 y 14-04) Presencia local (Artículo 10-05)
Nivel de Gobierno:	Estatal (Estado de Yucatán)
Medida:	Reglamento del Servicio de Transporte de Carga en el Estado de Yucatán, Diario Oficial, septiembre 20, 1983, Capítulo II, Artículos 7 y 10 Reglamento de Tránsito en las Carreteras del Estado de Yucatán, Diario Oficial, abril 29, 1959, Capítulo IV, Artículo 55, fracción II
Descripción:	Servicios transfronterizos e Inversión Se requiere concesiones o permisos para prestar los servicios públicos de transporte. Para el otorgamiento de la concesión de transporte público de carga se requiere, si se trata de una persona física, ser mexicana por nacimiento y domiciliada en el Estado. Si se trata de una sociedad, deberá comprobarse por medio de su escritura constitutiva que está integrada en su totalidad por mexicanos por nacimiento y constituida conforme a las leyes del país. Es causa de revocación perder la nacionalidad mexicana, cuando el concesionario, sea persona física; cuando se trate de sociedad, cuando deje de estar constituida conforme se indica anteriormente. Las personas físicas o morales que soliciten permiso de ruta para la explotación de los servicios públicos de transporte deberán ser de nacionalidad mexicana.
Calendario de Reducción:	Ninguno

Sector:	Transporte
Subsector :	Transporte terrestre
Clasificación Industrial:	CMAP 711201 Servicio de autotransporte de materiales de construcción CMAP 711202 Servicio de autotransporte de mudanzas CMAP 711203 Otros servicios de autotransporte especializado de carga CMAP 711204 Servicio de autotransporte de carga en general CMAP 711311 Servicio de transporte foráneo de pasajeros en autobús CMAP 711312 Servicio de transporte urbano y suburbano de pasajeros en autobús CMAP 711315 Servicio de transporte en automóvil de ruleteo CMAP 711316 Servicio de transporte de automóvil de ruta fija CMAP 711317 Servicio de transporte en automóvil de sitio CMAP 711318 Servicio de transporte escolar CMAP 711319 Servicio de alquiler de automóviles CMAP 711320 Otro tipo de transporte de pasajeros, incluye vehículos de tracción animal CMAP 973105 Servicio de grúa para vehículo
Tipo de Reserva:	Trato nacional (Artículos 10-04 y 14-04) Presencia local (Artículo 10-05)
Nivel de Gobierno:	Estatal (Estado de Yucatán)
Medida:	Reglamento del Servicio de Transporte de Carga en el Estado de Yucatán, Diario Oficial, septiembre 20, 1983, Capítulo II, Artículos 7 y 10 Reglamento de Tránsito en las Carreteras del Estado de Yucatán, Diario Oficial, abril 29, 1959, Capítulo IV, Artículo 55, fracción II
Descripción:	Servicios transfronterizos e Inversión Se requiere concesiones o permisos para prestar los servicios públicos de

	transporte.
	Para el otorgamiento de la concesión de transporte público de carga se requiere, si se trata de una persona física, ser mexicana por nacimiento y domiciliada en el Estado. Si se trata de una sociedad, deberá comprobarse por medio de su escritura constitutiva que está integrada en su totalidad por mexicanos por nacimiento y constituida conforme a las leyes del país. Es causa de revocación perder la nacionalidad mexicana, cuando el concesionario, sea persona física; cuando se trate de sociedad, cuando deje de estar constituida conforme se indica anteriormente.
	Las personas físicas o morales que soliciten permiso de ruta para la explotación de los servicios públicos de transporte deberán ser de nacionalidad mexicana.
Calendario de Reducción:	Ninguno

Sector:	Transporte
Subsector :	Transporte terrestre
Clasificación Industrial:	CMAP 711201 Servicio de autotransporte de materiales de construcción
	CMAP 711202 Servicio de autotransporte de mudanzas
	CMAP 711203 Otros servicios de autotransporte especializado de carga
	CMAP 711204 Servicio de autotransporte de carga en general
	CMAP 711311 Servicio de transporte foráneo de pasajeros en autobús
	CMAP 711312 Servicio de transporte urbano y suburbano de pasajeros en autobús
	CMAP 711315 Servicio de transporte en automóvil de ruleteo
	CMAP 711317 Servicio de transporte en automóvil de sitio
	CMAP 711318 Servicio de transporte escolar
	CMAP 711319 Servicio de alquiler de automóviles
	CMAP 973105 Servicio de grúa para vehículos
Tipo de Reserva:	Trato nacional (Artículos 10-04 y 14-04)
	Presencia local (Artículo 10-05)
Nivel de Gobierno:	Estatal (Estado de Zacatecas)
Medida:	Ley de Tránsito del Estado de Zacatecas, Periódico Oficial, enero 18, 1989, Capítulo VII, Artículos 17 y 20
Descripción:	Servicios transfronterizos e Inversión
	La concesión del servicio público de transporte es un acto discrecional, temporal y revocable del Ejecutivo del Estado, por medio del cual se faculta a las personas físicas o morales para prestar el mencionado servicio. Las concesiones se otorgarán a personas físicas mexicanas por nacimiento, preferentemente, originarias y residentes del estado y a las personas morales que estén constituidas y operando en el estado.
Calendario de Reducción:	Ninguno

ANEXO I
LISTA DE EL SALVADOR
SECCIÓN A

Sector:	Todos los sectores
Subsector:	
Clasificación Industrial:	
Tipo de Reserva:	Trato nacional (Artículo 14-04)
	Trato de nación más favorecida (Artículo 14-05)

Nivel de Gobierno:	Nacional
Medidas:	Código de Comercio, Artículo 358 Ley de La Superintendencia de Sociedades y Empresas Mercantiles; Título III, Sociedades Extranjeras, sus Sucursales o Agencias, Artículos 15, 18 y 22
Descripción:	Inversión Las sociedades extranjeras que deseen realizar actos de comercio en El Salvador o quieran establecer agencias o sucursales, deberán presentar solicitud de autorización a la Superintendencia por medio de apoderado general y especialmente constituido; además deberá constituir y mantener en el país un patrimonio suficiente para la actividad mercantil que desarrollará en la República. De acuerdo a los requisitos de ley, la oficina que ejerza la vigilancia del Estado, si lo estima conveniente, podrá conceder autorización para que la sociedad ejerza el comercio en la República. En este caso, señalará un plazo para que la sociedad inicie sus operaciones y ordenará la inscripción de la misma en el Registro de Comercio del lugar en que la empresa establezca su oficina principal. La excepción del trato de nación más favorecida sólo aplicará respecto a inversionistas o inversiones centroamericanas.
Calendario de Reducción:	Ninguno

Sector:	Todos los sectores
Subsector:	
Clasificación Industrial:	
Tipo de Reserva:	Trato nacional (Artículo 14-04) Trato de nación más favorecida (Artículo 14-05)
Nivel de Gobierno:	Nacional
Medidas:	Constitución de la República, Artículos 95 y 109
Descripción:	Inversión La propiedad de bienes rústicos no podrá ser adquirida por extranjeros en cuyos países de origen no tengan iguales derechos los salvadoreños, excepto cuando se trate de tierras para establecimientos industriales.
Calendario de Reducción:	Ninguno

Sector:	Todos los sectores
Subsector:	
Clasificación Industrial:	
Tipo de Reserva:	Trato nacional (Artículo 14-04) Trato de nación más favorecida (Artículo 14-05) Alta dirección empresarial y consejos de administración (Artículo 14-08)
Nivel de Gobierno	Nacional
Medidas:	Constitución de la República, Artículo 115 Ley Reguladora del Ejercicio del Comercio e Industria, Artículos 3 y 4 Reglamento de la Ley Reguladora del Ejercicio del Comercio e Industria, Artículos 2 y 10 Código de Comercio, Artículo 6
Descripción:	Inversión El comercio, la industria y la prestación de servicios en pequeño son patrimonio exclusivo de los salvadoreños por nacimiento y de los centroamericanos naturales, en consecuencia, los inversionistas extranjeros no tendrán acceso a dichas actividades. Los extranjeros no pueden desempeñar cargos de administrador, director, gerente o representante de empresas en pequeño, ya sean éstas comerciales, industriales o de servicio. La excepción del trato de nación más favorecida sólo aplicará respecto a

	inversionistas o inversiones centroamericanas.
Calendario de Reducción:	Ninguno

Sector:	Asociaciones cooperativas de producción
Subsector:	
Clasificación Industrial:	
Tipo de Reserva:	Trato nacional (Artículo 14-04)
Nivel de Gobierno:	Nacional
Medias:	Reglamento de la Ley General de Asociaciones Cooperativas; Título VI, Capítulo I, Artículo 84
Descripción:	Inversión En las asociaciones cooperativas de producción las tres cuartas partes cuando menos del número de asociados deberán ser salvadoreños.
Calendario de Reducción:	Ninguno

Sector:	Pesca
Subsector:	
Clasificación Industrial:	
Tipo de Reserva:	Trato nacional (Artículos 10-04 y 14-04) Trato de nación más favorecida (Artículos 10-03 y 14-05) Presencia local (Artículo 10-05)
Nivel de Gobierno:	Nacional
Medidas:	Constitución de la República, Artículo 115 Ley de Fomento y Garantía de la Inversión Extranjera, Artículo 5 Ley General de las Actividades Pesqueras, Artículos 25, 26, 28, 37, 38 y 40 Reglamento para la Aplicación de la Ley General de las Actividades Pesqueras, Artículos 30 y 32
Descripción:	Servicios transfronterizos e Inversión La pesca artesanal podrá ser ejercida exclusivamente por: a) personas naturales salvadoreñas y centroamericanas de origen residentes en el país; b) asociaciones cooperativas; c) sociedades mercantiles. Las sociedades mercantiles, para poder dedicarse a la pesca artesanal deberán comprobar que en la sociedad participan o tienen acciones en más del 90% naturales salvadoreños y que, más del 60% de sus socios, son de oficio pescadores artesanales. La pesca marítima tecnificada en las zonas de bajura para las especies pelágicas y demersales y la pesca tecnificada en la zona de altura para las especies demersales, podrán realizarla: a) las personas naturales salvadoreñas y centroamericanas de origen; b) asociaciones cooperativas; c) las sociedades mercantiles salvadoreñas en cuyo capital participan o tengan acciones en más del 50% personas salvadoreñas; esta última circunstancia deberá comprobarse por cualquier medio fehaciente de prueba, a juicio de la Dirección General. Los Gobiernos extranjeros no pueden participar, ni tener acciones en empresas que deseen dedicarse a la pesca artesanal, tecnificada en la zona de bajura para especies pelágicas y demersales; y en la zona de altura para especies demersales. Toda embarcación dedicada a la pesca artesanal y tecnificada deberá tener matrícula salvadoreña.
Calendario de educción:	Ninguno

Sector:	Pesca
Subsector:	Acuicultura
Clasificación Industrial:	
Tipo de Reserva:	Presencia local (Artículo 10-05)
Nivel de Gobierno:	Nacional
Medidas:	Ley General de las Actividades Pesqueras, Artículo 46
Descripción:	Servicios transfronterizos Cualquier persona natural o jurídica, extranjera con residencia definitiva en el país, podrá dedicarse a la acuicultura.
Calendario de Reducción:	Ninguno

Sector:	Servicios de comunicaciones
Subsector:	Servicios audiovisuales
Clasificación Industrial:	CPC 871. Servicios de publicidad CPC 96111. Servicios relacionados con actividades de promoción o publicidad CPC 9613. Servicios de radio y televisión
Tipo de Reserva:	Trato nacional (Artículo 10-04) Trato de nación más favorecida (Artículo 10-03) Requisitos de desempeño (Artículo 14-07)
Nivel de Gobierno:	Nacional
Medidas:	Decreto de las disposiciones para regular la explotación de obras de naturaleza intelectual por medios de comunicación pública y la participación de artistas salvadoreños en espectáculos públicos. Decreto Legislativo No. 239, de fecha 9 de junio de 1983, publicado en Diario Oficial N° 111, Tomo 279, de fecha 15 de junio de 1983 Decreto N° 18, Sustitución de los artículos 1 y 4 del Decreto Legislativo N° 239, de fecha 9 de junio de 1983, publicado en el Diario Oficial N° 7, Tomo 282, de fecha 10 de enero de 1984
Descripción:	Servicios transfronterizos e Inversión Los anuncios comerciales que se utilicen en los medios de comunicación pública del país, deberán ser producidos y grabados por elementos nacionales en un 90%. Los anuncios comerciales producidos o grabados por elementos centroamericanos, podrán ser utilizados en los medios de comunicación de El Salvador, toda vez que en el país en que se originen se compruebe la misma reciprocidad para con los anuncios comerciales producidos o grabados en El Salvador. Los anuncios comerciales que no llenen los requisitos mencionados en los dos incisos anteriores, sólo podrán ser transmitidos en los medios de comunicación pública del país, si son anuncios de productos, marcas o servicios internacionales importados o producidos en el país bajo licencia y mediante el pago de una cuota de compensación de cinco mil colones.
Calendario de Reducción:	Ninguno

Sector:	Servicios de comunicaciones
Subsector:	Servicios audiovisuales
Clasificación:	CPC 9613. Servicio de radio y televisión
Tipo de Reserva:	Trato nacional (Artículo 10-04)
Nivel de Gobierno:	Nacional
Medidas:	Reglamento para el Establecimiento y Operación de Estaciones Radiodifusoras, Artículos 16, 17 y 66`
Descripción:	Servicios transfronterizos Las estaciones radiodifusoras deberán ser manejadas por operadores responsables, salvadoreños de nacimiento debidamente autorizados.

	Para ser locutor de una radiodifusora se requiere ser ciudadano salvadoreño.
Calendario de Reducción:	Ninguno

Sector:	Servicios de comunicaciones
Subsector:	Servicios audiovisuales
Clasificación Industrial:	CPC 75241. Servicios de transmisión de programas de televisión CPC 75242. Servicios de transmisión de programas de radio
Tipo de Reserva:	Trato nacional (Artículo 14-04)
Nivel de Gobierno:	Nacional
Medidas:	Ley de Telecomunicaciones, Artículo 123
Descripción:	Inversión Las concesiones y licencias para los servicios de difusión de libre recepción, sólo se otorgarán a personas naturales por nacimiento o jurídicas salvadoreñas. En el caso de personas jurídicas salvadoreñas, el capital social deberá ser constituido por lo menos con el 51% de salvadoreños. Este capital social y sus reformas deberán ser reportados a la Superintendencia General de Electricidad y Telecomunicaciones (SIGET).
Calendario de Reducción:	Ninguno

Sector:	Servicios de distribución
Subsector:	Servicios de intermediarios, servicios comerciales al por mayor y al por menor
Clasificación Industrial:	CPC 622. Servicios comerciales al por mayor CPC 631. Servicios de venta al por menor de alimentos CPC 632. Servicios de venta al por menor de productos no comestibles
Tipo de Reserva:	Trato nacional (Artículos 10-04 y 14-04) Presencia local (Artículo 10-05)
Nivel de Gobierno:	Nacional
Medidas:	Constitución de la República, Artículo 95 Ley para el Establecimiento de Tiendas Libres en los Puertos Marítimos de El Salvador, Artículo 5
Descripción:	Servicios transfronterizos e Inversión Los permisos para organizar centros o establecimientos comerciales en los puertos marítimos del país los concederá el Ministro de Hacienda. La ubicación de los pabellones destinados a tal fin la decidirá la Comisión Ejecutiva Portuaria Autónoma (CEPA). Las personas naturales o jurídicas podrán solicitar los permisos a que se refiere el inciso anterior. Las primeras deberán ser salvadoreñas, mayores de edad y de responsabilidad y honradez comprobadas. En la concesión de los permisos, se preferirá a los salvadoreños por nacimiento y a las personas jurídicas salvadoreñas.
Calendario de Reducción:	Ninguno

Sector:	Servicios de esparcimiento, culturales y deportivos (excepto los servicios audiovisuales)
Subsector:	Servicios de espectáculos (incluidos los de teatro, bandas y orquestas y circos)
Clasificación Industrial:	CPC 96191. Servicios artísticos de productores de teatro, grupos de cantantes, bandas y orquestas

	CPC 96192. Servicios proporcionados por autores, compositores, escultores, artistas del espectáculo y otros artistas, a título individual CPC 96194. Servicios de circos, parques de atracciones y otros servicios de atracciones similares CPC 96199. Otros servicios de espectáculos n.c.p.
Tipo de Reserva:	Trato nacional (Artículo 10-04)
Nivel de Gobierno:	Nacional
Medidas:	Ley de Migración, Artículos 62-A y 62-B Decreto Legislativo N° 382 de fecha 29 de mayo de 1970; publicado en el Diario Oficial N° 64, Tomo 227, de fecha 10 de abril de 1970 Decreto Ejecutivo N° 16 de fecha 12 de mayo de 1970; publicado en el Diario Oficial N° 87, Tomo 227, de fecha 18 de mayo de 1970
Descripción:	Servicios transfronterizos Se entiende por artista toda persona que actúa individualmente o en compañía de otra u otras, para la ejecución de música, canto, baile, locución, animación de espectáculos, sea que lo haga personalmente (en vivo), ante un público más o menos numeroso, o por medio de la radio o televisión. Ningún artista extranjero podrá ejercer actos remunerados de ninguna especie, sin que preceda autorización expresa del Ministerio del Interior, el cual oirá previamente la opinión ilustrativa del sindicato legalmente establecido (en el término de 15 días), correspondiente a la actividad artística a que se dedica el interesado. Los artistas extranjeros pagarán anticipadamente al sindicato respectivo un derecho de actuación equivalente al 10% de la remuneración bruta que perciban en el país, si no fuera posible el pago anticipado el contratista tendrá que rendir "caución" suficiente a favor del sindicato respectivo. Ningún artista o grupo de artistas extranjeros podrán actuar en el país por más I – SV – Sección A - 13 de 30 días consecutivos o por intervalos, dentro del plazo de un año contado desde el primer día de su actuación.
Calendario de Reducción:	Ninguno

Sector:	Servicios de esparcimiento, culturales y deportivos (excepto los servicios audiovisuales)
Subsector:	Servicios de espectáculos (incluidos los de teatro, bandas y orquestas y circos)
Clasificación Industrial:	CPC 96194. Servicios de circos, parques de atracciones y otros servicios de atracciones similares
Tipo de Reserva:	Trato nacional (Artículo 10-04)
Nivel de Gobierno:	Nacional
Medidas:	Decreto N° 122, de fecha 4 de noviembre de 1988, publicado en el Diario Oficial N° 219, Tomo 301, de fecha 25 de noviembre de 1988, Artículo 3 Decreto N° 193, de fecha 8 de marzo de 1989, publicado en el Diario Oficial N° 54, Tomo 302, de fecha 17 de noviembre de 1989, Artículos 1 y 2 Reglamento para la Aplicación de los Decretos Legislativos 122 y 193 Relativos a Empresas Circenses, Artículos 1 y 2
Descripción:	Servicios transfronterizos Todo circo extranjero que ingrese y desee trabajar en el territorio nacional deberá solicitar ante el Ministerio del Interior, la autorización correspondiente, la cual una vez concedida deberá hacerse del conocimiento de la Asociación Salvadoreña de Empresarios Circenses, (ASEC), antes que el circo inicie sus presentaciones. En caso de circos extranjeros o espectáculos similares, el derecho de actuación será del 2.5 % de la entrada bruta, que diariamente perciba en la taquilla, debiéndose liquidar y pagar por el sistema de retención. Todo circo extranjero está obligado a proporcionar a la ASEC, el 3% de

	la entrada bruta obtenida en la venta de boletos por cada presentación así como el 10% del ingreso total obtenido por la venta al público dentro del circo, de banderines, gorras, camisetas, globos, fotografías y otra clase de objetos. El circo extranjero deberá rendir caución suficiente a favor de la ASEC. Todo circo extranjero que ingrese al país, solo podrá trabajar en la ciudad de San Salvador, por un período de 15 días, prorrogable por una sola vez por otros 15 días más y deberá solicitar la autorización correspondiente ante el Ministerio del Interior, quien al emitirla deberá inmediatamente comunicarlo, antes de que I – SV – Sección A - 15 inicie su presentación el circo autorizado por la ASEC. Un circo extranjero que haya actuado en el país, solo podrá ingresar nuevamente después de transcurrido un año por lo menos de la fecha de salida del mismo.
Calendario de Reducción:	Ninguno

Sector:	Servicios de esparcimiento, culturales y deportivos (excepto los servicios audiovisuales)
Subsector:	Servicios de espectáculos (incluidos los de teatro, bandas y orquestas y circos)
Clasificación Industrial:	CPC 96191. Servicios artísticos de productores de teatro, grupos de cantantes, bandas y orquestas CPC 96192. Servicios proporcionados por autores, compositores, escultores, artistas del espectáculo y otros artistas, a título individual CPC 96194. Servicios de circos, parques de atracciones y otros servicios de atracciones similares CPC 96199. Otros servicios de espectáculos n.c.p.
Tipo de Reserva:	Trato nacional (Artículo 10-04) Requisitos de desempeño (Artículo 14-07)
Nivel de Gobierno:	Nacional
Medidas:	Decreto de las disposiciones para regular la explotación de obras de naturaleza intelectual por medios de comunicación pública y la participación de artistas salvadoreños en espectáculos públicos. Decreto Legislativo N°. 239, de fecha 9 de junio de 1983, publicado en Diario Oficial N° 111, Tomo 279 de fecha 15 de junio de 1983. Decreto N° 18, Sustitución de los artículos 1 y 4 del Decreto Legislativo N° 239, de fecha 9 de junio de 1983, publicado en el Diario Oficial N° 7, Tomo 282 de fecha 10 de enero de 1984.
Descripción:	Servicios transfronterizos e Inversión Cuando se trate de espectáculos públicos con la participación viva de artistas de cualquier género, la participación de nacionales, será en un 20% de los extranjeros que actúen en él.
Calendario de Reducción:	Ninguno

Sector:	Servicios de transportes
Subsector:	Servicios de transporte marítimo
Clasificación Industrial:	CPC 7211. Transporte de pasajeros CPC 7212. Transporte de carga CPC 7213. Alquiler de embarcaciones con tripulación CPC 7214. Servicios de remolque y tracción CPC 745. Servicios de apoyo relacionados con el transporte marítimo
Tipo de Reserva:	Trato nacional (Artículo 10-04) Presencia local (Artículo 10-05)
Nivel de Gobierno:	Nacional

Medidas:	Ley de Navegación y Marina, Artículos 10, 19, 20, 26, 27 y 32 Ley Reglamentaria de Marina, Artículos 87, 89, 93, 94, 97, 114, 128 y 129
Descripción:	Servicios transfronterizos La navegación y comercio de cabotaje entre puertos de la república, quedan reservados para las embarcaciones de bandera nacional no así entre puertos centroamericanos; pero también podrán ejercerlo las embarcaciones extranjeras que se sometan a las mismas condiciones impuestas a las de bandera nacional; quedando desde luego sujetas en todo a las leyes y reglamentos de la república. Para ser consideradas como nacionales las embarcaciones deben llenar las condiciones y requisitos siguientes: a) ser matriculadas; b) usar el pabellón nacional; c) ser mandadas por capitanes o patronos nacionales o nacionalizados; d) tener en su tripulación no menos del 80% de marinos salvadoreños. El dueño de una embarcación que quiera matricularla, deberá ser residente en la república. Los marineros que no pertenezcan a alguna tripulación de embarcaciones del tráfico y los peones cargadores que formen el gremio, se ocuparán del desembarque y transbordo de los productos, artefactos o mercaderías extranjeras o nacionales en los puertos habilitados de la república.
Calendario de Reducción:	Ninguno

Sector:	Servicios de transporte aéreo
Subsector:	Servicios aéreos especializados
Clasificación Industrial:	
Tipo de Reserva:	Trato nacional (Artículo 10-04) Trato de nación más favorecida (Artículo 10-03)
Nivel de Gobierno:	Nacional
Medidas:	Ley de Aeronáutica Civil, Artículos 60, 71 y 72
Descripción:	Servicios transfronterizos Para desarrollar servicios aéreos especializados se requiere de autorización, cuando estos sean de carácter permanente se requerirá del permiso de operación. Estos están sujetos a las pruebas de necesidad económica, la reciprocidad y a la política aérea nacional.
Calendario de Reducción:	Ninguno

Sector:	Servicios de transporte aéreo
Subsector:	Servicios de apoyo relacionados con el transporte aéreo
Clasificación Industrial:	CPC 746. Servicios auxiliares del transporte aéreo CPC 8868. Mantenimiento (los servicios de reparación y mantenimiento de aeronaves durante el período en que se retira una aeronave de servicio) - Pilotos, copilotos
Tipo de Reserva:	Trato nacional (Artículo 10-04) Trato de nación más favorecida (Artículo 10-03)
Nivel de Gobierno:	Nacional
Medidas:	Ley de Aeronáutica Civil, Artículos 22, 23 y 115
Descripción:	Servicios transfronterizos La convalidación o reconocimiento de licencias, certificados y autorizaciones expedidos por autoridades aeronáuticas extranjeras para el personal técnico aeronáutico a bordo de aeronaves o en tierra se realizará con base a los principios de reciprocidad. Las empresas que tengan sus bases de operaciones en El Salvador deberán operar sus aeronaves con pilotos al mando y copilotos de nacionalidad salvadoreña; pudiendo contratar pilotos extranjeros, siempre y cuando haya reciprocidad y éstos cumplan con los requisitos establecidos por la legislación vigente.

	Las empresas que a la fecha de establecer sus bases de operaciones en El Salvador se encuentren operando con extranjeros como pilotos al mando y copilotos, podrán seguir utilizando sus servicios mientras éstos reúnan los requisitos legales para la concesión de sus licencias.
Calendario de Reducción:	Ninguno

ANEXO I
LISTA DE EL SALVADOR
SECCIÓN B

Sector:	Servicios a las empresas
Subsector:	Servicios profesionales
Clasificación Industrial:	CPC 862. Servicios de contabilidad, auditoría y teneduría de libros CPC 86302. Servicios de preparación y revisión de impuestos de sociedades
Tipo de Reserva:	Trato nacional (Artículo 14-04) Requisitos de desempeño (Artículo 14-07) Alta dirección empresarial y consejos de administración (Artículo 14-08)
Nivel de Gobierno:	Nacional
Medidas Vigentes:	Código de Comercio
Descripción:	Inversión El Salvador se reserva el derecho de adoptar o mantener cualquier medida con respecto a la inversión en los servicios de contabilidad, auditoría y teneduría de libros así como los servicios de preparación y revisión de impuestos de sociedades.
Plazo:	2 años a partir de la entrada en vigor de este tratado

Sector:	Servicios de construcción
Subsector:	Trabajos de construcción
Clasificación Industrial:	CPC 511. Trabajos previos a la construcción en obras de edificación y construcción CPC 512. Construcción de edificios CPC 513. Trabajos generales de construcción en obras de ingeniería civil CPC 514. Montaje e instalación de construcciones prefabricadas CPC 515. Trabajos de construcción especializados CPC 516. Trabajos de instalación CPC 517. Trabajos de acabado de edificios
Tipo de Reserva:	Trato nacional (Artículo 14-04) Requisitos de desempeño (Artículo 14-07) Alta dirección empresarial y consejos de administración (Artículo 14-08)
Nivel de Gobierno:	Nacional
Medidas Vigentes:	
Descripción:	Inversión El Salvador se reserva el derecho de adoptar o mantener cualquier medida con respecto a la inversión relacionada con los trabajos de construcción listados en el elemento clasificación industrial.
Plazo:	2 años a partir de la entrada en vigor de este tratado

Sector:	Servicios de transporte
Subsector:	Servicios de transporte por carretera
Clasificación Industrial:	CPC 7121. Otros tipos de transporte regular de pasajeros

	CPC 7122. Otros tipos de transporte no regular de pasajeros
	CPC 7123. Transporte de mercancías
	CPC 7124. Alquiler de vehículos comerciales con conductor
	CPC 7441. Servicios de estaciones de autobuses
Tipo de Reserva:	Trato nacional (Artículo 14-04)
	Requisitos de desempeño (Artículo 14-07)
	Alta dirección empresarial y consejos de administración (Artículo 14-08)
Nivel de Gobierno:	Nacional
Medidas Vigentes:	
Descripción:	Inversión
	El Salvador se reserva el derecho de adoptar o mantener cualquier medida con respecto a la inversión en el subsector de servicios de transporte por vía terrestre, limitado a otros tipos de transporte regular de pasajeros, otros tipos de transporte no regular de pasajeros, transporte de mercancías, alquiler de vehículos comerciales con conductor y servicios de estaciones de autobuses.
	Plazo: 2 años a partir de la entrada en vigor de este tratado

ANEXO II
LISTA DE EL SALVADOR

Sector:	Servicios a las empresas
Subsector:	Servicios profesionales
Clasificación Industrial:	CPC 861, CPC 862, CPC 863, CPC 8671, CPC 8672, CPC 8673, CPC 8674,
	CPC 9312, CPC 932, CPC 93191, CPC 842 (limitado a profesionales en informática), CPC 8790 (limitados a los agentes aduanales y limitados a los profesores de parvularia, básica y bachillerato).
Tipo de Reserva:	Trato de nación más favorecida (Artículo 10-03)
	Trato nacional (Artículo 10-04)
	Presencia local (Artículo 10-05)
Descripción:	Servicios transfronterizos
	El Salvador se reserva el derecho de adoptar o mantener cualquier medida al comercio transfronterizo de servicios del subsector servicios profesionales
Medidas Vigentes:	

Sector:	Servicios de comunicaciones
Subsector:	Servicios audiovisuales
Clasificación Industrial:	CPC 75241. Servicios de transmisión de programas de televisión (incluye los servicios de satélite prestados directamente al cliente cuando el proveedor vende en bloque y de forma directa programas de televisión a viviendas particulares situadas en zonas alejadas)
	CPC 75242. Servicios de transmisión de programas de radio
Tipo de Reserva:	Trato de nación más favorecida (Artículo 10-03)
	Trato nacional (Artículo 10-04)
	Presencia local (Artículo 10-05)
Nivel de Gobierno:	Nacional
Descripción:	Servicios transfronterizos
	El Salvador se reserva el derecho de adoptar o mantener cualquier medida que restrinja la prestación transfronteriza de servicios audiovisuales, específicamente los servicios de red necesarios para la transmisión de señales de televisión independiente del tipo de tecnología (red) utilizada, incluyendo los servicios de satélite prestados directamente

	al cliente cuando el proveedor vende en bloque y de forma directa programas de televisión a viviendas particulares situadas en zonas alejadas; y los servicios de red necesarios para la transmisión de señales auditivas, como las emisiones de radio, las transmisiones de cable y los servicios de megafonía, durante los dos años posteriores a la entrada en vigor de este tratado. Transcurrido el plazo indicado en el párrafo anterior, las medidas vigentes a esa fecha estarán sujetas a las disposiciones establecidas en el artículo 10-06(1).
Medidas Vigentes:	

Sector:	Servicios de construcción
Subsector:	Trabajos de construcción
Clasificación Industrial:	CPC 511. Trabajos previos a la construcción en obras de edificación y construcción CPC 512. Construcción de edificios CPC 513. Trabajos generales de construcción en obras de ingeniería civil CPC 514. Montaje e instalación de construcciones prefabricadas CPC 515. Trabajos de construcción especializados CPC 516. Trabajos de instalación CPC 517. Trabajos de acabado de edificios
Tipo de Reserva:	Trato de nación más favorecida (Artículo 10-03) Trato nacional (Artículo 10-04) Presencia local (Artículo 10-05)
Nivel de Gobierno:	Nacional
Descripción:	Servicios transfronterizos El Salvador se reserva el derecho de adoptar o mantener cualquier medida que restrinja la prestación transfronteriza de servicios relacionados con los trabajos de construcción listados en el elemento clasificación industrial, durante los dos años posteriores a la entrada en vigor de este tratado. Transcurrido el plazo indicado en el párrafo anterior, las medidas vigentes a esa fecha estarán sujetas a las disposiciones establecidas en el artículo 10-06(1).
Medidas Vigentes:	

Sector:	Servicios de transporte
Subsector:	Servicios de transporte por carretera
Clasificación Industrial:	CPC 7121. Otros tipos de transporte regular de pasajeros CPC 7122. Otros tipos de transporte no regular de pasajeros CPC 7123. Transporte de mercancías CPC 7124. Alquiler de vehículos comerciales con conductor CPC 7441. Servicios de estaciones de autobuses
Tipo de Reserva:	Trato de nación más favorecida (Artículo 10-03) Trato nacional (Artículo 10-04) Presencia local (Artículo 10-05)
Descripción:	Servicios transfronterizos El Salvador se reserva el derecho de adoptar o mantener cualquier medida que restrinja la prestación transfronteriza de servicios en el subsector de servicios de transporte por vía terrestre, limitado a otros tipos de transporte regular de pasajeros, otros tipos de transporte no regular de pasajeros, transporte de mercancías, alquiler de vehículos comerciales con conductor y servicios de estaciones de autobuses, durante los dos años posteriores a la entrada en vigor de este tratado. Transcurrido el plazo indicado en el párrafo anterior, las medidas vigentes a esa fecha estarán sujetas a las disposiciones establecidas en el Artículo 10-06(1).

Medidas Vigentes:	

ANEXO III
SECCION A: ACTIVIDADES ECONOMICAS RESERVADAS A CADA PARTE
LISTA DE EL SALVADOR

El Salvador se reserva el derecho exclusivo de desempeñar y de negarse a autorizar el establecimiento de inversiones en las siguientes actividades:

1.   Emisión de la moneda

a)   Descripción de actividades:
El poder de emisión de especies monetarias corresponde exclusivamente al Estado Salvadoreño, el cual podrá ejercerlo directamente o por medio de un instituto emisor de carácter público.

b)   Medidas:

Constitución de la República, Artículo 111

2.   Servicios Postales

a)   Descripción de actividades:

La dirección suprema del servicio postal corresponde al poder ejecutivo.

b)   Medidas:

Reglamento de Correos, Artículo 1

ANEXO IV
LISTA DE EL SALVADOR

El Salvador exceptúa la aplicación del Artículo 14-05 (Trato de nación más favorecida), al tratamiento otorgado bajo aquellos acuerdos en vigor o firmados después de la fecha de entrada en vigor de este tratado, en materia de:

a)   aviación;
b)   pesca; o
c)   asuntos marítimos, incluyendo salvamento.

Para mayor certeza, el Artículo 14-05 no se aplica a ningún programa presente o futuro de cooperación internacional para promover el desarrollo económico.

*   *   *

AGREEMENT BETWEEN THE UNITED STATES OF AMERICA AND THE HASHEMITE KINGDOM OF JORDAN ON THE ESTABLISHMENT OF A FREE TRADE AREA [*]
[excerpts]

The Agreement between the United States of America and the Hashemite Kingdom of Jordan on the Establishment of a Free Trade Area was signed on 24 October 2000. It entered into force on the date of signature.

PREAMBLE

The Government of the United States of America ("United States") and the Government of the Hashemite Kingdom of Jordan ("Jordan"),

Desiring to strengthen the bonds of friendship and economic relations and cooperation between them;

Wishing to establish clear and mutually advantageous rules governing their trade;

Aspiring to promote their mutual interest through liberalization and expansion of trade between their countries;

Reaffirming their willingness to strengthen and reinforce the multilateral trading system as reflected in the World Trade Organization, and to contribute to regional and international cooperation;

Recognizing that Jordan's economy is still in a state of development and faces special challenges;

Recognizing the objective of sustainable development, and seeking both to protect and preserve the environment and to enhance the means for doing so in a manner consistent with their respective needs and concerns at different levels of economic development;

Recognizing that their relations in the field of trade and economic activity should be conducted with a view to raising living standards and promoting economic growth, investment opportunities, development, prosperity, employment and the optimal use of resources in their territories;

Desiring to foster creativity and innovation and promote trade in goods and services that are the subject of intellectual property rights;

Recognizing the need to raise public awareness of the challenges and opportunities offered by trade liberalization;

Wishing to raise the capacity and international competitiveness of their goods and services;

---

[*] *Source*: The Government of the United States and the Government of Jordan (2000). "Agreement between the United States of America and the Hashemite Kingdom of Jordan on the Establishment of a Free Trade Area"; available on the Internet (http://usembassy-amman.org.jo/FTA/FTATxt.html). [Note added by the editor.]

Desiring to promote higher labor standards by building on their respective international commitments and strengthening their cooperation on labor matters; and

Wishing to promote effective enforcement of their respective environmental and labor law;

HAVE AGREED AS FOLLOWS:

ARTICLE 1: ESTABLISHMENT OF A FREE TRADE AREA AND RELATIONSHIP TO OTHER AGREEMENTS

1.   The Parties to this Agreement, consistent with Article XXIV of the General Agreement on Tariffs and Trade 1994 ("GATT 1994") and Article V of the General Agreement on Trade in Services ("GATS"), hereby establish a free trade area in accordance with the provisions of this Agreement.

2.   The Parties reaffirm their respective rights and obligations with respect to each other under existing bilateral and multilateral agreements to which both Parties are party, including the Marrakesh Agreement Establishing the World Trade Organization ("WTO Agreement").

3.   This Agreement shall not be construed to derogate from any international legal obligation between the Parties that entitles a good or service, or the supplier of a good or service, to treatment more favorable than that accorded by this Agreement.

4.   Nothing in Article 17 shall be construed to authorize a Party to apply a measure that is inconsistent with the Party's obligations under the WTO Agreement.

ARTICLE 3: TRADE IN SERVICES

1.   This Article applies to measures by a Party affecting trade in services between the Parties.

2.

(a)   With respect to market access through the modes of supply identified in Article I of the GATS, each Party shall accord services and service suppliers of the other Party treatment no less favorable than that provided for under the terms, limitations, and conditions agreed and specified in its Services Schedule to Annex 3.1 to this Agreement.

In sectors where such market access commitments are undertaken, the measure which a Party shall not maintain or adopt either on the basis of a regional subdivision or on the basis of its entire territory, unless otherwise specified in its Services Schedule to Annex 3.1, are those measures defined in Article XVI:2(a)-(f) of the GATS.

(b)   In the sectors inscribed in its Services Schedule to Annex 3.1, and subject to any conditions and qualifications set out therein, each Party shall accord to services and service suppliers of the other Party, in respect of all measures affecting the supply of services, treatment no less favorable than that it accords to its own like services and service suppliers.

(c)

    (i)   Subject to subparagraph (c)(ii), any market access or national treatment commitment inscribed in a Party's Services Schedule to Annex 3.1 shall give rise to the same rights and obligations 2 between the Parties as if that commitment had been inscribed in that Party's scheduleof specific ommitments annexed to the GATS.3

    (ii)   The provisions of GATS that shall be construed to give rise to rights and obligations under this Article are: Articles IIIbis; VI:1, 2, 3, 5, 6; VII:1 & 2; VIII:1, 2, 5; IX; XI; XII; XIII:1; XIV; XV:2; XVI; XVII; XVIII; XX:2; and XXVII; Annex on Movement of Natural Persons Supplying Services under the Agreement; Annex on Financial Services; Annex on Air Transport, paragraphs 1, 2, 3, 4, 6; and Annex on Telecommunications, paragraphs 1-5.

3.   Jordan has listed, in its schedule annexed to the GATS, exemptions from most-favored-nation treatment that are based on a reciprocity requirement. Jordan confirms that the United States satisfies those reciprocity requirements specified in Annex 3.2.

4.

    (a)   Unless they are specifically defined in this Article or in the Services Schedules to Annex 3.1, terms used in this Article and such Services Schedules that are also used in the GATS shall be construed in accordance with their meaning in the GATS, mutatis mutandis.

    (b)   All references in this Article to the GATS are to the GATS in effect on the date of entry into force of this Agreement. If, after that date, a Party alters its schedule of specific commitments annexed to the GATS, the GATS is amended, or the results of the negotiations described in GATS Articles VI:4, X:1, XIII:2, or XV:1 enter into effect, this Article shall be amended, as appropriate, after consultations between the Parties.

    (c)   Reference in this Article to a provision of the GATS includes any footnote to that provision.

ARTICLE 4: INTELLECTUAL PROPERTY RIGHTS

1.   Each Party shall, at a minimum, give effect to this Article, including the following provisions:

    (a)   Articles 1 through 6 of the Joint Recommendation Concerning Provisions on the Protection of Well-Known Marks (1999), adopted by the Assembly of the Paris Union for the Protection of Industrial Property and the General Assembly of the World Intellectual Property Organization ("WIPO");

    (b)   Articles 1 through 22 of the International Convention for the Protection of New Varieties of Plants (1991) ("UPOV Convention");

    (c)   Articles 1 through 14 of the WIPO Copyright Treaty (1996) ("WCT") 4; and (d)　　Articles 1 through 23 of the WIPO Performances and Phonograms Treaty (1996) ("WPPT").5

2.　　Each Party shall make best efforts to ratify or accede to the Patent Cooperation Treaty (1984) and the Protocol Relating to the Madrid Agreement Concerning the International Registration of Marks (1989).

3.　　Each Party shall accord to nationals of the other Party treatment no less favorable than it accords to its own nationals with regard to the protection 6 and enjoyment of all intellectual property rights and any benefits derived therefrom, subject to the exceptions provided in this Article.

4.　　A Party may derogate from paragraph 3 in relation to its judicial and administrative procedures, including the designation of an address for service or the appointment of an agent within the jurisdiction of the other Party, only where such derogations are necessary to secure compliance with laws and regulations that are not inconsistent with the provisions of this Agreement and where such practices are not applied in a manner that would constitute a disguised restriction on trade.

5.　　The obligations under paragraphs 3 and 4 do not apply to procedures provided in multilateral agreements concluded under the auspices of WIPO relating to the acquisition or maintenance of intellectual property rights.

Trademarks and Geographical Indications

6.　　Trademarks shall include service marks, collective marks and certification marks, 7 and may include geographical indications.8

7.　　The owner of a registered trademark shall have the exclusive right to prevent all third parties not having the owner's consent from using in the course of trade identical or similar signs, including geographical indications, for goods or services which are related to those in respect of which the trademark is registered, where such use would result in a likelihood of confusion.

8.　　Article 6bis of the Paris Convention for the Protection of Industrial Property (1967) ("Paris Convention") shall apply, mutatis mutandis, to goods or services which are not similar to those identified by a well-known trademark, whether registered or not, provided that use of that trademark in relation to those goods or services would indicate a connection between those goods or services and the owner of the trademark and provided that the interests of the owner of the trademark are likely to be damaged by such use.

9.　　Neither Party shall require recordal of trademark licenses to establish the validity of the license or to assert any rights in a trademark.

Copyright and Related Rights

10.　　Each Party shall provide that all reproductions, whether temporary or permanent, shall be deemed reproductions and subject to the reproduction right as envisaged in the provisions embodied in WCT Article 1(4) and the Agreed Statement thereto, and WPPT Articles 7 and 11 the Agreed Statement thereto.

11.   Each Party shall provide to authors and their successors in interest, to performers and to producers of phonograms the exclusive right to authorize or prohibit the importation into each Party's territory of copies of works and phonograms, even where such copies were made with the authorization of the author, performer or producer of the phonogram or a successor in interest.

12.   Each Party shall provide to performers and producers of phonograms the exclusive right to authorize or prohibit the broadcasting and communication to the public of their performances or phonograms, regardless of whether the broadcast or communication is effected by wired or wireless means, except that a Party may provide exemptions for analog transmissions and free over-the-air broadcasts, and may introduce statutory licenses for non-interactive services that, by virtue of their programming practices, including both the content of their transmissions and their use of technological measures to prevent unauthorized uses, are unlikely to conflict with a normal exploitation of phonograms or performances.

13.   In applying the prohibition under Article 11 of the WCT and Article 18 of the WPPT on circumvention of effective technological measures that are used by authors, performers and producers of phonograms in connection with the exercise of their rights and that restrict unauthorized acts in respect of their works, performances and phonograms, each Party shall prohibit civilly and criminally the manufacture, importation or circulation of any technology, device, service or part thereof, that is designed, produced, performed or marketed for engaging in such prohibited conduct, or that has only a limited commercially significant purpose or use other than enabling or facilitating such conduct.9

14.   Each Party shall provide that any natural person or legal entity acquiring or holding any economic rights by contract or otherwise, including contracts of employment involving protected subject matter, may freely and separately transfer such rights by contract and shall be able to exercise those rights in its own name and enjoy fully benefits of such rights.

15.   Each Party shall issue appropriate laws, regulations, or other measures ("measures") providing that all government agencies use only computer software authorized for intended use.

Such measures shall actively regulate the acquisition and management of software for government use.

16.   Each Party shall confine limitations or exceptions to exclusive rights to certain special cases which do not conflict with a normal exploitation of the work and do not unreasonably prejudice the legitimate interests of the right holders.

Patents

17.   Subject to paragraph 18, patents shall be available for any invention, whether product or process, in all fields of technology, provided that it is new, involves an inventive step and is capable of industrial application.

18.   Each Party may exclude from patentability:

    (a)   inventions, the prevention within their territory of the commercial exploitation of which is necessary to protect ordre public or morality, including to protect human, animal or plant life or health or to avoid serious prejudice to the environment provided that such exclusion is not made merely because the exploitation is prohibited by their law;

(b)   diagnostic, therapeutic and surgical methods for the treatment of humans or animals.

19.   If a Party permits the use by a third party of a subsisting patent to support an application for marketing approval of a product, the Party shall provide that any product produced under this authority shall not be made, used or sold in the territory of the Party other than for purposes related to meeting requirements for marketing approval, and if export is permitted, the product shall only be exported outside the territory of the Party for purposes of meeting requirements for marketing approval in the Party or in another country that permits the use by a third party of a subsisting patent to support an application for marketing approval of a product.

20.   Neither Party shall permit the use of the subject matter of a patent without the authorization of the right holder except in the following circumstances:

(a)   to remedy a practice determined after judicial or administrative process to be anti-competitive;

(b)   in cases of public non-commercial use or in the case of a national emergency or other circumstances of extreme urgency, provided that such use is limited to use by government entities or legal entities acting under the authority of a government; or

(c)   on the ground of failure to meet working requirements, provided that importation shall constitute working.

Where the law of a Party allows for such use pursuant to sub-paragraphs (a), (b) or (c), the Party shall respect the provisions of Article 31 of TRIPS and Article 5A(4) of the Paris Convention.

21.   With regard to filing a patent application, when it is not possible to provide a sufficient written description of the invention to enable others skilled in the art to carry out the invention, each Party shall require a deposit with an "international depository authority," as defined in the Budapest Treaty on the International Recognition of the Deposit of Microorganisms for the Purposes of Patent Procedure (1980).

Measures Related to Certain Regulated Products

22.   Pursuant to Article 39.3 of TRIPS, each Party, when requiring, as a condition of approving the marketing of pharmaceutical or of agricultural chemical products that utilize new chemical entities, 10 the submission of undisclosed test or other data, or evidence of approval in another country, 11 the origination of which involves a considerable effort, shall protect such information against unfair commercial use. In addition, each Party shall protect such information against disclosure, except where necessary to protect the public, or unless steps are taken to ensure that the information is protected against unfair commercial use.

23. With respect to pharmaceutical products that are subject to a patent:

(a) each Party shall make available an extension of the patent term to compensate the patent owner for unreasonable curtailment of the patent term as a result of the marketing approval process.

(b) the patent owner shall be notified of the identity of any third party requesting marketing approval effective during the term of the patent.

Enforcement of Intellectual Property Rights

24. Each Party shall provide that, at least in cases of knowing infringement of trademark, copyright and related rights, its judicial authorities shall have the authority to order the infringer to pay the right holder damages adequate to compensate for the injury the right holder has suffered as a result of the infringement and any profits of the infringer that are attributable to the infringement that are not taken into account in computing such damages. Injury to the right holder shall be based upon the value of the infringed-upon item, according to the suggested retail price of the legitimate product, or other equivalent measures established by the right holder for valuing authorized goods.

25. Each Party shall ensure that its statutory maximum fines are sufficiently high to deter future acts of infringement with a policy of removing the monetary incentive to the infringer, and shall provide its judicial and other competent authorities the authority to order the seizure of all suspected pirated copyright and counterfeit trademark goods and related implements the predominant use of which has been in the commission of the offense, and documentary evidence.

26. Each Party shall provide, at least in cases of copyright piracy or trademark counterfeiting, that its authorities may initiate criminal actions and border measure actions ex officio, without the need for a formal complaint by a private party or right holder.

27. In civil cases involving copyright or related rights, each Party shall provide that the natural person or legal entity whose name is indicated as the author, producer, performer or publisher of the work, performance or phonogram in the usual manner shall, in the absence of proof to the contrary, be presumed to be the designated right holder in such work, performance or phonogram. It shall be presumed, in the absence of proof to the contrary, that the copyright or related right subsists in such subject matter. Such presumptions shall pertain in criminal cases until the defendant comes forward with credible evidence putting in issue the ownership or subsistence of the copyright or related right.

28. Each Party shall provide that copyright piracy involving significant willful infringements that have no direct or indirect motivation of financial gain shall be considered willful copyright piracy on a commercial scale.

Transition Periods

29. Each Party shall implement fully the obligations of this Article within the following time periods:

(a) With respect to all obligations in paragraphs 1(c), 1(d), and 10 through 16, two years from the date of entry into force of this Agreement. In addition, Jordan agrees to accede to and ratify the WCT and WPPT within two years from the date of entry into force of this Agreement.

(b)   With respect to all obligations in paragraph 1(b), six months from the date of entry into force of this Agreement. In addition, Jordan agrees to ratify the UPOV Convention within one year from the date of entry into force of this Agreement.

(c)   With respect to all obligations in paragraph 22, except the obligation in footnote 10, immediately from the date of entry into force of this Agreement.

(d)   With respect to all obligations under this Article not referenced in subparagraphs (a), (b) and (c), three years from the date of entry into force of this Agreement.

ARTICLE 5: ENVIRONMENT

1.   The Parties recognize that it is inappropriate to encourage trade by relaxing domestic environmental laws. Accordingly, each Party shall strive to ensure that it does not waive or otherwise derogate from, or offer to waive or otherwise derogate from, such laws as an encouragement for trade with the other Party.

2.   Recognizing the right of each Party to establish its own levels of domestic environmental protection and environmental development policies and priorities, and to adopt or modify accordingly its environmental laws, each Party shall strive to ensure that its laws provide for high levels of environmental protection and shall strive to continue to improve those laws.

3.   (a)   A Party shall not fail to effectively enforce its environmental laws, through a sustained or recurring course of action or inaction, in a manner affecting trade between the Parties, after the date of entry into force of this Agreement.

(b)   The Parties recognize that each Party retains the right to exercise discretion with respect to investigatory, prosecutorial, regulatory, and compliance matters and to make decisions regarding the allocation of resources to enforcement with respect to other environmental matters determined to have higher priorities. Accordingly, the Parties understand that a Party is in compliance with subparagraph (a) where a course of action or inaction reflects a reasonable exercise of such discretion, or results from a bona fide decision regarding the allocation of resources.

4.   For purposes of this Article, "environmental laws" mean any statutes or regulations of a Party, or provision thereof, the primary purpose of which is the protection of the environment, or the prevention of a danger to human, animal, or plant life or health, through:

(a)   the prevention, abatement or control of the release, discharge, or emission of pollutants or environmental contaminants;

(b)   the control of environmentally hazardous or toxic chemicals, substances, materials and wastes, and the dissemination of information related thereto; or

(c)   the protection or conservation of wild flora or fauna, including endangered species, their habitat, and specially protected natural areas in the Party's territory, but does not include any statutes or regulations, or provision thereof, directly related to worker safety or health.

ARTICLE 6: LABOR

1.   The Parties reaffirm their obligations as members of the International Labor Organization ("ILO") and their commitments under the ILO Declaration on Fundamental Principles and Rights at Work and its Follow-up. The Parties shall strive to ensure that such labor principles and the internationally recognized labor rights set forth in paragraph 6 are recognized and protected by domestic law.

2.   The Parties recognize that it is inappropriate to encourage trade by relaxing domestic labor laws. Accordingly, each Party shall strive to ensure that it does not waive or otherwise derogate from, or offer to waive or otherwise derogate from, such laws as an encouragement for trade with the other Party.

3.   Recognizing the right of each Party to establish its own domestic labor standards, and to adopt or modify accordingly its labor laws and regulations, each Party shall strive to ensure that its laws provide for labor standards consistent with the internationally recognized labor rights set forth in paragraph 6 and shall strive to improve those standards in that light.

4.

(a)   A Party shall not fail to effectively enforce its labor laws, through a sustained or recurring course of action or inaction, in a manner affecting trade between the Parties, after the date of entry into force of this Agreement.

(b)   The Parties recognize that each Party retains the right to exercise discretion with respect to investigatory, prosecutorial, regulatory, and compliance matters and to make decisions regarding the allocation of resources to enforcement with respect to other labor matters determined to have higher priorities. Accordingly, the Parties understand that a Party is in compliance with subparagraph (a) where a course of action or inaction reflects a reasonable exercise of such discretion, or results from a bona fide decision regarding the allocation of resources.

5.   The Parties recognize that cooperation between them provides enhanced opportunities to improve labor standards. The Joint Committee established under Article 15 shall, during its regular sessions, consider any such opportunity identified by a Party.

6.   For purposes of this Article, "labor laws" means statutes and regulations, or provisions thereof, that are directly related to the following internationally recognized labor rights:

(a)   the right of association;

(b)   the right to organize and bargain collectively;

(c)   a prohibition on the use of any form of forced or compulsory labor;

(d)   a minimum age for the employment of children;

(e)   and acceptable conditions of work with respect to minimum wages, hours of work, and occupational safety and health.

ARTICLE 7: ELECTRONIC COMMERCE

1.   Recognizing the economic growth and opportunity provided by electronic commerce and the importance of avoiding barriers to its use and development, each Party shall seek to refrain from:

(a)   deviating from its existing practice of not imposing customs duties on electronic transmissions;

(b)   imposing unnecessary barriers on electronic transmissions, including digitized products; and

(c)   impeding the supply through electronic means of services subject to a commitment under Article 3 of this Agreement, except as otherwise set forth in the Party's Services Schedule in Annex 3.1.

2.   The Parties shall also make publicly available all relevant laws, regulations, and requirements affecting electronic commerce.

3.   The Parties reaffirm the principles announced in the U.S.-Jordan Joint Statement on Electronic Commerce.

ARTICLE 8: VISA COMMITMENTS

1.   Subject to its laws relating to the entry, sojourn and employment of aliens, each Party shall permit to enter and to remain in its territory nationals of the other Party solely to carry on substantial trade, including trade in services or trade in technology, principally between the Parties.

2.   Subject to its laws relating to the entry, sojourn and employment of aliens, each Party shall permit to enter and to remain in its territory nationals of the other Party for the purpose of establishing, developing, administering or advising on the operation of an investment to which they, or a company of the other Party that employs them, have committed or are in the process of committing a substantial amount of capital or other resources.12

ARTICLE 11: BALANCE OF PAYMENTS

Should either Party decide to impose measures for balance of payments purposes, it shall do so in accordance with the Party's obligations under the WTO Agreement. In adopting such measures, the Party shall strive not to impair the relative benefits accorded to the other Party under this Agreement

ARTICLE 12: EXCEPTIONS

1.   For purposes of Article 2 of this Agreement, Article XX of GATT 1994 and its interpretative notes are incorporated into and made a part of this Agreement. The Parties

understand that the measures referred to in GATT 1994 Article XX(b) include environmental measures necessary to protect human, animal or plant life or health, and that GATT 1994 Article XX(g) applies to measures relating to conservation of living and non-living exhaustible natural resources.

2.   Nothing in this Agreement shall be construed:

    (a)   to require any Party to furnish or allow access to any information the disclosure of which it determines to be contrary to its essential security interests;

    (b)   to prevent any Party from taking any actions that it considers necessary for the protection of its essential security interests:

        (i)   relating to the traffic in arms, ammunition and implements of war and to such traffic and transactions in other goods, materials, services and technology undertaken directly or indirectly for the purpose of supplying a military or other security establishment,

        (ii)   taken in time of war or other emergency in international relations, or

        (iii)   relating to the implementation of national policies or international agreements respecting the non-proliferation of nuclear weapons or other nuclear explosive devices; or

    (c)   to prevent any Party from taking action in pursuance of its obligations under the United Nations Charter for the maintenance of international peace and security.

3.   Except as set out in this paragraph, nothing in this Agreement shall apply to taxation measures.

    (a)   Nothing in this Agreement shall affect the rights and obligations of either Party under any tax convention. In the event of any inconsistency between this Agreement and any such convention, that convention shall prevail to the extent of the inconsistency.

    (b)   Notwithstanding subparagraph (a), Article 2.3 and such other provisions of this Agreement as are necessary to give effect to Article 2.3 shall apply to taxation measures to the same extent as does Article III of the GATT 1994.

    (c)   Notwithstanding subparagraph (a), the national treatment commitment under Article 3.2 shall apply to taxation measures to the same extent as under the GATS, and the national treatment commitment under Article 3.2(b) shall apply to taxation measures to the same extent as if the Party had made an identical national treatment commitment under Article XVII of the GATS.

ARTICLE 13: ECONOMIC COOPERATION AND TECHNICAL ASSISTANCE

To realize the objectives of this Agreement and to contribute to the implementation of its provisions:

(a)   the Parties declare their readiness to foster economic cooperation; and

(b)   in view of Jordan's developing status, and the size of its economy and resources, the United States shall strive to furnish Jordan with economic technical assistance, as appropriate.

ARTICLE 15: JOINT COMMITTEE

1.   A Joint Committee is hereby established to supervise the proper implementation of this Agreement and to review the trade relationship between the Parties.

2.   The functions of the Joint Committee shall include, inter alia:

(a)   reviewing the general functioning of this Agreement

(b)   reviewing the results of this Agreement in light of the experience gained during its functioning and its objectives, and considering ways of improving trade relations between the Parties, and furthering the objectives of the Agreement, including through further cooperation and assistance;

(a)   facilitating the avoidance and settlement of disputes, including through consultations pursuant to Articles 17.1 (b) and 17.2 (a);

(b)   considering and adopting any amendment to this Agreement or modification to the commitments therein, provided that the adoption of such amendment or modification shall be subject to the domestic legal requirements of each Party;

(c)   developing guidelines, explanatory materials, and rules on the proper implementation of this Agreement, as necessary, and particularly: (i) guidelines and explanatory materials on the implementation of Annex 2.2, and (ii) rules for the selection and conduct of members of panels formed under Article 17, and model rules of procedure for such panels

(f)   at its first meeting, discussing the review performed by each Party of the environmental effects of this Agreement.

3.   Structure of the Joint Committee

(a)   The Joint Committee shall be composed of representatives of the Parties and shall be headed by (i) the United States Trade Representative and (ii) Jordan's Minister primarily responsible for international trade, or their designees.

(b)   The Joint Committee may establish and delegate responsibilities to ad hoc and standing committees or working groups, and seek the advice of non-governmental persons or groups.

4.   The Joint Committee shall convene at least once a year in regular session in order to review the general functioning of the Agreement. Regular sessions of the Joint Committee shall be held alternately in each country. Special meetings of the Joint Committee shall also be

convened within 30 days at the request of either Party and shall be held in the territory of the other Party, except as the Parties may otherwise agree. The Joint Committee shall establish its own rules of procedure. All decisions of the Joint Committee shall be taken by consensus.

5.   Recognizing the importance of transparency and openness, the Parties reaffirm their respective practices of considering the views of interested members of the public in order to draw upon a broad range of perspectives in the implementation of this Agreement.

6.   Each Party shall designate an office to serve as the contact point with regard to this Agreement. That office shall receive official correspondence related to this Agreement and provide administrative assistance to the Joint Committee and to dispute settlement panels established under Article 17.

ARTICLE 16: CONSULTATIONS

1.   The Parties shall at all times endeavor to agree on the interpretation and application of this Agreement, and shall make every attempt to arrive at a mutually satisfactory resolution of any matter that might affect its operation.

2.   Either Party may request consultations with the other Party with respect to any matter affecting the operation or interpretation of this Agreement. If a Party requests consultations with regard to a matter, the other Party shall afford adequate opportunity for consultations and shall reply promptly to the request for consultations and enter into consultations in good faith.

ARTICLE 17: DISPUTE SETTLEMENT

1.

    (a)   The Parties shall make every attempt to arrive at a mutually agreeable resolution through consultations under Article 17, whenever

        (i)   a dispute arises concerning the interpretation of this Agreement;

        (ii)   a Party considers that the other Party has failed to carry out its obligations under this Agreement; or

        (iii)   a Party considers that measures taken by the other Party severely distort the balance of trade benefits accorded by this Agreement, or substantially undermine fundamental objectives of this Agreement.

    (b)   A Party seeking consultations pursuant to subparagraph (a) shall submit a request for consultations to the contact point provided for under Article 15.6. If the Parties fail to resolve a matter described in subparagraph (a) through consultations within 60 days of the submission of such request, either Party may refer the matter to the Joint Committee, which shall be convened and shall endeavor to resolve the dispute.

    (c)   If a matter referred to the Joint Committee has not been resolved within a period of 90 days after the dispute was referred to it, or within such other period as the Joint Committee has agreed, either Party may refer the matter to a dispute settlement panel. Unless otherwise agreed by the Parties, the panel shall be composed of three members: each Party shall appoint one member, and the two appointees shall choose a third who will serve as the chairman.

(d)   The panel shall, within 90 days after the third member is appointed, present to the Parties a report containing findings of fact and its determination as to whether either Party has failed to carry out its obligations under the Agreement or whether a measure taken by either Party severely distorts the balance of trade benefits accorded by this Agreement or substantially undermines the fundamental objectives of this Agreement. Where the panel finds that a Party has failed to carry out its obligations under this Agreement, it may, at the request of the Parties, make recommendations for resolution of the dispute. The report of the panel shall be non-binding.

(e)

(i)   If the dispute settlement panel under this Agreement or any other applicable international dispute settlement mechanism under an agreement to which both Parties are Party has been invoked by either Party with respect to any matter, the mechanism invoked shall have exclusive jurisdiction over that matter.

(ii)   If a mechanism described in subparagraph (e)(i) fails for procedural or jurisdictional reasons to make findings of law or fact, as necessary, on a claim included in a matter with respect to which a Party has invoked such mechanism, subparagraph (e)(i) shall not be construed to prevent the Party from invoking another mechanism with respect to such claim.

2.

(a)   After a dispute has been referred to a dispute settlement panel under this Agreement and the panel has presented its report, the Joint Committee shall endeavor to resolve the dispute, taking the report into account, as appropriate.

(b)   If the Joint Committee does not resolve the dispute within a period of 30 days after the presentation of the panel report, the affected Party shall be entitled to take any appropriate and commensurate measure.

3.   The Parties, within 180 days after the entry into force of this Agreement, shall enter into discussions with a view to developing rules for the selection and conduct of members of panels and Model Rules of Procedure for panels. The Joint Committee shall adopt such rules. Unless the Parties otherwise agree, a panel established under this Article shall conduct its proceedings in accordance with the Model Rules of Procedure.

4.

(a)   A Party may invoke a panel under paragraph 1(c) of this Article for claims arising under Article 3 only to the extent that a claim arises with regard to a commitment that is inscribed in the Party's Services Schedule to Annex 3.1 to this Agreement, but is not inscribed in the Party's schedule of specific commitments annexed to the GATS. Such commitment may include a market access or national treatment commitment in a sector, a horizontal commitment applicable to a sector, or additional commitment.

(b)   Except as otherwise agreed by the Parties, a Party may invoke a panel under paragraph 1(c) of this Article for claims arising under Article 4 only to the extent that the same claim would not be subject to resolution through the WTO Understanding on Rules and Procedures Governing the Settlement of Disputes.

(c)   If a dispute involves both a claim described in subparagraph (a) or (b) and another claim, subparagraph 1(e) shall not prevent a Party from invoking another international dispute settlement mechanism with regard to such other claim. Nothing in this subparagraph shall allow a Party to invoke the dispute settlement mechanism of both this Article and another international dispute settlement mechanism with regard to the same claim.

ARTICLE 18: MISCELLANEOUS PROVISIONS

1.   Neither Party may provide for a right of action under its domestic law against the other Party on the ground that a measure of the other Party is inconsistent with this Agreement.

2.   For purposes of Articles 5 and 6, "statutes and regulations" means,

(a)   with respect to Jordan, an act of the Jordanian Parliament, or by-law or regulation promulgated pursuant to an act of the Jordanian Parliament that is enforceable by action of the Government of Jordan; and

(b)   with respect to the United States, an act of the United States Congress or regulation promulgated pursuant to an act of the U.S. Congress that is enforceable, in the first instance, by action of the federal government.

3.   The Annexes and Schedules to this Agreement are an integral part thereof.

4.   All references in this Agreement to GATT 1994 are to the GATT 1994 in effect on the date of entry into force of this Agreement.

ARTICLE 19: ENTRY INTO FORCE AND TERMINATION

1.   The entry into force of this Agreement is subject to the completion of necessary domestic legal procedures by each Party.

2.   This Agreement shall enter into force two months after the date on which the Parties exchange written notification that such procedures have been completed, or after such other period as the Parties may agree.

3.   Either Party may terminate this Agreement by written notification to the other Party.

This Agreement shall expire six months after the date of such notification.

IN WITNESS WHEREOF, the undersigned, being duly authorized by their respective Governments, have signed this Agreement.

Done at Washington, in duplicate, in the English language, this twenty-fourth day of October, 2000, which corresponds to this twenty-sixty day of Rajab, 1421. An Arabic language text shall be prepared, which shall be considered equally authentic upon an exchange of diplomatic notes confirming its conformity with the English language text. In the event of a discrepancy, the English language text shall prevail.

For the Government of the
United States of America

For the Government of the
Hashimite Kingdom of Jordan

*   *   *

1   For purposes of this Agreement, "schedule" shall include both the schedule and headnotes.

2   Nothing in this Article shall require a Party to take any action with regard to the WTO or a Council, Committee, Body, or the Ministerial Conference of the WTO.

3   The Parties acknowledge and accept that the commitments of the United States in financial services in subparagraphs 2(a) and 2(b) have been undertaken in accordance with the WTO Understanding on Commitments in Financial Services subject to the limitations and conditions set forth in the schedule of the United States.

4   Articles 1(4) and 6(2) of the WCT shall be excepted from this Agreement. Such exception shall be without prejudice to each Party's respective rights and obligations under the WCT, the Berne Convention for the Protection of Literary and Artistic Works (1971) ("Berne Convention") and the Agreement on Trade-Related Aspects of Intellectual Property Rights ("TRIPS").

5.   Articles 5, 8(2), 12(2), and 15 of the WPPT shall be excepted from this Agreement. Such exception shall be without prejudice to each Party's respective rights and obligations under the WPPT, the Berne Convention and TRIPS.

6.   For purposes of paragraphs 3 and 4, "protection" shall include matters affecting the availability, acquisition, scope, maintenance and enforcement of intellectual property rights as well as uses of intellectual property rights specifically covered by this Agreement.

7   Neither Party is obligated to treat certification marks as a separate category in national law, provided that such marks are protected.

8   A geographical indication shall be considered a trademark to the extent that the geographical indication consists of any sign, or any combination of signs, capable of identifying a good or service as originating in the territory of a Party, or a region or locality in that territory,

where a given quality, reputation or other characteristic of the good or service is essentially attributable to its geographical origin.

9   This provision does not require either Party to mandate that any consumer electronics, telecommunications or computing product not otherwise violating the prohibition be designed to affirmatively respond to any effective technological measure. Any violation of the prohibition shall be independent of any infringement of copyright or related rights.

10   It is understood that protection for "new chemical entities" shall also include protection for new uses for old chemical entities for a period of three years.

11   It is understood that, in situations where there is reliance on evidence of approval in another country, Jordan shall at a minimum protect such information against unfair commercial use for the same period of time the other country is protecting such information against unfair commercial use.

12   Paragraphs 1 and 2 of this Article render nationals of Jordan eligible for treaty-trader (E-1) and treaty-investor (E-2) visas subject to the applicable provisions of U.S. laws and corresponding regulations governing entry, sojourn and employment of aliens. They also guarantee similar treatment for U.S. nationals seeking to enter Jordan's territory.

13   A determination that an originating good is being imported as a result of the reduction or elimination of a duty provided for in this Agreement shall be made only if such reduction or elimination is a cause which contributes significantly to the increase in imports, but need not be equal to or greater than any other cause. The passage of a period of time between the commencement or termination of such reduction or elimination and the increase in imports shall not by itself preclude the determination referenced in this footnote. If the increase in imports is demonstrably unrelated to such reduction or elimination, the determination referenced in this footnote shall not be made.

*   *   *

AGREEMENT BETWEEN NEW ZEALAND AND SINGAPORE ON A CLOSER ECONOMIC PARTNERSHIP*

[excerpts]

The Agreement between New Zealand and Singapore on a Closer Economic Partnership was signed on 14 November 2000. It entered into force on 1 January 2001.

PART 6: INVESTMENT

Article 26
Scope and Coverage

1   This Part shall apply to all investments in goods and services.

2   Articles 28, 29 and 30 shall not apply to any measures affecting investments adopted or maintained pursuant to Part 5 to the extent that they relate to the supply of any specific service through commercial presence as defined in Article 16(n), whether or not they are covered by Annex 2.

Article 27
Definitions

For the purposes of this Agreement :

1   "Investments" include but are not limited to the following:

a)   movable and immovable property and other property rights such as mortgages, liens or pledges;

b)   shares, stocks, debentures, bank bills, deposits, securities, and similar interests in companies or enterprises (whether incorporated or unincorporated);

c)   claims to money or to any performance under contract having an economic value;

d)   intellectual property rights and goodwill;

e)   business concessions conferred by law or under contract, including any concession to search for, cultivate, extract or exploit natural resources;

---

* *Source*: The Government of New Zealand and the Government of Singapore (2000). "Agreement between New Zealand and Singapore on a Closer Economic Partnership"; Foreign Ministry, Government of New Zealand, available on the Internet (http://www.mft.govt.nz/foreign/regions/Singpdf/part1.pdf); and Ministry of Trade and Industry, Government of Singapore, available also on the Internet (http:// www. mti. gov. sg/ public/ economgmt/fta.cfm). [Note added by the editor.]

    f)   derivative instruments.

2   "Proceeds from investment" include but are not limited to the following:

    a)   profits, capital gains, dividends, royalties, interest and other current income accruing from an investment;

    b)   the proceeds from the liquidation of an investment;

    c)   loan payments in connection with an investment;

    d)   royalties, license fees, payments in respect of technical assistance, service and management fees;

    e)   payments in connection with contracts involving the presence of an investor's property in the territory of the other Party and payment in connection with contracts where remuneration depends substantially on the production, revenues or profits of an enterprise;

    f)   earnings of investors of a Party who work in connection with an investment in the territory of the other Party.

3   "Investor" means:

    a)   a natural person who resides in the territory of the other Party or elsewhere and who under the law of that other Party:

        (i)   is a national of that other Party; or

        (ii)   has the right of permanent residence in that other Party, in the case of a Party which accords substantially the same treatment to its permanent residents as it does to its nationals in respect of measures affecting investments, provided that that Party is not obligated to accord to such permanent residents more favourable treatment than would be accorded by the other Party to such permanent residents;

        or

    b)   any company, firm, association or body, with or without legal personality, whether or not incorporated, established or registered under the applicable laws in force in a Party; making or having made an investment in the other Party's territory.

Article 28
Most Favoured Nation Status

Except as otherwise provided for in this Agreement, each Party shall accord to investors and investments of the other Party, in relation to the establishment, acquisition, expansion, management, conduct, operation, liquidation, sale, transfer (or other disposition), protection and expropriation (including any compensation) of investments, treatment that is no less favourable than that it accords in like situations to investors and investments from any other State or separate customs territory which is not party to this Agreement.

Article 29
National Treatment

Except as otherwise provided for in this Agreement, each Party shall accord to investors and investments of the other Party in relation to the establishment, acquisition, expansion, management, conduct, operation, liquidation, sale, transfer (or other disposition), protection and expropriation (including any compensation) of investments, treatment that is no less favourable than that it accords in like situations to its own investors and investments.

Article 30
Standard of Treatment

Each Party shall accord to investors and investments of the other Party the better of the treatment required by Articles 28 and 29.

Article 31
Repatriation and Convertibility

1   Each Party shall allow investors of the other Party, on a non-discriminatory basis, to transfer and repatriate freely and without undue delay their investments and proceeds from investment. Each Party shall permit transfers to be made in a freely usable currency at the market rate of exchange prevailing on the date of transfer with respect to spot transactions in the currency to be transferred.

2   Notwithstanding paragraph 1, a Party may prevent a transfer through the equitable, non-discriminatory and good faith application of its laws relating to:

a)   bankruptcy, insolvency or the protection of the rights of creditors;

b)   issuing, trading or dealing in securities;

c)   criminal or penal offences, and the recovery of proceeds of crime;

d)   reports of transfers of currency or other monetary instruments; or

e)   ensuring the satisfaction of judgments in adjudicatory proceedings.

Article 32
Limitations

1   Articles 28, 29 and 30 shall not apply to:

a)   any limitation that is listed by a Party in Annex 3;

b)   an amendment to a limitation covered by paragraph (a) to the extent that the amendment does not decrease the conformity of the limitation with Articles 28, 29 and 30;

c)   any new limitation adopted by a Party, and incorporated into Annex 3, which does not affect the overall level of commitments of that Party under this Part; to the extent that such limitations are inconsistent with those Articles.

2   As part of the reviews of this Agreement provided for in Article 68, the Parties undertake to review at least every two years the status of the limitations set out in Annex 3 with a view to reducing the limitations or removing them.

3   A Party may, at any time, either upon the request of the other Party or unilaterally, remove in whole or in part limitations set out in Annex 3 by written notification to the other Party.

4   A Party may, at any time, incorporate a new limitation into Annex 3 in accordance with paragraph 1(c) of this Article by written notification to the other Party. On receiving such written notification, the other Party may request consultations regarding the limitation. On receiving the request for consultations, the Party incorporating the new limitation shall enter into consultations with the other Party.

Article 33
Subrogation

1   In the event that either Party (or any agency, institution, statutory body or corporation designated by it) as a result of an indemnity it has given in respect of an investment or any part thereof makes payment to its own investors in respect of any of their claims under this Part, the other Party acknowledges that the former Party (or any agency, institution, statutory body or corporation designated by it) is entitled by virtue of subrogation to exercise the rights and assert the claims of its own investors. The subrogated rights or claims shall not be greater than the original rights or claims of such investors.

2   Any payment made by one Party (or any agency, institution, statutory body or corporation designated by it) to its investors shall not affect the right of such investors to make their claims against the other Party in accordance with Article 34, in cases where the former Party elects not to exercise its subrogated rights or claims.

Article 34
Investment Disputes

1   Any legal dispute between an investor of one Party and the other Party arising directly out of an investment by that investor in the territory of that other Party shall, as far as possible, be settled amicably through negotiations between the investor and that other Party.

2   If the dispute cannot be resolved as provided for in paragraph 1 within 6 months from the date of request for negotiations then, unless the parties to the dispute agree otherwise, it shall, upon the request of either such party, be submitted to conciliation or arbitration by the International Centre for Settlement of Investment Disputes established by the Convention on the Settlement of Investment Disputes between the States and Nationals of Other States done at Washington on 18 March, 1965, provided that the other party does not withhold its consent under Article 25 of that Convention.

ANNEX 3

INVESTMENT LIMITATIONS

Introductory Note

1   Each Party has set out, pursuant to Article 32, the limitations established by it that do not conform with obligations imposed by:

    a)   Article 28 (most-favoured-nation status); and

    b)   Article 29 (national treatment).

2   Each limitation sets out the following elements:

    a)   "Type of Limitation" specifies the obligation referred to in paragraph 1 for which a limitation is necessary;

    b)   "Legal Citation" identifies the laws, regulations or other measures which are relevant to the limitation. A measure cited in the legal citation element:

        (i)   means the measure as amended, continued or renewed as of the date of entry into force of this Agreement, and

        (ii)   includes any subordinate measure adopted or maintained under the authority of and consistent with the measure;

    c)   "Description" sets out the non-conforming aspects of the measures for which the limitation is necessary, or the basis on which the limitation is applied to a sector.

ANNEX 3.1

Limitations of New Zealand

    A.   <u>All sectors</u>

Type of Limitation: National treatment (Article 29)

Legal Citation: Fisheries Act 1996
                       Overseas Investment Act 1973
                       Overseas Investment Act Regulations 1995
                       Overseas Investment Amendment Act 1998

Description: 1 Under the Overseas Investment Act Regulations, 1995, issued under the Overseas Investment Act 1973, Ministerial approval is required for the following investments by an overseas person:

a) acquisition or control of 25 per cent or more of any class of shares or voting power in a New Zealand entity where either the consideration for the transfer or the value of the assets exceeds NZ$50 million, unless an exemption exists or an authorisation is granted;

b) commencement of business operations, or acquisition of an existing business, including business assets, in New Zealand, where the total expenditure to be incurred in setting up or acquiring that business or those assets exceeds NZ$50 million, unless an exemption exists or an authorisation is granted;

c) acquisition, regardless of dollar value, of:

(i) 25 per cent or more of any class of shares or voting power in a New Zealand entity that owns commercial fishing quota or annual catch entitlement;

(ii) commercial fishing quota or annual catch entitlement; unless an exemption exists or an authorisation is granted

d) acquisition, regardless of dollar value of:

(i) New Zealand land outside of urban areas and exceeding five hectares or land wherever located worth more than NZ$ 10 million;

(ii) scenic reserve land (including land that encompasses or adjoins recreational, historic or heritage areas, the foreshore and lakes);

(iii) land over 0.4 hectares on specified off-shore islands;

(iv) any land on all other islands;

unless an exemption exists or an authorisation is granted;

e) acquisition, regardless of dollar value, of 25 percent or more of any New Zealand entity that owns or controls:

(i) New Zealand land outside of urban areas and exceeding five hectares or land wherever located worth more than NZ$ 10 million;

(ii) scenic reserve land (including historic or heritage areas, the foreshore and lakes);

(iii) land over 0.4 hectares on specified off-shore islands;

(iv) any land on all other islands;

unless an exemption exists or an authorisation is granted.

2 Ministers, in determining whether to grant approval, act in accordance with a screening regime (a non-legally binding description of which is appended to this Annex) which may be adjusted or replaced from time to time by New Zealand Government legislation, regulation or policy setting.

B.   Producer and Marketing Boards

Type of Limitation: National treatment (Article 29)

Legal Citation: Agriculture (Emergency Powers) Act 1934
                              Apple and Pear Export Regulations 1999
                              Apple and Pear Industry Restructuring Act 1999
                              Dairy Board Act 1961
                              Dairy Industry Restructuring Act 1999
                              Game Industry Board Regulation 1985
                              Hop Marketing Regulations 1939
                              Kiwifruit Export Regulations 1999
                              Kiwifruit Industry Restructuring Act 1999
                              Marketing Act 1936
                              Meat Board Act 1997
                              Pork Industry Board Act 1997
                              Primary Products Marketing Act 1953
                              Wool Board Act 1997

Description: More favourable treatment may be accorded to New Zealand nationals and permanent residents in respect of ownership of Producer and Marketing Board assets.

C.   Fishing

Type of Limitation: National treatment (Article 29)

Legal Citation: Fisheries Act 1996

Description: 1   Without the permission of the Minister of Fisheries, and subject to any conditions that he or she thinks fit to impose, no vessel owned or operated by an overseas person may be registered to carry out commercial fishing or fish carrying activities.

                              2   No vessel that is not a New Zealand ship will be used for commercial fishing within the territorial sea of New Zealand.

                              3   Foreign fishing vessels or fish carriers are required to obtain the approval of the Minister of Fisheries before entering New Zealand internal waters. If the Minister of Fisheries is satisfied that the vessel has undermined international conservation and management measures he or she may deny the vessel approval to enter New Zealand internal waters.

D.   Privatisation

Type of Limitation: National treatment (Article 29)

Legal Citation:

Description: More favourable treatment may be accorded to New Zealand nationals and permanent residents in respect of ownership of enterprises currently in State ownership.

347

E.   Overseas Company Reporting Requirements

Type of Limitation: National treatment (Article 29)

Legal Citation: Companies Act 1993
                               Financial Reporting Act 1993

Description: Overseas companies are required to prepare audited financial statements on an annual basis. Legislation also requires financial statements in relation to an overseas company's New Zealand business. The following companies are required to deliver annual audited financial statements to the Registrar of Companies for registration:

a)   issuers – i.e. those who have raised capital from the New Zealand public ;

b)   overseas companies;

c)   subsidiaries of companies or bodies corporate incorporated outside New Zealand;

d)   companies in which 25 per cent or more of the shares are held or controlled by:

(i)   a subsidiary of a company or body corporate incorporated outside New Zealand or a subsidiary of that subsidiary;

(ii)   a company or body corporate incorporated outside New Zealand;

(iii)   a person not ordinarily resident in New Zealand.

F.   All Sectors

Type of Limitation: National treatment (Article 29)

Legal Citation:

Description: More favourable treatment may be accorded to New Zealand nationals and permanent residents in the form of incentives or other programmes to help develop local entrepreneurs and assist local companies to expand and upgrade their operations.

G.   Services

Type of Limitation   National treatment (Article 29)
                              Most favoured nation status (Article 28)

Legal Citation:

Description: 1   Most favoured nation status and national treatment shall not apply where a services sector is not scheduled under Part 5.

2   Where a services sector is scheduled under Part 5, the terms, limitations, conditions and qualifications stated therein shall apply to investments in that sector.

3   Any horizontal commitments, limitations, conditions and qualifications scheduled under Part 5 shall apply to investments in the services sector concerned.

DESCRIPTION OF THE OVERSEAS INVESTMENT REGIME

1   The following is a brief, non legally binding, description of the criteria applied to overseas investment that requires approval under New Zealand's Overseas Investment Act 1973 and the Fisheries Act 1996. The criteria may be adjusted or replaced from time to time by Government legislation, regulation or policy setting. A more detailed description of the criteria is set out in the Overseas Investment Regulations 1995.

Non-Land (Prudential Criteria)

2   Ministers must be satisfied that prospective investors:

a)   have business experience and acumen;

b)   demonstrate a financial commitment to the investment;

c)   are of good character and do not have a criminal record that would prevent them from obtaining permanent residence in New Zealand.

Land and Fishing Quota

3   In addition to the applicable prudential criteria, in order to approve overseas investment in specific non-farm land and fishing quota, Ministers must consider whether the investment is in the national interest. In doing so, Ministers shall have regard to whether the investment is likely to result in:

a)   the creation of new job opportunities in New Zealand, or the retention of existing jobs in New Zealand that would otherwise be lost;

b)   the introduction to New Zealand of new technology or business skills;

c)   the development of new export markets, or increased export market access for New Zealand exporters;

d)   added market competition, greater efficiency, greater productivity, or enhanced domestic services, in New Zealand;

e)   the introduction of additional investment for development purposes;

f)   increased processing in New Zealand of primary products;

g)   in the case of an investment in land, whether an individual intends to reside permanently in New Zealand.

Additional Requirements for Farm Land

4   In addition to the prudential criteria, approval of overseas investment in farm land requires that the farm land has been offered for sale or acquisition on the open market to New Zealanders. Farm land is defined as land used exclusively or principally for the purpose of agricultural, horticultural, or pastoral purposes, or for the keeping of bees, poultry or livestock.

5   To approve overseas investment in farm land Ministers must also consider whether the overseas investment in farm land is in the national interest and likely to result in "substantial and identifiable benefits" to New Zealand. Ministers must have regard to the same matters as for fishing quota and other land and investment, as well as:

a)   whether experimental or research work will be carried out on the land;

b)   the proposed use of the land; and

c)   whether the overseas investor intends to farm the land for his or her own use and benefit, and is capable of doing so.

ANNEX 3.2

Limitations of Singapore

A.   <u>Services</u>

Type of Limitation: Most favoured nation status (Article 28)

Most favoured nation status (Article 28)

National treatment (Article 29)

Legal Citation:

Description: 1   Most favoured nation status and national treatment shall not apply where a services sector is not scheduled under Part 5.

2   Where a services sector is scheduled under Part 5, the terms, limitations, conditions and qualifications stated therein shall apply to investments in that sector.

3   Any horizontal commitments, limitations, conditions and qualifications scheduled under Part 5 shall apply to investments in the services sector concerned.

B.   All Sectors

Type of Limitation: National treatment (Article 29)

Legal Citation:

Description: More favourable treatment may be accorded to Singapore nationals and permanent residents in the form of incentives or other programmes to help develop local entrepreneurs/technopreneurs and assist local companies to expand and upgrade their operations.

C.   All Sectors

Type of Limitation: National treatment (Article 29)

Legal Citation: Companies Act, Cap 50 (1994)

Description: Compliance by Foreign Companies with the Companies Act as in establishing, reporting and filing of accounts.

a)   Commercial presence, right of establishment and movement of juridical persons are subject to compliance with the following provisions:

(i)   a foreigner who wishes to register a business firm must have a local manager who should be:

A)   a Singapore citizen;
B)   a Singapore permanent resident;
C)   a Singapore employment pass holder; or
D)   a dependent's pass holder and have written permission from the Singapore Immigration and Registration (SIR).

Provided that a foreigner who is a Singapore permanent resident or a Singapore employment pass holder or a dependent's pass holder with written permission from SIR can register a business without appointing a local manager;

ii)   every company must have at least 2 directors, and one of whom must be locally resident;

iii)   all branches of foreign companies registered in Singapore must have at least 2 locally resident agents. (To qualify as locally resident, a person should be either a Singapore citizen or Singapore permanent resident or Singapore employment pass holder or dependent's pass holder with written permission from SIR);

b)   establishment of a foreign company's branch is subject to the filing of necessary documents.

D.   All Sectors

Type of Limitation: National treatment (Article 29)

Legal Citation: Banking Act, Cap 19 (1985)
Directive on Housing Loans to Financial Institutions issued by the Monetary Authority of Singapore (MAS)
Residential Property Act, Cap 274 (1985)

Description: 1   Ownership of land:

a)   non-citizens cannot own land.

2   Ownership of property:

a)   non-citizens are restricted from purchasing landed property and residential property in a building of less than 6 levels;

b)   there are also restrictions on non-citizens owning Housing & Development Board (HDB) flats;

3   Housing loans:

a)   banks are:

(i)   not allowed to extend Singapore Dollar (S$) loans to non-Singapore citizens (excluding permanent residents) and non-Singapore companies for the purpose of purchasing residential properties in Singapore. A company incorporated outside Singapore or majority-owned by non-Singapore citizens and/or permanent residents is considered a non-Singapore company;

(ii)   allowed to extend only one S$ loan to permanent residents for the purchase of residential property which must be owner-occupied.

E.   All Sectors

Type of Limitation: National treatment (Article 29)

Legal Citation: Banking Act, Cap 19 (1985)

MAS Notice No. 757

Description: 1   Banks are not allowed to extend S$ credit facilities to non-residents[1] for the following purposes:

a)   speculating in the S$ currency and interest rate markets;

b)   financing third-party trade between countries not involving Singapore;

---

[1]   For the purposes of this MAS Notice 757, Singapore residents are: (i) Singapore citizens; (ii) individuals who are Singapore tax-residents; (iii) companies incorporated in Singapore which are jointly-owned or majority-owned by Singapore citizens; or (iv) overseas subsidiaries which are jointly-owned or majority-owned by Singapore citizens. All other persons are considered non-residents

c)   financing the acquisition of shares of companies not listed on the Stock Exchange of Singapore or Central Limit Order Book (CLOB);

d)   financing activities outside Singapore except when approved by MAS.

2   Banks must consult MAS before extending S\$ credit facilities to non-residents[22] for, inter alia:

a)   amounts exceeding S\$5 million for financing investments such as shares, bonds, deposits, and commercial properties;

b)   amounts exceeding S\$20 million via repurchase agreements of Singapore Government Securities with full delivery of collateral; and

c)   all activities not explicitly mentioned in the MAS Notice 757.

F.   <u>Printing & Publishing Manufacture & Repair of Transport Equipment Power/Energy</u>

Type of Limitation: National treatment (Article 29)

Legal Citation:

Description: More favourable treatment may be accorded to Singapore nationals and permanent residents in the above sectors.

G.   <u>Privatisation</u>

Type of Limitation: National treatment (Article 29)

Legal Citation:

Description: More favourable treatment may be accorded to Singapore nationals and permanent residents in respect of ownership of enterprises currently in Government ownership.

H.   <u>Government-Linked Companies</u>

Type of Limitation: Most favoured nation status (Article 28)

National treatment (Article 29)

Legal Citation:

Description: 1   Most favoured nation status and national treatment shall not apply to any corporate entities in which the Singapore Government is the majority shareholder or has a special share. Such corporate entities shall be permitted to limit the participation of foreign capital in terms of maximum percentage limit on foreign shareholding or the total value of individual or aggregate foreign investment.

2   The term 'special share' whether created by a corporate entity's articles of association, or by domestic law or administrative action, includes a paid-up share or any other share (whether ordinary, equity or otherwise) and any share that has

special voting or veto rights in respect of or entitles the holder to give or withhold consent or object to:

a)   the disposal of the whole or substantial part of the corporate entity's undertaking;

b)   the acquisition by any person of any specified percentage of the issued share capital of the corporate entity;

c)   the appointment of the board of directors, management and/or executive staff of the corporate entity;

d)   the winding up or dissolution of the corporate entity; or

e)   any change to the memorandum of association and/or articles of association of a corporate entity relating to the issue, ownership, transfer, cancellation and acquisition of shares of the corporate entity, appointment and dismissal of the board of directors, management and/or executive staff of the corporate entity.

I.   Manufacturing Sector

Type of Limitation: Most favoured nation status (Article 28)

National treatment (Article 29)

Legal Citation: Control of Manufacture Act, Cap 57 (1985)

Description: Statutory licensing requirements for the manufacture of goods, such as:

a)   firecrackers;
b)   drawn steel products;
c)   pig iron and sponge iron;
d)   rolled steel products;
e)   steel ingots, billets, blooms and slabs;
f)   beer and stout;
g)   CD, CD-ROM, VCD;
h)   DVD, DVD-ROM;
i)   chewing gum, bubble gum, dental chewing gum or any like substance;
j)   cigarettes;
k)   matches;
l)   cigars.

*   *   *

FREE TRADE AGREEMENT BETWEEN THE GOVERNMENT OF CANADA AND THE GOVERNMENT OF THE REPUBLIC OF COSTA RICA[*]
[excerpts]

> The Free Trade Agreement between the Government of Canada and the Government of the Republic of Costa Rica was signed on 23 April 2001.

PART THREE: SERVICES AND INVESTMENT

Chapter VIII: Services and Investment

Article VIII.1 General provisions

1.   The Parties recognise the increasing importance of trade in services and investment in their economies. In their efforts to gradually develop and broaden their relations, the Parties will co-operate in the WTO and plurilateral fora, with the aim of creating the most favourable conditions for achieving further liberalisation and additional mutual opening of markets for trade in services and investment.

2.   With a view to developing and deepening their relations under this Agreement, the Parties agree that within 3 years of the date of entry into force, they will review developments related to trade in services and investment, and consider the need for further disciplines in these areas.

3.   Upon request of either Party, the other Party shall endeavour to provide information on measures that may have an impact on trade in services and investment.

Article VIII.2 Investment

The Parties note the existence of the Agreement between the Government of Canada and the Government of Costa Rica for the Promotion and Protection of Investments, signed in San José, Costa Rica, on March 18, 1998 (APPI).

Article VIII.3 Services

1.   The Parties herein recognize the importance of their rights and obligations assumed in the General Agreement on Trade in Services (GATS).

2.   (a)   The Parties to this Agreement shall encourage bodies responsible for the regulation of professional services in their respective territories to:

---

[*]   Source: The Government of Canada and the Government of Costa Rica (2001). "Free Trade Agreement between the Government of Canada and the Government of the Republic of Costa Rica"; available on the Internet (http://www.sice.oas.org/Trade/cancr/English/cancr19e.asp#p3c8arVIII.1). [Note added by the editor.]

(i)   ensure that measures relating to the licensing or certification of nationals of the other Party are based on objective and transparent criteria, such as competence and the ability to provide a service; and

(ii)   cooperate with the view to developing mutually acceptable standards and criteria for licensing and certification of professional service providers.

(b)   The following elements may be examined with regard to the standards and criteria referred to in subparagraph (a)(ii):

    (i)   education - accreditation of schools or academic programs;

    (ii)   examinations - qualifying examinations for licensing, including alternative methods of assessment such as oral examinations and interviews;

    (iii)   experience - length and nature of experience required for licensing;

    (iv)   conduct and ethics - standards of professional conduct and the nature of disciplinary action for non-conformity with those standards;

    (v)   professional development and re-certification - continuing education and ongoing requirements to maintain professional certification;

    (vi)   scope of practice - extent of, or limitations on, permissible activities;

    (vii)   local knowledge - requirements for knowledge of such matters as local laws, regulations, language, geography or climate; and

    (vii)   consumer protection - alternatives to residency requirements, including bonding, professional liability insurance and client restitution funds, to provide for the protection of consumers.

(b)   These bodies should report on the result of their discussions related to the development of mutually acceptable standards mentioned in subparagraph (a)(ii) and, as appropriate, provide any recommendations to the Coordinators.

(c)   With respect to the recognition of qualification and licensing requirements, the Parties note the existence of rights and obligations with respect to each other under Article VII of the GATS.

(d)   For the purpose of this paragraph, professional services means services, the provision of which requires specialized post-secondary education, or equivalent training or experience, and for which the right to practice is granted or restricted by a Party, but does not include services provided by trades-persons or vessel and aircraft crew members.

*   *   *

PART FOUR

INVESTMENT-RELATED PROVISIONS IN ASSOCIATION AGREEMENTS, BILATERAL AND INTERREGIONAL COOPERATION AGREEMENTS

AGREEMENT ON TRADE, DEVELOPMENT AND COOPERATION BETWEEN THE EUROPEAN COMMUNITY AND ITS MEMBER STATES, OF THE ONE PART, AND THE REPUBLIC OF SOUTH AFRICA, OF THE OTHER PART *
[excerpts]

The Agreement on Trade, Development and Cooperation between the European Community and Its Member States, of the One Part, and the Republic of South Africa, of the Other Part was signed at Pretoria on 11 October 1999. It entered into force on 1 January 2000. The member States of the European Community are: Austria, Belgium, Denmark, Finland, France, Germany, Greece, Ireland, Italy, Luxembourg, the Netherlands, Portugal, Spain, Sweden and the United Kingdom.

TITLE III

TRADE RELATED ISSUES

SECTION B

RIGHT OF ESTABLISHMENT AND SUPPLY OF SERVICES

Article 29

Reconfirmation of GATS obligations

1.   In recognition of the growing importance of services for the development of their economies, the Parties underline the importance of strict observance of the General Agreement on Trade in Services (GATS), in particular its principle on most-favoured-nation treatment, and including its applicable protocols with annexed commitments.

2.   In accordance with the GATS, this treatment shall not apply to:

   (a)   advantages accorded by either Party under the provisions of an agreement as defined in Article V of the GATS or under measures adopted on the basis of such an agreement;

   (b)   other advantages accorded pursuant to the list of most-favoured-nation exemptions annexed by either Party to the GATS.

3.   The Parties reaffirm their respective commitments as annexed to the fourth Protocol to the GATS concerning basic telecoms and the fifth Protocol concerning financial services.

---

* *Source*: European Communities (1999). "Agreement on Trade, Development and Cooperation between the European Community and Its Member States, of the One Part, and the Republic of South Africa, of the Other Part", *Official Journal of the European Communities*, L 311, 04 December 1999, pp. 3- 297; available also on the Internet (http://europa.eu.int/eur-lex//en/lif/dat/1999/en_299A1204_02.html). [Note added by the editor.]

Article 30
Further liberalisation of supply of services

1.   The Parties will endeavour to extend the scope of the Agreement with a view to further liberalising trade in services between the Parties. In the event of such an extension, the liberalisation process shall provide for the absence or elimination of substantially all discrimination between the Parties in the services sectors covered and should cover all modes of supply including the supply of a service:

    (a)   from the territory of one Party into the territory of the other;

    (b)   in the territory of one Party to the service consumer of the other;

    (c)   by a service supplier of one Party, through commercial presence in the territory of the other;

    (d)   by a service supplier of one Party, through presence of natural persons of that Party in the territory of the other.

2.   The Cooperation Council shall make the necessary recommendations for the implementation of the objective set out in paragraph 1.

3.   When formulating these recommendations, the Cooperation Council shall take into account the experience gained by the implementation of the obligations of each Party under the GATS, with particular reference to Article V generally and especially paragraph 3(a) thereof covering the participation of developing countries in liberalisation agreements.

4.   The objective set out in paragraph 1 shall be subject to a first examination by the Cooperation Council at the latest five years after the entry into force of this Agreement.

SECTION C

CURRENT PAYMENTS AND MOVEMENT OF CAPITAL

Article 32
Current payments

1.   Subject to the provisions of Article 34, the Parties undertake to allow all payments for current transactions between residents of the Community and of South Africa to be made in freely convertible currency.

2.   South Africa may take the necessary measures to ensure that the provisions of paragraph 1, which liberalise current payments, are not used by its residents to make unauthorised capital outflows.

Article 33
Capital movements

1.   With regard to transactions on the capital account of balance of payments, the Community and South Africa shall ensure, from the entry into force of this Agreement, that capital relating to direct investments in South Africa in companies formed in accordance with current laws can move freely, and that such investment and any profit stemming therefrom can be liquidated and repatriated.

2.   The Parties shall consult each other with a view to facilitating and eventually achieving full liberalisation of the movement of capital between the Community and South Africa.

Article 34
Balance of payment difficulties

Where one or more Member States of the Community, or South Africa, is in serious balance of payments difficulties, or under threat thereof, the Community or South Africa, as the case may be, may, in accordance with the conditions established under the General Agreement on Tariffs and Trade and Articles VIII and XIV of the Articles of Agreement of the International Monetary Fund, adopt restrictions on current transactions which shall be of limited duration and may not go beyond what is necessary to remedy the balance of payments situation. The Community or South Africa, as the case may be, shall inform the other Party forthwith and shall submit to it as soon as possible a timetable for the elimination of the measures concerned.

SECTION D

COMPETITION POLICY

Article 35
Definition

The following are incompatible with the proper functioning of this Agreement, in so far as they may affect trade between the Community and South Africa:

(a)   agreements and concerted practices between firms in horizontal relationships, decisions by associations of firms, and agreements between firms in vertical relationships, which have the effect of substantially preventing or lessening competition in the territory of the Community or of South Africa, unless the firms can demonstrate that the anti-competitive effects are outweighed by pro-competitive ones;

(b)   abuse by one or more firms of market power in the territory of the Community or of South Africa as a whole or in a substantial part thereof.

Article 36
Implementation

If, at the entry into force of this Agreement, either Party has not yet adopted the necessary laws and regulations for the implementation of Article 35, in their jurisdictions it shall do so within a period of three years.

Article 37
Appropriate measures

If the Community or South Africa considers that a particular practice in its domestic market is incompatible with the terms of Article 35, and:

(a)   is not adequately dealt with under the implementing rules referred to in Article 36, or

(b)   in the absence of such rules, and if such practice causes or threatens to cause serious prejudice to the interests of the other Party or material injury to its domestic industry, including its services industry, the Party concerned may take appropriate measures consistent with its own laws, after consultation within the Cooperation Council, or after 30 working days following referral for such consultation. The appropriate measures to be taken shall respect the powers of the Competition Authority concerned.

Article 38
Comity

1.   The Parties agree that, whenever the Commission or the South African Competition Authority has reason to believe that anti-competitive practices, defined under Article 35, are taking place within the territory of the other authority and are substantially affecting important interests of the Parties, it may request the other Party's competition authority to take appropriate remedial action in terms of that authority's rules governing competition.

2.   Such a request shall not prejudice any action under the requesting authority's competition laws that may be deemed necessary and shall not in any way encumber the addressed authority's decision-making powers or its independence.

3.   Without prejudice to its respective functions, rights, obligations or independence, the competition authority so addressed shall consider and give careful attention to the views expressed and documentation provided by the requesting authority and, in particular, pay heed to the nature of the anti-competitive activities in question, the firm or firms involved, and the alleged harmful effect on the important interests of the aggrieved Party.

4.   When the Commission or the Competition Authority of South Africa decides to conduct an investigation or intends to take any action that may have important implications for the interests of the other Party, the Parties must consult, at the request of either Party and both shall endeavour to find a mutually acceptable solution in the light of their respective important interests, giving due regard to each other's laws, sovereignty, the independence of the respective competition authorities and to considerations of comity.

Article 39
Technical assistance

The Community shall provide South Africa with technical assistance in the restructuring of its competition law and policy, which may include among others:

(a)   the exchange of experts;

(b)   organisation of seminars;

(c)   training activities.

Article 40
Information

The Parties shall exchange information taking into account the limitations imposed by the requirements of professional and business secrecy.

SECTION F

OTHER TRADE-RELATED PROVISIONS

Article 45
Government procurement

1.   The Parties agree to cooperate to ensure that access to the Parties' procurement contracts is governed by a system which is fair, equitable and transparent.

2.   The Cooperation Council shall periodically review the progress made in this matter.

Article 46
Intellectual property

1.   The Parties shall ensure adequate and effective protection of intellectual property rights in conformity with the highest international standards. The Parties apply the WTO Agreement on Trade Related Aspects of Intellectual Property Rights (TRIPs) from 1 January 1996 and undertake to improve, where appropriate, the protection provided for under that Agreement.

2.   If problems in the area of intellectual property protection affecting trading conditions were to occur, urgent consultations shall be undertaken, at the request of either Party, with a view to reaching mutually satisfactory solutions.

3.   The Community and its Member States confirm the importance they attach to the obligations arising from the:

     (a)   Protocol to the Madrid Agreement concerning the International Registration of Marks (Madrid 1989);

     b)   International Convention for the Protection of Performers, Producers of Phonogram and Broadcasting Organisations (Rome 1961);

     (c)   Patent Cooperation Treaty (Washington 1979 as amended and modified in 1984).

4.   Without prejudice to the obligations arising from the WTO Agreement on TRIPs, South Africa could favourably consider accession to the multilateral conventions referred to in paragraph 3.

5.   The Parties confirm the importance they attach to the following instruments:

(a)   the provisions of the Nice Agreement concerning the International Classification of Goods and Services for the Purposes of the Registration of Marks (Geneva 1977 and amended in 1979);

(b)   Berne Convention for the Protection of Literary and Artistic Works (Paris Act, 1971);

(c)   International Convention for the Protection of New Varieties of Plants (UPOV) (Geneva Act, 1978);

(d)   Budapest Treaty on the International Recognition of the Deposit of Micro-organisms for the Purposes of Patent Procedure (1977 modified in1980);

(e)   Paris Convention for the Protection of Industrial Property (Stockholm Act, and amended in 1979) WIPO;

(f)   WIPO Copyright Treaty (WCT), 1996.

6.   In order to facilitate the implementation of this Article, the Community may provide, on request and on mutually agreed terms and conditions, technical assistance to South Africa in, among other things, the preparation of laws and regulations for the protection and enforcement of intellectual property rights, the prevention of the abuse of such rights, the establishment and reinforcement of domestic offices and other agencies involved in enforcement and protection, including the training of personnel.

7.   The Parties agree that for the purpose of this Agreement, intellectual property includes in particular copyright, including the copyright on computer programmes and neighbouring rights, utility models, patents, including biotechnical inventions, industrial designs, geographical indications, including appellations of origin, trade marks and service marks, topographies of integrated circuits, as well as the legal protection of databases and the protection against unfair competition as referred to in Article 10 bis of the Paris Convention for the Protection of Industrial Property and protection of undisclosed information on know-how.

TITLE IV

ECONOMIC COOPERATION

Article 51
Industry

The aim of cooperation in this area is to facilitate the restructuring and modernisation of the South African industry while fostering its competitiveness and growth and to create conditions favourable to mutually beneficial cooperation between South African and Community industry.

The aim of the cooperation shall be, inter alia:

(a)   to encourage cooperation between the Parties' economic operators (companies, professionals, sectoral and other business organisations, organised labour, etc.);

(b)   to back the efforts of South Africa's public and private sectors to restructure and modernise industry, under conditions ensuring environmental protection, sustainable development and economic empowerment;

(c)   to foster an environment which favours private initiatives, with the aim of stimulating and diversifying output for the domestic and export markets;

(d)   to promote improved utilisation of South Africa's human resources and industrial potential through, inter alia, the facilitation of access to credit and investment finance and support to industrial innovation, technology transfer, training, research and technological development.

Article 52
Investment promotion and protection

Cooperation between the Parties shall aim to establish a climate which favours and promotes mutually beneficial investment, both domestic and foreign, especially through improved conditions for investment protection, investment promotion, the transfer of capital and the exchange of information on investment opportunities.

The aims of cooperation shall be, inter alia, to facilitate and encourage:

(a)   the conclusion, where appropriate, between the Member States and South Africa of agreements for the promotion and protection of investment;

(b)   the conclusion, where appropriate, between the Member States and South Africa of agreements to avoid double taxation;

(c)   the exchange of information on investment opportunities;

(d)   work towards harmonised and simplified procedures and administrative practices in the field of investment;

(e)   support, through appropriate instruments, the promotion and encouragement of investment in South Africa and in the Southern African region.

Article 63
Services

The Parties agree to foster cooperation in the services sector in general and in the area of banking, insurance and other financial services in particular, through, inter alia:

(a)   encouraging trade in services;

(b)   exchanging, where appropriate, information on rules, laws and regulations governing the services sector in the Parties;

(c)   improving accounting, auditing, supervision and regulation of financial services and financial monitoring, for example through the facilitation of training schemes.

*   *   *

AGREEMENT BETWEEN THE GOVERNMENT OF THE REPUBLIC OF TURKEY AND THE GOVERNMENT OF THE UNITED STATES OF AMERICA CONCERNING THE DEVELOPMENT OF TRADE AND INVESTMENT RELATIONS[*]

The Agreement between the Government of the Republic of Turkey and the Government of the United States of America Concerning the Development of Trade and Investment Relations was signed on 29 September 1999. It entered into force on 11 February 2000.

The Government of the Republic of Turkey and the Government of the United States of America (individually a "Party" and collectively the (Parties"):

1)   .   Desiring to enhance the partnership, friendship, and spirit of cooperation between the two countries;

2)   Desiring to develop further both countries' international trade and economic interrelationship;

3)   Taking into account the membership of both countries in the World Trade Organization (WTO), and noting that this Agreement is without prejudice to the rights and obligations of the Parties under the Marrakech Agreement Establishing the World Trade Organization and the agreements, understandings, and other instruments relating thereto or concluded under the auspices of the WTO;

4)   Recognizing the importance of fostering an open and predictable environment for international trade and investment;

5)   Recognizing the benefits to each Party resulting from increased international trade and investment, and that trade-distorting investment measures and protectionism would deprive the Parties of such benefits;

6)   Recognizing the essential role of private investment, both domestic and foreign, in furthering growth, creating jobs, expanding trade, improving technology and enhancing economic development;

7)   Recognizing that foreign direct investment confers positive benefits on each Party;

8)   Acknowledging previous Agreements between the Republic of Turkey and the United States, and noting that this Agreement is without prejudice to the rights and obligations of the Parties under such Agreements;

---

[*]   *Source*: The Government of the United States and the Government of Turkey (1999). "Agreement between the Government of the Republic of Turkey and the Government of the United States of America Concerning the Development of Trade and Investment Relations", *Official Gazette of the Government of Turkey No. 23961, 11 February 2000*; available also on the Internet (http://www.turkey.org/business/TIFA-E.htm). [Note added by the editor.]

9)   Recognizing the increased importance of services in their economies and in their bilateral relations;

10)   Recognizing the need to eliminate non-tariff barriers in order to facilitate greater access to the markets of both countries;

11)   Recognizing the importance of providing adequate and effective protection and enforcement of intellectual property rights and of adherence to intellectual property rights conventions;

12)   Recognizing the significance to both countries' economic welfare of working toward the observance and promotion of internationally recognized core labor standards based on the principles underlying core ILO Conventions.

13)   Desiring to ensure that trade and environmental policies are mutually supportive in furtherance of sustainable development;

14)   Desiring to encourage and facilitate private sector contacts between the two countries;

15)   Recognizing the principles set forth in the Joint Communique of the Turkey-U.S. Joint Economic Commission of October 20-21, 1998 and the Memorandum of Understanding on establishing a mechanism of commercial consultation signed in Ankara on January 28,1998;

16)   Considering that it would be in their mutual interest to establish a bilateral mechanism to explore methods to liberalize trade and investment, including the negotiation of agreements to facilitate freer trade.

To this end, the Parties agree as follows:

ARTICLE ONE

The Parties affirm their desire to expand trade in products and services consistent with the terms of this Agreement. They shall take appropriate measures to encourage and facilitate in a mutually beneficial way the exchange of goods and services and to secure favorable conditions for long-term development and diversification of trade between their respective nationals and companies.

ARTICLE TWO

The Parties shall establish a Turkey-United States Council on Trade and Investment, "the Council," which shall be composed of representatives of both Parties. The Turkish side will be chaired by the Undersecretariat of Foreign Trade; and the U.S. side will be chaired by Office of the U.S. Trade Representative (USTR). Both Parties may be assisted by officials of other government entities as circumstances require. The Council will meet at least once a year on mutually accepted dates.

ARTICLE THREE

The objectives of the Council are to hold consultations on specific trade and investment matters of interest to the Parties; to identify agreements appropriate for negotiation; and to identify and work toward the removal of impediments to trade and investment.

ARTICLE FOUR

For the purpose of further developing bilateral trade and providing for a steady increase in the exchange of products and services, the Parties shall consider whether further agreements relating to trade, taxation, intellectual property, investment, labor and environmental issues and to any other matters agreed upon by the Parties would be desirable.

ARTICLE FIVE

1.   Either Party may raise for consultation between the Parties any investment matter not arising under the Treaty between the Parties concerning the Reciprocal Encouragement and Protection of Investments, signed in Washington on December 3, 1985, "the Investment Treaty", or any trade matter. Requests for consultation shall be accompanied by a written explanation of the subject to be discussed and consultations shall be held within 30 days of the request, unless the requesting Party agrees to a later date.

2.   This Agreement shall be without prejudice to the rights of either Party under its domestic law or under any other instrument to which either country is a party.

ARTICLE SIX

The present Agreement shall enter into force on the date on which the Parties exchange notification that each has completed the legal procedures necessary for this purpose.

ARTICLE SEVEN

The Parties agree to formulate an action agenda for the Council within 30 days of the entry into force of this Agreement.

ARTICLE EIGHT

The present Agreement shall remain in force for a period of five (5) years and thereafter its validity shall be automatically extended on a yearly basis, unless a written notice of termination is given by either Party six (6) months prior to the end of any such period.

IN WITNESS WHEREOF, the undersigned, being duly authorized by their respective governments, have signed this Agreement.

DONE at Washington this 29th day of September 1999, in duplicate in the Turkish and English languages, both texts being equally authentic.

*   *   *

AGREEMENT BETWEEN THE GOVERNMENT OF THE UNITED STATES OF AMERICA AND THE ARAB REPUBLIC OF EGYPT CONCERNING THE DEVELOPMENT OF TRADE AND INVESTMENT RELATIONS[*]

> The Agreement between the Government of the United States of America and the Arab Republic of Egypt Concerning the Development of Trade and Investment Relations was signed on 1 July 1999. It entered into force on the date of signature.

The Government of the United States of America and the Government of the Arab Republic of Egypt (individually a "party" and collectively the "parties"):

1)   Desiring to enhance the partnership, friendship, and spirit of cooperation between the two countries;

2)   Desiring to develop further both countries' international trade and economic interrelationship;

3)   Taking into account the membership of both countries in the World Trade Organization (WTO), and noting that this agreement is without prejudice to the rights and obligations of the parties under the Marrakesh Agreement establishing the World Trade Organization and the agreements, understandings, and other instruments relating thereto or concluded under the auspices of the WTO;

4)   Recognizing the importance of fostering and open and predictable environment for international trade and investment;

5)   Recognizing the benefits to each party resulting from increased international trade and investment, and that trade-distorting investment measures and protectionism would deprive the parties of such benefits;

6)   Recognizing the essential role of private investment, both domestic and foreign, in furthering growth, creating jobs, expanding trade, improving technology and enhancing economic development;

7)   Recognizing that foreign direct investment confers positive benefits on each party;

8)   Taking into account the treaty between the parties concerning the reciprocal encouragement and protection of investments, signed at Washington on September 29, 1982, "The Investment Treaty," and noting that this Agreement is without prejudice to the rights and obligations of the parties under The Investment Treaty;

---

[*]   *Source*: The Government of the United States and the Government of Egypt (1999). "Agreement between the Government of the United States of America and the Arab Republic of Egypt Concerning the Development of Trade and Investment Relations"; available on the Internet (http://www.usis.egnet.net/usis/agree1.htm). [Note added by the editor.]

9)   Recognizing the increased importance of services in their economies and in bilateral relations;

10)   Acknowledging the need to eliminate non-tariff barriers in order to facilitate greater access to the markets of both countries;

11)   Recognizing the importance of providing adequate and effective protection and enforcement of intellectual property rights and of adherence to the intellectual property rights conventions;

12)   Recognizing the significance to both countries' economic welfare of working toward the observance and promotion of internationally recognized core labor standards;

13)   Desiring to ensure that trade and environmental policies are mutually supportive in furtherance of sustainable development;

14)   Desiring to encourage and facilitate private sector contracts between the two countries;

15)   Recognizing the views mutually expressed in the Joint Statement of the U.S. Egyptian Partnership for Economic Growth and Development of May 3, 1998;

16)   Considering that it would be in their mutual interest to establish a bilateral mechanism to explore methods to liberalize trade and investment, including the negotiations of agreements to facilitate freer trade;

To this end, the parties agree as follows:

Article One

The parties affirm their desire to expand trade in products and services consistent with the terms of this agreement. They shall take appropriate measures to encourage and facilitate the exchange of goods and services and to secure favorable conditions for long-term development and diversification of trade between their respective nationals and companies.

Article Two

The parties shall establish a United States-Egypt Council on Trade and Investment which shall be composed of representatives of both parties. The Egyptian side be will chaired by the Ministry of Trade and Supply; and the U.S. side will be chaired by the office of the U.S. Trade Representative (USTR). Both parties will be assisted by officials of other government entities as circumstances require. The council will meet at such times as agreed by the two parties.

Article Three

The objectives of this Council are to hold consultations on specific trade matters, and those investment matters not arising under The Investment Treaty, of interest to the parties; to identify agreements appropriate for negotiation; and to identify and work toward the removal of impediments to trade and investment flows.

Article Four

For the purpose of further developing bilateral trade and providing for a steady increase in the exchange of products and services, the parties shall consider whether further agreements relating to trade, taxation, intellectual property and investment issues would be desirable.

Article Five

1)   Either party may raise for consultation between the parties any investment matter not arising under The Investment Treaty or any trade matter. Requests for consultations shall be accompanied by a written explanation of the subject to be discussed and consultations shall be held within 30 days of the request, unless the requesting party agrees to a later date.

2)   This Agreement shall be without prejudice to the rights of either party under its domestic law or under any other instrument to which either country is a party.

Article Six

This Agreement shall enter into force on the date of its signature by both parties.

Article Seven

This Agreement shall remain in force unless terminated by mutual consent of the parties or by either party upon six months written notice to the other party.

In witness thereof, the undersigned, being duly authorized by their respective governments, have signed this Agreement.

Done at Washington, D.C. this 1st day of July, 1999, in duplicate in the English and Arabic languages, both texts being equally authentic.

*   *   *

INVESTMENT INCENTIVE AGREEMENT BETWEEN THE GOVERNMENT OF THE UNITED STATES OF AMERICA AND THE ARAB REPUBLIC OF EGYPT[*]

The Investment Incentive Agreement between the Government of the United States of America and the Arab Republic of Egypt was signed on 1 July 1999. It entered into force on the date of signature.

AFFIRMING their common desire to encourage economic activities in Egypt that promote the development of the economic resources and productive capacities of Egypt; and

RECOGNIZING that this objective can be promoted through investment support provided by the Overseas Private Investment Corporation ("OPIC"), a development institution and an agency of the United States of America, in the form of investment insurance and reinsurance, debt and equity investments and investment guaranties;

HAVE AGREED as follows:

ARTICLE I

As used in this Agreement, the following terms have the meanings herein provided. The term "Investment Support" refers to any debt or equity investment, any investment guaranty and any investment insurance or reinsurance which is provided by the Issuer in connection with a project in the territory of Egypt. The term "Issuer" refers to OPIC and any successor agency of the United States of America, and any agent of either. The term "Taxes" means all present and future taxes, levies, imposts, stamps, duties and charges, whether direct or indirect, imposed in Egypt and all liabilities with respect thereto.

ARTICLE 2

The two Governments confirm their understanding, that the Issuer's activities are governmental in nature and therefore:

(a) The Issuer shall not be subject to regulation under the laws of Egypt applicable to insurance or financial organizations, but, in the provision of Investment Support, shall be afforded all rights and have access to all remedies of any such entity, whether domestic, foreign or multilateral.

(b) The Issuer, all operations and activities undertaken by the Issuer in connection with any Investment Support, and all payments, whether of interest, principal, fees, dividends, premiums or the proceeds from the liquidation of assets or of any other nature, that are made, received or guaranteed by the Issuer in connection with any Investment Support shall be exempt from Taxes,

---

[*] *Source*: The Government of the United States and the Government of Egypt (1999). "Investment Incentive Agreement between the Government of the United States of America and the Arab Republic of Egypt"; available on the Internet (http://www.usis.egnet.net/usis/agree2.htm). [Note added by the editor.]

whether imposed directly on the Issuer or payable in the first instance by others. Neither projects receiving Investment Support nor investors in such projects shall be exempt from Taxes by operation of this Article, provided, however, that any Investment Support shall be accorded tax treatment no less favorable than that accorded to the investment support of any other national or multilateral development institution which operates in Egypt. The Issuer shall not be subject to Taxes in connection with any transfer, succession or other acquisition which occurs pursuant to paragraph (c) of this Article or Article 3(a) hereof, but obligations for Taxes previously accrued and unpaid with respect to interests received by the Issuer shall not be extinguished as a result of such transfer, succession or other acquisition.

(c)   If the Issuer makes a payment to any person or entity, or exercises its rights as a creditor or subrogee, in connection with any Investment Support, the Government of Egypt shall recognize the transfer to, or acquisition by, the Issuer of any cash, accounts, credits, instruments or other assets in connection with such payment or the exercise of such rights, as well as the succession of the Issuer to any right, title, claim, privilege or cause of action existing, or which may arise, in connection therewith.

(d)   With respect to any interests transferred to the Issuer or any interests to which the Issuer succeeds under this Article, the Issuer shall assert no greater rights than those of the person or entity from whom such interests were received, provided that nothing in this Agreement shall limit the right of the Government of the United States of America to assert a claim under international law in its sovereign capacity, as distinct from any rights it may have as the Issuer pursuant to paragraph (c) of this Article.

ARTICLE 3

(a)   Amounts in the currency of Egypt, including cash, accounts, credits, instruments or otherwise,- acquired by the Issuer upon making a payment, or upon the exercise of its rights as a creditor, in connection with any Investment Support provided by the Issuer for a project in Egypt, shall be accorded treatment in the territory of Egypt no less favorable as to use and conversion than the treatment to which such funds would have been entitled in the hands of the person or entity from which the Issuer acquired such amounts.

(b)   Such currency and credits may be transferred by the Issuer to any person or entity and upon such transfer shall be freely available for use by such person or entity in the territory of Egypt in accordance with its laws.

ARTICLE 4

(a)   Any dispute between the Government of the United States of America and the Government of the Arab Republic of Egypt regarding the interpretation of this Agreement or which, in the opinion of either party hereto, presents a question of international law arising out of any project or activity for which Investment Support has been provided shall be resolved, insofar as possible, through negotiations between the two Governments. If, six months following a request for negotiations hereunder, the two Governments have not resolved the dispute, the dispute, including the question of 'Whether such dispute presents a question of international law, shall be submitted, at the initiative of either Government, to an arbitral tribunal for resolution in accordance with paragraph (b) of this Article.

(b)   The arbitral tribunal referred to in paragraph (a) of this Article shall be established and shall function as follows:

(i)   Each Government shall appoint one arbitrator. These two arbitrators shall by agreement designate a president of the tribunal who shall be a citizen of a third state and whose appointment shall be subject to acceptance by the two Governments. The arbitrators shall be appointed within three months, and the president within six months, of the date of receipt of either Government's request for arbitration. If the appointments are not made within the foregoing time limits, either Government may, in the absence of any other agreement, request the Secretary-General of the International Centre for the Settlement of Investment Disputes to make the necessary appointment or appointments. Both Governments hereby agree to accept such appointment or appointments.

(ii)   Decisions of the arbitral tribunal shall be made by majority vote and shall be based on the applicable principles and rules of international law. Its decision shall be final and binding.

(iii)   During the proceedings, each Government shall bear the expense of its arbitrator and of its representation in the proceedings before the tribunal, whereas the expenses of the president and other costs of the arbitration shall be paid in equal parts by the two Governments. In its award, the arbitral tribunal may reallocate expenses and costs between the two Governments.

(iv)   In all other matters, the arbitral tribunal shall regulate its own procedures.

ARTICLE 5

(a)   This Agreement shall enter into force on the date of signature.

(b)   This Agreement shall continue in force until six months from the date of a receipt of a note by which one Government informs the other of its intent to terminate this Agreement. In such event, the provisions of this Agreement shall, with respect to Investment Support provided while this Agreement was in force, remain in force so long as such Investment Support remains outstanding, but in no case longer than twenty years after the termination of this Agreement.

IN WITNESS WHEREOF, the undersigned, duly authorized by their respective Governments, have signed this Agreement

DONE at Washington, District of Columbia, United States of America, on the 1st Day of July, 1999, in duplicate, in the English language.

*   *   *

AGREEMENT CONCERNING THE DEVELOPMENT OF TRADE AND INVESTMENT BETWEEN THE GOVERNMENT OF THE REPUBLIC OF SOUTH AFRICA AND THE GOVERNMENT OF THE UNITED STATES OF AMERICA[*]

The Agreement Concerning the Development of Trade and Investment between the Government of the Republic of South Africa and the Government of the United States of America was signed on 18 February 1999. It entered into force on the date of signature.

PREAMBLE

The Government of the Republic of South Africa and the Government of the United States of America (hereinafter referred to individually as a "Party" and jointly as the "Parties"):

1.   Inspired by the strong desire to strengthen the ties of friendship and cooperation existing between the Parties;

2.   Committed to achieving economic development and meaningful integration of developing countries into the global economy;

3.   Recognizing the benefits to each Party resulting from increased trade and investment;

4.   Determined to work towards greater well-being for their peoples, through increased trade and investment;

5.   Convinced of the importance of reinforcing the flow of trade in goods and services;

6.   Recognizing the important role of agriculture and agricultural trade between our two countries;

7.   Desiring to ensure that trade and environmental policies are mutually supportive in furtherance of economic growth and sustainable development;

8.   Recognizing that foreign direct investment confers benefits on each Party;

9.   Recognizing the value of fostering a favorable environment for trade and investment between the Parties, including through the elimination of impediments to trade and the provision of adequate and effective protection of intellectual property rights;

10.   Reaffirming their commitment to respect and promote the fundamental rights of workers in both countries, based on the core conventions of the International Labor Organization;

---

[*]   *Source*: The Government of the United States and the Government of South Africa (1999). "Agreement Concerning the Development of Trade and Investment between the Government of the Republic of South Africa and the Government of the United States of America"; available on the Internet (http://www.ustr.gov/regions/africa/tifasaus.htm). [Note added by the editor.]

11.   Noting the membership of both countries in the World Trade Organization and accepting that this Agreement is without prejudice to each Party's rights and obligations under the agreements, understandings, and other instruments related to or concluded under the auspices of the WTO;

12.   Recognizing the positive and constructive role of the Trade and Investment Committee (TIC) of the Bi-National Commission (BNC), co-chaired by the US Secretary of Commerce and the South African Minister of Trade and Industry, in enhancing economic ties between the two countries;

13.   Taking into account the need to eliminate non-tariff barriers in order to facilitate greater access to the markets of both countries;

14.   Reaffirming their desire to resolve trade and investment problems and disputes through consultation and dialogue;

HEREBY AGREE as follows:

Article One
OBJECTIVES

The Parties will seek to:

(1)   Expand trade in goods and services between them, within the framework and terms of this agreement.

(2)   Take appropriate measures to encourage and facilitate the exchange of goods and services, and to secure favorable conditions for long-term development and diversification of trade between the two countries.

(3)   Encourage private sector investment between the two countries, as a means of furthering growth, job creation, and economic development, and, to this end, will promote an open and predictable environment for investment and facilitate expanded contacts between their respective private sectors.

Article Two
COUNCIL ON TRADE AND INVESTMENT

(1)   The Parties will establish a Council on Trade and Investment (The Council) which will be composed of representatives of both Parties. South Africa's side will be chaired by a representative appointed by the Department of Trade and Industry (DTI). The United States of America's side will be chaired by the Office of the United States Trade Representative (USTR). Each Chair may work with officials from other Government entities as circumstances require.

(2)   The function of the Council will be to ensure the fulfilment of the objectives of this Agreement, as set out in Article One, and to provide a forum for consultation and dialogue on specific trade and investment matters of interest to the Parties, as well as for identifying and working towards the removal of impediments to trade and investment flows. In this connection,

the Council will build on the work of and, when both Parties consider it appropriate, consult or cooperate with the TIC of the BNC.

(3)   The Council will meet at such times as will be agreed by the Parties.

Article Three
CONSULTATION AND COOPERATION

(1)   Either Party may, whenever it considers it appropriate, consult the civil society in its country, such as business, labor, consumer, environmental and academic groups, on matters related to the work of the Council. Either Party may, when it considers it appropriate, present the views of its civil society at meetings of the Council.

(2)   For the purposes of providing for the further expansion of bilateral trade and investment flows, the Parties will consider whether further agreements relating to taxation, intellectual property, and trade and investment issues would be desirable.

(3)   Either Party may, at any time, raise for consultation any trade or investment matter between the Parties. Requests for consultation will be accompanied by a written explanation of the subject to be discussed, and the consultations will be held within a reasonable time, the venue for which will be agreed between the Parties.

Article Four
FINAL CLAUSES

(1)   This Agreement is without prejudice to the rights and obligations of either Party under its domestic law or under any other agreements, conventions or other instruments to which either country is a party.

(2)   This Agreement may be amended through an exchange of notes between the Parties through diplomatic channels.

(3)   The Agreement will enter into force on the date of its signature by both Parties and will remain in force unless terminated by mutual consent of the Parties, or by either Party upon six months' written notice to the other Party.

IN WITNESS WHEREOF, the undersigned, being duly authorized by their respective Governments, have signed this Agreement.

DONE in duplicate at Cape Town, on 18 February 1999, in the English language.

*   *   *

AGREEMENT BETWEEN THE GOVERNMENT OF THE UNITED STATES OF AMERICA AND THE GOVERNMENT OF THE REPUBLIC OF GHANA CONCERNING THE DEVELOPMENT OF TRADE AND INVESTMENT RELATIONS [*]

The Agreement between the Government of the United States of America and the Government of the Republic of Ghana Concerning the Development of Trade and Investment Relations was signed on 26 February 1999. It entered into force on the date of signature.

The Government of the United States of America and the Government of the Republic of Ghana (individually a "Party" and collectively the "Parties"):

1) ⸳ Desiring to enhance the friendship and spirit of cooperation between the two countries;

2) Desiring to develop further both countries' international trade and economic interrelationship;

3) Taking into account the participation of both countries in the World Trade Organization (WTO), and noting that this Agreement is without prejudice to the rights and obligations of the Parties under the Marrakesh Agreement Establishing the World Trade Organization and the agreements, understandings, and other instruments relating thereto or concluded under the auspices of the WTO;

4) Recognizing the importance of fostering an open and predictable environment for international trade and investment;

5) Recognizing that it is desirable that trade and investment problems between the Parties should be resolved by mutual agreement;

6) Recognizing the benefits to each Party resulting from increased international trade and investment, and that trade and investment barriers would deprive the Parties of such benefits;

7) Recognizing the essential role of private investment, both domestic and foreign, in furthering growth, creating jobs, expanding trade, improving technology and enhancing economic development;

8) Recognizing that foreign direct investment confers positive benefits on each Party;

9) Recognizing the increasing importance of services in their respective economies and in their bilateral relations;

---

[*] *Source*: The Government of the United States and the Government of Ghana (1999). "Agreement between the Government of the United States of America and the Government of the Republic of Ghana Concerning the Development of Trade and Investment Relations"; available on the Internet (http://www.ustr.gov/regions/africa/ghana.htm). [Note added by the editor.]

10)   Taking into account the need to eliminate non-tariff barriers in order to facilitate greater access to the markets of both countries;

11)   Recognizing the importance of providing adequate and effective protection and enforcement of intellectual property rights, and taking into account each Party's obligations contained in the Agreement on Trade-Related Aspects of Intellectual Property Rights (TRIPS) and in intellectual property rights conventions;

12)   Desiring to further secure the observance and promotion of internationally recognized core labor standards and workers' rights, given the contribution that these afford to the economic well being of both Parties;

13)   Desiring to ensure that trade and environmental policies are mutually supportive in furtherance of sustainable development; and

14)   Considering that it would be in their mutual interest to establish a bilateral mechanism between the Parties for encouraging the liberalization of trade and investment between them.

To this end, the Parties agree as follows:

ARTICLE ONE

The Parties affirm their desire to expand trade in products and services consistent with the terms of this Agreement. They will take appropriate measures to encourage and facilitate the exchange of goods and services and to secure favorable conditions for long-term development and diversification of trade between their respective nationals and companies.

ARTICLE TWO

The Parties will establish a United States - Ghana Council on Trade and Investment ("the Council") which will be composed of representatives of both Parties. The United States of America's side of the Council will be chaired by the Office of the United States Trade Representative (USTR), while the Republic of Ghana's side of the Council will be chaired by the Ministry of Trade and Industry. Each Chair may be assisted by officials of other government entities in their respective countries as circumstances require.

ARTICLE THREE

The objectives of the Council are to hold consultations on specific trade and investment matters of interest to the Parties and the enhancement of trade and investment flows. The Council will also work toward the removal of impediments to such trade and investment flows.

ARTICLE FOUR

The Council will meet at such times and venues as agreed by the Parties.

ARTICLE FIVE

Either Party may seek the views of civil society, such as business, labor, consumer, environmental, and academic groups, on matters related to the work of the Council whenever the Party considers it appropriate.

ARTICLE SIX

For the purposes of further developing bilateral trade and investment and providing for a steady increase in the exchange of goods and services, the Parties will consider whether further agreements relating to trade, taxation, intellectual property, labor, transfer of technology, technical cooperation, and investment issues would be desirable.

ARTICLE SEVEN

Either Party may raise for consultation any trade or investment matter between the Parties. Requests for consultation will be accompanied by a written explanation of the subject to be discussed and consultations will be held within 90 days from the date of the written explanation unless otherwise agreed by the Parties.

Where a Party's specific measure or practice is the subject of discussion, initial consultations will normally be held in the territory of that Party, unless otherwise agreed.

This Agreement will be without prejudice to the rights of either Party under its domestic law or under any other instrument to which either country is a party.

ARTICLE EIGHT

Either Party may request a revision of this Agreement by giving a written notice to the other Party. Such a request will be responded to within six months from the date of submission. No revision of this Agreement will be valid unless it is agreed to and signed by both Parties.

ARTICLE NINE

Any dispute between the Parties relating to the implementation and interpretation of this Agreement will be resolved through consultations and negotiations.

ARTICLE TEN

This Agreement will become effective on the date of its signature and will remain effective unless terminated by mutual consent of the Parties or by either Party upon six months' written notice to the other Party.

IN WITNESS WHEREOF, the undersigned, being duly authorized by their respective governments, have signed this Agreement.

Done in duplicate at Washington, D.C., this 26th day of February 1999.

*   *   *

AGREEMENT BETWEEN THE UNITED STATES OF AMERICA AND THE SOCIALIST REPUBLIC OF VIETNAM ON TRADE RELATIONS[*]
[excerpts]

The Agreement between the United States of America and the Socialist Republic of Vietnam on Trade Relations was signed on July 2000.

The Government of the United States of America and the Government of the Socialist Republic of Vietnam (hereinafter referred to collectively as "Parties" and individually as "Party"),

Desiring to establish and develop mutually beneficial and equitable economic and trade relations on the basis of mutual respect for their respective independence and sovereignty;

Acknowledging that the adoption of and compliance with international trade norms and standards by the Parties will aid the development of mutually beneficial trade relations, and should be the underlying basis of those relations;

Noting that Vietnam is a developing country at a low level of development, is in the process of economic transition and is taking steps to integrate into the regional and world economy by, inter alia, joining the Association of Southeast Asian Nations (ASEAN), the ASEAN Free Trade Area (AFTA), and the Asia Pacific Economic Cooperation forum (APEC), and working toward membership in the World Trade Organization (WTO);

Having agreed that economic and trade ties and intellectual property rights protection are an important and necessary element in the strengthening of their bilateral relations; and

Being convinced that an agreement on trade relations between the Parties will best serve their mutual interests,

Have agreed as follows:

---

[*] *Source*: The Government of the United States of America and the Government of Vietnam (2000). "Agreement between the United States of America and the Socialist Republic of Vietnam on Trade Relations"; available on the Internet (http://www.ivietnam.com/Eng/business/Laws/trade/printable/ English/agreement.htm). [Note added by the editor.]

CHAPTER IV

DEVELOPMENT OF INVESTMENT RELATIONS

Article 1
Definitions

For the purpose of this Chapter, Annex H, the exchanged letters on Investment Licensing Regime, and, with respect to a covered investment, Articles 1 and 4 of Chapter VII:

1. "investment" means every kind of investment in the territory of a Party owned or controlled directly or indirectly by nationals or companies of the other Party, and includes investment consisting or taking the form of:

   A. a company or enterprise;

   B. shares, stock, and other forms of equity participation, and bonds, debentures, and other forms of debt interests, in a company;

   C. contractual rights, such as under turnkey, construction or management contracts, production or revenue sharing contracts, concessions, or other similar contracts;

   D. tangible property, including real property, and intangible property, including rights, such as leases, mortgages, liens and pledges;

   E. intellectual property, including copyrights and related rights, trademarks, patents, layout designs (topographies) of integrated circuits, encrypted program-carrying satellite signals, confidential information (trade secrets), industrial designs and rights in plant varieties; and

   F. rights conferred pursuant to law, such as licenses and permits;

2. "company" means any entity constituted or organized under applicable law, whether or not for profit, and whether privately or governmentally owned or controlled, and includes a corporation, trust, partnership, sole proprietorship, branch, joint venture, association, or other organization;

3. "company of a Party" means a company constituted or organized under the laws of that Party;

4. "covered investment" means an investment of a national or company of a Party in the territory of the other Party;

5. "state enterprise" means a company owned, or controlled through ownership interests, by a Party;

6. "investment authorization" means an authorization granted by the foreign investment authority of a Party to a covered investment or a national or company of the other Party;

7.   "investment agreement" means a written agreement between the national authorities of a Party and a covered investment or a national or company of the other Party that (i) grants rights with respect to natural resources or other assets controlled by the national authorities and (ii) the investment, national or company relies upon in establishing or acquiring a covered investment;

8.   "UNCITRAL Arbitration Rules" means the arbitration rules of the United Nations Commission on International Trade Law;

9.   "national" of a Party means a natural person who is a national of a Party under its applicable law;

10.   an "investment dispute" is a dispute between a Party and a national or company of the other Party arising out of or relating to an investment authorization, an investment agreement or an alleged breach of any right conferred, created or recognized by this Chapter, Annex H, the exchanged letters on Investment Licensing Regime, and Articles 1 and 4 of Chapter VII with respect to a covered investment;

11.   "non-discriminatory" treatment means treatment that is at least as favorable as the better of national treatment or most favored nation treatment;

12.   "ICSID Convention" means the Convention on the Settlement of Investment Disputes between States and Nationals of Other States, done at Washington, March 18, 1965; and

13.   "Centre" means the International Centre for Settlement of Investment Disputes Established by the ICSID Convention.

Article 2
National Treatment and Most-Favored Nation Treatment

1.   With respect to the establishment, acquisition, expansion, management, conduct, operation and sale or other disposition of covered investments, each Party shall accord treatment no less favorable than that it accords, in like situations, to investments in its territory of its own nationals or companies (hereinafter "national treatment") or to investments in its territory of nationals or companies of a third country (hereinafter "most favored nation treatment"), whichever is most favorable (hereinafter "national and most favored nation treatment"). Each Party shall ensure that its state enterprises, in the provision of their goods or services, accord national and most favored nation treatment to covered investments, subject to the provisions of paragraph 4.3 of Annex H.

2.   A.   A Party may adopt or maintain exceptions to the obligations of paragraph 1 in the sectors or with respect to the matters specified in Annex H to this Agreement. In adopting such an exception, a Party may not require the divestment, in whole or in part, of covered investments existing at the time the exception becomes effective.

        B.   The obligations of paragraph 1 do not apply to procedures provided in multilateral agreements concluded under the auspices of the World Intellectual Property Organization relating to the acquisition or maintenance of intellectual property rights.

Article 3
General Standard of Treatment

1.   Each Party shall at all times accord to covered investments fair and equitable treatment and full protection and security, and shall in no case accord treatment less favorable than that required by applicable rules of customary international law.

2.   Each Party shall in no way impair by unreasonable and discriminatory measures the management, conduct, operation and sale or other disposition of covered investments.

Article 4
Dispute Settlement

1.   Each Party shall provide companies and nationals of the other Party with an effective means of asserting claims and enforcing rights with respect to covered investments.

2.   In the event of an investment dispute, the parties to the dispute should attempt to resolve the dispute through consultation and negotiation, which may include the use of non-binding third-party procedures. Subject to paragraph 3 of this Article, if the dispute has not been resolved through consultation and negotiations, a national or company of one Party that is a party to an investment dispute may submit the dispute for resolution under one of the following alternatives:

      A.   to the competent courts or administrative tribunals of the Party in the territory of which the covered investment has been made; or

      B.   in accordance with any applicable, previously agreed dispute-settlement procedures; or

      C.   in accordance with the terms of paragraph 3.

3.   A.   Provided that the national or company concerned has not submitted the dispute for resolution under sub-paragraph 2.A or B, and that ninety days have elapsed from the date on which the dispute arose, the national or company concerned may submit the dispute for settlement by binding arbitration:

      (i)   to the Centre, if both Parties are members of the ICSID Convention and the Centre is available; or

      (ii)   to the Additional Facility of the Centre, if the Additional Facility is available; or

      (iii)   in accordance with the UNCITRAL Arbitration Rules; or

      (iv)   if agreed by both parties to the dispute, to any other arbitration institution or in accordance with any other arbitration rules.

      B.   A national or company, notwithstanding that it may have submitted a dispute to binding arbitration under sub-paragraph 3.A, may seek interim injunctive relief, not involving the payment of damages, before the judicial or administrative tribunals of a Party, prior to the institution of the arbitral proceeding or during the proceeding, for the preservation of rights and interests.

4.   Each Party hereby consents to the submission of any investment dispute for settlement by binding arbitration in accordance with the choice of the national or company under sub-paragraph 3.A(i), (ii), (iii) or the mutual agreement of both parties to the dispute under sub-paragraph 3.A(iv). This consent and the submission of the dispute by a national or company under sub-paragraph 3.A shall satisfy the requirement of:

A.   Article II of the United Nations Convention on the Recognition and Enforcement of Foreign Arbitral Awards, done at New York, June 10, 1958, for an "agreement in writing;" and

B.   Chapter II of the ICSID Convention (Jurisdiction of the Centre) and the Additional Facility Rules for written consent of the parties to the dispute.

5.   Any arbitration under sub-paragraph 3.A(ii), (iii) and (iv) shall be held in a state that is a party to the United Nations Convention on the Recognition and Enforcement of Foreign Arbitral Awards, done at New York, June 10, 1958.

6.   Any arbitral award rendered pursuant to this Chapter shall be final and binding on the parties to the dispute. Each Party shall carry out without delay the provisions of any such award and provide in its territory for the enforcement of such award. Each Party's enforcement of an arbitral award issued in its territory shall be governed by its national law.

7.   In any proceeding involving an investment dispute, a Party shall not assert, as a defense, counterclaim, right of set-off, or for any other reason, that indemnification or other compensation for all or part of the alleged damages has been received or will be received pursuant to an insurance or guarantee contract.

8.   For the purposes of this Article and of Article 25(2)(b) of the ICSID Convention with respect to a covered investment, a company of a Party that, immediately before the occurrence of the event or events giving rise to an investment dispute, was a covered investment, shall be treated as a company of the other Party.

Article 5
Transparency

Each Party shall ensure that its laws, regulations and administrative procedures of general application that pertain to or affect investments, investment agreements, and investment authorizations are promptly published or otherwise made publicly available.

Article 6
Special Formalities

This Chapter shall not preclude a Party from prescribing special formalities in connection with covered investments, such as a requirement that such investments be legally constituted under the laws and regulations of that Party, or a requirement that transfers of currency or other monetary instruments be reported, provided that such formalities shall not impair the substance of any of the rights set forth in this Chapter, Annex H, the exchanged letters on Investment Licensing Regime, and, with respect to a covered investment, Articles 1 and 4 of Chapter VII.

Article 7
Technology Transfer

Neither Party shall mandate or enforce, as a condition for the establishment, acquisition, expansion, management, conduct or operation of a covered investment, any requirement (including any commitment or undertaking in connection with the receipt of a government permission or authorization) to transfer technology, a production process or other proprietary knowledge except:

1.   when applying generally applicable environmental laws that are consistent with the provisions of this Agreement; or

2.   pursuant to an order, commitment or undertaking that is enforced by a court, administrative tribunal or competition authority to remedy an alleged or adjudicated violation of competition laws.

Article 8
Entry, Sojourn and Employment of Aliens

1.   Each Party shall permit nationals and companies of the other Party to transfer employees of any nationality, subject to the Party's laws relating to the entry and sojourn of aliens, to their operations in the territory of the Party in the event that those employees are executives or managers or possess specialized knowledge relating to those operations.

2.   Each Party shall permit nationals and companies of the other Party to engage, within the territory of that Party, top managerial personnel of their choice, regardless of nationality, subject to the Party's laws relating to the entry and sojourn of aliens.

3.   The foregoing paragraphs shall not preclude a Party from applying its labor laws, so long as they do not impair the substance of the rights granted under this Article.

Article 9
Preservation of Rights

This Chapter, Annex H, the exchanged letters on Investment Licensing Regime, and, with respect to a covered investment, Articles 1 and 4 of Chapter VII, shall not derogate from any of the following that entitle covered investments in like situations to treatment more favorable than that accorded herein:

- laws, regulations and administrative procedures, or administrative or adjudicatory decisions of a Party;
- international legal obligations; or, obligations assumed by a Party, including those contained in an investment agreement or investment authorization.

Article 10
Expropriations and Compensation for War Damages

1.   Neither Party shall expropriate or nationalize investments either directly or indirectly through measures tantamount to expropriation or nationalization ("expropriation") except for a public purpose; in a non-discriminatory manner; upon payment of prompt, adequate and effective compensation; and in accordance with due process of law and the general principles of treatment provided for in Article 3. Compensation shall be equivalent to the fair market value of the expropriated investment immediately before the expropriatory action was taken; be paid without delay; include interest at a commercially reasonable rate from the date of expropriation; be fully realizable; and be freely transferable at the prevailing market rate of exchange on the date of expropriation. The fair market value shall not reflect any change in value occurring because the expropriatory action had become known before the date of expropriation.

Each Party shall accord national and most favored nation treatment to covered investments as regards any measure relating to losses that investments suffer in its territory owing to war or other armed conflict, revolution, state of national emergency, insurrection, civil disturbance, or similar events.

3.   Each Party shall accord restitution, or pay compensation in accordance with paragraph 1, in the event that covered investments suffer from losses in its territory, owing to war or other armed conflict, revolution, state of national emergency, insurrection, civil disturbance, or similar events, that result from:

    A.   requisitioning of all or part of such investments by the Party's forces or authorities, or

    B.   destruction of all or part of such investments by the Party's forces or authorities that was not required by the necessity of the situation.

Article 11
Trade -Related Investment Measures

1.   Subject to the provisions of paragraph 2, neither Party shall apply any trade-related investment measures (TRIMs) which are inconsistent with the Agreement on Trade-Related Investment Measures of the WTO. The illustrative list of TRIMs set forth in the WTO Agreement on TRIMs ("the List") is contained in Annex I of this Agreement. TRIMs contained on the List will be considered inconsistent with this Article regardless of whether they are imposed in laws, regulations, or as conditions for individual investment contracts or licenses.

2.   The Parties agree to eliminate all TRIMs (including those contained in laws, regulations, contracts or licenses) which fall under sub-paragraphs 2(A) (trade balancing requirements) and 2(B) (foreign exchange controls on imports) of the List by the time this Agreement enters into force. Vietnam shall eliminate all other TRIMs no later than five years after the date of entry into force of the Agreement, or the date required under the terms and conditions of Vietnam's accession to the WTO, whichever occurs first.

Article 12
Application to State Enterprises

A Party's obligations shall apply to a state enterprise in the exercise of any regulatory, administrative or other governmental authority delegated to it by that Party.

Article 13
Future Negotiation of Bilateral Investment Treaty

The Parties will endeavor to negotiate a bilateral investment treaty in good faith within a reasonable period of time.

Article 14
Application to Covered Investments

The provisions of this Chapter, Annex H, the exchanged letters on Investment Licensing Regime, and Articles 1 and 4 of Chapter VII shall apply to covered investments existing at the time of entry into force as well as to those established or acquired thereafter.

Article 15
Denial of Benefits

Each Party reserves the right to deny to a company of the other Party the benefits of this Chapter and Chapter V of this Agreement if nationals of a third country own or control the company and

1.   the denying Party does not maintain normal economic relations with the third country; or

2.   the company has no substantial business activities in the territory of the Party under whose laws it is constituted or organized.

ANNEX H
VIETNAM

In accordance with the provisions in Article 2 of Chapter IV, the Government of the Socialist Republic of Vietnam reserves the right to adopt or maintain exceptions to national treatment in the following sectors and matters:

1.   Vietnam may adopt or maintain exceptions to the obligation to accord national treatment to covered investments in the sectors or with respect to the matters specified below:

Broadcasting, television; production, publication and distribution of cultural products; investment in insurance; banking; brokerage, dealership in securities and currency values, and other related services; mineral exploration and exploitation; construction, installation, operation and maintenance of telecommunication facility; construction and operation of inland water, sea and air ports; cargo and passenger transportation by railway, airway, road, sea and inland water-way transportation; fishing and fish catching; real estate business.

2.   Sectors in which Vietnam may require that an investment project be in conjunction with the development of local raw material sources:

Processing of paper, vegetable oil, milk, cane sugar, wood processing (except for projects using imported wood).

Such requirements for the development of local raw material sources in the above sectors may be maintained for up to 5 years from the entry into force of this Agreement.

3.   Sectors in which Vietnam may require that an investment project export at least 80% of products:

Cement production; paints and construction paints; toiletry tiles and ceramics; PVC and other plastics; footwear; clothing; construction steel; detergent powder; tires and inner tubes for automobile and motor bikes; NPK fertilizer; alcoholic products; tobacco; papers (including printing, and writing paper, photocopy).

Such requirements for exporting at least 80% of products in the above sectors may be maintained for up to 7 years from the entry into force of this Agreement.

4.   Except as otherwise provided in this Paragraph (including sub-paragraphs 4.1-4.6), the following exceptions to national treatment shall be applied to a covered investment of a national or company of the United States in all sectors, including but not limited to those sectors listed in paragraphs 1, 2 and 3 of this Annex:

4.1   Requirements on investment capital:

(a)   After the entry into force of this Agreement, nationals or companies of the United States shall be allowed to contribute, increase and reinvest capital in any currency, including Vietnamese currency originating from any lawful activity in Vietnam.

(b)   The following requirements may be maintained for up to 3 years from the entry into force of this Agreement:

(i)   Nationals or companies of the United States must contribute at least 30% of the legal capital of a joint venture unless a lower contribution is approved by the investment licensing agencies;

(ii)   The legal capital of a U.S.-owned enterprise shall not be less than 30% of investment capital unless a lower proportion is approved by the investment licensing agencies;

(iii)   A national or company of the United States that is a party to a joint venture with a Vietnamese national or company shall give a right of first refusal to the Vietnamese party with respect to the transfer of an interest in the joint venture. An enterprise in Vietnam that is 100% owned by U.S. nationals or companies shall give a right of first refusal to Vietnamese nationals or companies with respect to the transfer of any interest in the enterprise. In any such case, the right of first refusal may be exercised only if the offer of the Vietnamese national or company is the same in all material terms with an offer received from any third party, including with respect to purchase price, timing and method of payment. Any such transfer shall require the approval of the investment licensing agencies; and

      (iv)   Nationals or companies of the United States are not yet allowed to establish a joint stock company. An enterprise in Vietnam that is invested or owned by U.S. nationals or companies may not issue bonds or shares to the public in Vietnam.

    (c)   Nationals and companies of the United States shall not be permitted to acquire more than 30% of the shares of an equitized State enterprise.

4.2   Organization and management of joint ventures:

Vietnam may maintain the following requirements for up to 3 years from the entry into force of this Agreement:

    (a)   The General Director or First Deputy General Director must be Vietnamese citizens; and

    (b)   A limited number of the most important matters which relate to the organization and operation of the enterprise, comprising the appointment or dismissal of General Director, First Deputy General Director, Chief Accountant; amendments of and additions to the charter of the enterprise; approval of final annual financial statements and financial statement of capital construction; and loan for investment shall be decided on the basis of consensus.

4.3   Prices and fees of some goods and services under the State's control:

Vietnam is in the process of reforming its pricing system in order to develop a uniform set of fees and prices. With a view to creating a more attractive, non-discriminatory business environment, Vietnam shall:

    (a)   upon the entry into force of this Agreement, (i) refrain from imposing new or more onerous discriminatory prices and fees; and (ii) eliminate, discriminatory prices and fees for the installation of telephones, telecommunications services (other than the subscription charge for local telephone service), water, and tourist services;

    (b)   within two (2) years of the entry into force of this Agreement, eliminate, progressively, discriminatory prices and fees for registration of motor vehicles, international port charges, and for the subscription charge for local telephone service; and

    (c)   within four (4) years of the entry into force of this Agreement, eliminate, progressively, discriminatory prices and fees for all other goods and services including, without limitation, electricity and air transport.

4.4   Government subsidies and supports:

Government subsidies and supports granted to domestic enterprises, which include land allocation for investment projects, preferential credits, research and development and education assistance programs and other forms of Government supports, may not be made available to nationals or companies of the United States.

4.5   Ownership, use of land and residences:

(a)   Nationals and companies of the United States are not allowed to own land and residences. U.S. investors are allowed only to lease land for investment purposes.

(b)   U.S. enterprises are not yet allowed either to mortgage land use rights at foreign credit institutions operating in Vietnam or to transfer land use rights except for the case of transfers of invested assets associated with the land within the land lease period.

4.6   Notwithstanding the above reservations to national treatment for the ownership and use of land and residences, Vietnam shall create favorable conditions in exercising the mortgage and transfer of land use rights relating to covered investments including the elimination, within 3 years from the entry into force of this Agreement, of the restrictions on mortgage and transfer of land use rights mentioned in sub-paragraph 4.5(b).

ANNEX H
UNITED STATES

1.   The Government of the United States of America may adopt or maintain exceptions to the obligation to accord national treatment (8) to covered investments in the sectors or with respect to the matters specified below:

atomic energy; customhouse brokers; licenses for broadcast, common carrier, or aeronautical radio stations; COMSAT; subsidies or grants, including government-supported loans, guarantees and insurance; landing of submarine cables; and state and local measures as to which the United States may adopt or maintain exceptions to national treatment under any of its bilateral investment treaties signed between 1 January 1995, and the date of entry into force of this Agreement.

Most favored nation treatment shall be accorded in the sectors and matters indicated above.

2.   The Government of the United States of America may adopt or maintain exceptions to the obligation to accord national and most favored nation treatment to covered investments in the sectors or with respect to the matters specified below:

fisheries; air and maritime transport, and related activities; banking, insurance, securities, and other financial services; leasing of minerals and pipeline rights-of-way on government lands; and one-way satellite transmissions of direct-to-home (DTH) and direct broadcast satellite (DBS) television services and of digital audio services.

ANNEX I

TRIMs -- Illustrative List

1.   TRIMs that are inconsistent with the obligation of national treatment provided for in paragraph 4 of Article III of GATT 1994 include those which are mandatory or enforceable

under domestic law or under administrative rulings, or compliance with which is necessary to obtain an advantage, and which require:

A.   the purchase or use by an enterprise of products of domestic origin or from any domestic source, whether specified in terms of particular products, in terms of volume or value of local products, or in terms of a proportion of volume or value of its local production; or

B.   that an enterprise's purchases or use of imported products be limited to an amount related to the volume or value of local products that it exports.

2.   TRIMs that are inconsistent with the obligation of general elimination of quantitative restrictions provided for in paragraph 1 of Article XI of GATT 1994 include those which are mandatory or enforceable under domestic law or under administrative rulings, or compliance with which is necessary to obtain an advantage, and which restrict:

A.   the importation by an enterprise of products used in or related to its local production, generally or to an amount related to the volume or value of local production that it exports;

B.   the importation by an enterprise of products used in or related to its local production by restricting its access to foreign exchange to an amount related to the foreign exchange inflows attributable to the enterprise; or

C.   the exportation or sale for export by an enterprise of products, whether specified in terms of particular products, in terms of volume or value of products, or in terms of a proportion of volume or value of its local production.

CHAPTER V

BUSINESS FACILITATION

Article 1

1.   To facilitate business activity, and subject to the provisions of Chapters I (including Annexes A, B, C, D and E), III (including Annexes F and G) and IV (including Annexes H and I) of this Agreement, each Party shall:

A.   permit nationals and companies of the other Party to import and use, in accordance with normal commercial practices, office and other equipment, such as typewriters, photocopiers, computers and facsimile machines in connection with the conduct of their activities in the territory of such Party;

B.   subject to its laws and procedures governing immigration and foreign missions, permit, on a non-discriminatory basis and at market prices, nationals and companies of the other Party access to and use of office space and living accommodations;

C. subject to its laws, regulations and procedures governing immigration and foreign missions, permit nationals and companies of the other Party to engage agents, consultants and distributors of either Party, on prices and terms mutually agreed between the parties, for their production and covered investments;

D. permit nationals and companies of the other Party to advertise their products and services (i) through direct agreement with the advertising media, including television, radio, print and billboard, and (ii) by direct mail, including the use of enclosed envelopes and cards pre-addressed to that national or company;

E. encourage direct contact, and permit direct sales, between nationals and companies of the other Party and end-users and other customers of their goods and services, and encourage direct contacts with agencies and organizations whose decisions will affect potential sales;

F. permit nationals and companies of the other Party to conduct market studies, either directly or by contract, within its territory;

G. permit nationals and companies of the other Party to stock an adequate supply of samples and replacement parts for after-sales service for covered investment products; and

H. provide non-discriminatory access to governmentally-provided products and services, including public utilities, to nationals and companies of the other Party at fair and equitable prices (and in no event at prices greater than those charged to any nationals or companies of third countries where such prices are set or controlled by the government in connection with the operation of their commercial representations).

Article 2

For purposes of this Chapter, the term "non-discriminatory" means treatment that is at least as favorable as the better of national treatment or most favored nation treatment.

Article 3

In case of conflict between any provision of this Chapter and any provision of Chapters I (including Annexes A, B, C, D and E), III (including Annexes F and G) and IV (including Annexes H and I), the provision of the Chapters I, III and IV shall control to the extent of the conflict.

CHAPTER VI

TRANSPARENCY-RELATED PROVISIONS AND RIGHT TO APPEAL

Article 1

Each Party shall publish on a regular and prompt basis all laws, regulations and administrative procedures of general application pertaining to any matter covered by this Agreement.

Publication of such information and measures will be in a manner which enables governmental agencies, enterprises and persons engaged in commercial activity to become acquainted with them before they come into effect and to apply them in accordance with their terms. Each such publication shall include the effective date of the measure, the products (by tariff line) or services affected by the measure, and all authorities that must approve or be consulted in the implementation of the measure, and provide a contact point within each authority from which relevant information can be obtained.

Article 2

Each Party shall provide nationals and companies of the other Party with access to data on the national economy and individual sectors, including information on foreign trade. The provisions of this paragraph and the preceding paragraph do not require disclosure of confidential information which would impede law enforcement or otherwise be contrary to the public interest, or would prejudice the legitimate commercial interests of particular enterprises, public or private. For the purposes of this Agreement, confidential information that would prejudice the legitimate commercial interests of particular enterprises means specific information concerning the importation of a product that would have a significant adverse effect on the price or quantity available of such product, but shall not include information required to be disclosed under the agreements administered by the WTO.

Article 3

Each Party shall allow, to the extent possible, the other Party and its nationals the opportunity to comment on the formulation of laws, regulations and administrative procedures of general application that may affect the conduct of business activities covered by this Agreement.

Article 4

All laws, regulations and administrative procedures of general application referred to in paragraph 1 of this Article that are not published and readily available to other governments and persons engaged in commercial activities as of the date of signature of this Agreement will be made public and readily and quickly available. Only laws, regulations and administrative procedures of general application that are published and readily available to other governments and persons engaged in commercial activity will be enforced and enforceable.

Article 5

The Parties shall have or designate an official journal or journals and all measures of general application shall be published in such journals. The Parties will publish such journals on a regular basis and make copies of them readily available to the public.

Article 6

The Parties shall administer, in a uniform, impartial and reasonable manner all their respective laws, regulations and administrative procedures of general application of all the types described in paragraph 1 of this Article.

Article 7

The Parties will maintain administrative and judicial tribunals and procedures for the purpose, inter alia, of the prompt review and correction (upon the request of an affected person) of administrative action relating to matters covered by this Agreement. These procedures shall include the opportunity for appeal, without penalty, by persons affected by the relevant decision. If the initial right of appeal is to an administrative body, there shall also be the opportunity for appeal of the decision to a judicial body. Notice of the decision on appeal shall be given to the appellant and the reasons for such decision shall be provided in writing. The appellant shall also be informed of the right to any further appeal.

Article 8

The Parties shall ensure that all import licensing procedures, both automatic and non-automatic, are implemented in a transparent and predictable manner, and in accordance with the standards of the WTO Agreement on Import Licensing Procedures.

CHAPTER VII

GENERAL ARTICLES

Article 1 Cross-Border Transactions and Transfers

1.   Unless otherwise agreed between the parties to such transactions, all cross-border commercial transactions, and all transfers of currencies relating to a covered investment, shall be made in United States dollars or any other currency that may be designated from time to time by the International Monetary Fund as being a freely usable currency.

2.   In connection with trade in products and services, each Party shall grant to nationals and companies of the other Party the better of most-favored-nation or national treatment with respect to:

      A.   opening and maintaining accounts, in both local and foreign currency, and having access to funds deposited in financial institutions located in the territory of the Party;

      B.   payments, remittances and transfers of currencies convertible into freely usable currency at a market rate of exchange or financial instruments representative thereof, between the territories of the two Parties, as well as between the territory of that Party and that of any third country;

      C.   rates of exchange and related matters, including access to freely usable currencies.

3.   Each Party shall grant to covered investments of the other Party the better of national or most favored nation treatment with respect to all transfers into and out of each Party's territory. Such transfers include:

      •   contributions to capital;

- profits, dividends, capital gains, and proceeds from the sale of all or any part of the investment or from the partial

- or complete liquidation of the investment;

- interest, royalty payments, management fees, and technical assistance and other fees;

D.   payments made under contract, including a loan agreement;

E.   compensation pursuant to Article 10 of Chapter IV and payments arising out of an investment dispute.

4.   In all cases, treatment of cross-border transactions and transfers will be consistent with each Party's obligations to the International Monetary Fund.

5.   Each Party shall permit returns in kind to be made as authorized or specified in an investment authorization, investment agreement, or other written agreement between the Party and a covered investment or a national or company of the other Party.

6. Notwithstanding paragraphs 1 through 5, a Party may prevent a transfer through the equitable, non-discriminatory and good faith applications (including the seeking of preliminary relief, such as judicial injunctions and temporary restraining orders) of its law relating to:

A.   bankruptcy, insolvency or the protection of the rights of creditors;

B.   issuing, trading or dealing in securities, futures, options, or derivatives;

C.   reports or records of transfers;

D.   criminal or penal offenses; or

E.   ensuring compliance with orders or judgments in judicial or administrative proceedings.

The provisions of this Article relating to financial transfers shall not preclude:

A.   a requirement that a national or company (or its covered investment) comply with customary banking procedures and regulations, provided that they do not impair the substance of the rights granted under this Article;

B.   prudential measures in order to protect the interests of creditors and to ensure the stability and integrity of the national financial system.

Article 2 National Security

This Agreement shall not preclude a Party from applying measures that it considers to be necessary for the protection of its own essential security interests. Nothing in this Agreement shall be construed to require either Party to furnish any information, the disclosure of which it considers contrary to its essential security interests.

Article 3 General Exceptions

1.   Subject to the requirement that such measures are not applied in a manner which would constitute a means of arbitrary or unjustifiable discrimination between countries where like conditions prevail, or a disguised restriction on international trade, nothing in this Agreement shall be construed to prohibit the adoption or enforcement by either Party of measures:

   A.   with respect to Chapter I, Trade in Goods, necessary to secure compliance with laws or regulations not inconsistent with the provisions of this Agreement, including measures related to the protection of intellectual property rights and the prevention of deceptive practices;

   B.   with respect to Chapter I, Trade in Goods, referred to in Article XX of the GATT 1994; or with respect to Chapter III, Trade in Services, referred to in Article XIV of the GATS.

2.   Nothing in this Agreement shall preclude a Party from applying its laws in respect of foreign missions as set forth in applicable legislation.

3.   Nothing in this Agreement limits the application of any existing or future agreements between the Parties on trade in textiles and textile products.

Article 4 Taxation

1.   No provision of this Agreement shall impose obligations with respect to tax matters, except that:

   A.   Chapter I, other than Article 2.1 of such Chapter, shall apply only to taxes other than direct taxes as defined in paragraph 3 of this Article.

   B.   Within Chapter IV,

      i)   Articles 4 and 10.1 will apply with respect to expropriation; and

      ii)   Article 4 will apply with respect to an investment agreement or an investment authorization.

2.   With respect to the application of Chapter IV, Article 10.1, an investor that asserts that a tax measure involves an expropriation may submit that dispute to arbitration pursuant to Chapter IV, Article 4.3, provided that the investor concerned has first referred to the competent tax authorities of both Parties the issue of whether that tax measure involves an expropriation. However, the investor cannot submit the dispute to arbitration if, within nine months after the date of referral, the competent tax authorities of both Parties determine that the tax measure does not involve an expropriation.

3.   "Direct taxes" comprise all taxes on total income, on total capital or on elements of income or of capital, including taxes on gains from the alienation of property, taxes on estates,

inheritances and gifts, and taxes on the total amounts of wages or salaries paid by enterprises, as well as taxes on capital appreciation.

Article 5 Consultations

1.   The Parties agree to consult periodically to review the operation of this Agreement.

2.   The Parties agree to consult promptly as arranged through appropriate channels at the request of either Party to discuss any matter concerning the interpretation or implementation of this Agreement and other relevant aspects of the relations between the Parties.

3.   The Parties agree to establish a Joint Committee ("Committee") on Development of Economic and Trade Relations between Vietnam and the United States of America. The Committee's responsibilities shall include the following:

> A.   monitoring and securing the implementation of this Agreement and making recommendations to achieve the objectives of this Agreement;

> B.   ensuring that a satisfactory balance of concessions is maintained during the life of this Agreement;

> C.   serving as the appropriate channel through which the Parties shall consult at the request of either Party to discuss and resolve matters arising from interpretation or implementation of this Agreement; and

> D.   seeking and making proposals on the enhancement and diversification of economic and trade relations between the two countries.

4.   The Committee shall be co-chaired by representatives of the Parties at the ministerial level, and have members who are representatives from the relevant agencies concerned with the implementation of this Agreement. The Committee shall meet annually or at the request of either Party. The location of the meetings shall alternate between Hanoi and Washington D.C., unless the Parties agree otherwise. The organization and the terms of reference of the Committee shall be adopted by the Committee at its first session.

Article 6 Relationship between Chapter IV, Annex H, Exchanged Letters, and Annex G

As to any matter concerning investment in services not specified in Annex G, the provisions of Annex H shall apply. However, in the event of a conflict between a provision set forth in Chapter IV, Annex H, or exchanged letters on Investment Licensing Regime, and a provision set forth in Annex G, the provision set forth in Annex G shall prevail to the extent of the conflict. Annex H and exchanged letters on Investment Licensing Regime shall not be construed or applied in a manner that would deprive a Party of rights provided under Annex G.

Article 7 Annexes, Schedules and Exchanged Letters

The Annexes, Schedules, and the exchanged letters on Investment Licensing Regime to this Agreement constitute an integral part of this Agreement.

Article 8 Final Provisions, Entry into Force, Duration, Suspension and Termination

1.   This Agreement shall enter into force on the day on which the Parties have exchanged notifications that each has completed the legal procedures necessary for this purpose, and shall remain in force for three years.

2.   This Agreement shall be extended for successive terms of three years if neither Party notifies the other Party of its intent to terminate this Agreement at least 30 days before the end of a term.

3.   If either Party does not have domestic legal authority to carry out its obligations under this Agreement, either Party may suspend application of this Agreement, or, with agreement of the other Party, any part of this Agreement, including MFN treatment. In that event, the Parties will seek, to the fullest extent practicable under domestic law, to minimize unfavorable effects on existing trade relations between the Parties.IN WITNESS THEREOF, the undersigned, being duly authorized by their respective Governments, have signed this Agreement.

DONE at Washington D.C., in duplicate, this thirteenth day of July 2000, in the English and Vietnamese languages, each text being equally authentic.

*   *   *

1.   As used in this Agreement, the term "normal trade relations" shall have the same meaning as the term "most favored nation" treatment.

2.   This condition is understood in terms of number of sectors, volume of trade affected and modes of supply. In order to meet this condition, agreements should not provide for the a priori exclusion of any mode of supply.

3.   The term "relevant international organizations" refers to international bodies whose membership is open to the relevant bodies of at least all Members of the WTO.

4.   If a Party undertakes a market-access commitment in relation to the supply of a service through the mode of supply referred to in subparagraph 2(A) of Article 1 and if the cross-border movement of capital is an essential part of the service itself, that Party is thereby committed to allow such movement of capital. If a Party undertakes a market-access commitment in relation to the supply of a service through the mode of supply referred to in subparagraph 2(C) of Article 1, it is thereby committed to allow related transfers of capital into its territory.

5.   Subparagraph 2(C) does not cover measures of a Party which limit inputs for the supply of services.

6.   Specific commitments assumed under this Article shall not be construed to require either Party to compensate for any inherent competitive disadvantages which result from the foreign character of the relevant services or service supplier.

7.   Where the service is not supplied directly by a juridical person but through other forms of commercial presence such as a branch or a representative office, the service supplier (i.e. the

juridical person) shall, nonetheless, through such presence be accorded the treatment provided for service suppliers under this Chapter. Such treatment shall be extended to the presence through which the service is supplied and need not be extended to any other parts of the supplier located outside the territory where the service is supplied.

8.   With respect to the treatment accorded by a State, Territory or Possession of the United States, national treatment means treatment no less favorable than the treatment accorded thereby, in like situations, to investments of nationals of the United States resident in, and companies legally constituted under the laws and regulations of other States, Territories or Possessions of the United States.

*   *   *

ECONOMIC PARTNERSHIP, POLITICAL COORDINATION AND COOPERATION AGREEMENT BETWEEN THE EUROPEAN COMMUNITY AND ITS MEMBER STATES, OF THE ONE PART, AND THE UNITED MEXICAN STATES, OF THE OTHER PART[*]

[excerpts]

AND

DECISION NO 2/2001 OF THE EUROPEAN UNION AND MEXICO JOINT COUNCIL OF 27 FEBRUARY 2001 IMPLEMENTING ARTICLES 6, 9, 12(2)(B) AND 50 OF THE ECONOMIC PARTNERSHIP, POLITICAL COORDINATION AND COOPERATION AGREEMENT

[excerpts]

The Economic Partnership, Political Coordination and Cooperation Agreement between the European Community and Its Member States, of the One Part, and the United Mexican States, of the Other Part was signed on 8 December 1997. It entered into force on 1 January 2000. Decision No 2/2001 of the European Union and Mexico Joint Council of 27 February 2001 Implementing Articles 6, 9, 12(2)(b) and 50 of the Economic Partnership, Political Coordination and Cooperation Agreement was adopted on 27 February 2001. It entered into force on 1 March 2001. Annexes I, II and III, and Appendix I of Decision No 2/2001, are not published here; they are available from the same source. The member States of the European Community are: Austria, Belgium, Denmark, Finland, France, Germany, Greece, Ireland, Italy, Luxembourg, the Netherlands, Portugal, Spain, Sweden and the United Kingdom.

TITLE III
TRADE

Article 4
Objective

The objective of this Title is to establish a framework to encourage the development of trade in goods and services, including a bilateral and preferential, progressive and reciprocal liberalisation of trade in goods and services, taking into account the sensitive nature of certain products and service sectors and in accordance with the relevant WTO rules.

Article 6
Trade in services

In order to achieve the objective laid down in Article 4, the Joint Council shall decide on the appropriate arrangements for a progressive and reciprocal liberalisation of trade in services, in

---

[*] *Source*: European Communities (2000). "Economic Partnership, Political Coordination and Cooperation Agreement between the European Community and Its Member States, of the One Part, and the United Mexican States, of the Other Part", *Official Journal of the European Communities*, L 276, 28 October 2000, pp. 45-79; available also on the Internet (http://europa.eu.int/eur-lex/en/lif/dat/2000/en_200A1028_01.html). [Note added by the editor.]

accordance with the relevant WTO rules, in particular, Article V of the General Agreement on Trade in Services (GATS), and taking due account of the commitments already undertaken by the Parties within the framework of that Agreement.

Article 7

The decisions of the Joint Council referred to in Articles 5 and 6 of this Agreement in respect of trade in goods and services, shall adequately cover all these issues within a comprehensive framework and shall enter into force as soon as they have been adopted.

TITLE IV
CAPITAL MOVEMENTS AND PAYMENTS

Article 8
Capital movements and payments

The objective of this Title is to establish a framework to encourage the progressive and reciprocal liberalisation of capital movements and payments between Mexico and the Community, without prejudice to other provisions in this Agreement and further obligations under other international agreements that are applicable between the Parties.

Article 9

In order to achieve the objective laid down in Article 8, the Joint Council shall adopt the measures and timetable for a progressive and reciprocal elimination of restrictions on capital movements and payments between the Parties, without prejudice to other provisions in this Agreement and further obligations under other international agreements that are applicable between the Parties.

This decision shall include, in particular, the following matters:

(a)   the definition, content, extension and substance of the concepts included explicitly or implicitly in this Title;

(b)   capital transactions and payments, including national treatment, to be covered by the liberalisation;

(c)   scope of the liberalisation and transitional periods;

(d)   the inclusion of a clause allowing the Parties to maintain restrictions in this area justified on grounds of public policy, public security, public health and defence;

e)   the inclusion of clauses allowing the Parties to introduce restrictions in this area in case of difficulties in the operation of exchange-rate or monetary policy of one of the Parties, balance of payments difficulties or, in conformity with international law, the imposition of financial restrictions on third countries.

TITLE V
PUBLIC PROCUREMENT, COMPETITION, INTELLECTUAL PROPERTY AND OTHER TRADE-RELATED PROVISIONS

Article 10
Public procurement

1.   The Parties shall agree to the gradual and mutual opening of agreed government procurement markets on a reciprocal basis.

2.   In order to achieve this objective, the Joint Council shall decide on the appropriate arrangements and timetable. The decision shall include, in particular, the following matters:

(a)   coverage of the agreed liberalisation;
(b)   non-discriminatory access to the agreed markets;
(c)   threshold values;
(d)   fair and transparent procedures;
(e)   clear challenge procedures;
(f)   use of information technology.

Article 11
Competition

1.   The Parties shall agree on the appropriate measures in order to prevent distortions or restrictions of competition that may significantly affect trade between Mexico and the Community. To this end, the Joint Council shall establish mechanisms of cooperation and coordination among their authorities with responsibility for the implementation of competition rules. Such cooperation shall include mutual legal assistance, notification, consultation and exchange of information in order to ensure transparency relating to the enforcement of competition laws and policies.

2.   In order to achieve this objective, the Joint Council shall decide in particular, on the following matters:

(a)   agreements between undertakings, decisions by associations of undertakings and concerted practices between undertakings;

(b)   the abuse by one or more undertakings of a dominant position;

(c) mergers between undertakings;

(e)   state monopolies of a commercial character;

(f)   public undertakings and undertakings to which special or exclusive rights have been granted.

Article 12
Intellectual, industrial and commercial property

1.   Reaffirming the great importance they attach to the protection of intellectual property rights (copyright - including the copyright in computer programmes and databases - and neighbouring rights, the rights related to patents, industrial designs, geographical indications including designation of origins, trademarks, topographies of integrated circuits, as well as protection against unfair competition as referred to in Article 10a of the Paris Convention for the Protection of Industrial Property and protection of undisclosed information), the Parties undertake to establish the appropriate measures with a view to ensuring an adequate and effective protection in accordance with the highest international standards, including effective means to enforce such rights.

2.   To this effect, the Joint Council shall decide on:

(a)   a consultation mechanism with a view to reaching mutually satisfactory solutions in the event of difficulties in the protection of intellectual property;

(b)   the detailed measures to be adopted in pursuance of the objective set out in paragraph 1, taking into account in particular the relevant multilateral conventions on intellectual property.

TITLE VI

COOPERATION

Article 14
Industrial cooperation

1.   The Parties shall support and promote measures to develop and strengthen efforts to set in motion a dynamic, integrated and decentralised management of industrial cooperation in order to create a climate conducive to economic development, taking account of their mutual interests.

2.   Such cooperation shall focus in particular on:

(a)   strengthening contacts between both Parties' economic operators, by means of conferences, seminars, missions to seek out industrial and technical opportunities, round tables and general and sector-specific fairs, with a view to identifying and exploiting areas of mutual business interest and to boosting trade, investment and industrial cooperation and technology-transfer projects;

(b)   strengthening and extending the existing dialogue between both Parties' economic operators through the promotion of further consultation and coordination activities in order to identify and eliminate obstacles to industrial cooperation, to encourage respect for competition rules, to ensure the consistency of overall measures and to help industry adapt to market requirements;

(c)   promoting industrial cooperation initiatives in the context of the process of privatisation and liberalisation of both Parties in order to encourage investments by means of industrial cooperation between undertakings;

(d)   supporting modernisation, diversification, innovation, training, research and development and quality initiatives;

(e)   promoting the participation of both Parties in pilot projects and in special programmes according to their specific terms.

Article 15
Investment promotion

The Parties shall help to create an attractive and stable environment for reciprocal investment. Such cooperation shall take the form inter alia of:

(a)   arrangements for information, identification and dissemination relating to legislation and investment opportunities;

(b)   support for the development of a legal environment conducive to investment between the Parties, where appropriate, by the conclusion between the Member States and Mexico, of agreements to promote and protect investment and agreements to prevent double taxation;

(a)   the development of harmonised and simplified administrative procedures;

(d)   the development of mechanisms for joint investments, in particular, with the small and medium-sized enterprises of both Parties.

Article 16
Financial services

1.   The Parties undertake to establish cooperation in the financial services sector, in conformity with their laws, regulations and policies and in accordance with the rules and disciplines of the GATS, in light of their mutual interest and long and medium-term economic objectives.

2.   The Parties agree to work together both bilaterally and at the multilateral level to increase mutual understanding and awareness of their respective business environments and to bring about exchanges of information on financial regulations, financial supervision and control and other aspects of common interest.

3.   Such cooperation shall have the particular objective of encouraging improved and diversified productivity and competitiveness in the financial services sector.

TITLE VII

INSTITUTIONAL FRAMEWORK

Article 45
Joint Council

A Joint Council is hereby established which shall supervise the implementation of this Agreement. It shall meet at ministerial level, at regular intervals, and when circumstances require. It shall examine any major issues arising within the framework of this Agreement and any other bilateral or international issues of mutual interest.

Article 46

1.   The Joint Council shall consist of the Members of the Council of the European Union and Members of the European Commission on the one hand, and Members of the Government of Mexico, on the other.

2.   Members of the Joint Council may arrange to be represented, in accordance with the conditions laid down in its rules of procedure.

3.   The Joint Council shall establish its own rules of procedure.

4.   The Joint Council shall be presided in turn by a Member of the Council of the European Union and a Member of the Government of Mexico, in accordance with the provisions to be laid down in its rules of procedure.

Article 47

The Joint Council shall, for the purpose of attaining the objectives of this Agreement, have the power to take decisions in the cases provided for herein. The decisions taken shall be binding on the Parties which shall take the measures necessary to implement them. The Joint Council may also make appropriate recommendations.

It shall draw up the decisions and recommendations by agreement between the two Parties.

Article 48
Joint Committee

1.   The Joint Council shall be assisted in the performance of its duties by a Joint Committee composed of representatives of the members of the Council of the European Union and of the European Commission, on the one hand, and of representatives of the Government of Mexico on the other, normally at senior civil servant level.

In its rules of procedure the Joint Council shall determine the duties of the Joint Committee, which shall include the preparation of meetings of the Joint Council and how the Committee shall function.

2.   The Joint Council may delegate to the Joint Committee any of its powers. In this event the Joint Committee shall take its decisions in accordance with the conditions laid down in Article 47.

3.   The Joint Committee shall generally meet once a year, on a date and with an agenda agreed in advance by the Parties, in Brussels one year and Mexico the next. Special meetings may be convened by mutual agreement. The office of chairman of the Joint Committee shall be held alternately by a representative of each of the Parties.

Article 49
Other special committees

The Joint Council may decide to set up any other special committee or body to assist it in the performance of its duties.

In its rules of procedure, the Joint Council shall determine the composition and duties of such committees or bodies and how they shall function.

Article 50
Dispute settlement

The Joint Council shall decide on the establishment of a specific trade or trade related dispute settlement procedure compatible with the relevant WTO provisions in this field.

*   *   *

DECISION NO 2/2001 OF THE EUROPEAN UNION AND MEXICO JOINT COUNCIL OF 27 FEBRUARY 2001 IMPLEMENTING ARTICLES 6, 9, 12(2)(B) AND 50 OF THE ECONOMIC PARTNERSHIP, POLITICAL COORDINATION AND COOPERATION AGREEMENT[*]
[excerpts]

THE JOINT COUNCIL,

Having regard to the Economic Partnership, Political Coordination and Cooperation Agreement between the European Community and its Member States, of the one part, and the United Mexican States, of the other part (hereinafter "the Agreement"), and in particular articles 6, 9, 12 and 50 in conjunction with Article 47 thereof.

Mindful of their rights and obligations under the Marrakesh Agreement establishing the World Trade Organisation (hereinafter "the WTO").

---

[*] *Source*: European Communities (2001). "Decision No 2/2001 of the European Union and Mexico Joint Council of 27 February 2001 Implementing Articles 6, 9, 12(2)(b) and 50 of the Economic Partnership, Political Coordination and Cooperation Agreement"; *Official Journal of the European Communities*, L 070, 12 March 2001, pp. 7-50; available also on the Internet (http://europa.eu.int/eur-lex/en/lif/dat/ 2001/ en_ 201D0153.html). [Note added by the editor.]

Whereas:

(1)   Article 4 and 6 of the Agreement provide that the Joint Council shall decide on the arrangements for a progressive and reciprocal liberalisation of trade in services, in accordance with Article V of the General Agreement on Trade in Services (hereinafter "GATS").

(2)   Article 9 of the Agreement provides that the Joint Council shall adopt measures for the progressive liberalisation of investment and related payments between the Parties.

(3)   Article 12 of the Agreement stipulates that the Joint Council shall adopt measures with a view to ensure an adequate and effective protection of intellectual property rights.

(4)   Article 50 of the Agreement provides that the Joint Council shall establish a specific trade or trade related dispute settlement procedure.

(5)   In accordance with Article 60 of the Agreement, upon entry into force of that Agreement, the Decision 2/2000 of the Joint Council established by the Interim Agreement on trade and trade-related matters between the European Community, of the one part, and the United Mexican States, of the other part, is deemed to have been adopted by the Joint Council established by the Agreement. That decision implements the objectives laid down in Articles 5, 10, 11 and 12(2)(a) of the Agreement,

HAS DECIDED AS FOLLOWS:

TITLE I

GENERAL PROVISIONS

Article 1
Scope of the Decision

The Joint Council hereby lays down the necessary arrangements for implementing the following objectives of the Agreement:

(a)   the progressive and reciprocal liberalisation of trade in services, in conformity with Article V of GATS;

(b)   the progressive liberalisation of investment and related payments;

(c)   ensuring an adequate and effective protection of the intellectual property rights, in accordance with the highest international standards; and

(d)   establishing a dispute settlement mechanism.

TITLE II

TRADE IN SERVICES

Article 2
Coverage

1.   For the purposes of this Title, trade in services is defined as the supply of a service:

   (a)   from the territory of a Party into the territory of the other Party;

   (b)   in the territory of a Party to the service consumer of the other Party;

   (c)   by a service supplier of a Party, through commercial presence in the territory of the other Party;

   (d)   by a service supplier of a Party, through presence of natural persons in the territory of the other Party.

2.   This Title applies to trade in all services sectors with the exception of:

   (a)   audio-visual services;

   (b)   air services, including domestic and international air transportation services, whether scheduled or non-scheduled, and related services in support of air services, other than:

      (i)   aircraft repair and maintenance services during which an aircraft is withdrawn from service,

      (ii)   the selling and marketing of air transport services,

      (iii)   computer reservation system (CRS) services, and

   (c)   maritime cabotage.

3.   Maritime transport and financial services shall be governed by the provisions laid down in Chapters II and III, respectively, unless otherwise specified.

4.   Nothing in this Title shall be construed to impose any obligation with respect to government procurement.

5.   The provisions of this Title shall not apply to subsidies granted by the Parties.

CHAPTER I

GENERAL PROVISIONS

Article 3
Definitions

For purposes of this Chapter:

(a)   A federal, central or subcentral government includes any non-governmental body in the exercise of any regulatory, administrative or other governmental authority delegated to it by that federal, central and sub-central government;

(b)   "service suppliers" of a Party means any person of a Party that seeks to provide or provides a service;

(c)   "commercial presence" means:

   (i)   as regards nationals, the right to set up and manage undertakings, which they effectively control. This shall not extend to seeking or taking employment in the labour market or confer a right of access to the labour market of another Party,

   (ii)   as regards juridical persons, the right to take up and pursue the economic activities covered by this Chapter by means of the setting up and management of subsidiaries, branches or any other form of secondary establishment,

(d)   "subsidiary" means a juridical person which is effectively controlled by another juridical person;

(e)   a "Community juridical person" or a "Mexican juridical person" means a juridical person set up in accordance with the laws of a Member State of the Community or of Mexico, respectively, and having its registered office, central administration, or principal place of business in the territory of the Community or of Mexico, respectively;

   Should the juridical person have only its registered office or central administration in the territory of the Community or Mexico, respectively, it shall not be considered as a Community or a Mexican juridical person, respectively, unless its operations possess a real and continuous link with the economy of the Community or Mexico, respectively;

(f)   a "national" means a natural person who is a national of one of the Member States or Mexico according to their respective national legislations.

Article 4
Market Access

In those sectors and modes of supply which shall be liberalised pursuant to the decision provided for in Article 7 (3), and subject to any reservations stipulated therein, the measures which a Party shall not maintain or adopt are defined as:

(a) limitations on the number of services suppliers whether in the form of numerical quotas, monopolies, exclusive service suppliers or the requirements of an economic needs test;

(b) limitations on the total value of service transactions or assets in the form of numerical quotas or the requirement of an economic needs test;

(c) limitations on the total number of service operations or on the total quantity of service output expressed in the terms of designated numerical units in the form of quotas or the requirement of an economic needs test;

(d) limitations on the total number of natural persons that may be employed in a particular service sector or that a service supplier may employ and who are necessary for, and directly related to, the supply of a specific service in the form of numerical quotas or a requirement of an economic needs test;

(e) limitations on the participation of foreign capital in terms of maximum percentage limit on foreign shareholding or the total value of individual or aggregate foreign investment; and

(f) measures which require specific types of legal entities or joint ventures through which a service supplier of the other Party may supply a service.

Article 5
Most Favoured Nation Treatment

1.   Subject to exceptions that may derive from harmonisation of regulations based on agreements concluded by a Party with a third country providing for mutual recognition in accordance with Article VII of GATS, treatment accorded to services suppliers of the other Party shall be no less favourable than that accorded to like services suppliers of any third country.

2.   Treatment granted under other agreements concluded by one of the Parties with a third country which have been notified under Article V of GATS shall be excluded from this provision.

3.   If a Party enters into an agreement of the type referred to in paragraph 2, it shall afford adequate opportunity to the other Party to negotiate the benefits granted therein.

Article 6
National Treatment

1.   Each Party shall, in accordance with Article 7, grant to services and service suppliers of the other Party, in respect of all measures affecting the supply of services, treatment no less favourable than that it accords to its own like services and services suppliers.

2.   A Party may meet the requirement of paragraph 1 by according to services and service suppliers of the other Party, either formally identical treatment or formally different treatment to that it accords to its own like services and service suppliers.

3.   Formally identical or formally different treatment shall be considered to be less favourable if it modifies the conditions of competition in favour of services or service suppliers of the Party compared to like services or service suppliers of the other Party.

Article 7
Trade liberalisation

1.   As provided for in paragraphs 2 to 4, the Parties shall liberalise trade in services between themselves, in conformity with Article V of GATS.

2.   From the entry into force of this Decision, neither Party shall adopt new, or more, discriminatory measures as regards services or service suppliers of the other Party, in comparison with the treatment accorded to its own like services or service suppliers.

3.   No later than three years following the entry into force of this Decision, the Joint Council shall adopt a decision providing for the elimination of substantially all remaining discrimination between the Parties in the sectors and modes of supply covered by this Chapter (1). That decision shall contain:

> (a)   a list of commitments establishing the level of liberalisation which the Parties agree to grant each other at the end of a transitional period of ten years from the entry into force of this Decision;

> (b)   a liberalisation calendar for each Party in order to reach at the end of the ten-year transitional period the level of liberalisation described in subparagraph (a).

4.   Except as provided for in paragraph 2, Articles 4, 5 and 6 shall become applicable in accordance with the calendar and subject to any reservations stipulated in the Parties' lists of commitments provided for in paragraph 3.

5. The Joint Council may amend the liberalisation calendar and the list of commitments established in accordance with paragraph 3, with a view to remove or add exceptions.

Article 8
Regulatory carve-out

Each Party may regulate the supply of services in its territory, in so far as regulations do not discriminate against services and service suppliers of the other Party, in comparison to its own like services and service suppliers.

Article 9
Mutual recognition

1.   In principle no later than three years following the entry into force of this Decision, the Joint Council shall establish the necessary steps for the negotiation of agreements providing for the mutual recognition of requirements, qualifications, licenses and other regulations, for the purpose of the fulfilment, in whole or in part, by service suppliers of the criteria applied by each Party for the authorisation, licensing, operation and certification of service suppliers and, in particular, professional services.

2.   Any such agreement shall be in conformity with the relevant provisions of the WTO Agreement and, in particular, Article VII of GATS.

CHAPTER III

FINANCIAL SERVICES

Article 11
Definitions

In accordance with the terms of the Annex on Financial Services to the GATS and the GATS Understanding on Commitments in Financial Services, for purposes of this Chapter:

(a)   "Financial service" means any service of a financial nature offered by a financial service supplier of a Party. Financial services comprise the following activities:

A.   Insurance and insurance-related services:

1.   direct insurance (including co-insurance):

(a)   life;

(b)   non-life;

2.   reinsurance and retrocession;

3.   insurance inter-mediation, such as brokerage and agency; and

4.   services auxiliary to insurance, such as consultancy, actuarial, risk assessment and claim settlement services.

B.   Banking and other financial services (excluding insurance):

1.   acceptance of deposits and other repayable funds from the public;

2.   lending of all types, including consumer credit, mortgage credit, factoring and financing of commercial transaction;

3.   financial leasing;

4.   all payment and money transmission services, including credit, charge and debit cards, travellers cheques and bankers drafts;

5.   guarantees and commitments;

6.   trading for own account or for account of customers, whether on an exchange, in an over-the-counter market or otherwise, the following:

   (a)   money market instruments (including cheques, bills, certificates of deposits);

   (b)   foreign exchange;

   (c)   derivative products including, but not limited to, futures and options;

   (d)   exchange rate and interest rate instruments, including products such as swaps, forward rate agreements;

   (e)   transferable securities;

   (f)   other negotiable instruments and financial assets, including bullion;

7.   participation in issues of all kinds of securities, including underwriting and placement as agent (whether publicly or privately) and provision of services related to such issues;

8.   money broking;

9.   asset management, such as cash or portfolio management, all forms of collective investment management, pension fund management, custodial, depository and trust services;

10.   settlement and clearing services for financial assets, including securities, derivative products, and other negotiable instruments;

11.   provision and transfer of financial information, and financial data processing and related software by suppliers of other financial services;

12.   advisory, intermediation and other auxiliary financial services on all the activities listed in subparagraphs (1) through (11), including credit reference and analysis, investment and portfolio research and advice, advice on acquisitions and on corporate restructuring and strategy.

(b) "Financial service supplier" means any juridical person of a Party authorised to supply financial services. The term "financial service supplier" does not include a public entity.

(c) "New financial service" means a service of a financial nature, including services related to existing and new products or the manner in which a product is delivered, that is not supplied by any financial service supplier in the territory of a Party but which is supplied in the territory of the other Party.

(d) "Public entity" means:

1. A government, a central bank or a monetary authority, of a Party, or an entity owned or controlled by a Party, that is principally engaged in carrying out governmental functions or activities for governmental purposes, not including an entity principally engaged in supplying financial services on commercial terms; or

2. A private entity, performing functions normally performed by a central bank or monetary authority, when exercising those functions.

(e) "Commercial presence" means a juridical entity within a Party's territory for the supply of financial services and includes wholly or partly owned subsidiaries, joint ventures, partnerships, franchising operations, branches, agencies, representative offices or other organisations.

Article 12
Establishment of financial service suppliers

1. Each Party shall allow the financial service suppliers of the other Party to establish a commercial presence in its territory.

2. Each Party may require a financial service supplier of the other Party to incorporate under its own law or impose terms and conditions on establishment that are consistent with the other provisions of this Chapter.

3. No Party may adopt new measures as regards to the establishment and operation of financial service suppliers of the other Party, which are more discriminatory than those applied on the date of entry into force of this Decision.

4. No Party shall maintain or adopt the following measures:

(a) limitations on the number of financial service suppliers whether in the form of numerical quotas, monopolies, exclusive financial service suppliers or the requirements of an economic needs test;

(b) limitations on the total value of financial service transactions or assets in the form of numerical quotas or the requirement of an economic test;

(c) limitations on the total number of service operations or on the total quantity of service output expressed in the terms of designated numerical units in the form of quotas or the requirement of an economic needs test;

(d)   limitations on the total number of natural persons that may be employed in a particular financial service sector or that a financial service supplier may employ and who are necessary for, and directly related to, the supply of a specific financial service in the form of numerical quotas or a requirement of an economic needs test; and

(e)   limitations on the participation of foreign capital in the terms of maximum percentage limit on foreign shareholding or the total value of individual or aggregate foreign investment.

Article 13
Cross-border provision of financial services

1.   Each party shall allow the cross-border provision of financial services.

2.   No Party may adopt new measures as regards to the cross-border provision of financial services by financial service suppliers of the other Party which are more discriminatory as compared to those applied on the date of entry into force of this Decision.

3.   Without prejudice to other means of prudential regulation of the cross-border provision of financial services, a Party may require the registration of cross-border financial service suppliers of the other Party.

4.   Each Party shall permit persons located in its territory to purchase financial services from financial service suppliers of the other Party located in the territory of that other Party. This obligation does not require a Party to permit such suppliers to do business or carry on commercial operations; or to solicit, market or advertise their activities in its territory. Each Party may define the meaning of "doing business", "carry on commercial operations", "solicit", "market" and "advertise" for purposes of this obligation.

Article 14
National treatment

1.   Each Party shall grant to the financial service suppliers of the other Party, including those already established in its territory on the date of entry into force of this Decision, treatment no less favourable than that it accords to its own like financial service suppliers with respect to the establishment, acquisition, expansion, management, conduct, operation and sale or other disposition of commercial operations of financial service suppliers in its territory.

2.   Where a Party permits the cross-border provision of a financial service it shall accord to the financial service suppliers of the other Party treatment no less favourable than that it accords to its own like financial service suppliers with respect to the provision of such a service.

Article 15
Most favoured nation treatment

1.   Each Party shall accord to financial service suppliers of the other Party treatment no less favourable than it accords to the like financial service suppliers of a non Party.

2.   Treatment granted under other agreements concluded by one of the Parties with a third country which have been notified under Article V of GATS shall be excluded from this provision.

3.   If a Party enters into an agreement of the type referred to in paragraph 2, it shall afford adequate opportunity to the other Party to negotiate the benefits granted therein.

Article 16
Key personnel

1.   No Party may require a financial service supplier of the other Party to engage individuals of any particular nationality as senior managerial or other key personnel.

2.   No Party may require that more than a simple majority of the board of directors of a financial service supplier of the other Party be composed of nationals of the Party, persons residing in the territory of the Party, or a combination thereof.

Article 17
Commitments

1.   Nothing in this Chapter shall be construed to prevent a Party to apply:

(a)   any existing measure inconsistent with Articles 12 to 16 which is listed on Annex I; or

(b)   an amendment to any discriminatory measure referred to in subparagraph (a) to the extent that the amendment does not increase the inconsistency of the measure with Articles 12 to 16, as it existed immediately before the amendment.

2.   The measures listed in Annex I shall be reviewed by the Special Committee on Financial Services established under Article 23, with a view to propose to the Joint Council their modification, suspension or elimination.

3.   No later than three years following the entry into force of this Decision, the Joint Council shall adopt a decision providing for the elimination of substantially all remaining discrimination. That decision shall contain a list of commitments establishing the level of liberalisation which the Parties agree to grant each other.

Article 18
Regulatory carve out

Each Party may regulate the supply of financial services, in so far as regulations do not discriminate against financial service or financial service suppliers of the other Party in comparison to its own like financial services and financial service suppliers.

Article 19
Prudential carve out

1.   Nothing in this Chapter shall be construed to prevent a Party from adopting or maintaining reasonable measures for prudential reasons, such as:

> (a)   the protection of investors, depositors, financial market participants, policy-holders, policy-claimants, or persons to whom a fiduciary duty is owed by a financial service supplier;

> (b)   the maintenance of the safety, soundness, integrity or financial responsibility of financial service suppliers; or

> (c)   ensuring the integrity and stability of a Party's financial system.

2.   These measures shall not be more burdensome than necessary to achieve their aim, and shall not discriminate against financial service suppliers of the other Party in comparison to its own like financial service suppliers.

3.   Nothing in this Chapter shall be construed to require a Party to disclose information relating to the affairs and accounts of individual consumers or any confidential or proprietary information in the possession of public entities.

Article 20
Effective and transparent regulation

1.   Each Party shall make its best endeavours to provide in advance to all interested persons any measure of general application that the Party proposes to adopt in order to allow an opportunity for such persons to comment on the measure. Such measure shall be provided:

> (a)   by means of an official publication; or

> (b)   in other written or electronic form.

2.   Each Party's appropriate financial authority shall make available to interested persons its requirements for completing applications relating to the supply of financial services.

3.   On the request of an applicant, the appropriate financial authority shall inform the applicant of the status of its application. If such authority requires additional information from the applicant, it shall notify the applicant without undue delay.

4.   Each Party shall make its best endeavours to ensure that the Basle Committee's "Core Principles for Effective Banking Supervision", the International Association of Insurance Supervisors' "Key Standards for Insurance Supervision" and the International Organisation of Securities Commissions' "Objectives and Principles of Securities Regulation" are implemented and applied in its territory.

5.   The Parties also take note of the "Ten Key Principles for Information Exchange" promulgated by the Finance Ministers of the G7 Nations, and undertake to consider to what extent they may be applied in bilateral contacts.

Article 21
New financial services

Each Party shall permit a financial service supplier of the other Party to provide any new financial service of a type similar to those services that the Party permits its own financial service suppliers to provide under its domestic law in like circumstances. A Party may determine the juridical form through which the service may be provided and may require authorisation for the provision of the service. Where such authorisation is required, a decision shall be made within a reasonable time and the authorisation may only be refused for prudential reasons.

Article 22
Data processing

1.   Each Party shall permit a financial service supplier of the other Party to transfer information in electronic or other form, into and out of its territory, for data processing where such processing is required in the ordinary course of business of such financial service supplier.

2.   As far as the transfer of personal data is concerned, each Party shall adopt adequate safeguards to the protection of privacy and fundamental rights, and freedom of individuals in accordance with Article 41 of the Agreement.

Article 23
Special Committee on Financial Services

1.   The Joint Council hereby establishes a Special Committee on Financial Services. The Special Committee shall be composed of representatives of the Parties. The principal representative of each Party shall be an official of the Party's authority responsible for financial services set out in Annex II.

2.   The functions of the Special Committee shall include:

   (a)   supervising the implementation of this Chapter;

   (b)   considering issues regarding financial services that are referred to it by a Party;

   (c)   considering the application of measures listed by either Party in Annex I in order to propose to the Joint Council its modification, suspension or elimination, as appropriate;

   (d)   reviewing the provisions contained in this Chapter at such a time as either of the Parties may grant a third party more favourable access to its financial services market pursuant to the conclusion of a regional economic integration agreement compatible with Article V of GATS, with a view to proposing consequent modifications to this Chapter to the Joint Council; and

(e)   considering implementation of Article 16 of the Agreement.

3.   The Special Committee shall meet once a year on a date and with an agenda agreed in advance by the Parties. The office of chairman shall be held alternately. The Special Committee shall report to the Joint Committee the results of each annual meeting.

Article 24
Consultations

1.   A Party may request consultations with the other Party regarding any matter arising under this Chapter. The other Party shall give sympathetic consideration to the request. The Parties shall report the results of their consultations to the Special Committee on Financial Services at its annual meeting.

2.   Consultations under this Article shall include officials of the authorities specified in Annex II.

3.   Nothing in this Article shall be construed to require financial authorities participating in consultations to disclose information or take any action that would interfere with individual regulatory, supervisory, administrative or enforcement matters.

4.   Where a Party requires information for supervisory purposes concerning a financial service supplier in the other Party's territory, the Party may approach the competent financial authority in the other Party's territory to seek the information.

Article 25
Dispute settlement

Arbitrators appointed to panels established in accordance with Title V for disputes on prudential issues and other financial matters shall have the necessary expertise relevant to the specific financial service under dispute, as well as expertise or experience in financial services law or practice, which may include the regulation of financial institutions.

Article 26
Specific exceptions

1.   Nothing in this Chapter shall be construed to prevent a Party, including its public entities, from exclusively conducting or providing in its territory activities or services forming part of a public retirement plan or statutory system of social security, except when those activities may be carried out by financial service suppliers in competition with public entities or private institutions.

2.   Nothing in this Chapter applies to activities conducted by a central bank or monetary authority or by any other public entity in pursuit of monetary or exchange rate policies.

3.   Nothing in this Chapter shall be construed to prevent a Party, including its public entities, from exclusively conducting or providing in its territory activities or services for the account or with the guarantee or using the financial resources of the Party, or its public entities.

CHAPTER IV

GENERAL EXCEPTIONS

Article 27
Exceptions

1. The provisions of this Title are subject to the exceptions contained in this Article.

2. Subject to the requirement that such measures are not applied in a manner which would constitute a means of arbitrary or unjustifiable discrimination between countries where like conditions prevail, or a disguised restriction on trade in services, nothing in this Title shall be construed to prevent the adoption or enforcement by any Party of measures:

   (a) necessary to protect public morals or to maintain public order and public security;

   (b) necessary to protect human, animal or plant life or health;

   (c) necessary to secure compliance with laws or regulations which are not inconsistent with the provisions of this Title including those relating to:

      (i) the prevention of deceptive and fraudulent practices or to deal with the effects of a default on services contracts;

      (ii) the protection of the privacy of individuals in relation to the processing and dissemination of personal data and the protection of confidentiality of individual records and accounts;

      (iii) safety;

   (d) inconsistent with the objective of Article 6 and 14, provided that the difference in treatment is aimed at ensuring the effective or equitable imposition or collection of direct taxes in respect of services or service suppliers of the other Party.

3. The provisions of this Title shall not apply to the Parties' respective social security systems or to activities in the territory of each Party, which are connected, even occasionally, with the exercise of official authority.

4. Nothing in this Title shall prevent a Party from applying its laws, regulations and requirements regarding entry and stay, work, labour conditions, and establishment of natural persons (3) provided that, in so doing, it does not apply them in a manner as to nullify or impair the benefits accruing to the other Party under the terms of a specific provision of this Title.

TITLE III

INVESTMENT AND RELATED PAYMENTS

Article 28
Definitions

1.   For the purpose of this Title, investment made in accordance with the laws of the Parties means direct investment, investment in real estate and purchase and sale of any kind of securities, as defined in the OECD Codes of Liberalisation.

2.   Payments covered by this Title are those related to an investment.

Article 29
Payments related to investment

1.   Without prejudice to Articles 30 and 31, restrictions on payments related to investment between the Parties shall be progressively eliminated. The Parties undertake not to introduce any new restrictions on payments related to direct investment from the entry into force of this Decision.

2.   Restrictions on payments related to investments in the services sector which have been liberalised in accordance with Title II of this Decision shall be eliminated according to the same timetable.

Article 30
Exchange rate policy and monetary policy difficulties

1.   Where, in exceptional circumstances, payments related to investment between the Parties cause, or threaten to cause, serious difficulties for the operation of the exchange rate policy or monetary policy of a Party, that Party may take safeguard measures that are strictly necessary for a period not exceeding six months. The application of safeguard measures may be extended through their formal reintroduction.

2.   The Party adopting the safeguard measure shall inform the other Party forthwith and present, as soon as possible, a time schedule for their removal.

Article 31
Balance of payments difficulties

1.   Where one or more Member States or Mexico is in serious balance of payments difficulties, or under imminent threat thereof, the Community or the Member State concerned, or Mexico, as the case may be, may adopt restrictive measures with regard to payments, including transfers of proceeds from the total or partial liquidation of direct investment. Such measures shall be equitable, non-discriminatory, in good faith, of limited duration and may not go beyond what is necessary to remedy the balance of payments situation.

2.   The Community or the Member State concerned, or Mexico, as the case may be, shall inform the other Party forthwith and present, as soon as possible, a time schedule for their

removal. Such measures shall be taken in accordance with other international obligations of the Party concerned, including those under the WTO Agreement and the Articles of Agreement of the International Monetary Fund.

Article 32
Transfers

The liquidation and transfer abroad of any direct investment made in Mexico by Community residents or in the Community by Mexican residents, and of any profits stemming therefrom, shall not be affected by the provisions of Article 30.

Article 33
Investment promotion between the Parties

The Community and its Member States, within the scope of their respective competences, and Mexico shall aim to promote an attractive and stable environment for reciprocal investment. Such promotion should take the form, in particular, of:

(a)   mechanisms for information about and identification and dissemination of investment legislation and opportunities;

(b)   development of a legal framework favourable to investment on both sides, particularly through the conclusion, where appropriate, by the Member tates of the Community and Mexico of bilateral agreements promoting and protecting investment and preventing double taxation;

(c)   development of uniform and simplified administrative procedures; and

(d)   development of mechanisms for joint investments, in particular with the small and medium enterprises of both Parties.

Article 34
International commitments on investment

The Community and its Member States, within the scope of their respective competences, and Mexico recall their international commitments with regard to investment, and especially the OECD Codes of Liberalisation and OECD National Treatment Instrument.

Article 35
Review clause

With the view of the objective of progressive liberalisation of investment, the Community and its Member States, and Mexico affirm their commitment to review the investment legal framework, the investment climate and the flow of investment between their territories consistent with their commitments in international investment agreements not later than three years after the entry into force of this Decision.

TITLE IV

INTELLECTUAL PROPERTY

Article 36
Multilateral Conventions on Intellectual Property

1.   The Community and its Member States, on the one hand, and Mexico on the other hand, confirm their obligations arising from the following multilateral conventions:

(a)   Agreement on Trade-related Aspects of Intellectual Property Rights (TRIPs Agreement, 1994);

(b)   Paris Convention for the Protection of Industrial Property (Stockholm Act, 1967);

(c)   Berne Convention for the Protection of Literary and Artistic Works (Paris Act, 1971);

(d)   International Convention for the Protection of Performers, Producers of Phonograms and Broadcasting Organisations (Rome, 1961); and

(e)   Patent Cooperation Treaty (Washington, 1970, amended in 1979 and modified in 1984).

2.   The Parties confirm the importance they attach to the obligations arising from the International Convention for the Protection of New Varieties of Plants, 1978 (1978 UPOV Convention), or the International Convention for the Protection of New Varieties of Plants, 1991 (1991 UPOV Convention).

3.   At the entry into force of this Decision, the Member States of the Community and Mexico will have acceded to the Nice Agreement concerning the International Classification of Goods and Services for the purposes of the Registration of Marks (Geneva, 1977 and amended in 1979).

4.   Within 3 years of the entry into force of this Decision the Members States of the Community and Mexico will have acceded to the Budapest Treaty of the International Recognition of the Deposit of Micro-organisms for the Purposes of Patent Procedure (1977, modified in 1980).

5.   The Parties shall make every effort to complete the necessary procedures for their accession to the following multilateral conventions at the earliest possible opportunity:

(a)   the WIPO Copyright Treaty (Geneva, 1996); and

(b)   the WIPO Performances and Phonogram Treaty (Geneva, 1996).

TITLE V

DISPUTE SETTLEMENT

CHAPTER I

SCOPE AND COVERAGE

Article 37
Scope and coverage

1.   The provisions of this Title shall apply with respect to any matter arising from this Decision or from Articles 4, 5, 6, 7, 8, 9, 10 and 11 of the Agreement (hereinafter the "covered legal instruments").

2.   By way of exception, the arbitration procedure laid down in Chapter III shall not be applicable in the case of disputes concerning Article 9(2), 31(2) last sentence, 34 and 36 of this Decision.

CHAPTER II

CONSULTATION

Article 38
Consultation

1.   The Parties shall at all times endeavour to agree on the interpretation and application of the covered legal instruments and shall make every attempt through cooperation and consultations to arrive to a mutually satisfactory resolution of any matter that might affect their operation.

2.   Each Party may request consultations within the Joint Committee with respect to any matter relating to the application or interpretation of the covered legal instruments or any other matter that it considers might affect their operation.

3.   The Joint Committee shall convene within 30 days of delivery of the request and shall endeavour to resolve the dispute promptly by means of a decision. That decision shall specify the implementing measures to be taken by the Party concerned, and the period of time to do so.

CHAPTER III

ARBITRATION PROCEDURE

Article 39
Establishment of an arbitration panel

1.   In case a Party considers that a measure applied by the other Party violates the covered legal instruments and such matter has not been resolved within 15 days after the Joint Committee has convened pursuant to Article 38(3) or 45 days after the delivery of the request for a Joint Committee meeting, either Party may request in writing the establishment of an arbitration panel.

2.   The requesting Party shall state in the request the measure and indicate the provisions of the covered legal instruments that it considers relevant, and shall deliver the request to the other Party and to the Joint Committee.

Article 40
Appointment of arbitrators

1.   The requesting Party shall notify the other Party of the appointment of an arbitrator, and propose up to 3 candidates to serve as a chair. The other Party must then appoint a second arbitrator within 15 days, and propose up to 3 candidates to serve as a chair.

2.   Both Parties shall endeavour to agree on the chair within 15 days after the second arbitrator has been appointed.
3.   The date of establishment of the arbitration panel shall be the date on which the chair is appointed.

4.   If a Party fails to appoint its arbitrator pursuant to paragraph 1, such arbitrator shall be selected by lot from the candidates proposed. If the Parties are unable to agree on the chair within the time period referred to in paragraph 2, it shall be selected by lot within one week from the candidates proposed.

5.   If an arbitrator dies, withdraws or is removed, a replacement shall be selected within 15 days in accordance with the selection procedure followed to select him or her. In such a case, any time period applicable to the arbitration panel proceeding shall be suspended for a period beginning on the date the arbitrator dies, withdraws or is removed and ending on the date the replacement is selected.

Article 41
Panel reports

1.   The arbitration panel should, as a general rule, submit an initial report containing its findings and conclusions to the Parties not later than three months from the date of establishment of the arbitration panel. In no case should it do so later than five months from this date. Any Party may submit written comments to the arbitration panel on its initial report within 15 days of presentation of the report.

2.   The arbitration panel shall present to the Parties a final report within 30 days of presentation of the initial report.

3.   In cases of urgency, including those involving perishable goods, the arbitration panel shall make every effort to issue its final report to the Parties within three months from the date of establishment of the arbitration panel. In no case should it do so later than four months. The arbitration panel may give a preliminary ruling on whether a case is urgent.

4.   All decisions of the arbitration panel, including the adoption of the final report and of any preliminary ruling, shall be taken by majority vote, each arbitrator having one vote.

5.   The complaining Party may withdraw its complaint at any time before the final report has been issued. Such withdrawal is without prejudice to its right to introduce a new complaint regarding the same issue at a later point in time.

Article 42
Implementation of panel reports

1.   Each Party shall be bound to take the measures involved in carrying out the final report referred to in Article 41(2).

2.   The Party concerned shall inform the other Party within 30 days after the final report has been issued of its intentions in respect of its implementation.

3.   The Parties shall endeavour to agree on the specific measures that are required for implementing the final report.

4.   The Party concerned shall promptly comply with the final report. If it is impracticable to comply immediately, the Parties shall endeavour to agree on a reasonable period of time to do so. In the absence of such agreement, either Party may request the original arbitration panel to determine the length of the reasonable period of time, in light of the particular circumstances of the case. The ruling of the arbitration panel shall be given within 15 days from that request.

5.   The Party concerned shall notify to the other Party the measures adopted in order to implement the final report before the expiry of the reasonable period of time determined in accordance with paragraph 4. Upon that notification, any of the Parties may request the original arbitration panel to rule on the conformity of those measures with the final report. The ruling of the arbitration panel shall be given within 60 days from that request.

6.   If the Party concerned fails to notify the implementing measures before the expiry of the reasonable period of time determined in accordance with paragraph 4, or if the arbitration panel rules that the implementing measures notified by the Party concerned are inconsistent with the final report, such Party shall, if so requested by the complaining Party, enter into consultations with a view to agree on a mutually acceptable compensation. If no such agreement has been reached within 20 days from the request, the complaining Party shall be entitled to suspend only the application of benefits granted under the covered legal instruments equivalent to those affected by the measure found to violate the covered legal instruments.

7.   In considering what benefits to suspend, a complaining Party should first seek to suspend benefits in the same sector or sectors as that affected by the measure that the panel has found to

violate the covered legal instruments. A complaining Party that considers it is not practicable or effective to suspend benefits in the same sector or sectors may suspend benefits in other sectors.

8. The complaining Party shall notify the other Party of the benefits which it intends to suspend no later than 60 days before the date on which the suspension is due to take effect. Within 15 days from that notification, any of the Parties may request the original arbitration panel to rule on whether the benefits which the complaining Party intends to suspend are equivalent to those affected by the measure found to violate the covered legal instruments, and whether the proposed suspension is in accordance with paragraphs 6 and 7. The ruling of the arbitration panel shall be given within 45 days from that request. Benefits shall not be suspended until the arbitration Panel has issued its ruling.

9. The suspension of benefits shall be temporary and shall only be applied by the complaining Party until the measure found to violate the covered legal instruments has been withdrawn or amended so as to bring it into conformity with the covered legal instruments, or the Parties have reached agreement on a resolution of the dispute.

10. At the request of any of the Parties, the original arbitration panel shall rule on the conformity with the final report of any implementing measures adopted after the suspension of benefits and, in light of such ruling, whether the suspension of benefits should be terminated or modified. The ruling of the arbitration panel shall be given within 30 days from the date of that request.

11. The rulings provided for in paragraphs 4, 5, 8 and 10 shall be binding.

Article 43
General provisions

1. Any time period mentioned in this Title may be extended by mutual agreement of the Parties.

2. Unless the Parties otherwise agree, the arbitration panel proceedings shall be conducted in accordance with the Model Rules of Procedure set out in Annex III. The Joint Committee may amend the Model Rules of Procedure.

3. Arbitration proceedings established under this Title will not consider issues relating to each Party's rights and obligations under the WTO.

4. Recourse to the dispute settlement provisions of this Title shall be without prejudice to any possible action in the WTO framework, including dispute settlement action. However, where a Party has, with regard to a particular matter, instituted a dispute settlement proceeding under either Article 39(1) of this Title or the WTO Agreement, it shall not institute a dispute settlement proceeding regarding the same matter under the other forum until such time as the first proceeding has ended. For purposes of this paragraph, dispute settlement proceedings under the WTO Agreement are deemed to be initiated by a Party's request for a panel under Article 6 of the Understanding on Rules and Procedures Governing the Settlement of Disputes of the WTO.

TITLE VI

SPECIFIC DUTIES OF THE JOINT COMMITTEE WITH RESPECT TO TRADE AND OTHER TRADE RELATED MATTERS

Article 44

1.   The Joint Committee shall:

(a)   supervise the implementation and proper operation of this Decision, as well as of any other decision concerning trade and other trade related matters(4);

(b)   oversee the further elaboration of the provisions of this Decision;

(c)   undertake consultations pursuant to Article 38(2) and (3);

(d)   carry out any functions assigned to it under this Decision or under any other decision concerning trade or trade related matters;

(e)   assist the Joint Council in the performance of its functions regarding trade and other trade related matters;

(f)   supervise the work of all the special committees established under this Decision; and

(g)   report annually to the Joint Council.

2.   The Joint Committee may:

(a)   set up any special committees or bodies to deal with matters falling within its competence, and determine their composition and duties, and how they shall function;

(b)   meet at any time by agreement of the Parties;

(c)   consider any issues regarding trade and other trade related matters, and take appropriate action in the exercise of its functions; and

(d)   take decisions or make recommendations on trade and other trade related matters, in accordance with Article 48(2) of the Agreement.

3.   When the Joint Committee meets in order to perform any of the tasks conferred upon it by this Decision, it shall be composed of representatives of the members of the Council of the European Union and of the European Commission, on the one hand, and of representatives of the Government of Mexico, on the other, with a responsibility for trade and trade related matters, normally at senior civil servant level.

TITLE VII

FINAL PROVISIONS

Article 45
Entry into force

This Decision shall enter into force on the first day of the month following that in which it is adopted by the Joint Council.

Article 46
Annexes

The Annexes to this Decision, including the Appendixes to those Annexes, are an integral part thereof.

Done at Brussels, 27 February 2001.

For the Joint Council
The President

J. Castañeda

(1)   The Joint Council may decide to postpone the adoption of the decision provided for in this paragraph. Should this occur, the decision shall be adopted not later than one year after the conclusion of the negotiations mandated by Article XIX of GATS and in any event within a reasonable timeframe before the end of the ten-year transitional period.

(2)   Notwithstanding Article 3(e), shipping companies established outside the Community or Mexico and controlled by nationals of a Member State of the Community or Mexico, respectively, shall also be beneficiaries of the provisions of this Chapter, if their vessels are registered in accordance with their respective legislation, in that Member State or in Mexico and carry the flag of a Member State or Mexico.

(3)   In particular, a Party may require that natural persons must possess the necessary academic qualifications and/or professional experience specified in the territory where the service is supplied, for the sector of activity concerned.

(4)   The Parties understand that "trade and other trade related matters" includes any matter arising under this Decision and Titles III through V of the Agreement.

*   *   *

AGREEMENT BETWEEN THE GOVERNMENT OF THE UNITED STATES OF AMERICA AND THE GOVERNMENT OF THE FEDERAL REPUBLIC OF NIGERIA CONCERNING THE DEVELOPMENT OF TRADE AND INVESTMENT RELATIONS*

The Agreement between the Government of the United States of America and the Government of the Federal Republic of Nigeria Concerning the Development of Trade and Investment Relations was signed on 16 February 2000. It entered into force on the date of signature.

The Government of the United States of America and the Government of the Federal Republic of Nigeria (individually a "Party" and collectively the "Parties"):

1)   Desiring to enhance the friendship and spirit of cooperation between the two countries;

2)   Desiring to develop further both countries' international trade and economic interrelationship;

3)   Taking into account the participation of both countries in the World Trade Organization (WTO), and noting that this Agreement is without prejudice to the rights and obligations of the parties under the Marrakesh Agreement establishing the World Trade Organization and the agreements, understandings, and other instruments relating thereto or concluded under the auspices of the WTO;

4)   Recognizing the importance of fostering an open and predictable environment for international trade and investment;

5)   Recognizing that it is desirable that trade and investment problems between the Parties should be resolved by mutual agreement;

6)   Recognizing the benefits to each Party resulting from increased international trade and investment, and that trade and investment barriers would deprive the Parties of such benefits;

7)   Recognizing the essential role of private investment, both domestic and foreign, in furthering growth, creating jobs, expanding trade, improving technology and enhancing economic development;

8)   Recognizing that foreign direct investment confers positive benefits on each Party;

9)   Recognizing the increasing importance of services in their respective economies and in their bilateral relations;

---

* *Source*: The Government of the United States and the Government of Nigeria (2000). "Agreement between the Government of the United States of America and the Government of the Federal Republic of Nigeria Concerning the Development of Trade and Investment Relations"; available on the Internet (http://www.ustr.gov/regions/africa/ustifa.htm). [Note added by the editor.]

10)   Taking into account the need to eliminate non-tariff barriers in order to facilitate greater access to the markets of both countries;

11)   Recognizing the importance of providing adequate and effective protection and enforcement of intellectual property rights, and taking into account each Party's obligations contained in the Agreement on Trade-Related Aspects of Intellectual Property Rights (TRIPS) and in intellectual property rights conventions;

12)   Desiring to further secure the observance and promotion of internationally recognized core labor standards and workers' rights, given the contribution that these afford to the economic well-being of both Parties;

13)   Desiring to ensure that trade and environmental policies are mutually supportive in furtherance of sustainable development; and

14)   Considering that it would be in their mutual interest to establish a bilateral mechanism between the Parties for encouraging the liberalization of trade and investment between them.

To this end, the Parties agree as follows:

ARTICLE ONE

The Parties affirm their desire to expand trade in products and services consistent with the terms of this Agreement. They will take appropriate measures to encourage and facilitate the exchange of goods and services and to secure favorable conditions for long-term development and diversification of trade between their respective nationals and companies.

ARTICLE TWO

The Parties will establish a United States - Nigeria Council on Trade and Investment ("the Council") which will be composed of representatives of both Parties. The United States of America's side of the Council will be chaired by the Office of the United States Trade Representative (USTR), while the Federal Republic of Nigeria's side of the Council will be chaired by the Ministry of Commerce. Each chair may be assisted by officials of other government entities in their respective countries as circumstances require.

ARTICLE THREE

The objectives of the Council are to hold consultations on specific trade and investment matters of interest to the Parties and the enhancement of trade and investment flows. The Council will also work toward the removal of impediments to such trade and investment flows.

ARTICLE FOUR

The Council will meet at such times and venues as agreed by the Parties.

ARTICLE FIVE

Either Party may seek the views of civil society, such as business, labor, consumer, environmental, and academic groups, on matters related to the work of the Council whenever the Party considers it appropriate.

ARTICLE SIX

For the purposes of further developing bilateral trade and investment and providing for a steady increase in the exchange of goods and services, the Parties will consider whether further agreements relating to trade, taxation, intellectual property, labor, transfer of technology, technical cooperation, and investment issues would be desirable.

ARTICLE SEVEN

Either Party may raise for consultation any trade or investment matter between the Parties. Requests for consultation will be accompanied by a written explanation of the subject to be discussed and consultations will be held within 90 days from the date of the written explanation unless otherwise agreed by the Parties.

Where a Party's specific measure or practice is the subject of discussion, initial consultations will normally be held in the territory of that Party, unless otherwise agreed.

This Agreement will be without prejudice to the rights of either Party under its domestic law or under any other instrument to which either country is a Party.

ARTICLE EIGHT

Either Party may request a revision of this Agreement by giving written notice to the other Party. Such a request will be responded to within six months from the date of submission. No revision of this Agreement will be valid unless it is agreed to and signed by both Parties.

ARTICLE NINE

Any dispute between the Parties relating to the implementation and interpretation of this Agreement will be resolved through consultations and negotiations.

ARTICLE TEN

This Agreement will become effective on the date of its signature and will remain effective unless terminated by mutual consent of the Parties or by either Party upon six months' written notice to the other Party.

IN WITNESS WHEREOF, the undersigned, being duly authorized by their respective governments, have signed this Agreement.

DONE AT WASHINGTON THIS DAY OF FEBRUARY 16, 2000.

* * *

PARTNERSHIP AGREEMENT BETWEEN THE MEMBERS OF THE AFRICAN, CARIBBEAN AND PACIFIC GROUP OF STATES OF THE ONE PART, AND THE EUROPEAN COMMUNITY AND ITS MEMBER STATES, OF THE OTHER PART*
[excerpts]

The Partnership Agreement between the Members of the African, Caribbean and Pacific Group of States of the One Part, and the European Community and Its Member States, of the Other Part was signed at Cotonou, Benin, on 23 June 2000.

THE COTONOU AGREEMENT

FINAL ACT

PART 3: COOPERATION STRATEGIES

TITLE I: DEVELOPMENT STRATEGIES

CHAPTER 1: GENERAL FRAMEWORK

ARTICLE 19
Principles and objectives

1.   The central objective of ACP-EC cooperation is poverty reduction and ultimately its eradication; sustainable development; and progressive integration of the ACP countries into the world economy. In this context, cooperation framework and orientations shall be tailored to the individual circumstances of each ACP country, shall promote local ownership of economic and social reforms and the integration of the private sector and civil society actors into the development process.

2.   Cooperation shall refer to the conclusions of United Nations Conferences and to the objectives, targets and action programmes agreed at international level and to their follow up as a basis for development principles. Cooperation shall also refer to the international development cooperation targets and shall pay particular attention to putting in place qualitative and quantitative indicators of progress.

3.   Governments and non-State actors in each ACP country shall initiate consultations on country development strategies and community support thereto.

---

* *Source*: African, Caribbean and the Pacific States and the European Community (2000). "Partnership Agreement between the Members of the African, Caribbean and Pacific Group of States of the One Part, and the European Community and Its Member States, of the Other Part", *Official Journal of the European Communities,* L 317, 15 December 2000, P. 3; available also on the Internet (http://www.acpsec.org/gb/cotonou/accord1e.htm). [Note added by the editor.]

ARTICLE 20
The Approach

The objectives of ACP-EC development cooperation shall be pursued through integrated strategies that incorporate economic, social, cultural, environmental and institutional elements that must be locally owned. Cooperation shall thus provide a coherent enabling framework of support to the ACP's own development strategies, ensuring complementarity and interaction between the various elements. In this context and within the framework of development policies and reforms pursued by the ACP States, ACP-EC cooperation strategies shall aim at:

    a.   achieving rapid and sustained job-creating economic growth, developing the private sector, increasing employment, improving access to productive economic activities and resource, and fostering regional cooperation and integration;

    b.   promoting human and social development helping to ensure that the fruits of growth are widely and equitably shared and promoting gender equality;

    c.   promoting cultural values of communities and specific interactions with economic, political and social elements;

    d.   promoting institutional reforms and development, strengthening the institutions necessary for the consolidation of democracy, good governance and for efficient and competitive market economies; and building capacity for development and partnership; and

    e.   promoting environmental sustainability, regeneration and best practices, and the preservation of natural resource base.

2.   Systematic account shall be taken in mainstreaming into all areas of cooperation the following thematic or cross-cutting themes: gender issues, environmental issues and institutional development and capacity building. These areas shall also be eligible for Community support.

3.   The detailed texts as regards development cooperation objectives and strategies, in particular sectoral policies and strategies shall be incorporated in a compendium providing operational guidelines in specific areas or sectors of cooperation. These texts may be revised, reviewed and/or amended by the Council of Ministers on the basis of a recommendation from the ACP-EC Development Finance Cooperation Committee.

PART 3: COOPERATION STRATEGIES

TITLE I: DEVELOPMENT STRATEGIES

CHAPTER 2: AREAS OF SUPPORT

SECTION 1: ECONOMIC DEVELOPMENT

ARTICLE 21
Investment and private sector development

1.　Cooperation shall support the necessary economic and institutional reforms and policies at national and/or regional level, aiming at creating a favourable environment for private investment, and the development of a dynamic, viable and competitive private sector.

Cooperation shall further support:

　　a.　the promotion of public-private sector dialogue and cooperation;

　　b.　the development of entrepreneurial skills and business culture;

　　c.　privatisation and enterprise reform; and

　　d.　development and modernisation of mediation and arbitration systems.

2.　Cooperation shall also support improving the quality, availability and accessibility of financial and non-financial services to private enterprises, both formal and informal; by:

　　a.　catalysing and leveraging flows of private savings, both domestic and foreign, into the financing of private enterprises by supporting policies for developing a modern financial sector including a capital market, financial institutions and sustainable microfinance operations;

　　b.　the development and strengthening of business institutions and intermediary organisations, associations, chambers of commerce and local providers from the private sector supporting and providing non-financial services to enterprises such as professional, technical, management, training and commercial support services; and

　　c.　supporting institutions, programmes, activities and initiatives that contribute to the development and transfer of technologies and know-how and best practices on all aspects of business management.

3.　Cooperation shall promote business development through the provision of finance, guarantee facilities and technical support aimed at encouraging and supporting the creation, establishment, expansion, diversification, rehabilitation, restructuring, modernisation or privatisation of dynamic, viable and competitive enterprises in all economic sectors as well as financial intermediaries such as development finance and venture capital institutions, and leasing companies by:

a.   creating and/or strengthening financial instruments in the form of investment capital;

b.   improving access to essential inputs such as business information and advisory, consultancy or technical assistance services;

c.   enhancement of export activities, in particular through capacity building in all trade-related areas; and

d.   encouraging inter-firm linkages, networks and cooperation including those involving the transfer of technology and know-how at national, regional and ACP-EU levels, and partnerships with private foreign investors which are consistent with the objectives and guidelines of ACP-EC Development cooperation.

4.   Cooperation shall support microenterprise development through better access to financial and non-financial services; an appropriate policy and regulatory framework for their development; and provide training and information services on best practices in microfinance.

5.   Support for investment and private sector development shall integrate actions and initiatives at macro, meso and micro economic levels.

ARTICLE 23
Economic sector development

Cooperation shall support sustainable policy and institutional reforms and the investments necessary for equitable access to economic activities and productive resources, particularly:

a.   the development of training systems that help increase productivity in both the formal and the informal sectors;
b.   capital, credit, land, especially as regards property rights and use;

c.   development of rural strategies aimed at establishing a framework for participatory decentralised planning, resource allocation and management;

d.   agricultural production strategies, national and regional food security policies, sustainable development of water resources and fisheries as well as marine resources within the economic exclusive zones of the ACP States. Any fishery agreement that may be negotiated between the Community and the ACP States shall pay due consideration to consistency with the development strategies in this area;

e.   economic and technological infrastructure and services, including transport, telecommunication systems, communication services and the development of information society;

f.   development of competitive industrial, mining and energy sectors, while encouraging private sector involvement and development;

g.   trade development, including the promotion of fair trade;

h.   development of business, finance and banking; and other service sectors;

i.   tourism development; and

j.   development of scientific, technological and research infrastructure and services; including the enhancement, transfer and absorption of new technologies;

k.   the strengthening of capacities in productive areas, especially in public and private sectors.

ARTICLE 24
Tourism

Cooperation will aim at the sustainable development of the tourism industry in ACP countries and sub-regions, recognising its increasing importance to the growth of the services sector in ACP countries and to the expansion of their global trade, its ability to stimulate other sectors of economic activity, and the role it can play in poverty eradication.

Cooperation programmes and projects will support the efforts of ACP countries to establish and improve the countries legal and institutional framework and resources for the development and implementation of sustainable tourism policies and programmes, as well as inter alia, improving the competitive position of the sector, especially small and medium-sized enterprises (SMEs), investment support and promotion, product development including the development of indigenous cultures in ACP countries, and strengthening linkages between tourism and other sectors of economic activity.

PART 3: COOPERATION STRATEGIES

TITLE I: DEVELOPMENT STRATEGIES

CHAPTER 2: AREAS OF SUPPORT

SECTION 3: REGIONAL COOPERATION AND INTEGRATION

ARTICLE 28
General approach

Cooperation shall provide effective assistance to achieve the objectives and priorities which the ACP States have set themselves in the context of regional and sub-regional cooperation and integration, including inter-regional and intra-ACP cooperation. Regional Cooperation can also involve Overseas Countries and Territories (OCTs) and outermost regions. In this context, cooperation support shall aim to:

a.   foster the gradual integration of the ACP States into the world economy;

b.   accelerate economic cooperation and development both within and between the regions of the ACP States;

c.   promote the free movement of persons, goods, services, capital, labour and technology among ACP countries;

d.   accelerate diversification of the economies of the ACP States; and coordination and harmonisation of regional and sub-regional cooperation policies; and

e.   promote and expand inter and intra-ACP trade and with third countries.

ARTICLE 29
Regional economic integration

Cooperation shall, in the area of regional economic integration, support:

a.   developing and strengthening the capacities of:

i.   regional integration institutions and organisations set up by the ACP States to promote regional cooperation and integration, and

ii.   national governments and parliaments in matters of regional integration;

b.   fostering participation of Least Developed Countries (LDC) ACP States in the establishment of regional markets and sharing the benefits therefrom;

c.   implementation of sectoral reform policies at regional level;

d.   liberalisation of trade and payments;

e.   promoting cross-border investments both foreign and domestic, and other regional or sub-regional economic integration initiatives; and

f.   taking account of the effects of net transitional costs of regional integration on budget revenue and balance of payments.

PART 3: COOPERATION STRATEGIES

TITLE II: ECONOMIC AND TRADE COOPERATION

CHAPTER 1: OBJECTIVES AND PRINCIPLES

ARTICLE 34
Objectives

1.   Economic and trade cooperation shall aim at fostering the smooth and gradual integration of the ACP States into the world economy, with due regard for their political choices and development priorities, thereby promoting their sustainable development and contributing to poverty eradication in the ACP countries.

2.   The ultimate objective of economic and trade cooperation is to enable the ACP States to play a full part in international trade. In this context, particular regard shall be had to the need for the ACP States to participate actively in multilateral trade negotiations. Given the current level of development of the ACP countries, economic and trade cooperation shall be directed at enabling the ACP States to manage the challenges of globalisation and to adapt progressively to new conditions of international trade thereby facilitating their transition to the liberalised global economy.

3.   To this end economic and trade cooperation shall aim at enhancing the production, supply and trading capacity of the ACP countries as well as their capacity to attract investment. It shall further aim at creating a new trading dynamic between the Parties, at strengthening the ACP countries trade and investment policies and at improving the ACP countries' capacity to handle all issues related to trade.

4.   Economic and trade cooperation shall be implemented in full conformity with the provisions of the WTO, including special and differential treatment, taking account of the Parties' mutual interests and their respective levels of development.

ARTICLE 35
Principles

1.   Economic and trade cooperation shall be based on a true, strengthened and strategic partnership. It shall further be based on a comprehensive approach which builds on the strengths and achievements of the previous ACP-EC Conventions, using all means available to achieve the objectives set out above by addressing supply and demand side constraints. In this context, particular regard shall be had to trade development measures as a means of enhancing ACP States' competitiveness. Appropriate weight shall therefore be given to trade development within the ACP States' development strategies, which the Community shall support.

2.   Economic and trade cooperation shall build on regional integration initiatives of ACP States, bearing in mind that regional integration is a key instrument for the integration of ACP countries into the world economy.

3.   Economic and trade cooperation shall take account of the different needs and levels of development of the ACP countries and regions. In this context, the Parties reaffirm their attachment to ensuring special and differential treatment for all ACP countries and to maintaining special treatment for ACP LDCs and to taking due account of the vulnerability of small, landlocked and island countries.

PART 3: COOPERATION STRATEGIES

TITLE II: ECONOMIC AND TRADE COOPERATION

CHAPTER 2: NEW TRADING ARRANGEMENTS

ARTICLE 36
Modalities

1.   In view of the objectives and principles set out above, the Parties agree to conclude new World Trade Organisation (WTO) compatible trading arrangements, removing progressively barriers to trade between them and enhancing cooperation in all areas relevant to trade.

2.   The Parties agree that the new trading arrangements shall be introduced gradually and recognise the need, therefore, for a preparatory period.

3.   In order to facilitate the transition to the new trading arrangements, the non-reciprocal trade preferences applied under the Fourth ACP-EC Convention shall be maintained during the preparatory period for all ACP countries, under the conditions defined in Annex V to this Agreement.

4.   In this context, the Parties reaffirm the importance of the commodity protocols, attached to Annex V of this Agreement. They agree on the need to review them in the context of the new trading arrangements, in particular as regards their compatibility with WTO rules, with a view to safeguarding the benefits derived therefrom, bearing in mind the special legal status of the Sugar Protocol.

ARTICLE 38
Joint Ministerial Trade Committee

1.   A Joint ACP-EC Ministerial Trade Committee shall be established.

2.   The Ministerial Trade Committee shall pay special attention to current multilateral trade negotiations and shall examine the impact of the wider liberalisation initiatives on ACP-EC trade and the development of ACP economies. It shall make any necessary recommendations with a view to preserving the benefits of the ACP-EC trading arrangements.

3.   The Ministerial Trade Committee shall meet at least once a year. Its rules of procedure shall be laid down by the Council of Ministers. It shall be composed of representatives of the ACP States and of the Community.

PART 3: COOPERATION STRATEGIES

TITLE II: ECONOMIC AND TRADE COOPERATION

CHAPTER 3: COOPERATION IN THE INTERNATIONAL FORA

ARTICLE 39
General Provisions

1.   The Parties underline the importance of their active participation in the WTO as well as in other relevant international organisations by becoming members of these organisations and closely following their agenda and activities.

2.   They agree to cooperate closely in identifying and furthering their common interests in international economic and trade cooperation in particular in the WTO, including participation in setting and conducting the agenda in future multilateral trade negotiations. In this context, particular attention shall be paid to improve access to the Community and other markets for products and services originating in the ACP countries.

3.   They also agree on the importance of flexibility in WTO rules to take account of the ACP's level of development as well of the difficulties faced in meeting their obligations. They further agree on the need for technical assistance to enable the ACP countries to implement their commitments.

4.   The Community agrees to assist the ACP States in their efforts, in accordance with the provisions set out in this Agreement, to become active members of these organisations, by developing the necessary capacity to negotiate, participate effectively, monitor and implement these agreements.

PART 3: COOPERATION STRATEGIES

TITLE II: ECONOMIC AND TRADE COOPERATION

CHAPTER 4: TRADE IN SERVICES

ARTICLE 41
General Provisions

1.   The Parties underline the growing importance of services in international trade and their major contribution to economic and social development.

2.   They reaffirm their respective commitments under the General Agreement on Trade in Services (GATS), and underline the need for special and differential treatment to ACP suppliers of services;

3.   In the framework of the negotiations for progressive liberalisation in trade and services, as provided for in Article XIX of GATS, the Community undertakes to give sympathetic

consideration to the ACP States' priorities for improvement in the EC schedule, with a view to meeting their specific interests.

4.   The Parties further agree on the objective of extending under the economic partnership agreements, and after they have acquired some experience in applying the Most Favoured Nation (MFN) treatment under GATS, their partnership to encompass the liberalisation of services in accordance with the provisions of GATS and particularly those relating to the participation of developing countries in liberalisation agreements.

5.   The Community shall support the ACP States' efforts to strengthen their capacity in the supply of services. Particular attention shall be paid to services related to labour, business, distribution, finance, tourism, culture and construction and related engineering services with a view to enhancing their competitiveness and thereby increasing the value and the volume of their trade in goods and services.

PART 3: COOPERATION STRATEGIES

TITLE II: ECONOMIC AND TRADE COOPERATION

CHAPTER 5: TRADE-RELATED AREAS

ARTICLE 44
General Provisions

1.   The Parties acknowledge the growing importance of new areas related to trade in facilitating progressive integration of the ACP States into the world economy.

They therefore agree to strengthen their cooperation in these areas by establishing full and coordinated participation in the relevant international fora and agreements.

2.   The Community shall support the ACP States' efforts, in accordance with the provisions set out in this Agreement and the development strategies agreed between the Parties to strengthen their capacity to handle all areas related to trade, including, where necessary, improving and supporting the institutional framework.

ARTICLE 45
Competition Policy

1.   The Parties agree that the introduction and implementation of effective and sound competition policies and rules are of crucial importance in order to improve and secure an investment friendly climate, a sustainable industrialisation process and transparency in the access to markets.

2.   To ensure the elimination of distortions to sound competition and with due consideration to the different levels of development and economic needs of each ACP country, they undertake to implement national or regional rules and policies including the control and under certain conditions the prohibition of agreements between undertakings, decisions by associations of

undertakings and concerted practices between undertakings which have as their object or effect the prevention, restriction or distortion of competition. The Parties further agree to prohibit the abuse by one or more undertakings of a dominant position in the common market of the Community or in the territory of ACP States.

3.   The Parties also agree to reinforce cooperation in this area with a view to formulating and supporting effective competition policies with the appropriate national competition agencies that progressively ensure the efficient enforcement of the competition rules by both private and state enterprises. Cooperation in this area shall, in particular, include assistance in the drafting of an appropriate legal framework and its administrative enforcement with particular reference to the special situation of the least developed countries.

ARTICLE 46
Protection of Intellectual Property Rights

1.   Without prejudice to the positions of the Parties in multilateral negotiations, the Parties recognise the need to ensure an adequate and effective level of protection of intellectual, industrial and commercial property rights, and other rights covered by TRIPS including protection of geographical indications, in line with the international standards with a view to reducing distortions and impediments to bilateral trade.

2.   They underline the importance, in this context, of adherence to the Agreement on Trade-Related Aspects of Intellectual Property Rights (TRIPS) to the WTO Agreement and the Convention on Biological Diversity (CBD).

3.   They also agree on the need to accede to all relevant international conventions on intellectual, industrial and commercial property as referred to in Part I of the TRIPS Agreement, in line with their level of development.

4.   The Community, its Member States and the ACP States may consider the conclusion of agreements aimed at protecting trademarks and geographical indications for products of particular interest of either Party.

5.   For the purpose of this Agreement, intellectual property includes in particular copyright, including the copyright on computer programmes, and neighbouring rights, including artistic designs, and industrial property which includes utility models, patents including patents for bio-technological inventions and plant varieties or other effective sui generis systems, industrial designs, geographical indications including appellations of origin, trademarks for goods or services, topographies of integrated circuits as well as the legal protection of data bases and the protection against unfair competition as referred to in Article 10a of the Paris Convention for the Protection of Industrial Property and protection of undisclosed confidential information on know how.

6.   The Parties further agree to strengthen their cooperation in this field. Upon request and on mutually agreed terms and conditions cooperation shall inter alia extend to the following areas: the preparation of laws and regulations for the protection and enforcement of intellectual property rights, the prevention of the abuse of such rights by right-holders and the infringement of such rights by competitors, the establishment and reinforcement of domestic and regional offices and other agencies including support for regional intellectual property organisations involved in enforcement and protection, including the training of personnel.

ARTICLE 52
Tax Carve-out Clause

1.   Without prejudice to the provisions of Article 31 of Annex IV, the Most Favoured Nation treatment granted in accordance with the provisions of this Agreement, or any arrangement adopted under this Agreement, does not apply to tax advantages which the Parties are providing or may provide in the future on the basis of agreements to avoid double taxation or other tax arrangements, or domestic fiscal legislation.

2.   Nothing in this Agreement, or in any arrangements adopted under this Agreement, may be construed to prevent the adoption or enforcement of any measure aimed at preventing the avoidance or evasion of taxes pursuant to the tax provisions of agreements to avoid double taxation or other tax arrangements, or domestic fiscal legislation.

3.   Nothing in this Agreement, or in any arrangements adopted under this Agreement, shall be construed to prevent the Parties from distinguishing, in the application of the relevant provisions of their fiscal legislation, between taxpayers who are not in the same situation, in particular with regard to their place of residence, or with regard to the place where their capital is invested.

PART 4: DEVELOPMENT FINANCE COOPERATION

TITLE II: FINANCIAL COOPERATION

CHAPTER 7: INVESTMENT AND PRIVATE SECTOR DEVELOPMENT SUPPORT

ARTICLE 74

Cooperation shall, through financial and technical assistance, support the policies and strategies for investment and private sector development as set out in this Agreement.

ARTICLE 75
Investment promotion

The ACP States, the Community and its Member States, within the scope of their respective competencies, recognising the importance of private investment in the promotion of their development cooperation and acknowledging the need to take steps to promote such investment, shall:

   a.   implement measures to encourage participation in their development efforts by private investors who comply with the objectives and priorities of ACP-EC development cooperation and with the appropriate laws and regulations of their respective States;

   b.   take measures and actions which help to create and maintain a predictable and secure investment climate as well as enter into negotiations on agreements which will improve such climate;

c. encourage the EU private sector to invest and to provide specific assistance to its counterparts in the ACP countries under mutual business cooperation and partnerships;

d. facilitate partnerships and joint ventures by encouraging co-financing;

e. sponsor sectoral investment fora to promote partnerships and external investment;

f. support efforts of the ACP States to attract financing, with particular emphasis on private financing, for infrastructure investments and revenue generating infrastructure critical for the private sector;

g. support capacity building for domestic investment promotion agencies and institutions involved in promoting and facilitating foreign investment;

h. disseminate information on investment opportunities and business operating conditions in the ACP States; and

i. promote national, regional and ACP-EU private sector business dialogue, cooperation and partnerships, in particular through an ACP-EU private sector business forum. Support for operations of an ACP-EU private sector business forum shall be provided in pursuit of the following objectives:

  i. to facilitate dialogue within the ACP/EU private sector and between the ACP/EU private sector and the bodies established under the Agreement;

  ii. to analyse and periodically provide the relevant bodies with information on the whole range of issues concerning relations between the ACP and EU private sectors in the context of the Agreement or, more generally, of economic relations between the Community and the ACP countries; and

  iii. to analyse and provide the relevant bodies with information on specific problems of a sectoral nature relating to, inter alia, branches of production or types of products at regional or sub-regional level.

ARTICLE 76
Investment finance and support

1. Cooperation shall provide long-term financial resources, including risk capital, to assist in promoting growth in the private sector and help to mobilise domestic and foreign capital for this purpose. To this end, cooperation shall provide, in particular:

a. grants for financial and technical assistance to support policy reforms, human resource development, institutional capacity-building or other forms of institutional support related to a specific investment, measures to increase the competitiveness of enterprises and to strengthen the capacities of the private financial and non-financial intermediaries, investment facilitation and promotion and competitiveness enhancement activities;

b.   advisory and consultative services to assist in creating a responsive investment climate and information base to guide and encourage the flow of capital;

c.   risk-capital for equity or quasi-equity investments, guarantees in support of domestic and foreign private investment and loans or lines of credit on the conditions laid down in Annex II "Terms and Conditions of Financing" to this Agreement; and

d.   loans from the Bank's own resources.

2.   Loans from the Bank's own resources shall be granted in accordance with its statute and with the terms and conditions laid down in Annex II to this Agreement.

ARTICLE 77
Investment guarantees

1.   Investment guarantees are an increasingly important tool for development finance as they contribute to reducing project risks and inducing private capital flows.

Cooperation shall therefore ensure the increasing availability and use of risk insurance as a risk-mitigating mechanism in order to boost investor confidence in the ACP States.

2.   Cooperation shall offer guarantees and assist with guarantees funds covering risks for qualified investment. Specifically, cooperation shall provide support to:

a.   reinsurance schemes to cover foreign direct investment by eligible investors; against legal uncertainties and the major risks of expropriation, currency transfer restriction, war and civil disturbance, and breach of contract. Investors may insure projects for any combination of the four types of coverage;

b.   guarantee programmes to cover risk in the form of partial guarantees for debt financing. Both partial risk and partial credit guarantee shall be available; and

c.   national and regional guarantee funds, involving, in particular, domestic financial institutions or investors for encouraging the development of the financial sector.

3.   Cooperation shall also provide support to capacity-building, institutional support and participation in the core funding of national and/or regional initiatives to reduce the commercial risks for investors (inter alia guarantee funds, regulatory bodies, arbitration mechanisms and judiciary systems to enhance the protection of investments improving the export credit systems).

4.   Cooperation shall provide such support on the basis of complementary and added value with respect to private and/or public initiatives and, whenever feasible, in partnership with private and other public organisations. The ACP and the EC will within the framework of the ACP-EC Development Finance Cooperation Committee undertake a joint study on the proposal to set up an ACP-EC Guarantee Agency to provide and manage investment guarantee programmes.

ARTICLE 78
Investment protection

1.   The ACP States and the Community and its Member States, within the scope of their respective competencies, affirm the need to promote and protect either Party's investments on their respective territories, and in this context affirm the importance of concluding, in their mutual interest, investment promotion and protection agreements which could also provide the basis for insurance and guarantee schemes.

2.   In order to encourage European investment in development projects of special importance to, and promoted by the ACP States, the Community and the Member States, on the one hand and the ACP States on the other, may also conclude agreements relating to specific projects of mutual interest where the Community and European enterprises contribute towards their financing.

3.   The Parties also agree to introduce, within the economic partnership agreements, and while respecting the respective competencies of the Community and its Member States, general principles on protection and promotion of investments, which will endorse the best results agreed in the competent international fora or bilaterally.

PART 4: DEVELOPMENT FINANCE COOPERATION

TITLE III: TECHNICAL COOPERATION

ARTICLE 79

1.   Technical cooperation shall assist the ACP States in the development of national and regional manpower resources, the sustained development of the institutions critical for development success, including inter alia strengthening ACP consulting firms and organisations, as well as exchange arrangements involving consultants from both ACP and EU firms.

2.   Furthermore, technical cooperation, shall be cost-effective and relevant to the need for which it is intended, and shall also favour the transfer of know-how and increase national and regional capabilities. Technical cooperation shall contribute to the achievement of project and programme goals, including efforts to strengthen management capacity of the National and Regional Authorising Officers. Technical assistance shall:

   a.   be demand-driven and thus made available only at the request of the ACP State or States concerned, and adapted to recipient needs;

   b.   complement and support ACP efforts to identify their own requirements;

   c.   be monitored and followed up to guarantee effectiveness;

   d.   encourage the participation of ACP experts, consultancy firms and educational and research institutions in contracts financed from the Fund and identify ways of employing qualified national and regional personnel on Fund projects;

e.   encourage the secondment of ACP national cadres as consultants to an institution in their own country, or a neighbouring country, or to a regional organisation;

f.   aim at developing knowledge of national and regional manpower constraints and potential and establish a register of ACP experts, consultants and consultancy firms suitable for employment on projects and programmes financed from the Fund;

g.   support intra-ACP technical assistance in order to promote the exchange between the ACP States of technical assistance, management and professional expertise;

h.   develop action programmes for long-term institution building and staff development as an integral part of project and programme planning, account being taken of the necessary financial requirements;

i.   support arrangements to enhance the capacity of the ACP States to build up their own expertise; and

j.   give special attention to the development of the ACP States' capacities in project planning, implementation and evaluation, as well budget management.

3.   Technical assistance may be provided in all areas of cooperation and within the limits of the mandate of this Agreement. The activities covered would be diverse in scope and nature, and would be tailored to meet the needs of the ACP States.

4.   Technical cooperation may be either of a specific or a general nature. The ACP-EC Development Finance Cooperation Committee shall establish the guidelines for the implementation of technical cooperation.

ARTICLE 80

With a view to reversing the brain drain from the ACP States, the Community shall assist ACP States which so request to facilitate the return of qualified ACP nationals resident in developed countries through appropriate re-installation incentives.

PART 5: GENERAL PROVISIONS FOR THE LEAST-DEVELOPED, LANDLOCKED AND ISLAND ACP STATES (LDLICs)

CHAPTER 1: GENERAL PROVISIONS

ARTICLE 84

1.   To enable LDLICs to take full advantage of the opportunities offered by the Agreement so as to step up their respective rates of development, cooperation shall ensure special treatment for the least developed ACP countries and take due account of the vulnerability of landlocked and island ACP countries. It shall also take into consideration the needs of countries in post-conflict situations.

2.   Independently of the specific measures and provisions for the least-developed, landlocked and island countries in the different chapters of the Agreement, special attention shall be paid in respect of these groups as well as countries in post-conflict situations to:

   a.   the strengthening of regional cooperation;

   b.   transport and communications' infrastructure;

   c.   the efficient exploitation of marine resources and the marketing of products so produced and, in the case of landlocked countries, inland fisheries;

   d.   structural adjustment where account shall be taken of the level of development of these countries and equally, at the implementation stage, of the social dimension of adjustment; and

   e.   the implementation of food strategies and integrated development programmes.

PART 5: GENERAL PROVISIONS FOR THE LEAST-DEVELOPED, LANDLOCKED AND ISLAND ACP STATES (LDLICs)

CHAPTER 2: LEAST-DEVELOPED ACP STATES

ARTICLE 85

1.   The least-developed ACP States shall be accorded a special treatment in order to enable them to overcome the serious economic and social difficulties hindering their development so as to step up their respective rates of development.

2.   The list of least-developed countries is given in Annex VI. It may be amended by a decision of the Council of Ministers where:

   a.   a third State in a comparable situation accedes to this Agreement; and

b.   the economic situation of an ACP State changes considerably and durably to the extent that it needs to be included in the least-developed category or its inclusion in that category is no longer justified.

ARTICLE 86

The provisions adopted in respect of the least-developed ACP States are contained in the following Articles: 2, 29, 32, 35, 37, 56, 68, 84, 85.

PART 5: GENERAL PROVISIONS FOR THE LEAST-DEVELOPED, LANDLOCKED AND ISLAND ACP STATES (LDLICs)

CHAPTER 3: LANDLOCKED ACP STATES

ARTICLE 87

1.   Specific provisions and measures shall be established to support landlocked ACP States in their efforts to overcome the geographical difficulties and other obstacles hampering their development so as to enable them to step up their respective rates of development.

2.   The list of landlocked ACP States is given in Annex VI. It may be amended by decision of the Council of Ministers when a third State in a comparable situation accedes to the Agreement.

ARTICLE 88

The provisions adopted in respect of the landlocked ACP States are contained in the following Articles: 2, 32, 35, 56, 68, 84, 87.

PART 5: GENERAL PROVISIONS FOR THE LEAST-DEVELOPED, LANDLOCKED AND ISLAND ACP STATES (LDLICs)

CHAPTER 4: ISLAND ACP STATES

ARTICLE 89

1.   Specific provisions and measures shall be established to support island ACP States in their efforts to overcome the natural and geographical difficulties and other obstacles hampering their development so as to enable them to step up their respective rates of development.

2.   The list of island ACP States is given in Annex VI. It may be amended by decision of the Council of Ministers when a third State in a comparable situation accedes to the Agreement.

ARTICLE 90

The provisions adopted in respect of the island ACP States are contained in the following Articles: 2, 32, 35, 56, 68, 84, 89.

PART 6: FINAL PROVISIONS

ARTICLE 91
Conflict between this Agreement and other treaties

No treaty, convention, agreement or arrangement of any kind between one or more Member States of the Community and one or more ACP States may impede the implementation of this Agreement.

*   *   *

PART FIVE

PROTOTYPE BILATERAL INVESTMENT TREATIES

AGREEMENT BETWEEN THE GOVERNMENT OF THE KINGDOM OF CAMBODIA AND THE GOVERNMENT OF _____ CONCERNING THE PROMOTION AND PROTECTION OF INVESTMENTS[*]

The Government of the Kingdom of Cambodia and The Government of .... (hereinafter referred to as "Contracting Parties");

Bearing in mind the friendly and cooperative relations existing between the two countries and their peoples;

Intending to create favourable conditions for investments by nationals of one Contracting Party on the basis of sovereign equality and mutual benefit, and

Recognizing that the Agreement on the Promotion and Protection of such Investments will be conducive to the stimulation of investment activities in both countries;

Have agreed as follows:

ARTICLE I
DEFINITIONS

For the purpose of this Agreement:

1.   The term "investment" shall mean any kind of asset invested by investors of one Contracting Party in the territory of the other Contracting Party, in conformity with the laws and regulations of the latter, including, but not exclusively:

   a.   movable and immovable property as well as other rights such as mortgages, privileges, and guarantees and any other similar rights;

   b.   rights derived from shares, bonds or any other form of interest in companies or joint venture in the territory of the other Contracting Party;

   c.   claims to money or to any performance having a financial value;

   d.   intellectual property rights, including rights with respect to copyrights, patents, trademarks, trade names, industrial designs, technical processes, goodwill and know-how;

   e.   business concessions having an economic value conferred by law or under contract related to investment including concessions to search for or exploit natural resources.

   Any alteration of the form in which assets are invested shall not affect their character as an investment, provided that such alteration has also been approved or admitted under Article II.

---

[*]   *Source*: The Government of Cambodia, Ministry of Foreign Affairs. [Note added by the editor.]

2.   The term "investor" means national of one Contracting Party who invests in the territory of the other Contracting Party. The term "national" shall comprise with regard to either Contracting Party;

>   (i)   natural person having the nationality of that Contracting Party in accordance with its law; and

>   (ii)   legal persons constituted under the law of that Contracting Party.

3.   The term "without delay" shall be deemed that to be fulfilled if a transfer is made within such period as is normally required by international finance practices.

4.   "Territory" shall mean:

>   a.   In respect of ....:
>   The territory of the .... as defined in its laws.

>   b.   In respect of the territory of the Kingdom of Cambodia as defined in its laws.

ARTICLE II
PROMOTION AND PROTECTION OF INVESTMENTS

1.   Either Contracting Party shall encourage and create favourable conditions for investors of the other Contracting party to invest in its territory, and shall admit such capital in accordance with its laws and regulations.

2.   Investments of investors of either Contracting Party shall at all times be accorded fair and equitable treatment and shall enjoy adequate protection and security in the territory of the other Contracting Party.

ARTICLE III
MOST-FAVOURED-NATION PROVISIONS

1.   Each Contracting Party shall ensure fair and equitable treatment of the investments of investors of the other Contracting Party and shall not impair, by unreasonable or discriminatory measures, the operation, management, maintenance, use, enjoyment or disposal thereof by those investors. Each Contracting Party shall accord to such investment adequate physical security and protection.

2.   More particularly, each Contracting Party shall accord to such investments treatment which in any case shall not be less favourable than that accorded to investments of investors of any third state.

3.   If a Contracting Party has accorded special advantages to investors of any third state by virtue of agreements establishing customs unions, economic unions, monetary unions or similar institutions, that Contracting Party shall not be obliged to accord such advantages to investors of the other Contracting Party.

4.   The provision of this Agreement shall not apply to matters of taxation in the territory of either Contracting Party. Such matters shall be governed by any Avoidance of Double Taxation Treaty between the two Contracting Parties and the domestic laws of each Contracting Party.

ARTICLE IV
EXPROPRIATION

Each Contracting Party shall not take any measures of expropriation, nationalization, or otherwise subjected to any other measures having effect equivalent to nationalization or expropriation (hereinafter referred to as "expropriation") against the investments of an investor of the other Contracting Party except under the following conditions:

<ul>
<li>a. the measures are taken for a lawful purpose, for public interest and under due process of law;</li>
</ul>

<ul>
<li>b. the measures are non discriminatory;</li>
</ul>

<ul>
<li>c. the measures are accompanied by provisions for the payment of prompt, adequate and effective compensation. Such compensation shall amount to the fair market value of the investments affected immediately before the measures of expropriation became a public knowledge. Such market value shall be determined in accordance with internationally acknowledged practices and methods or, where such fair market value cannot be determined, it shall be such reasonable amount as may be mutually agreed between the Contracting Parties hereto, and it shall be freely transferable in freely usable currencies from the Contracting Party.</li>
</ul>

ARTICLE V
COMPENSATION FOR LOSSES

1.   Investors of one Contracting Party, whose investments in the territory of the other Contracting Party suffer losses owing to war or other armed conflict, revolution, a state of investor emergency, revolt, insurrection or riot in the territory of the latter Contracting Party, shall be accorded by the latter Contracting Party treatment, as regards restitution, indemnification, compensation or other settlement.

2.   The treatment shall not be less favourable than that which the latter Contracting Party accords to investors or investors of any third state.

ARTICLE VI
TRANSFER

1.   Each Contracting Party shall, subject to its laws and regulations, allow without unreasonable delay the free transfer of investments made by investors of the other Contracting Party. Such transfer shall include, in particular, though not exclusively:

<ul>
<li>a. profits, interests, dividends and other current income accruing from investments;</li>
</ul>

<ul>
<li>b. funds necessary:</li>
</ul>

(i)   for the acquisition of raw or auxiliary materials, semi fabricated or finished products; or

(ii)   to replace capital assets in order to safeguard the continuity of an investment;

c.   additional funds necessary for the development of an investment;

d.   funds in repayment of loans related to investments;

e.   royalties or fees;

f.   earning of natural persons;

g.   proceeds accruing from sale or liquidation of the investment;

h.   compensation for losses pursuant to Article 5;

i.   compensation for expropriation pursuant to Article 4;

2.   The exchange rate applicable to such transfer in the paragraph 1 of this Article shall be the rate of exchange prevailing at the time of remittance.

ARTICLE VII
SUBROGATION

If the investments of an investor of the one Contracting Party are insured against non-commercial risks under a system established by law, any subrogation of the insurer or re-insurer to the rights of the said investor pursuant to the terms of such insurance shall be recognized by the other Contracting Party, provided, however, that the insurer or the re-insurer shall not be entitled to exercise any rights other than the rights which the investor would have been entitled to exercise.

ARTICLE VIII
SETTLEMENT OF DISPUTES BETWEEN
INVESTORS AND THE CONTRACTING PARTY

1.   Any dispute between a Contracting Party and an investor of the other Contracting Party, concerning an investment of the latter in the territory of the former, shall be settled amicably through consultations and negotiations.

2.   If such a dispute cannot be settled within a period of six months from the date of the written notification by either party requested amicable settlement, the dispute shall, at the request of the investor concerned, be submitted either to the judicial procedures provided by the Contracting Party concerned or to international arbitration or conciliation.

3.   In case that the dispute is submitted to arbitration or conciliation the investor shall be entitled to refer the dispute to:

(a)   The International Center of Settlement of Investment Disputes for settlement by conciliation or arbitration under the Convention on the Settlement of Investment Disputes between States and Nationals of other States, opened for signature at Washington D.C, on 18 March 1965, in case both Contracting Parties have become the Parties to the Convention; or

(b)   An ad hoc tribunal to be established under the arbitration rules of the United Nations Commission on International Trade Law (UNCITRAL). An arbitral award shall be final and binding on both parties to the dispute.

(c)   Neither Contracting Party shall pursue through diplomatic channels any matter referred to arbitration until the proceeding have terminated or a contracting Party has failed to abide by or comply with the award rendered by an arbitral tribunal.

ARTICLE IX
SETTLEMENT OF DISPUTES BETWEEN THE CONTRACTING PARTIES CONCERNING INTERPRETATION AND APPLICATION OF THE AGREEMENT

1.   Disputes between the Contracting Parties concerning the interpretation or application of this Agreement should, if possible, be settled through diplomatic channels.

2.   If dispute between the Contracting Parties cannot thus be settled, it shall upon the request of either Contracting Party be submitted to an arbitral tribunal.

3.   Such an arbitral tribunal shall be constituted for each individual case in the following way. Within two months of receipt of the request for arbitration, each Contracting Party shall appoint one member of the tribunal. Those two members shall then select a national of a third State who on approval by the Contracting Parties shall be appointed Chairman of the Tribunal. The Chairman shall be appointed within two months from the date of appointment of the other two members.

4.   If within the period specified in paragraph 3 of this Article the necessary appointments have not been made, either Contracting Party may, in the absence of any other Agreement, invite the President of the International Court of Justice to make any necessary appointment. If the President is a national of either Contracting Party or if he is otherwise prevented from discharging the said function, the Vice-President shall be invited to make a necessary appointment. If the Vice-President is a national of either Contracting Party or he too is prevented from discharging the said function, the member of the International Court or Justice next in seniority that is not a national of either Contracting Party shall be invited to make the necessary appointment.

5.   An arbitral tribunal shall reach its decision by a majority of votes. Such decision shall be binding on both Contracting Parties. Each Contracting Party shall bear the cost of its own member of the Tribunal and of its representation in an arbitral proceedings; the cost of the Chairman and the remaining costs shall be borne in equal parts by the Contracting Parties. The Tribunal may, however, in its decision direct that a higher proportion of costs shall be borne by one of the two Contracting Parties, and its award shall be binding on both Contracting Parties. The Tribunal shall determine its own procedure.

ARTICLE X
APPLICABILITY OF THIS AGREEMENT

This Agreement shall apply to investments made in the territory of either Contracting Party in accordance with its laws and regulations concerning foreign investment any law amending or replacing it, but shall not apply to any dispute, claim or difference which arose before its entry into force.

ARTICLE XI
APPLICATION OF OTHER PROVISIONS

If the provisions of law of either Contracting Party or obligations under international law existing at present or established hereafter between the Contracting Parties in addition to the present Agreement contain a regulation, whether general or specific, entitling investments by investors of the other Contracting Party to a treatment more favourable than is provided for by the present Agreement, such regulation shall be the extent that it is more favourable prevail over the present Agreement.

ARTICLE XII
CONSULTATION AND AMENDMENT

1.   Either Contracting Party may request that consultations be held on any matter concerning this Agreement. The other Party shall accord sympathetic consideration to the proposal and shall afford adequate opportunity for such consultations.

2.   This Agreement may be amended at any time, if deemed necessary, by mutual consent of both Contracting Parties.

ARTICLE XIII
ENTRY INTO FORCE, DURATION AND TERMINATION

1.   The present Agreement shall enter into force thirty (30) days after the later date on which the Contracting Parties have notified each other that their constitutional requirements for the entry into force of this Agreement have been fulfilled. It shall remain in force for a period of ten (10) years and shall continue in force thereafter for another period of ten years and so forth unless, after the expiry of the initial period of ten years, either Contracting Party notifies in writing of its intention to terminate this Agreement. The notice of termination shall become effective one year after it has been received by the other Contracting Party.

2.   With respect to investments made or acquired prior to the date of termination of this Agreement, the provisions of this Agreement shall continue to be effective for a period of ten (10) years from the date of termination.

IN WITNESS WHEREOF, the undersigned, duly authorized thereto by their respective Governments, have signed this Agreement.

Done in duplicate at ………………….on …………...in Khmer, ……………. and English languages. All texts are equally authentic. If there is any divergence concerning the interpretation, the English text shall prevail.

FOR THE GOVERNMENT
OF THE KINGDOM OF CAMBODIA

....

FOR THE GOVERNMENT
OF ....

....

*   *   *

AGREEMENT BETWEEN THE GOVERNMENT OF THE REPUBLIC OF CROATIA AND THE GOVERNMENT OF THE _____ ON THE RECIPROCAL PROMOTION AND PROTECTION OF INVESTMENTS*

The Government of the Republic of Croatia and the Governemnt of the _____ (hereinafter the "Contracting Parties");

Desiring to promote greater economic cooperation between them, with respect to investment by investors of one Conctracting Party in the territory of the other Contracting Party;

Recognizing that agreement upon the treatment to be accorded to such investment will stimulate the flow of private capital and the economic development of the Contracting Parties;

Agreeing that a stable framework for investment will maximize effective utilization of economic resources and increase prosperity;

Having resolved to conclude the Agreement on the reciprocal promotion and protection of investments;

Have agreed as follows:

ARTICLE 1
Definitions

For the purposes of the Agreement:

1.   The term "investment" means every kind of asset established or acquired by investors of one Contracting Party in the territory of the other Contracting Party in accordance with its laws and regulations and shall include in particular, though not exclusively:

a)   movable and immovable property as well as any other rights in rem such as mortgages, liens, pledges, usufructs and similar rights;

b)   stock, shares, debentures and other forms of participation in companies;

c)   claims to money or to any performance having economic value, including every loan granted for the purpose of creating economic value;

d)   intellectual property rights including, but not limited to, copyrights and neighbouring rights, industrial property rights, trademarks, patents, industrial designs and technical processes, rights in plants varieties, know-how, trade secrets, trade names and goodwill;

---

*   *Source*: The Government of Croatia, Ministry of Foreign Affairs. [Note added by the editor.]

e)   rights to engage in economic and commercial activities conferred by law and by virtue of a contract, including concessions to search for, cultivate, extract or exploit natural resources.

Any change of the form in which asset is invested or reinvested shall not affect its character as an investment.

2.   The term "investor" means in respect of either Contracting Party:

a)   a natural person, a national of a Contracting Party who makes an investment in the territory of the other Contracting Party;

b)   a legal person incorporated, constituted or otherwise duly organised in accordance with the laws and regulations of one Contracting Party, having its seat and performing real business activity in the territory of the same Contracting Party and making an investment in the territory of the other Contracting Party;

3.   The term "returns" means income deriving from an investment and includes, in particular though not exclusively, profits, dividends, interests, capital gains, royalties, patents licence fees, and other fees. Reinvested returns shall enjoy the same treatment as the original investment.

4.   The term "without delay" shall mean such period as is normally required for the completion of necessary formalities for the transfer of payments. The said period shall commence on the day on which the request for transfer has been submitted and may on no account exceed one month.

5.   The term "freely convertible currency" means a currency which is widely traded in international foreign exchange markets and widely used in international transactions.

6.   The term "territory" means:

-       with respect to the Republic of Croatia: the territory of the Republic of Croatia as well as those maritime areas adjacent to the outer limit of the territorial sea including the seabed and subsoil over which the Republic of Croatia exercises, in accordance with international law, its sovereign rights and jurisdiction.

-       with respect to the _____:

ARTICLE 2
Promotion and admission of investments

1.   Each Contracting Party shall encourage and create favourable conditions for investors of the other Contracting Party to make investments in its territory and shall admit such investments in accordance with its laws and regulations.

2.   In order to encourage mutual investment flows, each Contracting Party shall endeavour to inform the other Contracting Party, at the request of either Contracting Party, on the investment opportunities in its territory.

3.   Each Contracting Party shall grant, whenever necessary, within the framework of its legislation, permits in connection with the investments in its territory, including authorisations for engaging top managerial and technical personnel of their choice, regardless of nationality.

4.   Each Contracting Party shall permit, subject to its laws, regulations and procedures affecting the entry, stay and work of natural persons, regardless of nationality, key personnel including top managerial and technical persons who are employed for the purposes of investments by an investor of the other Contracting Party, to enter, stay and work in its territory. Immediate family members (spouse and minor children) of such key personnel shall also be granted similar treatment with regard to the entry and temporary stay in the host Contracting Party.

ARTICLE 3
Protection of investments

1.   Each Contracting Party shall extend in its territory full protection and security to investments and returns of investors of the other Contracting Party. Neither Contracting Party shall hamper, by arbitrary, unreasonably or discriminatory measures, the development, management, maintenance, use, enjoyment, expansion, sale and if it is the case, the liquidation of such investments. Either Contracting Party shall observe any other obligation it may have entered into with regard to specific investments of investors of the other Contracting Party.

2.   Investments or returns of investors of either Contracting Party in the territory of the other Contracting Party shall be accorded fair and equitable treatment in accordance with international law and provisions of this Agreement.

3.   Each Contracting Party shall in its territory not impose mandatory measures on investments by investors of the other Contracting Party concerning purchase of materials, means of production, operation, transport, marketing of its products or similar orders having unreasonable or discriminatory effects.

4.   Each Contracting Party shall promptly publish, or otherwise make publicly available, its laws, regulations, procedures and administrative rulings and judicial decisions of general application as well as international agreements which may affect the investments of investors of one Contracting Party in the territory of the other Contracting Party.

ARTICLE 4
National treatment and most favoured nation treatment

1.   Neither Contracting Party shall accord in its territory to investments and returns of investors of the other Contracting Party a treatment less favourable than that which it accords to investments and returns of its own investors, or investments and returns of investors of any other third State, whichever is more favourable to the investors concerned.

2.   Neither Contracting Party shall accord in its territory to the investors of the other Contracting Party, as regards management, maintenance, enjoyment, use or disposal of their investment, a treatment which is less favourable than that which it accords to its own investors or to investors of any third State, whichever is more favourable to the investors concerned.

3.   The provisions of paragraph 1 and 2 of this Article shall not be construed so as to oblige one Contracting Party to extend to the investors of the other Contracting Party the benefit of any

treatment, preference or privilege which may be extended by the former Contracting Party by virtue of:

a)   any existing or future customs union or economic union, free trade area or similar international agreement,

b)   any international agreement or arrangement, completely or partially related to taxation,

to which either of the Contracting Party is or may become a Party in the future.

ARTICLE 5
Expropriation

1.   A Contracting Party shall not expropriate or nationalise directly or indirectly an investment in its territory of an investor of another Contracting Party or take any measure or measures having equivalent effect (hereinafter referred to as "expropriation") except:

a)   for a purpose which is in the public interest,

b)   on a non-discriminatory basis,

c)   in accordance with due process of law, and

d)   accompanied by payment of prompt, adequate and effective compensation.

2.   Compensation shall be paid without delay.

3.   Such compensation shall amount to the fair market value of the expropriated investment at the time immediately before the expropriation was taken or became publicly known, whichever is earlier.

4.   Such fair market value shall be expressed in a freely convertible currency on the basis of the market rate of exchange existing for that currency at the moment referred to in paragraph 2. of this Article. Compensation shall also include interest at a commercial rate established on a market basis for the currency in question from the date of expropriation until the date of actual payment.

5.   The investor, whose investments are expropriated, shall have the right to prompt review of its case by a judicial or other competent authority of that Contracting Party, valuation of its investments and payment of compensation in accordance with the principles set out in this Article.

ARTICLE 6
Compensation for damage or loss

1.   When investments made by investors of either Contracting Party suffer loss or damage owing to war or other armed conflict which is not a result of the activities of the Contracting Party to which the investors belong, civil disturbances, revolution, riot or similar events in the territory of the latter Contracting Party, they shall be accorded by the latter Contracting Party, treatment, as regards restitution, indemnification, compensation or any other settlement, not less

favourable than that that the latter Contracting Party accords to its own investors or to investors of any third State, whichever is most favourable to the investors concerned.

2.   Without prejudice to paragraph 1 of this Article, investors of one Contracting Party who in any of the events referred to in that paragraph suffer damage or loss in the territory of the other Contracting Party resulting from:

    a)   requisitioning of their property or part thereof by its forces or authorities;

    b)   destruction of their property or part thereof by its forces or authorities which was not caused in combat action or was not required by the necessity of the situation, shall be accorded a prompt restitution, and where applicable prompt, adequate and effective compensation for damage or loss sustained during the period of requisitioning or as a result of destruction of their property. Resulting payments shall be made in freely convertible currency without delay.

3.   Investor whose investments suffer damage or loss in accordance to paragraph 2. of this Article, shall have the right to prompt review of its case by a judicial or other competent authority of that Contracting Party and of valuation of its investments and payment of compensation in accordance with the principles set out in paragraph 2. of this Article.

ARTICLE 7
Transfers

1.   Each Contracting Party shall ensure that all payments relating to an investment in its territory of an investor of the other Contracting Party may be freely transferred into and out of its territory without delay. Such transfers shall include, in particular, though not exclusively:

    a)   the initial capital and additional amounts to maintain or increase an investment;

    b)   returns;

    c)   the amounts required for payment of expenses which arise from the operation of the investment under contract, loan repayments, payment of royalties, management fees, licence fees or other similar expenses;

    d)   proceeds from the sale or liquidation of all or any part of an investment;

    e)   payments of compensation under Article 5 and 6 of this Agreement;

    f)   payments arising out of the settlement of an investment dispute;

    g)   earnings and other remuneration of personnel engaged from abroad in connection with an investment.

2.   The nationals of each Contracting Party who have been authorized to work in the territory of the other Contracting Party in connection with an investment shall also be permitted to transfer an appropriate portion of their earnings to their country of origin.

3.   Transfers shall be made in a freely convertible currency at the rate applicable on the day transfers are made to spot transactions in the currency used.

4.   Each Contracting Party shall ensure that the interest at the commercial rate established on the a market basis for the currency in question is calculated together with compensation for the period starting from the occurrence of events under Articles 5 and 6 until the date of transfer of payment and payment will be effected in accordance with provisions of paragraphs 1 and 2 of this Article.

5.   Each Contracting Party shall ensure that the transfers will be made without delay, with no other expenses than the usual taxes and costs.

ARTICLE 8
Subrogation

If a Contracting Party or its designated agency makes a payment under an indemnity, guarantee or contract of insurance given in respect of an investment of an investor in the territory of the other Contracting Party, the latter Contracting Party shall recognise the assignment of any right or claim of such investor to the former Contracting Party or its designated agency and the right of the former Contracting Party or its designated agency to exercise by virtue of subrogation any such right and claim to the same extent as its predecessor in title.

ARTICLE 9
Application of other legal provisions

If the provisions of law of either Contracting Party or international obligations existing at present or established thereafter between the Contracting Parties in addition to the present Agreement, contain a rule, whether general or specific, entitling investments by investors of the other Contracting Party to a treatment more favourable than is provided for by the present Agreement, such rule shall, to the extent that it is more favourable, prevail over the present Agreement.

ARTICLE 10
Settlement of disputes between a Contracting Party
and an investor of the other Contracting Party

1.   Any investment dispute between a Contracting Party and an investor of the other Contracting Party shall be settled by negotiations.

2.   If a dispute under paragraph 1 of this Article cannot be settled within six (6) months of a written notification, the dispute shall be upon the request of the investor settled as follows:

  a)   by a competent court of the Contracting Party, or

  b)   by conciliation or arbitration by the International Centre for Settlement of Investment Disputes (ICSID), established by the Convention on the Settlement of Investment Disputes between States and Nationals of other States, opened for signature in Washington on March 18th, 1965. In case of arbitration, each Contracting Party, by this Agreement irrevocably consents in advance, even in the absence of an individual arbitral agreement between the Contracting Party and the investor, to submit any such dispute to this Centre. This consent implies the renunciation of the requirement that the internal administrative or judicial remedies should be exhausted; or

c)   by arbitration by three arbitrators in accordance with the Arbitration Rules of the United Nations Commission on International Trade Law (UNCITRAL), as amended by the last amendment accepted by both Contracting Parties at the time of the request for initiation of the arbitration procedure. In case of arbitration, each Contracting Party, by this Agreement irrevocably consents in advance, even in the absence of an individual arbitral agreement between the Contracting Party and the investor, to submit any such dispute to the tribunal mentioned.; or

d)   by arbitration in accordance with the Rules of Arbitration of the International Chamber of Commerce (ICC).

3.   The award shall be final and binding; it shall be executed according to the national law; each Contracting Party shall ensure the recognition and enforcement of the arbitral award in accordance with its relevant laws and other regulations.

4.   A Contracting Party which is a party to a dispute shall not, at any stage of conciliation or arbitration proceedings or enforcement of an award, raise the objection that the investor who is the other party to the dispute has received an indemnity by virtue of a guarantee in respect of all or a part of its losses.

ARTICLE 11
Settlement of disputes between
the Contracting Parties

1.   Disputes between the Contracting Parties concerning the interpretation or application of this Agreement shall be settled as far as possible by negotiations.

2.   If a dispute according to paragraph 1 of this Article cannot be settled within six (6) months it shall upon the request of either Contracting Party be submitted to an arbitral tribunal.

3.   Such arbitral tribunal shall be constituted <u>ad hoc</u> as follows: each Contracting Party shall appoint one arbitrator and these two arbitrators shall agree upon a national of a third State as their chairman. Such arbitrators shall be appointed within two (2) months from the date one Contracting Party has informed the other Contracting Party, of its intention to submit the dispute to an arbitral tribunal, the chairman of which shall be appointed within two (2) further months.

4.   If the periods specified in paragraph 3 of this Article are not observed, either Contracting Party may, in the absence of any other relevant arrangement, invite the President of the International Court of Justice to make the necessary appointments. If the President of the International Court of Justice is a national of either of the Contracting Parties or if he is otherwise prevented from discharging the said function, the Vice-President or in case of his inability the member of the International Court of Justice next in seniority should be invited under the same conditions to make the necessary appointments.

5.   The tribunal shall establish its own rules of procedure.

6.   The arbitral tribunal shall reach its decision in virtue of the present Agreement and pursuant to the rules of international law. It shall reach its decision by a majority of votes; the decision shall be final and binding.

7.   Each Contracting Party shall bear the costs of its own member and of its legal representation in the arbitration proceedings. The costs of the chairman and the remaining costs shall be borne in equal parts by both Contracting Parties. The tribunal may, however, in its award determine another distribution of costs.

ARTICLE 12
Application of the Agreement

This Agreement shall apply to investments made prior to or after the entry into force of this Agreement, but shall not apply to any investment dispute that may have arisen or any claim, which was settled before its entry into force.

ARTICLE 13
Entry into force

This Agreement shall enter into force on the thirtieth day following the date of receipt of the latter notification through diplomatic channels by which one Contracting Party notifies the other Contracting Party that its internal legal requirements for the entry into force of this Agreement have been fulfilled.

ARTICLE 14
Duration and denunciation

1.   This Agreement shall remain in force for a period of twenty (20) years and shall be extended thereafter for the following twenty (20) year periods unless, one year before the expiration of the initial or any subsequent period, one Contracting Party notifies the other Contracting Party of its intention to denounce the Agreement. In that case, the notice of denunciation shall become effective by the expiration of current period of twenty (20) years.

2.   In respect of investments made prior to the date when the notice of denunciation of this Agreement becomes effective, the provisions of this Agreement shall continue to be effective for a period of twenty (20) years from the date of denunciation of this Agreement.

IN WITNESS WHEREOF, the undersigned representatives, duly authorised thereto, have signed the present Agreement.

DONE at _____, on _____, in two originals, each in the Croatian, _____ and English language, both text being equally authentic. The text in the English language shall prevail in case of difference of interpretation.

FOR THE GOVERNMENT OF   **FOR THE GOVERNMENT OF**
THE REPUBLIC OF CROATIA   **THE _____**

*   *   *

IN THE NAME OF GOD

AGREEMENT ON RECIPROCAL PROMOTION AND PROTECTION OF INVESTMENTS BETWEEN THE GOVERNMENT OF THE ISLAMIC REPUBLIC OF IRAN AND THE GOVERNMENT OF _____ *

PREAMBLE

The Government of the Islamic Republic of Iran and the Government of the .... hereinafter referred to as the "Contracting Parties",

Desiring to intensify economic cooperation to the mutual benefit of both States;

Intending to utilize their economic resources and potential facilities in the area of investments as well as to create and maintain favourable conditions for investments of the nationals of the Contracting Parties in each others' territory and;

Recognizing the need to promote and protect investments of nationals of the Contracting Parties in each others' territory;

Have agreed as follows:

ARTICLE 1
DEFINITIONS

For the purpose of this Agreement, the meaning of the terms used therein are as follows:

1.   The term "investment" refers to every kind of property or asset, including the following, invested by the investors of one Contracting Party in the territory of the other Contracting Party in accordance with the laws and regulations of the other Contracting Party (hereinafter referred to as the host Contracting Party):

(a)   movable and immovable property as well as rights related thereto ;

(b)   shares or any kind of participation in companies ;

(c)   money and/or receivables;

(d)   industrial and intellectual property rights such as patent, utility models, industrial designs or models, trade marks and names, know-how and goodwill ;

(e)   rights to search for, extract or exploit natural resources.

---

*   *Source*: The Government of the Islamic Republic of Iran, Ministry of Foreign Affairs. [Note added by the editor.]

2.   The term "investors" refers to the following persons who invest in the territory of the other Contracting Party within the framework of this Agreement:

(a)   natural persons who, according to the laws of either Contracting Party,are considered to be its national and have not the nationality of the host Contracting Party.

(b)   legal persons of either Contracting Party which are established under the laws of that Contracting Party and their headquarters or their real economic activities are located in the territory of that Contracting Party.

3.   The term "returns" refers to the amounts legally yielded by an investment including profit derived from investments, dividends, royalities and fees.

4.   The term "territory" refers to areas under the soverignty or jurisdiction of either Contracting Party, as the case may be, including their maritime areas.

ARTICLE 2
PROMOTION OF INVESTMENTS

1.   Either Contracting Party shall encourage its nationals to invest in the territory of the other Contracting Party.

2.   Either Contracting Party shall, within the framework of its laws and regulations, create favourable conditions for attraction of investments of nationals of the other Contracting Party in its territory.

ARTICLE 3
ADMISSION OF INVESTMENTS

1.   Either Contracting Party shall admit investments of natural and legal persons of the of the other Contracting Party in its territory in accordance with its laws and regulations.

2.   When an investment is admitted, either Contracting Party shall, in accordance with its laws and regulations, grant all necessary permits for the realization of such an investment.

ARTICLE 4
PROTECTION OF INVESTMENTS

1.   Investments of natural and legal persons of either Contracting Party effected within the territory of the other Contracting Party, shall receive the host Contracting Party's full legal protection and fair treatment not less favourable than that accorded to investors of any third state who are in a comparable situation.

2.   If a Contracting Party has accorded or shall accord in future special advantages or rights to investor(s) of any third state by virtue of an existing or future agreement establishing a free trade area, a customs union, a common market or a similar regional organization and/or by virtue of an arrangement on the avoidance of double taxation, it shall not be obliged to accord such advantages or rights to investors of the other Contracting Party.

ARTICLE 5
MORE FAVOURABLE PROVISIONS

Notwithstanding the terms set froth in this Agreement, more favourable provisions which have beeen or may be agreed upon by either of the Contracting Parties with an investor of the other Contracting Party are applicable.

ARTICLE 6
EXPROPRIATION AND COMPENSATION

1.   Investments of natural and legal persons of either Contracting Party shall not be nationalized, confiscated, expropriated or subjected to similar measures by the other Contracting Party except such measures are taken for public purposes, in accordance with due process of law, in a non-discriminatory manner, and effective and appropriate compensation is envisaged. The amount of compensation shall be paid without delay.

2.   The amount of compensation shall be equivalent to the value of the investment immediately before the action of nationalization, confiscation or expropriation was taken.

ARTICLE 7
LOSSES

Investors of either Contracting Party whose investments suffer losses due to war, any armed conflict, revolution or similar state of emergency in the territory of the other Contracting Party shall be accorded by the other Contracting Party treatment no less favourable than that accorded to its own investors or to investors of any third country.

ARTICLE 8
REPATRIATION AND TRANSFER

1.   Each Contracting Party shall, in accordance with its laws and regulations, permit in good faith the following transfers related to investments referred to in this Agreement, to be made freely and without delay out of its territory:

(a)   returns;

(b)   proceeds from the sale and/or liquidation of all or part of an investment ;

(c)   royalties and fees related to transfer of technology agreement ;

(d)   sums paid pursuant to Articles 6 and /or 7 of this Agreement ;

(e)   loan installments related to an investment provided that they are paid out of such investment activities ;

(f)   monthly salaries and wages received by the employees of an investor who have obtained in the territory of the host Contracting Party, the corresponding work permits related to that investments ;

(g)   payments arising from a decision of the authority referred to in Article 12.

2.   The above transfers shall be effected in a convertible currency and at the current rate of exchange in accordance with the exchange regulations prevailing on the date of transfer.

3.   The investor and the host Contracting Party may agree otherwise on the mechanism of repatriation or transfers referred to in this Article.

ARTICLE 9
SUBROGATION

If a Contracting Party or its designated agency, within the framework of a legal system, subrogates an investor pursuant to a payment made under an insurance or guarantee agreement against non-commercial risks:

(a)   such subrogation shall be recognized by the other Contracting Party ;

(b)   the subrogee shall not be entitled to exercise any rights other than the rights which the investor would have been entitled to exercise ;

(c)   disputes between the subrogee and the host Contracting Party shall be settled in accordance with Article 12 of this Agreement.

ARTICLE 10
OBSERVANCE OF COMMITMENTS

Either Contracting Party shall guarantee the observance of the commitments it has entered into with respect to investments of natural or legal persons of the other Contracting Party.

ARTICLE 11
SCOPE OF THE AGREEMENT

This Agreement shall apply to investments approved by the competent authority of the host Contracting Party.

The competent authority in the Islamic Republic of Iran is "Organization for Investment, Economic and Technical Assistance of Iran (O.I.E.T.A.I.)" or any other authority which will succeed to it.

The competent authority in the .... is the "Ministry of Foreign Affairs".

ARTICLE 12
SETTLEMENT OF DISPUTES BETWEEN A CONTRACTING PARTY
AND INVESTOR (S) OF THE OTHER CONTRACTING PARTY

1.   If any dispute arises between the host Contracting Party and investor(s) of the other Contracting Party with respect to an investment, the host Contracting Party and the investor(s) shall primarily endeavour to settle the dispute in an amicable manner through negotiation and consultation.

2.   In the event that the host Contracting Party and the investor(s) can not agree within six months from the date of notification of the claim by one party to the other, either of them may

refer the dispute to the competent courts of the host Contracting Party or with due regard to their own laws and regulations to an arbitral tribunal of three members referred to in paragraph 5 below.

3. A dispute primarily referred to the competent courts of the host Contracting Party, as long as it is pending, cannot be referred to arbitration save with the parties agreement; and in the event that a final judgment is rendered, it cannot be referred to arbitration.

4. National courts shall not have jurisdiction over any dispute referred to arbitration. However, the provisions of this paragraph do not bar the winning party to seek for the enforcement of the arbitral award before national courts.

5. The host Contracting Party or the investor(s) of the other Contracting Party who desires to refer the dispute to the arbitration shall appoint an arbitrator through a written notice sent to the other Party. The other Party shall appoint an arbitrator within sixty days from the date of receipt of the said notice and the appointed arbitrators shall within sixty days from the date of the last appointment, appoint the umpire. In the event that each party fails to appoint its arbitrator within the mentioned period and/or the appointed arbitrators fail to agree on the umpire, each of the parties may request the Secretary General of the Permanent Court of Arbitration to appoint the failing party's arbitrator or the umpire, as the case may be. However the umpire shall be appointed from amongst nationals of a state having diplomatic relations with both Contracting Parties, at the time of appointment.

6. The arbitration shall be conducted according to the United Nations Commission on International Trade Law (UNCITRAL) rules.

ARTICLE 13
SETTLEMENT OF DISPUTES BETWEEN THE CONTRACTING PARTIES

1. All disputes arising between the Contracting Parties relating to the interpretation or application of this Agreement shall, in the first place, be settled amicably by consultation. In case of disagreement, either Contracting Party may, subject to its laws and regulations, while sending a notice to the other Party, refer the case to an arbitral tribunal of three members consisting of two arbitrators appointed by the Contracting Parties and an umpire.

In case the dispute is referred to the arbitral tribunal, either Contracting Party shall appoint an arbitrator within sixty days from the receipt of the notification and the arbitrators appointed by the Contracting Parties shall appoint the umpire within sixty days from the date of last appointment. If either Contracting Party does not appoint its own arbitrator or the appointed arbitrators do not agree on the appointment of the umpire within the said periods, each Contracting Party may request the President of the International Court of Justice, to appoint the arbitrator of the failing party or the umpire, as the case may be.

However the umpire shall be a national of a state having diplomatic relations with both Contracting Parties at the time of the appointment.

2. In case the umpire is to be appointed by the President of the International Court of Justice, if the President of the International Court of Justice is prevented from carrying out the said function or if he is a national of either Contracting Party, the appointment shall be made by

the vice-president of the International Court of Justice, and if the vice-president is also prevented from carrying out the said function or he is a national of either Contracting Party, the appointment shall be made by the senior member of the said court who is not a national of either Contracting Party.

3.   Each Contracting Party shall bear the costs of its own member of the tribunal or its representation in the arbitral proceedings; the cost of the umpire and remaining costs shall be borne by the Contracting Parties in equal parts. However, the tribunal may decide different proportions of costs to be borne by the two Contracting Parties.

4.   Subject to other provisions agreed by the Contracting Parties, the arbitral tribunal shall determine its procedure and the place of arbitration.

5.   The decisions of the arbitral tribunal shall be binding on the Contracting Parties.

ARTICLE 14
VALIDITY OF THE AGREEMENT

1.   This Agreement shall be approved/ratified by the competent authorities of each Contracting Party in accordance with their laws and regulations.

2.   This Agreement shall enter into force for a period of ten years after 30 days from the date of the last notification of either Contracting Party to the other Contracting party that it has fulfilled necessary measures in accordance with its laws and regulations for the entry into force of this Agreement. After the said period, this Agreement shall remain in force thereafter unless one of the Contracting Parties notifies the other Contracting Party in writing of its unwillingness to continue with it, six months prior to the expiration or termination thereof.

3.   After the expiration of the validity or termination of this Agreement its provisions shall apply to investments under this Agreement for a further period of ten years.

ARTICLE 15
LANGUAGE AND NUMBER
OF THE TEXTS

This Agreement is done in duplicate in the Persian, …….. and …….. languages, all texts being equally authentic. In case of divergence of interpretation the …….. text shall prevail.

Signed in ……………… on …………… corresponding to …………………… by representatives of the Government of the Islamic Republic of Iran and the Government of the ………………………

For the Government of the   For the Government of
Islamic Republic of Iran   ……………

*   *   *

AGREEMENT FOR THE ENCOURAGEMENT AND PROTECTION OF INVESTMENT BETWEEN _____ AND THE OPEC FUND FOR INTERNATIONAL DEVELOPMENT[*]

AND

LIST OF AGREEMENTS SIGNED BY THE OPEC FUND FOR INTERNATIONAL DEVELOPMENT WITH THIRD COUNTRIES

AGREEMENT, between the _____ (hereinafter called the Host Country) and the OPEC Fund for International Development (hereinafter called the OPEC Fund).

Whereas OPEC Member States, being conscious of the need for solidarity among all developing countries and aware of the importance of financial cooperation between them and other developing countries, have established the OPEC Fund to provide financial support to the latter countries, in addition to the existing bilateral and multilateral channels through which OPEC Member States extend financial assistance to other developing countries;

And whereas the OPEC Member States have, in addition, empowered the OPEC Fund to partake in the stimulation of capital flows thereto and, specifically, to assist in financing private sector activities involving entities located in the territories of other developing countries, including the Host Country, with a view to optimizing the aforementioned objective of financial cooperation;

And whereas the Host Country and the OPEC Fund being mindful that a stable framework for the envisaged investments will conduce to the effective utilization of economic resources and contribute towards the improvement of living standards; and, accordingly, have resolved to conclude an agreement for the encouragement and protection of such investment activities;

Now, therefore, the parties hereto hereby agree as follows:

ARTICLE I
DEFINITIONS

1.01   Wherever used in this Agreement, and unless the context otherwise requires, the following terms have the following meanings:

(a)   Investment" means every kind of investment owned or controlled directly or indirectly by the OPEC Fund in the territory of the Host Country and, without prejudice to the generality of the foregoing, includes investment consisting or taking the form of:

(i)   shares, stock, and other form of equity participation, and bonds, credits, debentures, and other forms of debt interests, in a company;

(ii)   tangible property, including real property; and intangible property, including rights, such as leases, mortgages, liens, pledges and rights to payment arising under any form of debt instrument of whatever nature;

---

[*]   *Source*: OPEC Fund for International Development (2001). [Note added by the editor.]

(iii)   contractual rights, such as those under construction or management contracts, production or revenue-sharing contracts, concessions, or other forms of contracts;

(iv)   rights conferred by or pursuant to law, such as licenses and permits; and

(v)   intellectual property, including copyrights and related rights, patents, industrial designs, as well as advisory services and confidential business information.

(b)   "Company" means any entity established under or pursuant to the Host Country's laws and regulations, whether or not wholly or partially owned or controlled privately or by the state or any organ thereof, including a corporation, partnership, sole or joint venture or proprietorship, association or any other organization.

(c)   "OPEC Fund" means the OPEC Fund for International Development established by the Member States of the Organization of the Petroleum Exporting Countries (OPEC) by virtue of the Agreement signed in Paris on January 28, 1976, as amended.

(d)   "Host Country" means the _____ , including all political or administrative subdivisions, and any agency or instrumentality thereof.

(e)   "Territory" means the territory of the Host Country, including its territorial sea as well as the exclusive economic zone over which the Host Country exercises sovereign rights for the purpose of exploring and exploiting, conserving and managing the natural resources, whether living or non-living, of the waters superjacent to the sea bed and of the sea bed and its sub-soil.

ARTICLE II
GENERAL PRINCIPLES

2.01   With respect to the establishment, acquisition, expansion, management, conduct, operation and sale or other disposition of investments, the Host Country shall accord treatment thereto no less favourable than that it accords, in like situations, to investments in its territory by any other multilateral development finance institution operating in the Host Country (hereinafter referred to as "most favoured party").

2.02   The Host Country shall ensure that its laws, regulations, administrative practices and procedures of general application, and adjudicatory decisions, that pertain to or affect investments are promptly published or otherwise made publicly available.

2.03   The Host Country shall provide effective means of asserting claims and enforcing rights with respect to investments and shall not in any way impair, by unreasonable or discriminatory measures, the management, conduct, operation, sale or other disposition of any such investment.

2.04   The Host Country shall at all times accord to investments in its territory fair and equitable treatment and full protection and security, and shall in no case accord less favourable treatment than that required by or under international law.

2.05   The Host Country shall pursuant to its laws and regulations accord to the OPEC Fund and its investments or, as the case may require, the officials, agents and other representatives of the OPEC Fund, treatment no less favourable than the Host Country accords to the most favoured party and its investments (hereinafter referred to as "most favoured party treatment"), and such treatment shall extend but not be limited to the issuance of visas or permits to enter and remain in its territory for the purpose of initiating, appraising, establishing or administering, winding up or otherwise terminating any investment or any other activity connected therewith located in its territory.

2.06   The most favoured party treatment shall not be construed so as to oblige the Host Country to extend to investments the advantages resulting from:

(a)   any existing or future customs or economic union, a free trade area or regional economic organization of which the Host Country is or becomes a member; or

(b)   without prejudice to Article VII, any international or bilateral agreement or arrangement relating wholly or mainly to taxation.

ARTICLE III
PRIOR NOTIFICATION OF INVESTMENT PROPOSAL

3.01   The OPEC Fund shall prior to each investment inform the Government of the Host Country about the envisaged investment in the form of a written project proposal. Such a proposal will contain a summary statement regarding the envisaged investment and will be forwarded by the OPEC Fund to the Minister of Finance, or other representative of the Host Country designated in that behalf, for further consideration.

3.02   The OPEC Fund shall not finance any investment in the territory of the Host Country if the Government of the Host Country objects to such financing.

ARTICLE IV
EXPROPRIATION

4.01   The Host Country shall not expropriate or nationalize an investment either directly or indirectly through measures tantamount to expropriation or nationalization except for a public purpose; in a non-discriminatory manner; upon payment of prompt, adequate and effective compensation; and in accordance with due process of law and the general principles of treatment provided for in Article II above.

4.02   Compensation shall be paid without delay and shall be equivalent to the fair market value of the expropriated investment immediately before the expropriatory action was taken; and be fully realizable and freely transferable. The fair market value of such investment shall not be adversely affected by any change in value occurring because the expropriatory action had become known before the date of expropriation or its implementation.

ARTICLE V
COMPENSATION FOR LOSSES

5.01   The Host Country shall accord most favoured party treatment to investments as regards any measure relating to losses that investments suffer in its territory owing to war or other armed conflict, revolution, state of national emergency, insurrection, civil disturbance or similar events.

5.02   The Host Country shall effect restitution, or pay compensation in accordance with Section 4.02 above, in the event that investments suffer losses in its territory, owing to war or other armed conflict, revolution, state of national emergency, insurrection, civil disturbance, or similar events, that result from:

(a)   requisitioning of all or part of such investment by the Host Country's forces or authorities; or

(b)   destruction of all or part of such investments by the Host Country's forces or authorities that was not required by the necessity of the situation.

ARTICLE VI
PAYMENTS AND TRANSFERS

6.01   The Host Country shall permit all transfers relating to an investment to be made without restrictions and without delay into and out of its territory. Such transfers include:

(a)   contributions to capital;

(b)   profits, capital gains, and proceeds from the sale of all or any part of the investment or from the partial or complete liquidation of the investment;

(c)   principal, interest, royalty payments, management fees, technical assistance and other fees;

(d)   payments made under a contract; and

(e)   compensation pursuant to Articles IV and V.

6.02   The Host Country shall permit transfers to be made in a freely convertible currency at the market rate of exchange prevailing on the date of transfer.

6.03   Notwithstanding sections 6.01 and 6.02, the Host Country may prevent a transfer through the equitable, non-discriminatory and good faith application of its laws relating to:

(a)   bankruptcy, insolvency or the protection of the rights of creditors;

(b)   issuing, trading or dealing in securities;

(c)   criminal or penal offences; or

(d)   ensuring compliance with orders or judgments in adjudicatory proceedings.

6.04   Notwithstanding Sections 6.01 and 6.02, transfers and other payments receivable by the OPEC Fund in respect of an investment may be subject to any generally applicable foreign exchange restrictions, regulations and controls in force in the Host Country arising from exceptional balance of payments difficulties of limited duration and in consonance with the exercise in good faith of powers conferred in that behalf by law.

ARTICLE VII
EXEMPTION FROM TAXATION

7.01   In compliance with the general principles set out in Article II and, in particular, the stipulations relating to most favoured party treatment, the OPEC Fund, its assets, property, operations, and any obligation or security issued or guaranteed by the OPEC Fund, and any other transactions undertaken by the OPEC Fund in connection with any investment in the territory of the Host Country, authorized by or pursuant to this Agreement, shall be immune from all taxation, levies or duties chargeable or otherwise imposed by, or in the territory of, the Host Country; and references in this Article to the OPEC Fund shall, *mutatis mutandis*, be construed as including references to the officials, agents and other representatives of the OPEC Fund specified in Section 2.05 above.

7.02   Notwithstanding Section 7.01, the reference therein to the officials, agents and other representatives of the OPEC Fund shall not include nationals and other third parties resident in the Host Country.

ARTICLE VIII
CONSULTATION

8.01   The parties to this Agreement agree to consult promptly, on the request of either, to resolve any dispute, controversy or claim in connection with this Agreement or the breach, termination or invalidity thereof or otherwise relating to the interpretation or application of this Agreement or the realization of the objectives of this Agreement.

ARTICLE IX
ARBITRATION CLAUSE

9.01   Any dispute, controversy or claim arising out of or relating to this Agreement or the breach, termination or invalidity thereof or otherwise relating to the interpretation or application of this Agreement, that is not resolved through consultations, shall be submitted upon request of either party to an arbitral tribunal for binding decision in accordance with the applicable rules of international law. In the absence of an agreement by the parties to the contrary, the UNCITRAL Arbitration Rules, in force and effect on the date of this Agreement, shall govern.

9.02   The Host Country and the OPEC Fund will each appoint one arbitrator and the two arbitrators so appointed shall together appoint the third arbitrator as chairman, failing which such third arbitrator shall be appointed by the International Court of Arbitration in Paris, France. Where the UNCITRAL Arbitration Rules do not provide for a particular situation, the arbitrators shall in their absolute discretion determine what course of action should be followed and the arbitrator's decision shall be final.

9.03   Any arbitration under this Agreement shall be held in a state (not being the Host Country or any Member State of the OPEC Fund) that is a party to the United Nations Convention on the

Recognition and Enforcement of Foreign Arbitral Awards, done in New York, United States of America, on June 10, 1958; and the English Language shall be used throughout the arbitral proceedings.

9.04   Each party to this Agreement hereby waives any right of sovereign immunity as to it and its property in respect of the enforcement and execution of any award rendered by an arbitral tribunal constituted under or pursuant to this Agreement.

ARTICLE X
GOVERNING LAW

10.01   This Agreement and all documents executed in connection therewith as well as their validity, enforcement, and interpretation, and all disputes arising thereunder, shall be governed by the applicable provisions of this Agreement and shall be supplemented by the applicable principles of international law and *ex aequo et bono*.

ARTICLE XI
MAINTENANCE OF OTHER RIGHTS
AND OBLIGATIONS

11.01   This Agreement shall not be construed so as to derogate from any obligations of the Host Country under the following measures, especially in cases where such measures entitle investments to treatment more favourable than that accorded by this Agreement, that is to say:

(a)   the laws and regulations, administrative practices or procedures, or administrative or adjudicatory decisions of the Host Country;

(b)   international legal obligations; or

(c)   any other obligations assumed by the parties to this Agreement, including those contained in an investment authorization or an agreement or other legally enforceable undertaking for or in connection with an investment.

ARTICLE XII
COMMUNICATIONS

12.01   Any notice or other communication required or permitted to be given or made under this Agreement shall be in writing. Such notice or communication shall, as appropriate for the concerned requirement, be deemed to have been duly given or made when it has been delivered by hand, mail, telex or telefax or other electronic means to the party to which it is required to be given or made, at the party's address specified below or at any other address as the party shall have specified in writing to the party giving the notice or making the communication.
For the Host Country:

The Minister of _____
Ministry of _____

_____

_____

For the OPEC Fund:

The Director-General
The OPEC Fund for International Development

ARTICLE XIII
ENTRY INTO FORCE,
DURATION AND TERMINATION

13.01   This Agreement shall enter into force following the receipt by the OPEC Fund of the instrument of ratification, a legal opinion or certification, or other documentary evidence of approval by the Host Country of this Agreement and upon the written certification by the OPEC Fund that all its internal legal requirements for the entry into force of this Agreement have been fulfilled.

13.02   This Agreement shall remain in force for a period of ten years and shall continue in force unless terminated in accordance with Section 13.03.

13.03   Each Party may terminate this Agreement at the end of the initial ten years period or at any time by giving one year's written notice to the other Party.

13.04   Notwithstanding the termination of this Agreement, all other provisions thereof, except those relating to the establishment of a new investment, shall continue to apply to any investments established or acquired prior to the date of its termination and remain in force for an additional period of ten years from the said date.

IN WITNESS whereof, the parties hereto, acting through their duly authorized representatives, have caused this Agreement to be signed in two copies in the English language, each considered an original and both to the same and one effect.

FOR THE _____ :

FOR THE OPEC FUND FOR INTERNATIONAL DEVELOPMENT:

_____

LIST OF AGREEMENTS SIGNED BY THE OPEC FUND FOR INTERNATIONAL DEVELOPMENT WITH THIRD COUNTRIES[*]

List of agreements signed by the OPEC Fund for International Development with third countries, 1 September 2001		
Country/territory	**Date of signature**	**Date of entry into force**
OPEC fund for International Development		
Mauritania	27 October 1999	30 June 2000
Turkmenistan	10 December 1999	Not yet in force
Cape Verde	8 February 2000	22 January 2001
Togo	4 April 2000, 26 April 2000[a]	26 January 2001
Bangladesh	19 May 2000	12 December 2000
Uganda	8 June 2000	7 August 2001
Yemen	23 June 2000	Not yet in force
Uzbekistan	11 August 2000	23 July 2001
Lebanon	23 September 2000	15 August 2001
Pakistan	24 October 2000	16 February 2001
Mali	7 November 2000	Not yet in force
Sudan	7 November 2000	29 June 2001
Cambodia	10 November 2000	Not yet in force
Bolivia	24 October 2000	Not yet in force
Mozambique	24 October 2000, 21 November 2000[a]	Not yet in force
Mauritius	13 December 2000, 12 January 2001[a]	27 August 2001
Burundi	22 January 2001, 30 January 2001[a]	Not yet in force
Jamaica	15 January 2001, 8 February 2001[a]	Not yet in force
Egypt	20 December 2000, 6 March 2001[a]	Not yet in force
Albania	20 February 2001, 9 March 2001[a]	Not yet in force
Syria	21 March 2001	Not yet in force
Palestine	17 May 2001	Not yet in force
Belize	4 May 2001, 14 May 2001[a]	Not yet in force
Gambia	19 December 2000, 22 January 2001[a]	23 July 2001
Paraguay	14 March 2001, 30 May 2001[a]	Not yet in force
Benin	4 May 2001, 20 June 2001[a]	Not yet in force
Maldives	4 May 2001, 28 June 2001[a]	Not yet in force
Seychelles	4 May 2001, 23 May 2001[a]	Not yet in force
Senegal	4 July 2001, 24 July 2001[a]	Not yet in force

---

[a] Signed by postal exchange.

*   *   *

---

[*]   *Source*: OPEC Fund for International Development (2001). [Note added by the editor.]

AGREEMENT BETWEEN THE REPUBLIC OF PERU AND THE _____ ON THE PROMOTION AND RECIPROCAL PROTECTION OF INVESTMENTS[*]

The Government of the Republic of Peru and the Government of ...., hereinafter designated as the 'Contracting Parties',

Desiring to intensify economic cooperation to the mutual benefit of both Contracting Parties,

For the purpose of creating and keep fair, equitable and favorable conditions for the investment made by investors of one of the Contracting Parties within the territory of the other Contracting Party, and

Recognizing that the subscription of an Agreement for the Promotion and Reciprocal Protection of Investments may encourage private economic initiative and increase the welfare of both peoples,

HAVE AGREED AS FOLLOWS:

Article 1
Definitions

For the purposes of this Agreement:

1.   "Investment" designates any kind of assets owned by an investor of one of the Contracting Parties, in the territory of the other Contracting Party and, in particular, though not exclusively, includes:

   a.   Shares, stocks and any other forms of equity participation in a company and in joint ventures; in accordance with domestic legislation;

   b.   Movable and immovable property as well as any other rights in rem, acquired or used to obtain economic benefits or other business purposes;

   c.   Loans, securities, rights to money or any other performance having an economic value directly related to an specific investment;

   d.   Intellectual and industrial property rights, such as copyrights and related rights, trademarks or trade brands, geographical indications, designs and industrial models, patents, layout designs (topograhies) of integrated circuits and plant breeder rights.

   e.   Concessions granted by law or under contract for the exercise of an economic activity, including concessions to prospect, search or exploit natural resources.

---

[*]   *Source*: The Government of Peru, Ministry of Foreign Affairs. [Note added by the editor.]

     f.   Reinvestments of profits, understood as investment of the profits in the same company where they were generated.

Any change in the form of an investment does not affect its character as an investment.

Investment does not mean:

     a.   a payment obligation, or granting of a loan to the State or to a State-owned company;

     b.   Loans to a company, when the due date thereof is under three years ;

     c.   claims to money exclusively derived from:

     ·   commercial contracts for the sale of goods or services by a national or company in the territory of one Party to a company in the territory of the other Party; or

     ·   any type of trade financing.

"Investor" designates:

     a.   individuals who have the citizenship of any of the Contracting Parties, according to their legislation; or

     b.   corporate bodies, including civil and commercial companies and other associations, which are incorporated or duly constituted in accordance with the applicable laws and regulations of one Contracting Party.

2.   "Earnings" designates the sums obtained or produced from an investment made in accordance with this Agreement, such as profits, interests, dividends and royalties.

3.   "Territory" designates, in addition to the areas contained within the land boundaries, the adjacent maritime zones and air space in which the Contracting Parties exercise sovereign rights and jurisdiction in accordance with their respective legislation.

Article 2
Investment Promotion and Protection

1.   Each Contracting Party shall promote within its territory investments made by investors of the other Contracting Party and shall admit them in accordance with its laws and regulations.

2.   Investments made by investors of one of the Contracting Parties within the territory of the other Contracting Party, in accordance with the laws and regulations of the latter, shall be entitled to the full protection and juridical security of this Agreement, in accordance with principles of international law.

3.   Each Contracting Party shall publicize and disseminate laws and regulations related to investments of investors of the other Contracting Party. Likewise, the Contracting Parties shall exchange information on investment opportunities in their territory in order to increase investment flows.

Article 3
Investment Treatment

1.   Each Contracting Party shall ensure fair and equitable treatment for investments made, in accordance with this Agreement, by investors of the other Contracting Party and shall not impair by arbitrary or discriminatory measures, the free management, utilization, use, enjoyment or disposal of such investments by investors of that Contracting Party.

2.   Each Contracting Party shall specifically grant to those investments a treatment that shall not be less favorable than that granted to investments of their own investors or to investments of investors of a third State, whichever may be more favorable to the investments of investors of the other Contracting Party.

3.   If from the legal provisions of one of the Contracting Parties or from any other agreed upon by the Contracting Parties beyond what was stipulated in this Agreement, contains a general or special regulation in accordance with which the investments of the investors of the other Contracting Party shall be granted a most favorable treatment than what was provided for in this Agreement, these regulations shall prevail over this Agreement, insofar as they are more favorable.

4.   The treatment agreed upon by this Article shall not extend to the benefits and advantages that one of the Contracting Parties grants to the nationals or companies of third States by virtue of agreements to avoid double taxation or other agreements on taxation matters.

5.   This treatment shall not extend to the privileges that either of the Contracting parties may grant to nationals or companies of third States because they are members of a customs or economic union, a common market or a free trade area or similar international agreements entered into with third States, including integration and border development agreements.

Article 4
Transfers

1.   Each Contracting party shall guarantee to the investors of the other Contracting Party the free transfer of payments related to an investment registered with the national competent agency, in particular but not exclusively:

    a.   the capital of the investment and of the reinvestments made in accordance with the laws and regulations of the receiving State;

    b.   all net profits;

    c.   the repayment of loans and other lendings defined in section c) of paragraph 1 of article 1 of this Agreement;

    d.   the proceeds of the sale or partial or total liquidation of the investment;

    e.   indemnities and compensations by virtue of Articles 5 and 6 of this Agreement;

    f.   payment resulting from settlement of disputes by virtue of Articles 8 and 9.

2.   Transfers shall be made in a freely convertible currency, without restriction or delay.

3.   Nevertheless the agreed in paragraphs 1 and 2, the Contracting Parties may hinder the transfer by the equitable and non discriminatory application of their legislation in the following cases:

   a.   bankruptcy, insolvency or protection of creditor's rights;

   b.   issuance, trade and transactions of securities;

   c.   criminal or administrative infringements;

   d.   guarantee of enforcement of decisions in administrative proceedings;

   e.   Non-compliance of obligations under prevailing tax laws;

   f.   Non-compliance of obligations under prevailing labour laws.

4.   Paragraphs 1 and 2 are subject to reasonable measures to be adopted or hold by each Party, by reasons of prudence in order to ensure the integrity and stability of its financial system.

5.   Notwithstanding paragraphs 1 and 2 of this Article, in cases of exceptional or serious difficulties in the balance of payments, each Contracting party shall have the right, to temporary limit transfers, in equitable and non discriminatory way and in accordance with principles internationally accepted.

Article 5
Expropriations

1.   Investments made by investors of one Contracting Party in the territory of the other Contracting Party shall not be expropriated, nationalized or subject to any other measures that have equivalent effects to expropriation or nationalization (hereinafter called "expropriation") except for reasons of national security or, public necessity, in a non-discriminatory basis and under due legal process.

2.   Such measures shall be taken along with provisions for the payment of a prompt, adequate and effective compensation. The amount of such compensation shall correspond to the fair value of the expropriated investment immediately before the date on which the expropriation is carried out or is declared, whichever occurs first. Such a fair value shall be expressed in a freely convertible currency at the exchange rate of the market in that moment. Compensation shall also include the interests at the banking rate in force, from the expropriation date up to the date of its effective payment.

3.   The investor whose investment is expropriated shall have the right to submit to review of judicial authorities or other competent authorities of the Contracting Party, its case and the compensation valuation, under the principles contained in this Article.

Article 6
Compensation for losses

The investors of one of the Contracting Parties whose investments have suffered losses due to a war or any other armed conflict, revolution, state of national emergency, state of siege, rebellion or other similar events in the territory of the other Contracting Party shall be treated by the latter not less favorable, that its own investors with regards to restitutions, compensations and indemnifications.

Article 7
Subrogation

1.   If one of the Contracting Parties or an authorized agent makes payments to its investors in accordance with a guarantee granted against non-commercial risks in regard to an investment in the territory of the other Contracting Party, the latter, without prejudice of the rights granted in Article 9, shall recognize the rights of the former Contracting Party or its agent or agency, authorized or designated, whether by legal provisions or by means of a juridical measure.

2.   Likewise, the other Contracting Party shall acknowledge the cause and scope of the subrogation by the former Contracting Party or agent authorized, in all these rights of the previous holder, granted in accordance with this Agreement.

Article 8
Settlement of Disputes between a Contracting Party and
an Investor of the other Contracting Party

1.   Disputes that may arise between one of the Contracting Parties and an investor of the other Contracting Party relating to investments made within the meaning of this Agreement shall, if possible, be settled in a friendly manner between the parties to the dispute.

2.   If a dispute that is within the meaning of paragraph 1 cannot be settled within a term of six months, counted from the date in which one of the parties to the dispute has delivered a notice in writing to the other Contracting Party, it shall be submitted at the request of one of them to:

     a.   The competent tribunal of the Contracting Party within whose territory the investment was made.

     b.   The international arbitration of the International Center for Settlement of Investment Disputes (ICSID), established pursuant the "Convention on the Settlement of Investment Disputes between States and Nationals of other States", opened for signature at Washington 18 March, 1965.

3.   Once the dispute has been submitted to the competent tribunal of the Contracting Party within whose territory the investment was made or to international arbitration, the choice of one or the other procedure shall be definitive.

4.   The arbitral decision shall be final and binding and each Party shall comply with it in accordance with its laws.

Article 9
Settlement of Disputes between the Contracting Parties

1.   Disputes between Contracting Parties concerning the interpretation or application of the provisions of this Agreement shall, if possible, be settled by the Contracting Parties through their diplomatic channels.

2.   If a dispute cannot be settled this way within a term of six months from the date in which one of the Parties to the dispute has notified on the dispute to the other Party, it shall be submitted, at the request of one of them, to an Arbitral Tribunal.

3.   The Arbitral Tribunal shall be constituted ad hoc. Each Contracting Party shall appoint one member and these two members shall agree to elect as Chairman a national of third State who shall be appointed by the both Contracting Parties. The members shall be appointed within a term of two months, and the Chairman, within a term of three months, after one of the Contracting Parties has notified the other Party that it wishes to submit the dispute to an Arbitral Tribunal.

4.   If the terms stipulated in paragraph 3 have not been met, and in the absence of any other agreement, either Contracting Party may invite the President of the International Court of Justice to make the necessary appointments. If the President is a national of either Contracting Party or is otherwise prevented from discharging the said function, the Vice-President shall be invited to make the necessary appointments. If the Vice-President is a national of either Contracting Party or is prevented from discharging the said function, the Member of the International Court of Justice who is ranked immediately below him and who is not a national of one of the Contracting Parties, shall be invited to make the necessary appointments.

5.   The Arbitral Tribunal shall reach its decisions by a majority of votes. Its decisions shall be final and binding. Each Contracting Party shall bear the costs of its own arbitrator, as well as the costs of its representation in the arbitral proceedings. The costs of the Chairman and the remaining costs shall be born equally by the two Contracting Parties. The Arbitral Tribunal shall determine its own procedure.

Article 10
Case of Interruption of Diplomatic or Consular Relations

The provisions of this Agreement shall continue to be fully applicable irrespectively of whether or not the Contracting Parties have diplomatic or consular relations.

Article 11
Application of the Agreement

1.   This Agreement shall apply to investments made by the investors of one Contracting Party in the territory of the other Contracting Party before or after the entry into force of this Agreement. It shall, however, not be applicable to disputes which have arisen to its entry into force.

2.   This Agreement shall not be applicable to disputes relating to events or actions taken and completed before its entry into force, even if the effects remain after that date.

Article 12
Entry into Force, Duration and Termination of the Agreement

1.   The Contracting Parties shall notify each other of the completion of their legal requirements for the entry into force of this Agreement.

2.   This Agreement shall enter into force thirty days after the date of the latter of the two notifications. It shall remain binding for fifteen years and shall be extended afterwards for an indefinite time unless one of the Contracting Parties gives written notice of its intention to terminate it, six months before it expires.

3.   After fifteen years have elapsed, the Agreement may be denounced at any time with prior notice of six months.

4.   For investments made before the date of termination of this Agreement, it shall continue to be in force for fifteen years after that date.

Article 13
Language

This Agreement drafted in duplicate, one in Spanish and the other in _____, each version being equally authentic.

In case of any divergence or interpretation, the Spanish text shall prevail.

IN WITNESS THEREOF, the undersigned, duly authorized thereto by their respective Governments, have signed this Agreement.

DONE at ...., on.............2000.

FOR THE REPUBLIC OF PERU   FOR ....

*   *   *

TREATY BETWEEN THE GOVERNMENT OF THE UNITED STATES OF AMERICA AND THE GOVERNMENT OF THE REPUBLIC OF _____ CONCERNING THE ENCOURAGEMENT AND RECIPROCAL PROTECTION OF INVESTMENT[*]

The Government of the United States of America and the Government of the Republic of .... (hereinafter the "Parties");

Desiring to promote greater economic cooperation between them, with respect to investment by nationals and companies of one Party in the territory of the other Party;

Recognizing that agreement upon the treatment to be accorded such investment will stimulate the flow of private capital and the economic development of the Parties;

Agreeing that a stable framework for investment will maximize effective utilization of economic resources and improve living standards;

Recognizing that the development of economic and business ties can promote respect for internationally recognized worker rights;

Agreeing that these objectives can be achieved without relaxing health, safety and environmental measures of general application; and

Having resolved to conclude a Treaty concerning the encouragement and reciprocal protection of investment;

Have agreed as follows:

ARTICLE I

For the purposes of this Treaty

(a)   "company" means any entity constituted or organized under applicable law, whether or not for profit, and whether privately or governmentally owned or controlled, and includes a corporation, trust, partnership, sole proprietorship, branch, joint venture, association, or other organization;

(b)   "company of a Party" means a company constituted or organized under the laws of that Party,

(c)   "national" of a Party means a natural person who is a national of that Party under its applicable law;

---

[*]   *Source*: The Government of the United States of America, Department of State. [Note added by the editor.]

(d)   "investment" of a national or company means every kind of investment owned or controlled directly or indirectly by that national or company, and includes investment consisting or taking the form of:

(i)   a company;

(ii)   shares, stock, and other forms of equity participation, and bonds, debentures, and other forms of debt interests, in a company;

(iii)   contractual rights, such as under turnkey, construction or management contracts, production or revenue-sharing contracts, concessions, or other similar contracts;

(iv)   tangible property, including real property, and intangible property, including rights, such as leases, mortgages, liens and pledges;

(v)   intellectual property, including:

copyrights and related rights;

patents,

rights in plant varieties,

industrial designs,

rights in plant varieties,

industrial designs,

rights in semiconductor layout designs,

trade secrets, including know-how and confidential business information,

trade and service marks, and

trade names; and

(vi)   rights conferred pursuant to law, such as licenses and permits;

(e)   "covered investment" means an investment of a national or company of a Party in the territory of the other Party;

(f)   "state enterprise" means a company owned, or controlled through ownership interests, by a Party;

(g)   "investment authorization" means an authorization granted by the foreign investment authority of a Party to a covered investment or a national or company of the other Party;

(h)   "investment agreement" means a written agreement between the national authorities of a Party and a covered investment or a national or company of the other Party that (i) grants rights with respect to natural resources or other assets controlled by the national authorities and (ii) the investment, national or company relies upon in establishing or acquiring a covered investment;

(i)   "ICSID Convention" means the Convention on the Settlement of Investment Disputes between States and Nationals of Other States, done at Washingto, March 18, 1965;

(j)   "Centre" means the International Centre for Settlement of Investment Disputes Established by the ICSID Convention; and

(k)   "UNCITRAL Arbitration Rules" means the arbitration rules of the United Nations Commission on International Trade Law.

ARTICLE II

1.   With respect to the establishment, acquisition, expansion, management, conduct, operation and sale or other disposition of covered investments, each Party shall accord treatment no less favorable than that it accords, in like situations, to investments in its territory of its own nationals or companies (hereinafter "national treatment") or to investments in its territory of nationals or companies of a third country (hereinafter "most favored nation treatment"), whichever is most favorable (hereinafter "national and most favored nation treatment"). Each Party shall ensure that is state enterprises, in the provision of their goods or services, accord national and most favored nation treatment to covered investments.

2.   (a)   A Party may adopt or maintain exceptions to the obligations of paragraph 1 in the sectors or with respect to the matters specified in the Annex to this Treaty. In adopting such an exception, a Party may not require the divestment, in whole or in part, of covered investments existing at the time the exception becomes effective.

       (b)   The obligations of paragraph 1 do not apply to procedures provided in multilateral agreements concluded under the auspices of the World Intellectual Property Organization relating to the acquisition or maintenance of intellectual property rights.

3   (a)   Each Party shall at all times accord to covered investments fair and equitable treatment and full protection and security, and shall in no case accord treatment less favorable than that required by international law.

       (b)   Neither Party shall in any way impair by unreasonable and discriminatory measures the management, conduct, operation, and sale or other disposition of covered investments.

4.   Each Party shall provide effective means of asserting claims and enforcing rights with respect to covered investments.

5.   Each Party shall ensure that its laws, regulations, administrative practices and procedures of general application, and adjudicatory decisions, that pertain to or affect covered investments are promptly published or otherwise made publicly available.

ARTICLE III

1.   Neither Party shall expropriate or nationalize a covered investment either directly or indirectly through measures tantamount to expropriation or nationalization ("expropriation") except for a public purpose; in a non-discriminatory manner; upon payment of prompt, adequate and effective compensations; and in accordance with due process of law and the general principles of treatment provided for in Article II, paragraph 3.

2.   Compensation shall be paid without delay; be equivalent to the fair market value of the expropriated investment immediately before the expropriatory action was taken ("the date of expropriation"; and be fully realizable and freely transferable. The fair market value shall not reflect any change in value occurring because the expropriatory action had become known before the date of expropriation.

3.   If the fair market value is denominated in a freely usable currency, the compensation paid shall be no less than the fair market value on the date of expropriation, plus interest at a commercially reasonable rate for that currency, accrued form the date of expropriation until the date of payment.

4.   If the fair market value is denominated in a currency that is not freely usable, the compensation paid – converted into the currency of payment at the market rate of exchange prevailing on the date of payment – shall be no less than;

    (a)   the fair market value on the date of expropriation, converted into a freely usable currency at the market rate of exchange prevailing on that date, plus

    (b)   interest, at commercially reasonable rate for that freely usable currency, accrued from the date of expropriation until the date of payment.

ARTICLE IV

1.   Each Party shall accord national and most favored nation treatment to covered investments as regards any measure relating to losses that investments suffer in its territory owing to war or other armed conflict, revolution, state of national emergency, insurrection, civil disturbance, or similar events.

2.   Each Party shall accord restitution, or pay compensation in accordance with paragraphs 2 through 4 of Article III, in the event that covered investments suffer losses in its territory, owing to war or other armed conflict, revolution, state of national emergency, insurrection, civil disturbance, or similar events, that result from:

    a)   requisitioning of all or part of such investments by the Party's forces or authorities, or

    b)   destruction of all or part of such investments by the Party's forces or authorities that was not required by the necessity of the situation.

ARTICLE V

1.   Each party shall permit all transfers relating to a covered investment to be made freely and without delay into and out of its territory. Such transfers include:

(a)   contributions to capital;

(b)   profits, dividends, capital gains, and proceeds form the sale of all or any part of the investment or from the partial or complete liquidation of the investment;

(c)   interest, royalty payments, management fees, and technical assistance and other fees;

(d)   payment made under a contract, including a loan agreement; and

(e)   compensation pursuant to Articles III and IV, and payments arising out of an investment dispute.

2.   Each Party shall permit transfers to be made in a freely usable currency at the market rate of exchange prevailing on the date of transfer.

3.   Each party shall permit returns in kind to be made as authorized or specified in an investment authorization, investment agreement, or other written agreement between the Party and a covered investment or a national or company of the other Party.

4.   Notwithstanding paragraphs 1 to 3, a Party may prevent a transfer through the equitable, non-discriminatory and good faith application of its laws relating to:

(a)   bankruptcy, insolvency or the protection of the rights of creditors;

(b)   issuing, trading or dealing in securities;

(c)   criminal or penal offenses; or

(d)   ensuring compliance with orders or judgements in adjudicatory proceedings.

ARTICLE VI

Neither Party shall mandate or enforce, as a condition for the establishment, acquisition, expansion, management, conductor operation of a covered investment, any requirement (including any commitment or undertaking in connection with the receipt of a governmental permission or authorization):

(a)   to achieve a particular level or percentage of local content, or to purchase, use or otherwise give a preference to products or services of domestic origin or from any domestic source;

(b)   to limit imports by the investment of products or services in relation to a particular volume or value of production, exports of foreign exchange earnings;

(c)   to export a particular type, level or percentage of products or services, either generally or to a specific market region;

(d)   to limit sales by the investment of products or services in the Party's territory in relation to a particular volume or value of production, exports or foreign exchanges earnings,

(e)   to transfer technology, a production process or other proprietary knowledge to a national or company in the Party's territory, except pursuant to an order, commitment or undertaking that is enforced by a court, administrative tribunal or competition authority to remedy an alleged or adjudicated violation of competition laws; or

(f)   to carry out a particular type, level or percentage of research and development in the Party's territory.

Such requirements do not include conditions for the receipt or continued receipt of an advantage.

ARTICLE VII

1.   (a)   Subject to its laws relating to the entry and sojourn of aliens, each Party shall permit to enter and to remain in its territory nationals of the other Party for the purpose of establishing, developing, administering or advising on the operation of an investment to which they, or a company of the other Party that employs them, have committed or are in the process of committing a substantial amount of capital or other resources.

(b)   Neither Party shall, in granting entry under paragrapl (a), require a labor certification test or other procedures of similar effect, or apply any numerical restriction.

2.   Each Party shall permit covered investments to engage top managerial personnel of their choice, regardless of nationality.

ARTICLE VIII

The Parties agree to consult promptly, on the request of either, to resolve any disputes in connection with the Treaty, or to discuss any matter relating to the interpretation or application of the Treaty or to the realization of the objectives of the Treaty.

ARTICLE IX

1.   For purposes of this Treaty, an investment dispute is a dispute between a Party and a national or company of the other Party arising out of or relating to an investment authorization, an investment agreement or an alleged breach of any right conferred, created or recognized by this Treaty with respect to a covered investment.

2.   A national or company that is a party to an investment dispute may submit the dispute for resolution under one of the following alternatives:

(a) to the courts or administrative tribunals of the Party that is a party to the dispute; or

(b) in accordance with any applicable, previously agreed dispute settlement procedures; or

(c) in accordance with the terms of paragraph 3.

3. (a) Provided that the national or company concerned has not submitted the dispute for resolution under paragraph 2(a) or (b), and that three months have elapsed form the date on which the dispute arose, the national or company concerned may submit the dispute for settlement b binding arbitration:

   (i) to the Centre, if the Centre is available; or

   (ii) to the Additional Facility of the Centre, if the Centre is not available; or

   (iii) in accordance with the UNCITRAL Arbitration Rules; or

   (iv) if agreed by both parties to the dispute to any other arbitration institution or in accordance with any other arbitration rules.

   (b) A national or company, notwithstanding that it may have submitted a dispute to binding arbitration under paragraph 3 (a), may seek interim injunctive relief, not involving the payment of damages, before the judicial or administrative tribunals of the Party that is a party to the dispute, prior to the institution of the arbitral proceeding or during the proceeding, for the preservation of its rights and interests.

4. Each Party hereby consents to the submission of any investment dispute for settlement by binding arbitration in accordance with the choice of the national or company under paragraph 3 (a) (i), (ii), and (iii) or the mutual agreement of both parties to the dispute under paragraph 3 (a) (iv). This consent and the submission of the dispute by a national or company under paragraph 3 (a) shall satisfy the requirement of:

(a) Chapter II of the ICSID Convention (Jurisdiction of the Centre) and the Additional Facility Rules for written consent of the parties to the dispute; and

(b) Article II of the United Nations Convention o n the Recognition and enforcement of Foreign Arbitral Awards, done at New York, June 10, 1958, for an "agreement in writing".

5. Any arbitration under paragraph 3 (a) (ii), (iii) or (iv) shall be held in a state that is a party to the United Nations Convention on the Recognition and Enforcement of Foreign Arbitral Awards, done at New York, June 10, 1958.

6. Any arbitral award rendered pursuant to this Article shall be final and binding on the parties to the dispute. Each Party shall carry out without delay the provisions of any such award and provide in its territory for the enforcement of such award.

7.   In any proceeding involving an investment dispute, a Party shall not assert, as a defense, counterclaim, right of set-off or for any other reason, that indemnification or other compensation for all or part of the alleged damages has been received or will be received pursuant to an insurance or guarantee contract.

8.   For purposes of Article 25 (2) (b) of the ICSID Convention and this Article, a company of a Party that, immediately before the occurrence of the event or events giving rise to an investment dispute, was a covered investment, shall be treated as a company of the other Party.

ARTICLE X

1.   Any dispute between the Parties concerning the interpretation or application of the Treaty, that is not resolved through consultations or other diplomatic channels, shall be submitted upon the request of either Party to an arbitral tribunal for binding decision in accordance with the applicable rules of international law. In the absence of an agreement by the Parties to the contrary, the UNCITRATL Arbitration Rules shall govern, except to the extent these rules are (a) modified by the Parties or (b) modified by the arbitrators unless either Party objects to the proposed modification.

2.   Within two months of receipt of a request, each Party shall appoint an arbitrator. The two arbitrators shall select a third arbitrator as chairman, who shall be a national of a third state. The UNCITRAL Arbitration Rules applicable to appointing members of three-member panels shall apply mutatis mutandis to the appointment of the arbitral panel except that the appointing authority referenced in those rules shall be the Secretary General of the Centre.

3.   Unless otherwise agreed, all submissions shall be made and all hearings shall be completed within six months of the date of selection of the third arbitrator, and the arbitral panel shall render its decisions within two months of the date of the final submissions or the date of the closing of the hearings, whichever is later.

4.   Expenses incurred by the Chairman and other arbitrators, and other costs of the proceedings, shall be paid for equally by the Parties. However, the arbitral panel may, at its discretion, direct that a higher proportion of the costs be paid by one of the Parties.

ARTICLE XI

This Treaty shall not derogate from any of the following that entitle covered investments to treatment more favorable that that accorded by this Treaty:

(a)   laws and regulations, administrative practices or procedures, or administrative or adjudicatory decisions of a Party;

(b)   international legal obligations; or

(c)   obligations assumed by a Party, including those contained in an investment authorization or an investment agreement.

ARTICLE XII

Each Party reserves the right to deny to a company of the other Party the benefits of this Treaty if nationals of a third country own or control the company and

(a)   the denying Party does not maintain normal economic relations with the third country; or

(b)   the company has no substantial business activities in the territory of the Party under whose laws it is constituted or organized.

ARTICLE XIII

1.   No provision of this Treaty shall impose obligations with respect to tax matters, except that:

(a)   Articles III, IX and X will apply with respect to expropriation; and

(b)   Article IX will apply with respect to an investment agreement or an investment authorization.

2.   With respect to the application of Article III, an investor that asserts that a tax measures involves an expropriation may submit that dispute to arbitration pursuant to Article IX, paragraph 3, provided that the investor concerned has first referred to the competent tax authorities of both Parties the issue of whether that tax measure involves an expropriation.

3.   However, the investor cannot submit the dispute to arbitration if, within nine months after the date of referral, the competent tax authorities of both Parties determine that the tax measure does not involve an expropriation.

ARTICLE XIV

1.   This Treaty shall not preclude a Party from applying measures necessary for the fulfillment of its obligations with respect to the maintenance or restoration of international peace or security, or the protection of its own essential security interests.

2.   This Treaty shall not preclude a Party from prescribing special formalities in connection with covered investments, such as a requirement that such investments be legally constituted under the laws and regulations of that Party. Or a requirement that transfers of currency or other monetary instruments be reported, provided that such formalities shall not impair the substance of any of the rights set forth in this Treaty.

ARTICLE XV

1.   (a)   The obligations of this Treaty shall apply to the political subdivisions of the Parties.

(b)   With respect to the treatment accorded by a State, Territory or possession of the United States of America, national treatment means treatment no less favorable that the treatment accorded thereby, in like situations, to investments of nationals of the United States of America resident in, and companies legally constituted under the laws and regulations of, other States, Territories or possessions of the United States of America.

2.   A Party may terminate this Treaty at the end of the initial ten year period or at any time thereafter by giving one year's written notice to the other Party.

ARTICLE XVI

1.   This Treaty shall enter into force thirty days after the date of exchange of instruments of ratification. It shall remain in force for a period of ten years and shall continue in force unless terminated in accordance with paragraph 2. It shall apply to covered investments existing at the time of entry into force as well as to those established or acquired thereafter.

2.   A Party may terminate this Treaty at the end of the initial ten year period or at any time thereafter by giving one year's written notice to the other Party.

3.   For ten years from the date of termination, all other Articles shall continue to apply to covered investments established or acquired prior to the date of termination, except insofar as those Articles extend to the establishment or acquisition of covered investments.

4.   The Annex shall form an integral part of the Treaty.

IN WITNESS WHEREOF, the respective plenipotentiaries have signed this Treaty.

Done in duplicate at [city] this [number] day of [month, year], in the English and [foreign] languages, each text being equally authentic.

FOR THE GOVERNMENT OF   FOR THE GOVERNMENT OF
THE UNITED STATES   ....
OF AMERICA

ANNEX

1.   The Government of the United States of America may adopt or maintain exceptions to the obligation to accord national treatment to covered investments in the sectors or with respect to the matters specified below:

> atomic energy; customhouse brokers; licenses for broadcast, common carrier, or aeronautical radio stations; COMSAT; subsidies or grants, including government-supported loans, guarantees and insurance; state and local measures exempt from Article 1102 of the North American Free Trade Agreement pursuant to Article 1108 thereof, and landing of submarine cables.

Most favored nation treatment shall be accorded in the sectors and matters indicated above.

2.   The Government of the United States of America may adopt or maintain exceptions to the obligation to accord national and most favored nation treatment to covered investments in the sectors or with respect to the matters specified below;

> fisheries; air and maritime transport, and related activities; banking, insurance, securities, and other financial services; and one-way satellite transmissions of direct-to-home (DTH) and direct broadcast satellite (DBS) television services and of digital audio services.

3.   The Government of the Republic of [country] may adopt or maintain exceptions to the obligation to accord national treatment to covered investments in the sectors or with respect to the matters specified below:

Most favored nation treatment shall be accorded in the sectors and matters indicated above.

4.   Notwithstanding paragraph 3, each Party agrees to accord national treatment to covered investments in the following sectors:

leasing of minerals and pipeline rights-of-way on government lands.

*   *   *

PART SIX

PROTOTYPE BILATERAL DOUBLE TAXATION TREATIES

CONVENTION BETWEEN THE UNITED STATES OF AMERICA AND _____ FOR THE AVOIDANCE OF DOUBLE TAXATION AND THE PREVENTION OF FISCAL EVASION WITH RESPECT TO TAXES ON INCOME*

The United States of America and ...., desiring to conclude a Convention for the avoidance of double taxation and the prevention of fiscal evasion with respect to taxes on income, have agreed as follows:

Article 1

GENERAL SCOPE

1.   This Convention shall apply only to persons who are residents of one or both of the Contracting States, except as otherwise provided in the Convention.

2.   The Convention shall not restrict in any manner any benefit now or hereafter accorded:

  a)   by the laws of either Contracting State; or

  b)   by any other agreement between the Contracting States.

3.   Notwithstanding the provisions of subparagraph 2(b):

  (a)   the provisions of Article 26 (Mutual Agreement Procedure) of this Convention exclusively shall apply to any dispute concerning whether a measure is within the scope of this Convention, and the procedures under this Convention exclusively shall apply to that dispute; and

  (b)   unless the competent authorities determine that a taxation measure is not within the scope of this Convention, the non-discrimination obligations of this Convention exclusively shall apply with respect to that measure, except for such national treatment or most-favored-nation obligations as may apply to trade in goods under the General Agreement on Tariffs and Trade. No national treatment or most-favored-nation obligation under any other agreement shall apply with respect to that measure.

  (c)   For the purpose of this paragraph, a "measure" is a law, regulation, rule, procedure, decision, administrative action, or any similar provision or action.

4.   Notwithstanding any provision of the Convention except paragraph 5 of this Article, a Contracting State may tax its residents (as determined under Article 4 (Residence)), and by reason of citizenship may tax its citizens, as if the Convention had not come into effect. For this purpose, the term "citizen" shall include a former citizen or long-term resident whose loss of such status had as one of its principal purposes the avoidance of tax (as defined under the laws of

---

*   *Source*: The Government of the United States (1996). "Convention between the United States of America and _____ for the Avoidance of Double Taxation and the Prevention of Fiscal Evasion with Respect to Taxes on Income "; available on the Internet (http://www.treas.gov/taxpolicy/t0txmod1.html). [Note added by the editor.]

the Contracting State of which the person was a citizen or long-term resident), but only for a period of 10 years following such loss.

5. The provisions of paragraph 4 shall not affect:

    a) the benefits conferred by a Contracting State under paragraph 2 of Article 9 (Associated Enterprises), paragraphs 2 and 5 of Article 18 (Pensions, Social Security, Annuities, Alimony, and Child Support), and Articles 23 (Relief From Double Taxation), 24 (Non-Discrimination), and 25 (Mutual Agreement Procedure); and

    b) the benefits conferred by a Contracting State under paragraph 6 of Article 18 (Pensions, Social Security, Annuities, Alimony, and Child Support), Articles 19 (Government Service), 20 (Students and Trainees), and 27 (Diplomatic Agents and Consular Officers), upon individuals who are neither citizens of, nor have been admitted for permanent residence in, that State.

Article 2

TAXES COVERED

1. The existing taxes to which this Convention shall apply are:

    a) in the United States: the Federal income taxes imposed by the Internal Revenue Code (but excluding social security taxes), and the Federal excise taxes imposed with respect to private foundations.

    b) in ....: ....
    ....

2. The Convention shall apply also to any identical or substantially similar taxes that are imposed after the date of signature of the Convention in addition to, or in place of, the existing taxes. The competent authorities of the Contracting States shall notify each other of any significant changes that have been made in their respective taxation laws or other laws affecting their obligations under the Convention, and of any official published material concerning the application of the Convention, including explanations, regulations, rulings, or judicial decisions.

Article 3

GENERAL DEFINITIONS

1. For the purposes of this Convention, unless the context otherwise requires:

    a) the term "person" includes an individual, an estate, a trust, a partnership, a company, and any other body of persons;

    b) the term "company" means any body corporate or any entity that is treated as a body corporate for tax purposes according to the laws of the state in which it is organized;

c)   the terms "enterprise of a Contracting State" and "enterprise of the other Contracting State" mean respectively an enterprise carried on by a resident of a Contracting State, and an enterprise carried on by a resident of the other Contracting State; the terms also include an enterprise carried on by a resident of a Contracting State through an entity that is treated as fiscally transparent in that Contracting State;

d)   the term "international traffic" means any transport by a ship or aircraft, except when such transport is solely between places in a Contracting State;

e)   the term "competent authority" means:

    (i)   in the United States: the Secretary of the Treasury or his delegate; and

    (ii)   in......................: ....;

f)   the term "United States" means the United States of America, and includes the states thereof and the District of Columbia; such term also includes the territorial sea thereof and the sea bed and subsoil of the submarine areas adjacent to that territorial sea, over which the United States exercises sovereign rights in accordance with international law; the term, however, does not include Puerto Rico, the Virgin Islands, Guam or any other United States possession or territory;

g)   the term .... means ....;

h)   the term "national" of a Contracting State, means:

    (i)   any individual possessing the nationality or citizenship of that State; and

    (ii)   any legal person, partnership or association deriving its status as such from the laws in force in that State;

i)   the term "qualified governmental entity" means:

    (i)   any person or body of persons that constitutes a governing body of a Contracting State, or of a political subdivision or local authority of a Contracting State;

    (ii)   a person that is wholly owned, directly or indirectly, by a Contracting State or a political subdivision or local authority of a Contracting State, provided (A) it is organized under the laws of the Contracting State, (B) its earnings are credited to its own account with no portion of its income inuring to the benefit of any private person, and (C) its assets vest in the Contracting State, political subdivision or local authority upon dissolution; and

    (iii)   a pension trust or fund of a person described in subparagraph (i) or (ii) that is constituted and operated exclusively to administer or provide pension benefits described in Article 19; provided that an entity described in subparagraph (ii) or (iii) does not carry on commercial activities.

2.   As regards the application of the Convention at any time by a Contracting State any term not defined therein shall, unless the context otherwise requires, or the competent authorities agree to a common meaning pursuant to the provisions of Article 25 (Mutual Agreement Procedure), have the meaning which it has at that time under the law of that State for the purposes of the taxes to which the Convention applies, any meaning under the applicable tax laws of that State prevailing over a meaning given to the term under other laws of that State

Article 4

RESIDENCE

1.   Except as provided in this paragraph, for the purposes of this Convention, the term "resident of a Contracting State" means any person who, under the laws of that State, is liable to tax therein by reason of his domicile, residence, citizenship, place of management, place of incorporation, or any other criterion of a similar nature.

    a)   The term "resident of a Contracting State" does not include any person who is liable to tax in that State in respect only of income from sources in that State or of profits attributable to a permanent establishment in that State.

    b)   A legal person organized under the laws of a Contracting State and that is generally exempt from tax in that State and is established and maintained in that State either:

        i)   exclusively for a religious, charitable, educational, scientific, or other similar purpose; or

        ii)   to provide pensions or other similar benefits to employees pursuant to a plan is to be treated for purposes of this paragraph as a resident of that Contracting State.

    c)   A qualified governmental entity is to be treated as a resident of the Contracting State where it is established.

    d)   An item of income, profit or gain derived through an entity that is fiscally transparent under the laws of either Contracting State shall be considered to be derived by a resident of a State to the extent that the item is treated for purposes of the taxation law of such Contracting State as the income, profit or gain of a resident.

2.   Where by reason of the provisions of paragraph 1, an individual is a resident of both Contracting States, then his status shall be determined as follows:

    a)   he shall be deemed to be a resident of the State in which he has a permanent home available to him; if he has a permanent home available to him in both States, he shall be deemed to be a resident of the State with which his personal and economic relations are closer (center of vital interests);

b)   if the State in which he has his center of vital interests cannot be determined, or if he does not have a permanent home available to him in either State, he shall be deemed to be a resident of the State in which he has an habitual abode;

c)   if he has an habitual abode in both States or in neither of them, he shall be deemed to be a resident of the State of which he is a national;

d)   if he is a national of both States or of neither of them, the competent authorities of the Contracting States shall endeavor to settle the question by mutual agreement.

3.   Where by reason of the provisions of paragraph 1 a company is a resident of both Contracting States, then if it is created under the laws of one of the Contracting States or a political subdivision thereof, it shall be deemed to be a resident of that State.

4.   Where by reason of the provisions of paragraph 1 a person other than an individual or a company is a resident of both Contracting States, the competent authorities of the Contracting States shall endeavor to settle the question by mutual agreement and determine the mode of application of the Convention to such person.

Article 5

PERMANENT ESTABLISHMENT

1.   For the purposes of this Convention, the term "permanent establishment" means a fixed place of business through which the business of an enterprise is wholly or partly carried on.

2.   The term "permanent establishment" includes especially:

a)   a place of management;

b)   a branch;

c)   an office;

d)   a factory;

e)   a workshop; and

f)   a mine, an oil or gas well, a quarry, or any other place of extraction of natural resources.

3.   A building site or construction or installation project, or an installation or drilling rig or ship used for the exploration of natural resources, constitutes a permanent establishment only if it lasts or the activity continues for more than twelve months.

4.   Notwithstanding the preceding provisions of this Article, the term "permanent establishment" shall be deemed not to include:

a)   the use of facilities solely for the purpose of storage, display or delivery of goods or merchandise belonging to the enterprise;

b) the maintenance of a stock of goods or merchandise belonging to the enterprise solely for the purpose of storage, display or delivery;

c) the maintenance of a stock of goods or merchandise belonging to the enterprise solely for the purpose of processing by another enterprise;

d) the maintenance of a fixed place of business solely for the purpose of purchasing goods or merchandise, or of collecting information, for the enterprise;

e) the maintenance of a fixed place of business solely for the purpose of carrying on, for the enterprise, any other activity of a preparatory or auxiliary character;

f) the maintenance of a fixed place of business solely for any combination of the activities mentioned in subparagraphs a) through e).

5.   Notwithstanding the provisions of paragraphs 1 and 2, where a person--other than an agent of an independent status to whom paragraph 6 applies-is acting on behalf of an enterprise and has and habitually exercises in a Contracting State an authority to conclude contracts that are binding on the enterprise, that enterprise shall be deemed to have a permanent establishment in that State in respect of any activities that the person undertakes for the enterprise, unless the activities of such person are limited to those mentioned in paragraph 4 that, if exercised through a fixed place of business, would not make this fixed place of business a permanent establishment under the provisions of that paragraph.

6.   An enterprise shall not be deemed to have a permanent establishment in a Contracting State merely because it carries on business in that State through a broker, general commission agent, or any other agent of an independent status, provided that such persons are acting in the ordinary course of their business as independent agents.

7.   The fact that a company that is a resident of a Contracting State controls or is controlled by a company that is a resident of the other Contracting State, or that carries on business in that other State (whether through a permanent establishment or otherwise), shall not constitute either company a permanent establishment of the other.

Article 6

INCOME FROM REAL PROPERTY (IMMOVABLE PROPERTY)

1.   Income derived by a resident of a Contracting State from real property (immovable property), including income from agriculture or forestry, situated in the other Contracting State may be taxed in that other State.

2.   The term "real property (immovable property)" shall have the meaning which it has under the law of the Contracting State in which the property in question is situated.

3.   The provisions of paragraph 1 shall apply to income derived from the direct use, letting, or use in any other form of real property.

4.   The provisions of paragraphs 1 and 3 shall also apply to the income from real property of an enterprise and to income from real property used for the performance of independent personal services.

5.   A resident of a Contracting State who is liable to tax in the other Contracting State on income from real property situated in the other Contracting State may elect for any taxable year to compute the tax on such income on a net basis as if such income were business profits attributable to a permanent establishment in such other State. Any such election shall be binding for the taxable year of the election and all subsequent taxable years unless the competent authority of the Contracting State in which the property is situated agrees to terminate the election.

Article 7

BUSINESS PROFITS

1.   The business profits of an enterprise of a Contracting State shall be taxable only in that State unless the enterprise carries on business in the other Contracting State through a permanent establishment situated therein. If the enterprise carries on business as aforesaid, the business profits of the enterprise may be taxed in the other State but only so much of them as are attributable to that permanent establishment.

2.   Subject to the provisions of paragraph 3, where an enterprise of a Contracting State carries on business in the other Contracting State through a permanent establishment situated therein, there shall in each Contracting State be attributed to that permanent establishment the business profits that it might be expected to make if it were a distinct and independent enterprise engaged in the same or similar activities under the same or similar conditions. For this purpose, the business profits to be attributed to the permanent establishment shall include only the profits derived from the assets or activities of the permanent establishment.

3.   In determining the business profits of a permanent establishment, there shall be allowed as deductions expenses that are incurred for the purposes of the permanent establishment, including a reasonable allocation of executive and general administrative expenses, research and development expenses, interest, and other expenses incurred for the purposes of the enterprise as a whole (or the part thereof which includes the permanent establishment), whether incurred in the State in which the permanent establishment is situated or elsewhere.

4.   No business profits shall be attributed to a permanent establishment by reason of the mere purchase by that permanent establishment of goods or merchandise for the enterprise.

5.   For the purposes of the preceding paragraphs, the profits to be attributed to the permanent establishment shall be determined by the same method of accounting year by year unless there is good and sufficient reason to the contrary.

6.   Where business profits include items of income that are dealt with separately in other Articles of the Convention, then the provisions of those Articles shall not be affected by the provisions of this Article.

7.   For the purposes of the Convention, the term "business profits" means income from any trade or business, including income derived by an enterprise from the performance of personal services, and from the rental of tangible personal property.

8.   In applying paragraphs 1 and 2 of Article 7 (Business Profits), paragraph 6 of Article 10 (Dividends), paragraph 3 of Article 11 (Interest), paragraph 3 of Article 12 (Royalties), paragraph 3 of Article 13 (Gains), Article 14 (Independent Personal Services) and paragraph 2 of Article 21 (Other Income), any income or gain attributable to a permanent establishment or fixed base during its existence is taxable in the Contracting State where such permanent establishment or fixed base is situated even if the payments are deferred until such permanent establishment or fixed base has ceased to exist.

Article 8

SHIPPING AND AIR TRANSPORT

1.   Profits of an enterprise of a Contracting State from the operation of ships or aircraft in international traffic shall be taxable only in that State.

2.   For the purposes of this Article, profits from the operation of ships or aircraft include profits derived from the rental of ships or aircraft on a full (time or voyage) basis. They also include profits from the rental of ships or aircraft on a bareboat basis if such ships or aircraft are operated in international traffic by the lessee, or if the rental income is incidental to profits from the operation of ships or aircraft in international traffic. Profits derived by an enterprise from the inland transport of property or passengers within either Contracting State, shall be treated as profits from the operation of ships or aircraft in international traffic if such transport is undertaken as part of international traffic.

3.   Profits of an enterprise of a Contracting State from the use, maintenance, or rental of containers (including trailers, barges, and related equipment for the transport of containers) used in international traffic shall be taxable only in that State.

4.   The provisions of paragraphs 1 and 3 shall also apply to profits from participation in a pool, a joint business, or an international operating agency.

Article 9

ASSOCIATED ENTERPRISES

1.   Where:

   a)   an enterprise of a Contracting State participates directly or indirectly in the management, control or capital of an enterprise of the other Contracting State; or

   b)   the same persons participate directly or indirectly in the management, control, or capital of an enterprise of a Contracting State and an enterprise of the other Contracting State, and in either case conditions are made or imposed between the two enterprises in their commercial or financial relations that differ from those that would be made between independent enterprises, then, any profits that, but for those conditions, would have accrued to one of the enterprises, but by reason of those conditions have not so accrued, may be included in the profits of that enterprise and taxed accordingly.

2. Where a Contracting State includes in the profits of an enterprise of that State, and taxes accordingly, profits on which an enterprise of the other Contracting State has been charged to tax in that other State, and the other Contracting State agrees that the profits so included are profits that would have accrued to the enterprise of the first-mentioned State if the conditions made between the two enterprises had been those that would have been made between independent enterprises, then that other State shall make an appropriate adjustment to the amount of the tax charged therein on those profits. In determining such adjustment, due regard shall be paid to the other provisions of this Convention and the competent authorities of the Contracting States shall if necessary consult each other.

Article 10

DIVIDENDS

1. Dividends paid by a resident of a Contracting State to a resident of the other Contracting State may be taxed in that other State.

2. However, such dividends may also be taxed in the Contracting State of which the payor is a resident and according to the laws of that State, but if the dividends are beneficially owned by a resident of the other Contracting State, except as otherwise provided, the tax so charged shall not exceed:

   a) 5 percent of the gross amount of the dividends if the beneficial owner is a company that owns directly at least 10 percent of the voting stock of the company paying the dividends;

   b) 15 percent of the gross amount of the dividends in all other cases.

   This paragraph shall not affect the taxation of the company in respect of the profits out of which the dividends are paid.

3. Subparagraph a) of paragraph 2 shall not apply in the case of dividends paid by a United States person that is a Regulated Investment Company or a Real Estate Investment Trust (REIT). In the case of a United States person that is a REIT, subparagraph b) of paragraph 2 also shall not apply, unless the dividend is beneficially owned by an individual holding a less than 10-percent interest in the REIT.

4. Notwithstanding paragraph 2, dividends may not be taxed in the Contracting State of which the payor is a resident if the beneficial owner of the dividends is a resident of the other Contracting State that is a qualified governmental entity that does not control the payor of the dividend.

5. For purposes of the Convention, the term "dividends" means income from shares or other rights, not being debt claims, participating in profits, as well as income that is subjected to the same taxation treatment as income from shares under the laws of the State of which the payor is a resident.

6.   The provisions of paragraphs 1 and 2 shall not apply if the beneficial owner of the dividends, being a resident of a Contracting State, carries on business in the other Contracting State, of which the payor is a resident, through a permanent establishment situated therein, or performs in that other State independent personal services from a fixed base situated therein, and the dividends are attributable to such permanent establishment or fixed base. In such case the provisions of Article 7 (Business Profits) or Article 14 (Independent Personal Services), as the case may be, shall apply.

7.   A Contracting State may not impose any tax on dividends paid by a resident of the other State, except insofar as the dividends are paid to a resident of the first-mentioned State or the dividends are attributable to a permanent establishment or a fixed base situated in that State, nor may it impose tax on a corporation's undistributed profits, except as provided in paragraph 8, even if the dividends paid or the undistributed profits consist wholly or partly of profits or income arising in that State.

8.   A corporation that is a resident of one of the States and that has a permanent establishment in the other State or that is subject to tax in the other State on a net basis on its income that may be taxed in the other State under Article 6 (Income from Real Property (Immoveable Property)) or under paragraph 1 of Article 13 (Gains) may be subject in that other State to a tax in addition to the tax allowable under the other provisions of this Convention. Such tax, however, may be imposed on only the portion of the business profits of the corporation attributable to the permanent establishment and the portion of the income referred to in the preceding sentence that is subject to tax under Article 6 (Income from Real Property (Immoveable Property)) or under paragraph 1 of Article 13 (Gains) that, in the case of the United States, represents the dividend equivalent amount of such profits or income and, in the case of ...., is an amount that is analogous to the dividend equivalent amount.

9.   The tax referred to in paragraph 8 may not be imposed at a rate in excess of the rate specified in paragraph 2 a).

Article 11

INTEREST

1.   Interest arising in a Contracting State and beneficially owned by a resident of the other Contracting State may be taxed only in that other State.

2.   The term "interest" as used in this Convention means income from debt-claims of every kind, whether or not secured by mortgage, and whether or not carrying a right to participate in the debtor's profits, and in particular, income from government securities and income from bonds or debentures, including premiums or prizes attaching to such securities, bonds or debentures, and all other income that is subjected to the same taxation treatment as income from money lent by the taxation law of the Contracting State in which the income arises. Income dealt with in Article 10 (Dividends) and penalty charges for late payment shall not be regarded as interest for the purposes of this Convention.

3.   The provisions of paragraph 1 shall not apply if the beneficial owner of the interest, being a resident of a Contracting State, carries on business in the other Contracting State, in which the interest arises, through a permanent establishment situated therein, or performs in that other State independent personal services from a fixed base situated therein, and the interest is attributable to

such permanent establishment or fixed base. In such case the provisions of Article 7 (Business Profits) or Article 14 (Independent Personal Services), as the case may be, shall apply.

4.   Where, by reason of a special relationship between the payer and the beneficial owner or between both of them and some other person, the amount of the interest, having regard to the debt-claim for which it is paid, exceeds the amount which would have been agreed upon by the payer and the beneficial owner in the absence of such relationship, the provisions of this Article shall apply only to the last-mentioned amount. In such case the excess part of the payments shall remain taxable according to the laws of each State, due regard being had to the other provisions of this Convention.

5.   Notwithstanding the provisions of paragraph 1:

a)   interest paid by a resident of a Contracting State and that is determined with reference to receipts, sales, income, profits or other cash flow of the debtor or a related person, to any change in the value of any property of the debtor or a related person or to any dividend, partnership distribution or similar payment made by the debtor to a related person, and paid to a resident of the other State also may be taxed in the Contracting State in which it arises, and according to the laws of that State, but if the beneficial owner is a resident of the other Contracting State, the gross amount of the interest may be taxed at a rate not exceeding the rate prescribed in subparagraph b) of paragraph 2 of Article 10 (Dividends); and

b)   Interest that is an excess inclusion with respect to a residual interest in a real estate mortgage investment conduit may be taxed by each State in accordance with its domestic law.

Article 12

ROYALTIES

1.   Royalties arising in a Contracting State and beneficially owned by a resident of the other Contracting State may be taxed only in that other State.

2.   The term "royalties" as used in this Convention means:

(a)   any consideration for the use of, or the right to use, any copyright of literary, artistic, scientific or other work (including computer software, cinematographic films, audio or video tapes or disks, and other means of image or sound reproduction), any patent, trademark, design or model, plan, secret formula or process, or other like right or property, or for information concerning industrial, commercial, or scientific experience; and

(b)   gain derived from the alienation of any property described in subparagraph (a), provided that such gain is contingent on the productivity, use, or disposition of the property.

3.   The provisions of paragraph 1 shall not apply if the beneficial owner of the royalties, being a resident of a Contracting State, carries on business in the other Contracting State through a permanent establishment situated therein, or performs in that other State independent personal

services from a fixed base situated therein, and the royalties are attributable to such permanent establishment or fixed base. In such case the provisions of Article 7 (Business Profits) or Article 14 (Independent Personal Services), as the case may be, shall apply.

4.   Where, by reason of a special relationship between the payer and the beneficial owner or between both of them and some other person, the amount of the royalties, having regard to the use, right, or information for which they are paid, exceeds the amount which would have been agreed upon by the payer and the beneficial owner in the absence of such relationship, the provisions of this Article shall apply only to the last-mentioned amount. In such case the excess part of the payments shall remain taxable according to the laws of each Contracting State, due regard being had to the other provisions of the Convention.

Article 13

GAINS

1.   Gains derived by a resident of a Contracting State that are attributable to the alienation of real property situated in the other Contracting State may be taxed in that other State.

2.   For the purposes of this Convention the term "real property situated in the other Contracting State" shall include:

a)   real property referred to in Article 6 (Income from Real Property (Immovable Property));

b)   a United States real property interest; and

c)   an equivalent interest in real property situated in ....

3.   Gains from the alienation of personal property that are attributable to a permanent establishment that an enterprise of a Contracting State has in the other Contracting State, or that are attributable to a fixed base that is available to a resident of a Contracting State in the other Contracting State for the purpose of performing independent personal services, and gains from the alienation of such a permanent establishment (alone or with the whole enterprise) or of such a fixed base, may be taxed in that other State.

4.   Gains derived by an enterprise of a Contracting State from the alienation of ships, aircraft, or containers operated or used in international traffic or personal property pertaining to the operation or use of such ships, aircraft, or containers shall be taxable only in that State.

5.   Gains from the alienation of any property other than property referred to in paragraphs 1 through 4 shall be taxable only in the Contracting State of which the alienator is a resident.

Article 14

INDEPENDENT PERSONAL SERVICES

1.   Income derived by an individual who is a resident of a Contracting State in respect of the performance of personal services of an independent character shall be taxable only in that State, unless the individual has a fixed base regularly available to him in the other Contracting State for

the purpose of performing his activities. If he has such a fixed base, the income attributable to the fixed base that is derived in respect of services performed in that other State also may be taxed by that other State.

2.   For purposes of paragraph 1, the income that is taxable in the other Contracting State shall be determined under the principles of paragraph 3 of Article 7.

Article 15

DEPENDENT PERSONAL SERVICES

1.   Subject to the provisions of Articles 16 (Directors' Fees), 18 (Pensions, Social Security, Annuities, Alimony, and Child Support) and 19 (Government Service), salaries, wages, and other remuneration derived by a resident of a Contracting State in respect of an employment shall be taxable only in that State unless the employment is exercised in the other Contracting State. If the employment is so exercised, such remuneration as is derived therefrom may be taxed in that other State.

2.   Notwithstanding the provisions of paragraph 1, remuneration derived by a resident of a Contracting State in respect of an employment exercised in the other Contracting State shall be taxable only in the first-mentioned State if:

   a)   the recipient is present in the other State for a period or periods not exceeding in the aggregate 183 days in any twelve month period commencing or ending in the taxable year concerned;

   b)   the remuneration is paid by, or on behalf of, an employer who is not a resident of the other State; and

   c)   the remuneration is not borne by a permanent establishment or a fixed base which the employer has in the other State.

3.   Notwithstanding the preceding provisions of this Article, remuneration described in paragraph 1 that is derived by a resident of a Contracting State in respect of an employment as a member of the regular complement of a ship or aircraft operated in international traffic shall be taxable only in that State.

Article 16

DIRECTORS' FEES

Directors' fees and other compensation derived by a resident of a Contracting State for services rendered in the other Contracting State in his capacity as a member of the board of directors of a company that is a resident of the other Contracting State may be taxed in that other Contracting State.

Article 17

ARTISTES AND SPORTSMEN

1.   Income derived by a resident of a Contracting State as an entertainer, such as a theater, motion picture, radio, or television artiste, or a musician, or as a sportsman, from his personal activities as such exercised in the other Contracting State, which income would be exempt from tax in that other Contracting State under the provisions of Articles 14 (Independent Personal Services) and 15 (Dependent Personal Services) may be taxed in that other State, except where the amount of the gross receipts derived by such entertainer or sportsman, including expenses reimbursed to him or borne on his behalf, from such activities does not exceed twenty thousand United States dollars ($20,000) or its equivalent in …….. for the taxable year concerned.

2.   Where income in respect of activities exercised by an entertainer or a sportsman in his capacity as such accrues not to the entertainer or sportsman himself but to another person, that income, notwithstanding the provisions of Articles 7 (Business Profits) and 14 (Independent Personal Services), may be taxed in the Contracting State in which the activities of the entertainer or sportsman are exercised, unless it is established that neither the entertainer or sportsman nor persons related thereto participate directly or indirectly in the profits of that other person in any manner, including the receipt of deferred remuneration, bonuses, fees, dividends, partnership distributions, or other distributions.

Article 18

PENSIONS, SOCIAL SECURITY, ANNUITIES, ALIMONY AND CHILD SUPPORT

1.   Subject to the provisions of Article 19 (Government Service), pension distributions and other similar remuneration beneficially owned by a resident of a Contracting State, whether paid periodically or as a single sum, shall be taxable only in that State, but only to the extent not included in taxable income in the other Contracting State prior to the distribution.

2.   Notwithstanding the provisions of paragraph 1, payments made by a Contracting State under provisions of the social security or similar legislation of that State to a resident of the other Contracting State or to a citizen of the United States shall be taxable only in the first-mentioned State.

3.   Annuities derived and beneficially owned by an individual resident of a Contracting State shall be taxable only in that State. The term "annuities" as used in this paragraph means a stated sum paid periodically at stated times during a specified number of years, under an obligation to make the payments in return for adequate and full consideration (other than services rendered).

4.   Alimony paid by a resident of a Contracting State, and deductible therein, to a resident of the other Contracting State shall be taxable only in that other State. The term "alimony" as used in this paragraph means periodic payments made pursuant to a written separation agreement or a decree of divorce, separate maintenance, or compulsory support, which payments are taxable to the recipient under the laws of the State of which he is a resident.

5.   Periodic payments, not dealt with in paragraph 4, for the support of a child made pursuant to a written separation agreement or a decree of divorce, separate maintenance, or compulsory

support, paid by a resident of a Contracting State to a resident of the other Contracting State, shall be exempt from tax in both Contracting States.

6.   For purposes of this Convention, where an individual who is a participant in a pension plan that is established and recognized under the legislation of one of the Contracting States performs personal services in the other Contracting State:

a)   Contributions paid by or on behalf of the individual to the plan during the period that he performs such services in the other State shall be deductible (or excludible) in computing his taxable income in that State. Any benefits accrued under the plan or payments made to the plan by or on behalf of his employer during that period shall not be treated as part of the employee's taxable income and shall be allowed as a deduction in computing the profits of his employer in that other State.

b)   Income earned but not distributed by the plan shall not be taxable in the other State until such time and to the extent that a distribution is made from the plan.

c)   Distributions from the plan to the individual shall not be subject to taxation in the other Contracting State if the individual contributes such amounts to a similar plan established in the other State within a time period and in accordance with any other requirements imposed under the laws of the other State.

d)   The provisions of this paragraph shall not apply unless:

(i)   contributions by or on behalf of the individual to the plan (or to another similar plan for which this plan was substituted) were made before he arrived in the other State; and

(ii)   the competent authority of the other State has agreed that the pension plan generally corresponds to a pension plan recognized for tax purposes by that State.

The benefits granted under this paragraph shall not exceed the benefits that would be allowed by the other State to its residents for contributions to, or benefits otherwise accrued under a pension plan recognized for tax purposes by that State.

Article 19

GOVERNMENT SERVICE

1.   Notwithstanding the provisions of Articles 14 (Independent Personal Services), 15 (Dependent Personal Services), 16 (Director's Fees) and 17 (Artistes and Sportsmen):

a)   Salaries, wages and other remuneration, other than a pension, paid from the public funds of a Contracting State or a political subdivision or a local authority thereof to an individual in respect of services rendered to that State or subdivision or authority in the discharge of functions of a governmental nature shall, subject to the provisions of subparagraph (b), be taxable only in that State;

b) such remuneration, however, shall be taxable only in the other Contracting State if the services are rendered in that State and the individual is a resident of that State who:

  i) is a national of that State; or

  ii) did not become a resident of that State solely for the purpose of rendering the services.

2. Notwithstanding the provisions of paragraph 1 of Article 18 (Pensions, Social Security, Annuities, Alimony, and Child Support):

a) any pension paid from the public funds of a Contracting State or a political subdivision or a local authority thereof to an individual in respect of services rendered to that State or subdivision or authority in the discharge of functions of a governmental nature shall, subject to the provisions of subparagraph (b), be taxable only in that State;

b) such pension, however, shall be taxable only in the other Contracting State if the individual is a resident of, and a national of, that State.

Article 20

STUDENTS AND TRAINEES

Payments received by a student, apprentice, or business trainee who is, or was immediately before visiting a Contracting State, a resident of the other Contracting State, and who is present in the first-mentioned State for the purpose of his full-time education at an accredited educational institution, or for his full-time training, shall not be taxed in that State, provided that such payments arise outside that State, and are for the purpose of his maintenance, education or training. The exemption from tax provided by this Article shall apply to an apprentice or business trainee only for a period of time not exceeding one year from the date he first arrives in the first-mentioned Contracting State for the purpose of his training.

Article 21

OTHER INCOME

1. Items of income beneficially owned by a resident of a Contracting State, wherever arising, not dealt with in the foregoing Articles of this Convention shall be taxable only in that State.

2. The provisions of paragraph 1 shall not apply to income, other than income from real property as defined in paragraph 2 of Article 6 (Income from Real Property (Immovable Property)), if the beneficial owner of the income, being a resident of a Contracting State, carries on business in the other Contracting State through a permanent establishment situated therein, or performs in that other State independent personal services from a fixed base situated therein, and the income is attributable to such permanent establishment or fixed base. In such case the provisions of Article 7 (Business Profits) or Article 14 (Independent Personal Services), as the case may be, shall apply.

Article 22

LIMITATION ON BENEFITS

1.   A resident of a Contracting State shall be entitled to benefits otherwise accorded to residents of a Contracting State by this Convention only to the extent provided in this Article.

2.   A resident of a Contracting State shall be entitled to all the benefits of this Convention if the resident is:

a)   an individual;

b)   a qualified governmental entity;

c)   a company, if

i)   all the shares in the class or classes of shares representing more than 50 percent of the voting power and value of the company are regularly traded on a recognized stock exchange, or

ii)   at least 50 percent of each class of shares in the company is owned directly or indirectly by companies entitled to benefits under clause i), provided that in the case of indirect ownership, each intermediate owner is a person entitled to benefits of the Convention under this paragraph;

d)   described in subparagraph 1(b) (i) of Article 4 (Residence);

e)   described in subparagraph 1(b) (ii) of Article 4 (Residence), provided that more than 50 percent of the person's beneficiaries, members or participants are individuals resident in either Contracting State; or

f)   a person other than an individual, if:

i)   On at least half the days of the taxable year persons described in subparagraphs a), b), c), d) or e) own, directly or indirectly (through a chain of ownership in which each person is entitled to benefits of the Convention under this paragraph), at least 50 percent of each class of shares or other beneficial interests in the person, and

ii)   less than 50 percent of the person's gross income for the taxable year is paid or accrued, directly or indirectly, to persons who are not residents of either Contracting State (unless the payment is attributable to a permanent establishment situated in either State), in the form of payments that are deductible for income tax purposes in the person's State of residence.

3.   a)   A resident of a Contracting State not otherwise entitled to benefits shall be entitled to he benefits of this Convention with respect to an item of income derived from the other State, if:

       i)   the resident is engaged in the active conduct of a trade or business in the first-mentioned State,

       ii)   the income is connected with or incidental to the trade or business, and

       iii)   the trade or business is substantial in relation to the activity in the other State generating the income.

b)   For purposes of this paragraph, the business of making or managing investments will not be considered an active trade or business unless the activity is banking, insurance or securities activity conducted by a bank, insurance company or registered securities dealer.

c)   Whether a trade or business is substantial for purposes of this paragraph will be determined based on all the facts and circumstances. In any case, however, a trade or business will be deemed substantial if, for the preceding taxable year, or for the average of the three preceding taxable years, the asset value, the gross income, and the payroll expense that are related to the trade or business in the first-mentioned State equal at least 7.5 percent of the resident's (and any related parties') proportionate share of the asset value, gross income and payroll expense, respectively, that are related to the activity that generated the income in the other State, and the average of the three ratios exceeds 10 percent.

d)   Income is derived in connection with a trade or business if the activity in the other State generating the income is a line of business that forms a part of or is complementary to the trade or business. Income is incidental to a trade or business if it facilitates the conduct of the trade or business in the other State.

4.   A resident of a Contracting State not otherwise entitled to benefits may be granted benefits of the Convention if the competent authority of the State from which benefits are claimed so determines.

5.   For purposes of this Article the term "recognized stock exchange" means:

a)   the NASDAQ System owned by the National Association of Securities Dealers, Inc. and any stock exchange registered with the U.S. Securities and Exchange Commission as a national securities exchange under the U.S. Securities Exchange Act of 1934; and

b)   [stock exchanges of the other Contracting State].

Article 23

RELIEF FROM DOUBLE TAXATION

1.   In accordance with the provisions and subject to the limitations of the law of the United States (as it may be amended from time to time without changing the general principle hereof), the United States shall allow to a resident or citizen of the United States as a credit against the United States tax on income

a)   the income tax paid or accrued to .... by or on behalf of such citizen or resident; and

b)   in the case of a United States company owning at least 10 percent of the voting stock of a company that is a resident of .... and from which the United States company receives dividends, the income tax paid or accrued to .... by or on behalf of the payor with respect to the profits out of which the dividends are paid.

         For the purposes of this paragraph, the taxes referred to in paragraphs 1(b) and 2 of Article 2 (Taxes Covered) shall be considered income taxes.

2.   In accordance with the provisions and subject to the limitations of the law of .... (as it may be amended from time to time without changing the general principle hereof), ... shall allow to a resident or citizen of........ as a credit against the .... tax on income

a)   the income tax paid or accrued to the United States by or on behalf of such resident of citizen;
         and

b)   in the case of a .... company owning at least 10 percent of the voting stock of a company that is a resident of the United States and from which the .... company receives dividends, the income tax paid or accrued to the United States by or on behalf of the payor with respect to the profits out of which the dividends are paid.

         For the purposes of this paragraph, the taxes referred to in paragraphs 1(a) and 2 of Article 2 (Taxes Covered) shall be considered income taxes.

3.   Where a United States citizen is a resident of ....:

a)   with respect to items of income that under the provisions of this Convention are exempt from United States tax or that are subject to a reduced rate of United States tax when derived by a resident of .... who is not a United States citizen, ... shall allow as a credit against .... tax, only the tax paid, if any, that the United States may impose under the provisions of this Convention, other than taxes that may be imposed solely by reason of citizenship under the saving clause of paragraph 4 of Article 1 (General Scope);

b)   for purposes of computing United States tax on those items of income referred to in subparagraph (a), the United States shall allow as a credit against United States tax the income tax paid to .... after the credit referred to in subparagraph (a); the credit so allowed shall not reduce the portion of the United States tax that is creditable against the .... tax in accordance with subparagraph (a); and

(c)   for the exclusive purpose of relieving double taxation in the United States under subparagraph (b), items of income referred to in subparagraph (a) shall be deemed to arise in .... to the extent necessary to avoid double taxation of such income under subparagraph (b).

Article 24

NON-DISCRIMINATION

1.   Nationals of a Contracting State shall not be subjected in the other Contracting State to any taxation or any requirement connected therewith that is more burdensome than the taxation and connected requirements to which nationals of that other State in the same circumstances, particularly with respect to taxation on worldwide income, are or may be subjected. This provision shall also apply to persons who are not residents of one or both of the Contracting States.

2.   The taxation on a permanent establishment or fixed base that a resident or enterprise of a Contracting State has in the other Contracting State shall not be less favorably levied in that other State than the taxation levied on enterprises or residents of that other State carrying on the same activities. The provisions of this paragraph shall not be construed as obliging a Contracting State to grant to residents of the other Contracting State any personal allowances, reliefs, and reductions for taxation purposes on account of civil status or family responsibilities that it grants to its own residents.

3.   Except where the provisions of paragraph 1 of Article 9 (Associated Enterprises), paragraph 4 of Article 11 (Interest), or paragraph 4 of Article 12 (Royalties) apply, interest, royalties, and other disbursements paid by a resident of a Contracting State to a resident of the other Contracting State shall, for the purpose of determining the taxable profits of the first-mentioned resident, be deductible under the same conditions as if they had been paid to a resident of the first-mentioned State. Similarly, any debts of a resident of a Contracting State to a resident of the other Contracting State shall, for the purpose of determining the taxable capital of the first-mentioned resident, be deductible under the same conditions as if they had been contracted to a resident of the first-mentioned State.

4.   Enterprises of a Contracting State, the capital of which is wholly or partly owned or controlled, directly or indirectly, by one or more residents of the other Contracting State, shall not be subjected in the first-mentioned State to any taxation or any requirement connected therewith that is more burdensome than the taxation and connected requirements to which other similar enterprises of the first-mentioned State are or may be subjected.

5.   Nothing in this Article shall be construed as preventing either Contracting State from imposing a tax as described in paragraph 8 of Article 10 (Dividends).

6.   The provisions of this Article shall, notwithstanding the provisions of Article 2 (Taxes Covered), apply to taxes of every kind and description imposed by a Contracting State or a political subdivision or local authority thereof.

Article 25

MUTUAL AGREEMENT PROCEDURE

1.   Where a person considers that the actions of one or both of the Contracting States result or will result for him in taxation not in accordance with the provisions of this Convention, he may, irrespective of the remedies provided by the domestic law of those States, and the time

limits prescribed in such laws for presenting claims for refund, present his case to the competent authority of either Contracting State.

2.   The competent authority shall endeavor, if the objection appears to it to be justified and if it is not itself able to arrive at a satisfactory solution, to resolve the case by mutual agreement with the competent authority of the other Contracting State, with a view to the avoidance of taxation which is not in accordance with the Convention. Any agreement reached shall be implemented notwithstanding any time limits or other procedural limitations in the domestic law of the Contracting States. Assessment and collection procedures shall be suspended during the pendency of any mutual agreement proceeding.

3.   The competent authorities of the Contracting States shall endeavor to resolve by mutual agreement any difficulties or doubts arising as to the interpretation or application of the Convention. In particular the competent authorities of the Contracting States may agree:

   a)   to the same attribution of income, deductions, credits, or allowances of an enterprise of a Contracting State to its permanent establishment situated in the other Contracting State;

   b)   to the same allocation of income, deductions, credits, or allowances between persons;

   c)   to the same characterization of particular items of income, including the same characterization of income that is assimilated to income from shares by the taxation law of one of the Contracting States and that is treated as a different class of income in the other State;

   d)   to the same characterization of persons;

   e)   to the same application of source rules with respect to particular items of income;

   f)   to a common meaning of a term;

   g)   to advance pricing arrangements; and

   h)   to the application of the provisions of domestic law regarding penalties, fines, and interest in a manner consistent with the purposes of the Convention.

           They may also consult together for the elimination of double taxation in cases not provided for in the Convention.

4.   The competent authorities also may agree to increases in any specific dollar amounts referred to in the Convention to reflect economic or monetary developments.

5.   The competent authorities of the Contracting States may communicate with each other directly for the purpose of reaching an agreement in the sense of the preceding paragraphs.

Article 26

EXCHANGE OF INFORMATION AND ADMINISTRATIVE ASSISTANCE

1.   The competent authorities of the Contracting States shall exchange such information as is relevant for carrying out the provisions of this Convention or of the domestic laws of the Contracting States concerning taxes covered by the Convention insofar as the taxation thereunder is not contrary to the Convention, including information relating to the assessment or collection of, the enforcement or prosecution in respect of, or the determination of appeals in relation to, the taxes covered by the Convention. The exchange of information is not restricted by Article 1 (General Scope). Any information received by a Contracting State shall be treated as secret in the same manner as information obtained under the domestic laws of that State and shall be disclosed only to persons or authorities (including courts and administrative bodies) involved in the assessment, collection, or administration of, the enforcement or prosecution in respect of, or the determination of appeals in relation to, the taxes covered by the Convention or the oversight of the above. Such persons or authorities shall use the information only for such purposes. They may disclose the information in public court proceedings or in judicial decisions.

2.   In no case shall the provisions of paragraph 1 be construed so as to impose on a Contracting State the obligation:

a)   to carry out administrative measures at variance with the laws and administrative practice of that or of the other Contracting State;

b)   to supply information that is not obtainable under the laws or in the normal course of the administration of that or of the other Contracting State;

c)   to supply information that would disclose any trade, business, industrial, commercial, or professional secret or trade process, or information the disclosure of which would be contrary to public policy (ordre public).

3.   Notwithstanding paragraph 2, the competent authority of the requested State shall have the authority to obtain and provide information held by financial institutions, nominees or persons acting in an agency or fiduciary capacity, or respecting interests in a person, including bearer shares, regardless of any laws or practices of the requested State that might otherwise preclude the obtaining of such information. If information is requested by a Contracting State in accordance with this Article, the other Contracting State shall obtain that information in the same manner and to the same extent as if the tax of the first-mentioned State were the tax of that other State and were being imposed by that other State, notwithstanding that the other State may not, at that time, need such information for purposes of its own tax. If specifically requested by the competent authority of a Contracting State, the competent authority of the other Contracting State shall provide information under this Article in the form of depositions of witnesses and authenticated copies of unedited original documents (including books, papers, statements, records, accounts, and writings), to the same extent such depositions and documents can be obtained under the laws and administrative practices of that other State with respect to its own taxes.

4.   Each of the Contracting States shall endeavor to collect on behalf of the other Contracting State such amounts as may be necessary to ensure that relief granted by the Convention from taxation imposed by that other State does not inure to the benefit of persons not entitled thereto.

This paragraph shall not impose upon either of the Contracting States the obligation to carry out administrative measures that would be contrary to its sovereignty, security, or public policy.

5.   For the purposes of this Article, the Convention shall apply, notwithstanding the provisions of Article 2 (Taxes Covered), to taxes of every kind imposed by a Contracting State.

6.   The competent authority of the requested State shall allow representatives of the applicant State to enter the requested State to interview individuals and examine books and records with the consent of the persons subject to examination.

Article 27

DIPLOMATIC AGENTS AND CONSULAR OFFICERS

Nothing in this Convention shall affect the fiscal privileges of diplomatic agents or consular officers under the general rules of international law or under the provisions of special agreements.

Article 28

ENTRY INTO FORCE

1.   This Convention shall be subject to ratification in accordance with the applicable procedures of each Contracting State. Each Contracting State shall notify the other as soon as its procedures have been complied with.

2.   The Convention shall enter into force on the date of the receipt of the later of such notifications, and its provisions shall have effect:

   a)   in respect of taxes withheld at source, for amounts paid or credited on or after the first day of the second month next following the date on which the Convention enters into force;

   b)   in respect of other taxes, for taxable periods beginning on or after the first day of January next following the date on which the Convention enters into force.

Article 29

TERMINATION

1.   This Convention shall remain in force until terminated by a Contracting State. Either Contracting State may terminate the Convention by giving notice of termination to the other Contracting State through diplomatic channels. In such event, the Convention shall cease to have effect:

   a)   in respect of taxes withheld at source, for amounts paid or credited after the expiration of the 6 month period beginning on the date on which notice of termination was given; and

b) in respect of other taxes, for taxable periods beginning on or after the expiration of the 6 month period beginning on the date on which notice of termination was given.

IN WITNESS WHEREOF, the undersigned, being duly authorized thereto by their respective Governments, have signed this Convention.

DONE at _____ in duplicate, in the English and .... languages, both texts being equally authentic, this ..... day <u>of (month)</u>, 19....

*   *   *

AGREEMENT BETWEEN THE GOVERNMENT OF ZIMBABWE AND _____ FOR THE AVOIDANCE OF DOUBLE TAXATION AND THE PREVENTION OF FISCAL EVASION WITH RESPECT TO TAXES ON INCOME AND CAPITAL GAINS[*]

The Government of the Republic of Zimbabwe

AND

The ....

Desiring to conclude an Agreement for the avoidance of double taxation and the prevention of fiscal evasion with respect to taxes on income and capital gains, have agreed as follows:

Article 1
PERSONAL SCOPE

This Agreement shall apply to persons who are residents of one or both of the Contracting States.

Article 2
TAXES COVERED

1.   The existing taxes to which this Agreement shall apply are:

(a)   in ....

(hereinafter referred to as ....;

(b)   in Zimbabwe:

(i)   the income tax;

(ii)   the non-resident shareholders' tax;

(iii)   the non-residents' tax on interest;

(iv)   the non-residents' tax on fees;

(v)   the non-residents' tax on royalties;

(vi)   the capital gains tax; and

(vii)   the residents' tax on interest;

(hereinafter referred to as "Zimbabwean tax").

---

[*]   *Source*: The Government of Zimbabwe, Ministry of Finance. [Note added by the editor.]

---

2.   The Agreement shall apply also to any identical or substantially similar taxes which are imposed after the date of signature of the Agreement in addition to, or in place of, the existing taxes. The competent authorities of the Contracting States shall notify each other of any significant changes which have been made in their respective taxation laws.

Article 3
GENERAL DEFINITIONS

1.   For the purposes of this Agreement, unless the context otherwise requires:

    (a)   (i)   the term ....means the ....and,

        (ii)   the term "Zimbabwe" means the Republic of Zimbabwe;

    (b)   the terms "a Contracting State" and "the other Contracting State" mean .... or Zimbabwe, as the context requires;

    (c)   the term "company" means any body corporate or any entity which is treated as a company or body corporate for tax purposes;

    (d)   the term "competent authority" means:

        (i)   in ...., or his authorised representative; and

        (ii)   in Zimbabwe, the Commissioner of Taxes or his authorised representative;

    (e)   the terms "enterprise of a Contracting State" and "enterprise of the other Contracting State" mean respectively an enterprise carried on by a resident of a Contracting State and an enterprise carried on by a resident of the other Contracting State;

    (f)   the term "international traffic" means any transport by ship, aircraft or road or rail transport vehicle operated by an enterprise of a Contracting State except when the ship, aircraft or road or rail transport vehicle is operated solely between places in the other Contracting State;

    (g)   the term "national" means:

        (i)   any individual possessing the nationality of a Contracting State;

        (ii)   any legal person or association deriving its status as such from the laws in force in a Contracting State; and

    (h)   the term "person" includes an individual, an estate, a trust, a company and any other body of persons which is treated as an entity for tax purposes.

2.   As regards the application of the Agreement by a Contracting State any term not defined therein shall, unless the context otherwise requires, have the meaning which it has under the law of that State concerning the taxes to which the Agreement applies.

Article 4
RESIDENT

1.   For the purposes of this Agreement, the term "resident of a Contracting State" means any person who, under the laws of that State, is liable to tax therein by reason of his domicile, residence, place of management or any other criterion of a similar nature.

2.   Where by reason of the provisions of paragraph 1 of this Article an individual is a resident of both Contracting States, then his status shall be determined as follows:

   (a)   he shall be deemed to be a resident of the State in which he has a permanent home available to him; if he has a permanent home available to him in both States, he shall be deemed to be a resident of the State with which his personal and economic relations are closer (centre of vital interests);

   (b)   if the State in which he has his centre of vital interests cannot be determined, or if he does not have a permanent home available to him in either State, he shall be deemed to be a resident of the State in which he has an habitual abode;

   (c)   if he has an habitual abode in both States or in neither of them, he shall be deemed to be a resident of the State of which he is a national;

   (d)   if he is a national of both States or of neither of them, the competent authorities of the Contracting States shall settle the question by mutual agreement.

3.   Where, by reason of the provisions of paragraph 1 of this Article, a person other than an individual is a resident of both Contracting States, then it shall be deemed to be a resident only of the state in which its place of effective management is situated.

Article 5
PERMANENT ESTABLISHMENT

1.   For the purposes of this Agreement, the term "permanent establishment" means a fixed place of business through which the business of an enterprise is wholly or partly carried on.

2.   The term "permanent establishment" shall include especially:

   (a)   a place of management,

   (b)   a branch,

   (c)   an office,

   (d)   a factory,

   (e)   a workshop, and

   (f)   a mine, an oil or gas well, a quarry or any other

   (g)   place of extraction of natural resources.

3.   The term "permanent establishment" likewise encompasses:

(a)   a building site, a construction, assembly or installation project or supervisory activities in connection therewith; and

(b)   the furnishing of services, including consultancy services, by an enterprise through employees or other personnel engaged by the enterprise for such purposes, but only where activities of that nature continue (for the same or a connected project) within a Contracting State for a period or periods aggregating more than 183 days within any twelve-month period commencing or ending in the year of assessment concerned.

4.   Notwithstanding the preceding provisions of this Article, the term "permanent establishment" shall be deemed not to include:

(a)   the use of facilities solely for the purpose of storage, display or delivery of goods or merchandise belonging to the enterprise;

(b)   the maintenance of a stock of goods or merchandise belonging to the enterprise solely for the purpose of storage, display or delivery;

(c)   the maintenance of a stock of goods or merchandise belonging to the enterprise solely for the purpose of processing by another enterprise;

(d)   the maintenance of a fixed place of business solely for the purpose of purchasing goods or merchandise, or of collecting information, for the enterprise;

(e)   the maintenance of a fixed place of business solely for the purpose of carrying on, for the enterprise, any other activity of a preparatory or auxiliary nature;

(f)   the maintenance of a fixed place of business solely for any combination of activities mentioned in subparagraphs (a) to (e) of this paragraph, provided that the overall activity of the fixed place of business resulting from this combination is of a preparatory or auxiliary character.

5.   Notwithstanding the provisions of paragraphs 1 and 2 of this Article where a person - other than an agent of an independent status to whom paragraph 6 of this Article applies - is acting on behalf of an enterprise and has, and habitually exercises, in a Contracting State an authority to conclude contracts in the name of the enterprise, that enterprise shall be deemed to have a permanent establishment in that State in respect of any activities which that person undertakes for the enterprise, unless the activities of such person are limited to those mentioned in paragraph 4 of this Article which, if exercised through a fixed place of business, would not make this fixed place of business a permanent establishment under the provisions of that paragraph.

6.   An enterprise shall not be deemed to have a permanent establishment in a Contracting State merely because it carries on business in that State through a broker, general commission agent or any other agent of an independent status, provided that such persons are acting in the ordinary course of their business.

7.   The fact that a company which is a resident of a Contracting State controls or is controlled by a company which is a resident of the other Contracting State, or which carries on business in that

other State (whether through a permanent establishment or otherwise), shall not of itself constitute either company a permanent establishment of the other.

Article 6
INCOME FROM IMMOVABLE PROPERTY

1. Income derived by a resident of a Contracting State from immovable property (including income from agriculture or forestry) situated in the other Contracting State may be taxed in that other State.

2. The term "immovable property" shall have the meaning which it has under the law of the Contracting State in which the property in question is situated. The term shall in any case include property accessory to immovable property, livestock and equipment used in agriculture and forestry, rights to which the provisions of general law respecting landed property apply, usufruct of immovable property and rights to variable or fixed payments as consideration for the working of, or the right to work, mineral deposits, sources and other natural resources. Ships and aircraft shall not be considered as immovable property.

3. The provisions of paragraph 1 of this Article shall also apply to income derived from the direct use, letting or use in any other form of immovable property and to income from the alienation of such property.

4. The provisions of paragraphs 1 and 3 of this Article shall also apply to the income from immovable property of an enterprise and to income from immovable property used for the performance of independent personal services.

Article 7
BUSINESS PROFITS

1. The profits of an enterprise of a Contracting State shall be taxable only in that State unless the enterprise carries on business in the other Contracting State through a permanent establishment situated therein. If the enterprise carries on business as aforesaid, the profits of the enterprise may be taxed in the other State but only so much of them as is attributable to that permanent establishment.

2. Subject to the provisions of paragraph 3 of this Article, where an enterprise of a Contracting State carries on business in the other Contracting State through a permanent establishment situated therein, there shall in each Contracting State be attributed to that permanent establishment the profits which it might be expected to make if it were a distinct and separate enterprise engaged in the same or similar activities under the same or similar conditions and dealing wholly independently with the enterprise of which it is a permanent establishment.

3. In determining the profits of a permanent establishment, there shall be allowed as deductions those deductible expenses which are incurred for the purposes of the business of the permanent establishment, including executive and general administrative expenses so incurred, whether in the State in which the permanent establishment is situated or elsewhere.

4.   Insofar as it has been customary in a Contracting State to determine the profits to be attributed to a permanent establishment on the basis of an apportionment of the total profits of the enterprise to its various parts, nothing in paragraph 2 of this Article shall preclude that Contracting State from determining the profits to be taxed by such an apportionment as may be customary. The method of apportionment adopted shall, however, be such that the result shall be in accordance with the principles contained in this Article.

5.   No profits shall be attributed to a permanent establishment by reason of the mere purchase by that permanent establishment of goods or merchandise for the enterprise.

6.   For the purposes of the preceding paragraphs of this Article, the profits to be attributed to the permanent establishment shall be determined by the same method year by year unless there is good and sufficient reason to the contrary.

7.   Where profits include items of income which are dealt with separately in other Articles of this Agreement, then the provisions of those Articles shall not be affected by the provisions of this Article.

Article 8
INTERNATIONAL TRAFFIC

1.   Profits of an enterprise of a Contracting State from the operation or rental of ships, aircraft, rail or road transport vehicles in international traffic and the rental of containers and related equipment which is incidental to the operation of ships, aircraft, rail or road transport vehicles in international traffic shall be taxable only in the Contracting State in which the place of effective management of the enterprise is situated.

2.   If the place of effective management of a shipping enterprise is abroad a ship or boat, then it shall be deemed to be situated in the Contracting State in which the home harbour of the ship or boat is situated, or, if there is no such home harbour, in the Contracting State of which the operator of the ship or boat is resident.

3.   The provisions of paragraph 1 of this Article shall also apply to profits from the participation in a pool, a joint business or an international operating agency.

Article 9
ASSOCIATED ENTERPRISES

1.   Where

   (a)   an enterprise of a Contracting State participates directly or indirectly in the management, control or capital of an enterprise of the other Contracting State and

   (b)   the same persons participate directly or indirectly in the management, control or capital of an enterprise of a Contracting State and an enterprise of the other Contracting State and in either case conditions are made or imposed between the two enterprises in their commercial or financial relations which differ from those which would be made between independent enterprises, then any profits which would, but for those conditions, have accrued to one of the enterprises, but, by reason of those conditions, have not so accrued, may be included in the profits of that enterprise and taxed accordingly.

2.   Where a Contracting State includes in the profits of an enterprise of that State - and taxes accordingly - profits on which an enterprise of the other Contracting State has been charged to tax in that other State and the profits so included are profits which would have accrued to the enterprise of the first-mentioned State if the conditions made between the two enterprises had been those which would have been made between independent enterprises, then that other State may make an appropriate adjustment to the amount of tax charged therein on those profits. In determining such adjustment, due regard shall be had to the other provisions of this Agreement and the competent authorities of the Contracting States shall if necessary consult each other.

Article 10
DIVIDENDS

1.   Dividends paid by a company which is a resident of a Contracting State to a resident of the other Contracting State may be taxed in that other State.

2.   However, such dividends may also be taxed in the Contracting State of which the company paying the dividends is a resident and according to the laws of that State, but if the beneficial owner of the dividends is a resident of the other Contracting State, the tax so charged shall not exceed:

(a)   .... per cent of the gross amount of the dividends if the beneficial owner is a company which controls directly or indirectly at least 25 per cent of the capital of the company paying the dividends;

(b)   .... per cent of the gross amount of the dividends in all other cases.

The provisions of this paragraph shall not affect the taxation of the company in respect of the profits out of which the dividends are paid.

3.   The term "dividends" as used in this Article means income from shares or other rights participating in profits (not being debt-claims), as well as income from other corporate rights which is subjected to the same taxation treatment as income from shares by the laws of the Contracting State of which the company making the distribution is a resident.

4.   The provisions of paragraphs 1 and 2 of this Article shall not apply if the beneficial owner of the dividends, being a resident of a Contracting State, carries on business in the other Contracting State of which the company paying the dividends is a resident, through a permanent establishment situated therein, or performs in that other State independent personal services from a fixed base situated therein, and the holding in respect of which the dividends are paid is effectively connected with such permanent establishment or fixed base. In such case the provisions of Article 7 or Article 15, as the case may be, shall apply.

5.   Where a company which is a resident of a Contracting State derives profits or income from the other Contracting State, that other State may not impose any tax on the dividends paid by the company, except insofar as such dividends are paid to a resident of that other State or insofar as the holding in respect of which the dividends are paid is effectively connected with a permanent establishment or a fixed base situated in that other State, nor subject the company's undistributed

profits to a tax on undistributed profits, even if the dividends paid or the company undistributed profits consist wholly or partly of profits or income arising in such other State.

Article 11
INTEREST

1.   Interest arising in a Contracting State and paid to a resident of the other Contracting State may be taxed in that other State.

2.   However, such interest may also be taxed in the Contracting State in which it arises and according to the laws of that State, but if the beneficial owner of the interest is a resident of the other Contracting State, the tax so charged shall not exceed per cent of the gross amount of interest.

3.   The term "interest" as used in this Article means income from debt-claims of every kind, whether or not secured by mortgage and whether or not carrying a right to participate in the debtor's profits, and in particular, income from government securities and income from bonds or debentures, including premiums and prizes attaching to such securities, bonds or debentures. Penalty charges for late payment shall not be regarded as interest for the purposes of this Article.

4.   The provisions of paragraphs 1 and 2 of this Article shall not apply if the beneficial owner of the interest, being a resident of a Contracting State, carries on business in the other Contracting State in which the interest arises, through a permanent establishment situated therein, or performs in that other State independent personal services from a fixed base situated therein, and the debt-claim in respect of which the interest is paid is effectively connected with such permanent establishment or fixed base. In such case, the provisions of Article 7 or Article 15, as the case may be, shall apply.

5.   Interest shall be deemed to arise in a Contracting State when the payer is a resident of that State. Where, however the person paying the interest, whether he is a resident of a Contracting State or not, has in a Contracting State a permanent establishment or a fixed base in connection with which the indebtedness on which the interest is paid was incurred, and such interest is borne by such permanent establishment or fixed base, then such interest shall be deemed to arise in the State in which the permanent establishment or fixed base is situated.

6.   Where, by reason of a special relationship between the payer and the beneficial owner or between both of them and some other person, the amount of the interest, having regard to the debt-claim for which it is paid, exceeds the amount which would have been agreed upon by the payer and the beneficial owner in the absence of such relationship, the provisions of this Article shall apply only to the last-mentioned amount. In such case, the excess part of the payments shall remain taxable according to the laws of each Contracting State, due regard being had to the other provisions of this Agreement.

Article 12
ROYALTIES

1.   Royalties arising in a Contracting State and paid to a resident of the other Contracting State may be taxed in that other State.

2.   However, such royalties may also be taxed in the Contracting State in which they arise and according to the laws of that State, but if the beneficial owner of the royalties is a resident of the

other Contracting State, the tax so charged shall not exceed ..... per cent of the gross amount of the royalties.

3.   The term "royalties" as used in this Article means payments of any kind received as a consideration for the use of, or the right to use, any copyright of literary, artistic or scientific work (including cinematograph films and films, and other means of production used for radio or television broadcasting), any patent, trade mark, design or model, plan, secret formula or process, or for information concerning industrial, commercial or scientific experience.

4.   The provisions of paragraphs 1 and 2 of this Article shall not apply if the beneficial owner of the royalties, being a resident of a Contracting State, carries on business in the other Contracting State in which the royalties arise, through a permanent establishment situated therein, or performs in that other State independent personal services from a fixed base situated therein, and the right or property in respect of which the royalties are paid is effectively connected with such permanent establishment or fixed base. In such case, the provisions of Article 7 or Article 15, as the case may be, shall apply.

5.   Royalties shall be deemed to arise in a Contracting State when the payer is a resident of that State. Where, however, the person paying the royalties, whether he is a resident of a Contracting State or not, has in a Contracting State a permanent establishment or a fixed base in connection with which the obligation to pay the royalties was incurred, and such royalties are borne by such permanent establishment or fixed base, then such royalties shall be deemed to arise in the State in which the permanent establishment or fixed base is situated.

6.   Where, by reason of a special relationship between the payer and the beneficial owner or between both of them and some other person, the amount of the royalties, having regard to the use, right or information for which they are paid, exceeds the amount which would have been agreed upon by the payer and the beneficial owner in the absence of such relationship, the provisions of this Article shall apply only to the last-mentioned amount. In such case, the excess part of the payments shall remain taxable according to the laws of each Contracting State, due regard being had to the other provisions of this Agreement.

Article 13
TECHNICAL FEES

1.   Technical fees arising in a Contracting State and paid to a resident of the other Contracting State may be taxed in that other State.

2.   However, such technical fees may also be taxed in the Contracting State in which they arise and according to the laws of that State, but if the beneficial owner of the technical fees is a resident of the other Contracting State, the tax so charged shall not exceed .... per cent of the gross amount of the technical fees.

3.   The term "technical fees" as used in this Article means payments of any kind to any person, other than to an employee of the person making the payments, in consideration for any service of an administrative, technical, managerial or consultancy nature, unless the payment is the reimbursement of actual expenses incurred by that person with respect to the service.

4.   The provisions of paragraphs 1 and 2 of this Article shall not apply if the recipient of the technical fees, being a resident of a Contracting State, carries on business in the other Contracting

State in which the technical fees arise, through a permanent establishment situated therein, or performs in that other State independent personal services from a fixed base situated therein, and the technical fees are effectively connected with such permanent establishment or fixed base. In such case, the provisions of Article 7 or Article 15, as the case may be, shall apply.

5.   Technical fees shall be deemed to arise in a Contracting State when the payer is a resident of that State. Where, however, the person paying the technical fees, whether he is a resident of a Contracting State or not, has in a Contracting State a permanent establishment or a fixed base in connection with which the obligation to pay the technical fees was incurred, and such technical fees are borne by the permanent establishment or fixed base, then such technical fees shall be deemed to arise in the State in which the permanent establishment or fixed base is situated.

6.   Where, by reason of a special relationship between the payer and the beneficial owner or between both of them and some other person, the amount of the technical fees paid exceeds the amount which would have been agreed upon by the payer and the beneficial owner in the absence of such relationship, the provisions of this Article shall apply only to the last-mentioned amount. In such case, the excess part of the payments shall remain taxable according to the laws of each Contracting State, due regard being had to the other provisions of this Agreement.

Article 14
CAPITAL GAINS

1.   Gains derived by a resident of a Contracting State from the alienation of immovable property referred to in Article 6 and situated in the other Contracting State may be taxed in that other State.

2.   Gains from the alienation of movable property forming part of the business property of a permanent establishment which an enterprise of a Contracting State has in the other Contracting State or of movable property pertaining to a fixed base available to a resident of a Contracting State in the other Contracting State for the purpose of performing independent personal services, including such gains from the alienation of such a permanent establishment (alone or with the whole enterprise) or of such a fixed base, may be taxed in that other State.

3.   Gains from the alienation of ships, aircraft or road or rail transport vehicles operated in international traffic by an enterprise of a Contracting State and movable property pertaining to the operation of such ships, aircraft or road or rail transport vehicles shall be taxable only in that State.

4.   Gains derived by a resident of a Contracting State from the alienation of shares in a company which is a resident of the other Contracting State may be taxed in that other State.

5.   Gains from the alienation of any property other than that referred to in the preceding paragraphs of this Article, shall be taxable only in the Contracting State of which the alienator is a resident.

Article 15
INDEPENDENT PERSONAL SERVICES

1.   Income derived by an individual who is a resident of a Contracting State in respect of professional services or other activities of an independent character shall be taxable only in that State unless he has or had a fixed base regularly available to him in the other Contracting State for the purpose of performing his activities. If he has or had such a fixed base, the income may be taxed in the other State but only so much of it as is attributable to that fixed base.

2.   The term "professional services" includes especially independent scientific, literary, artistic, educational or teaching activities as well as the independent activities of physicians, lawyers, engineers, architects, dentists and accountants.

Article 16
DEPENDENT PERSONAL SERVICES

1.   Subject to the provisions of Articles 17, 19 and 20, salaries, wages and other similar remuneration derived by a resident of a Contracting State in respect of an employment shall be taxable only in that State unless the employment is exercised in the other Contracting State. If the employment is so exercised, such remuneration as is derived therefrom may be taxed in that other State.

2.   Notwithstanding the provisions of paragraph 1 of this Article, remuneration derived by a resident of a Contracting State in respect of an employment exercised in the other Contracting State shall be taxable only in the first-mentioned State if:

   (a)   the recipient is present in the other State for a period or periods not exceeding in the aggregate 183 days in the calendar year concerned, and

   (b)   the remuneration is paid by, or on behalf of, an employer who is not a resident of the other State; and

   (c)   the remuneration is not borne by a permanent establishment or fixed base which the employer has in the other State.

3.   Notwithstanding the preceding provisions of this Article, remuneration derived in respect of an employment exercised aboard a ship, aircraft or road or rail transport vehicle operated in international traffic by an enterprise of a Contracting State, shall be taxable only in that State.

Article 17
DIRECTORS' FEES

Directors' fees and other similar payments derived by a resident of a Contracting State in his capacity as a member of the board of directors of a company which is a resident of the other Contracting State may be taxed in that other State.

Article 18
ENTERTAINERS AND SPORTSPERSONS

1.   Notwithstanding the provisions of Articles 7, 15 and 16, income derived by a resident of a Contracting State as an entertainer such as a theatre, motion picture, radio or television artiste, or a musician, or as a sportsperson, from his personal activities as such exercised in the other Contracting State, may be taxed in that other State.

2.   Where income in respect of personal activities exercised by an entertainer or a sportsperson in his capacity as such accrues not to the entertainer or sportsperson himself but to another person, that income may, notwithstanding the provisions of Articles 7, 15 and 16, be taxed in the Contracting State in which the activities of the entertainer or sportsperson are exercised.

Article 19
PENSIONS AND ANNUITIES

1.   Subject to the provisions of paragraph 2 of Article 20, pensions and other similar remuneration for past employment, and annuities, arising in a Contracting State and paid to a resident of the other Contracting State, may be taxed in the first-mentioned State.

2.   The term "annuity" means a stated sum payable periodically at stated times during life or during a specified or ascertainable period of time under an obligation to make the payments in return for adequate and full consideration in money or money's worth.

3.   Notwithstanding the provisions of paragraph 1 of this Article, pensions paid and other payments made under a public scheme which is part of the social security system of a Contracting State, a political subdivision or a local authority thereof shall be taxable only in that State.

Article 20
GOVERNMENT SERVICE

1.   (a)   Salaries, wages and similar remuneration, other than a pension, paid by a Contracting State or a political subdivision or a local authority thereof to. an individual in respect of services rendered to that State or subdivision or authority shall be taxable only in that State.

        (b)   However, such salaries, wages and other similar remuneration shall be taxable only in the other Contracting State if the services are rendered in that State and the individual is a resident of that State who:

                (i)   is a national of that State; or

                (ii)   did not become a resident of that State solely for the purpose of rendering the services.

2.   (a)   Any pension paid by, or out of funds created by, a Contracting State or a political subdivision or a local authority thereof to an individual in respect of services rendered to that State or subdivision or authority shall be taxable only in that State.

(b)   However, such pension shall be taxable in the other Contracting State if the individual is a resident of, and a national of, that State.

3.   The provisions of Articles 16, 17 and 19 shall apply to salaries, wages and similar remuneration, and to pensions, in respect of services rendered in connection with a business carried on by a Contracting State or a political subdivision or a local authority thereof.

Article 21
STUDENTS, APPRENTICES AND BUSINESS TRAINEES

A student, apprentice or business trainee who is present in a Contracting State solely for the purpose of his education or training and who is, or immediately before being so present was, a resident of the other Contracting State, shall be exempt from tax in the first-mentioned State on payments received from outside that first-mentioned State for the purposes of his maintenance, education or training.

Article 22
OTHER INCOME

Items of income arising in a Contracting State which are not dealt with in the foregoing Articles of this Agreement may be taxed in that State.

Article 23
ELIMINATION OF DOUBLE TAXATION

Double taxation shall be eliminated as follows:

1.   (a)   In................, Zimbabwean tax paid by residents of .... in respect of income taxable in Zimbabwe, in accordance with the provisions of this Agreement, shall be deducted from the taxes due according to .... fiscal law. Such deduction shall not, however, exceed an amount which bears to the total ....tax payable the same ratio as the income concerned bears to the total income.

       (b)   In Zimbabwe subject to the provisions of the law of Zimbabwe regarding the allowance as a credit against Zimbabwean tax of the tax payable in a territory outside Zimbabwe (which shall not affect the general principle hereof) .... tax payable, whether directly or by deduction, in respect of taxable income or chargeable gains from sources within................. shall be allowed as a credit against any Zimbabwean tax computed by reference to the same taxable income or chargeable gains by reference to which the .... tax is computed.

2.   For the purposes of paragraph 1 of this Article, the term "Zimbabwean tax payable" shall be deemed to include any amount which would have been payable as Zimbabwean tax but for an exemption or reduction of tax granted under Zimbabwean laws relating to incentives for the promotion of economic development in Zimbabwe which were in force on the date of signature of this Agreement or any other provisions which may subsequently be introduced in modification of or in addition to those laws so far as they are of a substantially similar character.

Article 24
NON-DISCRIMINATION

1.   Nationals of a Contracting State shall not be subjected in the other Contracting State to any taxation or any requirement connected therewith which is other or more burdensome than the taxation and connected requirements to which nationals of that other State in the same circumstances are or may be subjected. This provision shall notwithstanding the provisions of Article 1, also apply to persons who are not residents of one or both of the Contracting States.

2.   The taxation on a permanent establishment which an enterprise of a Contracting State has in the other Contracting State shall not be less favourably levied in that other State than the taxation levied on enterprises of that other State carrying on the same activities.

3.   Enterprises of a Contracting State, the capital of which is wholly or partly owned or controlled, directly or indirectly, by one or more residents of the other Contracting State, shall not be subjected in the first-mentioned State to any taxation or any requirement connected therewith which is other or more burdensome than the taxation and connected requirements to which other similar enterprises of that first-mentioned State are or may be subjected.

4.   Nothing in this Article shall be construed as obliging a Contracting State to grant to residents of the other Contracting State any personal allowances, reliefs and reductions for taxation purposes on account of civil status or family responsibilities which it grants to its own residents.

5.   The provisions of this Article shall apply to taxes which are the subject of this Agreement.

Article 25
MUTUAL AGREEMENT PROCEDURE

1.   Where a person considers that the actions of one or both of the Contracting States result or will result for him in taxation not in accordance with this Agreement, he may, irrespective of the remedies provided by the domestic law of those States, present his case to the competent authority of the Contracting State of which he is a resident or, if his case comes under paragraph 1 of Article 24, to that of the Contracting State of which he is a national. The case must be presented within three years from the first notification of the action resulting in taxation not in accordance with the provisions of the Agreement.

2.   The competent authority shall endeavour, if the objection appears to it to be justified and if it is not itself able to arrive at a satisfactory solution, to resolve the case by mutual agreement with the competent authority of the other Contracting State, with a view to the avoidance of taxation which is not in accordance with the Agreement.

3.   The competent authorities of the Contracting States shall endeavour to resolve by mutual agreement any difficulties or doubts arising as to the interpretation or application of the Agreement. They may also consult together for the elimination of double taxation in cases not provided for in the Agreement.

4.   The competent authorities of the Contracting States may communicate with each other directly for the purpose of reaching an agreement in the sense of the preceding paragraphs.

Article 26
EXCHANGE OF INFORMATION

1.   The competent authorities of the Contracting States shall exchange such information as is necessary for carrying out the provisions of this Agreement or of the domestic laws of the Contracting States concerning taxes covered by the Agreement insofar as the taxation thereunder is not contrary to the Agreement. The exchange of information is not restricted by Article 1. Any information received by a Contracting State shall be treated as secret in the same manner as information obtained under the domestic laws of that State and shall be disclosed only to persons or authorities [including courts and administrative bodies] concerned with the assessment or collection of, or the determination of appeals in relation to, the taxes covered by the Agreement. They may disclose the information in public court proceedings or in judicial decisions.

2.   In no case shall the provisions of paragraph 1 of this Article be construed so as to impose on a Contracting State the obligation:

(a)   to carry out administrative measures at variance with the laws or administrative practice of that or of the other Contracting State;

(b)   to supply information which is not obtainable under the laws or in the normal course of the administration of that or of the other Contracting State;

(c)   to supply information which would disclose any trade, business, industrial, commercial or professional secret or trade process, or information, the disclosure of which would be contrary to public policy.

Article 27
MEMBERS OF DIPLOMATIC MISSIONS AND CONSULAR POSTS

Nothing in this Agreement shall affect the fiscal privileges of members of diplomatic missions or consular posts under the general rules of international law or under the provisions of special agreements.

Article 28
ASSISTANCE IN RECOVERY

1.   The Contracting States shall, to the extent permitted by their respective domestic law, lend assistance to each other in order to recover the taxes referred to in Article 2 as well as interest and penalties with regard to such taxes, provided that reasonable steps to recover such taxes have been taken by the Contracting State requesting such assistance.

2.   Claims, which are the subject of requests for assistance, shall not have priority over taxes owing in the Contracting State rendering assistance and the provisions of paragraph 1 of Article 26 shall also apply to any information which, by virtue of this Article, is supplied to the competent authority of a Contracting State.

3.   It is understood that unless otherwise agreed by the competent authorities of both Contracting States,

(a)   ordinary costs incurred by a Contracting State in providing assistance shall be borne by that State,

(b)   extraordinary costs incurred by a Contracting State in providing assistance shall be borne by the other State and shall be payable regardless of the amount collected on its behalf by the first mentioned State.

As soon as a Contracting State anticipates that extraordinary costs may be incurred, it shall so advise the other Contracting State and indicate the estimated amount of such costs.

Article 29
ENTRY INTO FORCE

1.   Each of the Contracting States shall notify through diplomatic channels the other the completion of the procedures required by its law for the bringing into force of this Agreement. The Agreement shall enter into force on the date of the later of these notifications.

2.   The provisions of the Agreement shall apply:

(a)   with regard to taxes withheld at source, in respect of amounts paid or credited on or after the first day of the second month next following the date upon which the Agreement enters into force; and

(b)   with regard to other taxes, in respect of years of assessment beginning on or after the first day of January next following the date upon which the Agreement enters into force.

Article 30
TERMINATION

1.   This Agreement shall remain in force until termination by one of the Contracting States. Either Contracting State may terminate the Agreement, through the diplomatic channel, by giving notice of termination on or before June 30th in any calendar year beginning after the expiration of five years from the date of entry into force of the Agreement.

2.   In such event the Agreement shall cease to apply:

(a)   with regard to taxes withheld at source, in respect of amounts paid or credited after the end of the calendar year in which such notice is given; and

(b)   with regard to other taxes, in respect of years of assessment beginning after the end of the calendar year in which such notice is given.

IN WITNESS WHEREOF the undersigned, duly authorized to that effect by their respective Governments, have signed this Agreement.

DONE in duplicate at .... this............day of ....

FOR THE GOVERNMENT OF

THE REPUBLIC OF ZIMBABWE

FOR THE GOVERNMENT OF

THE REPUBLIC OF

*   *   *

SELECTED UNCTAD PUBLICATIONS ON TRANSNATIONAL CORPORATIONS AND FOREIGN DIRECT INVESTMENT

(For more information, please visit www.unctad.org/
en/pub on the web.)

A. Individual studies

World Investment Report 2001: Promoting Linkages. 386 p. Sales No. E.01.II.D.12 . $ 49.00 Selected materials available also from http://www.unctad.org/wir.

World Investment Report 2001: Promoting Linkages. An overview. 73 p. Free of charge.

Ten Years of World Investment Reports: The Challenges Ahead. Proceedings of an UNCTAD special event on future challenges in the area of FDI. UNCTAD/ITE/Misc.45. Free of charge. Available from http://www.unctad.org/wir.

World Investment Report 2000: Cross-border Mergers and Acquisitions and Development. 368 p. Sales No. E.99.II.D.20. $45. Selected materials available also from http://www.unctad.org/wir/contents/wir00content.en.htm.

World Investment Report 2000: Cross-border Mergers and Acquisitions and Development. An Overview. 75 p. Free-of-charge. Available also from http://www.unctad.org/wir/contents/ wir00content.en.htm.

World Investment Report 1999: Foreign Direct Investment and the Challenge of Development. 536 p. Sales No. E.99.II.D.3. $45. Selected materials available from http://www.unctad.org/wir/contents/ wir99content.en.htm.

World Investment Report 1999: Foreign Direct Investment and Challenge of Development. An Overview. 75 p. Free-of-charge. Available also from http://www.unctad.org/wir/contents/ wir99content.en.htm.

World Investment Report 1998: Trends and Determinants. 430 p. Sales No. E.98.II.D.5. $45. Selected materials available from http://www.unctad.org/ wir/contents/ wir98content.en.htm.

World Investment Report 1998: Trends and Determinants. An Overview. 67 p. Free-of-charge. Available also from http://www.unctad.org/ wir/contents/wir98content.en.htm.

World Investment Report 1997: Transnational Corporations, Market Structure and Competition Policy. 420 p. Sales No. E.97.II.D.10. $45. Selected materials available from http://www.unctad.org/wir/contents/ wir97content.en.htm.

World Investment Report 1997: Transnational Corporations, Market Structure and Competition Policy. An Overview. 70 p. Free-of-charge. Available also from http://www.unctad.org/wir/contents/ wir97content.en.htm.

World Investment Report 1996: Investment, Trade and International Policy Arrangements. 332 p. Sales No. E.96.II.A.14. $45. Selected materials available from http://www.unctad.org/ wir/contents/ wir96content.en.htm.

World Investment Report 1996: Investment, Trade and International Policy Arrangements. An Overview. 51 p. Free-of-charge. Available also from http://www.unctad.org/wir/contents/ wir96content.en.htm.

World Investment Report 1995: Transnational Corporations and Competitiveness. 491 p. Sales No. E.95.II.A.9. $45. Selected materials available from http://www.unctad.org/wir/ contents/wir95content.en.htm.

World Investment Report 1995: Transnational Corporations and Competitiveness. An Overview. 51 p. Free-of-charge. Available also from http://www.unctad.org/wir/ contents/wir95content.en.htm.

World Investment Report 1994: Transnational Corporations, Employment and the Workplace. 482 p. Sales No. E.94.II.A.14. $45. Selected materials available from http://www.unctad.org/wir/contents/wir94content.en.htm.

World Investment Report 1994: Transnational Corporations, Employment and the Workplace. An Executive Summary. 34 p. Free-of-charge. Available also from http://www.unctad.org/wir/contents/ wir94content.en.htm.

World Investment Report 1993: Transnational Corporations and Integrated International Production. 290 p. Sales No. E.93.II.A.14. $45. Selected materials available from http://www.unctad.org/wir/contents/ wir93content.en.htm.

World Investment Report 1993: Transnational Corporations and Integrated International Production. An Executive Summary. 31 p. ST/CTC/159. Free-of-charge. Available also from http://www.unctad.org/ wir/ contents/wir93content.en.htm.

World Investment Report 1992: Transnational Corporations as Engines of Growth. 356 p. Sales No. E.92.II.A.19. $45. Selected materials available from http://www.unctad.org/wir/ contents/wir92content.en.htm.

World Investment Report 1992: Transnational Corporations as Engines of Growth: An Executive Summary. 30 p. Sales No. E.92.II.A.24. Free-of-charge. Available also from http://www.unctad.org/wir/contents/ wir92content.en.htm.

World Investment Report 1991: The Triad in Foreign Direct Investment. 108 p. Sales No.E.91.II.A.12. $25. Full version is available also from http://www.unctad.org/wir/ contents/wir91content.en.htm.

World Investment Directory. Vol. VII (Parts I and II): Asia and the Pacific. 646 p. Sales No. E.00.II.D.11.

World Investment Directory. Vol. VI: West Asia. 192 p. Sales No. E.97.II.A.2. $35.

World Investment Directory. Vol. V: Africa. 508 p. Sales No. E.97.II.A.1. $75.

World Investment Directory. Vol. IV: Latin America and the Caribbean. 478 p. Sales No. E.94.II.A.10. $65.

World Investment Directory 1992. Vol. III: Developed Countries. 532 p. Sales No. E.93.II.A.9. $75.

World Investment Directory 1992. Vol. II: Central and Eastern Europe. 432 p. Sales No. E.93.II.A.1. $65. (Joint publication with the United Nations Economic Commission for Europe.)

World Investment Directory 1992. Vol. I: Asia and the Pacific. 356 p. Sales No. E.92.II.A.11. $65.

Investment Policy Review of Ecuador. 117 p. UNCTAD/ITE/IPC/Misc.2. Forthcoming. Summary available from http://www.unctad.org/en/docs/ poiteipcm2sum.en.pdf.

Investment and Innovation Policy Review of Ethiopia. 115 p. UNCTAD/ITE/IPC/Misc.4. Forthcoming. Advance copy available from http://www.unctad.org/en/docs/ poiteipcm4.en.pdf.

Investment Policy Review of Mauritius. 84 p. Sales No. E.01.II.D.11. $22. Advance copy available from http://www.unctad.org/en/docs/poiteipcm1.en.pdf.

Investment Policy Review of Peru. 108 p. Sales No. E.00.II.D. 7. $22. Summary available from http://www.unctad.org/en/docs/ poiteiipm19sum.en.pdf.

Investment Policy Review of Uganda. 75 p. Sales No. E.99.II.D.24. $15. Summary available from http://www.unctad.org/en/docs/ poiteiipm17sum.en.pdf.

Investment Policy Review of Egypt. 113 p. Sales No. E.99.II.D.20. $19. Summary available from http://www.unctad.org/en/docs/ poiteiipm11sum.en.pdf.

Investment Policy Review of Uzbekistan. 64 p. UNCTAD/ITE/IIP/Misc. 13. Free-of-charge. Full version available also from http://www.unctad.org/ en/docs/poiteiipm13.en.pdf.

(Presentation of the Investment Policy Reviews is available from http://www.unctad.org/en/pub/investpolicy.en.htm.)

FDI in Least Developed Countries at a Glance. 150 p. UNCTAD/ITE/IIA/3. Free of charge. Full version available also from http://www.unctad.org/en/pub/poiteiiad3.en.htm.

Foreign Direct Investment in Africa: Performance and Potential. 89 p. UNCTAD/ITE/IIT/Misc. 15. Free of charge. Full version available also from http://www.unctad.org/ en/docs/poiteiitm15.pdf.

International Investment Instruments: A Compendium, vol. IV. 319 p. Sales No. E.00.II.D.13. $55, vol. V. 505 p. Sales No. E.00.II.D.14. $55.

International Investment Instruments: A Compendium*.* Vol. I. 371 p. Sales No. E.96.II.A.9; Vol. II. 577 p. Sales No. E.96.II.A.10; Vol. III. 389 p. Sales No. E.96.II.A.11; the 3-volume set, Sales No. E.96.II.A.12. $125.

Bilateral Investment Treaties 1959-1999 143 p. UNCTAD/ITE/IIA/2, Free-of-charge. Available only in electronic version from http://www.unctad.org/ en/pub/poiteiiad2.en.htm.

Bilateral Investment Treaties in the Mid-1990s*,* 314 p. Sales No. E.98.II.D.8. $46.

TNC-SME Linkages for Development: Issues-Experiences-Best Practices*. Proceedings of the Special Round Table on TNCs, SMEs and Development, UNCTAD X, 15 February 2000, Bangkok, Thailand.* 113 p. UNCTAD/ITE/TEB1. Free-of-charge.

Handbook on Foreign Direct Investment by Small and Medium-sized Enterprises: Lessons from Asia*.* 200 p. Sales No. E.98.II.D.4. $48.

Handbook on Foreign Direct Investment by Small and Medium-sized Enterprises: Lessons from Asia. Executive Summary and Report of the Kunming Conference*.* 74 p. Free-of-charge.

Small and Medium-sized Transnational Corporations. Executive Summary and Report of the Osaka Conference*.* 60 p. Free-of-charge.

Small and Medium-sized Transnational Corporations: Role, Impact and Policy Implications*.* 242 p. Sales No. E.93.II.A.15. $35.

Measures of the Transnationalization of Economic Activity*.* 93 p. Sales No. E.01.II.D.2. $20.

The Competitiveness Challenge: Transnational Corporations and Industrial Restructuring in Developing Countries*.* 283 p. Sales No. E.00.II.D.35. $42.

Integrating International and Financial Performance at the Enterprise Level*.* 116 p. Sales No. E.00.II.D.28. $18.

FDI Determinants and TNCs Strategies: The Case of Brazil*.* 195 p. Sales No. E.00.II.D.2. $35. Summary available from http://www.unctad.org/en/pub/psiteiitd14.en.htm.

The Social Responsibility of Transnational Corporations*.* 75 p. UNCTAD/ITE/IIT/Misc. 21. Free of charge. Out of stock. Full version available only from http://www.unctad.org/en/docs/poiteiitm21.en.pdf.

Conclusions on Accounting and Reporting by Transnational Corporations*.* 47 p. Sales No. E.94.II.A.9. $25.

Accounting, Valuation and Privatization*.* 190 p. Sales No. E.94.II.A.3. $25.

Environmental Management in Transnational Corporations: Report on the Benchmark Corporate Environment Survey*.* 278 p. Sales No. E.94.II.A.2. $29.95.

Management Consulting: A Survey of the Industry and Its Largest Firms. 100 p. Sales No. E.93.II.A.17. $25.

Transnational Corporations: A Selective Bibliography, 1991-1992. 736 p. Sales No. E.93.II.A.16. $75.

Foreign Investment and Trade Linkages in Developing Countries. 108 p. Sales No. E.93.II.A.12. $18.

Transnational Corporations from Developing Countries: Impact on Their Home Countries. 116 p. Sales No. E.93.II.A.8. $15.

Debt-Equity Swaps and Development. 150 p. Sales No. E.93.II.A.7. $35.

From the Common Market to EC 92: Regional Economic Integration in the European Community and Transnational Corporations. 134 p. Sales No. E.93.II.A.2. $25.

The East-West Business Directory 1991/1992. 570 p. Sales No. E.92.II.A.20. $65.

Climate Change and Transnational Corporations: Analysis and Trends. 110 p. Sales No. E.92.II.A.7. $16.50.

Foreign Direct Investment and Transfer of Technology in India. 150 p. Sales No. E.92.II.A.3. $20.

The Determinants of Foreign Direct Investment: A Survey of the Evidence. 84 p. Sales No. E.92.II.A.2. $12.50.

Transnational Corporations and Industrial Hazards Disclosure. 98 p. Sales No. E.91.II.A.18. $17.50.

Transnational Business Information: A Manual of Needs and Sources. 216 p. Sales No. E.91.II.A.13. $45.

The Financial Crisis in Asia and Foreign Direct Investment: An Assessment. 101 p. Sales No. GV.E.98.0.29. $20.

Sharing Asia's Dynamism: Asian Direct Investment in the European Union. 192 p. Sales No. E.97.II.D.1. $26.

Investing in Asia's Dynamism: European Union Direct Investment in Asia. 124 p. ISBN 92-827-7675-1. ECU 14. (Joint publication with the European Commission.)

World Economic Situation and Prospects 2001. 51 p. Sales No. E.01.II.C.2. $15. (Joint publication with the United Nations Department of Economic and Social Affairs.)

International Investment towards the Year 2002. 166 p. Sales No. GV.E.98.0.15. $29. (Joint publication with Invest in France Mission and Arthur Andersen, in collaboration with DATAR.)

International Investment towards the Year 2001. 81 p. Sales No. GV.E.97.0.5. $35. (Joint publication with Invest in France Mission and Arthur Andersen, in collaboration with DATAR.)

Liberalizing International Transactions in Services: A Handbook. 182 p. Sales No. E.94.II.A.11. $45. (Joint publication with the World Bank.)

The Impact of Trade-Related Investment Measures on Trade and Development: Theory, Evidence and Policy Implications. 108 p. Sales No. E.91.II.A.19. $17.50. (Joint publication with the United Nations Centre on Transnational Corporations.)

Transnational Corporations and World Development. 656 p. ISBN 0-415-08560-8 (hardback), 0-415-08561-6 (paperback). £65 (hardback), £20.00 (paperback). (Published by International Thomson Business Press on behalf of UNCTAD.)

Companies without Borders: Transnational Corporations in the 1990s. 224 p. ISBN 0-415-12526-X. £47.50. (Published by International Thomson Business Press on behalf of UNCTAD.)

The New Globalism and Developing Countries. 336 p. ISBN 92-808-0944-X. $25. (Published by United Nations University Press.)

B. IIA Issues Paper Series
(Executive summaries are available from http://www.unctad.org/iia.)

Illicit Payments. 93 p. Sales No. E.01.II.D

Home Country Measures. 93 p. Sales No. E.01.II.D

Host Country Operational Measures. 109 p. Sales No E.01.II.D.

Social Responsibility. 91 p. Sales No. E.01.II.D.4. $15.

Environment. 105 p. Sales No. E.01.II.D.3. $15.

Transfer of Funds. 65 p. Sales No. E.00.II.D.38. $10.

Employment. 69 p. Sales No. E.00.II.D.15. $10.

Taxation. 111 p. Sales No. E.00.II.D.5. $15.

International Investment Agreements: Flexibility for Development. 176 p. Sales No. E.00.II.D.6. $15.

Taking of Property. 70 p. Sales No. E.00.II.D.4. $12.

Trends in International Investment Agreements: An Overview. 121 p. Sales No. E.99.II.D.23. $ 12.

Lessons from the MAI. 43 p. Sales No. E.99.II.D.26. $ 10.

National Treatment. 75 p. Sales No. E.99.II.D.16. $12.

Fair and Equitable Treatment. 76 p. Sales No. E.99.II.D.15. $12.

Investment-Related Trade Measures. 52 p. Sales No. E.99.II.D.12. $12.

Most-Favoured-Nation Treatment 54 p. Sales No. E.99.II.D.11. $12.

Admission and Establishment. 49 p. Sales No. E.99.II.D.10. $12.

Scope and Definition. 80 p. Sales No. E.99.II.D.9. $12.

Transfer Pricing. 58 p. Sales No. E.99.II.D.8. $12.

Foreign Direct Investment and Development. 70 p. Sales No. E.98.II.D.15. $12.

C.   Serial publications

Current Studies, Series A

No. 30.*Incentives and Foreign Direct Investment*. 98 p. Sales No. E.96.II.A.6. $30. [Out of print.]

No. 29.*Foreign Direct Investment, Trade, Aid and Migration*. 100 p. Sales No. E.96.II.A.8. $25. (Joint publication with the International Organization for Migration.)

No. 28.*Foreign Direct Investment in Africa*. 119 p. Sales No. E.95.II.A.6. $20.

No. 27.*Tradability of Banking Services: Impact and Implications*. 195 p. Sales No. E.94.II.A.12. $50.

No. 26.*Explaining and Forecasting Regional Flows of Foreign Direct Investment*. 58 p. Sales No. E.94.II.A.5. $25.

No. 25.*International Tradability in Insurance Services*. 54 p. Sales No. E.93.II.A.11. $20.

No. 24.*Intellectual Property Rights and Foreign Direct Investment*. 108 p. Sales No. E.93.II.A.10. $20.

No. 23.*The Transnationalization of Service Industries: An Empirical Analysis of the Determinants of Foreign Direct Investment by Transnational Service Corporations*. 62 p. Sales No. E.93.II.A.3. $15.

No. 22.*Transnational Banks and the External Indebtedness of Developing Countries: Impact of Regulatory Changes*. 48 p. Sales No. E.92.II.A.10. $12.

No. 20.*Foreign Direct Investment, Debt and Home Country Policies*. 50 p. Sales No. E.90.II.A.16. $12.

No. 19.*New Issues in the Uruguay Round of Multilateral Trade Negotiations*. 52 p. Sales No. E.90.II.A.15. $12.50.

No. 18.*Foreign Direct Investment and Industrial Restructuring in Mexico*. 114 p. Sales No. E.92.II.A.9. $12.

No. 17.*Government Policies and Foreign Direct Investment*. 68 p. Sales No. E.91.II.A.20. $12.50.

ASIT Advisory Studies (formerly Current Studies, Series B; the full list is available from http://www.unctad.org/asit/ASIT%20Studies.htm.)

No. 16. *Tax Incentives and Foreign Direct Investment: A Global Survey.* 180 p. Sales No. E.01.II.D.5. $23. Summary available from http://www.unctad.org/asit/resumé.htm.

No. 15. *Investment Regimes in the Arab World: Issues and Policies*. 232 p. Sales No. E/F.00.II.D.32. $39.

No. 14. *Handbook on Outward Investment Promotion Agencies and Institutions*. 50 p. Sales No. E.99.II.D.22. $ 15.

No. 13. *Survey of Best Practices in Investment Promotion.* 71 p., Sales No. E.97.II.D.11. $ 35.

No.12. *Comparative Analysis of Petroleum Exploration Contracts.* 80 p. Sales No. E. 96.II.A.7. $35.

No.11. *Administration of Fiscal Regimes for Petroleum Exploration and Development.* 45 p. Sales No. E. 95.II.A.8.

No.10. *Formulation and Implementation of Foreign Investment Policies: Selected Key Issues.* 84 p. Sales No. E. 92.II.A.21. $12.

No.9. *Environmental Accounting: Current Issues, Abstracts and Bibliography.* 86 p. Sales No. E. 92.II.A.23.

UNCTAD-International Chamber of Commerce Series of Investment Guides (Summary of the Series is available from http://www.unctad.org/en/pub/investguide.en.htm.)

An Investment Guide to Mozambique: Opportunities and Conditions. Forthcoming.

An Investment Guide to Uganda: Opportunities and Conditions. 76 p. UNCTAD/ITE/IIT/Misc. 30. Free of charge. Full version available also from http://www.unctad.org/en/docs/poiteiitm30.en.pdf. (Joint publication with the International Chamber of Commerce.)

An Investment Guide to Bangladesh: Opportunities and Conditions. 66 p. UNCTAD/ITE/IIT/Misc.29. Free-of-charge. Full version available also from http://www.unctad.org/en/docs/poiteiitm29.en.pdf. (Joint publication with the International Chamber of Commerce.)

Guide d'investissement au Mali. 108 p. UNCTAD/ITE/IIT/Misc.24. Free-of-charge. Full version available also from http://www.unctad.org/fr/docs/ poiteiitm24.fr.pdf. (Joint publication with the International Chamber of Commerce, in association with PricewaterhouseCoopers.)

An Investment Guide to Ethiopia: Opportunities and Conditions. 69 p. UNCTAD/ITE/IIT/Misc.19. Free-of-charge. Full version available also from http://www.unctad.org/en/docs/poiteiitm19.en.pdf. (Joint publication with the International Chamber of Commerce, in association with PricewaterhouseCoopers.)

D. Journals

Transnational Corporations (formerly *The CTC Reporter*).

Published three times a year. Annual subscription price: $45; individual issues $20.

United Nations publications may be obtained from bookstores and distributors throughout the world. Please consult your bookstore or write to:

United Nations Publications

Sales Section
United Nations Office at Geneva
Palais des Nations
CH-1211 Geneva 10
Switzerland
Tel: (41-22) 917-1234
Fax: (41-22) 917-0123
E-mail: unpubli@unorg.ch

OR

Sales Section
Room DC2-0853
United Nations Secretariat
New York, NY 10017
U.S.A.
Tel: (1-212) 963-8302 or (800) 253-9646
Fax: (1-212) 963-3489
E-mail: publications@un.org

All prices are quoted in United States dollars.

For further information on the work of the Division on Investment, Technology and Enterprise Development, UNCTAD, please address inquiries to:

United Nations Conference on Trade and Development
Division on Investment, Technology and Enterprise Development
Palais des Nations, Room E-10054
CH-1211 Geneva 10, Switzerland
Telephone: (41-22) 907-5651
Telefax: (41-22) 907-0194
E-mail: natalia.guerra@unctad.org

QUESTIONNAIRE

International Investment Instruments: A Compendium

Volume VI

In order to improve the quality and relevance of the work of the UNCTAD Division on Investment, Technology and Enterprise Development, it would be useful to receive the views of readers on this publication. It would therefore be greatly appreciated if you could complete the following questionnaire and return it to:

Readership Survey
UNCTAD Division on Investment, Technology and Enterprise Development
United Nations Office in Geneva
Palais des Nations
Room E-9123
CH-1211 Geneva 10
Switzerland
Fax: 41-22-907-0194

1. Name and address of respondent (optional):

_____

_____

2. Which of the following best describes your area of work?

Government	○	Public enterprise	○
Private enterprise	○	Academic or research institution	○
International organization	○	Media	○
Not-for-profit organization	○	Other (specify) _____	

3. In which country do you work? _____

4. What is your assessment of the contents of this publication?

Excellent	○	Adequate	○
Good	○	Poor	○

5. How useful is this publication to your work?

Very useful ○   Of some use ○   Irrelevant ○

6. Please indicate the three things you liked best about this publication:

_____

_____

_____

7. Please indicate the three things you liked least about this publication:

_____

_____

_____

8. Are you a regular recipient of *Transnational Corporations* (formerly *The CTC Reporter*), UNCTAD-DITE's tri-annual refereed journal?

Yes　　　　　　○　　　　　　　　　　　　　　　　No　　　　○

If not, please check here if you would like to receive
a sample copy sent to the name and address you have
given above　　　　　　　　　　　　　　　　　　　　　　○

*　　*　　*